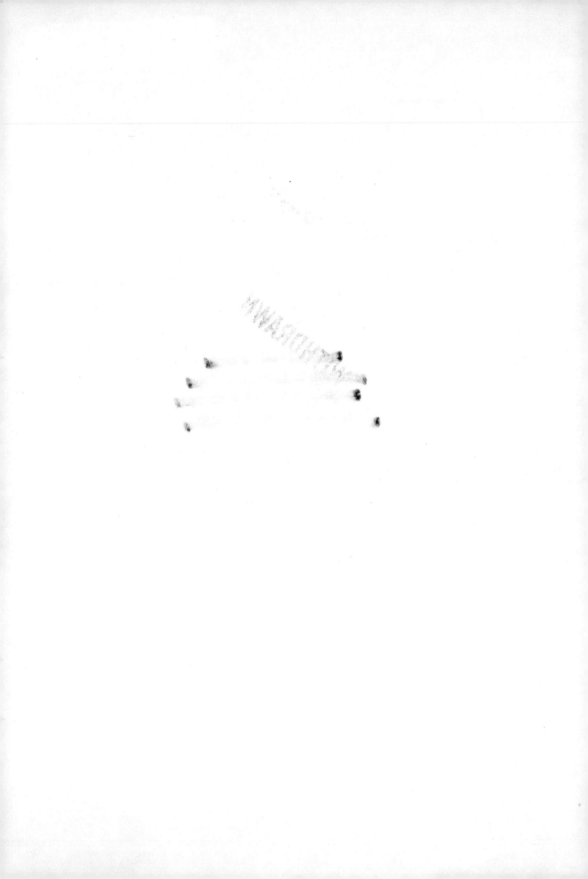

SYSTEMS
AND
THEORIES
IN
PSYCHOLOGY

McGraw-Hill Series in Psychology

CONSULTING EDITOR

Norman Garmezy

Adams: Human Memory
Berlyne: Conflict, Arousal, and Curiosity
Bernstein and Nietzel: Introduction to Clinical Psychology
Blum: Psychoanalytic Theories of Personality
Bock: Multivariate Statistical Methods in Behavioral Research
Brown: The Motivation of Behavior
Campbell, Dunnette, Lawler, and Weick: Managerial Behavior, Performance, and
    Effectiveness
Crites: Vocational Psychology
D'Amato: Experimental Psychology: Methodology, Psychophysics, and Learning
Dollard and Miller: Personality and Psychotherapy
Ferguson: Statistical Analysis in Psychology and Education
Fodor, Bever, and Garrett: The Psychology of Language: An Introduction to
    Psycholinguistics and Generative Grammar
Forgus and Melamed: Perception: A Cognitive-Stage Approach
Franks: Behavior Therapy: Appraisal and Status
Gilmer and Deci: Industrial and Organizational Psychology
Guilford: Psychometric Methods
Guilford: The Nature of Human Intelligence
Guilford and Fruchter: Fundamental Statistics in Psychology and Education
Guion: Personnel Testing
Hetherington and Parke: Child Psychology: A Contemporary Viewpoint
Hirsh: The Measurement of Hearing
Hjelle and Ziegler: Personality Theories: Basic Assumptions, Research, and
    Applications
Horowitz: Elements of Statistics for Psychology and Education
Hulse, Egeth, and Deese: The Psychology of Learning
Hurlock: Adolescent Development
Hurlock: Child Development
Hurlock: Developmental Psychology: A Life-Span Approach

SYSTEMS
AND
THEORIES
IN
PSYCHOLOGY

FOURTH EDITION

Melvin H. Marx

Georgia State University,
Professor Emeritus
University of Missouri

W. A. Cronan-Hillix

Professor of Psychology
San Diego State University

Boston, Massachusetts   Burr Ridge, Illinois
Dubuque, Iowa   Madison, Wisconsin   New York, New York
San Francisco, California   St. Louis, Missouri

McGraw-Hill

A Division of The McGraw·Hill Companies

SYSTEMS AND THEORIES IN PSYCHOLOGY

Printed and bound by Book-mart Press, Inc.

　　9 BKM BKM 9 9 8

This book was set in Times Roman by J. M. Post Graphics, Corp.
The editor was James D. Anker;
the production supervisors were Phil Galea and Louise Karam;
the cover was designed by Scott Chelius.
Project supervision was done by The Total Book.

See Acknowledgments on pages 490—494.
Copyrights included on this page by reference.

Library of Congress Cataloging-in-Publication Data

Marx, Melvin Herman.
　Systems and theories in psychology.

　(McGraw-Hill series in psychology)
　Bibliography; p.
　Includes index.
　1. Psychology—Philosophy.　I. Cronan-Hillix, W. A.
(William Allen).　　II. Title.　　III. Series.
BF38.M38　1987　　150.19　　86-15167
ISBN 0-07-040680-4

CONTENTS

PART 2 CONTEMPORARY THEORIES

PREFACE

The two-part organization of this book that was introduced in the third edition is retained in this one. However, two chapters have been added, one has been dropped, and others have been reorganized. Most of these changes have been suggested by the gracious responses we received to our survey of previous users, or by the criticisms of students at San Diego State University, Michigan State University, or Georgia State University, or by reviewers of earlier versions of this revision. We are grateful to all of them.

The added chapters are on cognitive psychology and on our "social relations"; the missing chapter is the one on personality, which our users told us too often overlapped with the more extensive coverage given to the subject in existing courses on personality theory. The major organizational changes include the combination of Gestalt theory and field theory into a single chapter, which we hope will itself be a better Gestalt; the juxtaposition of Hull and Tolman in a chapter on theoretical controversy; the moving of other S-R developments into a separate augmented chapter; and a thorough rewriting of the chapter on mathematical and computer influences, which now increasingly emphasizes the latter. We have tried very hard, with the help of our critics, to eliminate stylistic difficulties and unnecessary verbiage. We have added photographs of some of our most famous subjects, and hope that readers will enjoy them as much as we do. The results of more recent scholarship have, of course, been included to the extent that we could manage.

In some cases, we received contradictory advice, and could not make the requested changes in both directions at one. Some of our respondents loved signal detectability theory, and others disliked it intensely. The same went for Robert Watson's prescriptions; some wanted more thorough coverage of them so that they would be more useful, and others wanted them eliminated. We responded in much the same way in both cases; signal detectability theory was relegated to an appendix at the end of the chapter, and the coverage of prescriptions was increased and made more systematic, but was placed in end notes after each chapter. In both cases, those who wish to do so can use the materials, and others can easily ignore them.

Our objectives in this edition are the same as in the prior editions: to give the psychology major and the new graduate student a broad perspective on the most important systems and theories in psychology. An important part of this is a presentation of the continuity between historical and contemporary developments, and we believe we have made this connection better in this edition than we have previously. It is our hope that this integrated approach will help students to understand the relationships among the bits and pieces to which they are sometimes exposed in more specialized coursework.

We owe debts to so many students and reviewers that we cannot mention all of them by name. However, Janet Avanzato took apart Chapter 1 with a dissecting needle, and thereby helped us to reassemble it in a much better form. John Mueller stepped out from behind his reviewer's mask of anonymity so that he could give us extra help. Sharon Lynes offered help so persistently that we allowed her the tedium of many of our worst reference searches. Our appreciation to these three for their emotional support, as well as for their contributions to the manuscript, requires special mention.

We also wish to thank the following reviewers who helped in the preparation of this edition: Wesley Zaynor, Kent State University; James L. Pate, Georgia State University; M. B. Fletcher, Carson-Newman College; Alan Boneau, George Mason University; Dirk W. Mosig, Kearney State College; W. H. Jack, Franklin Pierce College; Brad Davis, Loma Linda University; and John Adamopoulos, Indiana University at South Bend.

Like all textbook writers, we owe a great debt to our wives, Terry Cronan-Hillix and Kay Marx, for lending their gracious assistance through all phases of manuscript preparation, as well as for their patient forebearance in coping with our occasionally excessive preoccupation with the manuscript. One of us is also grateful to his wife for lending him her name, as he has now become W. A. Cronan-Hillix. Finally, we are grateful to our series of McGraw-Hill editors—David Serbun, Stephanie Happer, and James D. Anker—who have provided guidance throughout the planning and preparation of the manuscript.

Melvin H. Marx
W. A. Cronan-Hillix

SYSTEMS
AND
THEORIES
IN
PSYCHOLOGY

MAJOR FIGURES IN THE FORMATION AND DEVELOPMENT OF SIX PSYCHOLOGICAL SYSTEMS

	1870	1880	1890	1900	1910	1920	1930	1940	1950	1960
STRUCTURALISM	Wundt	Titchener								
FUNCTIONALISM	James		Dewey	Angell			Carr Woodworth	McGeoch	Melton Underwood	
ASSOCIATIONISM		Ebbinghaus		Pavlov		Bekhterev	Thorndike	Guthrie		Estes
BEHAVIORISM				Meyer		Watson Weiss	Hunter Tolman	Skinner Hull Miller	Spence	
GESTALT THEORY	Mach	von Ehrenfels				Wertheimer Koffka	Köhler			
PSYCHOANALYSIS		Breuer Freud	Adler Rank Jones Jung Ferenczi				Horney Sullivan	Fromm		

PART **ONE**

SYSTEMS

In Part One we discuss the nature of psychological systems. After a brief examination of the history and philosophy of science, we turn to the emergence of psychology from its philosophical and physiological background. Six classic systems of psychology are then presented. The origins of each system are indicated. Then the major characteristics, contributions, and fate of the system are treated. Criticisms and defenses are contrasted for each system. A general outline based on systematic issues proposed by McGeoch (1933) guides the discussion of each system, and the dimensions of R. I. Watson (1967) provide a systematic way to approach the major commitments of each system. Use of these frameworks should make comparisons between different approaches easier to understand and remember and may help us to decide whether modern psychology has advanced significantly relative to these earlier systems. The table at the left shows the major figures associated with each system.

SYSTEMS OF PSYCHOLOGY

THE STUDY OF HISTORY

History is whatever has already happened. It is the moment that just passed, as well as the one that passed 100 years ago. The daily newspaper is history seen through a narrow slit. So is the news on television. Most textbooks in psychology are a kind of specialized history, with the width of the slit increased to about 40 years. In the past, students of psychology sometimes felt that they did not need to study history (Cole, 1984). However, in psychology, as in politics, those who do not know history are condemned to repeat its errors. Psychologists may once have thought that a brash young science in a brash new country was too busy with the present to worry much about the past. That point of view makes no sense, especially since our nation has celebrated its bicentenial and confronted the grim realities of the nuclear age. We are now very certain that we need all the knowledge of the past we can get to help ensure the future.

History teaches us that the present is only one point on a continuum of change. Our answers to questions will be replaced by others, as ours have replaced earlier answers. Psychology's questions last much longer than its answers, and a study of history is therefore more a study of questions than of answers. It is essential that we recognize the nature and value of our questions.

In the past, psychology in the United States has been shorter on professional historians than on history. That situation has changed as the history of psychology has become an active professional discipline. The *Journal of the History of the Behavioral Sciences* began publication in 1964, providing psychology's historians with a special outlet for their research articles as well as with a rallying point. In 1969, the International Society for the History of the Behavioral and Social Sciences organized and

3

began its meetings, which each year increase in size, level of scholarship, and excitement.

With the greater part of its history unexplored, psychology has begun to attract historians who are not psychologists. Michael Sokal was one of the first historians who specialized in the history of psychology. He has written (Sokal, 1971) about one of our leading early American psychologists, James McKeen Cattell, with some of his material coming from a treasure trove of historical papers which he found at the Cattell home.

Other scientists also regard the study of the history of their disciplines as important. For example, Beveridge (1957), who is a biologist, says:

> In recent years more and more attention is being given to the study of the history of science and every scientist ought to have at least some knowledge of this subject. It provides an excellent corrective to ever-increasing specialization and broadens one's outlook and understanding of science. There are books which treat the subject not as a mere chronicle of events but with an insight which gives an appreciation of the growth of knowledge as an evolutionary process. There is a vast literature dealing with the philosophy of science and the logic of scientific method. Whether one takes up this study depends upon one's personal inclinations, but, generally speaking, it will be of little help in doing research. (pp. 11–12)

Beveridge thus saw the history of science, which studies how science *has* proceeded, as useful. He thought that philosophy of science, which tells us how science *should* proceed, was much less useful. However, much has happened since Beveridge expressed his opinion on these subjects. Further study of the history of science has dramatically changed many people's opinions about the philosophy of science. It now appears that the two subjects can hardly be studied separately. A study of the history of science is as valuable for the philosopher of science as Beveridge thought it was for the scientist. And it is impossible to *understand* the history of science without knowing the issues raised by philosophers of science.

ORIENTING ATTITUDES TOWARD THE STUDY OF HISTORY

Historians have been reporting events for a very long time; for example, Thucydides was an Athenian historian who worked in the fifth century B.C., and there were historians before him. As we would expect, historians have evolved ideas about how they should approach their subject matter and about the factors that are important in determining the direction of historical change.

E. G. Boring discussed two of these ideas about historical change in his classic history textbook of 1950. *Zeitgeist* was one of Boring's favorite words; literally, it means "time spirit" or, more meaningfully, "the spirit of the times." In making the historical connection, however, "Zeitgeist" became rich in connotation; it referred to a view of history which contrasted with the "great man" view. The Zeitgeist view resembles a Marxist historical determinism, implying that the spirit of the times determines that a certain scientific advance will be made when the time is right. Great people *seem* to be responsible for great advances, but that is an appearance only. If one great person did not appear, another would step forward. Thus Newton and Leibniz both invented calculus independently at nearly the same time, and it matters little which of them was more instrumental in the discovery. It would have mattered very little if *neither* of them had invented it, for then someone else would have done so at nearly the same time. In fact, Newton's teacher, Isaac Barrow, had been close to the discovery himself and had started Newton in the right direction. Thus Barrow was a part of the Zeitgeist.

In contrast with this deemphasis on the importance of individuals, the "great person" theory of history says that great people do matter and that they are in fact responsible for scientific advance. An advocate of this view might say, "It may be true that an advance can only be made when the time is right, but everything you claim is based on the assumption that there are always plenty of great people. Surely Leibniz and Newton were to some extent interchangeable with respect to one particular finding; but take away Leibniz and Newton, and Darwin and Wallace, and Young and Helmholtz, and so on, and you will see that science does not advance!"

Boring calls the theory of those who emphasize the Zeitgeist naturalistic, as opposed to the personalistic theory of those who emphasize the great person. We do not have to choose one of these theories and reject the other. We are realistic enough to recognize the importance of cultural and intellectual preparation in paving the way for any scientific advance; to that extent, we are naturalistic theorists. But it is inspirational to study great people, and reading their work may help us to new discoveries.

Another distinction, and a very important one, has been made between the *historicist* and *presentist* approaches to the study of history. The historicist is interested in understanding each period in its own terms, applying only concepts, beliefs, attitudes, and possibilities that were available during the historical period being studied. The interest of the presentist is in using a knowledge of history in order to understand the present.

Historicists sometimes regard presentists as naive and think them likely to neglect important differences between past and present in making interpretations. An extreme example of the kind of error historians are apt to commit is the joke about the tourist, recently returned from Greece, who was boasting about the fabulous old coin he had purchased for a song on the Athenian black market for antiquities; he had cleverly smuggled it out of the country right in his pants pocket along with his other change. "It's priceless," he bragged, "pure gold, and coined in 469 B.C.!" "How could you tell when it was coined?" asked his skeptical friend. "Easy," came the quick reply, "the date was right on it!"

Few of us are so careless that we would fail to note that no Greek of the fifth century B.C. could know that Christ would be born several hundred years later. Not all historical interpretations, however, are so easily kept straight; for example, someone might forget that Charles Darwin had some terrible problems with the theory of evolution because he was completely unaware of the genetic principles already discovered by Mendel. Other problems of historical scholarship can be far more difficult, particularly when a translator must be interposed between the original writer and the historian. Either the translator or his reader might easily impute concepts to the original writer that were not developed until many generations later. Julian Jaynes (1976) believes that we misunderstand the mentality of ancient Greece because translators impute meanings to Greek words which they did not then have.

We have largely presentistic interests. We do not, of course, advocate poor scholarship, although the best scholarship is produced by those trained in the disciplines of history. We will do our best to avoid buying too much intellectual coin that is labeled "B.C." Even the purest historicism as practiced by the best scholars has its own trap for the unwary; it is possible to be buried so deeply in the dusty past that one loses sight of the present. The ideal historical scholar, it seems to us, accepts and interprets the past correctly, and on its own terms, both because the past has its own interest and charm and because it is only by understanding the past on its own terms that one has any hope of extracting wisdom that applies to the present. However, the ultimate use of historical knowledge lies in its present and future application. Thus the hope of presentists lies with historicism, and the uses of historicism lie in presentism.

If one accepts this position, then one must appreciate and respect the people who have played a role in psychology's history. We agree with Boring (1950) when he says, "The Greeks were as intelligent as we—there is no evidence that two millennia of evolution have improved man in the dimension in respect of which he excels the great apes" (p. 6). There is not even any evidence that our intelligence is greater than that of Cro-Magnon humans, whose brains were at least as large as ours. We owe much of our present success to the intelligence of our predecessors and to the achievements of human culture resulting from it, foremost among which is the development of science.

Unfortunately, we do not always fully appreciate the contributions of those who got us where we are. We may think that our current science is better than that of our predecessors, partly because history is likely to be written from the point of view of currently popular prejudices.

HOW SHOULD THE PRACTICE OF SCIENCE BE VIEWED?

Only five years after Beveridge made his statements about the history and philosophy of science, Thomas Kuhn (1962) created an upheaval in thinking about these two disciplines with his book *The Structure of Scientific Revolutions*. Philosophers of science reacted in about the same way as hornets do when their nests are whacked with a stick—with a great busy, angry, defensive buzzing. Kuhn claimed to be reporting what science was really like, after studying the history of science. What was this picture of science which was so remarkable, so upsetting, and so long concealed right under everyone's nose?

Kuhn said that science developed by alternately constructing and destroying *paradigms*. The concept of paradigm was critical in Kuhn's thinking and he evidently meant a lot of things by it. Margaret Masterman (1970) found twenty-one different usages of the term in his book! Although Kuhn later (1970) responded to such criticisms by making his definition of paradigm more limited and more precise, we will follow his earlier, less precise usage. It is richer in connotation and we find it more helpful in understanding the history of psychology.

A paradigm in Kuhn's inclusive sense involved nearly everything necessary for doing science, all the way from a particular set of metaphysical assumptions "at the top" through commitments to apparatus and experimental procedures "at the bottom." Between the top and the bottom are particular theories of the subject matter, including particular examples of solved problems (paradigmatic examples) as a very important component.

It therefore takes a lot of components to make up a paradigm, and Kuhn demanded that paradigms achieve a certain level of quality as well as quantity. A point of view, no matter how much it includes, is not a paradigm unless its accomplishments are impressive enough to attract the allegiance of essentially all the practitioners of that branch of science. Usually the accomplishments must be practical rather than merely theoretical; Kuhn says that effective calendars and bombs are the kinds of results which have attracted practitioners. If we look at the present budget for physics and realize how much of it depends on bombs, we will understand what Kuhn meant. In a similar vein, a system of psychology would probably attract enough adherents to become a paradigm if advocates of the position showed that they could bring an end to war!

In order for a paradigm to be attractive enough, the procedures it advocates have to be precise and clearly communicated and its predictions must be clear and unequivocal. Such a paradigm is very useful indeed. It tells the scientist what problems are worth studying and how they should be studied. A host of research projects are at the fingertips of every proponent of the paradigm. As Kuhn says, the paradigm presents puzzles, much like crossword puzzles, and, like the creator of the crossword puzzle, it "guarantees" that the puzzle has a solution.

Understandably, a paradigm may come to be regarded with some fondness by its beneficiaries. Textbooks and histories will come to rationalize and glorify the paradigm, intentionally or not. Writers feel justified in concentrating on those developments which led to our current "correct" view. Little attention is devoted to false starts, so the process as described appears more rational than it really was. Textbooks also have a duty to summarize current knowledge efficiently, and there seems to be little point in reporting inferior alternative views.

Given this background, it is not surprising that those nurtured within the paradigm come to accept it without bothering much about the preconceptions involved—to accept it, so to speak, unconsciously. Neither is it surprising that the paradigm is not given up easily; when occasional findings do not accord with the expectations demanded by the paradigm, they are easily shrugged off as experimental errors, mistakes in observation, or, as a last resort, unimportant exceptions not affecting the essential correctness of the paradigm.

As long as a paradigm is accepted and scientists can work in this comfortable "puzzle-solving" way, Kuhn says that science is in a "normal" period. Unfortunately for exponents of the easy life, the paradigm contains the seeds of its own destruction. Those seeds are nurtured by the necessary precision of the paradigm. On the one hand, the precision is an absolutely necessary feature, because imprecise and nonpredictive statements are not attractive to scientists. On the other hand, no body of scientific theory and practice has ever been so perfect that it never makes mistakes in prediction. These unexpected outcomes, which Kuhn calls "anomalies," eventually become so frequent and so obvious that, despite powerful resistance, they intrude upon the consciousnesses of the practitioners of the paradigm.

At this point, the paradigm goes into a "crisis" phase. During the crisis, the practitioners try desperately to patch up the old paradigm and perhaps still deny the reality of the unwanted results. The assumptions of the paradigm, unquestioned and unconsciously accepted during the period of normal science, suddenly are challenged and must be made explicit and defended.

Other scientists, mostly either new to the science or from some other discipline, start to propose alternative paradigms. Eventually one of the new paradigms will triumph by successfully solving some of the problems presented by the anomalies. It may not solve all of the problems, nor is it likely to be as well developed when it is first proposed as the old paradigm has become. Nevertheless, the new paradigm is more promising because the old paradigm is no longer completely tenable; thus the new one wins out. It does not necessarily do so by converting all the proponents of the old paradigm; however, new people in the field tend to be attracted to the new paradigm, and the old scientists will, after all, die off and become a part of history.

Examples of alternative paradigms are Ptolemaic astronomy, the old earth-centered view, and Copernican astronomy, which places the sun at the center of the solar system. Two other paradigms are Newtonian physics and Einsteinian physics. In both of these cases of paradigm shift there were great difficulties in forcing the acceptance of the new paradigm, and only obvious anomalies, according to Kuhn's view, were sufficient to bring about the paradigm switch. These changes in the fundamental beliefs of a whole science constituted what Kuhn calls a scientific revolution, and gave his book its title, *The Structure of Scientific Revolutions*.

We can now see why Kuhn's book brought about such a buzzing and humming among historians of science. The traditional view of science had always been that it was carried out at a perfectly objective level. Scientists were supposed to hold opinions very lightly and abandon them at the first sign of error. Anyone familiar with the acrimonious controversies between scientists would recognize this description as a gross misrepresentation of the actual behavior of scientists. Yet somehow few before Kuhn had so clearly pointed out how subjective and conservative our procedures were. There is still great controversy over the importance of subjectivity. However, one of the most prominent proponents of the more idealistic view, Karl Popper (1970), said that Kuhn forced him to realize that something like normal science has played a much larger role than he had previously suspected.

Kuhn's picture of science also leads to other fundamental conclusions. Most important, he sees great difficulty in defining and justifying scientific progress. It is not usually clear that a new paradigm is superior to the one that it replaces. The problems attacked and the natures of the solutions are likely to be so different that it is not easy to compare paradigms on the dimension of "goodness." The world is seen *differently*, but it is not necessarily seen *better*. Taken on its own terms, in its own time, the old paradigm was not less "scientific" than the newer one is.

Although Kuhn seems to have directed us much closer to the truth about the nature of the scientific quest, no view is ever complete or final. Gholson and Barker (1985) discuss the modifications of the picture of scientific development suggested by Lakatos (1970) and Laudan (1977). Lakatos believed that Kuhn made two basic errors. First, it was not typical for a science to have only a single paradigm; there were usually two or more competing "research programmes" which existed simultaneously. Second, members of two research traditions could talk meaningfully to one another, and the same data could be used to test competing theories. These two basic errors led Kuhn into a third error, the belief that progress in science was more a subjective than an objective matter. Lakatos believed that surviving research programs were those that handled the data better and were thus more progressive than their competitors.

Laudan's position was more in agreement with that of Lakatos, and he added his own belief that research traditions gradually change their core assumptions and are therefore more flexible than Kuhn would have us believe. Evolution, not revolution, is the typical mode of scientific change.

These disagreements by Lakatos and Laudan are, however, relatively minor corrections to the picture of scientific development painted by Kuhn, and his work provides us with the background we need for placing psychology's traditional schools and systems in perspective.He has told us that paradigmatic science proceeds through two phases: *normal* and *revolutionary*. In this analysis the period of crisis is regarded as a mere transition between the two. There is, however, another genuinely different kind of activity, *preparadigmatic science,* which one might or might not regard as truly scientific. Kuhn regarded preparadigmatic science as a kind of fumbling activity, more like making an almanac of unrelated facts than like science. Its practitioners were searching for a way to approach and formulate their problems—even a way to identify them. The preparadigmatic period is therefore marred by disagreements about every aspect of the fundamentals of scientific activity. This is a period of schools, and each school claims to have the light and the way. Yet no school can produce the evidence required to convince others of the correctness of its claim.

Kuhn believes that the social and behavioral sciences have been in this preparadigmatic period. It is always difficult to achieve sufficient perspective to say precisely where one *is;* but it is quite easy to see that Kuhn is correct about where psychology *was*. Let us therefore look at the nature of the classic schools and systems of psychology and at the service they provide as we wait for a paradigm.

SCHOOLS AND SYSTEMS OF PSYCHOLOGY

While Kuhn denied us paradigms, he said that preparadigmatic sciences were guided by something like a paradigm, although he did not say what it was. That "something like a paradigm" has typically been called a *school* of psychology, if we were paying attention to a group of associated psychologists. It was more likely to be called a *system* of psychology if we were paying attention to a group of ideas that were brought together to form a coherent set of beliefs about psychology. These schools or systems were, therefore, very like Kuhn's paradigms in that each one furnished the necessary principles for directing the psychologist's study of the subject matter in a way that would efficiently further knowledge.

Such a system would therefore have to provide statements about what the subject matter in question is or ought to be. Decisions about the subject matter would be related to positions on more philosophical issues, such as the question of the nature of mind and body. Psychologists also need to know how the subject matter should be studied. What organisms will be useful in revealing general principles? This problem is most often expressed in the form of the question, What can the study of animals tell us about people? Also, what general and specific methods will help to uncover the secrets of psychology? Should these methods be applied in laboratory or field? What sort of equipment is necessary? And so it goes through a host of questions and answers which, just as in the case of the paradigm, involve problems ranging all the way from the metaphysical to the mundane.

The directive statements of schools are, however, not often overtly stated. The process of acculturation in psychology, as in paradigmatic sciences or in the general culture, is far more subtle. A student would rarely be told "I, your teacher, am a functionalist, and I'm going to try to see that you become one too." The exception to this rule is psychoanalysis, a school of thought into which one is very explicitly indoctrinated. This is not to say that, in individual cases, students may not face a systematic indoctrination process into some other school. More often, however, the student simply observes how things are done, and much of the training involves imitation during a sort of apprenticeship. After training, most members of the profession simply think of themselves as psychologists and not as members of a particular school. They may even think that psychology is no longer divided into schools.

There is good reason to think that some approaches to psychology remain isolated from others. Krantz (1972) marshaled evidence indicating that operant psychologists form a school. For one thing, the *Journal of the Experimental Analysis of Behavior (JEAB)* cites itself, rather than some other source, quite often. That is evidence of some degree of isolation. It is certainly clear that operant psychology has many of the properties to be expected of a school, or even of a paradigm. It includes law, application, instrumentation, a kind of theory, and a general philosophy, and it has solved problems. It also presents additional problems and hence stimulates research, to an extent that should warm Kuhn's heart.

We are not saying that operant psychology constitutes a paradigm simply because it shares many paradigmatic characteristics; certainly the operant approach has not been adopted by all psychologists. The cognitive approach is a strong and increasingly popular alternative to operant psychology, and it has its own paradigm-like features. If we accept Lakatos's "correction" to Kuhn, with the possibility of two or more competing research programs, we could view these two approaches as such alternative coexisting paradigms.

In Part Two of this book, we will return to contemporary psychology. Meanwhile, we will take a look at six classic systems of psychology, each of which had its own ideas about how psychology ought to proceed. The central contentions of each of these systems make the directive function of psychological systems quite clear. The systems are listed in the order in which they originated.

Associationism   The psychologist should study the principles of association of ideas (or of words or of stimulus-response connections), analyzing complex events into simpler ones as the most direct road to understanding.

Structuralism   The psychologist should study the contents of consciousness through the method of experimental introspection, searching always for the irreducible elements which make up consciousness.

Functionalism   Psychology must be concerned primarily with the functions of mind and behavior in adapting the organism to the environment.

Psychoanalysis   The core of psychology is motivation, much of it unconscious and sexual, and it must be studied through its manifestations in dreams, errors, symptoms, and associations.

Behaviorism   The psychologist must study the behavior of the organism through strictly objective methods; consciousness cannot be part of the data of psychology.

Gestalt   The psychologist can arrive at useful and meaningful laws only through the study of significant wholes; premature analysis is disastrous.

In every school of psychology, classic or contemporary, there is continuing interplay between the systematic philosophical content of the school and the empirical findings encountered as the directive policies of the school are followed. Sometimes the findings even precede and give rise to the policies, rather than the other way around. Gestalt psychology, for example, originated when its founders said that the results of some experiments on apparent movement required laws relating to the whole stimulus field for any reasonable explanation. Empirical, theoretical, methodological, and philosophical statements tend to become interrelated (or perhaps just confused), so that the amalgam becomes "the system." This process seems to be precisely analogous in this respect to what Kuhn meant in his inclusive early view of paradigms.

So far, we have put more stress on the similarities between the classic systems of psychology and Kuhn's paradigms than we have on the differences. To prevent giving a distorted view, we ought now to look more closely at the hierarchy of commitments, from the most abstract at the top to the most concrete at the bottom, and see where paradigm-system differences are most likely to be found.

At the top, we find very general presuppositions in both cases, and these may be difficult or impossible to prove. Some of the presuppositions may even be common to physics and psychology; for example, scientists in both disciplines would be likely to believe that the universe is governed by laws that are humanly knowable and that these knowable laws are constant as we change places or as time passes. This kind of presupposition is particularly likely to escape examination because it is so appealing and seems so necessary to all scientific work. Such suppositions are metaphysical, because they cannot be confirmed directly through any physical observations, and they are certainly metatheoretical, because they are too general to serve as theories of any particular subject matter. Every discipline accepts such presuppositions, and more mature disciplines with paradigms would not be expected to differ systematically or fundamentally from less mature disciplines at the level of these very general presuppositions. One would, of course, hope that there would be progressive refinements of these presuppositions as all science matures.

At a slightly lower level of abstraction, one finds a set of presuppositions tailored to a particular subject matter but still at too high a level of abstraction to be part of any theory of the subject matter. For example, the assumption that psychology ought to study consciousness rather than behavior (or vice versa) is not a theoretical proposition, but it poses a problem which is relevant to psychology rather than to physics or chemistry. Again, the more mature sciences need and use similar presuppositions, and paradigms and systems probably do not differ drastically in the "goodness" of this type of metatheoretical assumption.

Systems and paradigms differ most at the theoretical level. Mature sciences have theories specific and predictive enough that both impressive successes and impressive failures (anomalies) can occur. Without such theories, neither normal science nor crises can occur. In less developed sciences, the theories are usually not precise enough to be disprovable; hence they cannot be "right" in any significant way either.

Systems do not lack data. Paradigms organize data better, and more developed sciences may collect more reliable data. However, the differences at this most concrete level are not nearly as dramatic as those at the level of theory. We therefore conclude that systems and paradigms differ primarily in that the former lack the unifying force of strong, precise, well-developed theories.

DESCRIBING AND EVALUATING SYSTEMS OF PSYCHOLOGY

Without an organizing framework, the facts of history sometimes seem to merge into a mass of unrelated details. How can one arrange the study of systems so that it makes sense, becomes useful, and remains in memory? We believe that three steps are necessary. First, the system must be described carefully. Its positive assertions must be presented in an organized manner. Second, the assertions of the system must be related to enduring issues in psychology and in its parent sciences, most directly philosophy and physiology. Third, the position of the system on these issues must be compared to the positions of other systems on the same issues.

We are fortunate to have guidelines for each of the steps in our discussion of systems.

1 John A. McGeoch (1933) wrote an article on the criteria for a psychological system. These criteria form an outline of basic issues which must be addressed by a system. We will discuss six of these areas for each of the classic systems: definition of psychology, postulates, mind-body position, nature of the data, principles of connection, and principles of selection.

These are critical issues for a system to face. For example, a system must decide what the subject matter for study will be. Thus it must define psychology, and in doing so it faces several questions. Does psychology study consciousness or behavior, or both? How much emphasis should be placed on psychology as applied science, and how much on psychology as pure science? How much attention should be given to physiological knowledge and techniques, and how much to more strictly behavioral approaches?

The question of "postulates" relates to the positive assertions of the system. In psychology, the postulates will not be so rigorous as mathematical postulates; never-theless, every system makes assumptions, and a part of the study of the system must necessarily be a study of the fundamental theses accepted by the system. Two of the most important postulates for psychological systems would concern the nature of the mind-body relationship and the nature of the data, McGeoch's third and fourth areas. Finally, a system must select and connect the entities with which it works, McGeoch's last two points.

2 Robert I. Watson (1967) made a careful study of enduring issues in psychology and in philosophical and scientific studies which preceded psychology, all the way back to the seventeenth century. He isolated eighteen current issues which were already of interest then. They will be presented in more detail in the next section. The concerns of every system of psychology can be related to many of these issues.

3 Fuchs and Kawash (1974) and Coan (1979) studied the opinions of historians about the positions of systems, or of individual psychological theorists, on issues derived from or similar to those isolated by Watson. These systematized opinions are the best information we have about the important differences between the prominent systems, or theoretical viewpoints, in the history of psychology. The dimensions along which these differences lie will also be described in the following section.

Watson's Prescriptive System

R. I. Watson (1909–1980) accepted Kuhn's judgment that the social and behavioral sciences had not yet developed a sufficiently precise, successful, and unified set of beliefs, theories, and practices to justify the application of the name of paradigm. He then asked himself how we have kept from flying off in all directions, indulging in random and fruitless activity. Psychology admittedly has had plenty of controversy, flaws, and false starts, but it nevertheless seems to have made progress. Psychologists think that they have a pretty good idea of what they are doing. What, in the absence of a paradigm, directs our efforts?

Watson's answer was that our efforts are given direction by a set of persistent questions which are seen as important by most psychologists. Watson, like Kuhn, arrived at his position after an intensive study of the history of his discipline. He identified eighteen questions which could be expressed as dimensions, with extreme opinions about each question represented as the polar extremes of the dimension and intermediate opinions represented as intermediate positions on the dimension. The list of dimensions is given in Table 1-1, as taken from Watson (1967, pp. 436–437). All the words describing poles of the prescriptions are defined in the Glossary at the back of this book.

These prescriptions have a more philosophical tone than one might expect, given the fact that they were intended as a replacement for the paradigms of more mature sciences. However, one must remember that psychology was born of philosophy and even the older sciences continue to have their philosophical side. Accordingly, Watson went back to the philosophers of the seventeenth century to see if he could find in their work the origins of the problems he had identified in a study of the psychology

TABLE 1-1
THE PRESCRIPTIONS OF PSYCHOLOGY ARRANGED IN CONTRASTING PAIRS

Conscious mentalism–Unconscious mentalism
    Emphasis on awareness of mental structure or activity—emphasis on unawareness
Contentual objectivism—Contentual subjectivism
    Psychological data viewed as behavior of individual–viewed as mental structure or activity of individual
Determinism–Indeterminism
    Human events completely explicable in terms of antecedents—not completely explicable
Empiricism–Rationalism
    Major, if not exclusive, source of knowledge is experience—is reason
Functionalism–Structuralism
    Psychological categories are activities—are contents
Inductivism–Deductivism
    Investigations should begin with facts or observations—should begin with assumed established truths
Mechanism–Vitalism
    Activities of living are completely explicable by physiochemical constituents—are not so explicable
Methodological objectivism–Methodological subjectivism
    Use of methods open to verification by another competent observer—not so open
Molecularism–Molarism
    Psychological data most aptly described in terms of relatively small units—in terms of relatively large units
Monism–Dualism
    Fundamental principle or entity in the universe is of one kind—is of two kinds, mind and matter
Naturalism–Supernaturalism
    Nature requires for its operations and explanation only the principles found within it—requires transcendent guidance as well
Nomotheticism–Idiographicism
    Emphasis on discovering general laws—on explaining particular events or individuals
Peripheralism–Centralism
    Stress on psychological events taking place at periphery of body—within the body
Purism–Utilitarianism
    Seeking of knowledge for its own sake—for its usefulness in other activities
Quantitativism–Qualitativism
    Stress on knowledge which is countable or measurable—on that which is different in kind or essence
Rationalism–Irrationalism
    Emphasis on data supposed to follow dictates of good sense and intellect—intrusion or domination of emotive and conative factors upon intellectual processes
Staticism–Developmentalism
    Emphasis on cross-sectional view—on changes with time
Staticism–Dynamicism
    Emphasis on enduring aspects—on change and factors making for change

of 1965. That is excellent for our purposes, for it means that these problems will be useful in comparing old and new views of psychology.

Are Watson's prescriptions all there is to the historical story? Of course not. Watson would have been the first to deny that they are. There is always an element of arbitrariness in any such list, and Watson must have wondered whether he should add still other dimensions. A favorite candidate of ours would be a dimension labeled "People are inherently evil—People are inherently good," with a parenthetical explanation like "People suffer from original sin and are innately hostile and aggressive—People are noble savages perverted by society." Certainly one could trace disagreements on this question from biblical times to the present, with psychology contributing at least its fair share to the controversy. You are free to suggest your own favorite dimension, as we have, or a whole new set. Nevertheless, Watson's list represents a thoughtful and useful analysis.

One very interesting use of Watson's prescriptions is as a sort of personality profile to describe individuals and schools that are important in the history of psychology. Your own "psychological personality profile" can be obtained by making a list numbered from 1 through 18, corresponding to Watson's eighteen prescriptive dimensions. Think of each of Watson's dimensions as a range from 1 to 5. For example, in the case of Watson's first dimension, the belief that the only thing psychologically important is the mental structure or activity of which a person is consciously aware would be represented by a 1; if, by way of contrast, you believed that unconscious processes were important and awareness completely insignificant, you would write a 5 by the number for the first dimension. Intermediate opinions on the dimensions would be represented by intermediate numbers. This is a very worthwhile exercise for any psychologist, since it both familiarizes one with Watson's prescriptions and makes one aware of one's own beliefs—sometimes in surprising ways!

It is more difficult and more problematic to rate the positions of schools on these dimensions than to rate the opinions of individuals. An individual presumably has only one opinion at any given time, although it may be hard enough to decide exactly what it is, even when the individual is oneself. When the individual is someone else, known only through his or her writing, it is much more difficult, especially when the opinions of important historical figures often change over time. When a whole school made up of many individuals with varying opinions is given a unified single rating, one should not take the results too seriously. Luchins and Luchins (1981) even suggested that the prescriptions "do not apply" to Gestalt psychology, but we do not believe that the difficulties encountered by their students justify such an extreme conclusion.

Factor Analytic Studies of Systems

Kawash and Fuchs (1974) asked psychologists with a professional interest in the history of their discipline to rank systems on Watson's prescriptions and then factor-analyzed the results to see how Watson's dimensions are interrelated. In doing so, they separated each dimension into two parts. They did not want to assume that the prescriptions were really represented by dimensions connecting two opposite poles. For example, looking at the first prescription, conscious mentalism–unconscious mentalism, Fuchs and Kawash allowed for the possibility that one system of psychology might emphasize both conscious and unconscious mentalism, while another might deny both. Thus Fuchs and Kawash asked their respondents to rate the emphasis each school placed on the thirty-six factors obtained by listing the names of the ends of Watson's eighteen prescriptions.

Coan (1979) did several studies of the theoretical orientations of psychologists. One of the studies resembled that of Fuchs and Kawash. Coan asked psychologists to rate the theoretical emphases of famous psychologists on thirty-four variables which were rather like the thirty-six poles of Watson's prescriptions. For theorists between 1880 and 1950, his factor analysis revealed six first-order factors: subjectivism–objectivism, holism–elementarism, qualitative orientation–quantitative orientation, personal orientation–apersonal orientation, dynamic orientation–static orientation, and endogenism–exogenism. Thus Coan, like Fuchs and Kawash before him, ends up with bipolar dimensions as a result of his factor analysis, although he begins with unipolar descriptive words.

It is unfortunate that the names of Coan's factors are not the same as those of the Fuchs and Kawash factors. However, idiographicism is very closely related to a personal orientation, and molarism is certainly very similar to holism. The other dimensions also cover much similar ground, and the two sets of factors together can guide us in our comparisons of systems.

For the sake of our own interest and that of the reader, we have rated six classic schools of psychology on each of Watson's dimensions. Thus we carried out a task similar to the one carried out by those who participated in the Fuchs and Kawash or Coan study, but we followed Watson in his assumption that the prescriptions could be regarded as bipolar dimensions. The results are presented in Table 1-2. If you find that you disagree dramatically with our rating of a school on a dimension, you should probably examine the basis for your rating. There is nothing unusual about disagreements, especially when one considers the difficulties in making such ratings. The discovery of disagreements serves a very useful purpose if it forces one to marshal good arguments, based on facts, for one's opinion.

SUMMARY AND CONCLUSIONS

The history of psychology is attracting ever-increasing interest. It is now recognized as a legitimate field of study within psychology, and several university psychology departments accept dissertations on the history of the discipline.

The historicistic-presentistic distinction reminds us that history must be understood on its own terms if we are to apply its lessons to the present, and the naturalistic-personalistic distinction reminds us that great people operate in the context of their culture, which has a powerful effect on what the science of a period can accomplish.

In part because of the work of Thomas Kuhn, the great significance of the study of history for the philosophy of science has come to be widely appreciated. Philosophy of science directs and reflects the history of science. Kuhn's emphasis is on reflection, but the emphasis of many of his critics (e.g., Popper, 1970) is on direction. Some philosophers, like Feyerabend (1970), take the extreme view that there is nothing consistent to reflect and thus there are no rules to use in directing scientists.

In Kuhn's more practical picture, the key concept is the paradigm, a concrete achievement including theory, law, instrumentation, and application, which unifies a scientific discipline around agreed-upon fundamentals. During periods of normal science, paradigms make specific predictions and suggest researchable problems; normal

TABLE 1-2
MEAN JUDGMENTS OF THE POSITIONS OF SIX PSYCHOLOGICAL SYSTEMS ON EACH OF WATSON'S EIGHTEEN PRESCRIPTIVE DIMENSIONS

Watson's dimensions	Mean ratings					
	Associationism	Structuralism	Functionalism	Behaviorism	Gestalt theory	Psychoanalysis
Mentalism: conscious versus unconscious	2.2	1.2	2.5	4.4	2.3	4.8
Content: objective versus subjective	3.2	4.9	2.1	1.1	3.8	4.2
Determinism–indeterminism	1.3	2.2	2.2	1.1	2.2	1.1
Empiricism–rationalism	1.1	1.7	2.2	1.3	3.2	3.6
Functionalism–structuralism	2.4	4.8	1.1	1.5	3.7	3.1
Inductivism–deductivism	1.5	3.2	1.9	1.7	4.1	4.3
Mechanism–vitalism	1.4	2.0	3.0	1.1	2.9	2.3
Methods: objectivism versus subjectivism	1.9	5.0	2.0	1.1	3.7	4.6
Molecularism–molarism	1.2	1.6	3.2	1.3	4.8	3.3
Monism–dualism	3.3	4.6	4.1	1.1	4.1	4.2
Naturalism–supernaturalism	2.3	1.6	1.4	1.1	2.4	1.9
Nomotheticism–idiographicism	1.3	1.2	2.9	1.0	4.1	3.1
Peripheralism–centralism	2.5	4.4	2.2	1.1	4.7	4.6
Purism–utilitarianism	1.6	1.1	4.9	3.2	2.2	4.6
Quantitativism–qualitativism	1.9	3.2	2.1	1.6	4.7	4.6
Rationalism–irrationalism	1.9	2.0	3.1	4.0	2.8	4.8
Staticism–developmentalism	3.1	1.3	4.1	2.8	2.3	3.6
Staticism–dynamicism	2.6	1.4	4.6	2.6	4.2	4.6

science works out these paradigmatic puzzles. In this process, it is certain that inexplicable observations (anomalies) will occur, forcing a period of crisis for the paradigm. Science then enters a revolutionary phase, and a new, more promising, paradigm eventually replaces the old one. Although Lakatos and Laudan, among others, have proposed modifications to the Kuhnian view of scientific change, the latter continues to provide a good framework within which the history of science may be studied.

According to Kuhn, psychology and the social sciences are not yet developed enough to have paradigms. Robert I. Watson agreed but pointed out that psychology employs a set of shared problems (which he labeled "prescriptions") in a similar role, to guide the development of our science. These prescriptions are prominent concerns of the various schools, or systems, of psychology. They can therefore be used as a framework for comparing the intellectual commitments of the various classic systems of psychology, as well as for understanding our own positions with respect to these earlier systems.

Systems of psychology are like paradigms in that they include a whole range of commitments, from very abstract "world views" to very concrete decisions about the best way to perform experiments and with what instruments. Systems are unlike paradigms in that they have not yet managed to achieve theories adequate in scope and precision to synthesize psychology's array of impressive concrete results or to facilitate the production of ever more effective new research.

An efficient study of the systems of psychology should take advantage of the historical scholarship of people like Kuhn, Watson, McGeoch, Fuchs and Kawash, and Coan. Our study will involve three phases: a purely descriptive study of the content of a system, guided by McGeoch and keeping in mind Kuhn's picture of scientific development; a placement of each system within the context of philosophical problems, guided by Watson; and a comparison of each system with others on important dimensions, guided by Coan and by Fuchs and Kawash.

FURTHER READINGS

Kuhn's *The structure of scientific revolutions* (1962, 1970) is so central to understanding what modern philosophers of science are talking about that everyone should read it. In addition, Kuhn writes so clearly and entertainingly that he provides no excuse for not reading him. R. I. Watson's "Psychology: A prescriptive science" (1967) provides a full explanation of the relationship of his prescriptions to Kuhn's thinking and to psychology. Hillix and Marx, in their *Systems and theories in psychology: A reader* (1974), reprint Watson's article and an article by Kuhn, "Historical structure of scientific discovery," along with other relevant readings. For those who are motivated enough to want both sides of several issues in the philosophy of science (Kuhn's side and Popper's side, roughly speaking), the more advanced book edited by Musgrave and Lakatos (1970), *Criticism and the growth of knowledge,* is truly excellent. Among other stimulating articles, it includes the one by Masterman mentioned earlier, a superb anti-Kuhnian article by Lakatos, and a reply to his critics by Kuhn. Gholson and Barker (1985) review the recent history of the Kuhnian controversy and show how the various positions might handle the relationship between behavioral and cognitive psychology.

Ludy Benjamin's *Teaching history of psychology: A handbook* (1981) is a rich source of sources of information about the history of psychology and can be read with interest and profit by students as well as by teachers. Coan's book, *Psychologists: Personal and theoretical pathways* (1979), contains studies of the theoretical orientations of contemporary psychologists as well as of historical figures and is a good example of how work that starts out as a historical study can end up in the present.

THE EMERGENCE OF PSYCHOLOGY

Kuhn's view of science emphasizes three phases—preparadigmatic, normal, and revolutionary—with the crisis period a transition between normal and revolutionary science. The history of psychology can also be viewed as having passed through three partially overlapping phases of development. In the first phase, there was no separate discipline of psychology; in the second, psychology was clearly preparadigmatic in Kuhn's sense; and in the third phase, beginning after World War II, there has been movement toward the achievement of a near-paradigm in several areas of psychology.

Psychology's roots lie in the earliest period, and we must therefore begin our study by tracing the development of ideas that helped psychology to emerge as an independent discipline. We will then outline some concrete problems that motivated, and lent a particular form to, the new science.

THE GROWTH OF SCIENTIFIC IDEAS

Table 2-1 is a summary of the contributions of some of the people who developed the scientific ideas that led to a science of psychology. Some of those in the table contributed directly to psychology, but many contributed only indirectly via what they did for general philosophical or scientific progress. Some of the ancient birth and death dates are approximate; the historical record is sometimes incomplete. In addition, multiple calendar changes challenge scholars who determine the dates for ancient events. It is interesting to notice how rapidly your mind is asked to roam over the centuries as your eye wanders from the beginning of this table to its end, and to imagine the life of a person lying within the short dash between birth and death dates.

Many historians have noted the apparently stepwise progress of the sciences. Those

TABLE 2-1
SUMMARY OF MAJOR CONTRIBUTIONS TO THE DEVELOPMENT OF PSYCHOLOGY

Person	Approximate birth and death dates	Contribution
Philosophy		
Thales	Sixth century B.C.	Naturalistic explanation; universe composed of water
Pythagoras	Sixth century B.C.	Mysticism and mathematics; Pythagorean theorem
Socrates	ca. 470–399 BC.	Idealistic philosopher; deductive approach
Democritus	ca. 460–370 B.C.	Universe composed of atoms; reductionistic account of complex phenomena
Plato	427–347 B.C.	Rationalistic, dualistic approach
Aristotle	384–322 B.C.	Rationalistic and observational methods; classification system for biology; laws of associative memory
Euclid	ca. 300 B.C.	Developer of geometry
Roger Bacon	ca. 1214–1294	Emphasis on free empirical observation
Francis Bacon	1561–1626	*Novum organum:* gave philosophical support to empirical science
Descartes	1596–1650	Dualistic interactionism; action of body is mechanistic
Locke	1632–1704	Opposed Descartes's innate ideas; used associationistic principles
Leibniz	1646–1716	Activity as basic; degrees of consciousness; coinventor of calculus
Berkeley	1685–1753	Experience as only source of knowledge; subjective idealism
La Mettrie	1709–1751	Mechanistic explanation applied to human behavior
Hume	1711–1776	Analysis of causality; origins of ideas of God and self in experience
Kant	1724–1804	Importance of native abilities in ordering the data of experience
Science		
Hippocrates	ca. 460–380 B.C.	"Father of medicine"; an excellent observer; naturalistic view of the human being
Archimedes	ca. 287–212 B.C.	First well-known experimental physicist
Herophilus and Erasistratus	Third century B.C.	First inference of distinction between sensory and motor nerves
Ptolemy	Second century A.D.	Alexandrian astronomer; his view of earth as center of universe held for centuries
Galen	Second century A.D.	Famous physician and anatomist; performed animal experiments
Copernicus	1473–1543	Polish astonomer who placed sun at center of solar system, thus changing the view of the place of human beings in the universe

(Cont.)

TABLE 2-1—*Continued*

Person	Approximate birth and death dates	Contribution
	Science	
Vesalius	1514–1564	First thorough treatise on human anatomy
Galileo	1564–1642	Reestablished observation as final court of appeal; made astronomical and physical discoveries
Kepler	1571–1630	Mathematical description of planetary orbits
Harvey	1578–1657	Demonstrated the circulation of the blood
Van Leeuwenhoek	1632–1723	First effective microscope; discoverer or identifier of protozoa, bacteria, and human sperm
Newton	1642–1727	Coinventor of calculus; set pattern of physics for 200 years
Linnaeus	1707–1778	Binomial system of biological classification
Bessel	1784–1846	Astronomer at Königsberg; worked out personal equations and thus posed a problem for psychology
Weber	1795–1878	Pioneer physiologist; formulated "Weber's law"
J. Müller	1801–1858	Comprehensive handbook of physiology; doctrine of specific energies of nerves
Fechner	1801–1887	His *Elemente der Psychophysik* believed by some to mark beginning of experimental psychology; modified Weber's law
Darwin	1809–1882	*The origin of species:* primary publication on evolution
Bernard	1813–1878	Concept of the internal environment
Helmholtz	1821–1894	Eminent physiologist; first experimental measurement of speed of nerve impulse; theories of hearing and seeing
Galton	1822–1911	Work in eugenics, statistics, individual differences; set many problems for psychology
Wundt	1832–1920	Founder of first psychological laboratory at University of Leipzig (1879)

treating subjects farthest from humans seem to have had the earliest beginning, and those closest to our immediate affairs the most recent. Psychology was one of the last sciences to develop; astronomy and physics were the first. Archimedes, in the third century B.C., was in some ways a sophisticated physicist. In the early seventeenth century, Kepler's mathematical description of the motions of the planets around the sun was the culmination of a long line of astronomical discoveries. The human body was investigated long before there was a science for the human "mind." Harvey, in 1628, described the circulation of the blood, about 250 years before Ebbinghaus did his pioneer work on memory.

Several reasons have been suggested for this long scientific neglect of human behavior. One is the sanctity of humans as maintained by human institutions, which hindered seeing a person as a natural phenomenon. Another is the complexity of human beings. A third may be that it is often easiest to be objective about the things that concern us least, and we are very concerned with ourselves. Finally, it is easy to think that, by virtue of being human ourselves, we already know about all we need to know about people. After all, hasn't everyone read the works of those who know humanity, from Shakespeare to Schulz, in whose comic strip Lucy offers Charley Brown psychiatric help for a price? Thus in saying that the study of people has been neglected, we mean only that the scientific study of people as a formal discipline got a late start.

Explanation: External and Internal

There was a time in human history when events were typically explained in terms of forces outside the scope of observable natural events. For example, Norse mythology explained storms by saying that the warrior of the gods was angry, and Homer explained victory in war in terms of the favoritism of the Greek gods. From the scientific point of view, there are two basic things wrong with these explanations: (1) They refer the explanation to unobservables, and (2) the events used as explanations do not fit within the same context as the events to be explained; there is thus no apparent logical connection between the alleged causes and their consequences. Such explanations are therefore called external, as opposed to internal.

It is not always easy to tell whether or not a particular explanation is internal. The extremes are often easy to classify. Theological explanations of natural events are external, and accepted scientific accounts are usually internal. However, some of the most sophisticated scientific explanations need some justification before they can be qualified as internal. These are the explanations that depend on postulated but unobserved entities like genes, stimulus elements, or quarks. Most scientists accept explanations couched in terms of such concepts as internal because they or their effects are potentially observable, are "observed" indirectly, or have implications for observations at another level. In addition, the *logical* connection between the unobserved entities and the surface observations is clear and explicit. Questions arise, however, if it is not clear that the concept is formulated so that it is potentially observable, if the supposed indirect observation can be accounted for in other ways, or if the implications from the deductive system containing the concept are not clear.

Although there are still people who explain disasters in terms of "the wrath of God," scientific explanation does not have recourse to such descriptions. Thales, a Greek philosopher of the sixth century B.C., is sometimes given credit for initiating attempts to explain natural events in terms of other natural events; he explained the nature of matter in terms of a single basic natural element, water. Democritus soon after explained matter in terms of basic particles called atoms, and modern science still holds to a similar concept. Whether these men really deserve credit for the swing toward internal explanation, however, is not important; the important thing is that science as we know it depends on the use of explanations which belong within the same natural framework as the observables to be explained.

The naturalistic philosophy of Thales and Democritus was followed by the idealistic skepticism of Socrates and Plato. Ingenious as it was, that skeptical philosophy may have contributed to the disappearance of Greek culture. Extreme pessimism has never been a productive attitude, and Greek skepticism combined pessimism with doubts about the reliability of our knowledge of the external world.

When the Roman culture, like the Greek, went into decline, the ensuing Middle Ages showed little concern for internal types of explanations or for scientific problems; perhaps the attitude was that great interest in natural events was bad for the soul, and the soul was definitely more important. An example of the external thinking that was predominant in the Middle Ages is the typical treatment of convulsions by flogging: such action was thought to drive out of the body the demons or evil spirits that were considered to be responsible for convulsive behavior. Today, of course, such treatment is not used, because convulsive behavior is generally viewed as determined by organic conditions within the body (a truly internal explanation). Convulsive electroshock is used in the treatment of psychosis, with explanations of its effectiveness which are hardly more satisfying than evil spirits; however, we are *seeking* an internal explanation, and the effectiveness of the shock is verified by empirical checks on the outcomes of treatment.

In denigrating external explanations, we are not assuming that the implications of such explanations *necessarily* lead to ineffective treatments. People are frequently "right for the wrong reasons." For example, modern work demonstrates that punishment may serve a purpose in eliminating undesirable behaviors. That would lead us to believe that a medieval treatment, flogging, administered every time an "evil spirit" was seen affecting someone's behavior, might occasionally lead to the apparent elimination of undesirable behavior.

Watson gives an interesting case in which a more correct conclusion followed from a kind of evidence we would find altogether unacceptable, while an inferior conclusion about the same issue was derived from an attempt at "internal" explanation, based on observational evidence. Watson (1963) says of Aristotle's views:

> In identifying life with the psyche and this, in turn, with the heart, he also rejects the Platonic doctrine of the brain as the organ of the soul. He used as one argument for doing so the fact that he found the brain to be insensible to direct stimulation. It is ironical that Plato was right for the wrong reasons. Plato assigned reason to the brain on the basis of several irrelevant reasons typical of which is the fact that the brain was the part of man nearest the heavens. Aristotle, on the other hand, was wrong for the "right," i.e., naturalistic reasons. (p. 52)

If some right decisions follow from the wrong theories, the theories have a greater life expectancy than if all decisions turn out badly. The phrenologists of the nineteenth and early twentieth centuries believed that our talents were reflected in the bumps on our skulls. If a person was diagnosed as having an inadequate bump in the area responsible for algebra, the phrenologist would recommend practicing algebra. That may have been good advice for increasing algebraic proficiency. If advice that followed from phrenological theory worked, the theory might be regarded as confirmed. And, indeed, it did take phrenology a long time to disappear.

Such examples demonstrate the fact that observations cannot logically confirm theories; they can only disconfirm them. In scientific practice, however, theories are seldom rejected because of a single disconfirmation. They can almost always be saved by finding a flaw in the observation or in the relationship between the observation and the theory. Even if these modes of rescue fail, most theories are complex enough that a change in a part of a theory will bring it into line with the observation and the bulk of the theory can be saved. Thus when observations seem to disconfirm a theory, the theory is not likely to be rejected immediately.

When observations are consistent with theory, the scientist may behave as though the theory were truly confirmed, even though the logician knows that affirming the consequent B in a statement of the form "If A, then B" does nothing toward proving that the antecedent A is true. If an observation occurs as a theory says it should, confidence in the usefulness of the theory increases, despite the illogicality of the increase in confidence. There is a kind of reasonableness in the theoretician's delight when the predictions of a theory are confirmed; the theory, after all, has been demonstrated to be "right" with respect to the observation. If many correct predictions of observations B are made from theory A, then the theory is regarded as successful, even though its correctness can never be logically demonstrated.

Reliance on Observation

Parallel with the use of internal explanation was an increasing reliance on observation. Most of the earlier Greek thinkers relied more on rationalistic methods than is the case in the modern era. For example, Euclid early developed a deductive geometry, and Pythagoras and his followers had a mystic belief in the efficacy of numbers. Socrates and Plato lent support to a rationalistic approach, Socrates with his logical questioning procedure and Plato with his emphasis on the importance of the ideal world, which he regarded as a higher form than the real world. Both questioned the senses as the source of truth and thus helped to turn the tide against what is now regarded as an essential feature of the scientific method: a primary reliance on observation.

Aristotle was one early thinker who used observational as well as rational methods. He was an advocate of logic and reasonableness, but he valued the evidence of the senses over the dictates of logic and the claims of "authorities," for whom he had little respect. His own authority, however, was accepted during the Middle Ages at the expense of observational methods.

Such science as there was during the medieval period was largely in the East. It remained for the Renaissance, beginning (by the most common convention) with Galileo Galilei (1564–1642) and his contemporaries, to renew European interest in natural science. Galileo was instrumental in renewing the scientific attitude toward observation and authority. He relied, for example, upon observation of the time of fall of bodies of unequal weight rather than upon the authoritative statement that heavy bodies fall faster than light ones. This is not to say, however, that Galileo made no use of a rationalistic and deductive approach. Some of Galileo's observations may even have been tainted by his rationally derived expectations, so that they turned out better than they should have.

Pure empiricists and pure rationalists are both as rare as golden fleeces, however hard empiricists or rationalists may try to push the powers of their own methods to their limits. Francis Bacon (1561–1626), in his *Novum organum* of 1620, did try to push empiricism to its limits. He said that science should work strictly by induction, piling observation upon observation until general facts emerge from specific facts. From our objective vantage point, it is clear that Bacon's extreme position was more useful as an antidote against too much rationalism than as a complete description of scientific procedure. Without the intervention of rational human beings, facts do not organize themselves into theories, laws, or Bacon's "general facts" or even make themselves into specific facts. They just lead to confusion. It seems that empiricists like Bacon have to take human rationality for granted, as a kind of implicit assumption which makes empiricism possible.

The English empiricists who came after Bacon tried to follow his approach to its logical conclusion. Locke denied the innate ideas attributed to humans by thinkers like Socrates and Descartes. Berkeley denied that we could be sure of the existence of the external world, since we have only experience to go on. He returned the external world to us only slightly used by assuming that God existed and would not deceive us about the external world. However, his skeptical position was philosophically more convincing than his retreat and has therefore been more influential. Finally, Hume applied empiricistic thinking to the notion of causality and maintained that all we really know about the "causal" connections between events is that some events are invariably contiguous in space and time. Our notion of causality is based on this observation. Chapter 3 discusses this issue further.

Over in the quiet German university town of Königsberg, all this empiricism finally stirred up a tremendous philosophical counterattack. Immanuel Kant was, as he later said, awakened from his dogmatic slumbers by Hume's empiricism. As it turned out, he was stirred into action in time to become one of the greatest philosophers of all time. Although he never in his 80 years of life traveled more than a few miles from his native Königsberg, he embarked upon great voyages of the mind. He believed that the empiricists were right in their claim that knowledge could come only through experience but that their picture was woefully inadequate in that they gave no explanation of how experience itself could be possible. The human mind could not be the *tabula rasa*, the blank sheet, that the empiricists supposed it to be. There had to be organizing principles, or all would be confusion. Kant proposed a compromise theory in which experience remains the teacher but needs a student who already has the ability to organize that experience. Kant's statements about the specific things that are given prior to experience —things like space, time, and unity—are no longer very important. However, the fundamental problem of just what *is* given remains today. Psychologists like Piaget, who try to find out how the mind of the child develops, the ethologists who try to discover how humans and animals organize experience, and the physiological psychologists who try to find out what information is extracted by nerve nets are all working on a modern version of the Kantian problem.

As we have said above, there is no such thing as a purely rationalistic or a purely empiricistic approach, nor is there a clear-cut line of demarcation between the two approaches. Francis Bacon, in his "discarding" of the rationalistic approach, had to use rationalistic methods in his arguments. The most empirically minded, "hardheaded" scientists eventually make general statements based on their observations and hence depend on the rationalistic method. On the other hand, rationalistic philosophers probably use empirical observations as a source of the plausible assumptions with which they begin.

The scientific usefulness of rationalistically derived conclusions depends on their consonance with observations. Although there is no pure approach and no clear method of classifying the techniques of particular individuals as more rationalistic than empirical or vice versa, we believe it is reasonable to say that science relies most on what observationally is, not on what rationally ought to be. Even that statement is an oversimplification, for there is never any final arbiter of truth, and there may be very serious questions about "what is."

Simplification

Thales and Democritus tried to simplify the apparent complexity of nature by appealing to simpler elements and to assumptions which allowed them to derive the observed complexity from the assumed simplicity. Their attempts were also reductionistic, since they reduced complexity by explanations depending on the existence of phenomena at a different, "lower" level; for example, Democritus supposed humans to be built of particles much like those which compose other forms of matter. Physiological psychologists make similar reductionistic statements when behavioral data are explained in terms of physiological events. It does not follow that a reductionistic account will also necessarily be a simple account, or even the simplest available. Reductionistic explanations do at least offer a potential economy of concepts, since a single concept can serve at more than one level of explanation. These economies may serve as the basis for choice between otherwise equivalent theories. Turner (1967) says:

> When we turn to the idea of a hierarchy of explanation, we especially realize that there is a guidance implicit within scientific invention. One seeks not only an explanation of a particular set of events but also a theoretical construction that itself is derivable from within some still more basic science. Chemical explanations, for example, were conceived in terms wholly unique to the phenomenology of chemistry itself. But the advantages and the guidance of atomic constructions are now all too apparent. Geneticists could have continued to think in terms of the gross characteristics of genotypes, but the molecular model of biochemistry offered explanations of the duplicative powers of the genes. And psychology can continue to build hypothetico-deductive models in learning theory, knowing (perhaps unconsciously) that issues of alternative theories will be resolved by developments in neuropsychology. (pp.178–179)

In a later book (1971), Turner continues to favor reductionism but discusses the issues in much greater detail. For example, he considers various alternative routes that might be taken in a reductionistic program: linguistic reduction, in which the concepts at one level are translated into concepts at another; mechanical reduction (through computer simulation); and neurological reduction. Despite all the heroic efforts at reductionism, there is not a single case in which a complex human behavior can be completely explained, using the concepts of neurophysiology. There seems to be little immediate danger that psychologists will be put out of business! We are not unique in this respect; there is no science which is, at this time, completely explained in terms of a more basic science.

However, there are many examples of reductionistic explanations which are dramatically successful within limited areas. One such instance is accounting for the reproduction of living things in terms of molecular genetics. In psychology, partial accounts of behavioral problems (for example, those associated with Down's syndrome) can also be given by referring to genetic structures. We know a great deal about what areas of the brain are associated with language functions, although we do not yet know how any of these areas carry out their functions. We can confidently expect more, and more complete, examples of the success of reductionistic approaches in the future. But reductionism is not the only approach to simplicity; scientists continue to look for simpler laws and theories, whether or not they involve different levels of explanation.

The Place of Humans in Nature

The Greeks regarded human beings as simply part of nature. Many of the Greek philosophers would probably have agreed that human behavior is lawful and predictable, just like the behavior of inanimate natural objects. Philosophers of the Middle Ages, however, took a different view. Human beings were regarded as creatures with a soul, possessed of a free will which set them apart from ordinary natural laws and subject only to their own willfulness and perhaps to the rule of God. Such a creature, being free-willed, could not be an object of scientific investigation.

Even the human body was regarded as sacrosanct. Anatomists had to double as grave robbers, and that made anatomy a highly risky, or very expensive, occupation. The strictures against observation slowed the development of anatomy and medicine for centuries and allowed incredible misconceptions to persist for over a thousand years. A science of psychology could not flourish in such an atmosphere.

René Descartes (1596–1650) started a trend which favored psychological research. He regarded the human body as a machine which moves and behaves in predictable ways if we know what the "inputs" are. A predictable system is a researchable system. Such a view made at least dead (soulless) bodies accessible to scientific investigation; animals, since Descartes regarded them as soulless, were also accessible. He salvaged free will for humans by giving them a soul which was free and which decided the actions of the body.

The idea that human beings might be objects of scientific study was furthered by Julien Offray de la Mettrie (1709–1751). He was convinced, apparently largely by the deterioration of his own thought processes during a fever, that a person was altogether a machine, with both mind and body dependent upon physical events. He espoused this view, despite strong opposition, until his early death from poisoning.

The analogy between human beings and machines, to which Descartes and La

Mettrie contributed, is a good example of the kind of partial analogy which starts persistent controversy. It is clear that human beings are not identical to any existing machine either in their construction or in their mode of operation. Descartes and La Mettrie, both brilliant thinkers, cannot have overlooked this glaring fact. Neither can other mechanistic thinkers. All of them support a limited likeness between the human being and a machine. Human beings construct machines and understand them fairly well; machine behavior can be predicted. Human beings, although neither constructed nor understood by themselves, are like machines in that they are influenced by their construction, and they should in principle be predictable like machines. Critics of the "mechanistic" position attack the complete, unintended analogy of the mechanist as often as the more limited analogy intended.

There was still resistance to viewing humans within a deterministic, natural framework when Charles Darwin (1809–1882) advanced his theory of organic evolution. Evolution itself was not a new idea, but Darwin buttressed the evolutionary theory with so much evidence that it took the scientific community by storm. It restored the continuity between humans and other animals which Descartes had denied when he attributed a soul to humans alone. It also contradicted the biblical account of creation. Theologically based opposition aroused a heated controversy which still persists. Today there is little questioning by scientists of the correctness of the general outlines of evolutionary theory. Evolution is a fact for nearly all of the scientific community, but a few fringe scientists and many people in the lay community continue to fight for equal time in the schools for a creationist account of life on earth.

Acceptance of evolutionary theory has made the science of psychology more acceptable by making it more plausible than ever to view human behavior as lawful. It has also made the study of animals an important part of that science; the assumed continuity between animals and humans supports the belief that knowledge gained in the study of animals will have significance for human behavior.

Let us take a moment to pass the first part of this chapter in review. We have seen that psychology developed late, perhaps because it is complex but also because people tended to see themselves as religious objects, to be subjective, and to think that they knew about humankind by virtue of being human. They also resisted any intrusion into the privacy of their mental processes.

All science tended to develop around the ideas of internal explanation, reliance on observation, and simplification. As humans were placed in the context of nature by virtue of being viewed as more deterministic and as more continuous with other animal forms, it became possible to apply the other scientific ideas to the study of humans as well, and most of the obstacles were cleared from the path that led to psychology. However, an absence of obstacles is not a science. There had to be reasons for starting a new kind of study. Those reasons were provided by the existence of a set of problems, to which we now turn.

SCIENCE AND SPIRITISM

It is instructive to examine a page out of the long book of controversy about "paranormal" phenomena as a test case for the ideas we have just presented about the history of science. The story involves an American connection to Wilhelm Wundt, who is often considered the father of psychology. The incident occurred just when Wundt was preparing his laboratory for its formal launching in 1879, but after he had started it on an informal basis in 1875.

In 1877 a famous medium from the United States, Henry Slade, visited Leipzig (Marshall & Wendt, 1980). Slade's claim to fame was his ability to "receive messages" allegedly written on slate tablets by the spirits of the dead. Slade had confessed to fraud in the United States, and had also been convicted of fraud in an English court a few weeks after arriving in England in 1876. However, that conviction was overturned on a technicality.

Despite the accusations of fraud, Slade came to Leipzig in November 1877. One of Slade's supporters was J. F. C. Zöllner, an astrophysicist who had been instrumental in convincing the authorities at Leipzig that Wundt should receive the call to their university. Zöllner promptly brought Slade to his home as a guest and steadfastly supported him in the controversy that quickly ensued about the legitimacy of Slade's claim to supernormal powers.

All of this put Wundt in a very delicate predicament. He owed much to Zöllner, yet he was unwilling to accept spiritism. William James distinguished between the softheaded and hardheaded attitude toward science (the sheep and the goats), and it is clear that Wundt ran with the goats.

Zöllner wanted to tie spiritism into a scientific framework, and he thought that spirit writing between slates that were tied together in three dimensions was possible if spirits could move in a fourth dimension. It followed that four-dimensional beings could tie knots in a string which was secured at both ends in our three-dimensional space. Slade's "spirits" produced the knots during a seance, as demanded by the theory.

A man named Ulrici heard of these demonstrations and accepted them as validating Slade's spiritism. It was Ulrici's publication of his conclusions that stung Wundt into action. In 1879, he wrote a long reply challenging Ulrici's judgment.

Wundt had attended at least one, and possibly two, of Slade's seances. In his attack on Ulrici, Wundt described one of them, during which Slade had produced spirit writing both in English and in German, the latter, however, in "a defective German as if written by an American or Englishman." Slade had told Wundt that he was himself a medium "of a strong power." Wundt comments wryly, "I myself must say that never in my life have I encountered events which would confirm this diagnosis" (Marshall & Wendt. 1980, p. 162).

The stated reasons for Wundt's rejection of Ulrici's conclusions about Slade were that the authorities to whom Ulrici appealed—among them, Weber and Fechner—were not authorities in the field of spiritism. The appropriate authorities, Wundt said, are other mediums. He said that Ulrici should have become expert in prestidigitation (sleight of hand) before he allowed himself to conclude that Slade was not producing his results through trickery. Scientists might be unusually poor observers in such a situation, Wundt argued, because they are used to trusting their subjects, and the possibility of deceit is not something they usually need to consider. But that is the very issue in evaluating spiritism.

Wundt also mentioned in his description of the seance that Slade would not allow an observer outside the circle of people directly involved in the seance. Slade explained that the spirits did not respond under these conditions. Thus we see not just an absence of control in the observations, but an impaired ability to make adequate objective observations of the events in question.

Wundt said that hearsay evidence should not be accepted unless the observer was a trustworthy master *of the field in question*. Furthermore, the reported observation should not contradict other firmly grounded facts. He knew of no example in science in which a new fact was completely contrary to all natural laws. A belief in spiritism required abandonment of the very laws of causality.

Beyond his serious arguments, Wundt allowed himself to have a bit of fun. He asked what one would conclude about the dead if Slade were correct. Well, said Wundt, "We must conclude that the souls of the dead are slaves to living men, mostly Americans, who permit spirits to carry out only silly tasks like clapping, knocking, and lifting tables. The souls of the dead are *intellectually* pitiable, judging from the content of the slate messages which are composed of higher and lower nonsense, mostly lower" (Marshall & Wendt, 1980).

Zusne and Jones (1982) provide a quotation from David Hume (1776) which sums up Wundt's attitude. Hume said "The knavery and folly of men are such a common phenomenon that I should rather believe the most extraordinary events to arise from their concurrence, than admit of a single violation of the laws of nature." (p. 362)

Thus the study of the kinds of claims that now fall into the province of parapsychology precedes and follows the existence of psychology as a formal science. Zusne and Jones trace a good part of this history, which seems prone to repeat itself, with variations, from generation to generation. Uri Geller has replaced Henry Slade, and spiritism is less popular than other forms of parapsychology.

If Wundt had accepted the claims of Slade, he would have been rejecting some of the ideas which, we claim, were necessary prerequisites if psychology were to become a science. One idea was accepted by those who supported spiritism, as well as by those who opposed it: truth is determined by observation. If observations conclusively demonstrated the existence of spiritism, then existing scientific laws would simply not apply to it. The laws, not the observations, would have to be overthrown. And if the laws of causality are overthrown, then there is little prospect that the behavior of human beings will be lawful. However, it is difficult to convince scientists of the validity of observations not made under controlled conditions. It seems to the skeptic all too convenient that the phenomena of parapsychology so often are said to disappear exactly when the key method of science appears: when observations are made under controlled conditions.

In his rejection of spiritism, Wundt demonstrated his acceptance of the ideas which underlie science and which made possible the emergence of psychology as a science. Let us turn to that legacy of problems to which Wundt and others applied the methods of the new science.

PSYCHOLOGY'S LEGACY OF PROBLEMS

Psychology inherited most of its problems from philosophy and physiology; for that reason it is often said that philosophy was the mother of psychology and physiology the father, or vice versa. Some of the problems passed on to psychology were of such a nature that no immediate scientific resolution was possible, but research was stimulated as scientists tried to find the answers to these elusive questions. We shall consider four problem areas: the mind-body problem, the physiology of perception, the reaction-time problem, and questions related to individual differences.

The Mind-Body Problem

The ghostly apparitions of dreams may have convinced people that there was more to human beings than met the physical eye. The writing of Plato shows that the thinking of his time divided humans into two components. Descartes's dualistic views did not differ greatly from Plato's. Most philosophers concede that both systems can be reconciled, sometimes with some forcing, into Christian theology, which also split man into two components, body and soul. Kantor (1963) reviews the evidence that Plato should not be construed in this dualistic way. In any case, some unobservable component is necessary if human immortality is logically to be maintained, since the observable portions of human beings are mortal.

If a person has both a mind and a body, then the question naturally arises, "What is the relationship between the two parts?" A long tradition of thought made the question inevitable. Before psychology ever had a formal beginning as a science, a German physicist, Gustav Theodor Fechner (1801–1887), started work on the problem. It was his intention to write equations that described the functional relationships between the psychic and physical realms. The result which he believed he found is the Weber-Fechner law, so named because E. H. Weber had already expressed much the same psychophysical relationship in a simpler, more primitive form. Boring (1950, p. 483) has questioned whether Fechner really intended to take a dualistic position, but certainly his problem was stated in dualistic terms. For example, in his *Elemente der Psychophysik* (1860), Fechner said he was concerned with "the exact science of the functional relations or relations of dependency between body and mind." In order to demonstrate these functional relations, it is necessary to have two separate things to measure. Fechner thought he was measuring two different things: On the one side he had the stimulus which acted on the body; on the other side he had the sensation, which he thought of as a mental event. Fechner wished to demonstrate the identity of the two kinds of events, but it was difficult to reunite the two aspects which had been separated by assumption. He wanted to demonstrate empirically an identity that philosophers, using rationalistic methods, had been alternately proving and disproving for hundreds of years.

The major mind-body positions that have been taken by philosophers are classified and summarized in Table 2-2. It would be wise to adopt a certain amount of skepticism about our classification; it is not always clear that the different positions are really different or that we have made the correct decisions about where a given philosopher should be placed. For example, psychophysical parallelism is supposed to assume two separate underlying kinds of reality, while the double-aspect view is supposed to assume two "processes" which are both aspects of one underlying reality. But what if a philosopher is not certain whether the two processes are different enough to "prove" the existence of two kinds of reality? We have already admitted that Fechner's position

TABLE 2-2
MAJOR PHILOSOPHICAL SOLUTIONS TO THE MIND-BODY PROBLEM
(An early important exponent of each position is identified in parentheses, with the approximate date of his contributions.)

Dualism*	
Cartesian interactionism (Descartes, 1641)	Two separate and interacting processes assumed
Psychophysical parallelism (Spinoza, 1665)	Two separate, independent, but perfectly correlated processes assumed
Occasionalism (Malebranche, 1675)	Two separate and independent processes assumed; correlated by the intervention of God

Monism†	
Materialism (Democritus, 400 B.C.)	A single underlying physical reality assumed
Subjective idealism (Berkeley, 1710)	A single underlying mental or spiritual reality assumed
Phenomenalism (Hume, 1740)	There are neither minds nor bodies as far as can be known; only ideas resulting from sense impressions exist

Compromises	
Double-aspect view (Russell, 1915)	Two processes assumed to be a function of one underlying reality
Epiphenomenalism (Hobbes, 1658)	Mind assumed to be a noncausal by-product of body

*Any point of view implying a basic difference between mind and body and therefore a relationship to be explained.
†Any point of view ignoring either mind or body or subsuming both under the same rubric.

is not clear. Furthermore, another of psychology's historians, Sahakian (1975), says that Spinoza did not assume two separate and independent realities. Some commentators have classified Wundt as a parallelist, while others claim him for dual-aspect theory.

Although not all solutions are as confusing as parallelism and dual-aspect theory, it is probably best to regard our scheme as a set of logical possibilities into which individual solutions may fit with more or less forcing. The scheme is not even exhaustive; who decreed that there were only two realities? What if there were material things, unconscious mind, and conscious mind, in all sorts of possible relationships? It might suit the fancy of some to add superconsciousness, or an immortal soul. Such positions, with more than two kinds of reality, would be called pluralisms.

There is, in any case, no known scientific method for deciding among the suggested solutions to the mind-body problem. Early psychologists nevertheless felt it necessary to take some stand on the problem. Then for several decades it became fashionable to reject the problem as meaningless. Philosophers and psychologists alike repeatedly "proved" that the question was nonsensical in the first place. However, it is not easy to dismiss a question which has so titillated the curiosity of humankind for at least 25 centuries. We are seldom satisfied when someone answers our questions with, "That's a poor question; ask me another." Today, whether it is meaningless or meaningful, soluble or insoluble, the mind-body problem is coming back into the consciousness of psychologists. The word *mind,* which was virtually taboo between about 1920 and 1950 in many circles, has come back into the psychological vocabulary so much that it is almost a buzzword. We shall return to the mind-body problem repeatedly in the later chapters; here let us merely remember that the problem was bequeathed to us in the beginning by philosophy.

The Psychology of Perception

Other scientists, notably physiologists, were interested in another relationship, that between physiological processes and perception. The German physiologist Hermann Ludwig Ferdinand von Helmholtz (1821–1894) is the most famous of those interested in this relationship; he adopted Thomas Young's (1773–1829) color theory and developed his own theory of hearing. Helmholtz, along with the English empiricists, believed that all knowledge depends upon sensory experience. If this is our assumption, then the problem of sensory physiology is also the problem of epistemology—the problem of the origins, nature, and limitations of knowledge. Physiological findings then have philosophical implications.

Helmholtz tried to refute Kant's statement that there is innate knowledge. Kant believed that the axioms of geometry were known independently of any experience of them. Helmholtz asked whether we would have developed the same geometry if we had inhabited the inside surface of a hollow sphere. His belief was that different axioms would have been demanded by different experiences.

If the views of Helmholtz and Kant are viewed only in broad outline, however, the two differ less than they may have thought. Although Kant is categorized with nativists and Helmholtz with empiricists, Kant did admit the role of experience. Helmholtz recognized the need for some basic mental faculties to exist in order that the mind be able to develop the concept of space out of the raw materials of experience. There is, of course, a considerable difference in emphasis. Empiricists, by virtue of their philosophy, want to observe and thus want observable things to be as important as possible. The nativist tends to be a rationalist, and it is convenient for rationalists if the uncertain stuff of experience can be assigned as small a role as possible.

It is easier to see the relationship between the philosophical questions of epistemology and the psychological and physiological problems of perception if we pretend for a moment that we are philosophers. We will then want to ask the question: "What kind of knowledge-gathering machine is a human being?" Or alternatively, "What information-gathering equipment does a human being have, and how does it work?" The answers to such questions had to come from a study of the special senses. As in the case of the mind-body problem, we are still seeking the answers, but the workings of the special senses are open to empirical observation, and the answers are coming.

The Reaction-Time Problem

The new science of psychology took over a second problem with epistemological implications. F. W. Bessel, an astronomer, read about an unfortunate incident which had occurred at Greenwich Observatory in 1796 (see Boring, 1950). An assistant's readings did not agree with the readings made by the head astronomer. Maskelyne, the boss, fired Kinnebrook, the assistant. Bessel, some 20 years after the event, realized that the incident might involve a mystery as well as a misfortune. Seeing a mystery lying under your nose is virtually the hallmark of the great scientist. Bessel saw that the error might have been caused by a difference in the time required for two different observers to react to information presented to different senses—for the readings were complex, and the observer had to coordinate a sound with the movement of a celestial body past a marker.

Bessel checked his hunch by comparing the times at which he recorded star transits with the times at which other astronomers under the same conditions recorded them. There were discrepancies in nearly all cases. Bessel then tried to write "personal equations," or correction terms, which would reduce all the readings to a common basis. However, it was obvious that there could be no absolute standard of correctness where the human observer was concerned. Our knowledge was once again shown to depend upon observers and their methods of observing and recording. If the determination of the time at which a star crosses a line is subject to error, then it seems logical that more complex judgments and observations must be even more subject to error. The philosophical point, however, did not provide the sense of urgency; it was the fact that the theoretical problems of epistemology were shown to be real, practical problems that stimulated Bessel and others after him to action. One can well imagine the difference in effect between the philosophers' general lament that one cannot be certain of anything and the astronomers' panic because nobody's readings agreed with anyone else's!

Donders, a Dutch physiologist, and his students developed this general problem. They assumed that complex tasks were made up of a set of simpler components. If the simple operations are carried out one after another, the time for a complex task is the sum of the times for the simpler operations which make up the complex task. The times for a whole set of simple operations could be established by subtracting the times for simpler tasks from those for more complex tasks. For example, Donders asked subjects to respond as quickly as possible with a single response to a single stimulus. Then he asked them to perform a more complex task: to respond in one way to one stimulus and in another way to a second stimulus. He assumed that the second task required the same operations as the first, plus the operation of "choice." Thus the time for choice could be obtained by subtracting the time for the simpler reaction from that for the more complex reaction.

When Wundt established the first laboratory of psychology, he took over this subtractive procedure. Like Donders, he hoped to use a whole hierarchy of tasks varying in complexity and thereby to discover the time required for the mental operations of sensing, perceiving, discriminating, and the like. Although he sometimes differed from Donders in his beliefs about which operations were included in a complex task, he did not question the assumption that complex tasks are performed via a sequence of simpler operations. Few psychologists would still hold this view. It is not clear that perceiving simply involves sensing *plus* something else. The whole nature of the process may change as the task is progressively complicated, or "elementary" operations may be carried out in parallel. The subtractive procedure becomes, in either case, invalid. Nevertheless, S. Sternberg (1966a,b) and others have used procedures highly reminiscent of the subtractive procedure to great advantage in a host of recent experiments (see Chapter 13).

Individual Differences

Two fields of study that have remained extremely important up to the present day are individual differences and statistics, the latter initially taken over and developed by psychology as a method for studying these differences. Much of the American acceptance of psychology may be attributed to the effectiveness of aptitude testing, which is part of the study of individual differences.

Sir Francis Galton (1822–1911) pioneered both in the development of statistics and in the study of individual differences. He developed the technique of correlation in connection with his inheritance studies. He was led to it by the observation that children typically regress toward the mean relative to their parents in such characteristics as height and intelligence; that is, children of extremely tall or short, or bright or stupid, parents tend to be closer to the norm in these characteristics than their parents. Correlation is symbolized by r because of its development in association with the phenomenon of regression.

The major factor underlying the development of Galton's interests was the Darwinian theory of evolution. Galton, who was Darwin's cousin, was interested in a practical problem: the improvement of the race through eugenics. In order to manipulate heredity, he needed to know how traits were inherited. This type of practical concern was in the direct line of conceptual descent that led from evolution to American functionalism. Stress on the organism's adjustment to the environment as a determining condition of survival or nonsurvival became a primary concern of psychology. The intellectual ferment produced by the theory of evolution raised questions that led directly to Galton's interest in individual differences, to mental testing and the statistical evaluation of differences, and to the flourishing of functionalism in the United States.

The theory of evolution also had implications for people's views of the philosophical controversy between rationalism and empiricism. Previously, most rationalists had had to buttress their positions by postulating some kind of far-fetched preestablished harmony between the constituion of the world and the human being's ideas about it. How could it happen that people possess correct innate ideas about the world in which they live? It is not intellectually satisfying to explain by saying that God gives ideas to humans. One would still want to know just how that was managed. The evolutionary point of view suggested that the rational side of the human being was molded into harmony with the world by the pressures of evolution. We can, according to this argument, count on the outcomes of rational analysis because humans, through evolution, have come to think the right things about the world. If thought has implications for action, then people who were mistaken about the world presumably took the wrong courses of action and failed to reproduce their genes. Those who were "rational" passed on their genes, and thus a tendency to think correct thoughts, to their progeny. In this way, evolution solidifies the effects of the world on humans into a kind of physiological rationalism.

PSYCHOLOGY'S INITIAL SUBJECT MATTER

Wilhelm Wundt was a physiologist with a medical degree. He had been trained in a strong scientific tradition, partly as an assistant to one of the world's greatest scientists, Helmholtz. Considering this personal background and the problems we have been discussing, one would expect that Wundt's laboratory would study problems of epistemology, reaction time, and sensation and perception, use experimental techniques in approaching all of these problems, and top everything off with a double helping of physiology. The only real surprise is with the topping: Wundt called his psychology an experimental physiological psychology, but there was almost no significant physiological experimentation. Watson (1963, p. 249; 1971, pp. 275–276) noted that Wundt did monitor pulse and breathing rates in studies of feeling; however, such measures did not play a critical role in Wundt's system.

Perhaps psychology felt the need of physiology in the beginning primarily for its prestige. Physics and mathematics have often been invoked by psychologists for similar reasons, and controversies have raged about whether the alleged dependence of psychology on the better-established disciplines is good or bad. In any case, Wundt seems to have done well by pointing to a presumed continuity with physiology, while he worked on problems so different that there was no doubt that psychology was an independent discipline.

Wundt was able to justify avoiding physiological experimentation because of his philosophical position on the mind-body problem. He believed that the mind and body run parallel courses and that one cannot say that bodily events cause mental events; external events simply give rise to certain bodily processes and, at the same time, to parallel mental processes. He thought that the primary task of psychology was to discover the elementary conscious processes, the manner of their connection, and the laws determining their connection. Since mind and body are parallel, the simplest way to do this, in Wundt's opinion, was to make a direct study of the mental events through the method of introspection. Psychology might later turn to the question of just what bodily processes accompany given mental processes, but that problem was secondary. This aspect of Wundt's thought has a modern parallel. Skinner, among others, has insisted that the *direct* study of *behavior* is more likely to be profitable than the attempt to relate it to physiological processes.

Wundt thus brought a kind of dualism to psychology. He also brought a strong belief in the experimental method. His research was laboratory inspection, not armchair introspection. He intended to rule metaphysical speculation out of psychology. He was constantly looking for experimental ways to attack mental processes. Wundt's experimentalism implied that he had accepted certain ideas which had developed within science and had to be accepted before a science of psychology could become a reality: the necessity for internal explanation, the reliance on observation, and the placement of the human being within the realm of the scientifically knowable. His search for the elements of consciousness also showed his scientific preference for simplicity.

The Leipzig laboratory, officially founded in 1879, also took over many of the specific problems that were waiting for psychology. The reaction-time problem has already been mentioned. Problems in sensation and perception were taken over from Helmholtz, Fechner, and others.

There was less at Leipzig to remind one of psychology's predecessors on the other side of the channel. Only through a brash American student, James McKeen Cattell, did the Leipzig laboratory turn out any work on Galton's problem of individual differences. Wundt, with prophetic accuracy, called Cattell's interest *ganz amerikanisch* (entirely, or typically, American). It has indeed turned out to be America's armies, schools, and industries that have placed the greatest emphasis on testing individuals for most efficient placement.

SUMMARY AND CONCLUSIONS

Several scientific ideas had to develop within science before psychology could emerge: that explanation of an event should be sought within the same system as the one within which the event occurred, that observation is the arbiter of scientific truth, and that human beings are part of the natural order. It follows that human behavior can be studied scientifically to determine the laws governing it.

Certain problems were bequeathed to psychology because of its immediate prehistory within science and philosophy. Among them were relating the mental and physical aspects of the human being, explaining the physiology of perception and the contents of perception, determining the basis for the "personal equation," and analyzing individual differences and heredity.

In this context, Wilhelm Wundt founded the first formal laboratory of psychology at the University of Leipzig in 1879. Although Wundt took over all of the problems mentioned above, he paid less attention to physiology than might have been expected. He had a powerful, even extreme, bias in the direction of experimentation, and he set out to apply that method to the analysis of consciousness.

FURTHER READINGS

The following books are classic works on the general history of science: Conant's *On understanding science: A historical approach* (1947) and *Harvard case histories in experimental science* (1957); Butterfield's *The origins of modern science: 1300–1800* (1957); and Sarton's *A guide to the history of science* (1952). Boring's *A history of experimental psychology* (1950) and Watson's *The great psychologists from Aristotle to Freud* (3rd ed, 1971) are highly recommended as sources of information about the history of psychology; however, so many good books have appeared and are appearing that the best advice may be to browse through the library shelves in the primary areas where history of psychology is found and see what looks particularly congenial or provocative. The many volumes of *History of psychology in autobiography,* which started to appear in 1930 and continue to appear periodically, are very interesting, in addition to providing valuable insights about how careers in psychology are made. Herrnstein and Boring's *A source book in the history of psychology* (1965) provides selected classics from the time of Aristotle up to the time of McDougall for students who like their history firsthand. Hillix and Marx (1974) in *Systems and theories in psychology: A reader* provide original readings coordinated with the present text, along with brief biographies for each of the men represented there. Chapter 2 of Ludy Benjamin's *Teaching history of psychology: A handbook* is a review of a variety of sources, including biographical sources, general sources, and journals publishing research in the field. It is therefore a "key to the library" for those wanting more information. The Marshall and Wendt chapter "Wilhelm Wundt, spiritism, and the assumptions of science" is a fascinating account of Wundt's involvement in the Slade incident; it appears in *Wundt studies,* the 1980 book edited by Bringmann and Tweney. In their *Anomalistic psychology* (1982) Zusne and Jones treat parapsychological research at much greater length, along with other peculiar phenomena, many of which are fascinating to a very wide audience.

ASSOCIATIONISM

Although Wundt founded the first recognized psychological laboratory, associationism developed earlier as a philosophy and as an identifiable psychological position. Many of its principles were used directly or in modified form by later schools, including Wundt's. Even Freudian psychoanalysis, which is in many ways so different from associationism, uses free association as one of its key methods. Thus there is a sense in which associationism precedes Wundt's structuralism both *chronologically* and *intellectually*. We shall therefore take associationism as our first system for discussion.

Associationism is really more a principle than a school of psychology. The principle of association derives from epistemological questions within philosophy. The epistemological question "How do we know?" is answered by empiricist philosophers, "Through the senses." Immediately the next question arises: "Then where do our complex ideas come from, since they are not directly sensed?" The answer to this second question gives the first principle of association: "Complex ideas come from the association of simpler ideas."

Since associationism thus has its roots in philosophy, its history extends back into antiquity. Table 3-1 lists the names of the most important figures in this tradition; note that we list Aristotle as our first associationist. The influence of associationism continues right up to today, and some of its guiding principles survive almost unchanged.

The British empiricists, although they were philosophers rather than psychologists, were as close to forming an associationistic "school" as any group. Their attempt to explain mental activity led to the statement of the several factors important in establishing associations. In our description of the development of British empiricism, we shall attempt to show the continuity of thinking in which empiricism and associationism were fused. Although these philosophers were concerned more with epistemological than with psychological problems, they anticipated later psychological developments in their attempts to apply the results of empirical observation to the solution of philosophical problems.

TABLE 3-1
IMPORTANT FIGURES IN ASSOCIATIONAL PSYCHOLOGY

Antecedent influences	Associationists		Contemporary representatives
	Founder	Developers	
Aristotle (384–322 B.C.)	David Hartley (1705–1757)	Thomas Brown (1778–1820)	William K. Estes, (1919–)
		James Mill (1773–1836)	
Thomas Hobbes (1588–1679)		John S. Mill (1806–1873)	
John Locke (1632–1704)		Alexander Bain (1818–1903)	
George Berkeley (1685–1753)		Hermann Ebbinghaus (1850–1909)	
David Hume (1711–1776)		Ivan P. Pavlov (1849–1936)	
		Vladimir M. Bekhterev (1857–1927)	
		Edward L. Thorndike (1874–1949)	
		Edwin R. Guthrie (1886–1959)	

Bishop George Berkeley (1685–1753), British empiricist philosopher.

Edward Lee Thorndike (1874–1949) American psychologist whose studies of instrumental conditioning were a prototype of associationism.

Historically, associationistic concepts have served as substitutes for more detailed learning theories. Three men stand out as the greatest contributors to this aspect of the associationistic movement.

Hermann Ebbinghaus caused a profound shift in the application of associationistic principles. Prior to his studies on the learning and forgetting of nonsense syllables, the tendency had been to begin with the associations already formed and attempt to infer backward to the process of formation. Ebbinghaus began at the beginning by studying the formation of the associations; it was thus possible for him to control the conditions under which the associations were formed and to make the study of learning scientific. He could then turn to the study of memory, secure in his knowledge of when and how the associations under study had been formed.

The second man, I. P. Pavlov, the great Russian physiologist, has primary responsibility for shifting the kind of association studied to S-R connections rather than ideas. His research on the conditioned reflex helped to objectify psychology.

The third contributor, E. L. Thorndike, developed an extensive account of psychological phenomena along associationistic lines. We shall treat his system most fully as the representative of associationism.

It is difficult to single out modern associationistic systematists, since they do not belong to any cohesive school. One is considered an associationist to the extent that one uses associationistic principles; but associationistic principles pervade recent and contemporary psychology, so we must select "associationists" according to their tendency to treat associationistic principles as primary.

BRITISH EMPIRICISM

The British empiricists used the same principles of association that had been suggested centuries before by Aristotle. He had suggested that items which are similar or opposite or contiguous tend to be associated with one another. The last principle, contiguity, comes closest to winning universal acceptance: If two things are experienced closely in time, they are likely to be associated. Similarity and contrast are accepted by some and rejected by others. The only principle of association added to Aristotle's list by the British empiricists was the principle of causality suggested by Berkeley and treated at length by Hume.

Table 3-2 summarizes the principles of association accepted by the most important figures within the associationistic movement. The first major figure in the associationistic tradition after Aristotle, Thomas Hobbes (1588–1679) was a political philosopher who helped to found British empiricism. He saw reason as the dominant guiding factor in human behavior; however, he took a strongly deterministic, mechanical view. Mental content was accounted for by recourse to sensory data only, eliminating the need for innate ideas as an explanation. The lawful succession of ideas was held to be responsible for all thought and action. Hobbes accounted for this succession in terms of association by contiguity. If an idea had previously been followed by another idea, it would tend to lead to the contiguous idea.

John Locke (1632–1704) reputedly "invented" an associationistic position independently of Hobbes, and he is usually regarded as the founder of British empiricism

TABLE 3-2
PRINCIPLES OF ASSOCIATIONISM

Author	Date	Principles			
		Contiguity	Similarity	Contrast	Causality
Aristotle	ca. 330 B.C.	X	X	X	
Thomas Hobbes	1651	X			
John Locke	1700	X	X		
George Berkeley	1733	X	X		
David Hume	1739	X	X		X
David Hartley	1749	X			
James Mill	1829	X			
John Stuart Mill	1843	X	X		
Alexander Bain	1855	X	X		
Herbert Spencer	1855	X	X		

because his position was clearer and more complete (see Boring, 1950, p. 169). We will see that the "founder" of a school or the "inventor" of an idea is frequently not the first person to have had a relevant inspiration, but the first person who does a thorough and attention-getting job with that inspiration.

Locke spent the early years of his adult life in politics, notably as the private secretary of the man who became the Earl of Shaftesbury. The Earl went alternately into and out of power, and so of course did Locke. That was not a propitious beginning for a philosopher. Locke's great book, *An essay concerning human understanding*, did not appear until 1690, when he was 57. It might never have appeared had not the Earl fallen completely from favor and died in exile in 1675; history would then have had little to say about a lifelong private secretary to an earl.

Locke's main concern in his *Essay* was the validity of knowledge. He said that all knowledge comes from experience, either through the senses or through reflection on sensory data. This extreme empiricism, denying any innate knowledge, was a return to the Aristotelian notion of the tabula rasa. This blank tablet was a symbol for the blank infant mind, on which sensory experience was presumed to be recorded. As such, it represented an attack on Descartes' belief in innate ideas.

Locke's ideas on association were also similar to Aristotle's. He added a chapter entitled "Of the association of ideas" to the fourth edition of the *Essay*, in which he pointed out that ideas are combined in experience according to principles very much like those of similarity and contiguity. However, his emphasis on association was not great, and he certainly did not stress it as a universal principle underlying the connection of ideas. He believed that ideas are ordinarily tied together by "natural" connections, and he clearly implied that associationistic principles are useful primarily for the explanation of abnormal connections.

Locke's intimations on the nature of associations led to subsequent formulations by Berkeley, Hume, and Mill. Berkeley made association more inclusive in scope; Hume characterized it as a "gentle force"; and James Mill made it into an inexorable principle of connection. Within the tradition of associationism the human mind started out free except for a little accidental determination, with Locke, and ended up completely determined, with Mill.

Locke also started a trend with his special theory of primary and secondary qualities, which he thought were the basis for sensory "ideas." According to this dichotomy, primary properties are those which inhere in bodies. They offer the main avenue between the mind and the external world. Properties such as solidity, figure (shape), motion, and number are representative of this category. Secondary properties, such as colors, sounds, and tastes, were said not to belong to objects but were instead considered functions of the mind itself. This distinction was soon destroyed by Berkeley but reappeared as the problem of distinguishing between psychology and physics. As we shall see later, Wundt made this distinction by saying that physics studies mediate experience while psychology studies immediate experience. Titchener, who brought Wundtian psychology to America, said that physics studies experience as independent of the experiencing organism, while psychology studies experience as dependent on the experiencing organism. The three men were all making a very similar point; each was dealing with the contribution of the experiencer to the experience from his own perspective.

George Berkeley (1685–1753) was Locke's intellectual successor. Although he was born 53 years later than Locke, his most important philosophical work appeared only 20 years after Locke's; Berkeley published his *An essay toward a new theory of vision* (1709) and *Principles of human knowledge* (1710) when he was about 25.

Berkeley wondered patronizingly how Locke could have seen so much when he was so old. As a matter of fact, Locke had been working on his problem for 20 years before he published, so perhaps he was not so very old while he was developing his position.

We should not leave the impression, because of Berkeley's comments on Locke's age as contrasted with his own precocity, that Berkeley was nothing but a brash and brilliant young man. Berkeley had a powerful religious and social sensibility. He wanted to found a university in the New World, and he was promised the money to do so by George II. As a consequence of this, Berkeley came to this side of the Atlantic and spent three years in Newport, Rhode Island. Because George II never came through with the money to found the planned university in Bermuda, Berkeley's time was wasted, as far as his original plans were concerned. Berkeley then returned to England until 1834, when he became Bishop of Cloyne in County Cork in Ireland.

Americans nevertheless benefited from his brief stay in the United States; Berkeley left his American home and land to Yale, and his books to Harvard. We honor his efforts in this country through the name of the city of Berkeley, California and the university, which, somewhat ironically, is one of the greatest universities in the New World, the kind of university which Berkeley did not manage to found in Bermuda.

Philosophically, Berkeley was a subjective idealist. For him, mind was the ultimate reality. This position is represented by the famous Latin phrase *esse est percipi* (to be is to be perceived). For Berkeley the main problem was not the relation of mind to matter (Descartes) or how matter generates mind (Locke), but how mind generates matter. The first question was how mind could generate a *belief* in matter, since the existence of matter could not be conclusively demonstrated. One could know only one's own mental contents.

All of this was consistent with, and probably motivated by, Berkeley's religious convictions. It would have pleased him to undermine materialism and atheism and to support religious belief. However, the logical consequence of his position is solipsism (the belief that there is only one mind, one's own, in which all else, including other minds, exists only as ideas). Thus an unreconstructed subjective idealism is a poor foundation for belief in anything beyond oneself.

Berkeley was an active and ingenious psychological thinker. He used tactile and kinesthetic sensations to break down the distinction Locke had made between primary and secondary qualities. Berkeley pointed out that the alleged primary qualities are really also functions of perception. Nothing can be known without the mediation of the senses, even motion or solidity. This argument is congruent with Berkeley's philosophical idealism. He believed that visual depth perception depends upon experience. He stressed tactile and kinesthetic sensations and their association with ocular movements in looking at near and far objects; this complex association then became "depth." Such reasoning was a specific psychological attempt to answer the general philosophical question of how mind generates matter. It shows Berkeley inverting the materialistic practice of taking the external world for granted and asking how we come to know about it. Berkeley regarded the data of consciousness as beyond doubt, and the problem was to account for complex ideas, like those of space and external objects.

In line with his theological background, Berkeley attempted to explain the stability, independence, and order of external objects by bringing in the all-perceiving mind of God. His metaphysical position is humorously presented in the following limerick (quoted in Russell, 1945, p. 648, and attributed to Ronald Knox):

There was a young man who said, God
Must think it exceedingly odd
If he finds that this tree
Continues to be
When there's no one about in the Quad.

Reply

Dear Sir:

Your astonishment's odd:
I am always about in the Quad.
And that's why the tree
Will continue to be,
Since observed by
Yours faithfully,
God.

David Hume (1711–1776), the next great British empiricist, was, like Berkeley, brilliantly precocious. His *A treatise on human nature* (1886; first published 1739–1740), on which his reputation was mainly based, appeared in three volumes when Hume was 28 and 29. Unlike Berkeley, Hume seems never to have become too concerned with the welfare of others; he was too busy seeking fame for himself. He never received an adequate measure of fame, according to his own high standards in such matters, until after the publication of his *History of England* (1748), which was phenomenally successful.

While Hume may have been irritating as a person, he was even more irritating as a philosopher. It was his skepticism about the existence of the external world that stimulated the caustic Samuel Johnson (1709–1784) to a famous nonverbal refutation. Boswell reports that he once asked Johnson how he could refute Hume's position on the existence of the external world. Johnson said, "I refute it thus," and kicked a rock. Opinions vary about the adequacy of Johnson's answer, but nobody denies that it makes a good story.

In his writing, Hume made a distinction between more vivid *impressions* (what we would call sensations or perceptions) and less vivid *ideas* (what we would call images or recollections). We will see that a similar distinction was made by Wundt and the structuralists when they began their "analysis of the mind." Their application of introspection to complex mental processes had an easy compatibility with the empiricistic and associationistic tradition. The epistemological question of the empiricist philosophers, "Where do complex ideas come from?" was attacked directly by the structuralists through introspection.

Hume also applied his analytic skill to one of the three principles of association he "discovered," the principle of cause and effect. He found that this principle was closely related to the principle of contiguity and that cause and effect did indeed come into being as an idea only if the cause had been contiguous with the effect. In addition, the cause invariably had to be followed by the effect.

Superficially, it seems that Hume reduced cause and effect to contiguity via his analysis, but the case is not simple. N. K. Smith (1949), who made a thorough study of Hume's position, concludes that Hume believed that the principle of cause and effect retained its independence despite its close relationship to temporal and spatial contiguity. However, cause and effect were not to be found existing in the things observed, but only in the mind of the observer. Since Hume did not believe that the existence of the external world could be demonstrated, the fact that causality did not exist there cannot be used as an argument against its independent existence.

Cause and effect, then, might seem to be a complex idea, one which might have been reduced to simpler ideas had Hume been so inclined. This view, too, is mistaken. Turner (1967) says of Hume's position: "We find, then, that *causation, resemblance, and contiguity* are the relations by which we associate ideas. As such, these relations have no existential significance; they represent activities of the imagination, and not ideas reducible in any way to impressions" (p. 34). One must conclude that Hume retained three distinct principles of association.

Finally, Hume's skeptical and antimetaphysical biases have been enormously influential. His famous paragraph from *An enquiry concerning human understanding* (1748/1902) reads:

When we run over libraries, persuaded of these principles, what havoc must we make? If we take in our hand any volume; of divinity or school metaphysics, for instance; let us ask, *Does It Contain Any Abstract Reasoning Concerning Quantity or Number?* No. *Does It Contain Any Experimental Reasoning Concerning Matter of Fact and Existence?* No. Commit it then to the flames; for it can contain nothing but sophistry and illusion. (p. 165)

Hume's viewpoint in this quotation is similar to that of modern positivism and operationism, which have also tried to rid science of metaphysics.

ASSOCIATIONISM AS A SYSTEMATIC DOCTRINE

Associationism as a system growing out of empiricism was "founded" in the eighteenth century by a scholarly physician, David Hartley (1705–1757). He took Locke's chapter title "The association of ideas" and made it his thesis. Hartley developed his psychology around associations, thus making associationism, for the first time, a formal doctrine with a name.

In contrast with the earlier politically active philosophers like Hobbes and Locke, Hartley led a relatively unexciting, orderly, and leisurely life. His single major publication was *Observations on man, his duty, and his expectations* (1749). He was much influenced by Newton and Locke. His conceptualization was similar to earlier, less elaborated speculation by Hobbes which used motion as an explanatory concept in brain activity; Hartley postulated vibratory actions within the nervous system corresponding to ideas and images. More intense vibrations were sensations, and less intense vibrations were ideas.

Hartley thus gave a physiological interpretation to Hume's distinction between impression and idea. He was a thoroughgoing mechanist in the spirit of Newton, and all of mental life was to be accounted for in terms of physical vibrations and their associations with one another. In this respect, Hartley furthered the development of an analytic, mechanistic, and reductionistic psychology; we have come to think of these tendencies as typical of the associationistic approach.

Since vibrations take a little while to die out, sensations persist after removal of the stimulus. Hartley offered his vibrations and their persisting "vibratiuncles" as a substitute for the then-current view of flow of animal spirits in tubular nerves. Contiguity was stressed as the principle of association, and associationistic principles were used to explain the details of visual depth perception as well as diverse other phenomena, such as emotional pleasure and pain and the meaning of words.

The next important development in associationism was produced by Thomas Brown (1778–1820) in Scotland. Brown rephrased Hartley's principles as principles of suggestion. This was a maneuver to get around the objections of his predecessors in the orthodox Scottish school to associationism and its analytic tendencies. Brown's predecessors were Thomas Reid (1710–1796) and Dugald Stewart (1753–1828), and their religious beliefs would not allow them to accept the skeptical and mechanistic explanations of a Hume or Hartley. However, there was little real difference between what Brown was saying and what the British empiricists had been saying about the basic principles of mental activity.

Brown is notable because of his emphasis on secondary principles of association. He was concerned with the problem of the selection, in a train of ideas, of the single idea that actually occurred when there were several that might occur. In this sense, he was interested in the problem of improving prediction. He presented several factors that might account for the selection of a particular idea: the number of times it had been associated with the preceding mental content, how recently the association had previously occurred, the vividness of the original idea, its duration, and the number of other ideas now present which had connections with the idea and thus added to its associative strength. Analogs to several of Brown's principles appear in much more recent learning theories. Modern concepts like number of trials, recency, and stimulus summation parallel Brown's secondary principles.

James Mill (1773–1836) presented one of the most extreme associationistic positions. His *Analysis of the phenomena of the human mind* (1829), published after 7 years of summer-vacation writing, presents Mill's "mental mechanics." He held that the law of association could account for the most complex mental experience. The idea of "every thing," for example, presumably contains all lesser ideas and is simply their sum. Mill said that simple ideas coalesced to form more complex ones, which might through long usage become so consolidated that they appeared as a single idea. Once the complex idea appeared in this way, it might in turn coalesce with other ideas to form even more complex ideas. Mill's position was the ultimate in simplicity, if not in accuracy, because of his use of simple addition and of contiguity as the single principle of association.

John Stuart Mill (1806–1873) was James Mill's son. They are the most potent philosophical father-son combination we will encounter. James sat John Stuart down at the table with him while he was writing the *History of India* and started his infant son reading Greek at the age of 3. John Stuart's educational accomplishments, with his father as his only schoolmaster, read like something out of Ripley's "Believe it or not;" by the time he was 12 he had gone through geometry, algebra, and Latin and turned his interest to scholastic logic. Through all of this his perfectionistic father continued to point out how he could and should be a better student, and John Stuart was expected to tutor his eight brothers and sisters.

With this background, it is not surprising that John Stuart did not deviate greatly from the psychological doctrines of his associationistic father. However, John Stuart did change the "mental mechanics" of his father slightly, into a kind of "mental chemistry." John Stuart Mill believed that ideas lose their original identity when they fuse into more complex ideas by association. He accepted his father's notion of coalescence of ideas in association but believed that very rapid combinations result in a loss of some parts. As he put it:

> The laws of the phenomena of the mind are sometimes analogous to mechanical, but sometimes also to chemical laws. When many impressions or ideas are operating in the mind together, there sometimes takes place a process of a similar kind of chemical combination. When impressions have been so often experienced in conjunction, that each of them calls up readily and instantaneously the ideas of the whole group, those ideas sometimes melt and coalesce into one another, and appear not several ideas but one; in the same manner as when the seven prismatic colors when they rapidly follow one another *generate* white; so it appears

to me that the Complex Idea, formed by the blending together of several simpler ones, should, when it really appears simple (that is, when the separate elements are not consciously distinguishable in it) be said to *result from,* or be *generated by,* the simple ideas, not to *consist of them. . . . These are cases of mental chemistry: in which it is* possible to say that the simple ideas generate, rather than that they compose, the complex ones. (J. S. Mill, 1843/1956, p. 558)

The younger Mill also discussed how mind creates matter, the problem posed by Berkeley. Mill attributed the power of expectation to the human mind. This gave humans the ability to expect certain sensations to be possible, given other sensations which arose from a particular "object." Mill named this set of expectations *permanent possibilities of sensation.* He thought that these possibilities adequately explained human belief in the material world. We shall see the same general problem reappear later as the problem of meaning in Titchener's psychology.

Alexander Bain (1818–1903), only 12 years younger than John Stuart Mill, carried on in the associationistic tradition. Bain was nominally a logician at Aberdeen, Scotland, but he was closer than anyone else we have discussed to being a formal psychologist. Bain had little help with his academic career, and he had difficulty in securing Scottish university professorships. He finally moved into London circles with John Stuart Mill. He published a comprehensive and systematic two-volume psychology text which relied heavily on associationism, *The senses and the intellect* (1855; republished 1886), and *The emotions and the will* (1859). Although at first slow to sell, these books were ultimately very successful, requiring several revisions and remaining the standard psychological texts in Britain for almost 50 years. They were a kind of physiological psychology. In 1876 Bain founded the first psychological journal, *Mind.* He supported it financially until 1892; it is still being published.

Bain developed a well-defined set of laws of association. Contiguity and similarity were the two principles Bain used to account for the formation of associations. In addition, there was a kind of summation effect, whereby "associations that are individually too weak to operate the revival of a past idea, may succeed by acting together" (1886, p. 544). And there was a principle of creativity, whereby "by means of Association, the mind has the power to form *new* combinations or aggregates, *different* from any that have been presented to it in the course of experience" (1886, p. 570). Bain thus accepted both Thomas Brown's secondary principle that associative strength is increased when several ideas work together and J. S. Mill's notion of the generation of complex ideas. Bain also proposed a version of the law of effect, according to which the strength of associations depended partially upon the consequences which followed their occurrence. He even discussed a version of trial-and-error learning and emphasized the role of chance in bringing about correct responses. His discussion is similar to that of Thorndike, who, as we will see later in this chapter, made trial-and-error learning and the law of effect the cornerstones of his theory of learning. He is also like Thorndike in that he accepted Darwin's work and thus some of the ideas that became the cornerstones of functional psychology.

Bain contributed to both the professional and intellectual development of psychology. Because he was himself a psychologist and because he founded the first journal of psychology, he completed the transformation of philosophical empiricism into psychological associationism. This transformation was abetted by the bridge that he built between the association of ideas and physiology.

British associationism left a legacy of the utmost significance to the newly developing experimental science of psychology. A major part of this significance lay in the methodological point of view which associationism developed and refined. The stimulus-response type of thinking and experimenting grew out of it. Once Hartley and Bain had made the connection between physiology and the mind, generations of psychologists were led to replace simple ideas with simple reflexes as their favored units.

We now turn to the kind of associationism that emerged during the last decades of the nineteenth century. Association of ideas was gradually replaced, in psychology, by association of stimuli and responses. The shift was related to the transition of psychology, so long a part of philosophy, into an empirical and natural science in its own right.

THE ASSOCIATION OF STIMULUS AND RESPONSE

Ebbinghaus's Invention of the Nonsense Syllable

Hermann Ebbinghaus (1850–1909) was an extremely capable German experimentalist who made the first thoroughly empirical study of association, or learning. His major interest was in memory, and he published (1885) the first systematic laboratory investigation of memory. He wanted to arrange the conditions of learning so that he could study the precise nature of memory. In order to do that, he devised the nonsense syllable in an effort to minimize the effects of associations formed prior to the beginning of his study.

The first nonsense syllables consisted simply of two consonants separated by a vowel (e.g., WOY, XAM, CIR). Ebbinghaus thought that he would be able to obtain more reliable memory curves if his learned materials were more homogeneous than ordinary words, whose associations with other words from prior learning would vary widely. Ebbinghaus found a negatively accelerated recall curve when the number of syllables retained was plotted as a function of time. Although it is now agreed that there is no such thing as "*the* learning curve," many recall curves approximate the Ebbinghaus form.

Ebbinghaus's contribution was particularly important because he was able to show that orderly results could be obtained by carefully controlled objective procedures, even in such complex and variable subject matter areas as human learning and memory. The first laboratory application of strict associationistic principles in the field of learning was a milestone in the history of scientific psychology.

Some skeptics have said "Yes, and the invention of the nonsense syllable was also a milestone in the history of boredom, of the kind that William James had in mind when he said that this kind of psychology could never have been produced in a country whose natives could be bored!" But James was referring to the type of work done by Fechner, not by Ebbinghaus. Ebbinghaus did get his idea for quantifying the study of memory after reading Fechner's work (1860) on quantification of psychophysics; however, James admired Ebbinghaus's work, which was a prototype for sound empirical investigation.

The skeptics are correct only on the surface. Nonsense syllables *are* dull, but that misses the point. Science often progresses by learning brilliant things from dull situations. How interesting is a linear accelerator or a cloud chamber? As things-in-themselves, they would bore us silly in a short time. And how interesting is it to watch a pigeon, a relatively stupid animal, pecking buttons in a little box? The charm of all these situations, including the nonsense-syllable situation, is that they tell us something about nature that we did not know before. And each of these situations is very rich in possibilities, in that amazing numbers of different manipulations can be studied within a single controlled environment. The invention of that environment was Ebbinghaus's genius and his contribution to psychology.

The next person we will look at made a similar contribution and had the good fortune to have a long life in which he could study the situation he created.

Pavlov's Discovery of the Conditioned Reflex

Ivan P. Pavlov (1849–1936) was born the son of a clergyman in Ryazan in central Russia, and at first he seemed destined for the priesthood. Instead, he moved to St. Petersburg and studied at the university there. One of his teachers was Mendeleev, the leading systematizer of the periodic table of elements. Pavlov received a medical degree in 1883, and soon after he spent time studying with Ludwig at Leipzig, where one assumes he would have had a chance to become acquainted with Wundt. Pavlov returned to St. Petersburg in 1890 as a professor of pharmacology at the Military Medical Institute. In 1895 he was elected to the professorship in physiology, where he remained until his death in 1936, attaining in 1924 the title of Director of the Physiological Institute for the Russian Academy of Science.

Ivan P. Pavlov (1849–1936), Russian physiologist and investigator of classical conditioning, shown with colleagues and one of his dogs.

In 1904, Pavlov was awarded a Nobel prize for his investigations of glandular and neural factors in digestion. In 1902, however, he had made an accidental discovery which was destined to change entirely the direction of his scientific career and to have a profound and lasting effect upon the development of psychological science.

Pavlov had developed an apparatus which made it possible to hold and measure the amount of saliva secreted by a dog under various conditions of feeding. The apparatus consisted of a calibrated glass tube inserted through a fistula in the animal's cheek. Pavlov went to some lengths to ensure a very high degree of control over environmental stimuli in the laboratory situation. The animal was harnessed in the apparatus within a relatively isolated experimental chamber, with recording devices outside. Pavlov's striking discovery consisted of his noting the persistent occurrence of *anticipatory* salivary flow. That is, the stimuli previously associated with the feeding of the animal (e.g., the approach of the attendant or the sight of the food dish) came to initiate salivation in animals as their training proceeded.

Pavlov was not the first person who observed such reflexes. One of history's lessons is that almost no one ever discovers something completely new. Robert Whytt (1763) had noted the existence of conditioned reflexes long before Pavlov. An American named Twitmyer also discovered conditioned reflexes (1905) but was assured that they were of no interest and so never followed up on his discovery. Pavlov also knew of the work of Sechenov (1829–1905), who had published a book, *Reflexes of the brain* (1863), which accounted for complex behavior in terms of basic reflexes, much as Pavlov later came to account for it.

Pavlov's greatness thus consisted, in part, in his ability to see the importance of a phenomenon which seemed unimportant on the surface. Another of history's lessons is that this is often the case. Röntgen discovered x-rays because he saw great significance in a little clouding on some film plates which should not have been cloudy. Pavlov saw great importance in a little saliva which kept trickling into his collection vials prematurely. The scientist, like the poet, may need to be able to see the universe in a flower.

Pavlov's thinking about the implications of his findings for the adaptive behavior of the animal culminated in a program of active research. The program was designed to lead to new insights concerning the physiology of the brain. The term *conditioned reflex* was used to express the acquired nature of the stimulus-response relationship.

Pavlov's interest in cortical functions is indicated in his choice of terms to describe the processes he investigated. One example is *irradiation,* implying a presumed spreading excitatory brain function. His research program was devoted to an exhaustive analysis of the factors involved in conditioning. The assumption was that an investigation of this simple kind of reflexive learning would allow him to penetrate some of the mysteries of the so-called higher mental processes.

Pavlov continued his research on the conditioned reflex throughout the remaining years of his long life. His environmental emphasis accorded extremely well with Marxist ideology, so he prospered as well after the revolution as before. Pavlov's conditioned reflexes were products of the environment. The implication was that the abilities of humans were determined by environmental influences, not by hereditary differences. Such thinking was music to communist ears.

Pavlov was able to develop a very complete system of psychology; even language was included as the "second signal system," to supplement the ordinary conditioned reflex, the first signal system. In his later years, Pavlov also turned his attention to the problems of abnormal behavior. He thought, for example, that catatonic schizophrenia was a matter of protective inhibition, which occurred to keep the organism from being overstimulated. Other psychoses were given similar speculative explanations.

It is somewhat ironic that Pavlov's great influence has been in psychology, a discipline toward which he never felt too kindly (see Pavlov, 1932), rather than in the area of brain physiology, with which he wished to be associated. This "injustice" has not occurred because of any perversity on the part of either physiologists or psychologists. Pavlov was more honored by psychologists simply because he was doing psychological work. Although his theoretical constructs sounded physiological, they were almost exclusively inferences from *behavioral* observations. Irradiation, the example we mentioned above, may sound like something that occurs in the cortex. However, it was known only through the observation of the behavioral phenomenon which we now call *stimulus generalization.* Kimble (1967) has given a very clear exposition of this facet of Pavlov's thought.

The details of Pavlov's work are beyond the scope of this book. For some of his own reports, in translation, see Pavlov (1927, 1928, 1941, 1955).

Pavlov's research represents a completion of the shift of the concept of association from its historical application to ideas to the relations between stimuli and entirely objective and highly quantifiable glandular secretions and muscular movements. John B. Watson, the founder of behaviorism, may have known of Pavlov's work through the latter's 1906 article in *Science,* which was the first article on the conditioned reflex that Pavlov published in English. Certainly Watson later made important use of Pavlov's research to support his own position. Pavlov is thus not just an associationist; he is also an extremely important antecedent of behaviorism.

Interest in Pavlov continues to be high, both in Russia and in the United States. Brozek (1973) reviewed the Pavlovinization of Russian psychology during the 1950s, when it became the official Russian psychology. Active research on the conditioned reflex, particularly in Russia, has filled in many of the physiological details which were generally missing from Pavlov's own research. There is little doubt that Pavlov performed or inspired, both directly and indirectly, more psychological research than any other single person up to the present time.

Bekhterev and Motor Conditioning

The third major figure in the shift of associationism away from ideas and toward overt behavior is Vladimir M. Bekhterev (1857–1927). His most significant contribution was the motor conditioned response. Pavlov's research had been almost entirely with glandular secretions, whose direct influence on overt behavior seemed somewhat restricted. Bekhterev, a Russian contemporary and rival of Pavlov, extended the conditioning principle to the striped musculature. His major research procedure involved the application of shock to the paw of a dog or the hand of a person following the presentation of a conditioned stimulus, such as a buzzer (Bekhterev, 1913). Bekhterev's findings were in general agreement with those of Pavlov; that is, after a number of pairings of the conditioned and unconditioned stimuli, the elicited movement was made when the conditioned stimulus was presented alone. No radically new principles were needed to account for conditioning of responses of the striped musculature.

Bekhterev had studied psychology under Wundt at Leipzig and was much more concerned with psychology than Pavlov was. His *reflexology* became a dominant theme in Russian psychology. Although American psychologists have preferred his motor conditioning techniques to Pavlov's salivary conditioning, they have found Pavlov's comprehensive experimentation and conceptualization more stimulating. Consequently, Bekhterev is regarded as having played a less important role than Pavlov in the development of associationism as a laboratory technique. However, he, like Pavlov, is an important precursor to behaviorism, as well as a prominent user of objective associationistic principles.

Thorndike's Connectionism

Thorndike's Life   The systematic stimulus-response psychology of Edward Lee Thorndike (1874–1949) was the closest approach, besides Pavlov's, to a complete and purely associationistic system since James Mill's. Although Thorndike started no school of psychology in the sense that Wundt or even Pavlov did, his mode of thinking was thoroughly associationistic. We can trace the logical evolution of associationism through Thorndike directly to behaviorism as practiced by J. B. Watson and B. F. Skinner. We will therefore treat Thorndike's connectionism as our example of a fully developed associationism.

Thorndike, like many famous men of science in the late nineteenth century, was the son of a minister (Joncich, 1968). His early life involved one move after another, as his Methodist father was shifted from church to church in the New England area. Despite these moves, Thorndike remained a brilliant student. He began his college career at Wesleyan University in Middletown, Connecticut, where he earned high marks and honors. Then he proceeded to Harvard, where he studied under William James. Because Harvard could not furnish the young graduate student any laboratory space for his experiments, James took Thorndike's chickens and other animals under his own wing in the basement of his home.

After 2 years at Harvard, Thorndike transferred to Columbia to study under James McKeen Cattell. That represented a move from a basement to an attic, where, after considerable negotiation, space was found for Thorndike to continue his experiments. What his life during this year was like may be best reflected in one of his letters to Elizabeth Moulton, whom he later married:

> A mouse just ran across my foot. A lot of rats are gnawing the bureau; three chicks are sleeping within a yard of me; the floor of my room is all over tobacco and cigarette ends and newspapers and books and coal and a chicken pen and the cats' milk dish and old shoes, and a kerosene can and a broom which seems rather out of place. It's a desolate hole, this flat of mine. (Joncich, 1968, p. 125)

Despite his limited laboratory resources and personal funds, Thorndike completed and published his dissertation in 1898, after a single year at Columbia. All of his animal research, including studies of maze learning in chickens and of escape from puzzle boxes by cats and dogs, was summarized in *Animal intelligence: An experimental study of the associative processes in animals*. The first part of the title was identical to that of Romanes's popular book on comparative psychology; perhaps Thorndike intended his title as an ironic reflection of Romanes's, since his dissertation minimized the intelligence of animals whereas Romanes had maximized it.

Thorndike's dissertation was later republished (1911), with new material added on associative learning in chicks, fish, and monkeys. Long before that, however, it had become a classic, and its young author (he was only 24 when he received his Ph.D.) had moved on to begin his professional career.

Thorndike's first job was in the education department of Western Reserve University in Cleveland. Thorndike, who had an elitist attitude toward educational institutions, was not very happy there. At the end of his first year, he seized an opportunity to return to Teachers College, Columbia University, where he spent the remainder of one of the most productive careers ever enjoyed by any psychologist.

Thorndike (1936) reveals a typically associationistic attitude in his description of that career, a description that is deterministic, environmentalistic, and passive in its view of the organism—in this case, of the scientist himself:

> The motive for my first investigations of animal intelligence was chiefly to satisfy requirements for courses and degrees. Any other topic would probably have served me as well. . . . I have recorded my beginning as a psychologist in detail because it illustrates what is perhaps the most general fact about my entire career as a psychologist later, namely, its responsiveness to outer pressure or opportunity rather than to inner needs. . . . Obviously I have not "carried out my career," as the biographers say. Rather it has been a conglomerate, amassed under the pressure of varied opportunities and demands. (pp. 265–266)

This self-portrait of "Thorndike the passivist" may very well have been exaggerated to show how well his own behavior fit his theory. His use of the word *conglomerate* even suggests that a career is a sum of parts, much as James Mill might have characterized a complex idea as a sum of simpler ones.

Boice (1977) relates an incident which portrays another side of Thorndike's personality. Thorndike had about 10 minutes left before he had to teach a class. He wondered aloud whether the interests of science would be better served if he used the 10 minutes to prepare for the class or if he used it to compute another correlation. "I think I'll compute another correlation," he concluded, and proceeded to do so. It does not appear from this incident that Thorndike always succumbed to external pressures, although in this case his students may have wished that he had.

Thorndike formally retired from Teachers College in 1939, after exactly four decades, but he contributed actively to psychology for another 10 years until his death in 1949. Much of his time was spent in the study of human learning and education, partly because the shift from animal learning to human learning had been suggested by Cattell.

Thorndike's System   There is no single, comprehensive account of Thorndike's system of connectionism. This is understandable: Thorndike did not think of himself as a systematist, or of his thinking and writing as contributing to a school. However, many of his key papers and chapters from books are collected in *Selected writings from a connectionist's psychology* (1949), which therefore probably offers the best single source of information about his work. Much of the following discussion and evaluation comes from that source.

Definition of Psychology   Thorndike's own opinion on definitions is suggested by his statement, "Excellent work can surely be done by men with widely different notions of what psychology is and should be, the best work of all perhaps being done by men such as Galton, who gave little or no thought to what it is or should be" (1949, p. 9). We could conclude from this, if we did not already know it, that Thorndike was no self-conscious systematist. We must therefore try to infer Thorndike's definition of psychology from what is implicit in his writing. Thorndike was a functionalist in his emphasis on the utilitarian aspects of psychology, and he could as well be classified as a functionalist as an associationist. However, psychology for him was first and foremost the study of stimulus-response connections or bonds. If a psychologist makes use of associations, and little else, in his account of mind and behavior, then we regard that person as an associationist. Thorndike seems to fit that mold.

However, Thorndike's conceptions of such associations went beyond the simple connections between discrete, molecular, and highly localized events sometimes assumed by his critics to be characteristic of his thinking. The following excerpt indicates the scope of his interpretation of connections and indirectly gives us a picture of what Thorndike (1949) considered to be the subject matter of psychology:

> Connections lead from states of affairs within the brain as well as from external situations. They often occur in long series wherein the response to one situation becomes the situation producing the next response and so on. They may be from parts or elements or features of a situation as well as from the situation as a whole. They may be largely determined by events preceding their immediate stimuli or by more or less of the accompanying attitude, even conceivably by his entire makeup and equipment. They lead to responses of readiness and unreadiness, awareness, attention, interest, welcoming and rejecting, emphasizing and restraining, differentiating and relating, directing and coordinating. The things connected may be subtle relations or elusive attitudes and intentions. (p. 81)

Postulates   Although explicit statements of postulates, like a definition of psychology, are not available in Thorndike's writing, some of his implicit assumptions are clear. Probably the most fundamental one is that behavior can be analyzed into associations of the kind described by him in the quotation given above. Another is that behavioral processes are quantifiable. He said that if something exists, it must exist in some amount, and that if it exists in some amount, then it can be measured. An interesting indication of the extent to which Thorndike was inclined to practice his preaching on this topic is his estimate, given in his autobiographical sketch (1949), that he had "probably spent well over 20,000 hours in reading and studying scientific books and journals" (p. 7).

Mind-Body Position   Thorndike was too much the matter-of-fact utilitarian to be much concerned with the mind-body problem, and he adopted no formal mind-body position. He stated (1949): "Under no circumstances, probably, could I have been able or willing to make philosophy my business" (p. 2). (In saying this, Thorndike seems to be suggesting that there are limitations on the power of arbitrary connections!) His common use of the words *mind* and *mental* therefore has no implication for a mind-body view, for he was not interested in philosophy. This usage indicates merely that Thorndike was relaxed about the use of ordinary language. He has been regarded by many as a behaviorist, but the following quotation shows that he had no deep prejudices about the possible existence or power of the mental realm:

> The real absurdity is to settle beforehand *what mind or matter can cause without empirical study of the phenomena of the connection between mind and body*. No one proves that causation is impossible between heterogeneous orders of being just by *saying so in a loud voice*. And the psychologist who affirms without other reason that because the mind moves the particles of the brain, it must be material, like a pumpkin, has a mind which is enough like a pumpkin to partially justify him. (Joncich, 1968, p.139)

This Thorndikian statement on the mind-body problem, written while he was a student at Columbia, is very much like William James's position in his *Principles of psychology* in 1890. Since Thorndike was fresh from studying with James, it is not surprising to encounter the Jamesian echo, with its implied dualism. However, the fairest thing to say about Thorndike's mind-body position is probably that he preferred to remain unaware of it.

What is also clear is that the young Thorndike was already fixed in that most scientific of attitudes, *an absolute reliance on observation as the arbiter of truth*. Thus, no matter how unlikely it might seem for "heterogeneous orders of being" to interact with one another, one simply had to find out by observation whether or not it happened. Quite clearly, Thorndike was an empiricist, not a rationalist.

Nature of the Data Thorndike's data were predominantly objective and very often quantified. We mentioned his estimate of the amount of time he spent reading. His research on the "goodness" of cities is a better illustration of how he used quantification professionally. Thorndike's own succinct summary of this research follows:

> It seemed to me probable that sociology would profit by studying the differences of communities in the same way that psychology studies the differences of individuals. Therefore I collected nearly 300 items of fact concerning each of 310 cities, studied their variations and intercorrelations, computed for each city three scores for the general goodness of life for good people for each city (G), for the personal qualities of its residents (P), and for their per capita income (I), and studied the causes of the differences among cities in G. (1949, pp. 10–11)

Principles of Connection Thorndike's best-known and most controversial contribution to psychological theory is his *law of effect*. In his early research with animals in puzzle boxes, he had been impressed with the gradual learning of the correct response and the gradual elimination of the incorrect ones. Thorndike argued that if animals *thought*, then there should be sudden changes in their performance, and he saw none.

Although Thorndike's view of learning has almost always been characterized as *trial-and-error*, actually Thorndike saw it more as a matter of *accidental success*. That is, it is the correct responses, not the errors, that lead to fixation of the response to be learned. *Exercise*, or frequency of occurrence, was accorded some strengthening powers, but not as much as occurred with the addition of success. He published the following formal statement:

Any act which in a given situation produces satisfaction becomes associated with that situation, so that when the situation recurs the act is more likely than before to recur also. Conversely, any act which in a given situation produces discomfort becomes disassociated from the situation, so that when the situation recurs the act is less likely than before to recur. (Thorndike, 1905, p. 203)

After extensive research on human learning (1931, 1932), Thorndike decided that the role of punishment or dissatisfaction was not at all comparable to the positive action of reward. He therefore revised his law of effect to give the predominant role to reward; punishment, he said, serves mainly to make the organism try something else rather than directly to dissociate the response from the situation.

Thorndike was cautious about basing conclusions concerning the effects of punishment on the ineffectiveness of the mild punishments he tried (like saying "wrong" following a number guessed by a subject). Nevertheless, he unwittingly gave rise to one of the most incredible psychological dogmas of the twentieth century: that punishment is ineffective in eliminating responses. This dogma is contrary to so much evidence, naturalistic as well as experimental, that it is harder to believe than the idea that the earth is flat. Presumably sensible psychologists were heard to say that punishment was really ineffective, because its effects might disappear after the punishment was withdrawn; these same psychologists marveled at the power of reinforcement, despite the well-established phenomenon of extinction when reinforcement was withdrawn!

The ineffectiveness of punishment remained dogma to many within the psychological community until at least the 1950s. It is still possible to find psychologists who maintain that punishment is never effective, although it is to be hoped that they are a vanishing breed. This is *not,* of course, to say that punishment is to be encouraged as a widespread technique or that it is always effective; in some situations even intensely aversive stimuli are ineffective in reducing the frequency of responses, and punishment may have undesirable side effects. Questions about the utility and desirability of punishment are quite justified, but they do not justify the assertion that punishment cannot be effective in suppressing or eliminating responses.

Two additional points should be made in this connection. First, Thorndike himself did not generalize from his results to the ineffectiveness of all punishers. A careful reading of Thorndike should have kept anyone from attributing such a dogma to him. The second point is that one cannot expect traditional views to be universally correct anyway. History gives us mistakes along with correct decisions, and we must find out which is which. Thorndike himself showed an almost cavalier disregard for authority, and we, in our turn, should question his hypotheses.

Thorndike suggested a cerebral function, the so-called confirming reaction (1933b), as the physiological basis of reinforcement. This suggestion implies the possibility of direct reinforcement through brain stimulation, which Olds (1955) later discovered. The suggestion was not closely connected to Thorndike's strictly behavioral program, but he was not timid about physiological speculation. He never took his own speculations very seriously, and they were not critical either for his experimentation or for his theorizing.

Nevertheless, one should not overlook Boring's insightful comment on the neat compatibility between the neuron theory which emerged in the last half of the nineteenth century and the associationistic theory which preceded and followed it. Boring (1950) says in part:

> The scheme of mind for which the associationists stood is a mental arrangement that much resembles this physical arrangement of the brain. For the associationists, mind is composed of an infinitude of separate ideas, just as the brain is constituted of an infinitude of cells. But these ideas are bound together into more complex ideas or into higher mental processes by a huge number of associations, just as the nerve cells are connected by fibers. . . . The important point is that the new picture of the brain, arrived at unpsychologically by discoveries in histological technique, nevertheless bore a close resemblance to the new picture of the mind that associationism yielded. (pp. 69–70)

The relevance of Boring's comments to Thorndike's connectionism is obvious.

In 1933, Thorndike reported an extension of his theory of reinforcement. He had discovered (1933a) what he called an "independent experimental proof of the strengthening after-effect" (p. 2). He labeled it the "spread of effect." It appeared that *nonrewarded* stimulus-response connections close to the rewarded connection acquired some strengthening from reinforcement. The closer the nonrewarded connection was to the rewarded one, the greater the strengthening. For example, a subject was asked to guess which number, from 0 through 9, went with each of a series of letters. One of the numbers was called "right," the others "wrong." Numbers guessed to letters in the vicinity of the one called right were more often repeated on subsequent trials. The observed strengthening was greater than the strengthening that would be produced by exercise alone.

Although the empirical data in support of this phenomenon have been amply verified, Thorndike's interpretation has not been generally accepted (Marx 1956; Bower & Hilgard, 1981). Alternative explanations in terms of guessing repeated *sequences* of responses, and other types of bias, were not adequately considered by Thorndike. However, it may yet be that an automatic strengthening effect, not dependent on cognitive factors, will be demonstrated. If it is, Thorndike's general reinforcement theory will look more attractive. Some published research has suggested that Thorndike's basic explanation may be correct (Bottenberg, Marx, & Pavur, 1976; Marx, 1957a, b, 1978, 1981; Marx, Marx, & Homer, 1981; Marx, Pavur, & Seymour, 1977; Postman, 1961). A great deal of research went into attempts to determine the reasons for the very small effects observed.

Hilgard's (1948) initial evaluation was that the spread of effect was crucial for Thorndike's position, as indicated by his statement that "for Thorndike, the spread of effect is the last line of defense. If it fails, there is little of theoretical interest left in what were once the dominant laws of learning" (p. 46). Subsequently, Hilgard and Bower downplayed the significance of the issue. However, in their most recent edition of *Theories of learning* (Bower & Hilgard, 1981), they have concluded, "That so much experimental effort went into deciding the 'reality' of this effect illustrates the allure of a critical theoretical issue" (p. 35).

Principles of Selection Stimulus-response associations account for differential attention to stimuli and for the selection of behavior, as well as for its acquisition.

Thorndike's (1913) recognition of the problem of selection in behavior is clearly given in the following excerpt from his *Psychology of learning:*

> All man's learning, and indeed all his behavior, *is selective.* Man does not, in any useful sense of the words, ever absorb, or re-present, or mirror, or copy, a situation uniformly. He never acts like a *tabula rasa* on which external situations write each its entire contribution, or a sensitive plate which duplicates indiscriminately whatever it is exposed to, or a gal-vanometer which is deflected equally by each and every item of electrical force. Even when he seems most subservient to the external situation—most compelled to take all that it offers and to do all that it suggests—it appears that his sense organs have shut off important features of the situation from influencing him in any way comparable to that open to certain others, and that his original or acquired tendencies to neglect and attend have allotted only trivial power to some and greatly magnified that of others. (pp. 111–112)

Thorndike interpreted problems of selective behavior, such as creativity in thinking, in terms of the same set of principles he applied to all learning, as indicated in this statement from the same source (1913):

> A closer examination of selective thinking will show that no principles beyond the laws of readiness, exercise, and effect are needed to explain it; that it is only an extreme case of what goes on in associative learning as described under the "piecemeal" activity of situations; and that attributing certain features of learning to mysterious faculties of abstraction or reasoning gives no real help toward understanding or controlling them.
>
> It is true that man's behavior in meeting novel problems goes beyond, or even against, the habits represented by bonds leading from gross total situations and customarily abstracted elements thereof. One of the two reasons therefor, however, is simply that the finer, subtle, preferential bonds with subtler and less often abstracted elements go beyond, and at times against, the grosser and more usual ones. One set is as much due to exercise and effect as the other. The other reason is that in meeting novel problems the mental set or attitude is likely to be one which rejects one after another response as their unfitness to satisfy a certain desideratum appears. What remains as the apparent course of thought includes only a few of the many bonds which did operate, but which, for the most part, were unsatisfying to the ruling attitude or adjustment.(pp. 112–113)

If the elimination of mystery is the essence of science, we see Thorndike in this quotation expressing himself as the essential scientist. We can also see his kinship with his forebears in the associationistic tradition: Locke, with his wish to eliminate the mysteries of innate ideas; Berkeley, with his attempt to solve the mystery of space perception; and Hume, who wished to consign all mysterious nonsense to the fire. Certainly the strength of science lies just here, and perhaps its weaknesses lie here too. Either way, Thorndike and the associationists are squarely in the middle of the scientific tradition.

CRITICISMS OF CONNECTIONISM

Elementarism

The essence of an associationistic position is that it is elementaristic. It was through their empiricism, elementarism, and analytic attitude that the British empiricists furthered psychology's progress as a science. It was through his acceptance of these attitudes, as manifested in his specificity, matter-of-factness, and attention to detail, that Thorndike made his most important contributions. Yet no approach to science can please everyone, and those who wanted psychology to pay immediate attention to the "big picture" were quick to attack Thorndike.

Thorndike's theory of transfer of training (Thorndike & Woodworth, 1901) is the epitome of his elementarism. The theory was that improved efficiency at one task, acquired as a result of training, would transfer to another task only insofar as the two tasks had "identical elements." The greater the number of identical elements, the greater the transfer of efficiency from one task to another. This is a simple and specific view, one that is open to experimental attack through the manipulation of the number of elements that are similar. It has therefore certainly been a theory of some value. However, in some situations it has appeared that some principle was learned which transferred perfectly to other tasks whose individual elements were quite different. Thus the theory requires at least some qualifications before it can be accepted as a complete theory of transfer. Gates (1942), in his carefully documented defense of connectionism, pointed out that Thorndike's elements were never intended to mean only the narrowest S-R connections; rather, they might include such things as "principles." "Identical," too, might be modified slightly to allow for degrees of similarity and to allow the theory more flexibility.

Modern theories of transfer are much more complex and detailed than Thorndike's, are pretty much limited to the prediction of list learning, and are still wrong. The rightness or wrongness of the identical elements theory, however, is not the issue. All current theories are probably "wrong" to some extent, but if they lead to clarification, experimentation, and progress in understanding the phenomena to which they apply, they are good theories. Science seems to proceed fastest and most surely when it works on small, researchable problems. Thorndike's elementarism led him and others to work on such problems.

Trial-and-Error Learning

Thorndike has been attacked for his emphasis on the randomness of learning, as implied in his characterization of learning as a trial-and-error process. His insistence on accepting only the simplest bases for animal learning and behavior led his critics to believe that Thorndike saw animals as stupid. Köhler (1947) and other Gestaltists have been especially active critics of all aspects of Thorndike's connectionism. The Gestaltists have suggested that learning in puzzle boxes and mazes necessarily appears to be random, stupid, and undirected because the animal cannot get an overview of the whole situation. The animal appears stupid because the situation is stupid, not because the animal is lacking in intelligence.

Thorndike's supporters might offer several defenses against such criticism. First, the behavior of the animal in the puzzle box is by no means altogether random or stupid. Much of the early behavior is directed at the exit, rather than at the device arbitrarily selected by the experimenter to release the animal. Such behavior is not stupid; it is intelligent in terms of the animal's past experience. Second, there may be a considerable amount of trial-and-error behavior which is not observed or recorded in the more open, less controlled situations which allow the animal an overview of the problem. Open situations do not guarantee that one will observe intelligence; they may just make it less likely that one will see the stupidity that is there. It may be that Thorndike's better controlled situation was more suited to reveal clearly the nature of the basic learning process. Third, and last, there is plenty of evidence from outside the puzzle box to show that learning can be slow, random, blind, and continuous rather than fast, intelligent, and sudden. The psychological clinic, the counseling situation, and the personal experiences of most of us provide many cases which seem to exemplify connectionistic rather than Gestalt learning processes, stupidity rather than insightful brilliance. Criticisms of Thorndike's description of learning should be tempered by these considerations.

Exercise

The sufficiency of frequency of occurrence, or the exercise principle per se, was seriously and tellingly questioned by the Gestalt critics. They made such a strong case that Thorndike (1935) revised his learning theory to add a new principle, *belongingness*. The evidence against exercise came partly from experiments which showed that contiguous terms are not necessarily associated in ordinary learning situations. For example, suppose that a subject has learned a set of paired associations such as A–1, B–2, C–3, D–4. These have been presented in the order indicated. The subject responds perfectly with response terms 1, 2, etc., to stimulus terms A, B, etc. However, if the subject is given one of the response terms, say 2, as a stimulus, he or she does not readily respond with the learned stimulus term that actually followed, in this case C. But C followed 2 just as closely in time as 2 followed B. A similar situation holds for successive sentences, such as "John is tired," "Jim is hurt." Here the connections John–tired and Jim–hurt are more readily formed and remembered than the connection tired–Jim, even though here again the purely physical relationship of the latter two terms is more nearly contiguous. Obviously something beyond mere contiguity in these cases is required for an effective association, and belongingness is the concept Thorndike used. He held that it is an important modifying condition of the strength of associations but not essential to the formation of associations.

Thorndike's own research (1932, p. 184) gave further evidence against the sufficiency of the old law of exercise. Subjects attempting to draw lines of a certain specified length while blindfolded did not show improvement even with many repeated trials. Thorndike's general conclusion was that exercise is a framework within which other conditions, such as effect, can operate.

Law of Effect

The oldest of Thorndike's contributions has been attacked by behaviorists as well as by Gestalt critics. First, some behaviorists objected to what they felt was a mentalistic and subjective concept; they interpreted "effect" to mean pleasurable sensations or something similar. Earlier versions of the law of effect, for example by Herbert Spencer, had included pleasure and pain as the critical features of the consequences of behavior.

Thorndike met this challenge (1913, p. 2) by pointing out that *he* meant by a satisfying state of affairs simply a state of affairs which the animal did nothing to avoid, often doing things which maintained or renewed it. By an annoying state of affairs he meant one which the animal often did something to end. Thorndike was not proposing a hedonism; he meant effect (on the response), not affect (a feeling).

Once it became clear that Thorndike was defining terms by referring to their effects on behavior, he was subjected to the accusation that his law was circular. Critics said that acquisition of response would have to be measured in order to determine whether or not the state of affairs was satisfying, and acquisition was just what the law of effect was intended to explain. If justified, this charge would show that Thorndike was saying, "If an animal will learn when its behavior is followed by a given state of affairs, it will learn when its behavior is followed by this state of affairs." This criticism is not fully justified, for the operations that Thorndike specified for satisfaction and annoyance were different operations from those which constituted a test of new learning. Once satisfiers and annoyers have been determined in some standard situation, they can be used in other situations to test their efficacy as reinforcers *of learning*. Such tests will be tests of the law of effect. The question, then, becomes one of how *generally* a given effect will reinforce behavior. Meehl (1950) made this point very forcefully.

Another criticism has been that Thorndike assumed that the satisfier or annoyer had to act backward upon a connection which had already occurred in order to strengthen it. However, it is just as easy to assume that the reinforcer acts upon the persisting traces from the stimulus and response that preceded the satisfaction or annoyance. Neobe-havioristic Hullian theory (Hull, 1952) has a specific postulate about stimulus traces which assumes that the action of a reinforcer depends upon its temporal relationship to the stimulus traces. This is simply a more sophisticated statement of Thorndike's position. There is no necessary retroaction implied by Thorndike's law of effect.

The automaticity of the strengthening by effect has also been questioned. Thorndike believed that learning could occur independently of any consciousness about what was being learned or why it was being learned (Thorndike & Rock, 1934). He was particularly gratified by the discovery of the spread-of-effect phenomenon (1933a), since even the most ardent of his critics would not attempt to explain the strengthening of *errors* as an intelligent or purposive process. The extent to which Thorndike was correct in his emphasis on automaticity cannot yet be determined, for this is still, 50 years later, a matter for debate. There is a considerable body of empirical evidence on both sides. It is interesting, however, that something very much like Thorndike's hypothesized "OK," or confirmatory, reaction is suggested by the intracranial self-stimulation technique (N. E. Miller, 1958; Olds, 1955). Electrical stimulation of certain brain areas apparently has an automatic reinforcing effect on preceding responses.

Mechanistic Determinism

Our last example concerns the widespread feeling that mechanistic science, such as that represented by Thorndikian connectionism, destroys human values. Thorndike (1949) had a characteristic answer to this kind of objection. Here is the way he posed the problem:

We must consider one final objection to using the methods of science in the world of values. Science, according to a very popular view, deals with a fatalistic world in which men, their wants and ideals, are all parts of a reel which unwinds year by year, minor whirls in a fixed dance of atoms. Values can have no place in such a world, and efforts to attain them by science must fail.

The truth of the matter, which is rather subtle, may best be realized by considering what I have elsewhere called the paradox of science, which is that scientists discover "causal" sequences and describe the world as one where the same cause will always produce the same effect, in order to change that world into a form nearer their heart's desire. Man makes the world a better home for man and himself a more successful dweller in it by discovering its regular unchangeable modes of action. He can determine the fate of the world and his own best, not by prayers or threats, but by treating it and himself by the method of science as phenomena, determined, as far as he can see, by their past history. (pp. 346–347)

And here, in a nutshell, is his solution:

Thus, at last, man may become ruler of himself as well as of the rest of nature. For strange as it may sound man is free only in a world whose every event he can understand and foresee. Only so can he guide it. We are captains of our own souls only insofar as they act in perfect law so that we can understand and foresee every response which we will make to every situation. Only so can we control our own selves. It is only because our intellects and morals—the mind and spirit of man—are a part of nature, that we can be in any significant sense responsible for them, proud of their progress, or trustful of their future. (1949, p.362)

THE CONTRIBUTIONS OF THORNDIKE

Thorndike's 50 years of professional activity at Teachers College were among the most productive that have ever been recorded by one person. Quantitatively, he accumulated a bibliography which at his death in 1949 had reached the amazing total of 507 items (Lorge, 1949). Many of the items were long books and monographs, and many were stuffed full of quantitative data. Thorndike worked and published in a remarkably wide range of fields. He started the systematic laboratory investigation of animal learning, produced the first complete associationistic learning theory, proceeded to an exhaustive analysis of human learning, as a result of which he revised his learning theory, became an active leader in the area of mental testing and educational practices, pioneered in the application of quantitative measures to sociopsychological problems, and contributed to the development of new techniques in the field of lexicography. It is amazing that one man could crowd such accomplishments into a lifetime!

Thorndike brought to all of these fields the same direct and factual approach that was so generally characteristic of his thinking. He was able to cut through to the heart of a problem with a minimum of the verbiage and double-talk found in many writers. Whatever one may think of some of his ideas, and whatever their eventual fate, we cannot fail to admire the freshness and perseverance of attack that he brought to the discipline.

Systematically, Thorndike's influence has declined, first as a contentious behaviorism took over in the 1920s, and more recently as the more sophisticated versions of neobehaviorism have emerged. But his work remains a bulwark of associationism, especially in the fields of animal and human learning and of educational psychology. Still, in 1981, Bower and Hilgard in their often-revised classic, *Theories of learning,* treat Thorndike's connectionism as their first theory of learning. They recognize the decline of interest in his system. However, they seem to share Tolman's (1938) much earlier judgment on the importance of Thorndike as the standard, the point from which learning theories begin:

> The psychology of animal learning—not to mention that of child learning—has been and still is primarily a matter of agreeing or disagreeing with Thorndike, or trying in minor ways to improve upon him. Gestalt psychologists, conditioned-reflex psychologists, sign-gestalt psychologists—all of us here in America seem to have taken Thorndike, overtly or covertly, as a starting point. (p. 11)

Nearly 50 years later, Thorndike and Tolman are gone. Yet B. F. Skinner's psychology is a kind of enduring monument to Thorndike's system, so close is their intellectual resemblance. We will discuss Skinner in more detail in a later chapter; but most of our readers will already have recognized that operant psychology relies very heavily upon a detailed working out of the law of effect. Operant psychologists generally share Thorndike's determinism and his belief that effect acts automatically. Thus, as long as operant psychology lives, Thorndike's psychology lives.

CONTEMPORARY ROLE OF ASSOCIATIONISM

In its broad outlines, associationism is practically synonymous with an orthodox interpretation of science. It is a belief that the primary job of science is to relate phenomena, to look for reliable functional relationships. This is a methodological characteristic that it shares with all systems, but particularly with functionalism.

Thus Thorndike could well have been considered a pioneer functionalist. But there is some justification for separating associationism in general, and Thorndike in particular, from functionalism. The functionalist puts greater emphasis on adaptation to the environment than does the associationist. In addition, functionalists may study this adaptation on a scale of evolutionary time, while associationists tend to limit their study to the life of the individual organism.

Finally, most associationists use a more restricted set of concepts than functionalists. They explain behavior by using a limited set of variables. Older associationists attempted to explain complex thought and behavior as *nothing but* the association of ideas. Thorndike was the very prototype of this type of thinking, believing that behavior was explicable on the basis of nothing but stimulus-response connections, inherited and acquired. Present-day association theorists tend to be more cautious in their objectives and to apply their limited set of concepts to an area much smaller than the total behavior of organisms. They are therefore *restrictive* in two ways: they restrict their conceptual framework, and they restrict its scope. Thorndike, like most earlier associationists, was restrictive only in the first way.

Today finding the relationship between *variables,* if not between stimuli and responses, is recognized as a fundamental task of science. Functional analysis is conceptually related to the analytic attitude of associationists. However, exactly what is to be related remains one of the critical problems for psychology. Thorndike's answer emphasized the wide range of possible stimulus and response factors. One thing that Thorndike was *not* restrictive about was his definition of "stimulus" and "response!" Whether or not a strict S-R associationism can be effectively applied to explain the broad range of overt behaviors still remains in doubt, but refined varieties of associationism continue to show promise.

There are four interrelated lines of current development. First, research on the conditioned reflex continues, especially in Russia (Cole & Maltzman, 1969; Razran, 1971), although there is certainly plenty of activity in other places as well (see Estes, 1975). The Russian work in the tradition of Pavlov and Bekhterev has reached a height of sophistication which surprises most western observers. In the United States, Gregory Razran (1949) adapted Pavlov's procedure for application to human subjects by using cotton dental plugs to collect saliva. The amount of salivation can be quantified by weighing the plugs before and after each trial. Razran used this procedure to study conditioning involving verbal stimuli. The galvanic skin response and conditioned eye blink are other popular responses used in human conditioning (see, for example, Kimmel, 1966).

Second, the neobehavioristic stimulus-response theory of Hull and his many followers and collaborators represents an important continuing influence. Here again interest has been mainly in the field of learning, animal as well as human. Kenneth Spence (1956, 1960) was one of the foremost users of a rather strict associationism (see Chapter 10). A more flexible kind of S-R associationism is seen in the work of Neal Miller and John Dollard (Dollard & Miller, 1950; N. E. Miller & Dollard, 1941). They extended S-R concepts into the fields of learning and abnormal behavior. Miller (1959) continued to liberalize the use of S-R concepts in more recent publications and aroused a tremendous interest in biofeedback with his operant conditioning of visceral and glandular responses (Miller, 1969).

A third line is evident in Guthrie's theory (Guthrie, 1935, 1952) and in the mathematizing of this kind of theory in Estes' statistical association theory (Estes, 1950, 1959b). Guthrie presents associationism in its boldest and most restrictive modern form, since the simple principle of contiguity between stimulus and response is used as the fundamental law of learning. Within learning theory, Guthrie has been, almost single-handedly, an articulate supporter of a simple contiguity position. He saw learning as a matter of associations and nothing else. Estes' mathematical theorizing has given rigorous quantitative expression to this view. Estes later (1959b) indicated some acceptance of reinforcement as a descriptive concept, if not as an explanatory principle.

Finally, there are some versions of associationism which are less orthodox than the preceding but which have enjoyed vigorous success. Two important examples are the learning theories of Tolman and Skinner. Tolman's purposive behaviorism (1932) is a cognitive type of learning theory that stresses association between stimuli—a sign-Gestalt or sign-significate theory. We have already discussed the close philosophical kinship between Thorndike and Skinner. The most important distinction between Skinner's position and that of a typical associationist is that Skinner places little emphasis on the *stimulus*-response relationship; he is far more concerned with the response-

reinforcement relationship; this, too, will be further discussed in Chapters 10 and 11, where we return to more recent theories that derive from the associationistic tradition.

SUMMARY AND CONCLUSIONS

In this chapter we have traced associationism from its origins in British empiricism, where the important tradition of association of ideas was elaborated, through its modification to deal with the formation of associations, to its emergence in Pavlov's and Thorndike's work as an association of stimulus and response. We have treated Thorndike's connectionism as the representative of associationism, although it was not developed by him as a self-consciously systematic position. We have indicated the most important criticisms of connectionism, the answers that can be given to them, and our evaluation of the importance of Thorndike's work. We have indicated briefly the role of associationism in contemporary psychology. If we regard associationism as implying the study of functional relationships between variables discovered through analysis, then associationism represents at least one phase in the development of any science.

It is clear that associationism has played a key role in the development of psychology, whatever the ultimate fate of the theories which build upon it as a necessary and sufficient principle. Some kind of associationism is certainly necessary. Whether or not associationism will be sufficient as a learning theory is more doubtful. It is remarkable that so ancient and simple a notion should continue to be useful. Its long viability attests to its vitality, especially when one considers that careful empirical tests since the times of Ebbinghaus and Pavlov have failed to reveal fundamental inadequacies in the approach. These tests have become increasingly precise and rigorous as mathematical modelers have taken advantage of the quantitative opportunities encouraged by the approach to make exact predictions of experimental outcomes. It will be interesting to see whether or not associationistic concepts will continue, as they have for some time, to serve as the central core of mathematical learning theory. Alleged logical proofs of inadequacies in the associationist position have not yet deterred investigators from continuing to carry out investigations inspired by the associationistic approach.

FURTHER READINGS

Boring's treatment in his *History of experimental psychology* (1950) remains a recommended source of information about the most important British empiricists and associationists. *A source book in the history of psychology* (1965), edited by Herrnstein and Boring, provides beautifully selected, organized, and introduced readings from the British empiricists and related theorists in the early part of the twentieth century. In our own readings, *Systems and theories in psychology: A reader* (Hillix & Marx, 1974), we offer a set of selections coordinated with this text, some of which of course accompany the present chapter. Turner's *Philosophy and the science of behavior* (1967) gives a sophisticated and admiring analysis of the British empiricists and demonstrates their immediate contemporary significance. *A handbook of contemporary Soviet psy-*

chology (1969), edited by Cole and Maltzman, is still one of the best books for those who would like to gain access to the Russian conditioning literature. The American literature can be accessed through any contemporary book on learning, but *Theories of learning* (1981) by Bower and Hilgard remains the classic among them, and Thorndike and many theorists to be treated later in this book can be found there as a bonus. We have already indicated that the easiest direct access to Thorndike's system is through his *Selected writings from a connectionist's psychology* (1949). For Thorndike's life, see Joncich's *The sane positivist: A biography of Edward L. Thorndike* (1968). She may tell you a little more than you want to know about Thorndike's New England, especially its institutions of learning, but she also constructs a finely detailed picture of her subject.

END NOTES

Dimensional Descriptions of Associationism

Conscious Mentalism–Unconscious Mentalism The early associationists put considerable emphasis on conscious mentalism, since they were concerned with sensations and ideas, both of which were thought to be elements found in consciousness. Later associationists, like Pavlov and Thorndike, were quite different. They stayed away from consciousness as an explanatory mechanism. Pavlov said that he first accounted for conditioning in terms of conscious connections but found that the concept of consciousness soon failed him. Thorndike emphasized the automatic, and presumably unconscious, action of the law of effect. Thus the two associationists who played the most prominent roles in our account of associationism tried to reject mentalism of whatever kind.

Contentual Objectivism–Contentual Subjectivism This dimension also underwent a shift over time. The earliest associationists attended to ideas and so emphasized subjective contents. The later ones, beginning with Ebbinghaus and progressing to Pavlov and Thorndike, shifted their attention to objective behavior. The shift was so radical that it extended virtually from one extreme to the other.

Determinism–Indeterminism The typical associationist has always tended toward determinism, in keeping with the analytic scientific character of this position.

Empiricism–Rationalism Thorndike was typical of the tradition with his extreme empiricism; he never went back on his early pronouncement that he was unprepared to reject *anything,* even something so unlikely to many as mind-body interaction, without empirical trial. And the British empiricists, from whom the associationistic tradition sprang, were *named* for their adherence to empiricism.

Structuralism–Functionalism For this fifth prescription, the assignment is less clear. The older philosophical associationists may have leaned toward structuralism.

What was in the mind seemed of more interest than what it was there for or its relationships to prior conditions. The later theorists, Pavlov and Thorndike, were more concerned with the adaptive functions of S-R connections, reflecting some evolutionary influence.

Inductivism–Deductivism This dimension presents almost no problems. From Francis Bacon to B. F. Skinner, all associationists have tried to "go down the line" with inductivism. We would have to go all the way back to Aristotle to find a problem. He was a user of inductive procedures, but he also lent his name to "Aristotelian logic," which is certainly a deductive procedure. Thus, although we do not believe in pure inductivists or deductivists, the associationists came as close as they could!

Mechanism–Vitalism This dimension is also no problem. The associationists always tried to eliminate all extraneous conceptual baggage, and thus they would not wish to admit that life had special properties. They were mechanists to the core.

Methodological Objectivism–Methodological Subjectivism Here we see the same shift from subjective to objective that we saw for the first two of Watson's prescriptions. Pavlov and Thorndike were especially noteworthy as early objectivists in their methods.

Molecularism–Molarism This is another very clear choice. Associationism began by being molecular and ended in exactly the same way, with no notable molarists in between. Molecularism, along with empiricism, goes a long way toward *defining* associationism. Without the breakdown of complex situations into smaller, molecular units, there would be nothing to associate. The only thing that changed was the subject matter, from ideas to behaviors.

Monism–Dualism It is impossible to make a representative rating for monism versus dualism. Locke was a dualist with his primary qualities that presumably existed in the external world and his secondary qualities that existed only in the mind. Berkeley and Hume, although they were formally subjective idealists and therefore monists, seemed to have difficulty in giving up on the existence of the external world. Pavlov and Thorndike, although they made little use of consciousness in their own thinking, did not seem secure in eliminating the internal world. Modern associationists like Skinner have little use for an internal world, but there is at least a tolerance for dualism in most associationists.

Naturalism–Supernaturalism Associationism has been almost completely naturalistic from the beginning. The only possible exception was Bishop Berkeley, and it's hardly fair to count him.

Nomotheticism–Idiographicism It is always confusing to deal with this issue. The usual explanation of the dimension says that nomotheticism puts the emphasis on discovering general laws and that idiographicism puts the emphasis upon accounting for the behavior of particular events or individuals. But the minute one asks how general laws can be *discovered,* it appears that it can only be through the study of individual cases to which the general laws would presumably apply. Further, when one asks how general laws can be tested, if and when they are discovered, the answer is that they can be tested by seeing whether or not they predict the outcomes of individual events.

On the other side of the coin, we would argue that one can give a scientifically satisfactory account of an individual event only by showing how it was explained by general laws. In the case of human beings, a description of an individual personality makes sense only when it is put in the context of other human beings. For example, it would tell us nothing to hear that an individual scored 47 on a test of assertiveness unless one knew something about how other people scored. Thus idiographic study seems to depend on nomothetic analysis, and vice versa. Falk (1956) wrote a long review which covered just this single muddled issue, and we cannot unravel all the strands of the argument here. But it does seem clear that the distinction between idiographicist and nomotheticist is a matter of degree rather than of kind.

There are two clearer questions related to the nomothetic-idiographic issue which can be more easily answered than whether a system is nomothetic or idiographic. (1) Does the scientist primarily make intensive studies of individuals (more idiographic) or survey-type studies of many individuals (more nomothetic)? (2) Is the information gathered to be used primarily in understanding individual cases (more idiographic) or in understanding statistical tendencies in aggregations of people (more nomothetic)? We believe that associationism has had a nomothetic flavor, which became more intense with Thorndike than it had ever been earlier. He seemed very concerned with quantifying, computing reliable statistics, and predicting *general* trends.

Centralism–Peripheralism On this dimension, associationism moved toward peripheralism as interest shifted from ideas to S-R connections, and methodology shifted from introspection to objective observation.

Purism to Utilitarianism Similar movement occurred on this dimension. British empiricists were concerned with philosophical problems, and their analysis of ideas suggested no immediate applications. However, Pavlov would have liked to cure schizophrenics by using his conditioning techniques, and Thorndike was deeply concerned with the educational process. This shift parallels the shift in the whole field of psychology, which for the most part started out without immediate aspirations to application but developed them increasingly as the field gained some expertise in applied areas.

Quantitativism–Qualitativism Associationism has always tended toward quantitativism. Even breaking down ideas into smaller units is an invitation to counting, and Pavlov was devoted to counting drops of saliva. For Thorndike quantification was a veritable obsession.

Rationalism–Irrationalism We would not like to imply that there is anything irrational about associationism or any other school. But of course that is not the meaning of the dimension. The question is, "To what extent is behavior determined by rational thought and to what extent by other factors?" Locke, very early in the tradition, began a trend to irrationalism by accounting for some peculiar behaviors in terms of unusual associations. For example, he suggested that one might fear the dark because one's nurse told ghoulish stories about events in the night. Thorndike put much stronger emphasis on such accidental influences, to the extent that he claimed that errors might even "irrationally" be strengthened by proximity to reinforcement. Pavlov's strong environmentalism, with an organism's conditioned responses depending on the exigencies of its conditioning history, placed him also on the side of irrationalism.

Staticism–Developmentalism   The empiricistic, associationistic view of epistemology makes it developmental. Organisms necessarily change over time because the organism is critically influenced by the environment which it happens to encounter. Despite this philosophical developmentalism, the most important associationists have done few long-term studies of development and hence have been less extreme developmentalists than they "should" have been.

Staticism–Dynamicism   Finally, the contrast between staticism and dynamicism is related to the previous polarity, but in this last case the focus is more on a general fluidity versus permanence, and the fluidity might be manifested within a shorter period of time than the periods of interest in studying development. On this dimension, modern associationists have not been very dynamic. There is a tendency to assume that associations coerce rather fixed behaviors and endure for a substantial time.

Of Watson's eighteen prescriptive dimensions, four seem to be most critical in fixing the nature of associationism. They are empiricism, molecularism, determinism, and quantitativism.

Associationism Compared to Other Systems

We now turn to the dimensions that Coan (1979) found most useful in distinguishing among psychological theorists. Taking the first three dimensions together because associationism occupies extreme, and related, positions on all of them, we find that well-developed associationism has been highly objective, elementaristic, and quantitative. This attitude on these three factors constitutes what Coan calls the *analytic* orientation; and associationism is nothing if it is not analytic. Thus we will see that associationism tends to be more analytic than other systems to be presented later.

Three factors making up a second set are also related. On them, associationism tends to take an apersonal orientation, to emphasize exogenistic (environmental) factors, and to be somewhat static. Although the position on this last factor is not extreme, the three attitudes go together to make up the *structural* attitude. Thus we would rate associationism (as we have already said in placing it on Watson's dimensions) as somewhat structural.

Finally, Coan calls a position which is structural and analytic a *restrictive* orientation. Again, we have already described associationism as quite restrictive on somewhat different grounds. Associationism as a system thus appears as a "hard-nosed," restrictive system with the analytic attitude which has been characteristic of the established sciences. It also tends to be more static and structural than other systems, although in this respect its position is slightly less extreme.

STRUCTURALISM

Edward Bradford Titchener (1867–1927), the English student of Wundt who became America's most prominent structuralist psychologist.

Wilhelm Maximilian Wundt (1832–1920), at about the time he came to Leipzig.

The highly developed introspective psychology called *structuralism* was first developed in Germany by Wilhelm Wundt (1832–1920). It is represented in its American form by the work of E. B. Titchener. In 1898, Titchener sharpened and dramatized the structural-functional distinction which had been made by James in 1884. Titchener thus effectively named both systems (see R. I. Watson, 1968, pp. 397–399). He pointed out the analogy between the type of psychology he favored and the study of structure in biology.

Titchener's system was a direct descendant of the system his mentor, Wundt, had developed at Heidelberg and Leipzig. During the early years of psychology in Germany, Wundt's psychology was virtually *the* psychology. Its purpose was the introspective analysis of the human mind. To many who examined Wundt's position, it appeared that psychology was to be a kind of chemistry of consciousness. The primary task of the psychologist was to discover the nature of elementary conscious experiences and their relationships to one another. Introspection by a highly trained person was thought to be the necessary tool. Table 4-1, on the facing page, lists the most important persons in structuralism.

Structuralism has been extremely significant in three ways. First, Wundt gave psychology a strong scientific impetus. He got the name *psychology* attached for the first time to a *scientific* endeavor. He gained formal academic recognition for psychology, giving it an identity clearly separated from the two main parental fields, physiology and philosophy. Second, structuralism provided a thorough test of the classic introspective method as the key method for psychology. Third, it provided a strong and clear orthodoxy against which the functional, behavioristic, and Gestalt forces could organize their resistance. The newer schools arose from a progressive

TABLE 4-1
IMPORTANT FIGURES IN STRUCTURALISM

| | Structuralists | |
Antecedent influences	Pioneers and founders	Developers of related positions
Franz Brentano (1838–1917)	Wilhelm Wundt, Leipzig (1832–1920)	Carl Stumpf, Berlin (1848–1936)
Gustav Fechner (1801–1887)	Edward B. Titchener, Cornell (1867–1927)	G.E. Müller, Göttingen (1850–1934)
H.L.F. von Helmholtz (1821–1894)		Oswald Külpe, Würzburg (1862–1915)
		K.M. Dallenbach, Illinois (1887–1971)
		J.P. Nafe, Washington University (St. Louis) (1888–1970)
		E.G. Boring, Harvard (1886–1968)

Wundt, founder of the first formal psychology laboratory at Leipzig in 1879, in the laboratory with his colleagues.

reformulation and final discarding of the basic structural problems. In turn, each new school formed its own caricature of the structuralist position, just as newspaper cartoonists caricature politicians with whose views they disagree. We must therefore take special pains to get behind these caricatures as we turn to the study of the psychologies of Wundt, with whom institutional psychology began, and Titchener, who brought his own interpretation of Wundtian psychology to America.

WUNDT AS THE FOUNDER OF STRUCTURALISM

It has been customary in America to cite Titchener as the founder of structural psychology. He named it, developed it, and buttressed it against functional and behavioral trends. However, Titchener's system was a derivation of (but not necessarily an improvement on) the system of Wilhelm Maximilian Wundt, under whom Titchener had studied for 2 years in Leipzig. Wundt himself was a self-conscious systematizer and the "father" of the new experimental psychology. He formally established the first laboratory for psychology at the University of Leipzig (now Karl Marx University) in 1879, 4 years after he had opened it informally. His influence on psychology was far greater than that of Titchener or, for that matter, any one of his students.

However, Titchener furnished the eyes through which Americans saw structural psychology. We give Titchener greater coverage later in this chapter because he is more accessible to us, because his position was more limited and therefore clearer, and because he was the main channel through which the Wundtian influence flowed to America. Titchener and his students *were* structural psychology in America. This does not imply any sort of subordinate stature for Wundt. On the contrary, Wundt was the more innovative, more productive, and more influential man.

Wundt's Life

Wundt was born the fourth child of a country pastor and his wife in Neckarau, Germany. Before the young Wundt was a year old, he contracted malaria, and the family moved to the small farming community of Leutershausen for the sake of his health (Bringmann, Bringmann, & Balance, 1980). The family never had much money, particularly after Wundt's father suffered a stroke and, from his meager salary, had to pay assistants to do much of his work. Wundt was an inveterate daydreamer and did little work in school. Friedrich Müller, his father's assistant, befriended and tutored Wundt, but the tutoring did not "take" very well because of Wundt's daydreaming.

When Wundt left home for high school, his habits of study and his academic background were so poor that he failed the first year. The second year he changed schools, and his older brother and a friend were able to prod him out of daydreaming and into study. Although Wundt modestly claimed that his marks were not very good, they were in fact excellent from that time on. He made friends and developed interests in reading and in the intellectual life. He could not afford to go to the university and so chose medical school instead. When he finished, he made the top score in the medical board examinations for his district in 1855.

Soon after, Wundt was allowed to teach courses (but with no salary) at the University of Heidelberg. However, he had hardly begun when he became deathly ill with tuberculosis and had to take an extended "vacation," during which he wrote his first book while he recuperated. Productivity in the face of adversity came to typify Wundt, who in later life wrote at an incredible pace despite having no vision in one eye and limited vision in the other.

In 1858, Wundt began a 7-year stint as the assistant of Hermann Helmholtz (1821–1894), in which position he received a small salary. During this period, he also wrote and did research. The writing prospered sufficiently that Wundt was able to resign his position as Helmholtz's assistant and live on the income from his books.

While he was Helmholtz's assistant, Wundt was also politically active. In 1866, he was elected a representative to the Second Chamber of the Baden Parliament from Heidelberg (Bringmann, Bringmann, & Balance, 1980). After 3 years, he resigned his position, pleading incompatibility between political and academic work and claiming that the issues with which he was most concerned had been happily resolved. After that time, his political activity was minimal.

In 1871 Wundt finally was appointed to a salaried position at Heidelberg, but the salary was a pittance. He also taught Helmholtz's course in physiology that summer, receiving more money for that than his own salary for the year. All of this made it possible for him to marry Sophie Mau in 1872, when he was 40 years old. Their first child was Eleonore, and the second was Max. Their third child, Lilli, died quite young. Her death was, so far as we know, the only deep personal tragedy that Wundt had to endure after he left Heidelberg.

In 1872, Wundt's prodigious efforts finally earned him a call to a chair in Zurich. The very next year, the more prestigious University of Leipzig made Wundt an offer which he was quick to accept. He had been less than comfortable in Switzerland, and the opportunities there seemed limited. Wundt was to remain in Leipzig as a revered teacher and researcher for 47 years, lecturing to packed auditoriums until he was well into his eighties.

Soon after he arrived in Leipzig, Wundt began to work toward the laboratory which later made him famous around the world. He brought illustrations and demonstrations with him when he came, and by December 1879 work on the first official psychological dissertation had begun in his fateful little room on the top floor of the "convict" building.

To the outsider, it must have seemed that Wundt's psychology was to be a sort of experimental mental chemistry. Many were reminded of John Stuart Mill's picture of the development of complex ideas. Wundt's enterprise received a boost from the triumphs in chemistry itself, particularly those of Mendeleev. In 1871, Mendeleev had revised his periodic table of the elements, first published in 1869, and had predicted from this table the existence of three new, as yet undiscovered, elements. In 1875 the first of the three, germanium, was discovered; in 1879, the year in which Wundt founded his laboratory, the second, scandium, was discovered.

Wundt tried to repudiate the chemical analogy to his psychology, saying that the two sciences were different in most respects. He did, however, acknowledge that they were similar in that the properties of a combination of elements or processes could not be predicted from a knowledge of the elements. Despite Wundt's general disavowal of the chemical analogy, his critics certainly, and potential students probably, saddled his psychology with the name of mental chemistry.

Even at this distance in time and space, we should be able to imagine the intense excitement and high hopes experienced by students who thought they might observe the development of a veritable periodic table of the mind. Students flocked to Leipzig from as far away as America and Japan. It was considered imperative to follow Wundt's course once one had arrived in eastern Germany. Although some, like America's cynical and backbiting Granville Stanley Hall, were disillusioned, most retained a fervor and intensity of purpose which are appropriate when one is part of a new enterprise of high moment.

Wundt lived to the age of 88, dying in 1920. Yet he probably never realized the extent to which the new science was to bear his stamp. It appears that about half of America's psychologists trace their academic lineage back to Wundt (Hillix & Broyles, 1980; Weigel & Gottfurcht, 1972). Although Wundt supervised only 14 dissertation students from America (Tinker, 1980), those students founded laboratories and preempted American psychology, with the help of a few imports like Titchener from England and Münsterberg from Germany. Thus only half of the field was left for all of Wundt's competitors, including people like William James, Carl Stumpf, and Alexius Meinong. Wundt had created an institutionalized version of psychology which was capable of self-replication, and that was the key to his tremendous success.

One of his students, Edward M. Weyer (1921) expressed the kernel of this idea concisely when asked about Wundt's greatest contribution. He said, "With all modesty and no claim to greatness, we psychologists in America, his followers, might say he contributed *us* and our psychological laboratories."

Wundt's Psychology

Wundt had many antecedents. Some of them were discussed in Chapter 2. We find other antecedents in the phenomenological tradition. Turner (1967, p. 60) defines phenomenology as a philosophy which regards the entities of experience as possessing an irreducible integrity of their own. Kant, in his *Critique of pure reason,* developed a part of the phenomenological viewpoint. He believed that whatever is known is *phenomenon* and that knowing requires an appearance in consciousness. Knowledge was thus restricted by Kant to appearances. This doctrine is still accepted in modern phenomenology; for example, Lauer (1965) says: "If we are to know what anything is—and this the phenomenologist will do—we must examine the consciousness we have of it; if this does not give us an answer, nothing will" (p. 7). Thus we might summarize the essence of phenomenology as the belief that our most reliable knowledge is the knowledge we have of our own conscious experiences.

In 1856, Lazarus and Steinthal first distinguished between phenomenology and psychology (see Capretta, 1967). They asserted that the former is concerned with a description of the phenomena of mental life, while the latter seeks to establish causal explanations of these phenomena. Thus when Wundt appeared on the scene, opinions were already being expressed on the relationship of phenomenology to psychology. Although Wundt accepted some of the foundation assumptions of phenomenology, he was not temperamentally a phenomenologist. He thought that psychology needed laboratory experimentation carried out by trained observers, not just the careful observations of phenomenologists.

Wundt's philosophy was neither materialistic nor spiritualistic. He opposed the latter type of view because he thought it tried to base a science of mental experience on speculations about a "thinking substance." He opposed materialism because he did not think a science of mind could be developed solely through physical investigations of the brain. Wundt felt that the study of mind must be a science of experience, agreeing on this point with the phenomenologists. Thus Wundt supported the existence of a science of psychology quite independent of biology and physiology.

Wundt believed, however, that psychology must have an experimental side. Schultz (1969) quotes Boring as saying: "The application of the experimental method to the problem of mind is the great outstanding event in the history of the study of the mind, an event to which no other is comparable" (epigraph). Wundt was the man responsible for this unparalleled event. Here is some of what he had to say on the subject:

> It is experiment, then, that has been the source of the decided advance in natural science, and brought about such revolutions in our scientific views. Let us now apply experiment to the science of mind. We must remember that in every department of investigation the experimental method takes on an especial form, according to the nature of the facts investigated. In psychology we find that only those mental phenomena which are directly accessible to physical influences can be made the subject matter of experiment. We cannot experiment upon mind itself, but only upon its outworks, the organs of sense and movement, which are functionally related to mental processes. (Wundt, 1894, p. 10)

The subject matter of psychology was to be *immediate* experience, as contrasted to *mediate* experience. By mediate experience Wundt meant experience used as a way to find out about something other than the experience itself. This is the usual way in which we use experience in gaining knowledge about the world. We say "The *leaf* is green"; the emphasis implies that our primary interest is in the leaf, rather than in the fact that we are experiencing green.

Immediate experience for Wundt was experience *as such,* and the task of psychology was the study of this immediate experience in itself. If we attempt to describe directly the *experience* we have in connection with a toothache, we are concerned with immediate experience. However, if, in conjunction with a dentist, we *use* the experience to find out about the location of the cavity which causes the toothache experience, we have switched to mediate experience. The experience is roughly the same, whatever use we may make of it. Our purposes, and hence possibly the aspects of the experience to which we attend, are, however, subject to change. A change in purpose may alter the nature of the experiences which *follow* the change in purpose.

The physicist is therefore interested only in mediate experience, but the Wundtian psychologist studies immediate experience. The method of study was to be *introspection,* or, in a rough German translation, *Selbstbeobachtung* (self-observation). However, Wundt made it absolutely clear that his version of introspection was *not* to be *mere* self-observation. Introspection was to be the *controlled* observation of the contents of consciousness under experimental conditions. Nonexperimental introspection was useless for scientific purposes. Wundt (1910) clarified his position in the preface to his *Principles of physiological psychology:*

> All accurate observation implies that the object of observation (in this case the psychical process) can be held fast by the attention, and any changes that it undergoes attentively followed. And this fixation by the attention implies, in its turn, that the observed object is independent of the observer. Now it is obvious that the required independence does not obtain in any attempt at a direct self-observation, undertaken without the help of experiment. The endeavor to observe oneself must inevitably introduce changes into the course of mental events—changes which could not have occurred without it, and whose usual consequence is that the very process which was to have been observed disappears from consciousness. In the first place, it (the experimental method) creates external conditions that look towards the production of a determinate mental process at a given moment. In the second place, it makes the observer so far master of the general situation, that the state of consciousness accompanying this process remains approximately unchanged. (p. 45)

Wundt thought that mind and body were parallel, but not interacting, systems. Blumenthal (1980) and Richards (1980) classify Wundt as an identity theorist, with mind and body being two aspects of the same underlying reality. Boring (1950) sees Wundt as a dualist, and van Hoorn and Verhave (1980) classify Wundt as a parallelist. It does not much matter whether we regard Wundt as an identity theorist (which he claimed to be) or as a parallelist (which is implied by the nature of his work). In either case, it is justifiable to take the point of view of the psychologist, to study that aspect of reality (if one is an identity theorist) or that component of reality (if one is a parallelist) which is designated by the term "mind." In either case, mind does not *depend* on the body, and it can be studied directly. Wundt's psychology was called *physiological psychology* (by which Wundt meant experimental psychology), but the task of relating mental events to their bodily parallels could wait until later. Wundt's experimentalism involved a very modern emphasis on the manipulation and control of variables, and that aspect of his psychology has remained an unshakable foundation of scientific psychology over the years.

Despite his emphasis on experimentation, Wundt (1910) did not think that it was the only road to psychological knowledge:

> We may add that, fortunately for the science, there are other sources of objective psycho- logical knowledge, which become accessible at the very point where the experimental method fails us. . . . In this way, experimental psychology and ethnic psychology form the principal departments of scientific psychology at large. They are supplemented by child and animal psychology, which in conjunction with ethnic psychology attempt to resolve the problems of psychogenesis. Workers in both these fields may, of course, avail themselves within certain limits of the advantages of the experimental method. But the results of experiment are here matters of objective observation only, and the experimental method accordingly loses the peculiar significance which it possesses as an instrument of introspection. (p. 5)

Thus Wundt had a broader view of the field of psychology than is usually attributed to him. Individual psychology included experimental psychology and child psychology; comparative psychology included animal psychology and ethnic psychology (van Hoorn & Verhave, 1980). Moreover, Wundt did not simply talk about such topics as ethnic psychology. He published *ten volumes* of his *Völkerpsychologie* (1900–1920) when he was in his seventies.

Wundt did, for the most part, "simply talk" about child and animal psychology. His *Lectures on human and animal psychology* (1894) devotes only 26 of its 454 pages to animal psychology. Wundt's publications and those of his students indicate that he felt that those aspects of psychology had a lower priority. However, it is unjust to criticize a man for narrowness when, as an unparalleled pioneer in his field, he published thousands of pages and taught thousands of students in a career unexcelled for productivity, in fields ranging from the psychology of language to the history of law and morality! No one person can do everything, but Wundt probably came as close as any psychologist has ever come.

Although Wundt's treatment of psychology was sometimes narrow, there is probably a greater narrowness in the modern psychologist's picture of Wundt's psychology. We typically stereotype or parody the position of every important historical figure, but Wundt receives cruel and unusually unjust treatment. He was German, he was "old-fashioned," and he is seldom appreciated to the extent he deserves.

Anderson (1971) presents evidence of this lack of appreciation. He submitted a list of Wundt's statements to a group of graduate students, who were to match these quotations with the names of a group of outstanding figures in the history of psychology, one of whom was Wundt. In no case was one of Wundt's quotations attributed to him most often by the students! The students presumably thought that the statements were too modern, or too experimental, or statistical, or behavioral, to have come from the "old-time introspectionist," Wilhelm Wundt.

For Wundt, the task for experimental psychology *was* the analysis of consciousness. However, his attitude toward consciousness left some room for ambiguity. He explicitly talked about mental *process,* not mental *contents* (1894): "As a matter of fact, ideas, like all other mental experiences, are not *objects,* but *processes, occurrences*" (p. 236).

The view of psychology as the science that searches for elementary processes was a difficult one. The opponents of Wundtian psychology were quick to accuse him of a static elementarism: of regarding the contents of consciousness as though they were stationary, structural elements. The name *existentialism* was sometimes affixed to the school because critics said that the elements of consciousness were regarded as existing just as physical objects exist. Boring's (1950) description of the naming of structural psychology is a beautiful summary of the general treatment accorded to Wundt's psychology, as practiced by Titchener, in the United States: "The enemies of this orthodox psychology name it, but always in accordance with what they most dislike in it" (p. 431).

Blumenthal (1980), Danziger (1979), and O'Donnell (1979) are three authors who have stressed the American misinterpretations of Wundt and some of the possible reasons for them. For example, Wundt laid great stress on the *active* nature of the human mind and yet was treated by Boring as though he opposed *voluntarism,* which was in reality a key concept in Wundt's system. The many distortions of Wundt should remind us of the presentistic versus historicistic dichotomy described in Chapter 1. However, there is no need to assume that all such distortions are matters of intention.

We should not be surprised when Titchener suggests that Wundt was influenced in his experimental attitudes by John Stuart Mill (Tweney & Yachanin, 1980), since the Englishman Titchener was familiar with the work of both men. All of us find it easy to assume, without having any direct evidence, that other people have been subject to the same influences that we have. This, as applied to historical figures, is a good example of presentism.

New and more accurate historical studies have begun to bring Wundt out of the historical shadows to which he was relegated by functionalism, Gestalt psychology, and behaviorism. His psychology has again become a subject of intense study and controversy.

The older Wundt would perhaps be glad that he was not around to see these disputes. He probably would not have cared about the opinions of his critics. If he had any tendency to feel insecure, he could remember the fact that he had taught 24,000 students in his lectures over the years and had written more pages of psychology than any of his detractors. His last assistant, Friedrich Sander, said (Bringmann, Balance, & Evans, 1975) that Wundt as an old man was mellow, tired of controversy, and fond of anecdote, the sort of grandfather that we would all like to have; and he *was* the professional "grandfather" that we psychologists *did* have.

OTHER EUROPEAN PSYCHOLOGISTS

Wundt was the most important systematizer and organizer in the early, formative days of psychology, but there were other psychologists in Europe. We have alluded briefly to two important predecessors in Leipzig when Wundt arrived there, Ernst Heinrich Weber and Theodor Gustav Fechner.

Weber and Fechner each made controlled observations of the sensitivity of human observers to stimulation. Between them they formulated the Weber-Fechner law, which is still probably the single instance that most quickly springs to mind when any psychologist is challenged to produce a lawful relationship within our field. Weber cast the law in a simple form, stating that the amount of increase in a stimulus which was required in order for an observer to note the change was a constant proportion of the initial stimulus, rather than an absolute amount of change. Fechner cast the law in its more sophisticated logarithmic form.

However, it is the method of study which is important, not the law per se. Wundt worked on similar problems of psychophysics when he established his own laboratory. Tinker (1980) estimated that 70 percent of the 186 dissertations produced in Wundt's laboratory had sensation and perception as their subject matter. It is therefore reasonable to regard the lion's share of problems treated by Wundt and his students as having derived from the work of Weber and Fechner. In addition, 9 percent of the dissertations treated problems of method, and some of these were concerned with psychophysical methods. Thus these two men were probably the most direct contributors both to the problems and to the critical methodological core—the experimental method—of the new psychology of Wundt and, after him, Titchener.

Other psychologists in Europe followed Wundt's lead more or less closely, and still others sprang from quite a different lineage. Few of them disagreed, during the early period, about the importance of introspection for psychology. Boring (1953), in tracing the history of introspection, claimed that none of these early psychologists thought of themselves especially as *introspectionists*. They were simply *psychologists,* regarding the importance of introspection as axiomatic. The only arguments were about the details of the method.

Franz Brentano (1838–1917) was among the most influential non-Wundtians because of the diverse effects he had within psychology. He was originally trained for the priesthood but took a doctoral degree in philosophy and taught this subject on university appointments first at Würzburg and later at Vienna. He resigned his priesthood because he could not accept the doctrine of the infallibility of the Pope. He was known as a great Aristotelian, and he influenced Gestalt psychology and psychoanalysis. He was recognized as a competitor to Wundt and Titchener, but his psychology proved to be less concrete and less popular than theirs.

Brentano's name is associated with *act psychology,* the major tenet of which is that psychology should study mental acts or processes rather than mental contents. He believed that mental acts always *refer* to objects; for example, if we regard hearing as the mental act, it always refers to something heard. In this case, the truly mental event is the hearing, which is an act and not a content. If we see a color, again it is the seeing which is mental, not the thing seen. For Brentano, colors and sounds—contents—are not a proper part of a psychology of the mind. It is easy to see that Brentano's position insulated him against the charges of elementarism which were leveled, fairly or not, at Wundt.

Brentano's *Psychologie* (1874) was the most important of his psychological publications. He was a philosopher first and a scientist second, while Wundt was the opposite. In addition, Brentano was an empiricist rather than an experimentalist. He established no laboratory and manipulated no variables, and this fact may have restricted the number of psychologists who spread Brentano's approach. Brentano influenced structural psychology more by his opposition than by competitive positive contributions. He also had a strong influence on the development of the phenomenological tradition, through Stumpf and others.

Carl Stumpf (1848–1936) was Wundt's major direct competitor. In 1894 he was awarded the outstanding professorship in German psychology at the University of Berlin. At that time Wundt, as dean of German psychologists, seemed the logical choice. It has long been rumored that the opposition of Helmholtz prevented Wundt from getting the appointment. However, historians have been unable to find any direct evidence to support the rumor, and it is known that Helmholtz wrote Wundt a favorable letter of recommendation for at least one position.

Stumpf was strongly influenced by Brentano. Brentano's position on phenomenology may have encouraged Stumpf in his acceptance of a less rigorous type of introspection than that considered acceptable by Wundt. Stumpf and Wundt aired their difference of opinion about tones in an acrimonious argument published in a series of journal articles. The key question turned out to be whether one should accept the judgments of highly trained introspectors (Wundt) or those of trained and expert musicians (Stumpf). The disagreement was what one might expect between a man who took a more phenomenological view and Wundt, who insisted on a more analytic and controlled type of introspection.

It was one of Stumpf's students, Husserl, who is usually credited with starting phenomenology as a formal doctrine. Husserl, however, had studied earlier with Brentano, and that association may have done more than his association with Stumpf to nurture his phenomenological views.

Stumpf's laboratory at Berlin never rivaled Wundt's in scope or intensity of research, but there were still many research projects. Stumpf's special field was audition, and his true love was music. Also, there were brilliant students at Berlin who were destined to be of great importance in the development of psychology, notably the three founders of Gestalt psychology, Wertheimer, Köhler, and Koffka; Kurt Lewin, the great field theorist who is a father of social psychology; and Max Meyer, who was an early behaviorist. Stumpf, like Brentano, was more notable for his differences from Wundt than for his similarities to him, but he did accept without serious question the use of introspection.

One of the most capable and productive experimental psychologists of the period in Germany was G. E. Müller (1850–1934). He spent some 40 years directing the laboratory at Göttingen. His major work was in the fields of memory, psychophysical methodology, and vision. With Pilzecker, he developed the interference theory of forgetting. They called the interference of new learning with old *retroactive inhibition,* a term which has never gone out of use. Müller even suggested the concept of *consolidation* in memory, a concept which was revived much later to account for postshock amnesia in passive avoidance learning experiments. Müller also extended Hering's theory of color vision and refined Fechner's techniques in psychophysics; many psychologists have heard of the Müller-Urban weights, numbers used as correction factors in analyzing psychophysical data.

More than Wundt or Stumpf, Müller succeeded in breaking free from philosophy and metaphysics, both of them his own early interests. In this way he was perhaps similar to Titchener, who struggled to free himself of what he perceived as the encumbering concern with philosophy.

Another important early psychologist, Oswald Külpe (1862–1915), was a fellow student of Titchener's in Wundt's laboratory. Külpe also worked for a shorter time with Müller at Göttingen. Although Külpe and Titchener were friends at Leipzig, they later had fundamental disagreements. Titchener did not follow Wundtian orthodoxy to the letter, but he was far more traditional than Külpe.

The first part of Külpe's psychological career was spent in more or less "classical" research efforts. He published a textbook (1895) which was quickly translated by Titchener. Külpe tried to include only experimental facts which had been obtained by careful introspection. Very soon after that, he went to Würzburg, where he directed a series of ingenious and provocative introspective experiments on thought. Classical introspection, according to the interpretation given these experiments, was incomplete. The expected continuity in thinking was not contained in the orthodox introspective analysis. The Würzburg interpretation of the results was that there were *impalpable awarenesses* which did not appear in consciousness as contents usually do. (One wonders at the implication that most conscious contents are *palpable*.) Külpe suggested that these impalpable awarenesses should be regarded as *functions* and included as genuine conscious data. This was a synthesis of the views of Brentano and Wundt, if one included both contents and functions and viewed the latter as identical to the acts of Brentano.

Külpe made a direct contribution to Titchener's thinking when he distinguished psychology from physics on a different basis from Wundt's. For Külpe and Titchener, psychology was distinguished by its concern with the dependence of experience upon the experiencing organism. Both men apparently borrowed this distinction from the philosophers Mach and Avenarius, although its relationship to Locke's distinction between primary and secondary qualities is also clear. The Machian influence pulled Külpe, as it did Titchener, toward positivism (Danziger, 1979).

TITCHENER'S STRUCTURALISM

Titchener's Life

Edward Bradford Titchener (1867–1927) was a native of the English town of Chichester. After receiving an education in England which included training as a physiologist, he joined the students who were flocking to the new mecca of psychology, Leipzig. He studied with Wundt for 2 years, from 1890 to 1892, when he came to the United States. Wundt left an indelible impression on Titchener. Titchener's student, E. G. Boring, the influential historian of psychology, may have exaggerated the imprint of Wundt on Titchener, but there can be no doubt that there is a strong continuity between the psychologies of the two men.

Titchener's apparent Germanism of personality has become a legend: his autocratic attitude, the formality of his lectures in academic robes, and even his bearded, Germanic appearance. Every lecture was a dramatic production, with the staging carefully prepared by assistants. The presentation began precisely on time, with Titchener sweeping onto the stage in his robes, continued through demonstrations orchestrated by Titchener, who was flanked by his able assistants, and ended with the last sentence of a polished lecture in near coincidence with the end of the hour.

Legend has had it that Titchener was as remarkably Germanic intellectually as he was in personality. There were other non-German students whose exposure to Wundt was more protracted than Titchener's but whose deviations from the line of orthodoxy laid down by Wundt were far more marked. Some of these more rebellious students came from America and returned to America. Perhaps the English culture from which Titchener came provided better nourishment for Wundtian views than did the practical-minded American spirit. Wundt owed something to the English empiricists, and Titchener in England had been influenced by them to the extent that he may have exaggerated their influence on Wundt. It is also possible that Americans saw Germanism in Titchener's personality and intellect where they should have seen just the proper Englishman.

Titchener spent all of his years in the United States at Cornell University. During most of those years he was a power to be reckoned with, despite the fact that his brand of psychology was not popular for long with the pragmatic Americans. However, the greater popularity of the functional and behavioral schools, and perhaps simple fatigue, gradually took their toll. In 1920, he wrote a touching letter to his ex-student Pillsbury, who was then at the University of Michigan. The letter could serve as a symbol for the fate of Titchener's psychology, and makes us gasp at the fate meted out to this dedicated scholar and scientist. He says, in part, in replying to an invitation to visit Pillsbury at Michigan:

> It was most decent of you to think of me; there is no pleasure quite like that of being believed in by one's old students. I wish very much that I could say yes. I have often wanted to come to Ann Arbor, and see your surroundings and your workshop, but I can't accept the invitation. The straight fact is that I have no clothes. We stripped ourselves in 1914, and ran ourselves into debt for a time when the U.S. came into the war; and now we are living from hand to mouth. . . . I have literally bought no clothes with the exception of three suits of underwear— since 1914. . . . Here appearance doesn't matter, because people are used to one, and in lecturing a gown covers a multitude of sins. . . . My wife is in like case: I asked her what was the last thing she bought, and she said a hat in 1916! (Unpublished letter to Walter Pillsbury, 1920)

Thus this very proper and decent Englishman, somewhat lost first in Germany and then in the United States for the last two-thirds of his life, approached the end of his career wearing a threadbare suit under his outwardly forbidding academic robes. At this distance in time, we can feel pride for him and for ourselves as his academic descendants. His poverty was brought about, not just by a low academic salary, but by his contributions to his family in the United States and England, and by the fact that he was forced to support his laboratory largely out of his own pocket during the war years.

During the last years of his life, Titchener gradually turned away from psychology to numismatics (coin collecting). He died relatively young in 1927, probably as the result of a brain tumor. He left behind such high goals of scholarship that E. G. Boring, his best-known student, was later to say that there were no scholars in American psychology. A likely guess is that Boring was measuring himself and others against the standards of Titchener.

Titchener's Psychology

We must now turn from Titchener's life to his work. One of his major themes was the unity of science. It seemed self-evident to him that all sciences were erected upon the same foundation: the world of human experience. When this world was observed in different ways, different sciences evolved. For example, Titchener believed that just as physics evolved when people began to view the world as a vast machine, so did psychology evolve when they looked at it as a mind, a set of experiences subject to psychological laws. To illustrate this idea of scientific unity further, at various junctures he drew analogies between the then nascent science of psychology and the more established sciences of biology, physics, and chemistry.

Titchener (1910) maintained that the hallmark of scientific method was observation, which in his view subsumed experimentation. He saw an experiment as an observation that could be repeated, isolated, and varied, thereby ensuring clarity and accuracy. He then distinguished between the physical science type of observation (looking at) and psychological observation or introspection (looking within).

States of consciousness were the proper objects of this psychological study. Titchener (1898) launched structural psychology as a system in the United States in his paper "The postulates of a structural psychology," partly as follows:

> We may inquire into the structure of an organism, without regard to function—by analysis determining its component parts, and by synthesis exhibiting the mode of its formation from the parts. . . .
>
> We find a parallel to morphology in a very large portion of "experimental" psychology. The primary aim of the experimental psychologist has been to analyze the structure of the mind; to ravel out the elemental processes from the tangle of consciousness, or (if we may change the metaphor) to isolate the constituents in the given conscious formation. His task is a vivisection, but a vivisection which shall yield structural, not functional results. He tries to discover, first of all, what is there and in what quantity, not what it is there for. (pp. 449–450; as presented in Dennis, 1948, p. 366)

It is difficult to tell from this quotation just what Titchener thought about mind and consciousness. He changes metaphor, self-consciously, in midsentence. From the context it seems that the bulk of his work fits the second metaphor, although he, like Wundt, always speaks of consciousness as composed of processes rather than of elements when he is trying to be most rigorous. Yet by analogy he lends reality status to consciousness, since the word *structure* and the biological attitude toward morphology lend such reality status.

It is not even safe to assume, however, that this founder of America's brand of structuralism rejected functionalism. On this subject, R. I. Watson (1968) says:

> Description of Titchener's system of psychology is sometimes oversimplified. He was a structuralist, critics said, meaning that the static elements of experience were his concern, as contrasted with functional study of the process of experience which had been espoused by James and others. This is simply not true. There is no doubt he utilized functional material; and the findings of psychophysics, which formed one major segment in his system, are readily viewed as depending upon the functions of discrimination and estimation. Unequivocally, he accepted the existence of a functional aspect of psychology. (p. 393)

Still, a stubborn critic might claim that the quotation from Titchener, above, shows that he *regretted* the existence of functional psychology, even though he *recognized* it.

Consciousness was defined by Titchener as the sum total of a person's experiences as they are *at any given time*. Mind was regarded as the sum total of a person's experiences considered as dependent on the person, *summed from birth to death*. Thus:

> "Mind" is understood to mean simply the sum total of mental processes experienced by the individual during his lifetime. Ideas, feelings, impulses, etc., are mental processes; the whole number of ideas, feelings, impulses, etc., experienced by me during my life constitutes my "mind." (Titchener 1899, p. 12)

Titchener also listed three problems for psychology that were similar to Wundt's:

> The aim of the psychologist is three-fold. He seeks (1) to analyze concrete (actual) mental experience into its simplest components, (2) to discover how these elements combine, what are the laws which govern their combination, and (3) to bring them into connection with their physiological (bodily) conditions. (1899, p. 15)

Titchener modified Wundt's distinction between psychology and physics much as Külpe did. He could not agree with Wundt that physics studied mediate experience and psychology immediate experience; he thought, in keeping with his ideas on the unity of science, that all experience was immediate. The distinction between fields must be made on the basis of different *attitudes* toward the same basic subject matter. Thus the physicist studied the experience as independent of the experiencing person, while the psychologist studied the experience as it *depended on* the experiencing person.

One might object that Bessel (see Chapter 2) and the astronomers who followed him were quite concerned with the dependence of experience upon the nature of the experiencing observer, and that the physicists Titchener refers to might also be prepared to evince concern. His reply might be that the physicist's concern with the role of the observer is expressed only in order that observations could again be made completely reliable and independent of the observer. Bessel studied the reactions of observers so that he could try to develop "personal equations" which allowed him to *eliminate* the differences among observers. Thus the interest of physicists and astronomers in the dependence of experiences upon persons is a perfect illustration of their basic attitude, rather than an exception to it.

Titchener's concept of *stimulus error* was related to the distinction between psychology and physics. By stimulus error Titchener meant the error of paying attention to, and reporting on, the known properties of the stimulus, rather than paying attention to and reporting the sensory experience itself. This is probably the most important and the most obvious error made by untrained introspectors. Titchener pointed out that this tendency to describe the conscious state in terms of the stimulus rather than of the experience per se is beneficial and necessary in everyday life. All of us, therefore, grow up with strong habits of this kind, since responses to the objective character of the stimulus are ordinarily the effective ones. But such strong habits must be unlearned if one is to become an adequate psychological observer, and the only way to do this is through a new and intensive learning effort. Thus the trained introspector is one who learns to ignore objects and events as such and to concentrate instead on the pure conscious experience.

The use of a reduction screen in visual research offers a good illustration of this situation. If an experimenter permits a subject to see a stimulus object and also the illumination impinging upon it, the subject reports that a piece of white paper is white even if it is very dimly illuminated and is actually reflecting less light energy to the eye than, say, a piece of coal under bright illumination. The common judgment of untrained subjects is that the paper is brighter than the coal. This illustrates the stimulus error. The error can be eliminated by means of a reduction screen, which permits the subject to see only a small part of the stimulus object through a peephole. Such a device prevents subjects from seeing either the nature of the object or the amount of illumination, and now their judgment follows the "true" character of the isolated sensory experience. A piece of white paper dimly illuminated is called dark gray, and a piece of black coal brightly illuminated is called light gray.

Judgments made with a reduction screen are more in accord with the physical energies of the stimuli, although they are less accurate descriptions of the reflectivities of the coal and the paper. Neither type of judgment need be viewed as more true in any ultimate sense. The structuralists wanted the description that correlated most closely with the *local* situation. Titchener felt that a kind of functional reduction screen needed to be built into each psychological introspector through extensive practice. Physicists and all other scientists make the stimulus error as a matter of course. They wish to report on observations in such a way that their reports agree with the objective character of the stimulus, regardless of any local or momentary effects that may presently be determining their perception of the stimulus. Only introspective psychologists want to know the pure character of the present experience.

Titchener thought that psychology ought to study experience as it seems to exist when we try to detach it from learning; that is, we should refuse to attribute meaning to it. These undesirable meanings become attached to stimuli through learning, and our reactions to the stimuli so directly incorporate the related experiences that the "percept" is no longer a product of the stimulus only.

Titchener exorcised child psychology and animal psychology from the main body of psychology, which we saw that Wundt did not do. Titchener did not deny that the study of the behavior of children and animals would yield valuable information; he just denied that the information would be *psychological* information. Titchener did not apparently for that reason discourage the study of these topics. One of his prize students, Margaret Floy Washburn, published a book entitled *The animal mind* (1908), and Titchener respected and befriended John B. Watson, whose behaviorism represented the antithesis of Titchener's own interests.

Wundt's experimentalism was expressed in more exaggerated form by Titchener. He seems to have been more insistent than Wundt that psychology be *pure*. Applied science seemed to Titchener a contradiction, where to Wundt it had only been premature. Scientists, as Titchener saw it, must keep themselves free of considerations about the practical worth of what they are doing. He accordingly never accepted the applied work by Cattell and others, which we will discuss in the next chapter, as making any important contribution to psychology. He decried the notion that the function of psychology was to find ways of ministering to sick minds. He was caustic about the possibility of becoming a psychologist through the process of untrained, morbid self-examination.

Titchener's mind-body position was similar to Wundt's in that both saw mental and physical events as running along parallel courses, whether that was because there were two types of reality paralleling one another, or because there were two views of the same reality. The latter view is more consistent with Titchener's insistence on one kind of consciousness toward which one might take different points of view. Philosophy did not interest Titchener as it had Wundt. He boasted about psychology's new freedom from philosophical speculation. In Titchener we see the full-blown scientific tendency to view philosophy as irrelevant and to carry Hume's antimetaphysical attitude into laboratory practice. Where there had been a tendency in Wundt to use scientific results philosophically, in Titchener the results were only to be plowed back into further *scientific* progress.

THE METHODOLOGY OF STRUCTURALISM

The primary technique of investigation for Titchener, even more than for Wundt, was introspection. Titchener's introspection was an even more highly formalized and practiced procedure than Wundt's had been. Introspection, according to Titchener, could be carried on scientifically only by exceptionally well-trained observers.

One instance of his feelings about naïve observers is given in a discussion of phenomenology:

> In the present connection, I mean, by a phenomenological account of mind, an account which purports to take mental phenomena at their face value, which records them as they are "given" in everyday experience; the account furnished by a naïve, common-sense, non-scientific observer, who has not yet adopted the special attitude of the psychologist. . . . It is more than doubtful whether, in strictness, such an account can be obtained. (1912a, p. 489)

It is clear that Titchener did not favor the use of untrained observers, nor did he at this time favor phenomenology as science.

It is difficult for us untrained observers to say just what it is that the trained observers learned to do, but we must try if we are to understand what introspective psychology was about. Our difficulties are increased because introspection changed as the years passed. Titchener thought that introspection was becoming more refined and more generally applicable with the passage of time. He commented (1912a): "Our graduate students—far better trained, it is true, than we were in our generation—sit down cheerfully to introspective tasks such as we had not dreamed of" (p. 427). One wonders what these marvelous, hitherto undreamed-of, tasks may have been like. Probably Titchener was allowing himself a little too much hyperbole in a moment of euphoria, but no doubt he needed to believe in the continuing evolution of introspective methods.

Still—although we are told that the graduate students were getting better at something—we have few hints as to what that was. The introspective method, like Kuhn's paradigms, doubtless had to be absorbed more than learned from books. We are told that introspection is to be the direct observation of consciousness, of mental processes. In this connection, Titchener (1912b) said: "The course that an observer follows will vary in detail with the nature of the consciousness observed, with the purpose of the experiment, with the instruction given by the experimenter. Introspection is thus a generic term, and covers an indefinitely large group of specific methodological procedures" (p. 485).

Thus even Titchener seems not to have had an easy time in finding a satisfactory definition of introspection. He fell back on a specification of the experimental conditions. This is commendable in its operationalism but shares the usual difficulty of operational definitions: generalization does not come easily. Are there then no commonalities among the different applications of the term "introspection"? Surely there is a self-consciousness about introspection, an awareness of observing?

Not according to Titchener. He says (1912a): "*In his attention to the phenomena under observation, the observer in psychology, no less than the observer in physics, completely forgets to give subjective attention to the state of observing*" (p. 443). Titchener, and Wundt before him, recognized that self-consciousness might interfere with the phenomena under observation and thus invalidate the results. We will discuss this kind of problem later in the chapter as we evaluate the criticisms of introspection.

If the above description of introspection is accurate and complete, we would seem to have little to question. The psychologist's report would be just like the physicist's report of the same thing. But Titchener was speaking of a *trained* introspector. Thus the key differences between the physicist and the psychologist must result from the training process. What happens to observers as they undergo training? We note that they give verbal reports from the beginning. Physicists also accept verbal reports and undergo training in observation. Nobody denies that we may get interesting results in physics or psychology by accepting the reports of others about the things they have seen. Others accept our reports as we accept theirs. The only reservation is that all of us must be able to tell exactly what we mean, by pointing to an instance if necessary.

The observer learning to introspect, however, is in a different kind of circumstance. Words that are meaningful are not accepted. A structural psychologist is not interested scientifically in the statement "I see a table," for "table" is a "meaning word," based on preknowledge about the aggregation of visual and tactile sensations by which we might identify the table. The structural psychologists believed that they were interested in the aggregate of sensations arising in connection with the table as stimulus as a *meaningless* aggregate. They did not want the aggregate summarized in a meaning word. Their interest was in the direct contents of experience, not in the inferences made on the basis of the contents.

So an observer who said *table* was cautioned against making the stimulus error and presumably was eventually able to exclude this type of word from his or her professional vocabulary. What words are left, then? Are only such words left as have no external referents, but referents only in experience? These are again difficult questions. Wundt and Titchener alike emphasized that the external conditions must be carefully controlled so that the contents of consciousness could be precisely determined and so that more than one observer could experience the same thing and thus cross-check the results of the experiment.

We can then say that a workable vocabulary should be possible, based on the commonalities in experience under the carefully controlled conditions. After all, how else do we agree even on meaningful words like "table"? It is reasonable to suppose that we check that part of our experience which consistently occurs in conjunction with the use of the word "table" by others. This is, of course, an oversimplification in that processes of abstraction and generalization are also involved in determining whether or not the object in question has a relatively flat upper surface, legs attached underneath, and so on. But it should be *easier,* not *harder,* to determine whether or not *green,* or some other simpler sensation, was present!

Therefore, it seems possible to create a language usage of the type the structuralists required. However, it may be easier to correlate words with objects than with experiences; we seem to be able to use words that refer to objects more reliably than those that refer to experiences. Perhaps it is more difficult than we think for introspectors to isolate that aspect of their manifold experience to which a particular word should apply. Certainly two introspectors cannot reach agreement in a difficult case by pointing to something external, as they can in the case of objects. That would again be making the stimulus error. Fingers cannot point directly into the remoter reaches of the world of experience. The findings of introspection could not always be agreed upon, even given very careful control of conditions. Perhaps the descriptions given of experience depend as much upon the presuppositions of the introspector as upon the nature of his or her sensations.

Had it been possible to secure sufficient scientific agreement on introspective statements of findings, the structural school might still be a vital force today. That it was not possible we shall see later. Meanwhile, we will try to delineate introspection a little more clearly.

Introspection may be more, but it is at least this: a generic term for several types of observation carried out in psychology. Titchener has taught us that different investigators may use different kinds of introspection. For example, psychologists at Cornell and Würzburg used slightly different varieties. The Cornell variety was carried out under laboratory conditions, with both external stimulation and instructions carefully determined by the investigator. Only those subjects were used who had been carefully trained by the experimenter or by another investigator who was versed in the same method. The training included the admonition to observe the contents of experience and report on them. It included discouraging the use of "meaning" words or "thing" words. The use of words considered appropriate for describing mental processes was encouraged.

We reproduce below a part of an account of an introspective experiment. It conveys something of the flavor of the introspective method, presumably as approved by Titchener, since the report appeared in "his" journal. The two observers (Os), C. and P., had been instructed to report their memory images following stimulation by geometric shapes of different colors. E. Murray's (1906) account of some of the findings follows:

1 Introspections.   Manner of appearance of image. As a rule, the memory image appears spontaneously at the beginning of the recording period, or in the preceding after image period. Thereafter it returns at irregular intervals, which usually grow longer toward the end of the minute. On a few occasions, C. reports, the image was apparently evoked by chance twitches of the eyeball or eyelid, by inspiration, or, automatically, by rhythmic pressure of the key. Occasionally, also, the observer reports a faint anxiety at the momentary failure of the image, and a temptation to summon it by movement of the eyes (O. C.), by steady fixation, or by recall of detail after detail (O. P.).

2 Localization of image.   The memory image usually appears in the same direction and at the same distance as did the original. P. distinguishes it from the sensory after image by its position outwards on the screen (the after image appearing "on the eyelids"), and remarks that "Its appearance is often accompanied by the feeling of turning toward it." Occasionally it seems to be situated "in the head," but in this case its distinctness is materially lessened.

That this localization is correlated with the presence of motor elements, actual or ideated, has abundant evidence. Thus C., noting that the memory image usually appears as an object with spacial relations, states that in this case "the feeling of accommodation" is present, with "tendency to move the eyes and locate the image directly in space." The less real this feeling (of accommodation and convergence), the less distinct the image. Thus, toward the end of the recording period (C. sometimes reports), the images become less vividly "visual," are accompanied by almost no tendency to fixation, and are localized, not in any definite portion of the visual field, but vague, "in the head,"—a type of image described by C. as "more subjective," or "more purely memorial."

It seems probable that P. also refers to the muscular sensations attending fixation in her less concretely phrased account of the semispontaneous recall of images. "I seem to turn my attention toward the place where I expect the image to appear. If I hold my attention on this place, several more images are likely to follow." And again, "my attention vacillates about the place on the board where the image is expected, then settles down, and below unfolds the image, sometimes indistinctly, but as the attention turns more decidedly toward it growing in vividness."

3 *Incompleteness of image*.   Images are rarely complete. The lower right hand portion is most often missing, and the upper left hand portion the most distinct,—a condition possibly correlated with the characteristic grouping of matter on the printed or written page, and the acquired habit of attending primarily to the upper left hand word. In cases *where the outline is complete, it is often doubtful whether* there are not gaps in the main body of the figure. Whether complete or incomplete in relation to the original, the image is usually reported as flashing in and out as a whole, without growth or alteration. (pp. 230–231)

Several points emerge from this description of reports on introspective observations. First, the reports clearly are about experiences rather than about stimuli; for example, the incompleteness of the images is something that is not correlated with the properties of the stimuli. Second, the introspective reports relate some stimulus elements or processes to others; the occurrence of the images is correlated with sensations of movement or of thinking about such movement. Third, a discussion of the stimuli is completely missing from the accounts; no geometric stimuli, or even colors, are mentioned in the description here. Fourth, there is some mention of the relationship of the images to external conditions and habits, in this case position in space, and reading habits.

After this examination of the problems in defining introspection, one may have less tendency to laugh at the sometimes futile definitional efforts of those who are still vitally concerned with introspection. Natsoulas (1970) shrugs off the problem in this way: "Here 'introspection' is a relatively neutral term for the process(es) whereby one arrives on the spot at introspective awarenesses" (p. 90).

EMPIRICAL PROPOSITIONS

In science, not only do observations determine theory, but also theory determines observations. This was as true of structuralism as of any other system, despite the fact that structuralists did their best to allow observations to exert a maximum effect on their scientific propositions.

The three basic elements of consciousness are probably good demonstrations of this proposition. *Sensations, images, and feelings* came all the way down from the English empiricist philosophers through Wundt to Titchener, who retained them nearly to the end of his life. The elements were long thought to be basic and incapable of further analytic reduction. It is fair to ask to what extent these elements were *discovered in* consciousness and to what extent they depended upon philosophical, linguistic, or theoretical considerations. We will return to this question later.

Sensations were thought to be the elements of perception, and images the elements of ideas. Images differed from sensations primarily by being less vivid, less clear, less intense, and sometimes less prolonged. Both images and sensations had certain basic attributes. For Wundt, there were only two attributes: intensity and quality. Titchener expanded the list to four: intensity, quality, attensity, and protensity.

For both men quality had its usual meaning of a difference in kind. Titchener defined attensity as synonymous with clarity, except that it was the type of clarity that varies with attention rather than with the objective characteristics of the stimulus. Intensity had its usual meaning of strength, and protensity referred to duration in time of the sensation or image. Some sensory modalities produced sensations which had the additional property of *extensity* in space.

Titchener saw that it was not easy to distinguish image from sensation but held that there was at least a quantitative difference. For example, there would be a point along the intensity dimension at which image became strong enough to be sensation or sensation became weak enough to be image.

An experiment by Perky (1910) at Cornell illustrated the difficulty of deciding what was image and what was sensation. Subjects told to "project" a banana on a blank screen did not report the appearance of a dim picture of a banana actually flashed on the screen but attributed the sensation to their unusually clear imagery at that time. Other subjects told to observe the actual banana failed to report when it was turned off, apparently maintaining an image strong enough to be confused with the previous dim sensation.

We should note that Perky was distinguishing between image and sensation on the basis of the presence or absence of an objective stimulus. This is not a distinction on the basis of conscious contents, and in some sense it is inconsistent from the point of view of a structuralist. However, this is always the procedure actually used to decide whether some conscious content is an image or a sensation; namely, one asks whether or not a stimulus is present which correlates with the sensation.

In any case, Perky's experiment cast doubt on the possibility of making the sensation-image distinction solely on the basis of the characteristics of conscious contents. As a result, there was a tendency to speak more about the attributes of sensations and less about images. Boring (1950, p. 201) cites a similar experiment by Schaub (1911) as providing more convincing evidence that images might be more intense than weak sensations. Thus enduring beliefs about the nature and number of conscious elements were beginning to erode.

Even earlier, the Würzburg psychologists got into heated controversy with Titchener on the subject of "imageless thought," which they claimed to have discovered. The admission of such an entity would have necessitated a revision of Titchener's view that images are the elements of thoughts. Accordingly, he rejected (as Kuhn would say we should expect he would) the views of Külpe and his students. The latter were joined in the defense of imageless thought by Binet in France and by the functionally oriented Woodworth at Columbia University. Titchener suspected that all of their results might have been caused by faulty—that is, incomplete—introspection. He did not find any clear evidence for this upstart element, this imageless thought. He had no use for impalpable awarenesses. His subjects did not confirm Woodworth's findings. Titchener's verdict was that the so-called thought element was probably an unanalyzed complex of kinesthetic sensations and images, which were always difficult to find in consciousness. The "will" element was also excluded. An *act of will* was simply a complex of images forming ideas in advance of action.

Titchener was able to bring attention into his system by equating it with clarity of sensation. He found in some subjects only a two-part breakdown of clarity, into central and clear versus peripheral and unclear; in other subjects, there was a multistep progression from clear to unclear.

Titchener rejected Wundt's tridimensional theory of feeling. Of the three dimensions pleasant-unpleasant, strained-relaxed, and excited-calm, he retained only the first. He reduced the other two to sensations and images, especially kinesthetic. They were therefore not to be regarded as special characteristics of feeling; in fact, they were not feeling at all.

Later, Titchener eliminated even the last remaining attribute of feelings (Henle, 1974). Nafe (1927) was the last of a series of students of Titchener who searched for the sensory differences between pleasantness and unpleasantness. Nafe believed that he had found the answer that Titchener wanted: pleasantness was a "bright pressure" located in the trunk at a higher level than the "dull pressure" of unpleasantness. Nafe suggested that vascular changes might be responsible for these sensations. If this point of view is accepted, then affect retains no independent properties. Sensation is all.

We now have examined several "empirical" propositions which had systematic relevance for Titchener. In addition, there are more directly empirical results (outcomes of experiments) which were generally accepted by the structuralists. Some of these results do not depend on any peculiarities of structuralist metaphysics or methodology and are acceptable to any psychologist regardless of systematic beliefs. For example, Titchener's first "empirical" chapter in *An outline of psychology* (1899) is entitled "The quality of sensation." In it are examined the qualities of visual, auditory, olfactory, gustatory, and other sensations. Each examination of these qualities is based on a relevant experiment or demonstration. The methodology of these observations is objective enough to satisfy psychologists of any persuasion, even though they might not be interested in that type of experiment for themselves.

STRUCTURALISM AS A SYSTEM

Definition of Psychology

Titchener's definition of psychology was "The analytic study of the generalized adult normal human mind through introspection." As we have seen, he excluded child and animal psychology, though Wundt had not. The "generalized" adds the implication that Titchener was not interested in individual differences, and Wundt seems to have shared his indifference on that subject. The qualifier "normal" excludes the mentally disturbed and defective from study—which ignores the interests of most modern clinical psychologists.

Basic Postulates

The term "postulates" refers to statements which are to be taken as unquestionable by some individual or group. Postulates in a formal logical sense serve as a basis from which other statements, called theorems, can be derived. Psychology has made relatively little use of postulates of this latter kind, and structural psychology was no exception to this rule. We have to come much closer to the present to find exceptions. Nevertheless, postulates in the first sense have long been a concern of psychologists. Again, the structuralists were no exception. For proof, we need only recall the title of Titchener's 1898 paper, "The postulates of a structural psychology."

What sorts of postulates, then, have traditionally concerned psychologists? Most of them have been the "high level" assumptions which guide the behavior of the psychological investigator. For example, the definition of psychology given above serves to direct investigation, and definitions cannot be directly tested. The reader can find other examples of this kind in our discussion of the goals and methods of Wundt and Titchener.

There are, however, still other kinds of statements which have been called postulates. These statements *seem* to rest upon an empirical foundation, rather than to be simply assumed, and are claimed to be universally supported by the relevant observations. We quote Titchener's paper (1898) directly for structuralist examples:

> We set out from a point of universal agreement. Everyone admits that *sensations* are elementary mental processes. There is, it is true, diversity of opinion as to the range of contents that the term shall cover. . . . The divergence, however, is not serious. Once more, we set out from a point of universal agreement. "There are two indispensable determinants of every psychical element, quality and intensity." (as cited in Shipley, 1961, pp. 233, 236)

We have mentioned that Titchener himself wished to add attensity and protensity to the list of "indispensable determinants." It was thus true that the "basic postulates" of structuralism underwent changes. There is no true set of underlying assumptions, or of universally supported statements, which can be cited. Because the postulates that did exist were not formal, logical postulates, it is not possible to make any statement about their number, sufficiency, or adequacy. These are the properties which a logician would analyze in a logical system, but none of the traditional psychological systems can support such an analysis.

There are, nevertheless, guiding principles which certainly seem to have been accepted by structuralists. The greatness of Wundt is based on the fact that he insisted on two of the basic "postulates" of science: that one ought to use both (1) *analysis* and (2) *control* as primary methods in psychology. Titchener excluded other methods as unscientific, although Wundt had not. Titchener could not affirm too strongly that psychology had won its fledgling wings and was independent of metaphysics. Knowledge was to be empirical, not a priori. Mind and consciousness were assumed to be useful concepts and to constitute the proper province for psychological study. Introspection was assumed to be a valid method for that study. This method required extended study and training for its efficient use. Consistency and law were assumed to hold for the realm of consciousness. Mind and body were thought to be parallel systems.

Nature of the Data

To summarize the previous discussion: Titchener believed that the primary data of psychology must be obtained by means of introspection and under strict experimental conditions. Wundt thought that the experimental method could be supplemented when necessary through some kinds of careful field observations. His final system included comparative psychology, which was made up of animal psychology and ethnic psychology. Both Wundt and Titchener would have argued that their data were as *objective* as any data in psychology. The "subjective" tag was applied by their critics, not by them. Today a controversy about the objectivity of data might be settled by computing the reliability of the judgments made. The intuitive analog of this reliability analysis, made long before the age of the computer, consigned introspective data to the subjective category. It is not certain that this judgment was justified.

Mind-Body Position

The Wundt and Titchener positions on the mind-body issue have been discussed, if not decided. We might add another quotation from Titchener (1899) which supports the view that he was an identity theorist: "The metaphysics to which Science points us is rather a metaphysics in which both matter and spirit disappear, to make way for the unitary conception of *experience*" (p. 366). This quotation sounds like a monism of experience, which could either be an idealism (consciousness is the only reality) or an identity theory (which does not take a position on what *kind* of reality experience is, mental or physical). Titchener's view is similar to that of Mach, of whose ideas Titchener was fond. Mach also emphasized experience as the basis of all science. Titchener (1910) later elaborated his position. He pointed out that the common-sense conception of mind leads to dead-end questions:

> Where, for instance, on that view, does the body end and the mind begin? Do the senses belong to mind or to body? Is the mind always active and the body always passive? Do body and mind ever act independently of each other? Questions such as these arise at once; but it is a hard matter to answer them. Parallelism has no logical pitfalls of this kind. (p. 14)

We conclude that it does not matter whether Wundt and Titchener were identity theorists or parallelists, but it is important that they were one or the other.

Principles of Connection

The problem of connection was a secondary one for Titchener. He first needed to work out the nature of the elements to be connected. We have seen that he gradually simplified his system, first eliminating some of the properties of feelings and finally eliminating feelings completely as a separate category of experience. Even before he eliminated feelings, he accepted the likelihood that there was no clear demarcation in experience between sensations and images. We will see that, as judged by one of his students, he had arrived at a rather different view of the nature of the problem of psychology at the end of his life. We might say that he spent most of his professional life in working out the preliminaries, in deciding how the task of psychology should be approached. Thus he had little time to spend on the problem of connections.

To the extent that he did concern himself with connections, Titchener explained them largely by the concepts of association. He reworded the principle of association by contiguity as his main law of association (1910):

> Let us try . . . to get a descriptive formula for the facts which the doctrine of association aims to explain. We then find this: that, whenever a sensory or imaginal process occurs in consciousness, there are likely to appear with it (of course, in imaginal terms) all those sensory and imaginal processes which occurred together with it in any earlier conscious present. . . . Now the law of contiguity can, with a little forcing, be translated into our own general law of association. (Titchener, 1910, pp. 378–379)

Titchener's law of association furnished him with a principle of successive connection; that is, item A tends to elicit item B immediately afterward. There remained the problem of connection of the elements within the cross section which is consciousness. This was to be solved by the presentation of the laws of synthesis. This task never seems to have been completed. From his discussion, it is clear that Titchener (1910) recognized the difficulty of synthesis, that the elements did not simply sum to the unitary experience which was there in the first place:

> If the conscious elements were "things," the task of reconstruction of an experience would not be difficult. We should put the simple bits of mind together, as the bits of wood are put together in a child's puzzle-map or kindergarten cube. But the conscious elements are "processes"; they do not fit together, side by side and angle to angle; they flow together, mix together, overlapping, reinforcing, modifying or arresting one another, in obedience to certain psychological laws. (p. 17)

This quotation should make us hesitant to classify Titchener as a static elementalist. Titchener seems here to be describing mind as quite dynamic. Nevertheless, he was never able to give the laws of synthesis whose existence he seemed to be guaranteeing in the last sentence of the quotation. His first task of analysis was never finished.

A further kind of connection for Titchener to explain was the problem of meaning. How does meaning become connected to sensation? He regarded this question as belonging outside of psychology but decided to answer it anyway. His answer was the well-known *context theory*. The meaning of a sensation, according to his theory, was simply the context in which it occurred in consciousness. A simple sensation does not have meaning; it gets meaning only from the other sensations or images accompanying it. The context of the sensation, which is its meaning, is a result of past experience with the sensation. The meaning is the result of associations between past sensations or images. What we call *meaning* is simply the totality of sensation accompanying the meaningful sensation:

No sensation means; a sensation simply goes on in various ways, intensively, clearly, spatially, and so forth. All perceptions mean. . . . For us, therefore, meaning may be mainly a matter of sensations of the special senses, or of images, or of kinesthetic or other organic sensations, as the nature of the situation demands. Of all its possible forms, however, two appear to be of especial importance: kinesthesis and verbal images. . . . But is meaning always conscious meaning? Surely not; meaning may be carried in purely physiological terms. (1910, pp. 367–369)

Principles of Selection

The basic problem of explaining why certain stimuli are selected in consciousness was handled by the use of the concept of attention, which was reduced to sensory clarity. Titchener initially believed that there were two degrees of clarity, but one of his students at Cornell, L. R. Geissler (1909), found that subjects could rate up to ten gradations along a numerical scale. Wirth, at Leipzig, produced similar findings.

According to Titchener (1908), there are three general stages of attention: (1) native, involuntary primary attention, where native factors like the intensity and quality of the sensory experience determine attention, along with involuntary attentive set or perhaps novelty; (2) voluntary secondary attention after the novelty wears off—this stage is difficult to get through in terms of attempting to maintain attention at a high level of clarity; and (3) derived primary, or habitual, attention, which is the ultimate objective; the attention is again involuntary, this time because of its history of learned development rather than because of native, unlearned factors.

As stages, these three conditions were obviously intended to be viewed as continuous rather than as clearly separable. An example of this continuity in stages is the development of interest in reading a certain kind of subject matter, such as that in a psychology text. Originally, attention will be held by factors like novelty and expectations generated by presuppositions concerning benefits to be gained by reading. As reading progresses, negative or inhibitory factors may develop as the student encounters unfamiliar terminology and difficult expositions and perhaps also as some expectations are disappointed. The second stage will thus appear, and the student will find it difficult to keep the material clear in consciousness. Fixation at this stage of attention is a serious problem in education and may partly account for academic difficulty and student complaints. If this troublesome stage can be survived, according to Titchener's account, the third stage will emerge. Then familiarity with the material will come to maintain a certain level of attention. In Titchener's view, reaching this stage of derived involuntary attention was an important objective of education.

CRITICISMS OF STRUCTURALISM

Such was the system called structuralism. It made many positive contributions to the science of psychology. Psychology became a science with an existence apart from metaphysics, with a careful experimental method and a nucleus to organize around. Within this framework, structuralists contributed many experimental findings. But structuralism, like any system seen by its opponents as "orthodox," made one of its greatest contributions by providing a target for the darts of criticism. They were not long in coming.

Introspection

The severest attack on structuralism was on the introspective method. Many of the criticisms were recognized as weaknesses by Wundt and Titchener, and they tried to remedy or prevent these weaknesses. The following points were debated.

Introspection must always be retrospection, since it takes time to report on a state of consciousness. Forgetting is rapid, especially immediately after having an experience, so that some of the experience may be lost. It is also possible that the necessity for retrospection will lead to embellishment, especially if the introspector has a vested interest in a theory that will be affected by the experimental results.

This objection was answered by using only well-trained observers working with time intervals that were very short and by postulating a *primary mental image,* a kind of mental echo which was assumed to preserve the experience for the introspector until it could be reported. If the report is made within the limits of this immediate memory, before conscious attention has changed, then little of value will be lost.

A second difficulty recognized by structuralists and critics alike is that the act of introspecting may change the experience drastically. The classic example is introspecting on the experience of anger. If the state is attended to, it tends to disintegrate and might disappear completely. Thus the measuring technique interferes with the experience, as it does in the case of the physicist measuring subatomic particles. A somewhat analogous situation in the social sciences is encountered by the cultural anthropologist who wishes to observe the habits and customs of some other culture. The presence of the anthropologist changes the behavior of the subjects. The undesirable effects of such an intrusion can be minimized if the observer remains in a household for a long time. The subjects should gradually return to their normal behaviors. But this result, like that of bringing introspection into the mental household, can be accomplished only by long and arduous effort. In the case of the mental household, the final state of affairs may be affected by the training process. Wundt postulated that what was observed became quite independent of the introspective process as training proceeded, but Titchener apparently did not take quite so strong a position. He did, however, feel that the experienced observer became unconscious of the act of observation after long practice.

A third difficulty is that psychologists relying on the introspective method at different laboratories were not getting comparable results. Boring (1953) provides examples of contradictory results coming from different laboratories. This difficulty *in practice* tends to confirm the above difficulties *in principle*. We have said earlier that we could see no insuperable obstacles to developing a language to describe introspective experiences, given control over the external elicitors of sensation. However, lack of agreement on results indicates that it was not *practically* possible to devise an adequate language or set of procedures. Titchener maintained that agreement would be reached eventually, presumably when all introspectors had learned to do their work as accurately and carefully as those at Cornell. For whatever reasons, introspection went out of favor before agreement was reached.

A fourth argument was perhaps the most decisive. There was growing evidence that some data which should belong in psychology could not be obtained by introspection. We have seen that Titchener himself recognized unconscious meanings. The Würzburg school pressed for the recognition of imageless thoughts; it looked suspiciously as though thought went on, blithely oblivious of the "fact" that it "could not occur" independently of the elements that introspective analysis had revealed. The psychoanalysts claimed that they had demonstrated beyond reasonable doubt that *unconscious* influences played a role in maladjustment and even in everyday motivation. The animal psychologists were getting interesting results despite the fact that animals could not introspect. All of these developments made it appear that the key structuralist *method,* like Titchener's definition of psychology, excluded too much that should be included in the field. The rising tide of objection pitched over the wall of structuralist orthodoxy and tore it down, leaving room for other problems and other methods. Introspection was found wanting as the exclusive psychological method.

Many critics jumped to the conclusion that since introspection was not everything, it was nothing. It is indeed difficult to define introspection; but it is also difficult to define *psychology* exactly, and we do not reject its study on that ground. It is unwise to issue blanket condemnations of something because it is undefined. There is always a possibility that some aspects of a vaguely defined method will prove useful.

In the present case, it should be noted that data which were gathered by introspection, broadly defined, have always been used in psychology. We have dramatic instances in which introspection gave us information about physiological processes and structures long before these processes and structures could be observed with other methods. For example, a three-color theory of vision was proposed by Thomas Young (1802) and worked out in detail by Helmholtz over 100 years before microscopic techniques became refined enough to reveal three fundamental types of color receptors within the retina. We believe that the usefulness of some type of introspection is far from ended. Introspection still has its place, despite the fate of the system which leaned too heavily upon it. If by introspection we mean the use of experience and the verbal reports based on this experience, then introspection, as Titchener noted, is simply coextensive with science and will presumably always be used.

Other Objections

There were other objections besides those that pertained to method. The narrowness of structural psychology was attacked. Compartmentalization was one of Titchener's favorite pastimes. He seemed to prefer putting an area of investigation into a non-psychological category to claiming it as a new province for psychology. When Watson started publishing the results of his behavioral studies, Titchener said that they were interesting but they were *not* psychology. Even physiological psychology, for Titchener, was a subsidiary problem to be attacked later. We can imagine how unpopular his views were to a growing band of enthusiastic and ambitious young scientific imperialists! They wanted to appropriate as much of the world for themselves as possible, not leave it for someone else. Titchener's conception of what psychology *ought not* do was too much for them to endure.

In addition, even within its limited domain, structuralism was castigated for its artificiality and its emphasis on analysis. These perceived shortcomings were most vigorously attacked by the Gestaltists, who deplored the loss that they thought must be engendered by analysis. They believed in the primacy of wholes with properties which could never be recovered by any synthesis of elements. For them, the primary method was phenomenological observation, not the analytic introspection of Titchener.

In order to clarify one final objection, let us recall an incident which was reported by James McKeen Cattell, an American who was Wundt's first assistant. Cattell had brought the study of individual differences to Leipzig, and Wundt reportedly declared the problem *ganz Amerikanisch* (entirely, or typically, American). Since the problem arose out of evolutionary thought through an Englishman, Sir Francis Galton, Wundt's comment—if he really made it—was not literally true, but a deeper truth is, in any case, reflected: that the American temperament was more pragmatic than the European at that time. Thus when Titchener brought his narrow version of Wundt's psychology to America, the reaction of Americans tended to be symmetrical to Wundt's. His kind of psychology was regarded as *ganz Deutsch*. The "pure science" aspect of structuralism had too little appeal. What difference did the elements of experience make in initiating and guiding action? Beginning with William James in America, the question was: "What is the function of consciousness in adjustment?" Since structuralism did not propose to give answers to that, or to any other, practical question, it never won the hearts of many Americans. If it had, all other obstacles, all criticism, might have been overcome. The fatal objection to any system is that its program is not attractive enough.

THE FATE OF STRUCTURALISM

The structuralistic view of consciousness was somewhat ambiguous. Critics claimed that structuralists approached consciousness as though it had a real existence independent of the body. This led to the alternative name *existentialism* for the school. This name now appears to have been an unfortunate choice, since it may lead to confusion between Wundtian and Titchenerian structuralism and modern varieties of existentialism, to which it bears only a remote resemblance. Today existentialism would be associated with names like that of Jean Paul Sartre.

The search for the elements of consciousness led to almost as much confusion. One conclusion was that there was but one established element, sensation. In Titchener's posthumous publication *Systematic psychology: Prolegomena* (1929), he concluded that introspective psychology deals exclusively with sensory materials. Its problem was reconceived as an examination of the *dimensions* of the one element.

In this reformulation of its problem, structural psychology may be said at the same time to have solved its original problem and to have arrived exactly nowhere. The problem of searching for elements had been eliminated; there seemed to be no laws of combination of elements to look for, since there was but one element to work with.

This logical cul-de-sac was brilliantly foreshadowed by James (1890) in Chapter 9 of his *Principles of psychology:*

> It is astonishing what havoc is wrought in psychology by admitting at the outset apparently innocent suppositions, that nevertheless contain a flaw. The bad consequences develop themselves later on, and are irremediable, being woven through the whole texture of the work. The notion that sensations, being the simplest things, are the first things to take up in psychology is one of these suppositions. The only thing which psychology has a right to postulate at the outset is the fact of thinking itself, and that must first be taken up and analyzed. If sensations then prove to be amongst the elements of the thinking, we shall be no worse off as respects them than if we had taken them for granted at the start. (p. 224)

Although this is fine critical writing, the astute reader has noticed that even James smuggled in the assumption that thinking had elements! And that assumption, perhaps, is more deadly than the further assumption that *given* that there are elements, sensations are among them.

Evans (1972) points out that Titchener's attitude toward phenomenological descrip tion underwent a gradual change, as did his other beliefs. Although Titchener is often portrayed as a rigid traditionalist, he modified his system just as other psychologists have modified theirs. In 1925, he had unbent to the extent of saying, "Phenomenology is not yet, is not of itself, experimental psychology; but it provides today a safe and sure mode of approach to the analysis of our psychological subject matter; and our recourse to it, our realization of its promise may perhaps be taken as a sign of adolescence" (Evans, 1972, p. 179). Had Titchener lived longer, there is no way to tell how far he might eventually have modified his systematic beliefs to make them more compatible with Gestalt psychology or with functionalism. There is no indication, however, that he could ever have accepted behaviorism, with its denial that con sciousness could be the subject matter of psychology. For Titchener, behaviorism was not a school of *psychology* at all!

Time was running out for structural psychology as it ran out for Titchener. He had withdrawn from the mainstream of psychology as the years passed. He resigned from the American Psychological Association early in his career because it refused to punish someone that Titchener believed had plagiarized one of his translations. He then formed his own group, the Society of Experimental Psychologists. His early burst of produc tivity in this country produced about nine papers per year for the first 7 years, but the rate declined thereafter.

His personal relationships were as variable as his professional life. He went through a fierce period in his relationship with Thorndike after ripping apart the latter's book (Joncich, 1968). Paradoxically, he was a loyal friend of J. B. Watson, sticking with him through his declaration of behaviorism and his forced resignation from Johns Hopkins. Finally, the battles were too much, and the old warrior seemed gradually to withdraw from his students and his field even as his brand of psychology became less and less popular.

E. G. Boring's book *The physical dimensions of consciousness* (1933) was in effect the death throe of structuralism. As a prominent student of Titchener and in some ways his most likely successor, Boring in 1933 was actually concerned chiefly with correlating conscious and physiological processes. This had been Titchener's third problem for psychology. Boring (1933) seems still to have been trying to salvage whatever he could of the structuralist systematic position:

> The doctrine of conscious dimensions, which I believe without proof to be essentially Titchener's way of meeting the challenge of Gestalt psychology and the anti-atomists, seems to me very important and the correct approach to the adequate description of mind. However, I am not willing to stress the doctrine as much as some of its friends would like, because I believe that categories of description, whether they be the psychological dimensions of quality and intensity or the physical dimensions of space, mass and time, are scientifically arbitrary and temporary, matters of the convenience or economy of description. One does not attempt to discover conscious elements, attributes, or dimensions, one makes them up and uses them as phenomenological exigencies require. (p. vii)

At this point, Boring was trying to wed structuralism to the increasing scientific and logical sophistication of his vantage point in time. He recognized the arbitrariness of scientific concepts and the importance of verbal convention even in the communication of introspective results. Yet the influence of Titchener was still strong a mere 6 years after his death, and Boring was fighting to salvage consciousness as a fit subject of scientific investigation.

Four years later, he had given up the struggle. He examined the definition of consciousness and the role of private experience. He concluded that private experience could not be scientifically useful until it became public; therefore, it was defined out of science. After arriving at "an awareness of an awareness" as the closest approximation to a definition of consciousness, he had this to say about it:

> Having understood, tough-minded rigorous thinkers will, I think, want to drop the term *consciousness* altogether. A scientific psychology is scarcely yet ready to give importance to so ill defined a physiological event as an awareness of an awareness. This concept might never have come to the fore had not people tried to interpret others in terms of their own "private" minds—that egocentric Copernican distortion which properly leads to desolate solipsism. (Boring, 1937, p. 458)

Thus Boring furnished first the capstone, then the tombstone, of structuralism. He who might have become the last defender of Titchener's brand of psychology became an overseer of its final demise. Structuralism as a unitary systematic force is dead. For us, it is but a dim memory of our psychological past, of the vibrant hope that led brilliant young scientists from distant shores to Leipzig and later attracted many fine American students to Cornell. Those who went did not return empty-handed or empty-headed; they returned with the idea of laboratories and with instruments to help in establishing them, and that aspect of structuralism conquered the psychological world.

Yet the psychological system that was once so dominant died of neglect. Sad. Had Titchener broadened Wundt's system rather than narrowing it, we might see today a greater conceptual continuity between past and present in psychology. As it happened, systematic evolution was too slow, and structuralism was replaced rather than reshaped.

Meanwhile, the phenomenological tradition lives on. We have seen that Titchener was beginning to recognize its contributions to psychology. Husserl had posited the individual's potential for grasping the "essence" or "central core" of reality, which he thought lies in consciousness. Sartre carried through Husserl's ideas of essences and concluded that phenomena are not appearances of objects but rather are the beings which objects leave in appearing to consciousness. He regards consciousness as the opposite of objectivity (Lauer, 1965).

Clearly this existential talk is not the kind that could have come from Wundt and Titchener. However, we should not forget that there is one fundamental similarity: the belief that an understanding of consciousness is central to an understanding of the human condition. And, lest we conclude that this is a problem of interest only to philosophers and quaintly outmoded psychologists, let us look at a quotation from a modern and controversial biologist: "The evolution of the capacity to simulate seems to have culminated in subjective consciousness. Why this should have happened is, to me, the most profound mystery facing modern biology" (Dawkins, 1976, p. 63).

SUMMARY AND CONCLUSIONS

Structuralism, which was regarded by E. B. Titchener as the one true psychology, was named by him in 1898, although all of the fundamentals of the system had been worked out by Wilhelm Wundt. Its problems began as the search for the basic conscious elements or processes, their mode and laws of connection, and their relation to the nervous system. Its chief method was to be experimental introspection, conceived by Wundt as the study of immediate experience and by Titchener as the study of experience as dependent upon the experiencing organism. Both Wundt and Titchener thought the experimental method indispensable for psychology. The structural school succeeded in winning academic recognition for psychology as an independent science, with the official founding of Wundt's laboratory in Leipzig in 1879 a landmark date. Psychology was regarded as an empirical science having some features of natural science and some of social science, according to Wundt's scheme.

Structuralism was criticized primarily for its methodology and the narrowness of its conception of psychology; animal and applied psychology were ignored in practice if not in principle. The critics prevailed, and modern psychology gratefully acknowledges the awesome historical debt owed to structuralism, while rejecting most of its systematic tenets. About half of America's psychologists are Wundtian by descent, but not by conviction. We do accept the preeminence of the experimental method, and we recognize that some forms of introspection are still important. Interest in consciousness and "mind" as subject matters is making a strong comeback, but most of the systematic formulations of structuralism are of historical interest only.

FURTHER READINGS

Wundt's *Principles of physiological psychology* (1910) gives a good picture of the structuralist position at that time, as the reader has seen in the quotations in the present chapter. This book, supplemented by Titchener's paper "Postulates of a structural psychology" (1898) and Boring's "History of introspection" (1953), yields an understanding of the general tenor of structuralist psychology early in the present century. There has been a great resurgence of interest in Wundt scholarship, part of which was inspired by the coming of the centennial of the founding of Wundt's laboratory; a good entree into this modern scholarship is the book edited by Bringmann and Tweney, *Wundt studies* (1980). This renewal in interest has been accompanied by a resurgence in *appreciation* of Wundt which is of at least equal scope.

It is an interesting exercise to browse through issues of the *American Journal of Psychology* printed prior to Titchener's death in 1927. They give a less biased and more balanced view of what structuralists were doing than we can give here. Titchener's *Text-book of psychology* (1910), Boring's *The physical dimensions of consciousness* (1933), and his article "A psychological function is the relation of successive differentiations of events in the organism" (1937) will finish off a picture of how structuralism developed and why it disappeared. R. I. Watson's *The great psychologists from Aristotle to Freud* (1971) provides interesting material about every classical system treated in the present book, as does Boring's *A history of experimental psychology* (1950). However, one should not accept Boring or anyone else as the last word on structuralism, especially since the school has become a topic of lively contemporary controversy. A reading of Blumenthal's "Wilhelm Wundt—Problems of interpretation" (1980) ought to leave one in the properly ambivalent mood.

END NOTES

Dimensional Descriptions of Structuralism

Structuralism is one of the easier schools to place in the framework of dimensions provided by Watson. Systems that take extreme positions, and that we tend to caricature more because we are less familiar with their details, are easier to rate.

Conscious Mentalism–Unconscious Mentalism Watson's first dimension is a good example; structuralism is the prototypical case of a system that emphasizes conscious mentalism. Its philosophy and its method were designed to make conscious mentalism accessible as the primary subject matter for psychology.

Content: Objectivism vs. Subjectivism Structuralists emphasized content that we would regard as subjective; in R. I. Watson's words, "psychological data viewed as . . . mental structure or activity of individual." This is quite clear and also relates to the previous dimension.

Determinism–Indeterminism Both Wundt and Titchener were deterministic in their views. However, Wundt's emphasis on *voluntarism* as a key part of his system opened the door for critics to claim that there was an indeterministic aspect of his system. This is a problem faced by all voluntarists, even though they typically believe that voluntary choices are also ultimately determined by their antecedents.

Empiricism–Rationalism Wundt and Titchener were empiricists, but again critics might claim that their system contained some "excess baggage" of rationalistic assumptions, perhaps that sensations were elements of consciousness or that introspection was the preferred method of psychological investigation. However, no system, regardless of how empiricistic it is, can proceed without such assumptions.

Functionalism–Structuralism   Titchener clearly placed structuralism on the structuralist end of the dimension! Wundt's position was less extreme, and Titchener was probably not as far to the structuralist "right" as most people would place him.

Inductivism–Deductivism   There is no doubt that structuralism was inductive; the sensitivity of the system to empirical results shows that it was no grand, fixed system of deductions but a scientific system designed to be changed in response to the demands of data.

Mechanism–Vitalism   Although structuralism might not be acknowledged as such by its opponents, it was quite mechanistic in its approach. We have seen that Wundt was very opposed to allowing supernatural entities to play a role in the science of psychology, and he was exposed to Helmholtz's antivitalism early in his career. Titchener was no different.

Methods: Objectivism vs. Subjectivism   We tend to place structuralism far out on the methodologically subjective end of this dimension, but the structuralists would not have rated *themselves* that way. They went to great pains to use objective methodology on a subjective subject matter. How far they succeeded is a matter for debate.

Molecularism–Molarism   The analytic character of structuralism is scarcely debatable, even if we accept the structuralists' contention that they were not looking for existential *elements* of consciousness. At the least, they were "unraveling processes," which involves a molecular, not a molar, approach.

Monism–Dualism   We have spent enough time trying to decide whether or not the structuralist mind-body approach involved dualistic assumptions. Let us credit them with tending toward monism, if that is the preferred bias in modern psychology.

Naturalism–Supernaturalism   Nearly all systems of psychology have been naturalistic. Structuralism was no exception.

Nomotheticism–Idiographicism   Structuralism was extremely nomothetic. Wundt was uninterested, to say the least, in individual differences, and we saw Titchener writing the words "generalized" and "normal" right into the definition of psychology. We will not find a school with a more radical position on this dimension.

Peripheralism–Centralism   The structuralists were centralists to the core. Images and sensations and feelings are not visible at the periphery, and again the position is clear.

Purism–Utilitarianism   The structuralists emphasized pure science to the nearly complete exclusion of applied science. This position was deadly for them in America, even though the puristic attitude is not uncommon among university researchers in other systems and other disciplines.

Quantitativism–Qualitativism   On this dimension the structuralist position is less extreme. Both quantity and quality were considered important. Much of the instrumentation developed within this tradition was designed for the sake of quantification. Titchener wrote manuals for both the quantitative and qualitative sides of experimental practice. Thus a nice solid middle-of-the-road position is indicated for this dimension.

Rationalism–Irrationalism   Structuralism made relatively little room for the intrusion of irrational factors into intellectual processes. Thus its position must be far toward the rational side.

Staticism–Developmentalism   With respect to this next to last prescription, the extreme cross-sectional nature of most structural research makes it static. Great pains were taken to try to *eliminate* changes with time rather than to study them.

Staticism–Dynamicism   The same considerations apply, although to a less extreme degree, to this second type of staticism contrast. The emphasis on interactions between conscious processes that coexist at a given moment provides for some incursion of dynamic factors. Our caricature of the goals and methods of structuralism usually places it in too extreme a position on this dimension. Both Wundt and Titchener laid great verbal stress on the dynamic features of consciousness.

Coan's Factors

We can begin by pointing out that structuralism, like associationism, was a restrictive school. In some sense, the restrictions of structuralism were more extreme, since the range of application of psychology was seen as smaller, at least by Titchener. However, the concepts used in explanations were somewhat less limited than those of associationism; we have seen that Titchener tended to incorporate associationistic principles as *part* of his system. Both schools were highly analytic, and structuralism was, as its name implies, more structural than any other system.

Despite its clear position on each dimension, structuralism does not fit into Coan's set of factors as neatly as we might like. Most restrictive systems tend to be objective, at the level of first-order factors. Structuralism was not. Structuralism is more elementaristic than most and may tend a touch more toward the quantitative than toward the qualitative. It is certainly more apersonal and static than most systems. Finally, it is, as Coan expects for restrictive and structural systems, exogenistic.

FUNCTIONALISM

INTRODUCTION

Functionalism was the first school of psychology to achieve its fullest expression in America. Its development there began with William James, who has been ranked as the greatest American psychologist (Becker, 1959). Part of the early strength of functionalism came from its opposition to structuralism, just as later part of the strength of behaviorism derived from its opposition both to structuralism and to the less extreme functionalism.

Functionalism was never a clearly differentiated systematic position. Woodworth (1948) said: "A psychology that attempts to give an accurate and systematic answer to the question 'What do men do?' and 'Why do they do it?' is called a *functional psychology*" (p. 13). Woodworth made the point that functionalism, as he saw it, was an eclectic and nondogmatic position, but his statement was not an adequate definition of functionalism. Though its definition must remain fittingly loose, we can at least add that a functionalist is characteristically concerned with the uses of the organism's behavior and consciousness in its adaptation to its environment. The functionalist also studies functional relationships between antecedents and behavior or consciousness; here *function* is used in its mathematical sense. American psychology, influenced by evolutionary theory and a practical spirit, has been concerned with the utilities of consciousness and behavior. Thus it has tended to be functional.

Table 5-1 shows that three groups of psychologists contributed to the development of functionalism. The *pioneers* were early psychologists who laid the groundwork for functionalism by opening up new fields of inquiry, such as child psychology, animal behavior, and the testing of individual differences. The *founders*, John Dewey and James Angell, developed functionalism as a system and gave it the status of a school

TABLE 5-1
IMPORTANT FIGURES IN AMERICAN FUNCTIONAL PSYCHOLOGY

British antecedent influences	American functionalists		
	Pioneers	Founders	Developers
Individual differences, mental tests, statistics			
Sir Francis Galton (1822–1911)	George T. Ladd (1842–1921), Yale	John Dewey (1859–1952), Chicago (Columbia)	Robert S. Woodworth (1869–1962), Columbia
	Edward W. Scripture (1964–1945), Yale		
	James McKeen Cattell (1860–1944), Columbia		
	G. Stanley Hall (1844–1924), Clark		
Evolutionary theory			
Charles Darwin (1809–1882)	James Mark Baldwin (1961–1934), Princeton	James R. Angell (1869–1949), Chicago	Harvey Carr (1873–1954), Chicago
Herbert Spencer (1820–1903)	William James (1842–1910), Harvard		
Animal behavior			
George John Romanes (1848–1894)	Edward L. Thorndike (1874–1949), Columbia		
C. Lloyd Morgan (1852–1936)			

at the University of Chicago. The *developers*, Harvey Carr and Robert S. Woodworth, elaborated and developed a more mature system.

Three primary antecedent influences, all British, are also shown in Table 5-1. Charles Darwin (1872/1909), studied animal behavior in addition to developing the theory of organic evolution (1859). Herbert Spencer (1855) produced the first textbook of psychology written from a strictly evolutionary perspective. Darwin's cousin Sir Francis Galton initiated the scientific study of human capacity, with stress on individual differences. Romanes and Morgan studied animal behavior from the evolutionary perspective and thereby began the modern study of comparative psychology. James, Hall, and Baldwin were strongly influenced by evolutionary theory. Carr was more interested in animal studies than was his most direct predecessor, Angell. Baldwin, Ladd, and Scripture all helped to set the stage for an American functional psychology, but their contributions were not fundamental enough to require treatment here. Early in his career, E. L. Thorndike had strong interests in animal research, and he was

William James (1842–1910), philosopher and pioneer psychologist. James founded an informal laboratory at about the same time as Wundt, and played a leading role in the early development of American functional psychology.

Harvey Carr (1873–1954), Chairman of the Department of Psychology at the University of Chicago during functional psychology's period of greatest popularity.

influenced by both James and Cattell, so he was important to functionalism as well as to associationism.

John B. Watson and Walter Hunter were products of the Chicago school of functionalism who went on to become behaviorists and so are not included in the table. However, Hunter guided a small but productive laboratory in doing research with a functionalist flavor at Brown University. Bergmann (1956) regarded Watson as the last and greatest functionalist, despite his espousal of behaviorism, so Hunter and Watson both deserve mention in this overview.

It seems that we have a rule of systematic evolution: Most of the Americans who studied with Wundt—notably Cattell and Hall—returned to the United States and moved in a functional direction. Students of functionalists, like Thorndike, Watson, and Hunter, moved further in the direction of objectivism and became behaviorists or near-behaviorists. Of course, one generation of organisms or of systematists does not evolve very far; but the direction of change was clear.

ANTECEDENTS OF FUNCTIONALISM

Charles Darwin (1809–1882) created one of the greatest controversies in intellectual history, one whose reverberations have not yet died out. Darwin's theory of evolution shook religion to its foundations.

Ironically, Darwin was such a cautious scientist, not to say a timid and withdrawn recluse, that he might never have published and started the controversy had Alfred Russell Wallace (1823–1913) not sent him a report which outlined the same theory of evolution on which Darwin had been working for 20 years. As Irvine (1963) said:

> Wallace's next letter, containing the famous paper on evolution and natural selection, struck him like a bombshell. Within a single week, while lying ill with malarial fever in the jungles of the Malay peninsula, Wallace had leaped from his earlier position to Darwin's most advanced conclusions. What Darwin had puzzled and wondered and worried and slaved over with infinite anxiety and pain for two decades, Wallace had investigated and explained— far less elaborately but still to precisely the same result—in some three years. The familiar ideas, the older man could not help noticing, were conveyed with un-Darwinian force and clarity. (pp. 98–99)

Characteristically, Darwin was unable to resolve the dilemma presented by his receipt of Wallace's paper. Two friends of his, Lyell and Hooker, resolved it for him by reading both Wallace's report and a sketch of Darwin's ideas before the same meeting of the Linnaean Society. It is to the credit of both Darwin and Wallace that they were lifelong friends, their mutual respect emerging unscathed from a situation which could have become extremely acrimonious.

Darwin did not personally respond to the furor which arose over his theory and which rose to a climax with the 1859 publication of *The origin of species*. When unpleasantness threatened, he always found it necessary to withdraw to the safety of a spa for the sake of his uncertain health. The battle fell to the lot of Thomas Henry Huxley (1825–1895), Darwin's fierce, brilliant friend and fellow biologist. That Huxley eventually carried the day for evolution, at least with the scientific community, is now history.

Despite his eccentricities, Charles Darwin was functionalism's most important antecedent. He was an acute observer of animal behavior as well as of animal morphology. His theory established a continuity between human beings and animals that was necessary to justify the extended study of animal psychology. Finally, the evolutionary emphasis on adaptation to the environment was imported directly as an "explanation" of behavior via instinct, and perhaps indirectly as the principle of reinforcement.

Sir Francis Galton (1822–1911) was inspired by his cousin Darwin to study the problem of heredity in human beings. It was his aristocratic wish to control heredity, but first he had to demonstrate its effectiveness as a way to improve the species. He was led by this necessity to study the inheritance of human intelligence, of which Galton himself is said to have had a great deal; Boring (1950, p. 461) says that Galton's IQ was estimated at 200. Such quasi-quantitative estimates are, of course, just amusing nonsense; however, if they are not taken too seriously they can remind us that in studying intellectual history we are studying the exploits of brilliant people.

Galton's *Hereditary genius* (1869/1883) contained studies of individual differences in intelligence. We have already noted briefly how the "*ganz Amerikanisch*" Cattell followed up in this area; it was not long before the field of mental testing was opened up, to come into full blossom in the testing of recruits for the U.S. Army during World

War I. Mental testing has done a great deal to justify the existence of psychology during our childhood years, although objections to it are now beginning to plague our adulthood. For some reason—and we will discuss one possible reason very soon—Galton has received relatively little credit from American psychologists for his accomplishments.

George John Romanes (1848–1894) and C. Lloyd Morgan (1852–1936) are important to psychology because of their work in the field of animal behavior. Each represents an attitude toward the relationship between humans and the lower animals. Darwin was castigated by theologians because of their belief that he was bringing humanity down to the level of the animals; they admitted apelike ancestry only with great, high-collared resistance. From the contemporary point of view, however, it appears that both Darwin and Romanes were overgenerous in the other direction. They were disarmingly willing to attribute human faculties to animals. Morgan would have none of their childish enthusiasm and demanded strict evidence before according *either* humans or animals a "higher" phyletic faculty on the basis of a particular performance. Romanes and Morgan thus defined a polarity which is still visible, but both men encouraged an interest in and study of animals.

As humanity has become more aware of the ecology of "spaceship Earth," interest in animals has hit an all-time peak. Popular television portrays animals as having abilities that make the claims of Romanes seem ultraconservative, including a morality that puts their human friends to shame. In the opposite direction, we have hosts of books likening humans to everything from apes to zebras and accounting for our problems by pointing to the origins of our aggression, or sexuality, or territoriality, in our animal past (Ardrey, 1961, 1966, 1970; Lorenz, 1966; D. Morris, 1968, 1969; Tiger, 1969). However controversial some of these efforts may be, they indicate a deep acceptance within the popular consciousness of the evolutionary perspective. The theory of evolution was a necessary intellectual step in preparing us to see ourselves as a part of all nature and thus to have a serious and beneficent concern for all nature.

Herbert Spencer (1820–1903) had a somewhat different perspective on nature; he saw evolution as a continuous battle of tooth and claw, with the victory going to the stronger. He thought that society must not interfere with the human part of this battle by helping the weak; it was nature's law that the weak must perish. Spencer was, in a slightly different guise, expressing Galton's eugenic concern with the betterment of the species. The reputations of both men have been worsened by this aspect of their thought; that is the reason we referred to earlier, in connection with Galton's receiving less credit than he seemingly deserves. The notion of eugenics has never been popular in democratic societies and is even less popular now since Hilter attempted to "improve the species" by murdering millions of Jews. Selective breeding is practiced systematically with animals but not with people. Thus Spencer and Galton, both brilliant men and strong supporters of evolutionary theory, probably did as much to impede the development of functional psychology as they did to advance it.

Spencer would be featured even in a catalog of eccentric geniuses. He anticipated Darwin with a theory of evolution which had the misfortune of being Lamarckian and thus not influential for long. Also unfortunately for him, Spencer did not tend to base his views on a thorough perusal of the facts. According to Irvine (1963):

No modern thinker has read so little in order to write so much. He prepared himself for his *Psychology* chiefly by perusing Mansel's *Prologomena Logicae* and for his *Biology* by going through Carpenter's *Principles of comparative psychology*. He produced a treatise on sociology without reading Comte, and a treatise on ethics without apparently reading anybody. . . . He had discovered that his "head sensations," with their attendant ramifications, were due to an impaired circulation of blood to the brain. . . . Some of the most abstruse chapters of the *Psychology* were dictated . . . during the intervals of a tennis game near London. His rational life had not become less eccentric with the passing of years. (pp. 287–288)

Despite his eccentricities, of which the foregoing gives but a hint, Spencer produced the first completely evolutionary psychology. Darwin specifically mentions Spencer's *The principles of psychology* (1855) as laying down the lines along which evolutionary psychology must develop. It is small wonder that Darwin favored Spencer's ideas, since Spencer made a virtual religion of continuity. Continuity between animals and humans was the key to evolution. Spencer made it the key to the development of consciousness out of living materials and the key to the development of living materials out of inanimate nature. This was a transfer of a biological problem into the realm of psychology and made Spencer's psychology the first functional psychology. Darwin's appreciation of Spencer was expressed in his *The origin of species* (1859), published 4 years *after* Spencer's psychology. Thus we see that, paradoxically, there was an evolutionary psychology 4 years before the first extensive treatment of evolution in biology.

Spencer, unlike the more cautious Darwin, did not hesitate to make broad characterizations of evolutionary theory and to draw analogies to society (Spencer, 1961; first published 1873). His influence was accordingly pronounced, if not always favorably regarded, in social thought, sociology, and social psychology (Hofstadter, 1955). Spencer saw clearly that the kinds of changes that occur through learning in the life of the individual could occur through selection in the life of the species. Unfortunately, he decided that associations acquired by the individual organism could be genetically transmitted; that is, he believed that Lamarck was correct. He had been persuaded of Lamarck's correctness by reading the arguments against Lamarck's theory, which indicates that Spencer's stubbornness did not always pay off. Had Spencer rejected Lamarck, or even suspended judgment, he might have been considered a great psychologist rather than one among many of functionalism's antecedents. Even so, the idea of referring evolutionary changes and changes with learning to a common framework but with a different time scale is a very important one (see Fisher, 1966, for a discussion). It is very attractive intellectually to refer learning and evolution to a common *mechanism* as well as to a common framework. Much effort has been expended in trying to implicate genetic materials like DNA and RNA in the learning process, but the results are, so far, unconvincing.

THE PSYCHOLOGY OF WILLIAM JAMES

James's Life

William James founded functionalism as a system, but not as a school, in his two-volume work *The principles of psychology* (1890). The book was a classic virtually before it was published, since much of the book had appeared in periodical form as the chapters were completed. R. I. Watson (1968) is among those who have pointed out that the book is still read by people who have no necessity to do so—a rare tribute for a book intended as an introduction to psychology! As we have already mentioned, James was also voted the greatest American psychologist by his fellow psychologists (Becker, 1959).

James was born into a family of charming eccentricity. His grandfather, the "elder William," had amassed a fortune estimated at 3 million dollars (Perry, 1935), a truly magnificent sum at that time. As a result, none of the heirs needed to work, and they were free to travel in Europe, move from place to place in America, and indulge their intellectual proclivities as they wished. All of this William's father, the "elder Henry," proceeded to do. He had lost a leg as a result of an accident, and this may have led him, with his fiery temperament, more into the life of the mind and religious pursuits than would otherwise have been the case. His children, including the younger William James, thus had highly irregular, but unusually urbane, educations. There must have been something good about this unusual upbringing, since the two older children, William and his one-year-younger brother Henry, were both persons of genius. As the eldest, William did not hesitate to give Henry advice on how to write his articles and novels—advice which, perhaps fortunately, the younger brother did not always follow. However, psychologists have long been fond of saying that William James was a psychologist who wrote like a novelist, while Henry was a novelist who wrote like a psychologist.

As a result of the exigencies of his education, William was exposed to much of the intellectual ferment of his time. He had plenty of opportunity to express his genius for finding out what he was not. He studied art for a year and decided that he was no artist, went collecting with the great naturalist Louis Agassiz and discovered that he was no collector, and went through the course of study for an M.D. with many interruptions because of poor health, only to find that he was no doctor. James (1890) must have had himself in mind when he wrote:

> There is a happy moment for fixing skill in drawing, for making boys collectors in natural history, and presently dissectors and botanists; then for initiating them into the harmonies of mechanics and the wonders of physical and chemical law. Later, introspective psychology and the metaphysical and religious mysteries take their turn; and, last of all, the drama of human affairs and worldly wisdom in the widest sense of the term. In each of us a saturation-point is soon reached in all these things. (II, p. 401)

Despite his tendencies to saturate quickly, James obtained an appointment from Harvard to teach anatomy, which gave him an opportunity to teach physiological psychology and to establish a small demonstration laboratory in 1875, at almost exactly the time that Wundt was doing the same thing in Leipzig. Soon thereafter, he embarked on his last great adventure in finding out what he was not. He started writing his great 1400-page *The principles of psychology* (1890), which led him upon its completion to decide that there was really no such thing as a science of psychology. He then turned increasingly to philosophy (he had been at least a closet philosopher throughout his life) and was soon successful in getting Hugo Münsterberg to come to Harvard and assume the responsibilities connected with the psychological laboratory. After

Münsterberg's arrival in 1897, James continued to write prolifically, and his *Talks to teachers* of 1899 and *Varieties of religious experience* of 1902 are of great interest to psychologists.

As a young man, James was almost devastatingly handsome. That could not have detracted from his popularity, but his personality was also urbane and enthusiastic, traits which come through in his writing. Joncich (1968) says of James that "the last book he read was always a great work and the last person seen a wonderful man" (p. 434). Considering what James said about the Fechnerian type of psychology (we will look more closely at that in a moment), Joncich may have been engaging in a bit of hyperbole. James also at one time called Herbert Spencer an ignoramus and said that he had no ability to work out anything in detail. But Joncich is essentially correct; James was enthusiastic even about his dislikes and no doubt was happy whenever he found something on which to exercise them.

Such a personality did not lead James to be a great experimentalist. His contribution to the development of psychology was through his ability to synthesize psychological principles suggested by the experiments of others, to make intuitive guesses where knowledge was missing, and to present the results in an incredibly attractive verbal package.

Chronologically, James belongs between Wundt (who was 10 years his senior) and Titchener (25 years his junior). As has been pointed out (Heidbreder, 1933), he both precedes and succeeds Titchener, in the sense that his ideas reach further back into the past for metaphysical roots and at the same time have lost so little of their freshness that James is still not only readable but also surprisingly modern, although necessarily not in all details. He had an unusual talent for being practical, readable, interesting, and popular—and at the same time commanding scientific respect.

To read James's *Principles* is to accompany him on a voyage of intellectual discovery. Although his writing is full of facts, there is little of the fact collector in James, and even less of the dogmatist. He leads his readers through the rough terrain of fundamental psychology with a sure eye for the obstacles and landmarks. He shows no mercy for those he believes misguided but is generous to the ingenious, even when he thinks they are wrong. It is not a journey with an end; the last sentence of his book (1890, II) is "And the more sincerely one seeks to trace the actual course of *psychogenesis,* the steps by which as a race we may have come by the peculiar mental attributes which we possess, the more clearly one perceives 'the slowly gathering twilight close in utter night' " (p. 688). Such honesty, even though depressing, is disarming and could be recommended even today.

James as a Critic

James disliked what he considered to be the narrowness, artificiality, and pointlessness of the Wundtian tradition in psychology. Thus he played an important role in the more general protest that the functionalists were later to make. It is best to let James speak for himself, as in the following two quotations from the *Principles,* to demonstrate the forcefulness of his criticism as well as the fluency and persuasiveness of his literary style. Of Fechner, for example, James (1890) said:

But it would be terrible if even such a dear old man as this could saddle our Science forever with his patient whimsies, and, in a world so full of more nutritious objects of attention, compel all future students to plough through the difficulties, not only of his own works, but of the still drier ones written in his refutation. (I, p. 549)

And, speaking more generally of the subsequent Wundtian psychology:

Within a few years what one may call a microscopic psychology has arisen in Germany, carried out by experimental methods, asking of course every moment for introspective data, but eliminating their uncertainty by operating on a large scale and taking statistical means. This method taxes patience to the utmost, and could hardly have arisen in a country whose natives could be *bored*. Such Germans as Weber, Fechner, Vierordt, and Wundt obviously cannot; and their success has brought into the field an array of younger experimental psychologists, bent on studying the *elements* of the mental life, dissecting them out from the gross results in which they are embedded, and as far as possible reducing them to quantitative scales. The simple and open method of attack having done what it can, the method of patience, starving out, and harassing to death is tried, the Mind must submit to a regular *siege*, in which minute advantages gained night and day by the forces that hem her in must sum themselves up at last into her overthrow. There is little of the grand style about these new prism, pendulum, and chronograph-philosophers. They mean business, not chivalry. What generous divination, and that superiority in virtue which was thought by Cicero to give a man the best insight into nature, have failed to do, their spying and scraping, their deadly tenacity and almost diabolic cunning, will doubtless some day bring about. (1890, I, pp. 192ff.)

One should not be misled into thinking that James criticized only members of other schools, however. Some of his harshest criticisms were reserved for his predecessor in the field of evolutionary psychology, the English "ignoramus" Herbert Spencer. Another example should make this point quite clear. In discussing Spencer's attempt to derive consciousness from inanimate matter which does not possess it, James says (1890, I) " 'Nascent' is Mr. Spencer's great word. In showing how at a certain point consciousness must appear upon the evolving scene this author fairly outdoes himself in vagueness" (p. 148).

The Positive Program

James was not merely a clever critic of elementarism and Wundtian introspectionism. On the contrary, he had an extensive positive program for psychology. While he himself preferred not to experiment, he recognized the value and the necessity of the experimental method, for psychology as well as for the older disciplines. More broadly, however, the keynote of his program is his emphasis on *pragmatism*, which implies that the validation of any knowledge must be in terms of its consequences, values, or utilities. Useful knowledge for psychology, James felt, would come from a study of behavior as well as consciousness, of individual differences as well as generalized principles, of emotion and nonrational impulses as well as intellectual abilities.

Underlying this kind of study was the general assumption that psychology must study *functions*—that psychology is a part of biological science and that human beings must be considered in their adaptation and readaptation to the environment. In keeping with the newly influential evolutionary theory, James felt that human behavior, and especially the mind, must have had some function to have survived. The effects of James's early medical training are also evident throughout his writing. He said (1890, I) "This book, assuming that thoughts and feelings exist and are vehicles of knowledge, thereupon contends that psychology when she has ascertained the empirical correlation of the various sorts of thought or feeling with definite conditions of the brain, can go no farther—can go no farther, that is, as a natural science" (p. vi). James thus tackled at the outset the very problem which the parallelistic views of Wundt and Titchener were designed to avoid: the relationship between mind and body. As to his own philosophy, James is quite explicit (1890, I): *The psychologists's attitude towards cognition* will be so important in the sequel that we must not leave it until it is made perfectly clear. *It is a thoroughgoing dualism.* It supposes two elements, mind knowing and thing known, and treats them as irreducible" (p.218).

James carried his attempt to relate mind and brain throughout his book, which is filled with illustrations of brain structures and with hypothetical diagrams depicting one or another aspect of neural or conscious activity. We do not wish to overemphasize the contrast, but James, more than Wundt, carried his medical education over into his program for psychology. One of James's most famous theoretical contributions, the James-Lange theory of emotion, is another example of this tendency, since James makes the sensory feedback from bodily actions the focal point of the emotional process.

Both Wundt and James relied heavily upon introspection as a tool of psychological research. Wundt was much more the experimentalist; James felt himself temperamentally unfitted to be a laboratory man, but philosophically he was committed to the experimental approach, and he encouraged some of his students to circumvent his deficiency in this respect by studying with Wundt.

Considering that he did little research, James had kept up wonderfully well with the status of psychology as of 1890. He treated the difficult and important problems of his time in depth and with remarkable astuteness; for example, he reviewed all of the evidence for and against Lamarckian evolution, including Weismann's famous experiment in which he cut off the tails of mice for generations without any effect on the lengths of the tails of the offspring. James rejected, apparently with complete assurance, evidence which at first thought surely proves the inheritance of acquired characteristics. He developed a surprisingly complete account of adaptation, bringing in instinct, habit, memory, attention, choice, and the relationships among all of them. Some of the material is quite striking; many modern readers would be surprised to read in James (1890, II):

> If a chick is born in the absence of the hen, it "will follow any moving object. And, when guided by sight alone, they seem to have no more disposition to follow a hen than to follow a duck or a human being. Unreflecting lookers-on, when they saw chickens a day old running after me," says Mr. Spalding, "and older ones following me for miles, and answering to my whistle, imagined that I must have some occult power over the creatures: whereas I had simply allowed them to follow me from the first. There is the instinct to follow; and the ear, prior to experience, attaches them to the right object."
>
> But if the man presents himself for the first time when the instinct of *fear* is strong, the

phenomena are altogether reversed. Mr. Spalding kept three chickens hooded until they were nearly four days old, and thus describes their behavior:

"Each of them, on being unhooded, evinced the greatest terror to me, dashing off in the opposite direction whenever I sought to approach it. . . . Whatever might have been the meaning of this marked change in their mental constitution—had they been unhooded on the previous day they would have run to me instead of from me—it could not have been the effect of experience; it must have resulted wholly from changes in their own organizations". (p. 396)

The source of the quote within James's quote is Spalding's article in Macmillan's magazine, written in 1873. One need hardly comment that the phenomenon of imprinting is here clearly described, along with the critical period. James uses these phenomena, along with others, to develop his laws of the relationships between instinct and habit, and thus of adaptation to the environment.

James on Consciousness

The breadth of James's view on consciousness, when contrasted with that of Titchener, is especially instructive as a cue to the difference between the structural and functional approaches to psychology. First, James pointed out the *characteristics* of consciousness, which are studied only by psychology: It is *personal,* individualistic—belongs only to a single person; it is *forever changing*—is essentially a process and should be studied first as such (his famous phrase "stream of consciousness" was coined to express this property); it is *sensibly continuous*—in spite of gaps, individual identity is always maintained; it is *selective*—it chooses, with attention providing the relevance and continuity for choice; and it occurs in *transitive* as well as *substantive* form.

This last point, the dichotomy between clear content and so-called fringe states of consciousness, is one of James's more noteworthy emphases. James held that transitive conscious processes are less easily noticed but are very important and that they had not been given sufficient credit or study. He thought that all ideas enter consciousness as transitive, marginal in attention, and often fleeting and that they may or may not then proceed to substantive form, in which the idea has more stability, more "substance." In any case, transitive or fringe ideas (as of unfamiliarity, relation, and the like) account for much meaning and behavior. The other characteristics of consciousness make it a unique personal possession which helps us to reach goals by *acting* in ever-changing ways on ever-changing content.

Second, James emphasized the *purpose* of consciousness. Here, as suggested above, he was much influenced by the new evolutionary theory and felt that consciousness must have some biological use or else it would not have survived. Its function is to make the human being a better-adapted animal—to enable humans to choose. Conscious choice is to be contrasted with habit, which becomes involuntary and nonconscious. Consciousness tends to become involved when there is a *new* problem, the need for a *new* adjustment. Its survival value, as James (1890) reasoned, is in relationship to the nervous system: "The distribution of consciousness shows it to be exactly such as we might expect in an organ added for the sake of steering a nervous system grown too complex to regulate itself" (p. 144).

Third, James thought that psychology had to study the conditions of consciousness. In contrast to Titchener, with his psychophysical parallelism, James felt that consciousness could not be considered apart from the body. In the *Principles,* James examined in detail the mind-body solutions of his time and found that he had to reject them all. However, his functional view of consciousness implied an interactionism; how could consciousness "control" the nervous system unless it could interact with it?

James's speculations about ideo-motor action seem to confirm this interpretation. James said that sensory processes tend to express themselves in motor processes unless something inhibits them; thus it is to be expected that any idea, unless inhibited by other ideas, will lead more or less directly to action. James's own example of the value of this hypothesis was that if one has trouble getting out of bed in the morning, one has simply to keep getting up in mind and clear out all conflicting ideas. He said that one would soon find oneself standing up.

We have mentioned that James experienced the usual textbook writer's dissatisfaction with his product, saying when he finished that his book proved only "that there is no such thing as a science of psychology" and that psychology is still in "an antescientific condition" (Boring, 1950, p. 511). Yet even today James seems to have an incredible modernity. Herrnstein and Boring (1965, pp. 483–495) reprinted the selection from James in which he had brilliantly refuted the same sorts of behavioristic arguments that were presented by John B. Watson about 25 years later. This demonstrates not only that such issues were already in the air before 1890 but also that James could write at a high pitch of incisiveness, recognizing and surgically treating the most critical methodological issues. We shall see the same Jamesian abilities again when we look for the antecedents of Gestalt psychology.

It would be easy to conclude that William James was perfect, completely prescient and above the limitations of his time. However, even James had feet which could be trapped in the clays of culture, as the following excerpt (1890, II) shows:

> We observe an identical difference between men as a whole and women as a whole. A young woman of twenty reacts with intuitive promptitude and security in all the usual circumstances in which she may be placed. Her likes and dislikes are formed; her opinions, to a great extent, the same that they will be through life. Her character is, in fact, finished in its essentials. How inferior to her is a boy of twenty in all these respects! His character is still gelatinous, uncertain what shape to assume, "trying it on" in every direction. Feeling his power, yet ignorant of the manner in which he shall express it, he is, when compared with his sister, a being of no definite contour. But this absence of prompt tendency in his brain to set into particular modes is the very condition which insures that it shall ultimately become so much more efficient than the woman's. The very lack of preappointed trains of thought is the ground on which general principles and heads of classification grow up; and the masculine brain deals with new and complex matter indirectly by means of these, in a manner which the feminine method of direct intuition, admirably and rapidly as it performs within its limits, can vainly hope to cope with. (pp. 368–369)

We can imagine that the great man, brilliant as he was, would be happy that he need not try to defend these remarks in today's world. And thus we close our description of America's greatest psychologist by noting that he, too, was only human.

We shall now take a brief look at other early American psychologists who were important parts of the functional tradition. It is a peculiarity of our history that, after James, there was a tendency for functional psychology to become less functional as it developed. No one can be certain why this happened; however, we can advance a reasonable hypothesis. Functional psychology is a child of evolutionary theory, and the basic focus of such a psychology should be on the adaptation of the organism to its environment. Keeping that in the center of our attention requires continuing study of the organism *in its environment*. However, most of the pioneers of American functionalism had some exposure to Wundt, with his emphasis on pure science and on the almost exclusive virtues of the experimental approach, which puts the organism in the rather unnatural environment of the laboratory. Thus functionalism in the period between James and quite recent times has tended to be an uneasy marriage between an evolutionary *philosophy* and an experimental *methodology*. When there were conflicts in this marriage, it usually turned out that methodology was the head of the household.

PIONEER AMERICAN FUNCTIONALISTS

G. Stanley Hall

Granville Stanley Hall (1844–1924) was a kind of hybrid psychologist, combining features of Wundt and James. He took the first American doctorate in psychology under James in 1878; then he went to Leipzig to study for two additional years under Wundt, lived next door to Fechner, and studied physiology under Ludwig. Very soon after his return, he founded one of the first psychological laboratories at Johns Hopkins University, in 1883. We should not push Hall's hybrid side too far, however; he was not too much of an experimentalist and made most of his contribution to psychology via the eminently practical administrative route. But before we go on with that story, let us take a look at Hall's early life.

Hall was born in Ashfield, Massachusetts, the son of a man who farmed after Hall's birth, although he had earlier spent time as a schoolteacher (Ross, 1972). Hall's mother and father shared strong religious convictions, which had a great deal to do with Hall's going to Williams College to prepare for the ministry. He then went to Union Theological Seminary to complete his preparations. There he turned toward philosophy, and he soon left for Germany, where he studied at the University of Berlin until, upon running out of money, he returned to Union and finished his divinity degree. However, he had been irreparably tainted by liberalism by his contact with philosophy, and he managed to preach for only 10 weeks before resolving his religious conflicts sufficiently to turn toward an academic career.

Hall was 34 by the time he got his degree from James at Harvard. With no acceptable employment in view, he was more or less forced to return to Germany for further study. This time he went to Leipzig and Wundt. Soon after his return, a job opened up at Johns Hopkins, where he later became the head of the department and founded a laboratory in 1883. At Hopkins he had both John Dewey and James McKeen Cattell as students; the latter felt that Hall was not honest with him, having first denied him a fellowship and having then denied responsibility for the decision.

Group at Clark University, Worcester, Mass., September 1909: 1 Franz Boas, 2 E. B. Titchener, 3 William James, 4 William Stern, 5 Leo Burgerstein, 6 G. S. Hall, 7 Sigmund Freud, 8 C. G. Jung, 9 Adolf Meyer, 10 H. S. Jennings, 11 C. E. Seashore, 12 Joseph Jastrow, 13 J. M. Cattell, 14 E. F. Buchner, 15 E. Katzenellenbogen, 16 Ernest Jones, 17 A. A. Brill, 18 W. H. Burnham, 19 A. F. Chamberlain, 20 Albert Schinz, 21 J. A. Magni, 22 B. T. Baldwin, 23 F. L. Wells, 24 G. M. Forbes, 25 E. A. Kirkpatrick, 26 Sandor Ferenczi, 27 E. C. Sanford, 28 J. P. Porter, 29 Sakyo Kanda, 30 Kikoso Kakise, 31 G. E. Dawson, 32 S. P. Hayes, 33 E. B. Holt, 34 C. S. Berry, 35 G. M. Whipple, 36 Frank Drew, 37 J. W. A. Young, 38 L. N. Wilson, 39 K. J. Karlson, 40 H. H. Goddard, 41 H. I. Klopp, 42 S. C. Fuller.

Granville Stanley Hall (1844–1924), as the President of Clark University, was responsible for planning the Clark Conference of 1909 at which this photograph was taken. Many of America's most famous psychologists attended this conference and were introduced to psychoanalysis by Freud, Jung, and Ferenczi.

In 1888, when Hall was only 44, he was appointed president of a university to be created at Worcester, Massachusetts, which would be called Clark University after its founder and benefactor. Hall and the trustees decided that it should be a graduate university devoted largely to research. Clark somewhat reluctantly agreed to their decision but kept tight control over the school's finances.

Hall proved to be an extreme autocrat as the university president. He was both secretive and peremptory with his faculty and paid them the minimum possible wage. However, he made Clark an interesting place to be for the first few years, imposing few teaching requirements and providing good equipment and working conditions for research. Hall seemed to have a genuine respect for research and for the "community of scholars" he had assembled.

The good side of Hall and of Clark University was not long able to balance the bad, and when the University of Chicago came into existence, it raided Clark's distinguished faculty:

> In the end, two-thirds of all those of faculty rank and 70 percent of the student body left Clark in the spring of 1892. Half of those went directly to the University of Chicago. Out of the ruins of Clark, Chicago had the foundation of distinguished departments in physics, chemistry, biology, and mathematics. When the university opened that fall, five of its thirty-one full professors were Clark men. Clark was left with only one distinguished department, psychology. (Ross, 1972, p. 227)

At almost the same time, Hall was engaged in controversies with many leaders of American psychology, so many that Ross devotes a chapter to his "professional quarrels." We cannot cover those quarrels here but will let the perceptive William James summarize Hall's personality, as he did in a letter of 1893 to Hugo Münsterberg:

> I am not altogether surprised that you have all come to grief in your negotiations with Hall, his personal psychology is a very queer and tortuous one, containing, however, elements of sincere devotion to truth. He hates clearness—clear formulas, clear statements, clear understandings; and mystification of some kind seems never far distant from everything he does. Yet I think he does not mean to deceive, nor is he a liar in any vulgar meaning of the term. He shrinks with an instinctive terror from any explanation that is definitive and irrevocable, and hence comes to say and do things that leave an avenue open to retreat—at bottom it is all connected with timidity in him—as a *dreamer* he is bold, when it comes to acting, he wills-and-wills-not. But what I least like in his journal and other writings of his as president, is the religious cant he finds it necessary to throw in. Yet in a certain sense even that is not insincerely meant! He has too complicated a mind! (quoted in Ross, 1972, pp. 240–241)

With his personality, it was surprising that Hall should have played such an important role in the development of American psychology, particularly since his role was much more that of an administrator than that of a scientist. Hall claimed that the word "evolution" was the touchstone for his psychology, which was much more the study of psychomotor processes than the study of consciousness. Yet, though Hall was clearly a functional psychologist, he was never able to express his psychological views in any complete and systematic way as James did in his *Principles*.

Let us turn, at last, from what Hall was not and did not do to what he did do. In

1887, the year before he became president of Clark, he founded the *American Journal of Psychology*. In 1891, he founded the *Pedagogical Seminary* (now the *Journal of Genetic Psychology*). This journal was one symptom of his interests in pedagogical psychology and the so-called "child study movement," areas in which Hall first became interested when he could not find employment more to his liking after he returned from his last sojourn in Germany. In 1892, the same year that Titchener arrived in America, the American Psychological Association was planned in a conference in Hall's study, and Hall became its first president.

Hall was also instrumental in developing scientific psychology in the United States, first through his development of the department at Johns Hopkins and then through his formation and nurturing of the department at Clark. The psychology department was the only one that managed to survive, nearly intact, the near-destruction of Clark University in 1892. Later, Hall used the new developments in psychoanalysis to the great credit of psychology and Clark University. In 1909, Clark celebrated its twentieth anniversary. Hall managed to bring Freud, Jung, and Ferenczi, three of the leading psychoanalysts, to Clark for the celebration. Naturally, with such bait, the event was also attended by many of America's most famous psychologists—William James in the year before his death, Hall himself, Titchener, and Cattell. This illustrious gathering probably contained more famous psychologists than any other group up to that time.

Hall continued to develop new areas in psychology, proceeding from child psychology, where he popularized the use of the questionnaire as a research tool, through adolescent psychology, where his two huge volumes of *Adolescence* (1904) are probably his most influential publications, and on into the psychology of old age, publishing *Senescence* (1922), appropriately, at the age of 78! In addition, he worked in the fields of applied psychology, educational psychology, sex (after his discovery of Freud), religious psychology, and even alimentary sensations. His book *Jesus, the Christ, in the light of psychology* (1917) represented a revival of his early theological interests.

Hall thus stimulated interest and activity in a variety of fields, in addition to playing his part as an administrative leader. All of his fields of interest were more applied than those studied by the structuralists, but Hall's students were not inspired by him to research careers. Although Hall turned out eighty-one Ph.D.s at Clark (many more than the fifty-four produced at Cornell by Titchener), fewer of them became prominent in psychology. Lewis Terman, long an American leader in the field of testing and individual differences, is probably the best known of them.

James McKeen Cattell

We have already met James McKeen Cattell (1860–1944) as the bold young American who, as Wundt (1921) reported, appointed himself Wundt's first assistant. Sokal (1981) tries to rob us of this pleasant story by showing that Cattell was *appointed* assistant in Wundt's laboratory, but there seems to be no necessary conflict between the two accounts of Cattell's assistantship. Wundt's story has the advantage, as we shall see, of being consistent with Cattell's lack of awe in the presence of authority figures.

Cattell's father, William Cattell, was the long-time president of Lafayette College, and he always did his best to support and promote the career of his son. Perhaps this close relationship with a college president gave Cattell too easy a familiarity with those who occupied such positions. James graduated from Lafayette in 1880 and spent two years traveling in England and Germany before returning to Johns Hopkins with a fellowship in 1882. While there, he worked with G. Stanley Hall, with the result— from Cattell's point of view, at least—that Hall wished to appropriate Cattell's work but did not wish to renew his fellowship.

Cattell thus turned to Wundt and Leipzig, where he was more appreciated. Wundt later referred to Cattell as a colleague rather than a student. The respect was reciprocated. Cattell received his Ph.D. under Wundt in 1886 and then spent the better part of two years in scholarly work at Cambridge before returning to the United States to found a laboratory at the University of Pennsylvania. His stay there was brief, and he moved to Columbia University in 1891, where he founded a second laboratory. He was there when Thorndike arrived with his basketful of trained chickens, hatched and educated in the James's basement. At Columbia Cattell was instrumental in developing one of the best-respected and most productive departments of psychology in the United States.

Unfortunately, Cattell was also engaged in antagonizing the president of Columbia University, Nicholas Murray Butler (Sokal, 1981). Cattell was on exactly the opposite side of this issue from his former teacher, G. Stanley Hall; Cattell was pressing for faculty governance of the university, the very thing that Hall resisted at Clark. Finally, in 1917, Cattell was discharged from the university because he objected to sending conscripts to Europe. There is little doubt that President Butler welcomed this justification for removing a pesky faculty member from his staff. Cattell remained understandably bitter about his discharge until the end of his life.

Cattell, unlike J. B. Watson when he was discharged (see the following chapter), did not have to turn to entirely new ventures. He had already rescued *Science* magazine from near bankruptcy and made it profitable, and he kept that journal in the family until after he died. He established the Psychological Corporation and, with James Mark Baldwin, founded the *Psychological Review* in 1894. He published the periodical biographical publication *American Men of Science,* the magazine *The Scientific Monthly,* and the educational weekly *School and Society*. All of these ventures contributed both to Cattell's financial support and to the development of psychology, particularly its practical side.

As a psychologist, Cattell never lived up to his promise as a research scientist. Much of his time at Columbia was spent in the development and promotion of mental tests. He began giving such tests to Columbia students in the 1890s, before the Binet-Simon scale had been developed. In this venture, Cattell was in the right field but with the wrong methods. Perhaps he had been unduly influenced during his stay in England by Sir Francis Galton; in any case, Cattell's measures were largely either anthropometric like Galton's or measures of very simple tasks, such as reaction time. It was not long before it was shown that Cattell's measures were poorly related to each other and to school performance. The Binet-Simon measures, based on much more complex performances, clearly surpassed Cattell's measures, and a large part of Cattell's professional effort went down the drain. His discharge from Columbia essentially ended his scientific prospects, although he did continue some activity in the field of individual differences and capacity, working mostly through the Psychological Corporation.

THE FOUNDING OF FUNCTIONALISM

It is traditional to date the founding of functionalism as a school in 1894, when John Dewey and James Angell came to teach at the new University of Chicago. Both had earlier been at the University of Michigan, where Angell had studied with Dewey. Had they stayed in Michigan, functionalism would probably have started a few hundred miles farther east than it did.

Those founding years must have been exciting ones, as psychology skipped and leapfrogged its way west, only a hundred years or so after the covered wagons had gone the same way. Cattell had founded a laboratory at Pennsylvania before turning back east to Columbia; Max Meyer was about to go to Missouri, and Harry Wolfe already had a laboratory at Nebraska; Titchener was ensconced at Cornell, and Hall was hanging on at what remained of Clark. It was fitting that Dewey and Angell be accorded the honor of founding a new school at a new university in a new nation.

Many of psychology's pioneers were very well acquainted with one another. Angell had studied not only under Dewey, but also under James, before proceeding to study with Erdmann in Halle, Germany. We have seen that Dewey had studied under G. S. Hall, that Hall had studied under James, and Cattell under Hall as well as Wundt, and that Cattell was waiting at Columbia for Thorndike, who arrived after studying with William James. The functionalists and fellow travelers were an exciting and close-knit coterie of brilliant psychologists and philosophers during those early years, and it is no wonder that they had the intellect and the persistence to start American psychology off in its own direction.

John Dewey

John Dewey (1859–1952), a philosopher, educator, and psychologist, was one of the truly eminent Americans of this century. We have seen that he studied with Hall at Hopkins, where he took his doctorate. He taught at Minnesota, as well as at Michigan, before going to the University of Chicago. It was Dewey who sent Angell from Michigan to Harvard to study with James, before rejoining him at Chicago to "found" functionalism there.

Sometimes we are surprised at the many interrelationships between prominent figures in the early history of psychology. Our supply of eminent psychologists is today so great, and their dispersal over such a wide area, that it is impossible for them all to know each other. In the early days of psychology, nearly all American psychologists who held Ph.D.s were concentrated on our east coast, and we are only now talking about their migration west. And we should not visualize past meetings of the American Psychological Association as though they occurred in a great hall in which there were signs saying "Structuralists register and meet here," "Functionalists register and meet here," and so on. Psychologists, then as now, simply met with other psychologists, whatever their systematic persuasions. There was and is much mingling, and particularly in the early period, well-known psychologists knew each other's work well.

Personal relationships have never paralleled systematic preferences anyway, so it is certainly good that conferences have never been segregated by school. Titchener would have missed his friend John B. Watson, except that Titchener had nothing to do with the American Psychological Association after its first years and would not have gone to a convention anyway. Dewey and his old teacher Hall would have been uncomfortable meeting in the functionalist room, because the two disliked each other intensely. Dewey would rather have shared his feelings with Wundt, who was very angry with Hall for having written a biography of Wundt which Wundt described as "fabricated from beginning to end." In fact, a large crowd might have met at a room labeled "Those who dislike G. S. Hall meet here." Personal likes and dislikes might be almost as good an organizing principle for studying the history of schools as the systems actually in use.

To return to Dewey, we would have found him in 1886 happy with the publication of his new book, *Psychology*. His happiness was justified, because the book was at first very popular; but that popularity was destined to be short-lived, for, as we have already said, James's *Principles* was destined to appear in 1890, and it was a book against which no other text could compete.

Ten years after his book appeared, Dewey (1896) published a short paper that was to become a true classic: "The reflex arc concept in psychology." This paper is considered a very significant landmark in the beginning of the functionalist movement. Dewey objected to the reflex-arc analysis, which broke behavior down into separate stimulus and response units and assumed that the sensory and motor nerves that participate in reflexes thus behave separately. According to the reflex-arc schema, the behavior chain can be broken down into (1) an afferent, or sensory, component initiated by the stimulus and mediated by the sensory nerves; (2) a central, or associative, component mediated by the spinal cord and the brain; and (3) an efferent, or motor, component mediated by motor nerves and culminating in a response. This schema is still in widespread use.

Dewey took examples from William James and Mark Baldwin to show the inadequacies of a formulation of behavior in terms of reflexes. Dewey's new formulation was more organismic. He viewed behavior as a *total coordination* which adapted the organism to a situation. He thus followed in the spirit of James's view of the continuity of consciousness, rather than James's view of reflex action.

Dewey regarded stimulus and response as convenient abstractions rather than as realities, and he pointed out the necessity for having a response before we can meaningfully say that we have a stimulus. The overall reflex is not a composition made of a stimulus succeeded by a response, for there is no such successive relationship involved. The stimulus-response distinction is artificial; it is a result of the holding over of the old mind-body dualism. It is a bit of a shock to think of Dewey making this "modern" claim in 1896.

The two main points that can be abstracted from Dewey's paper are (1) that behavior should be considered in relationship to its function and (2) that molar units of analysis should be used. The first point marked the beginning of the Chicago school of functional psychology, and the second was a Gestalt point made 20 years before Gestalt psychology existed.

The functional side of Dewey's (1896) paper is revealed in the following statement:

> The fact is that stimulus and response are not distinctions of existence, but teleological distinctions, that is, distinctions of function, or part played, with reference to reaching or maintaining an end. . . . There is simply a continuously ordered sequence of acts, all adapted in themselves and in the order of their sequence, to reach a certain objective end, the reproduction of the species, the preservation of life, locomotion to a certain place. The end has got thoroughly organized into the means. (pp. 365–366)

Unfortunately, the reflex-arc paper was one of the last of Dewey's contributions to psychology proper. During his stay at Chicago, he worked mostly in education and philosophy. He laid out the program for the progressive education movement in an address, "Psychology and social practice" (1900), delivered upon his retirement as president of the American Psychological Association. Dewey remained the titular head of this movement until his death. He, more than anyone else, was responsible for the application of pragmatism in education—the notion that education is life, learning is doing, and teaching should be student-centered rather than subject-centered. We should not hold Dewey responsible for the occasional excesses of his followers in the progressive education movement. Leaders are seldom asked by their followers to approve new interpretations and applications before they are put into practice. Dewey simply paid the usual price for fame in being saddled with the errors of others. In 1904, Dewey went to Columbia University Teachers College as professor of philosophy, and he remained there for the rest of his career.

Dewey, like William James, was always the philosopher in reality, whatever academic title he happened to be assuming at the time. Thus his importance to psychology does not come primarily from his direct contributions to the subject matter. He is remembered for his stimulation of others, particularly through his delineation of the philosophical foundations of functionalism and of their applications in education.

James Rowland Angell

One of the men most influenced by Dewey was J. R. Angell (1869–1949). Angell's interest in academic life was first awakened by reading Dewey's *Psychology,* and Angell later studied under Dewey at the University of Michigan. His father was president of that institution, and it was there that he received his M.A. with a major in philosophy.

After studying with Dewey, Angell went to Harvard to study with James for a time, after which he departed for Germany. He hoped to study with Wundt, but the laboratory was full, and he settled for a semester at Berlin and then one at Halle with Erdmann. With his thesis in philosophy nearly finished, Angell received an offer to assume a teaching position immediately at the University of Minnesota. Accepting the position would make it possible for him to marry his fiancee of four years. At that point, Angell showed his true evolutionary heritage by returning posthaste to Minnesota; he never found the time in a hectic life to obtain his Ph.D., although he later received honorary doctorates. Angell spent only one year at Minnesota before receiving an offer from the University of Chicago, where he would be rejoining his beloved teacher, John Dewey. That was an offer that he could not refuse, and it resulted in a move that produced a school of psychology.

Angell arrived in Chicago in 1894. His first paper, with A. W. Moore (1896), appeared in the same volume of *Psychological Review* as Dewey's reflex-arc paper. It was an experimental study of reaction times. The Angell-Moore paper attempted to resolve the controversy between Titchener and Baldwin. Titchener had held that re-action times are faster when the subject concentrates on the response (motor condition). Baldwin had claimed that, on the contrary, they are faster when the subject concentrates on the stimulus (sensory condition). Angell and Moore reported that there were wide individual differences in reaction times among naive subjects, with some giving faster sensory times (supporting Baldwin), but that with continuing practice motor times generally became faster (supporting Titchener). This resolution pointed up the basic differences between the structuralist position, with its emphasis on the highly trained observer, and the developing functionalist position, with its acceptance of data from naive as well as from trained observers.

In his paper replying to criticism of his type of psychology, Titchener borrowed from James the term *structural psychology* as opposed to *functional psychology*. The terms structural and functional were used as the basis of the newly defined "isms" in psychology. Titchener was thus responsible for the naming of both systems.

As we have already observed, Titchener was fighting a losing battle. As the century ended, developments in educational psychology, animal psychology, mental testing, and related fields were helping to strengthen the basic functionalist position. It was James Angell who became the leading champion of the new trend. He published a paper on the relations between structural and functional psychology (1903), a textbook (1904), and finally the clearest expression of the functionalist position in his 1906 address as president of the American Psychological Association, "The province of functional psychology" (1907):

> Functional psychology is at the present moment little more than a point of view, a program, an ambition. It gains its vitality primarily perhaps as a protest against the exclusive excellence of another starting point for the study of the mind, and it enjoys for the time being at least the peculiar vigor which commonly attaches to Protestantism of any sort in its early stages before it has become respectable and orthodox. The time seems ripe to attempt a somewhat more precise characterization of the field of functional psychology than has as yet been offered. (pp. 61, 94)

Angell proceeded in his address to outline three separate conceptions of functional psychology. First, functionalism might be considered a psychology of mental opera-tions in contrast to a psychology of mental elements. This view presents a direct antithesis between the structuralist and functionalist positions. From the functionalist point of view, Angell notes, the complete answer to the questions "What?"with respect to the mind must include answers to the corollary questions "How?" and "Why?" Second, functionalism might be considered the psychology of the fundamental utilities of consciousness. Angell presents in this second connection a view very similar to James's, with the mind functioning to mediate between the organism and its environment and becoming active primarily in accommodating to the novel situation. Third, functionalism might be considered the psychology of psychophysical relations. Here functionalism is the psychology of the total relationship of organism to environment, including all mind-body functions. This third view leaves open the study of nonconscious, habitual behavior.

Angell believed that the first and second views were too narrow. Each of them restricted functionalism to the study of conscious experience, and the first put too much emphasis on opposition to structuralism. The third view was most satisfactory, although Angell felt that the three views of functionalism were interdependent.

At Chicago, Angell got the department of psychology separated from the department of philosophy and became its chairman when Dewey left for Columbia. He made it a center for functional studies, with the help of outstanding students like John B. Watson and Harvey Carr, among others. Then, after much agonizing, Angell left Chicago to head the Carnegie Corporation. Not long after, Angell received another offer that he could not refuse, to become president of Yale University. He occupied that position with distinction from 1921 until his retirement in 1937. The pressures of administration made it inevitable that he give up his active role in psychology during those years.

THE CHICAGO SCHOOL: HARVEY CARR

It was also inevitable that psychology should miss the leadership of a man like Angell, but he was replaced by another able, albeit quiet, modest, and often underrated man, Harvey Carr (1873–1954). Carr, as a country boy from Indiana, did not have an easy time in making his way to the University of Chicago. He very gradually developed intellectual interests, first attending preparatory school and 2 years of college at DePauw University. He then fell ill and had to stay out of school while he recovered first his health and then his financial equilibrium by teaching in a nearby country school. Carr was then able to return to school at the University of Colorado for his bachelor's degree and to stay there for his master's degree. From there he went to Chicago to study experimental psychology, and obtained his Ph.D. there in 1905 at the age of 32. However, he was offered no job to go with his degree and had to scrounge for one, which found him teaching in a high school in Texas for a year. Then, after teaching at the Pratt Institute for 2 years, he returned to the University of Chicago to take the place of the departing J. B. Watson on the faculty when the latter went to Johns Hopkins. Harvey Carr had finally found a place, and he had earned it "the old-fashioned way," with a lot of hard work and persistence. Like G. S. Hall, he was into his mid-thirties before he was well embarked on a career in psychology.

Eleven years after he returned to Chicago, Carr took over Angell's position as head of the psychology department, although the appointment was not formalized for two additional years. McKinney (1978) described Carr in the early 1930s as a democratic leader who fulfilled his duties without a full-time secretary or even a private telephone. McKinney continued:

Carr, held in special regard by most of the graduate students, was my first choice. To me he was like a favorite uncle: warm, friendly, teasing at times, oblivious to everyone when he was preoccupied. He was a quiet, apparently happy family man who came to the office regularly and did his work unostentatiously. He was no academic prima donna, but was quite comfortable in the background; he seemed emotionally mature and unpretentious. (p. 143)

Life had always seemed to keep Harvey Carr waiting, but finally his contributions were recognized, and it was under Carr that Chicago functionalism flourished and took on as much definition as it ever had. Therefore we have chosen to consider Carr's position in some detail, as being a good representative of the functionalist position.

Chicago under Carr did not encourage much fuss about systems of psychology. What was being done at Chicago was regarded as *the* psychology of the time, and there was apparently little need felt for formal systematizing. Marx (1963, pp. 14ff.) has placed functional theorizing between the extremes of the large-scale deductive approach and the purely inductive approach. The functionalists have tended to construct very limited theories which stayed close to data. In this respect, they anticipated the modern trend toward miniature mathematical systems. Since they paid little attention to comprehensive theoretical systems, they had no need to ignore any "competing" approach to psychology.

The functionalists also felt that other "new" systematic positions like behaviorism, Gestalt psychology, and psychoanalysis had little to offer. These movements were regarded as exaggerated, overdramatized emphases on limited aspects of psychology. Thus the behaviorists' stress on overt behavior was merely taking up where the functionalists had already more quietly broken ground. The Gestalt psychologists were emphasizing points about the stimulus field which the functionalists had been investigating all the while. The psychoanalysts were pointing to the great importance of motivation, a concept that had been basic all along to the functionalist study of purposive and adaptive behavior. Thus the functionalists believed that the new schools added little to what their own all-embracing psychology had always included in its scope.

We will discuss Carr's functionalism as it was described in his 1925 textbook *Psychology*. Carr's central theme is organismic adjustment, which makes him a functionalist in the broadest sense.

Definition of Psychology

Psychology is the study of *mental activity,* which is the generic term for adaptive behavior. According to Carr (1925, pp. 72ff.), the adaptive act is a key concept for psychology. It involves three essential phases: (1) a motivating stimulus, (2) a sensory situation, and (3) a response that alters the situation to satisfy the motivating conditions. The motive is a stimulus that dominates the behavior of the organism until the organism reacts in such a way that the stimulus is no longer effective. Motives, as thus defined, are conceived of not as necessary to behavior but as directive forces that in general determine what we do. There are three ways in which a motive may be resolved by an adaptive act: The act may remove the stimulus, disrupt it by introducing a stronger stimulus, or resolve it through sensory adaptation to the stimulus.

Carr thought that both psychology and physiology studied adaptive behavior. The two disciplines were to be distinguished in terms of the kinds of variables each studied. Carr (1925) made the distinction thus:

Psychology is concerned with all those processes that are directly involved in the adjustment of the organism to its environment, while physiology is engaged in the study of vital activities such as circulation, digestion, and metabolism that are primarily concerned with the maintenance of the structural integrity of the organism. (p. 7)

Carr (1925) regarded consciousness as an artificial abstraction "that has no more independent existence than the grin of a Cheshire cat" (p. 6). Thus consciousness was an unfortunate reification, something that was supposed to exist, whereas all that exists in reality is a set of processes. The concept of consciousness is similar to other abstract concepts like intelligence, willpower, and crowd mind. Since it was a mere abstraction, consciousness could not play an active role in adapting the organism to the environment. It could not account for behavior. Thus we see Carr moving to a position between that of the earlier functionalists and that of the behaviorists.

Although Carr recognized the abstract nature of consciousness and the difficulties of subjective observation, he did not exclude introspective study from psychology. Of objective and subjective study, he says:

Each mode of observation possesses certain advantages and limitations. . . . Introspection gives us a more intimate and comprehensive knowledge of mental events. Some mental events cannot be objectively apprehended. . . . Introspection often reveals the motives and considerations derived from past experience that influence us in any particular act. . . .
Naturally the use of the subjective method must be confined to subjects of training and ability. Psychology must thus rely upon the objective method in the study of animals, children, primitive peoples, and many cases of insanity. (pp. 7–9)

Postulates

The postulates of functionalism, like those of all early psychological systems, were not explicitly stated. However, several assumptions stand out clearly:

1 Behavior is intrinsically adaptive and purposive.

2 All sensory stimuli affect behavior—not just motives, as defined above. For Carr, there was no absolute difference between a motive and any other stimulus; a motive might become an ordinary stimulus after it was resolved as a motive.

3 All activity is initiated by some sort of sensory stimulus; no response occurs without a stimulus.

4 Each response modifies the stimulus situation. Behavior, as earlier pointed out by Dewey, is essentially a continuous and coordinated process.

Functionalism also had several quasi-postulational methodological preferences. Two that seemed characteristic of the Chicago school, although they do not derive from the evolutionary perspective, were that the experiment is clearly to be preferred to naturalistic observation and that learning is the key area for study. Thus functionalism as it developed historically in the United States tended toward environmentalism, when, philosophically, we might have expected it to tend toward nativism.

Mind-Body Position

Here Carr followed Dewey, rather than James, and minimized the problem (see Chapter 2 for a summary of mind-body positions). He felt that there was no need for a detailed solution because there was no real problem. The psychophysical integrity, or integration, of the organism was simply assumed. Functionalism thus tends to adopt either a monistic or a double-aspect position but has no strong position of any kind. The earlier functionalists, like Angell, might tend toward a parallelism, or they might take an interactionist position as William James did in his early writing. However, Carr did not think that psychology, as an empirical and natural science, needed to concern itself with metaphysical problems. He did point out the inadequacy of psychophysical parallelism as adopted by Titchener, and the general functionalist position was in turn vigorously attacked by Watson as being in reality interactionist. Angell had earlier made the point that an epiphenomenal position must be rejected if one accepts the functionalist belief that consciousness has adaptive value.

Nature of the Data

Although, in its stress on organismic adjustment to the environment, functionalism had a behavioristic flavor, it did not eliminate introspection as a method of obtaining data. Its data were thus both objective and subjective, with increasing stress on the objective as functionalism aged.

There are ample studies of animals in the functionalist experimental literature to illustrate the use of objective data. On the other side, Carr's interests in perception and thinking illustrate his use of concepts that might not fit within a behavioristic framework. *Perception* as Carr used the word referred to the apprehension of the immediate environment through current stimuli. *Thinking* referred to apprehension of a situation that was not immediately present in the environment. Introspective data were acceptable in the study of either.

In this respect we see Carr in a position that mystified many psychologists. He accepted introspective data but denied the usefulness of consciousness as a scientific concept. No doubt he resolved the difficulty for himself by assuming that introspection did not consist of a study of a reified "consciousness." It simply reported on perfectly objective states of affairs, like the distances of objects (in studies of space perception) or the firing of neural circuits (in studies of learning, thinking, and the like).

Principles of Connection

The principles of connection are the principles of learning and as such were the heart of the functionalist research program. Learning, basically, was a process of establishing associative connections or of organizing elements of behavior through association into new and larger units. Most functionalists, like Carr, were willing to take over associationistic principles in their explanations of learning. Much of the work that followed from the Chicago tradition could not be distinguished from work that might have followed directly from the associationistic tradition. Notable examples are the verbal learning work done by McGeoch, Melton, and Underwood. Their work on nonsense syllables follows logically from the work of Ebbinghaus, who has already been discussed as an associationist. The diffuse "schools" of associationism and functionalism are often difficult to distinguish, which probably means that for some individuals, like Thorndike, it does not much matter whether they are classified as functionalists or associationists.

The functionalists usually preferred the *relative* approach to the interpretation of learning. They avoided what Carr called the "quest for constants" and emphasized instead a *dimensional* analysis through structuring a total learning situation into specific continua which could be measured. As Underwood put it (1949): "When any phenomenon can be demonstrated reliably (consistently) to vary in amount with respect to some specific characteristic, we have a *dimension*" (p. 7). His books on experimental psychology (1957, 1966) generally illustrate the functional approach. Carr's student and friend J. A. McGeoch (1942) also provided an excellent example of the functionalist approach to problems of learning. The position taken on the problem of the learning curve, which was a controversial and apparently exciting issue to the early generations of experimental psychologists, is representative. Until dimensional analyses could be completed, the functionalist was willing to accept gracefully the fact that there is no curve that can be called *the* learning curve. There is too much dependence of results upon the influence of the specific situation.

Functionalist research has dealt with factors influencing the rate and course of learning rather than with the basic nature of the learning process. It has also dealt with problems of retention and transfer. McGeoch's (1942) attitude typified the usual atheoretical stand. He accepted the empirical law of effect as an adequate explanatory principle and refused to take a stand on the theoretical necessity of effect. A summary of functionalist learning theory and research was given by Hilgard (1956) and by Hilgard and Bower (1975). In a more recent edition, they characterize functionalism in terms of its methodological approach to learning and other problems. They say that functionalism "was a loose confederation of methodological ideas, but the central goal was to perform a detailed experimental analysis of important psychological skills or tasks. Thus, the guiding idea was to dissect any given task, such as serial verbal learning, into a number of components or constituent skills, and to analyze those experimentally" (Bower & Hilgard, 1981, pp. 134–135).

Thus, in the eyes of many, the experimental and analytic ideas which we think of as more typical of structuralism and associationism dominated the functionalist program. One might even say that this analytic tendency subverted the more organismic position of Dewey and the evolutionary approach from which functionalism initially derived.

Principles of Selection

The main agents of behavior selection for Carr were *attention, motives,* and *learning*. Attention was conceived of as a preliminary act or sensorimotor adjustment. Its major function was to facilitate perception. Motives, defined as persistent stimuli, were thought to direct action and thus to have a major role in determining which behavior occurs. Learning operates in three main ways: (1) Some adaptive mechanisms must necessarily be acquired through experience; (2) as adjustive mechanisms are thus acquired, other aspects of the stimulating situation come to be associated with the response (as in conditioning) and thus capable of eliciting it; and (3) certain associations are imposed by society (for example, fear of the dark or of thunderstorms and dislike of particular ethnic groups).

THE COLUMBIA SCHOOL: ROBERT S. WOODWORTH

Robert Sessions Woodworth (1869–1962) was born in Massachusetts, the son of a minister and a schoolteacher; he spent six years in Iowa, six in a small Connecticut village, and the balance of his early youth in Boston. He studied mathematics and taught it in high school. He studied psychology and philosophy with James and Royce at Harvard, took a Ph.D. with Cattell, and studied physiology for five years, last with Sherrington at Liverpool, before finally making a decision for psychology. By that time, Woodworth was 34 years old, about as old as G. S. Hall and Harvey Carr had been at the beginnings of their professional careers. Nevertheless, he had nearly sixty active years ahead of him when he returned to Columbia University to be with his "old" professor, James McKeen Cattell, head of Columbia's psychology department.

Woodworth was one of psychology's most remarkable men. His professional career began at about the time that Thorndike was working with his chickens and cats, and ended in the modern era. Woodworth received the first American Psychological Foundation Gold Medal Award in 1956; published *Dynamics of behavior* in 1958, when he was 88; and started revising his popular *Contemporary schools of psychology* (1964), no doubt in the midst of a busy schedule of other activities. It was jokingly said at the 1956 convention of the American Psychological Association that Woodworth, then 86, was having an affair with his secretary. Although this comment was not intended to reflect Woodworth's behavior accurately, it did accurately reflect the genial and loving awe accorded Woodworth and his continuing accomplishments. It is amusing in this context to recall that Murchison got Woodworth to write his autobiography for the 1932 edition of *A history of psychology in autobiography;* it is assumed that such an autobiography is a backward look, shared by a person at or near the end of a professional career. Woodworth was obviously a person who spent little time in looking back. When he wrote that premature autobiography he still had nearly half of his career before him. Anyone who wanted to detail Woodworth's accomplishments *after* 1932 would have more material to cover than most of us generate in all of our professional lives.

Woodworth's systematic viewpoint was first expressed in his *Dynamic psychology* (1918). There are many resemblances between Woodworth's position and that of the Chicago functionalists (we have already had an opportunity to see that Angell and Woodworth shared a fondness for asking how and why things happened). However, Woodworth developed his position independently of the Chicago functionalists. His kind of psychology owed less to the analytic tradition of the associationists, and Woodworth was never quite as fond of the nonsense syllable experiment as were his compatriots at Chicago. He was truer than the Chicagoans to his evolutionary foundations. Both Boring (1950) and Hilgard (1956) treated Woodworth as a functionalist.

Woodworth shares antecedents with Chicago's functionalists: James and Dewey, Hall and Cattell. His system, like that of other functionalists, is moderate, eclectic, and unassuming, with no pretensions to finality or completeness. All these related functionalist views are experimentally oriented, with little general theoretical superstructure. Woodworth's functionalist eclecticism is extreme, as he tried to take the best features from all systems. Mowrer (1959) tells a story about Woodworth which illustrates this attitude:

> There is a story, perhaps apocryphal, to the effect that a colleague once good-naturedly chided Professor Woodworth for having "sat on the fence" during much of his professional lifetime, instead of getting down and becoming involved in prevailing controversy. To which Woodworth, after a moment's reflection, is supposed to have replied: "I guess I have, as you say, sat on the fence a good deal. But you have to admit one gets a good view from up there—and besides, it's cooler!" (p. 129)

This point of view may not be true of his 1958 book, but it is certainly true of Woodworth's earlier eclecticism; he tended to accept contributions irrespective of their origins. Even in Woodworth's last work (Woodworth and Sheehan, 1964), one gets the impression that he evaluated new publications as follows: "If it is good work, then it's functional. If it is functional, it is certainly acceptable."

Woodworth's dynamic psychology seemed to involve even less protest against Titchenerian structuralism than did the Chicago position. Woodworth accepted introspective techniques and sometimes defended them. Nevertheless, he thought that neither structuralism nor behaviorism provided an adequate methodology for psychology; we have already seen that Harvey Carr felt the same way. Woodworth was less influenced by associationism and a strict stimulus-response approach. The S-R theorists have often talked as though the stimulus led directly to a response, without mediation of the organism or dependence upon the organism to determine the response. This viewpoint is the basis for the complaint that much of psychology deals with the "empty organism." Woodworth "put the O back in psychology" by insisting that the formula for psychology should be S-O-R, not just S-R. He also relied heavily, even more than Carr, upon the concept of motivation. Perhaps because of his long-time study of physiology, Woodworth insisted upon considering the physiological events which underlie motivation as well as its behavioral manifestations.

The heart of Woodworth's system is his concept of *mechanism*, which has more or less the same meaning as Carr's *adaptive act*. Mechanisms for Woodworth were purposive responses or sets of responses. He made the same distinction as Sherrington (1906/1947) between preparatory and consummatory reactions. The former prepare for oncoming reactions, while the latter carry out the intention. Thus we must open our mouths (preparatory reaction) before we can receive food and swallow (consummatory reaction).

Drives for Woodworth were closely related to mechanisms. Although drives are generally defined as internal conditions that activate mechanisms, Woodworth preferred to think of internal drive processes as being themselves kinds of responses. The reverse was also true: mechanisms, the overt behavioral ways in which drives are satisfied, could become drives. Woodworth felt that practically all mechanisms could become drives and thus run under their own power, so to speak. G. W. Allport (1937) later advanced a similar idea in his theory of the "functional autonomy of motives."

A later contribution of Woodworth offers another illustration of this kind of thinking. This is his suggestion that the act of perceiving is intrinsically reinforcing, which was proposed in an unpretentious paper entitled "Reinforcement of perception" (Woodworth, 1947). Perception is here interpreted as an adaptive behavior whose successful performance is reinforcing without the operation of either extrinsic drive conditions or extrinsic reward conditions. This paper and his latest book seemed to put him more in the cognitive camp than in the S-R reinforcement camp, since he did not see any necessity for external reinforcing operations in order for behavior to be maintained.

CRITICISMS OF FUNCTIONALISM

Definition

Some critics have said that functionalism was not well enough defined to constitute a meaningful system. C. A. Ruckmick (1913), a Titchener-trained psychologist, objected to the vague and vacillating use of the term *function*. He found it used in two senses: first, to mean an activity or a use, and second, in the mathematical sense, to indicate a dependence of one variable on another (a functional relationship). Although the functionalists may have used the word function in more than one way, there is nothing wrong with that if the two usages are both acceptable and are not confused. The functionalists wanted to keep the best of two worlds in their multiple definitions. They retained an evolutionary point of view (first definition above) at the same time that they emphasized their "scientific" reliance on experimentation, which seeks functional relationships between independent and dependent variables (second definition above). Carr said, correctly we believe, that the mathematical meaning could be shown to include the others. This meaning of "function" is so general that there is nothing peculiarly functional (in the sense of functional psychology) about it.

Applied Science

The fact that functionalists, with their many interests in useful activities, did not distinguish carefully between pure and applied science was disturbing to some of the early critics. Contemporary psychologists take a position much like that of the functionalists. Pure and applied scientists use the same essential scientific procedures and can be distinguished only by the intent of the investigator (that is, the extent to which he or she has an application in mind). Many important basic relationships have been discovered as a result of strictly applied efforts, and some of the *most* important applied findings have been incidental results of pure research. Thus the contemporary position would be that the pure-applied distinction is not in itself very important, and the functionalist should not be criticized for deemphasizing the distinction.

Teleology

The functionalists were accused of using the ultimate consequences of behavior to explain behavior. In the absence of relevant evidence, such an explanation would be *teleological*. We have seen Dewey talking about the end getting thoroughly organized into the means, but such a statement, based on evolutionary thinking, is not teleological. Certainly Woodworth and Carr were careful to disclaim teleology and to postulate only current stimuli as causal. Carr recognized that an explanation in terms of the effects of behavior would be incomplete at best. It would tend to stop investigation before the detailed nature of the relationship between the stimulating situation, the physiology of the organism, and the behavior was worked out.

The tree-climbing behavior of certain larvae may be taken as an example. Their climbing has the effect of taking them up where the leaves are. Thus the behavior may be an important factor in the survival of the species; but if we say that they climb up the trees *in order to* eat the leaves, we are giving a teleological explanation that tells us little if anything about why the individual organism behaves as it does. As Carr (1925) said, "Each act must be explained in terms of the immediate situation and the animal's organization in reference to it" (p. 81). Thus, if we can show that the larvae always move up a gradient toward greater brightness, and this leads them to crawl up the tree, we have escaped from the illusory finality of the teleological explanation and are on the way to an explanation of the behavior in terms of proximate factors.

There is some similarity between the teleological accusation made against the functionalist and the accusation made against Thorndike and other reinforcement theorists that their explanation of reinforcement requires that a cause work backward to an effect that preceded it in time. In the case of both "instincts" and "behaviors learned through the action of reinforcement," however, the cause acts forward in time. When only the fittest survive, the effect is to select behaviors that are already adaptive (those larvae that crawl toward light have an advantage over those that do not). When reinforcement occurs, the effect is seen on subsequent trials and is presumed to be mediated through effects on activity contemporaneous with or following the reinforcement.

Because the problem of teleology so often comes up in any discussion of the marvelous adaptations of organisms to their environments, let us try to examine the question with the use of an analogy from another field. Assume that a believer in teleology points to the heavens and notes how beautifully the planets are adapted to their "task" of revolving about the sun. How could this have happened unless the orbits were *designed* to fulfill the final purpose, revolution around the central star? The answer of the consistent nonteleologist is simply that any planet or planetary component which got into the wrong orbit either fell into the sun or fell away from it. The "fittest" planets survived.

So it is with organisms. We see only the survivors, most of them marvelously fitted to their environments. Again, we cannot conclude that any mechanism beyond selection was needed to lead them to their present adaptation. If teleology were involved, we should not have seen the many extinctions that have recently occurred and the many endangered species which now exist. Apparently selection has occurred since the origin of life, and it continues.

Eclecticism

Because functionalists have generally been willing to accept so many different kinds of problems and techniques of investigation, they have often been accused of being vapid and nondescript eclectics. Kuhn (1962/1970) would probably take a broad eclecticism as a sure indication that psychology was languishing in a preparadigmatic state. Henle (1957) criticized the eclecticism of functionalism, directing her attention mostly to Woodworth. She maintained that an eclectic tended to accept the good features of contradictory positions at the expense of blurring the distinctions between them.

Henle was speaking of a theoretical eclecticism. She maintained that when there are alternative deductive systems for arriving at empirical statements, we cannot afford to fall between them. If we do, we have no genuine deductive capacity. Thus the eclectic must either choose a theory or devise one. However, there are other *levels* of eclecticism and other eclectic positions regarding theories.

First, one may be an eclectic at the level of rules for theory building as well as at the level of theory itself. That is, one may accept, say, both Gestalt and behavioristic methods and do work typical of both schools. Both subjective and objective data may be used. An eclecticism of methodology can be called a *metatheoretical eclecticism*. At the present stage of development in psychology, a tolerant but skeptical metatheoretical eclecticism may well be desirable. We have already seen how too narrow a metatheory contributed to the downfall of structuralism. To fail to attack problems because they do not fit into a particular methodological framework is to invite disaster. Only the most basic and general premises of science are well established enough to accept without much thought, and they will be reexamined if scientific progress demands it.

Even at a theoretical level, some kinds of eclecticism may be safe. The eclectic may use each theory for deductions within its area of application, admiring successes and regretting failures and trying all the time to correct them. Some eclectics may accept *no* theory rather than many, and they are freer to do so if they are not adherents to any system. The atheoretical system is becoming less popular with the general recognition that theories are necessary in order to organize knowledge and make prediction possible. In addition, the eclectic misses some of the stimulation, as well as the acrimony, of controversy.

Functionalists typically take a more inductive viewpoint than have the exponents of most systems. They have tended to pay less attention to the construction of theory than to empirical investigations. Thus, if one does not like eclecticism, one is justified in criticizing functionalism. Henle is such a critic. For others, however, eclecticism is grounds for compliments rather than criticisms. Certainly the eclecticism of the functionalists should not be mistaken for soft-mindedness or weakness. On the contrary, functionalists tend to be astute and tough-minded critics.

Finally, there is a different defense against those who bemoan eclecticism. It is that functionalism is not *necessarily* eclectic. One can easily imagine an eclectic *structuralism* under the quiet and modest Carr and a rigid theoretical functionalism under the autocratic Titchener. The point is that eclecticism depends on the personalities of a school's leaders as well as on the metatheoretical precepts of the school. There is nothing in functionalism to make it permanently atheoretical, nor is there any stipulation that it must forever have a wider range of experimental interests than other schools. Eclecticism has a subsidiary and partly accidental relationship to the functionalist position.

THE CONTRIBUTIONS OF FUNCTIONALISM

Because functionalism has been so moderate and lacking in presumption, it is easy to underestimate the importance of its contribution to psychology. It has erected no fancy theories and has not been much of a school or system, in a formal sense. However, functionalism has always been mainstream American psychology. It has never had to apologize for overlooking anything. Its early opposition to structuralism enlarged the conception of psychology just as the embryonic outlines of the new discipline were emerging. Functionalism very literally gave birth to behaviorism, in the person of one of its students, John B. Watson; the details of that birth will be presented in the next chapter.

The experimental contributions of functionalists have been most impressive; we have seen that, if anything, the functionalists were too dominated by the experimental ideal. They pioneered in studies of learning, animal as well as human; in psychopathology; in mental testing; and in genetic and educational psychology. The studies of functionalists have led to the development of applied psychology, which is perfectly consistent with the functionalists' pragmatism. Without the mental testers and applied psychologists, and without the clinical side of psychology to which functionalism contributed, psychology today would be a much more limited, and probably less interesting, discipline.

As to research, two products may be cited as classical illustrations of the patient and systematic functionalist approach. Woodworth's scholarly manual *Experimental psychology* (1938; Woodworth & Schlosberg, 1954) is a classic of its kind. It is a scientific handbook in the old style, dealing intensively and comprehensively with the data, methods, and theories connected with a large number of experimental settings. Just as James's *Principles* are still read, so the Woodworth handbooks are still consulted by experimental psychologists.

The other product is an extended series of studies, which several years ago had reached 24 in number, on the effects of distribution of practice on human verbal learning. They were carried out by Benton Underwood (1915–) and his associates (e.g. Underwood & Ekstrand, 1967). Underwood's persistent productivity in research nicely illustrates the functionalist tendency to deal intensively with interdependencies of empirical variables; this is the "dimensional analysis" mentioned earlier. This series of studies illustrates the difficulties, as well as the values, of the dimensional approach. Few scientists have had the patience to pursue research in a tightly restricted setting for such a long time, and even after these many years of functional study there is no end in sight for the dimensional analysis even of human verbal learning.

Among other functionalists who have actively conducted research were some of the Chicago graduates who worked under Carr. John McGeoch did an extensive set of human verbal learning and retention studies and had his own set of students and protégés, including A. W. Melton (1906–1978) and A. L. Irion (1918–), as well as Underwood. M. E. Bunch (1902–) had a long-time program of human and animal research on transfer and retention, and one of your present authors, M. H. Marx (1919–), was a Bunch student who carried on in his tradition before branching off into others. Fred McKinney (1908–1982) worked in mental health and counseling, after getting his Chicago degree and working on forgetting. He also worked in television instruction and the problem of values in teaching. These people have pursued empirical problems, many of them in applied areas, carefully and intensively, in a true functionalist tradition.

THE REBIRTH OF FUNCTIONALISM

Functionalism, in the broad sense of the term, is very strong today. Earlier we said that it was enjoying a renaissance, but on further reflection we decided that it had never had a dark age. Because of its eclectic and accepting nature, functionalism has never rejected anything, never ignored anything because metatheoretical considerations dictated that it was unimportant. Therefore functionalism has never had to apologize to anyone or for anything; many, if not most, American psychologists have simply continued on their quiet ways, following something resembling a functionalist program without thinking much about it.

If there is some resurgence in interest in functionalism, it is because of recent developments in genetics and evolutionary theory. These areas, as everyone knows, are in a period of extremely active growth, amid controversy about the application of molecular biology to the shaping of new forms of life. In 1973, in his introductory psychology textbook *Psychology: Man in perspective,* Arnold Buss expressed the opinion that evolutionary theory was the *only* theory sufficiently encompassing that one could organize all of psychology around it. Geneticists, ethologists, and sociobiologists have filled in so many pieces of the evolutionary puzzle that one *can* begin to believe that a comprehensive framework may be within reach, despite widespread controversy about many details of the picture. At the same time, a cognitive psychology is developing which, at every turn, combines introspective and objective data as it attempts to develop its view of human thinking. All of these developments are so consistent with functionalism that we can imagine genial smiles on the faces of James, Dewey, Angell, Woodworth, and Carr, as *their* broad kind of psychology emerges victorious.

SUMMARY AND CONCLUSIONS

Functionalism has been a loose and informal system, and its encompassing character made it the best representative of mainstream American psychology. Its major pioneers were William James, G. Stanley Hall, and James McKeen Cattell. We take John Dewey and James Angell as its "founders," although there was never any one event which could be identified as a founding. Harvey Carr at Chicago and Robert S.

Woodworth at Columbia were the early representatives of a developed functionalism. Carr was in a somewhat more analytic tradition, and Woodworth's dynamic psychology resembled more the molar approach of James and Dewey. Functionalism as a "movement" arose partially as a force opposing the structural psychology of Wundt and Titchener. It emphasized learning, mental testing, and other applied fields, which made functionalism appealing to the pragmatic American temperament. Although functionalism became a less self-conscious position as the need to oppose structuralism disappeared, its eclectic tendencies continued to fit many psychologists. Functionalism thus continued to go its unpretentious way during the heyday of behaviorism. Today the ascent of interest in evolutionary theory and the burgeoning growth in ethology, sociobiology, molecular biology, and cognitive theory, all of them consistent with a functional approach, have given a tremendous boost to a generally functional psychology.

Functionalism, especially as represented in the psychologies of Carr and Woodworth, relied heavily on experimentation; was more concerned with functional interrelationships of variables than with theoretical superstructures; accepted both introspective and behavioral data; stressed adaptive behavior and purposive, motivated activity within either an S-R (Carr) or an S-O-R (Woodworth) framework; and was always systematically eclectic while taking a tough-minded approach to experimental problems. Functionalists have made and will continue to make an important contribution to the advance of psychology as a science.

FURTHER READINGS

Our favorable allusions to Irvine's delightful *Apes, angels, and Victorians* (1963) should already have convinced the reader that it furnishes an easy entree to the people and the world who were functionalism's English antecedents. James's *Principles,* too, needs no further advertising from us as a source of information about our own legitimate American genius. Dewey's paper (1896) is brilliant, important, and blessedly short, since it is not easy reading even for the supposedly sophisticated among us. Carr's *Psychology* (1925) is, like Carr himself, simple and unpretentious and is probably the best representative of the Chicago position. For the Columbia development, Woodworth's early *Dynamic psychology* (1918) and later *Dynamics of behavior* (1958) are excellent sources. In addition, Woodworth's *Contemporary schools of psychology* (1948) is interesting because it shows how an eclectic functionalist viewed the competing schools. Woodworth's *Experimental psychology* (1938), revised by Woodworth and Schlosberg (1954), is worth a browse to see how systematic and careful functionalists were in their approach to methodological issues. The work of Underwood in *Psychological research* (1957) and of McGeoch in *Psychology of human learning* (1942) provides an excellent view of typically careful and persistent functionalist research on human verbal learning. Finally, there are several fascinating biographical sources of information about some of the greatest functionalists: Ralph Barton Perry's two-volume *The thought and character of William James* (1935), Dorothy Ross's *Stanley Hall: The psychologist as prophet* (1972) for the life of G. Stanley Hall, and Sokal's *An education in psychology: James McKeen Cattell's journal and letters from Germany and England, 1880–1888* (1981).

END NOTES

Dimensional Descriptions of Functionalism

Conscious Mentalism–Unconscious Mentalism   The functionalists from the be-ginning emphasized both conscious and unconscious mentalism. In doing so, they were moving away from the more extreme and exclusive structural emphasis on con-scious mentalism, and, despite their movement in this direction, functionalists never took the next step over to the other extreme, with the behaviorists. William James sometimes seemed to use consciousness to "explain" behavior, and sometimes did the reverse. Carr stayed away from consciousness as an explanatory mechanism. Thus the functionalists tended to take an intermediate, eclectic, perhaps too lukewarm, position on this dimension. If there is such a thing as a "perfect 3" on a scale of 1 to 5, functionalism should be it.

Content: Objective vs. Subjective   Almost all of the above reasoning applies just as well to this dimension. The evolutionary concerns of the functionalists guaranteed an interest in objective content greater than that of the structuralists and perhaps about equal to that of the "modal" associationist. But the functionalists did not abandon the use of introspection; if they had, they would have been behaviorists. Since they embraced a pragmatic philosophy and were more interested in learning and adaptive behavior than in fields like sensation and perception, we would place them somewhat toward the objective side.

Determinism vs. Indeterminism   Functionalists are generally within the broad scientific tradition which favors a deterministic position, although William James often toyed with the possibility that consciousness could "really" choose. Later functionalists were perhaps more toward the deterministic end of the continuum, and certainly the Darwinian heritage, with its reliance on chance mutations as the motor of evolution, encourages a deterministic view.

Empiricism–Rationalism   The functionalists were empiricists, as we see in their strong emphasis on learning, transfer, and memory in their experimental work. Their evolutionary background might have made them into rationalists, with knowledge more inherited than acquired. However, this did not happen to any of the leading functionalists, who tended to be almost as extreme in their empiricism as were the associationists to whom they were so closely related.

Functionalism vs. Structuralism   What can we say about this one? This is the prescription which names the school, and functionalists define the functional pole of this prescription, just as the Brooklyn Bridge is (partly) in Brooklyn. Their emphases on adaptation and on applied psychology are consistent with their functional orientation.

Inductivism–Deductivism   The functionalists are clearly inductivists, as we can see from the fact that they universally avoided the construction of extensive deductive systems. However, we should not put them at too extreme a position on this dimension, since they *were* interested in limited theories that applied to small areas, for example to particular experimental settings.

Mechanism–Vitalism Despite some accusations that they were teleological in their thinking—which might imply a vitalism—functionalists were fond of talking about, and thinking in terms of, mechanisms. Woodworth was a particularly good example in this respect, but Carr also recognized that the behavior of organisms rested exclusively on its organic foundation. As with most of these prescriptive issues, the functionalists did not seem to think it necessary to put a lot of stress on their mechanistic leanings and so managed, as usual, to seem middle-of-the-road.

Methods: Objective vs. Subjective This is another noncontroversial, neutral position to match their contentual objectivism–contentual subjectivism position perfectly.

Molecularism–Molarism The functionalists went from more molar beginnings toward a more molecular position. They were also more molar in their philosophical beliefs than in their experimental practices. We have seen that James and Dewey both anticipated Gestalt psychology with some of their pronouncements; but Carr and his students, who went in for a lot of dimensional analysis, rejoined the molecularistic tradition of the associationists.

Monism–Dualism William James sometimes took a dualistic position, but then James took both positions at some time or other on nearly *every* philosophical issue. Functionalists after James made a great issue of their monism, and James himself joined the monists in his later philosophical career.

Naturalism–Supernaturalism Functionalism found its origin in the naturalism of evolutionary theory, and if functionalism had a totem to which it prayed, that would have to be it. Thus, there is no doubt about its naturalism.

Nomotheticism–Idiographicism The relationship of functionalism to this dimension reminds one of its relationship to empiricism–rationalism; that is, functionalism should have been more idiographic than it actually was. Since genetic variety is a critical element in evolutionary theory, and early evolutionists like Galton quickly set out to study individual differences, one might expect that functionalists would be quite idiographic in their approach. But, as in the other cases of "dimensional surprise," functionalism took on a much more nomothetic cast when it came to America's laboratories. The interest in individual differences was never lost, but it was certainly diluted by other concerns, for example by the disappointing quest for "the" learning curve.

Peripheralism–Centralism Again, the functionalists had no need to take an extreme position. Their acceptance of both introspective techniques and behavioral observations allowed them to recognize the importance of both central and peripheral factors in the determination of behavior. We have seen that Woodworth helped psychology to refocus on the organism, which certainly took a little of the play away from peripheralism.

Purism–Utilitarianism An easy choice of utilitarianism here.

Quantitativism–Qualitativism The later functionalists were almost as quantitative in their orientation as were the associationists. This emphasis did not exist in James or Dewey, so we are again saved from having to place functionalism in an extreme position.

Rationalism–Irrationalism The functionalists recognized irrational determinants of behavior, but they never departed from James's belief that consciousness was a fighter for an end: the survival of the organism. We would regard this as a "rational" end, even though, philosophically, this goal might not be regarded as involving the highest rationality. Thus we would put the functionalists a little toward the irrationalistic end, but not far.

Staticism–Developmentalism The functionalists were developmentalists, as well they might have been. G. S. Hall pioneered in the field of genetic—that is, developmental—psychology, and, for every evolutionary psychologist, development of the species and of the individual had to be critical issues.

Staticism–Dynamicism Woodworth definitely stressed the dynamic causation of behavior, and Dewey and James made similar points. Other functionalists put less stress on fluidity, but we would still place functionalism well toward the dynamic end of this polarity.

Three dimensions which seem to be particularly important in describing functionalism are functionalism, utilitarianism, and molarism.

Functionalism Compared to Other Systems

We can now summarize functionalism's relationship to the systems we have already discussed by examining their relative positions on Coan's (1979) summary dimensions (p. 29). The first three dimensions are concerned with a distinction between an analytic and a synthetic approach. We have seen that associationism provides us with the epitome of an analytic approach. Functionalism would also be rated as an analytic system, but less extreme than associationism. Because its mature form put less stress on strictly objective data, functionalism was slightly less quantitative, and, as represented by some early functionalists, considerably less molecularistic. Nevertheless, functionalism as it developed in the United States, coming to emphasize dimensional analysis, fits better into an analytic than into a synthetic mold.

On Coan's second set of three dimensions, functionalism departs from associationism and from structuralism. Functionalism is more personal in orientation (it emphasized individual differences), more dynamic, and slightly more endogenistic. Thus functionalism, as we have already said, is functional, not structural.

Finally, considering all of Coan's dimensions together, we must ask whether or not functionalism would be regarded as a *restrictive* system. From everything that has been said before, we know that we cannot classify functionalism as being, overall, restrictive. It was too theoretically eclectic for that, and too eclectic with respect to the subject matters in which it was interested. However, functionalists generally *were* rather restrictive with regard to the scientific methodology which they felt to be appropriate; we would therefore not put functionalism far toward the fluid pole of the fluid–restrictive dimension.

BEHAVIORISM

John B. Watson founded behaviorism in the period just before World War I. It quickly became the most controversial of the active schools in America, assuming a prominent role both in psychology and in general cultural affairs. John Watson had one main positive and one main negative interest. He proposed a completely objective psychology. He wished to apply the techniques and principles of animal psychology to human beings. In this respect, he was a Darwinian. He insisted on the primacy of behavior, rather than of consciousness, as the source of psychological data. This positive aspect of behaviorism is called *methodological,* or *empirical,* behaviorism.

Watson's negative emphasis was his rejection of mentalistic concepts in psychology. He objected to the introspective psychology of Titchener and to Angell's functionalism. Watson claimed that Angell had kept an interactionistic bias and accepted introspective data. Watson wanted to free psychology of metaphysical concerns, but he himself took a metaphysical position by denying the existence of mind. This position on mind is called *metaphysical,* or *radical,* behaviorism. As one might expect, radical behaviorism has been even more controversial, and less widely accepted, than methodological behaviorism. Some have doubted that Watson himself believed it, just as many philosophers doubted that Hume or Berkeley really believed that the external world did not exist.

Behaviorism was dominant from about 1920 to about 1970. It earned the nickname of the "second force" in psychology, with its rival, psychoanalysis, as the first force. The "third force" was humanistic, phenomenological, and existential psychology, and it, together with the growing influence of cognitive psychology, today poses an increasing challenge to a strictly objective psychology.

TABLE 6-1
IMPORTANT FIGURES IN BEHAVIORISM

Antecedent Influences	Behaviorists		
	Pioneers	Founders	Developers
Evolution and Animal Behavior			
Charles Darwin (1809–1882)	James McKeen Cattell (1960–1944), Columbia	John B. Watson (1878–1958), Hopkins	Albert P. Weiss (1879–1931), Ohio State
C. Lloyd Morgan (1852–1936)	Edward L. Thorndike (1874–1949), Columbia		Walter S. Hunter (1889–1953), Brown
Jacques Loeb (1859–1924)			Karl S. Lashley (1890–1958), Chicago
Extensions of Mechanistic Explanations			
René Descartes (1596–1650)	Ivan P. Pavlov (1849–1936), St. Petersburg	Edward C. Tolman (1886–1961), California	
J.O. de La Mettrie (1709–1751)	Vladimir M. Bekhterev (1857–1927), St. Petersburg	Edwin R. Guthrie (1886–1959), Washington	
J. G. Cabanis (1757–1808)	James R. Angell (1869–1949), Chicago		
Positivism			
Auguste Comte (1798–1857)	Max Meyer (1873–1967), Missouri		Clark L. Hull (1884–1952), Yale
			B. F. Skinner (1904–), Harvard

Our discussion of behaviorism begins with the three major sources from which Watsonian behaviorism developed: the philosophical traditions of psychological objectivism (which probably were less important for Watson than the other two), animal psychology, and functionalism. We then describe the founding of behaviorism, outline Watson's system, with special emphasis on the mind-body issue, and consider some of the "secondary" characteristics of Watson's thinking. We continue with some of the other early behaviorists and describe criticisms of behaviorism. Finally, we review the factors responsible for the quick acceptance of behaviorism and evaluate Watson's contribution.

John Broadus Watson (1878–1958) was the first to formalize and popularize the behavioristic position and was the unquestioned leader of the school until he was forced out of Johns Hopkins in 1920.

Table 6-1 lists some of the people who were most important for behaviorism. We have already met James McKeen Cattell, Edward Lee Thorndike, James Angell, and the two Russian psychologists in our discussion of other schools. These men are not, therefore, pioneers of behaviorism in a strict sense, but they were among the early psychologists who emphasized objective methods.

EARLY TRENDS TOWARD PSYCHOLOGICAL OBJECTIVISM

There was already a long list of psychological objectivists before Watson appeared on the scene. Diserens (1925) reviewed the work of these objectivists, most of them philosophers. He described psychological objectivism as "any system in which the effort is made to substitute objective data and the universal method of science, direct observation, for subjective data and the special method of introspection" (p. 121).

We have already mentioned how Descartes and La Mettrie took some of the first steps toward the use of objective data in psychology. They extended mechanistic explanations to the human body and mind. Pierre Jean George Cabanis (1757–1808) continued this attempt to define mind fully in terms of objective factors, specifically in terms of physiological functions. One reason for his interest in such problems was that he was involved in the French Revolution and was asked to determine whether those beheaded by the guillotine were conscious after they were beheaded. Cabanis decided that consciousness depended upon the brain and that the twitching of the body was instinctual. The brain was the organ of mind as surely as the stomach was the organ of digestion. Because of his generally mechanistic position and fondness for physiological explanations, Cabanis is regarded by some as the father of physiological psychology.

Perhaps the most important name in this series is that of another Frenchman, Auguste Comte (1797–1857), who founded a movement called *positivism*. All varieties of positivism emphasize a demand for positive (that is, not debatable) knowledge. Unfortunately, there is a lot of disagreement about what kind of procedure produces such knowledge. Comte believed that positive knowledge could come only from public, objective observation. Introspection, which gives access only to private experience, or consciousness, could not provide valid knowledge. Comte denied the importance of the individual mind and vigorously criticized mentalism and subjective methodology.

According to Comte's epistemology, human critical thinking advanced through three stages. The first stage was theological, the second metaphysical, and the third ("highest") stage was positivistic, or scientific. Comte referred to traditional psychology as the last stage of theology, and in 1824 he described the method of introspection as follows (1824/1896): "In order to observe, your intellect must pause from activity, and yet it is this very activity you want to observe. If you cannot effect the pause, you cannot observe; if you do effect it, there is nothing to observe. The results of such a method are in proportion to its absurdity" (p. 11). We should remember that Comte wrote these words a half century *before* Wundt began to make extensive use of introspection at Leipzig, and about ninety years before John B. Watson publicly declared his behavioristic position; but they were sentiments with which Watson would have agreed.

More constructively, Comte emphasized two types of study of affective and intellectual functions: (1) determination with precision of the organic conditions upon which these functions depend and (2) observation of behavioral sequences. Watson also sought these two types of data. Many French and British materialists were followers of Comte on these points and carried on in his tradition.

LATER OBJECTIVISTS

In the late nineteenth and early twentieth century, functionalists and some other psychologists who were at most partial functionalists were leaning toward, or fully advocating, objectivity. We have already mentioned Cattell and Thorndike; Herrnstein (in J. B. Watson, 1967, pp. 18–20) argues that Thorndike's position was more like that of modern behaviorists than Watson's, because Thorndike's ideas about learning and reinforcement were more modern. In 1904, Cattell said (as quoted by Woodworth & Sheehan, 1964, p. 114): "It seems to me that most of the research work that has been done by me or in my laboratory is nearly as independent of introspection as work in physics or in zoology."

One of Watson's opponents, William McDougall (1871–1938), had defined psychology as the positive science of conduct. He made experimental observations on color discrimination in infants in 1901, and his books of 1905 and 1912 contain objective data. His 1912 volume was even named *Psychology: The study of behavior*. However, McDougall was an outspoken purposivist, accepted consciousness as real, and used introspective data. In short, he was the opposite of Watson in the most critical respects one can think of. He was certainly no rival to Watson in the formulation of an exclusively objective psychology.

Max Meyer (1873–1967) was a more serious candidate. He published *The fundamental laws of human behavior* in 1911, a book which reflects his thoroughgoing objectivism. That was two years before Watson published on the subject. By 1921, Meyer had indicated his behavioristic inclinations more overtly by titling another book *The psychology of the other one*. However, by this time Watson's contributions had already been universally recognized. Meyer was a "scientific isolate" (Esper, 1967) who feuded with his teacher, Carl Stumpf, and had exactly one Ph.D. student, A. P. Weiss. Meyer got himself fired from the University of Missouri because of a sex questionnaire in which he was only indirectly involved, with the incident compounded because of Meyer's self-righteous stubbornness.

We have also mentioned the Russian reflexology school, initiated by I. M. Sechenov and developed by Pavlov and Bekhterev. The latter entitled one of his books, originally published in Russia in 1910, *Objective psychology* (1913). Sechenov's *Reflexes of the brain* was originally published in monograph form in 1863 and in book form in 1873. This is amazing when one considers that Sechenov's basic philosophical and methodological position was nearly identical to Watson's in its objectivity. Sechenov illustrates the continuity from early through late objectivists to Watson's behaviorism.

ANIMAL PSYCHOLOGY

Evolutionary theory was tremendously important both in the development of psychology as a science and as a specific background factor determining the form of functional psychology. It also stimulated the study of animal psychology. Watson's involvement in the study of animal behavior may have been the most important single factor related to his formulation of the behavioristic position.

Animal psychology played a role in the controversy about evolutionary theory. Although Darwinian theory won quick acceptance among the majority of British intellectuals, it was violently opposed by the clergy and theologians. One of the most effective answers to their objections would be provided if mental continuity between humans and other animals could be demonstrated, much as Darwin had already demonstrated the physical continuities between animal and plant species. Thus if mind could be demonstrated in infrahuman organisms (contrary to Descartes's views), and its continuity with the human mind exhibited, Darwin would be vindicated.

Charles Darwin himself began the defense. His main theme in *Expression of emotions in man and animals* (1872) was that human emotional behavior is the result of the inheritance of behavior which was once useful but is now useless to human beings. Darwin drew upon a wealth of observations on animals for his examples. One of his most famous examples is the way people curl their lips in sneering. He held that to be a remnant of the baring of the canine teeth in rage by carnivorous animals. Another example of a behavioral remnant in another species is the tendency for dogs to turn in a circle several times before lying down. This was said to be a behavior held over from the dog's ancestors, to whom it was useful as a precautionary measure to frighten away snakes and the like and to flatten out a bed in grass or weeds.

George John Romanes has been mentioned as one of Darwin's personal friends who later used animal behavior in the defense of evolutionary theory. Romanes culled all kinds of literature for stories, scientific or popular, on animal behavior. People in many walks of life sent him their most remarkable anecdotes about animal intelligence. After he had accumulated a great mass of material, he wrote the first book on comparative psychology, *Animal intelligence* (1886). Romanes' method of gathering data is now called the *anecdotal method*. In spite of the fact that he had adopted explicit rules for using stories, Romanes was unable to avoid using some inadequately controlled observations, since he had no way of checking on the original sources. The

tendency to anthropomorphize—to read human motives and abilities into animal behavior—played into Romanes' hands, since his goal was the demonstration of continuity between humans and animals. Anthropomorphizing, like the anecdotal method,
is now thoroughly disapproved of in psychology, so Romanes is doubly damned. In
spite of the limitations of his methodology, Romanes deserves credit for stimulating
the initial development of comparative psychology. He prepared the way for the
experimental study of animal behavior, which followed shortly.

   C. Lloyd Morgan used a semiexperimental methodology and partly controlled observations in the field in his studies on animals. He is better known today for his
methodological contributions than for his substantive findings, and certainly his standards were more demanding than those of Romanes. Morgan adapted the law of
parsimony (also called, more picturesquely, *William of Occam's razor*) to comparative
psychology. In its original form, the law of parsimony stated that when either of two
hypotheses is consistent with the observed data, the simpler hypothesis must be preferred. As specialized for comparative psychology, "Lloyd Morgan's canon" states:
"In no case may we interpret an action as the outcome of the exercise of a higher
psychical faculty, if it can be interpreted as the outcome of the exercise of one which
stands lower in the psychological scale" (1899, p. 59). This dictum was intended to
counteract the tendency to anthropomorphize, and the point was well received (see
Newbury, 1954, for an extended discussion of Lloyd Morgan's canon in its various
interpretations).

   If one cannot anthropomorphize, how can the desired continuity be demonstrated?
One helpful rule is that Lloyd Morgan's canon should be applied to humans as well
as to animals. We have a tendency to "anthropomorphize" when interpreting the
behavior of other people, in the sense that we may give them too much credit for
higher mental functions. Romanes was demonstrating continuity by finding mind every-
where. Morgan also wished to demonstrate continuity, but he suggested that it might
be as easily done by demonstrating mind nowhere. In this contrast we see Romanes
"leveling up" and Morgan "leveling down." Morgan's appeal to simplicity and his
rejection of anthropomorphism were direct precursors of behaviorism.

   Morgan relied upon habit, rather than upon intelligence, as a major explanatory
factor. Trial-and-error learning was stressed. He assumed that human and subhuman
learning processes were continuous. Thorndike's laboratory experimentation was closely
related to Morgan's work in both content and outlook. Watson was also stimulated in
his animal research by reading Morgan's reports. All three men tried to explain learning
in terms of a few simple principles which apply to humans as well as to animals.
Others, like the Gestaltists, have been more like Romanes in tending to see insight,
which is characteristic of much human learning, in nonhuman animals.

   Lloyd Morgan's canon has been attacked by some psychologists. The critics claim,
correctly we believe, that in many cases the more complex of two alternative interpretations is the better one. However, this does not invalidate Morgan's canon or the
principle of parsimony; these rules apply only to cases in which all the alternative
explanations are about equally consistent with the available data. Naturally, if there
is a flaw in the simpler explanation, it is not acceptable. Then there is no issue at all.
But it is incumbent upon the proponent of the more complex account to show why

that account must be accepted over the simpler one. If that cannot be done, the simpler account is preferable. In all of this, however, we must recognize that it may not be simple to show which of the altenative accounts is simpler!

Jacques Loeb (1859–1924) is the next important figure we consider in the development of animal psychology. Loeb, a German biologist, came to the United States in 1891 and spent the greater part of his professional career here. Loeb is responsible for the wide acceptance of the concept of *tropism,* or forced movement, as an explanatory factor in animal behavior. (The word *taxis* is now more often used for the movement of a whole organism in response to some stimulus.) In a tropism, the response is a direct function of the stimulus and is in this sense *forced.* Loeb felt that all the behavior of the lowest of animal forms is tropistic and that a considerable proportion of the behavior of higher forms also is forced. One familiar example of a tropism is the apparently mechanical and irresistible movement of moths toward light (positive phototropism), even though flight directly into a flame results in their destruction. Of course, not many tropisms are so maladaptive.

Loeb was reacting against the anthropomorphic tendency which Romanes was thought to represent. Despite the fact that Loeb used tropistic factors to account for a great deal of the behavior of higher forms, he did not try to deal with human problems. He did, however, contribute to the question of consciousness by suggesting a way to determine whether or not a given organism was conscious. He said that an organism was conscious if it demonstrated associative memory. Certainly this is not a very demanding criterion; protozoa, for example, have been said to show evidence of associative learning. The question of what organisms are conscious can be given only an arbitrary answer. We can choose our definition of consciousness to suit our own taste, and there is no debating taste.

By the time of Loeb's pronouncements, the study of animal behavior within the biological sciences was becoming widespread. The biologists Thomas Beer, Albrecht Bethe, and Jacob J. von Uexkull supported Loeb's call for the elimination of psychological terms and the substitution of objective ones. Another biologist, H. S. Jennings, obtained evidence for the modifiability of behavior in the protozoan *Paramecium,* and he opposed Loeb's mechanistic interpretations of animal behavior. Hans Driesch also opposed Loeb and maintained a vitalistic position. That is, he maintained that living organisms differ qualitatively from nonliving matter and are not reducible to physicochemical reactions.

Other students of animal behavior included Sir John Lubbock, who was studying ants, wasps, and bees, and the Frenchmen J. Henri Fabre and Auguste Forel, who were also studying insects. Albrecht Bethe published a mechanistic interpretation of the social lives of ants and bees. Certainly animal psychology was by this time a going concern, although much of the study was not being done by psychologists. The pressure of these researches was pushing objective psychology to the fore some time before behavioristic psychology was founded as a school in America.

Watson, who studied under Loeb at the University of Chicago, was thoroughly exposed to this objective tradition within biology. Angell, who was Watson's primary adviser, discouraged him from doing a dissertation with Loeb because he did not regard Loeb as "safe." Angell's fears proved to be well-founded, when Watson left functionalism to found behaviorism. Watson was further exposed to biology at Johns Hopkins when, despite the fact that he went there as a full professor, he attended the courses of H. S. Jennings.

E. L. Thorndike was already working systematically with animals. Watson wanted to do some research on the effects of alcohol with Thorndike and stayed in close touch with him. Robert M. Yerkes (1876–1956) also began research with animals early, in 1900. Yerkes studied crabs, turtles, frogs, dancing mice, rats, worms, crows, doves, pigs, monkeys, apes, and finally humans. During Watson's early years in the field, he and Yerkes corresponded frequently about their research, long before they met face to face. Yerkes's research on apes was most significant. It is summarized in *Chimpanzees: A laboratory colony* (1943). Yerkes and Watson collaborated on the development of equipment and techniques for testing color vision in animals. However, Yerkes was no behaviorist, despite the fact that he did work in comparative psychology that was typically behaviorist in method. He was an admirer of Titchener, and he felt that the investigation of experience was one of psychology's most interesting problems. Yerkes's contribution to behaviorism was mainly that he strengthened the position of comparative psychology. He also strengthened the position of applied psychology via his contribution to the testing of Army recruits during World War I.

W. S. Small at Clark devised the first rat maze in the same year that Yerkes began his animal investigations, 1900. The albino rat was so well suited to being studied in the maze that it became the outstanding laboratory animal in psychology, and the rat-in-the-maze has continued to be a standard situation for the study of learning. Since the 1930s, the rat has shown that it is equally well adapted to life in the Skinner box (or, as Skinner prefers to call it, the operant chamber). Growth of the study of animals was so rapid between 1900 and 1911 that the *Journal of Animal Behavior* was founded then. Watson adopted Small's use of the maze with rats, although he criticized Small's experimental methods.

Finally, Margaret Floy Washburn, Titchener's first doctoral student and later president of the American Psychological Association, published a compendium of animal psychology (1908). The book was an analogical study of human and animal mental processes, but it contained much factual information and became a classic. Thus, some of the impetus for a behavioral psychology came from the camp of the structuralists. Watson's dislike for guessing what the rat was thinking finally led him to decide that he could get along without guessing what people were thinking.

AMERICAN FUNCTIONALISM ABOUT 1910

American functionalism was a third source of ideas that led toward behaviorism. The most prophetic functionalist was probably James Angell, with whom Watson was associated at Chicago before 1908. We have already met Angell as a founder of functionalism. He recognized that psychology, which had already accepted functionalism as a valid position, was moving further toward objectivity. He expressed himself at least twice to this effect before Watson's first published behavioristic pronouncements. In 1910, at the Minneapolis meetings of the American Psychological Association, Angell said:

But it is quite within the range of possibility, in my judgment, to see consciousness as a term fall into as marked disuse for everyday purposes in psychology as has the term soul. This will not mean the disappearance of the phenomena we call conscious, but simply the shift of psychological interest toward those phases of them for which some term like behavior affords a more useful clue. (1913, p. 255)

Two years later, at the Cleveland meetings of the association, he presented a paper on this topic which was written just before Watson's first systematic paper. He now spoke at greater length:

The comparative psychologists have from the first been vexed by the difficulty of ascribing to animals conscious processes of any specific kind in connection with intelligent behavior. . . . Obviously, for scientists engaged in this field of investigation, it would from many points of view be a material gain, in convenience at least, if the possible existence of consciousness might be forgotten and all animal behavior be described objectively. Nor has there been, so far as I am aware, any general objection to this proposal. . . . It is furthermore not unnatural that finding it practicable and convenient, as undoubtedly it is, to waive reference to consciousness in matters relating to animal behavior, the tendency should manifest itself to pursue a similar line of procedure in dealing with human conduct. This tendency does not so much represent any formally recognized program like that of our world-reforming realists, as it does a general drift occasioned by several different sources. Its informal and unselfconscious character is probably indicative of a more substantial and enduring basis than belongs to movements more carefully and more purposely nurtured. (1913, pp. 256ff.)

Boring (1950) summarized the situation in American psychology just before Watson's founding of behaviorism: "America had reacted against its German parentage and gone functional. . . . Behaviorism simply took from functionalism part but not all of the parental tradition . . . the times were ripe for more objectivity in psychology, and Watson was the agent of the times" (p. 642).

THE FOUNDING: JOHN B. WATSON

John Broadus Watson (1878–1958) was born on a farm near Greenville, South Carolina. His mother was very religious, his father was not, and Watson's personality may have been shaped by this conflict (Cohen, 1979). After his father left the family when Watson was 13, he showed a streak of rebelliousness. According to Watson's own account (1936), he never made more than a passing grade during his early years in school. He was twice arrested, once for discharging a firearm within the city limits of Greenville.

Watson attended Furman University in Greenville but apparently did not know what he would do afterward. During his last year, a professor whom he much admired stated that if a man ever handed in a paper backwards, he would fail him. Watson "accidentally" handed in his paper "backwards" (whatever that meant), was duly failed, and had to stay for an additional year of school. He got a master's degree instead of a bachelor's degree because of the extra year.

Watson next went to the University of Chicago, intending to study philosophy under John Dewey. Angell, however, soon preempted his interest and steered him into experimental psychology. Watson also studied physiology and neurology under H. H. Donaldson and Jacques Loeb. Angell and Donaldson discouraged Watson from doing a dissertation with Loeb and supervised his work themselves. Watson finished his Ph.D. work after just three years and three summers in 1903, the youngest man to receive a Ph.D. from Chicago up to that time (Watson, 1936). Part of the reason was that Watson had no money for entertainment and thus did nothing but work.

Although he had developed an undergraduate interest in philosophy and had taken some graduate work in it, that kind of thinking "wouldn't take hold" with Watson. He explained briefly:

> I got something out of the British School of philosophers—mainly out of Hume, a little out of Locke, a bit out of Hartley, nothing out of Kant, and strange to say, least of all out of John Dewey. I never knew what he was talking about then, and unfortunately for me, I still don't know. (1936, p. 274)

While at Chicago, Watson worked mainly with animal subjects. Some three decades later, he put his feelings this way:

> I never wanted to use human subjects. I hated to serve as a subject. I didn't like the stuffy, artificial instructions given to subjects. I always was uncomfortable and acted unnaturally. With animals I was at home. I felt that, in studying them, I was keeping close to biology with my feet on the ground. More and more the thought presented itself: Can't I find out by watching their behavior everything that the other students are finding out by using O's (observers). (1936, p. 276)

Watson's doctoral dissertation was accordingly done with animal subjects. It was directed jointly by Donaldson and Angell and involved correlating the increasing complexity of behavior in the young albino rat with the medullation of its central nervous system. Another piece of research completed at Chicago was his analysis of the sensory cues used by the rat in maze learning. Watson used the techniques of Small, Morgan, and Thorndike, although he believed that he had improved upon their experimental procedures. He concluded, after systematic elimination of the various senses, that kinesthesis (which he could not completely eliminate) was the most basic to maze learning. He observed that when the maze arms were shortened or lengthened, animals continued to turn at the places where alleys had been before.

In 1908, just before he was 30, Watson was offered the chair in psychology at Johns Hopkins University (Cohen, 1979). There he continued his experimental laboratory research on animals, took course work and laboratory work with Jennings, and established a research program with children at Phipps Psychiatric Clinic, working with psychiatrist Adolf Meyer.

According to his own statement, Watson had begun some time before to think in thoroughly objective terms. His animal researches at Chicago led him to his first behavioristic formulation in 1903 (J. B. Watson, 1929, preface). The colleague to whom he broached the idea was most likely Angell, who thoroughly disapproved despite his later sympathetic pronouncements quoted above. Apparently the chief objection at that time was that the formulation might apply to animals but not to human beings.

Watson's first public expression of his views came in a lecture given at Yale University in 1908, when he was again discouraged by his listeners. This time the chief objection seemed to be that his formulation was descriptive but not explanatory. Finally, in 1912, he gave a more definitive expression to his views in lectures at Columbia University. The first published polemic, a paper entitled "Psychology as the behaviorist views it," appeared the following year in the *Psychological Review* and marked the official launching of the behavioristic school in America.

Here is the essence of Watson's original position:

> Psychology as the behaviorist views it is a purely objective experimental branch of natural science. Its theoretical goal is the prediction and control of behavior. Introspection forms no essential part of its methods, nor is the scientific value of its data dependent upon the readiness with which they lend themselves to interpretation in terms of consciousness. The behaviorist, in his efforts to get a unitary scheme of animal response, recognizes no dividing line between man and brute. The behavior of man, with all its refinement and complexity, forms only a part of the behaviorist's total scheme of investigation. . . . The time seems to have come when psychology must discard all reference to consciousness; when it need no longer delude itself into thinking that it is making mental states the object of observation. (1913b, p. 158)

This first paper on behaviorism was followed shortly by a second one on the concepts of image and affect (Watson, 1913a). He reduced images to implicit language responses and affect to slight vascular changes in the genitalia. We shall see later that he was severely criticized for these reductions. These two early papers were combined into the introductory chapter of his first book, *Behavior: An introduction to comparative psychology,* which appeared in 1914. This book has been reissued (1967) with an introduction by R. J. Herrnstein, who shows very clearly how Watson first ignored and then embraced Pavlov. Herrnstein also outlines particularly well the relationship of Watson's thought to that of Tolman, Hull, and Skinner, all of whom—Skinner perhaps most—owe something to Watson.

In 1915 Watson was President of the American Psychological Association at the age of 37, an amazing age at which to receive that honor. Psychology was greeting behaviorism with open arms, showing an extraordinary willingness to embrace a new and radical viewpoint toward the science.

He had a brief stint in the army during World War I. His original assignment was to test pilots. Soon he was in trouble with one of his superiors and was sent to Texas to work on the military uses of homing pigeons (an ironic foreshadowing of Skinner's work on Project Pigeon during World War II). Finally, he got into more serious trouble because he criticized a worthless "test of balance" which was being used to select pilots. He was assigned to be sent behind enemy lines, where he would likely have been killed. Luckily for Watson, the war ended too soon for that to happen.

In 1919 Watson published another book, *Psychology from the standpoint of a behaviorist*. This volume completed the program outlined in his earlier papers. Objective methods were definitely extended into human behavioral problems. Verbal behavior was to be accepted as data, but introspection was rejected. Critics quickly made heated charges of inconsistency on this point. The book stressed developmental factors, and the 1924 revision gave detailed results of Watson's work at Johns Hopkins on infantile emotions and emotional conditioning.

Watson (1929) felt that psychology as a scientific discipline needed to make a complete break from the past. He declared:

> [Psychology] made a false start under Wundt . . . because it would not bury its past. It tried to hang on to tradition with one hand and push forward as a science with the other. Before progress could be made in astronomy, it had to bury astrology; neurology had to bury phrenology; and chemistry had to bury alchemy. But the social sciences, psychology, sociology, political science, and economics, will not bury their "medicine men." (p. 3)

Watson resigned from the faculty at Johns Hopkins before the beginning of the 1920–1921 school year. On November 20, 1920, Watson's wife, Mary Ickes Watson, sued him for "absolute divorce." Rosalie Rayner, the woman with whom Watson did his famous experimental work on infants, was named as correspondent in the divorce suit. On January 1, 1921, the *Baltimore Sun* reported that John B. Watson and Rosalie Rayner had been married on the previous Friday. Watson's own two-line account of these events is somewhat misleading: "All of this work came abruptly to a close with my divorce in 1920. I was asked to resign" (Watson, 1936, p. 279).

Cohen (1979) gives a consistent, although in some respects necessarily speculative, account of what really happened. Watson had written love letters to Rosalie. Mary Watson, who wished desperately to keep her husband, had found a love letter from Rosalie to her husband in one of his pockets. She therefore schemed to get those from John to Rosalie; she "befriended" Rosalie, eventually got a chance to search her room, and found the letters. One of Mary's brothers was Harold Ickes, who later became Franklin Roosevelt's Secretary of State; but, unfortunately for psychology, she had another brother, John, who "was, it seems, poor, dishonest, and greedy" (Cohen, 1979, p. 154). Cohen believes that John, after unsuccessfully trying to blackmail Rosalie's wealthy family, gave photocopies of some of Watson's love letters to President Goodnow of Johns Hopkins. After consulting some of his prominent faculty, including Watson's "friend" Adolf Meyer, Goodnow promptly sacked Watson, although he allowed it to be publicized as a resignation.

Not one of Watson's friends inside or outside of his university made any visible effort to defend him. He went penniless to New York City with no job or prospects. However, he had a sympathetic friend there, the sociologist William Thomas, who had been similarly sacked from Chicago for having transported a woman across state lines for immoral purposes. "Watson had done nothing so illegal or so geographic" (Cohen, 1979, p. 159). Thomas arranged for Watson to meet people at the J. Walter Thompson advertising agency, and Watson got a temporary job there. He did so well that he was soon earning $70,000 a year, a truly fabulous salary for the times. The last year at Johns Hopkins he had made about $4,500.

Watson had been forced out of academic life, and he was bitter about that and about the treatment he received from his friends and from other psychologists. His later books and writing were negatively reviewed by his erstwhile colleagues, who affected righteous intellectual airs toward their now commercialized compatriot. Of all Watson's friends, Titchener seemed least affected and most loyal. He maintained his correspondence with Watson for several years, despite his own declining health and influence. Only the New School for Social Research in New York City asked Watson to deliver lectures, and he had no offers of academic positions until it was far too late, after World War II had ended, and he was over 65.

For many years, Watson continued to supervise some research and to write books and popular articles. He did psychology a great service by convincing the public that psychology could be broadly applied to the real world, particularly in the fields of advertising and child rearing. His book *The psychological care of the infant and child* (1972, first published in 1928), made him something like the Dr. Spock of his generation. He wrote some twenty popular articles, spoke on radio shows, and gave lectures to many audiences. Watson had, from the beginning, been interested in the application of psychology, and circumstances forced him to practice what he might otherwise only have preached.

Watson's 1925 book, *Behaviorism,* probably received the most attention from the nonpsychological public. It contained a strong environmentalist position and a positive program for the improvement of human beings. His later work grew increasingly distant from its research foundations, and Watson himself was dissatisfied with the scientific adequacy of his later efforts, as stated in his autobiography of 1936.

Nothing new or significant was published by Watson following the mid-1920s. The man whose systematic pronouncements did so much to influence psychology gradually dropped completely out of professional activity. His intelligence and charm made him a great success in the world of business, and psychology's loss was Maxwell House Coffee's and Ponds Cold Cream's gain (those were two of the accounts on which he worked). Whatever our systematic position, we must regret the untimely and unnecessary loss of a figure whose vitality and clarity of expression commanded so much attention. Watson was relegated to the scientific scrap heap at 42, when many psychologists have just reached the height of their powers.

WATSONIAN BEHAVIORISM: SYSTEMATIC CRITERIA

Definition of Psychology

Psychology for Watson was "that division of natural science which takes human behavior—the doings and sayings, both learned and unlearned, of people as its subject matter" (1929, p. 4). No mention need be made of the psychic life or consciousness; these are "pure assumptions." Watson clearly included verbalization as a kind of behavior: "*Saying* is doing—that is, *behaving*. Speaking overtly or to ourselves (thinking) is just as objective a type of behavior as baseball" (1925, p. 6).

Watson's behaviorism had two specific objectives: to predict the response, knowing the stimulus, and to predict (really *postdict*) the stimulus, knowing the response. The terms *stimulus* and *response* represented for Watson broader concepts than their usual definitions allow:

> The rule, or measuring rod, which the behaviorist puts in front of him always is: Can I describe this bit of behavior I see in terms of "stimulus and response"? By stimulus we mean any object in the general environment or any change in the tissues themselves due to the

physiological condition of the animal, such as the change we get when we keep an animal from sex activity, when we keep it from feeding, when we keep it from building a nest. By response we mean anything the animal does—such as turning toward or away from a light, jumping at a sound, and more highly organized activities such as building a skyscraper, drawing plans, having babies, writing books, and the like. (1925, pp. 6–7)

Postulates

Watson's assumptions were stated directly and carefully, although not in formal postulational form. The major ones are:

1 Behavior is composed of response *elements* and can be successfully *analyzed* by natural scientific methods.

2 Behavior is composed *entirely* of glandular *secretions* and muscular *movements;* thus it is reducible ultimately to physicochemical processes.

3 There is an immediate response of some sort to every effective stimulus; every response has some kind of stimulus. There is thus a strict cause-and-effect *determinism* in behavior.

4 Conscious processes, if indeed they exist at all, cannot be studied *scientifically;* allegations concerning consciousness represent supernatural tendencies and, as hangovers from earlier prescientific theological phases of psychology, must be ignored.

A number of secondary assumptions, having to do with the nature of thinking, the role of the environment, and the like, are discussed in a later section because they are not central to the behaviorist argument.

Nature of the Data

The kind of data used by behaviorists has been indicated above. The data are always objective reports of muscular movements and glandular secretions, behaviors that occur in time and space. These behaviors must be, at least in principle, quantitatively analyzable, and stimulus-response relationships are the units of description (although they may be rather large-scale units, such as "building a skyscraper," and not merely "muscle twitches").

Principles of Connection

Here Watson adopted, at first, merely an older version of associationism, accepting the laws of frequency and recency minus the "effect" aspect that Thorndike had added. Apparently he saw in effect too much of the old mentalistic attitudes. Watson argued that the successful response must always occur and terminate the behavior. Thorndike replied that very often certain errors, such as entrance into the more popular blind alleys in a maze, were made more frequently than the corresponding correct response. Watson subsequently shifted his emphasis to classical conditioning as demonstrated in the laboratory by Pavlov and Bekhterev. He came to regard conditioning as the basis for all learning; the most complex habits could be conceived of as combinations and chainings of simpler reflexes. Woodworth noted (1948, p. 88) that in spite of Watson's enthusiasm for classical conditioning he apparently never recognized the very great similarity between Pavlovian reinforcement and Thorndikian effect. He continued to hold to an exercise law (frequency and recency factors) while accepting classical conditioning principles and even using them himself in his experiments on emotional conditioning in infants.

Principles of Selection

Watson assumed a large number of inherited reaction tendencies to stimulation and the "almost immediate" modification of these through conditioning into more and more complicated and individually differentiated tendencies. Thus he wrote:

> One of the problems of behaviorism is what might be called the ever increasing range of stimuli to which an individual responds. Indeed so marked is this that you might be tempted at first sight to doubt the formulation we gave above, namely that response can be predicted. If you will watch the growth and development of behavior in the human being, you will find that while a great many stimuli will produce a response in the new-born, many other stimuli will not. At any rate they do not call out the same response they later call out. For example, you don't get very far by showing a new-born baby a crayon, a piece of paper, or the printed score of a Beethoven symphony. . . . It is due to conditioning from earliest childhood on that the problem of the behaviorist in predicting what a given response will be is so difficult. (1925, p. 13)

Thus Watson maintained that selectivity of response and of the sufficient stimulus depends only on innate and acquired S-R connections. Selection does not constitute a unique problem. The older mentalistic concepts of purpose and value are eliminated as explanations.

The Mind-Body Problem

The mind-body solution proposed by Watson is at the heart of what has been called *radical* or *metaphysical behaviorism*. From about 1930 to 1950 this position even became almost noncontroversial, at least within psychology. However, the issue was revived (see Wann, 1964) by humanists, phenomenologists, and existentialists (the Third Force), and the wheel has come almost full circle, with consciousness almost a buzzword. Nevertheless, these critics have offered no convincing demonstration of a method for studying "mind" directly.

Many avowed behaviorists felt a need to take a strong position on the mind-body issue. They did not wish to study consciousness or mind and therefore denied its importance; their position was logical only if they accepted some appropriate mind-body position. Of the available positions (see Chapter 2), two were best fitted to their purposes. First, an epiphenomenal view would imply that consciousness had no causal efficacy and therefore held little interest for science. It might or might not attend bodily events and would not be of much importance. According to this position, mind would be comparable to a shadow; it would often, but not always, accompany and more or less follow the outlines of the physical object (body) to which it related but would itself have no substance and play no causal role.

Second, a completely physical monism would deny the very existence of mind and would serve the purposes of behaviorism admirably. Watson's early pronouncements were not clear on this point:

> Will there be left over in psychology a world of pure psychics, to use Yerkes' term? I confess that I do not know. The plans that I most favor for psychology lead practically to the ignoring of consciousness in the sense that that term is used by psychologists today. I have virtually denied that this realm of psychics is open to experimental investigation. I don't wish to go further into the problem at present because it leads inevitably over into metaphysics. If you will grant the behaviorist the right to use consciousness in the same way as other natural scientists employ it—that is, without making consciousness a special object of observation— you have granted all that my thesis requires. (1913b, p. 174)

Other expressions of a similar point of view may be found in papers by Walter Hunter and A. P. Weiss. Hunter (1926), for example, said:

> A brief inspection of the writings of any behaviorist will convince you that he is neither blind, deaf, anosmic, ageusic, or anaesthetic. He lives, and admits quite frankly that he lives, in the same world of objects and events which the psychologist and the layman alike acknowledge. Let us, therefore, hear no more from the psychologist that his opponent denies the existence of these things. (p. 89)

Weiss also accepted conscious processes as real, even if no more than epiphenomenal. He held that "consciousness (the totality of our sensations, images, and affections) is a purely personal experience and has no scientific value or validity unless it is *expressed* in some form of behavior, such as speech or other form of representation" (Weiss, 1917, p. 307). The general position here clearly stated is that the physical facts of behavior are sufficient; the "mental" correlates of these facts are unreliable and superfluous.

Acceptance of this methodological behaviorism put the behaviorist into the somewhat embarrassing position of admitting that experience exists, even if in a most shadowy manner, and yet cannot be attacked by scientific tools. Thus, faced with the dilemma of either admitting that there are some psychological facts which he cannot explain by natural scientific techniques or denying the existence of such alleged facts, the radical behaviorist, following Watson, chose the latter course: the denial that any conscious correlates of introspective reports existed.

By 1924 Watson chose this alternative. In his debate with McDougall (J. B. Watson & McDougall, 1929), Watson said that consciousness "has never been seen, touched, smelled, tasted, or moved. It is a plain assumption just as unprovable as the old concept of the soul" (p. 14). And, more at length:

> He then who would introduce consciousness, either as an epiphenomenon or as an active force interjecting itself into the physical and chemical happenings of the body, does so because of spiritualistic and vitalistic leanings. The Behaviorist cannot find consciousness in the test tube of his science. He finds no evidence anywhere for a stream of consciousness,

not even for one so convincing as that described by William James. He does, however, find convincing proof of an ever-widening stream of behavior. (p. 26)

Another early behaviorist, K. S. Lashley, likewise supported an extreme position. In his single excursion into such polemic, he wrote:

> There can be no valid objection by the behaviorist to the introspective method so long as no claim is made that the method reveals something besides body activity. . . . The attributes of mind, as definable on introspective evidence, are precisely the attributes of the complex physiological organization of the human body and a statement of the latter will constitute as complete and adequate an account of consciousness as seems possible from any type of introspective analysis. (1923, pp. 351–352)

This view reduces mind entirely to physiological functions and thus represents a radical behavioristic position.

There were several common behavioristic arguments against the existence of consciousness. First, they asked how the so-called gaps in consciousness, such as allegedly occur during sleep, can be explained. What is lost? What returns? There is no measurable, physical, loss. But there are behavior differences. For the behaviorist, unconsciousness simply meant that neural pathways were blocked off so that no stimulation could be reported.

Second, the behaviorists maintained that the stimulus is the important thing in introspection, not the alleged conscious correlates. Introspection is a way of reporting what has been learned by language training. Situations in which the "wrong" terms are learned are instructive. For example, if color-blind people call a "red" stimulus "gray," they are wrong only because it is not consistent with most other language reports on the stimulus.

Third, and most important, the behaviorists argued that the assumption of nonphysical events interacting with physical events clearly violates the conservation-of-energy principle. Physics tells us that energy is neither created nor destroyed in physical systems; it is only transformed. All the energy within physical systems can be accounted for physically. None is gained from or lost to any nonphysical system. If conscious events affected the body or its processes, they would have to do so by adding or subtracting energy or mass. But that is impossible, according to the conservation-of-energy principle. This principle should not be overthrown on the basis of philosophical dogma. Thus the fact of experiencing the allegedly mental process cannot influence even the muscular efforts necessary to speech. And if ideas *can* influence muscles, then they must themselves be physical events occurring in the nervous system—and they are therefore nonmental.

The radical behaviorist disposed of the major dualistic positions as follows. If mind exists, then it must either (1) affect behavior (interactionism) or (2) not affect behavior (parallelism). But if (1) is true, we have seen that the law of conservation of energy is violated. If (2) is true, how can one *say* that one has an "idea" unless so saying is induced by the "idea" itself, as according to (2) it cannot be. Thus ideas cannot be proved unless they affect the nervous system, in which case they are physical events.

Finally, the behaviorists insisted, the conservation-of-energy principle can be applied to the epiphenomenal view. If conscious correlates are accepted as strictly noncausal events, they must nevertheless be produced by physical events. But this means that energy is used to produce them; how else could physical events operate? Such expenditure of energy without demonstrable physical loss of energy or mass is likewise incompatible with generally accepted physical principles.

The radical behaviorist therefore turned to a strict physical monism, according to which "mental" is merely a description of the way the physical events function, and consciousness has no independent or unique existence.

WATSON'S EXPERIMENTAL PROGRAM

Although Watson's early work was with animals, the best example of his experimental program is the research he conducted on conditioning and reconditioning of emotional responses in infants. This work is also the best example of the application of conditioning techniques by any of the early behaviorists. It is described by Watson in the volume *Psychologies of 1925* (1926a).

Watson studied young infants to try to determine the kind and variety of congenital behavior which could be identified as presumably inherited. He states that "almost daily observation" was made of several hundred children through the first 30 days of postnatal life and of a smaller number for longer periods ranging into early childhood. The result of these observations was a catalog of the "birth equipment of the human young," as Watson called it. A long list of behaviors was developed, with objective descriptions for each, but the only experimental, or semiexperimental, observations at this time involved some work with twenty babies on the causal factors in handedness. Watson's conclusion (1926a) was that "there is no fixed differentiation of response in either hand until social usage begins to establish handedness" (p. 29).

Watson was also concerned with the genetic (longitudinal) study of the emotional life of the infant and child. Again the fully objective technique of behavior description was applied, this time intensively, to a sample of 3-year-olds. Watson found that most children of this age are shot through with useless and actually harmful emotional reactions. He was not content with what he described as the historically orthodox interpretation of such emotional behavior as inherited, and he saw the need for new experimental techniques. He soon discovered that children taken from typical homes did not make good subjects for the study of the origin of emotions. The obvious need for more controlled emotional backgrounds in infants was met by the use of "strong healthy children belonging to wet nurses in hospitals, and other children brought up in the home under the eye of the experimenters" (1926a, p. 42). With these subjects he instituted a prolonged series of simple tests, made primarily by the introduction of various kinds of animals, at the zoological park as well as in the laboratory. He was unable to find evidence of fear, and concluded that accounts of the inheritance of emotional responses to "frightening" stimuli were false.

One of the best-known contributions of this phase of his research program was Watson's description, as a result of further semiexperimental observations, of the basic conditions that could be depended upon to produce fear, rage, and love in infants. Watson found that fear was produced by loud sounds and sudden loss of support.

Rage resulted from hampering of bodily movement; and love, from tickling, rocking, patting, and stroking of the skin.

This pioneer research of Watson's constituted an advance which stimulated further research. Bridges (1932) questioned the ability to discriminate different emotions in the infant, and her results showed that the only sure distinction is between a generally excited state and a quiescent one. It is now generally conceded that infants' emotions cannot be judged reliably without knowledge of the stimulating situation (for example, if we know that the stimulus was a pinprick rather than stroking). Despite the modification of Watson's conclusions forced by later research, his basic point that infants show very few varieties of innate emotional behavior has not been contradicted.

From 1918 on, Watson reported, he conducted experiments designed to determine some of the factors underlying the acquisition and loss of emotional responses in children. "We were rather loath at first to conduct such experiments," he said, "but the need of this kind of study was so great that we finally decided to experiment upon the possibility of building up fears in the infant and then later to study practical methods for removing them" (1926b, p. 51). Watson found it possible to establish fear in a subject through a simple conditioning procedure, but it was more difficult than most secondary sources report. Once the fear was established, it spread, or generalized, to similar stimuli that had previously been neutral, in a manner comparable to that found for nonemotional conditioned responses.

Finally, Watson turned to the problem of eliminating conditioned fears. A variety of commonly used techniques was first tried experimentally on subjects in whom conditioned fears had been produced. Disuse, verbal appeal, frequent application of the feared stimulus, and the use of an unafraid model turned out to be ineffective. Then, in experimentation performed by Mary Cover Jones under Watson's direction, clear evidence for the effectiveness of the unconditioning, or reconditioning, technique was obtained from an infant named Peter, with whom intensive work was done. This was achieved by bringing in the conditioned fear stimulus at some distance, so as not to elicit the fear response, while the child was eating. After daily introductions of the stimulus (a rabbit) at progressively closer points on the long lunchroom table, the child was finally able to handle it without fear while continuing to eat. Generalized fear responses to similar objects were also found to be eliminated by this procedure.

Many years later, in reminiscing about this research and about Watson, Jones concluded her article with the mild comment: "We now use the term *behavior modification therapy* to describe the practical approach of John B. Watson and his followers. I welcome this opportunity to acknowledge with gratitude our indebtedness to this impressive figure in American psychology" (1974, p. 583).

There was about a thirty-year lag between Jones's report (1924) of the successful elimination of fear in Peter and the development of any significant body of work in behavior modification. This provides us with a chance to decide whether *Zeitgeist* theories or great man theories fit these facts best. Would it have made a difference in the time of development of behavior modification if John B. Watson had not been asked to resign his position as professor at Johns Hopkins some time before the beginning of the fall semester, 1920?

SECONDARY CHARACTERISTICS OF
WATSONIAN BEHAVIORISM

Today, the methodological characteristics of the behavioristic position are felt to be the most basic because of the continuing widespread acceptance of the methodological point and the growing rejection of other points. The secondary aspects of Watson's thinking are not implied by the word *behavioristic*. However, much of the attack on behaviorism has been directed at these secondary points, and they are often confused or mixed indiscriminately with the primary characteristics (see Koch, 1954, pp. 5–6).

It is safer to distinguish the critical and secondary propositions. For example, although it is natural for the behaviorist to view thinking as a peripheral process that is easily accessible to behavioral observation, it is not necessary to accept peripheralism in order to remain a methodological behaviorist. Characteristics like this one are treated as secondary. We shall discuss language development and thinking, the role of environmental factors in behavior, and determinism and personal responsibility as examples of secondary characteristics.

Language Development and Thinking

Because of its use as an example of a behavioristic interpretation of a mentalistic concept, the theory of language development plays a key role in behavioristic thinking. It goes as follows: First, many separate syllables are naturally produced by the normal vocimotor apparatus of any human child. The normal instigation for the first of such mouthings—for example, the common sound *da*—is probably some obscure stimulus. A *circular conditioned response* eventually becomes established as a result of the concurrence of the sound *da* with the saying of it. That is, infants hear *da* as they say it, and the sound itself becomes a conditioned stimulus to the saying—circular because it is self-perpetuating. The kind of babbling that is characteristic of early vocalization thus develops, with the infant stopping the sequence of repeated syllabling only when distracted by some other stronger stimulus or when fatigued. Second, the mother or some other adult hears this kind of babbling and repeats the sound, thus producing the conditioned stimulus and causing the child to repeat it. In this manner the child soon learns to imitate many of the sounds the mother makes, or at least to approximate them. Finally, the mother shows the child an object, such as a doll, while repeating the appropriate syllable. In this way new connections between visual stimuli and established sounds are developed. The further process of language development is a long-continued elaboration and refinement of this basic process.

Evidence for the soundness of this general interpretation was adduced from the case histories of deaf-mutes—babies born deaf whose initial babblings are not continued and who do not routinely learn to speak, presumably because they lack normal auditory conditioned stimuli. Also, with normal children, the behaviorist can point to the frequency with which parents use so-called baby talk in communicating with their infants.

In all this, the behaviorist takes pains to point out, there is nothing save brain connections and reconnections. No mental events are necessary. The child learns to say *blue* or *red* or *green,* or *loud* or *shrill* or *bass,* because of the conditioning of brain events and not because of sensory experience. Watson himself preferred to avoid the old terminology because he thought it was contaminated with mentalistic connotations, but Weiss and some of the less radical behaviorists were willing to use the old terms with new behavioristic meanings.

Watson extended this interpretation into the field of thinking, considered as implicit, or covert, behavior. Such behavior consists of tendencies toward muscular movements or glandular secretions that are not directly observable by the usual techniques of observation. They may nonetheless play an important role in activating or mediating other, more overt, behavior (e.g., *action currents* detectable in musculature by electronic devices). As language functions develop in young children from 2 years of age or so and on, much of their motor activity tends to be accompanied by a more or less complete language description. For example, little Sally will say "Sally eats"—or some approximation thereof—as she eats. Under parental and other adult pressures, however, a child is gradually forced to reduce this overt speech, which is generally regarded as unnecessary. It then tends to turn into silent speech, or thinking, in adulthood.

Past training in the form of conditioning accounts for both overt body behavior and language responses, overt as well as implicit. If the overt behavior aspects are inhibited, the implicit language responses may remain; the person is then said to be thinking. Thinking is thus primarily trial-and-error behavior of the laryngeal mechanism. Watson further pointed out that implicit language behavior might also be suppressed and thinking could continue in the form of either overt body activity or visceral reactions. A later Watsonian position thus was that we think with our whole bodies. Because of the poor connections between the visceral and the laryngeal series of muscle changes, visceral thinking responses are largely unverbalized. They may be involved in determining tendencies, hunches and intuitions, feelings of familiarity or unfamiliarity, certainty, and the like. Therefore, although thinking occurs primarily in verbal terms, it may also take other forms.

Watson's position on the control of unverbalized thinking is summarized in the following statement:

> I want to develop the thesis sometime that society has never been able to get hold of these implicit concealed visceral and glandular reactions of ours, or else it would have schooled them in us, for, as you know, society has a great propensity for regularizing all of our reactions. Hence most of our adult overt reactions—our speech, and movements of our arms, legs, and trunk—are schooled and habitized. Owing to their concealed nature, however, society cannot get hold of visceral behavior to lay down rules and regulations for its integration. It follows as a corollary from this that we have no names, no words with which to describe these reactions. They remain unverbalized. (1926b, p. 56)

Although Watson held an essentially peripheral theory of thinking, with stress on muscular reactions and tendencies toward them as the basis of thinking, other behaviorists carried the assumption of progressive suppression of muscular actions on to its logical conclusion. This means a central theory of thinking, with only brain states involved. B. F. Skinner's treatment of verbal behavior (1957) shows that Watson's behavioristic position regarding language and thinking remained alive for many years.

It is still held by some today. Recent multiple successes in teaching a rudimentary language to chimpanzees, orangutans, and at least one gorilla treat language as just another behavior that should be teachable to lower organisms once an appropriate communicative response is found. However, each organism has limitations on the complexity of the language which it can comprehend and produce.

Emphasis on the Environment

Although in his earlier writing Watson accepted the importance of inherited behavior tendencies, he increasingly emphasized the environment as the primary determiner of behavior. He declared that the concept of instinct was no longer needed in psychology, although he made it clear that he did not doubt the importance of inherited *structures*. Performance, then, was dependent upon the way in which the environment acted on such structures. The following example clarifies his position:

> The behaviorist would *not* say: "He inherits his father's capacity or talent for being a fine swordsman." He would say: "This child certainly has his father's slender build of body, the same type of eyes. . . . He, too, has the build of a swordsman." And he would go on to say: ". . . and his father is very fond of him. He put a tiny sword into his hand when he was a year of age, and in all their walks he talks sword play, attack, and defense, the code of duelling and the like." A certain type of structure plus early training—*slanting*—accounts for adult performance." (1926a, p. 2)

In his emphasis on the importance of environmental factors, Watson pointed to the very great variety of human traits and habits associated with different climates and different cultures. Although he recognized the limitations of available data, he felt that every normal human baby has within it essentially similar potentialities. This presumption led him to make predictions for which he has been strongly attacked. For example, he stated (1926a): "I would feel perfectly confident in the ultimately favorable outcome of careful upbringing of a *healthy, well-formed* baby born of a long line of crooks, murderers, thieves, and prostitutes. Who has any evidence to the contrary?" (p. 9). Then, admittedly going beyond the facts, Watson went on to state a challenge for which he is famous:

> I should like to go one step further tonight and say, "Give me a dozen healthy infants, well-formed, and my own specified world to bring them up in, and I'll guarantee to take any one at random and train him to become any type of specialist I might select—a doctor, lawyer, artist, merchant-chief, and yes, even into a beggarman and thief, regardless of his talents, penchants, tendencies, abilities, vocations and race of his ancestors." . . . Please note that when this experiment is made I am to be allowed to specify the way they are to be brought up and the type of world they have to live in. (1926a, p.10)

Determinism and Personal Responsibility

In the long-standing disagreement between science, with its acceptance of a strictly determined natural world, and theology and various types of philosophy, in which freedom of the will is generally accepted, there is no question at all about where

Watsonian behaviorism stands. Since all behavior, including that called *voluntary* and involving choices, is interpreted in physical terms, all acts are physically determined in advance.

Watson's own interest was less in the philosophical problem of determinism per se than in the consequent or corollary question of personal responsibility. Along with many other behavioristically inclined psychologists and sociologists, he argued against the assumption that individuals are personally responsible for their actions in the sense that they possess free will. The implications of this belief are especially important in relation to criminal behavior. The behaviorist would accept punishment of criminals as a part of a system of social control, but not on the basis of a theory of retribution. Instead of making errant individuals pay for violations, Watson would attempt to reeducate them. He conceded that if satisfactory reconditioning could not be achieved, the person might have to be kept under restraint or destroyed.

Watson himself developed a visionary program for social improvement, a so-called experimental ethics to be based on behaviorism. At the very end of his *Behaviorism,* he states:

> I think behaviorism does lay a foundation for saner living. It ought to be a science that prepares men and women for understanding the first principles of their own behavior. It ought to make men and women eager to rearrange their own lives, and especially eager to prepare themselves to bring up their own children in a healthy way. I wish I had time more fully to describe this, to picture to you the kind of rich and wonderful individual we should make of every healthy child; if only we could let it shape itself properly and then provide for it a universe in which it could exercise that organization—a universe unshackled by legendary folk lore of happenings thousands of years ago; unhampered by disgraceful political history; free of foolish customs and conventions which have no significance in themselves, yet which hem the individual in like taut steel bands. (1925, p. 248)

OTHER PROMINENT EARLY BEHAVIORISTS

Albert P. Weiss

Although Watson was without question the preeminent behaviorist, he had a number of important and sometimes vociferous supporters. One, Albert P. Weiss (1879–1931), was born in Germany but came to the United States at an early age. He was appointed assistant to Max Meyer, who himself had come from the University of Berlin. Meyer established the psychology laboratory at the University of Missouri in 1900. Meyer has already been mentioned as an early objectivist who antedated Watson. Weiss took his Ph.D. with Meyer at Missouri in 1916 and pursued an active career at Ohio State University. Weiss's *Theoretical basis of human behavior* was published in 1925. Weiss saw behavior as reducible to physicochemical terms. Psychology was thus a branch of physics. The first chapter of his book, for example, is entitled "The ultimate elements," and it consists of a discussion of the structure of matter, the nature of energy, the concept of force, and allied physical subjects.

Weiss was not merely a farfetched reductionist. On the contrary, he was among the most careful and ingenious of the early behaviorists, certainly more careful than

Watson in defining terms and developing concepts. A single example will illustrate the quality of his theoretical thinking: his attempt to explain voluntary activity (a problem whose resolution Watson did not attempt).

The problem for Weiss was to determine what kind of behavior is conditioned to the word *voluntary*. Whereas the mentalist says that the mind does the choosing, the behaviorist says that physiological brain states operate and that the term *voluntary* is applied when there is some conflict, or at least potential conflict, between the tendencies to action associated with different sets of stimuli. One set of stimuli eventually achieves a clear physiological channel, and the individual makes a "choice." This choice is determined by past experience as it has shaped brain connections. "Willpower," which is allegedly exercised on difficult choices, was for Weiss merely the spilling over of brain excitations into motor tensions which build up because they are not allowed immediate outlet. The effort of the "will" is assumed from the muscular contractions that are themselves by-products of brain action. Voluntary behavior is thus basically no different from other types but does have this apparent added characteristic of muscular tension.

Weiss regarded psychology as a biosocial discipline because of the nature of the variables with which it was concerned. He set up an experimental program of research on child behavior, but his early death prevented its consummation.

Edwin B. Holt

Edwin Holt (1873–1946) was influential mainly through his books, in which he gave strong philosophical support to behaviorism. As Boring (1950) has noted, Holt's greatest specific influence probably came through his stimulation of E. C. Tolman to combine purposivism and cognitive theory in his version of behaviorism. Holt published *The Freudian wish and its place in ethics* in 1915 and *Animal drive and the learning process* in 1931. Holt was a philosophical neorealist who attempted to integrate the essential parts of the behavioristic and psychoanalytic movements. He took his Ph.D. at Harvard in 1901 and subsequently taught both there and at Princeton.

Walter S. Hunter

Walter S. Hunter (1889–1953) made important methodological contributions to the field of animal learning. Like Watson, Hunter was trained in functionalism at Chicago. He took his Ph.D. with Angell and Carr in 1912. After teaching at the University of Texas, Kansas University, and Clark University, he went to Brown University and remained there for the rest of his life. At Brown, he developed and maintained a small but active department of experimentalists. His methodological innovations included the delayed-response and double alternation tasks, which were devised to investigate higher symbolic activities in animals. Hunter was interested primarily in laboratory research rather than in theory, but he nevertheless attempted to push a new name for the science of behavior: *anthroponomy* (1926). As with most terminological innovations, his was unsuccessful.

Karl S. Lashley

Karl Lashley (1890–1958) did his graduate work at the University of Pittsburgh and Johns Hopkins University, receiving his Ph.D. in psychology in 1914 at the latter. His major teaching appointments were at the Universities of Minnesota and Chicago and at Harvard University. He then became director, in 1942, of the Yerkes Laboratory of Primate Biology, the world-renowned chimpanzee research station at Orange Park, Florida. In this capacity he retained his professorship at Harvard because the two institutions were then administratively related.

Lashley's earliest research was performed in collaboration with the biologist H. S. Jennings and the behaviorist John B. Watson at Johns Hopkins. His research interests were broad, ranging from problems of size inheritance in paramecia to cerebral factors in migraine headaches (see Beach, Hebb, Morgan, & Nissen, 1960, for these and many of his other papers). The problem of brain function as related to behavior was his most important and most persistent interest and the one for which he is best known.

Lashley's interest in brain function was formed early in his training, but it was only in 1917, when he became associated with the eminent neurophysiologist Shepherd Ivory Franz, that he embarked upon research using ablation of the rat brain to determine localization of function.

It is unfortunate that those who do not know Lashley's work well almost inevitably remember him for his two vague principles with catchy names: *mass action* and *equipotentiality*. Even the meanings of these principles are not remembered precisely, for here is how Lashley summarized them:

> *Equipotentiality of parts.* The term "equipotentiality" I have used to designate the apparent capacity of any intact part of a functional area to carry out, with or without reduction of efficiency, the functions which are lost by destruction of the whole. This capacity varies from one area to another and with the character of the functions involved. It probably holds only for the association areas and for functions more complex than simple sensitivity or motor co-ordination.
>
> *Mass function.* I have already given evidence . . . that the equipotentiality is not absolute but is subject to a law of mass action whereby the efficiency of performance of an entire complex function may be reduced in proportion to the extent of brain injury within an area whose parts are not more specialized for one component of the function than for another. (1929, p. 25)

A careful reading of these principles makes any comment on their vagueness, or even perhaps on some circularity, unnecessary. One would certainly expect that a part which was "not more specialized for one component of the function than for another" would have to follow a principle of mass action! Krech (1962), in his excellent review of the problem of cortical localization, says that Lashley was aware of his own vagueness in stating these principles. Lashley probably stated the principles as definitely as the state of knowledge about brain mechanisms allowed.

Why, then, should Lashley be remembered? Pierre Flourens (1794–1867) had reached similar conclusions based on similar ablations about 100 years earlier. Lashley's unique contribution was that he brought far better, more analytical, *behavioral* techniques into cooperation with the best available physiological techniques. Lashley did not limit himself to the study of the effects of brain operations on naturally occurring behaviors, as Flourens had. He experimentally created behaviors in mazes and discrimination problems and then studied their retention and reacquisition after carefully planned ablations. His methodology was brilliant for his time, and his techniques excellent. He had been anticipated to some extent by his teacher, Franz, much as Isaac Newton was anticipated in the development of calculus by his teacher, Isaac Barrow; but both pupils went far beyond their teachers.

Despite the vagueness of his statements, there is no doubt that Lashley opposed the common belief in localization of function. The problem is by no means settled, but it appears likely that there is more localization than Lashley thought. We still understand too little of the structure of behavior to know, in most cases, what a "unitary function" might be. Until we know, we can reach no final solution to the localization problem.

The extent to which Lashley was recognized by nonpsychologists as well as by psychologists is suggested by the tribute paid him by the neurologist Stanley Cobb, who said (Beach et al., 1960) that in the early days at Hopkins, Lashley "fascinated us by the breadth of his interest and by his flair for ingenious and adventurous experimentation" (p. xvii). Cobb added: "During the next forty years, Lashley was to be the psychologist most frequently chosen by neurologists and psychiatrists to come to their meetings to give a paper or to discuss the papers of others" (Beach et al., 1960, p. xviii). He concluded by saying: "And so, in paying Karl Lashley our homage, we claim at least a tithe of his work for neurology!" (p. xx).

But it is, of course, not only for his neurological contributions that Lashley is honored in psychology. He also combined his behaviorism with a field orientation which made his views unique. In a twin introduction to the memorial volume of Lashley's selected papers (Beach et al., 1960), E. G. Boring reviewed these systematic views. In the same book, Lashley wrote that "it is the pattern and not the localization of energy on the sense organ that determines the functional effect" (p. 492); and, referring to brain action, "all of the cells of the brain are constantly active and are participating, by a sort of algebraic summation, in every activity" (p. 500).

Lashley's fascination with fields is also illustrated by his support for a pattern, or relational, interpretation of transposition learning, rather than for the S-R, or connectionistic, position. In his presidential address to the American Psychological Association in 1930, he attacked the simple connectionistic view. He later presented a novel alternative to the orthodox S-R interpretation of generalization and discrimination learning. The Lashley-Wade hypothesis is that differential training on several values of a stimulus dimension is necessary before generalization can occur. This denies the S-R assumption that reinforcement of a single stimulus value produces a generalization gradient. The controversy thus created stimulated a good deal of research. Kimble (1961, pp. 369ff.) wrote one review of the issue. Terrace (1966) later sided with Lashley and Wade: "A differential reinforcement procedure is necessary for the typical generalization gradient to emerge" (p. 339). Three years later, Kalish (1969) reached a compromise position after a thorough and thoughtful review of the evidence.

Although Lashley thus accepted a field-theoretical view of many problems, he remained an enthusiastic and committed behaviorist. He is thus a perfect example of a psychologist who rejected some of Watson's secondary beliefs while continuing to accept the central belief in methodological behaviorism.

Zing Yang Kuo

Z. Y. Kuo (1898–1970) was a Chinese psychologist who was trained in the United States, at Columbia University. He adopted an extremely environmentalistic position (Kuo, 1922/1924), far more radical than John B. Watson's. All alleged instincts were to be explained on the basis of inherited structure and environmental influences. Kuo did not rest his case on armchair speculation. He watched the development of behavior in the embryo chick by replacing part of the shell with a small transparent window (1932a–e). He found that much chick behavior which appeared to be instinctive is really learned during the embryonic period as a function of conditions within the egg. For example, the alternate stepping behavior of the normal newly hatched chick was shown to be dependent upon mechanically induced alternate limb movements inside the shell. Cramping from the yolk sac often acted as a stimulus to the movements. Kuo differed from Watson in that he preferred to think of continuities in behavior, rather than of conditioning, as a basic explanation of behavior changes.

In other research Kuo showed that cats' reactions to rats are not strictly determined by heredity but can be easily altered from the normal predatory form by appropriate experiences (1930/1938). These results all fit well with his environmentalism. Kuo concluded that inherited structures are important but that even these can be molded via environmental influences. He did not believe in any direct native behavior tendencies beyond those which are strictly the result of structural factors.

Kuo came back into print late in life (1967), after many years as a periodic refugee within his Chinese homeland. The stimulus was the then new ethological emphasis on inherited behaviors. By that time Kuo's views on exogenous and endogenous behaviors were considerably more moderate than they had been, but he continued to be both the environmentalist and the antimentalist. His book is interesting both because it is the product of a truly early behaviorist near the end of his life and because his brief recital of the woes he suffered in the maelstrom of the Chinese history of his time makes us appreciate our own stability a great deal more.

CONTEMPORARY BEHAVIORISTS

A list of contemporary psychologists who accept the behaviorist methodological point would be a long one indeed. There are four men, however, who have richly earned recognition for bridging the gap between Watson and the present. Their views were already important during Watson's lifetime, and they still are. These four men are E. C. Tolman (1886–1959), E. R. Guthrie (1886–1959), C. L. Hull (1884–1952), and B. F. Skinner (1904–). Their systems are discussed in more detail later in the present book. These men used Watson's behaviorism for the good that was in it and added their own personal contributions. In addition, we note in passing the important contributions of people like C. H. Graham (1951/1958) and W. R. Garner (Garner, Hake, & Eriksen, 1956) in applying a behavioristic approach in the experimental psychology of visual perception, and of D. O. Hebb (1949) and R. C. Davis (1953), who applied the approach in physiological psychology. The psychological science that has emerged because of the creative efforts of all these people is the kind of development that John B. Watson would have approved.

WATSONIAN BEHAVIORISM: CRITICISMS AND REPLIES

The critical attacks made upon Watson and his brand of behaviorism hit all aspects of the system, secondary as well as primary. Since we cannot consider them all, we shall discuss only those which relate to the methodological and metaphysical points that we think are most crucial. In addition, we present some comments on Watson's experimental ethics as examples of the criticisms of peculiarly Watsonian aspects of the position.

Methodological Behaviorism

Although psychology was reasonably well prepared for a stress on objectivity, not all psychologists were satisfied with Watson's pronouncements. An immediate objection was that Watson's extreme formulation left out important components of psychology. This point was made even by those who supported much of the objective program. Woodworth, for example, complained that the early behavioristic emphasis upon strict objectivity hindered the development of sensory and perceptual research, because it turned the attention of younger men away from this problem area. Acceptance by Watson of the "verbal report" was not satisfactory. For example, Woodworth criticized Watson for attempting to deal with the phenomena of afterimages. He said:

> The "phenomena" which Watson finds so interesting and valuable in the after-image experiment are the after-images themselves, not the subject's speech movements. We may conclude that verbal report is not a behavioristic method and that Watson's use of it is practically a confession of defeat for methodological behaviorism. (1948, p. 84)

A broader and more vigorous attack was made by McDougall, who presented himself as an earlier proponent and user of the strictly behavioristic experiment. McDougall's criticisms of this methodological incompleteness of Watson's position may be summarized in the statement that a completely objective approach cannot obtain an adequate account of (1) the functional relations of conscious experiences (e.g., their dependence on external or bodily conditions), (2) the accuracy of verbal report (e.g., whether or not a subject is malingering, as in military service), and (3) the meaningfulness of the verbal report (e.g., in regard to the analysis of dreams). He was particularly eloquent in regard to the incompleteness of the behavioristic account of the finer things in life, specifically music:

> I come into this hall and see a man on this platform scraping the guts of a cat with hairs from the tail of a horse; and sitting silently in attitudes of rapt attention are a thousand persons who presently break out into wild applause. How will the Behaviorist explain these strange incidents: How explain the fact that the vibrations emitted by the cat-gut stimulate

all the thousand into absolute silence and quiescence; and the further fact that the cessation of the stimulus seems to be a stimulus to the most frantic activity? Commonsense and psychology agree in accepting the explanation that the audience heard the music with keen pleasure, and vented their gratitude and admiration for the artist in shouts and handclappings. But the Behaviorist knows nothing of pleasure and pain, of admiration and gratitude. He has relegated all such "metaphysical entities" to the dust heap, and must seek some other explanation. Let us leave him seeking it. The search will keep him harmlessly occupied for some centuries to come. (J. B. Watson & McDougall, 1929, p. 63)

Watson would argue that McDougall and Woodworth, despite their objections, must use behavior as their datum. Whenever their metaphysics makes them try to use something else, they get into trouble. We find those who try to use consciousness as the basic datum involved in useless squabbles about what they find there. Consciousness is a tool for scientists, not an object of study. They use it to study *both* afterimages and concrete blocks but do not study it in itself.

As an example of the behavioristic attitude, consider a blind person who is interested in studying visual afterimages. Given someone to set up the equipment, this person could successfully conduct research by writing down the verbal responses emitted by an assistant and by subjects. Unable to use direct personal experience for obtaining data, a blind person would use the behavior of others. Those who *can* respond to light might use their own *responses* as data, but even they could not use their own *experience* as data. The blind person might have an advantage in some respects, since that person would be unbiased by personal responses to the stimuli. And, as Washburn (1908) early pointed out, the situation is the same for animals and for people other than ourselves—we are like the blind person who cannot see light, for we cannot see the consciousness of other organisms and thus must use their *behaviors* as a source of data.

On a somewhat different level of argument, Boring (1950) also criticized Watson for his acceptance of verbal report:

> Watson wished to let in discriminatory verbal report when it was accurate and verifiable, as it is, for instance, in the observation of difference tones, and to rule it out when it was unverifiable, as it is when it consists of statements about the nature of feeling or about the impalpable contents of imageless thinking. . . . The admission of verbal report was a damaging concession, for it made it appear that behaviorism was asking only for verbal changes and not for a reform in scientific procedures. (p. 645)

The modern behaviorist's answer to Boring is simply agreement. The central point of the whole behaviorist revolution was to use only verifiable data in psychology. The thing that furnishes such data is behavior and only behavior. Verbal behavior is certainly behavior, and it provides useful data if it is verifiable and repeatable. Not all behavior, and hence not all verbal behavior, furnishes useful data. The behaviorist is not under any obligation to accept data indiscriminately. Boring himself (1964) reported on a senseless controversy between Wundt and Stumpf concerning "whether a perceived tonal interval is bisected psychologically by the arithmetic or by the geometric mean of the tonal stimuli" (p. 683). The behaviorists believed, rightly or wrongly, that these disagreements arose partly because of the type of data used.

Woodworth and Sheehan (1964) present the basic enigma in two moderate, eloquently understated paragraphs which quietly communicate despair of a final answer:

> For one group of psychologists the proper content seemed reasonably to be man's conscious experience, which they held could be investigated through introspection. This is a method of self-observation which, as we shall see later, may take a variety of forms, ranging from the simple reporting of one's immediate sensory impression of a stimulus to long-extended probing, during analytical therapy, of one's emotional experiences. Unlike as these "introspections" may seem, they have in common a private quality which appears to distinguish them from the methods of physics or chemistry or biology. In these sciences any number of observers can report on what is visible in the test tube or under the microscope, whereas the psychological "experience" can be reported by only one observer.
>
> How real this distinction is remains a perplexing epistemological problem. Does each observer see in the test tube or under the microscope a bit of the real external world, or does each merely report on his subjective experience resulting from some emanations of the real world? If the latter is the case a sharp line cannot be drawn between the data of the "objective" sciences and the subjective data of psychology. In all cases the observing subject would be reporting the private content of his own "consciousness." (pp. 3–4)

O'Neil (1968) tried to clarify the behaviorist's position on consciousness by relating behaviorism to realism in philosophy, and he does succeed in showing that consciousness is not a problem for radical behaviorists, since they simply deny its existence; but it may remain a problem for others.

Watson's initial attempts to translate some of the older mentalistic concepts of psychology into behavioristic language have been criticized from two points of view. On the one hand, some have contended that the acceptance of any mentalistic terms weakened his strictly objective system. On the other hand, Heidbreder (1933) has taken Watson to task for: "a tendency to indulge in feats of translation, and apparently at times to regard translation as an explanation."

She continues:

> It is difficult, when reading some of the behavioristic accounts, to escape the impression that the writers regard it as an explanation to say that a wish is an organic set, that a meaning is a bodily attitude, that thoughts are language mechanisms. Yet little is added to the knowledge of wishes, meanings, and thoughts by these statements, which after all consist largely in taking over what is known about these happenings from common sense and the older psychology and devising, often not on the basis of known facts, some possible physiological explanation of them. (p. 275)

Although we agree with Heidbreder that Watson actually did little with such translations, we think they can be regarded as starting points in the objectification of psychological problems. While Watson was guilty as charged of premature enthusiasm, final evaluations of the success of the fully objective program must await more extensive applications of detailed research like that which Watson himself initiated on emotional conditioning in infants and children. No behaviorist would today rest content with purely verbal translations, and that is not what Watson intended either. The point is that the mentalistic terms as they had been used had no behavioral meaning, and the translation was really a definition of that meaning. The concept was not explained, but defined and made workable. Wishes and thoughts did not need translating; they needed *some* meaning that would be useful in a natural scientific framework. Skinner's book *Verbal behavior* (1957) makes its chief contribution through such a reformulation rather than through the presentation of new empirical results. This book presents many independent variables which might be useful in predicting verbal behavior. It does not, as one example, translate ideas into other terms; ideas are simply not part of the formulation. Watson was also often content to let mentalistic terms disappear rather than translate them into behavioristic concepts. This elimination of fruitless concepts and the hardheaded attitude toward the meanings of all terms were important contributions.

Another line of methodological criticism involved the charge that Watson was backtracking on his own restriction of psychology to observables by including implicit behavior tendencies, which were not directly observed albeit they were in theory observable. Woodworth, for example, complained that Watson, even while postulating such implicit behavior, restricted his own research on emotion to the directly observable overt aspects of behavior and made no effort to investigate the presumably important visceral components.

The answer to this objection is similar to the answer given to the previous objection. Certainly Watson, in his impatient enthusiasm to get to a new and thoroughly objective psychology, went beyond the available data in drawing conclusions and did not himself begin all the necessary research to back up his assumptions. Nevertheless, there is no necessary inconsistency in assuming implicit behavior tendencies while holding to a strictly objective systematic and experimental framework. No one can do everything. Attempts were made to observe implicit responses—for example, tongue, mouth, and larynx movements—in implicit speech, and much later even muscle potentials in deaf mutes. Watson's own research used observable responses for its data. It was only natural to make the explanatory system of behaviorism consistent with the data system, and the assumed implicit responses were not expected to *remain* unobserved.

This tendency to postulate unobserved entities can be seen throughout psychology. For example, Freud's explanation of subconscious processes grew out of the kind of data available to the psychoanalyst, and Hull's theory of learning was taken directly from experimental results. Watson's theorizing about internal changes, especially with emotion, seems amply vindicated by results of studies on the learning of visceral and glandular responses (N. E. Miller, 1969). Such is the success of this work that society may, after all, eventually be able to regularize these responses, the ones whose freedom from control Watson seemed to be bitterly celebrating in 1926.

E. C. Tolman criticized Watson for either leaving purpose out of his treatment of behavior or sneaking it in the back door. Tolman early criticized Watson's research on emotions, stating his criticism as follows:

> In short, our conclusion must be that Watson has in reality dallied with two different notions of behavior, though he himself has not clearly seen how different they are. On the one hand, he has defined behavior in terms of its strict underlying physical and physiological details. . . . We shall designate this as the *molecular* definition of behavior. And, on the other hand, he has come to recognize . . . that behavior, as such, is more than and different from the sum of its physiological parts. Behavior, as such, is an "emergent" phenomenon that

has descriptive and defining properties of its own. And we shall designate this latter as the *molar* definition of behavior. (1932, pp. 6–7)

Tolman's psychology is proof that he preferred the molar definition of behavior, that he thought that purposiveness must be introduced in order to have a useful psychology. Purpose generally alludes, in Tolman's usage, to some influence of the animal's behavior on the environment; for instance, we may speak of the purpose of an animal's behavior as being the release of a food pellet or the depression of a bar. Usually, the bending of a limb would not be considered a purposeful response, although it would be purposeful compared with the flexion of a muscle. Tolman contends that it is more useful to define responses in molar behavioral terms than in molecular physiological terms. Watson, like most psychologists before and after him, agreed in practice with this point. He wished to make the additional point that purposive behavior is in principle reducible to the physiological level, although he did not actually work on this level. Other behaviorists, like Guthrie (1952), have attempted to work on a more molecular (but still not physiological) level. If the problem of psychology is to explain the behavior of the animal in its environment, then it seems that a complete psychology must consider purpose as so defined. Tolman's quoted statement suggests that he believed that Watson recognized this kind of purposivism, since he rightfully accuses Watson of using the term *behavior* in both senses. However, Watson would not agree, nor would most contemporary behaviorists, that purpose as an explanatory concept in the McDougallian sense is legitimate.

The Gestalt psychologists have been vociferous in their complaints against the allegedly molecular brand of S-R psychology, as we shall see in the following chapter. But, again, a particularly telling argument came from within the behavioristic camp itself. As suggested above, K. S. Lashley was an avowed and enthusiastic behaviorist. His own research, however, convinced him that some of the secondary behavioristic assumptions were in error. As Lashley himself (1931) has told the story:

> I began life as an ardent advocate of muscle-twitch psychology. I became glib in formulating all problems of psychology in terms of stimulus-response and in explaining all things as conditioned reflexes. . . . I embarked enthusiastically upon a program of experiments to prove the adequacy of the motor-chain theory of integration. And the result is as though I had maliciously planned an attack upon the whole system. . . . The conditioned reflex turned out not to be a reflex, not the simple basic key to the learning problem. . . . In order that the concept of stimulus-response should have any scientific value it must convey a notion of how a particular stimulus elicits a particular response and no other. . . . When viewed in relation to the problems of neurology, the nature of the stimulus and of the response is intrinsically such as to preclude the theory of simple point-to-point connection in reflexes. (p. 14)

Watson's own research efforts were certainly not of the muscle-twitch variety with which he is so often identified. Much of the debate over behaviorism has resulted from the discrepancy between the behavioristic experimental program and the explanatory mechanisms within the theoretical framework which motivated the experiments. According to the framework, all complex behavior is reducible to combinations and chainings of simple reflexes and even to the terms of physics and chemistry. It is this kind of aspiration, rather than the experimental work, which is responsible for much of the opposition. But it would be a mistake to assume that behaviorism is inherently tied to a muscle-twitch view of psychology. It would be a mistake to believe that Lashley became less of a behaviorist because of his findings and the conclusions he drew from them. In the methodological sense, one can be a field theorist and a behaviorist at the same time; Tolman and Lashley are good demonstrations of that.

Metaphysical Behaviorism

Criticisms of Watson's rejection of the introspective technique were blunted by his acceptance of the verbal report as behavior, as indicated above. The argument that he was neglecting useful data was therefore not valid. The brunt of the critical attack upon his system was transferred to the metaphysical argument against interactionism and against his denial of the existence, and not merely the scientific usefulness, of mind.

Early attacks upon the extreme behavioristic position on mind were made by behaviorists and nonbehaviorists alike. Angell (1913), for example, cautioned:

> After all is said and done, something corresponding to consciousness in its vague common meaning does exist and it is within its compass that the problems of science arise. We must be cautious therefore that in seeking for bettered means of knowing human nature in its entirety we do not in effect commit the crowning absurdity of seeming to deny any practical significance to that which is its chief distinction—the presence of something corresponding to the term mind—the one thing of which the fool may be as sure as the wise man. (p. 267)

The behaviorist Hunter (1924) likewise expressed doubt about the radical position in his conclusion that "no mere denial of the existence of 'consciousness' can permanently win a wide following among psychologists" (p. 4). In this prediction Hunter would seem to have been borne out, since the radical behavioristic position on this particular issue has never been accepted by a majority of psychologists.

Some of the attacks on methodological behaviorism may be traced to the underlying assumption of the monistic metaphysical position. A good example is the criticism by Heidbreder (1933). She pointed out that if the behaviorist makes an outright denial of consciousness,

> He finds it extremely difficult to explain what he means by some of his terms. When he says that thinking is merely a matter of language mechanisms, or emotion an affair of visceral and glandular responses, he is at a loss to tell where he gets the terms "thinking" and "emotion." He cannot get them from his own awareness of his own inner speech or disturbed heart-beat, for, by hypothesis, such awareness is impossible. The heart and the larynx, to be sure, belong to the physical world, but one's immediate awareness of their action can be based only on one's personal and private sensations. Does the behaviorist mean, then, that a person cannot be aware of his own anger except by means of kymograph tracings, or blood-analysis, or some other evidence of his bodily reactions that is accessible to others as well as himself—by catching sight of his flushed face, in a mirror, for example, or by seeing directly his own clenched fist? (p.281)

Heidbreder (1933) also pointed out that "in actual practice, behaviorism rejects awareness that arises through the interoceptors and proprioceptors; awareness which arises through the exteroceptors it accepts without question. In this fact lies the clue to the acceptances and rejections that characterize behaviorism" (p. 218).

The behaviorist's reply would probably be to point out that it is difficult for anyone to say how one attributes meaning to words like *thinking* and *emotion*. Actually, the behaviorist would urge, they are not learned by some kind of connection to internal events; we learn to say "pain" in certain situations, such as when we observe blood on others or ourselves, or "thinking" when a problem has been presented and the person has not yet responded. We do not learn these things on the basis of the contents of our own consciousness alone; otherwise our language would be private. It is not surprising that the awareness which arises through the interoceptors is rejected, while that which arises through the exteroceptors is accepted. The language of interoceptors is based on private events, observable only by one individual. Science is a public enterprise, and only a public language about public events is appropriate for its subject matter.

A later criticism of Watson's extreme metaphysical position was presented by Bergmann (1956): "Watson's particular mistake was that in order to establish that there are no interacting minds, which is true, he thought it necessary to assert that *there are no minds,* which is not only false but silly" (p. 266). Bergmann suggests that Watson failed to keep out of philosophical trouble because he saw himself as a champion of the revolt not only against structuralism but also against functionalism; for this reason, presumably, he was not willing to stay with the more moderate metaphysical positions of the earlier systematists.

Bergmann's view probably represents a modal attitude toward Watson's metaphysics, although Watson's position by no means lacks contemporary supporters. Watson seems to have felt it necessary to do more than divorce psychology from metaphysics. Others within the school that he opposed had already tried to do that. He needed to destroy the very existence of mind in order to free psychologists from the methodological error of attempting to study this presumed entity. Part of Watson's contribution, then, is that he took a courageous and forceful metaphysical stand which, right or wrong, enabled him to lead psychologists out of the wilderness on the planks of his platform.

Criticisms of Secondary Properties

Watson's stand on determinism and personal responsibility as it related to his espousal of experimental ethics has been severely criticized. To begin with, it was pointed out that there is a paradox when a strict determinist talks as though he were trying to tell people what they should do—as though they could choose for themselves! A related argument is directed against the assumption by the behaviorist of a strict S-R interpretation of behavior, which is seen as mechanistic and therefore of dubious explanatory value in practical problems. McDougall, for example, said:

If all men believed the teachings of the mechanical psychology (and only beliefs that govern action are real beliefs) no man would raise a finger in the effort to prevent war, to achieve peace or to realize any other ideal. So I say that the mechanical psychology is useless and far worse than useless: it is paralyzing to human effort. (J. B. Watson & McDougall, 1929, pp. 71–72)

Before describing the behaviorist answer to such attacks, we should like to clarify one confusion that is well represented by the excerpt from McDougall. This is the confounding of determinism and mechanism. There is no good reason why a basically deterministic position should be any more mechanistic than nonmechanistic. It is true that people like Watson, who hold a mechanistic view, are also determinists; but so are most field theorists, at least those like Wolfgang Köhler and Kurt Lewin. They share the belief that behavior is lawful, but they diverge markedly with respect to the *type* of lawfulness involved. Mechanism involves a belief that organisms behave in a machinelike fashion, and it therefore implies a particular subtype of determinism. Determinism requires only that events occur according to *some* kind of natural law, and hence it is not necessarily mechanistic.

The behaviorist reply to McDougall's criticism would be that a position that poses practical difficulties is not necessarily wrong. It might be true that people cannot work for their own betterment, undesirable as this may seem. In addition, many opponents of determinism are not really for freedom of will, but for their own brand of determinism. A "good" determinism might be one controlled by some divine force. That is, individuals are free only so they can accept the fully determined rule of God.

Finally, the behaviorist would take note of one mistaken claim of those who hope to prove free will. The Heisenberg principle of uncertainty, or of limited measurability, has often been invoked as a proof that free will must exist for the human being, since it seems to exist for the electron. But the principle is simply a mathematical demonstration that given the properties of elementary particles it is impossible to measure precisely the position and momentum of an electron or of other low-mass constituents of the universe. There is disagreement within physics about the philosophical implications of Heisenberg's demonstration. Einstein, for example, never forsook a strictly deterministic picture of the behavior of even the electron. Even if behaviorists accepted their own positivistic medicine regarding the meaningfulness of determinacy in electrons (if you can't demonstrate it, it isn't true), they would still have a way out. Before the principle could be applied to behavioral problems, *behavioral* variables would have to be shown to be influenced by indeterminacy at the atomic level. It may be that indeterminacy at the atomic level disappears in going to the far more molar level of behavior. Certainly indeterminacy has only minute and utterly insignificant effects on molar *physical* events, such as the flight of golf balls or of space shuttles. A behaviorist's conclusion would be that there is no sound scientific basis for applying the Heisenberg principle to psychological problems.

We would like to add some final comments to this discussion. Determinism amounts to a kind of faith, since at best our knowledge can be only partially complete. A complete determinism cannot be demonstrated. This does not constitute support for the opposite contention, that there is free will; that cannot be demonstrated either. Our own position on this problem is that there will have to be more data, gathered with methods that we cannot even presently envisage, before a scientific position can be taken on the issue.

To return to the problem originally posed by the paradox of·the determinist attempting to influence people, we concede that there is no satisfactory answer to it. The determinist will probably agree with Thorndike's point of view (see Chapter 3): we are free only if our behavior is lawful; we can determine the behavior of other people and build a better world only if the world is predictable. Yet if everything is determined, including our efforts to make changes in nature, as we assume, the behaviorist can only hope that it is favorably determined, so that it will get better. Certainly McDougall's statement that mechanists (he really means determinists) will not raise a finger to prevent war, and so on, is false. Deterministic psychologists like Watson, Thorndike, and Skinner have worked very hard to make the world better. This is simply a matter of observation, and no philosophical supposings can contradict that.

Two other aspects of Watson's own individual position came under heavy attack. One was his environmentalism. There is nothing morally reprehensible about being an environmentalist—in fact, most environmentalists seem to be rather proud of it—but it is probably true that innate factors in behavior were unjustly neglected during the period of greatest ascendance of Watsonian behaviorism. We are now seeing a correction, with the rise of interest in ethology and sociobiology, together with renewed concern that the pendulum may have swung too far to the nativistic extreme.

The second attack was on Watson's use of S-R. His definitions were too casual and flexible and lent themselves easily to a certain amount of post hoc bending to account for results. To rebut these arguments, one can use the standard counters, that an infant science must sometimes exclude areas of study and be a bit cavalier about definitions if it is to get off the ground before it is paralyzed by inaction. Here, too, Watson's decisions can be defended because they produced results.

THE APPEAL OF BEHAVIORISM

The reponse to Watson's plea for complete objectivity in the methods and facts of psychology was far from predominantly negative. Both within psychology and without, he was greeted with acclaim of the kind often accorded outspoken men of great vision.

The primary reason for the appeal of Watsonian behaviorism was that American psychologists were ready and willing to leave the cramping confines of introspective study. Watson's call for an explicit extension of natural scientific methodology into the field of behavior was welcomed enthusiastically by many of the younger generation. An indication of the extent to which this enthusiasm went is given by E. C. Tolman (1927), who said:

> This paper should have been called "The frantic attempt of a behaviorist to define consciousness." In fact, the doctrine I shall present seems to me quite unprovable and to you it will no doubt seem something far worse. And yet so great is my faith that behaviorism

must ultimately triumph that I should rather present even the following quite doubtful hypothesis than hold my mouth and say nothing. (p. 433)

Tolman's faithful adherence to his doctrine shows that scientists do not always live up to their ideals of absolute objectivity! In Tolman's case, however, his disarmingly human honesty tells us that, at a higher level, he has reached the ultimate degree of objectivity required to recognize his own prejudices, and thus probably to counter them.

Strong supplementary support for the behavioristic doctrine came from the operational movement in physics, which was very quickly welcomed and adapted to psychology, and from the new positivism in philosophy as represented by the Vienna Circle. The relationships of these movements to behaviorism are well discussed by Stevens (1939). The relationship is roughly one of equivalence to methodological behaviorism. Each of the positions leads to an insistence upon the use of similar data and a similar attitude toward the data.

There are a number of secondary reasons for the striking success of Watson's call to arms. These have been well summarized by McDougall in his polemic directed against Watson. First, behaviorism was so simple as to be easily understood and undertaken, in contrast to Gestalt psychology and structuralism particularly; McDougall's further comment was that Watson's views

> abolish at one stroke many tough problems with which the greatest intellects have struggled with only very partial success . . . by the bold and simple expedient of inviting the student to shut his eyes to them, to turn resolutely away from them, and to forget that they exist. This naturally inspires in the breast of many young people, especially perhaps those who still have examinations to pass, a feeling of profound gratitude. (J. B. Watson & McDougall, 1929, pp. 41–42)

Second, in addition to its simplicity, Watsonian behaviorism had the advantage of being a peculiarly American product and so of being readily comprehended in the United States. Third, Watson's own forceful personality was a factor which helped him to spread the gospel.

Two additional factors were suggested by McDougall. Behaviorism was said to be attractive because some people are attracted by anything which is bizarre and preposterous. Also, some were attached to behaviorism out of pity for what they saw as Watson's misguided efforts, especially if they themselves were well informed. These explanations of behaviorism's appeal were more entertaining than serious; McDougall, although he seems to have regarded behaviorism as bizarre and misinformed enough, certainly showed it little pity. In this he was typical of behaviorism's opponents; there was little relenting on either side.

The response to Watson's appeal was in some ways even more striking outside psychology and the academic-scientific spheres. Woodworth (1948, pp. 93–94) gave some interesting specimen comments from newspaper and magazine reviews of Watson's *Behaviorism,* which called for social reforms. Most instructive are the brief quotations from the *New York Times* ("It marks an epoch in the intellectual history of man") and the *New York Herald Tribune* ("Perhaps this is the most important book ever written. One stands for an instant blinded with a great hope"). Woodworth concluded that Watson's behaviorism was "a religion to take the place of religion." There is no question but that in its fervor and faith it had some of the aspects of religion and that these were partly responsible for its great appeal.

Watson's environmentalism fitted well into the framework of our political system, whose self-evident truths include the claim that all are created equal. Watson's claim to be able to make anything of any healthy child supported the American dream that anyone can become president. Environmentalism has always been a more hopeful position than nativism, but the gap is rapidly narrowing as the hope of genetic engineering approaches reality. It would be ironic if, in the future, it were easier to correct our genetic deficiencies than to remedy our weaknesses through learning.

BEHAVIORISM'S CONTRIBUTIONS TO PSYCHOLOGY

Although he was severely criticized, John B. Watson made a great contribution to the development of scientific psychology. The primary contribution was his clear call for a strictly objective study of behavior. The influence of this call on psychology has been enormous. Methodological behaviorism has been so well absorbed into American psychology that it no longer need be argued. As Bergmann (1956) said: "Methodological behaviorism, like Functionalism, has conquered itself to death. It, too, has become a truism. Virtually every American psychologist, whether he knows it or not, is nowadays a methodological behaviorist" (p. 270).

An appreciably smaller number would care to be listed as Watsonian behaviorists. Many psychologists would still endorse Woodworth's 1924 comment:

> In short, if I am asked whether I am a behaviorist, I have to reply that I do not know, and do not much care. If I am, it is because I believe in the several projects put forward by behaviorists. If I am not, it is partly because I also believe in other projects which behaviorists seem to avoid, and partly because I cannot see any one big thing, to be called "behaviorism"— any one great inclusive enterprise binding together the various projects of the behaviorist into any more intimate union than they enjoy from being, each and severally, promising lines of work in psychology. (p. 264)

Even Watson's extreme metaphysical position, which was probably unnecessary, made a kind of contribution. Just as Titchener's strenuous effort to develop Wundtian structuralism gave a thorough American trial to that brand of psychology, so Watson's insistent laboring of the mind-body issue helped to establish the scientific fruitlessness of attending to that problem, at least at present. There is no necessary relationship between one's mind-body position and one's experimental or theoretical research. One's mind-body position is usually not specific enough to direct research; however, the type of research persons engage in may influence their mind-body position. The latter is easier to change, involving primarily verbal commitments rather than changes throughout a research program. Titchener wanted the issue to go away and let him do his research; Watson helped to eliminate the problem for a generation of experimenters. Recently, concern with the problem is again on the increase, but it still has little direct effect on research even in fields like psychosomatic medicine, where such an effect would be most plausible.

Watson's own contribution was primarily, as Boring (1950) put it, "as a dramatic polemicist and enthusiastic leader" (p. 645). In addition, we have described some examples of his important research, both with animals and with human young. Nevertheless, he contributed little by way of new technique or theory. Even his loosely formulated notions about thinking and language learning were mostly revisions of older ideas. Bergmann (1956) went so far as to say of Watson: "As I see him, Watson is above all a completer and a consummator—the greatest, though not chronologically the last, of the Functionalists" (pp. 267–268). It is difficult ever to say that anyone is an originator. But one who states issues for the first time clearly and unequivocally, as Watson did, is at least in this much an innovator. It is rare that anyone has as great an impact as Watson's upon the general method and formulation of a science.

Watson combined his own forceful personality, his extreme metaphysics, and his work in the laboratory to convince psychologists that they would be better off doing the type of work he advocated. It was as if he had said, "It is better to light one candle than to curse the darkness; better to do good behavioral studies in which we can be certain of what we have found than to introspect, and possibly end up with nothing."

Bergmann, as we have seen, thought Watson's most important contribution was his insistence that there are no interacting minds. We agree, but Bergmann's statement should be further clarified. It could, on the face of it, mean either (1) there are no minds that interact with bodies or (2) there are no minds that interact directly with each other. Bergmann and Watson would agree that both (1) and (2) are true. Even critics of behaviorism would probably accept (2). Minds could not interact except through extrasensory perception, which is not accepted by most psychologists. If (1) is also true, then, as Bergmann puts it, it must be possible in principle to predict the behavior of organisms given sufficient knowledge of three classes of antecedent variables: behavioral, physiological, and environmental. "Mental" variables are not included in predictive formulas.

Margaret Washburn believed that consciousness is a useful concept and introspection a useful method. Yet she would have agreed with the point of the preceding discussion in that she recognized that proof of the existence of consciousness in other organisms rests only upon an analogy. In other words, there are no interacting minds! Mind in others must remain an inference based upon behavioral observations.

The great import of the Watsonian revolution in psychology was thus to clarify and elaborate the point that the only interaction of minds is through physical events like words or other behavioral cues. Since Watson wished to relegate the mystical minds to the dust heap, we would do him more justice to say that *organisms* interact only through physical processes. Since science is made by human organisms, and since they have defined science as *public* knowledge, the subject matter of science must be observable by more than one member of the species. It must be *objective*.

In conclusion, Watson's own comments on his contributions are interesting. We quote both from his first polemic statement and from what is probably his last professional word:

In concluding, I suppose I must confess to a deep bias on these questions. I have devoted nearly twelve years to experimentation on animals. It is natural that such a one should drift into a theoretical position which is in harmony with his experimental work. Possibly I have put up a straw man and have been fighting that. There may be no absolute lack of harmony between the position outlined here and that of functional psychology. I am inclined to think, however, that the two positions cannot be easily harmonized. Certainly the position I advocate is weak enough at present and can be attacked from many standpoints. Yet when all this is admitted I still feel that the considerations which I have urged should have a wide influence upon the type of psychology which is to be developed in the future. (Watson, 1913b, p. 175)

And, in his brief autobiographical statement (1936), Watson concluded:

I still believe as firmly as ever in the general behavioristic position I took overtly in 1912. I think it has influenced psychology. Strangely enough, I think it has temporarily slowed down psychology because the older instructors would not accept it wholeheartedly, and consequently they failed to present it convincingly to their classes. The youngsters did not get a fair presentation, hence they are not embarking wholeheartedly upon a behavioristic career, and yet they will no longer accept the teachings of James, Titchener, and Angell.

    I honestly think that psychology has been sterile for several years. We need younger instructors who will teach objective psychology with no reference to the mythology most of us present-day psychologists have been brought up upon. When this day comes, psychology will have a renaissance greater than that which occurred in science in the Middle Ages. I believe as firmly as ever in the future of behaviorism—behaviorism as a companion of zoology, physiology, psychiatry, and physical chemistry. (p. 281)

SUMMARY AND CONCLUSIONS

Behaviorism, like all other schools, has a long past. It goes back directly to Descartes, who viewed the body as a complex machine. Watson's real contribution was the consistency and extremity of his basic viewpoint; he simplified and made objective the study of psychology by denying the scientific usefulness of mind and consciousness. He espoused a metaphysics to go with his methodology and felt it necessary to deny the existence as well as the utility of consciousness. His methodological point is still accepted, either wittingly or unwittingly, by nearly all experimental psychologists. Many other psychologists also are methodological behaviorists, but there is a growing counterforce in the form of phenomenological, existential, and humanistic types of psychology.

    Watson's metaphysical point, like most metaphysical points within science, is neither accepted nor rejected for scientific purposes, but is regarded as irrelevant. There is little evidence that a mind-body position affects the work done by psychologists. Rather, scientists seem more likely to adopt a mind-body position which harmonizes with the work they are already doing.

    Watson's secondary positions on issues like environmentalism and peripheralism have encouraged research. However, they are now regarded as preliminary formulations and have little current relevance. This should not be taken to mean that there is no longer controversy about environmentalism versus nativism; in fact, this issue is now being contested with renewed ferocity.

The reasons for the acceptance of Watsonian behaviorism are related to the clarity and force of Watson as a person. The close relationship of his psychology to the American tradition also made his credo more acceptable in the United States. Contemporaneous and somewhat later developments in physics (operationism) and philosophy (positivism) accorded so well with behaviorism that the conjunction of the three movements added force to all. The confining influence of structuralism also added impetus to any movement that was away from it.

Criticisms of behaviorism have been and continue to be vociferous. They have swept away most of the excesses of behaviorism and changed its form markedly. Metaphysical behaviorism, many of Watson's secondary tenets, and any mechanistic views that were associated with too rigid an S-R reflex formulation have largely disappeared. The foundation stone, behavioristic methodology, has stubbornly resisted and is a solid and apparently permanent contribution of John B. Watson. However, a stone is not a house, and a methodological restriction is not a complete system; so today, just as there is no structuralism, there is no great single system called *behaviorism*.

FURTHER READINGS

Diserens's (1925) paper on psychological objectivism is a classic historical treatment of behaviorism's antecedents, and it requires little modification today. The most useful primary publications are Watson's *Behaviorism* (1930), Meyer's *Psychology of the other one* (1921), and Weiss's *Theoretical basis of human behavior* (1925). Watson's *Behavior: An introduction to comparative psychology* was reprinted with a valuable new introduction by Herrnstein (1967). Tolman's *Purposive behavior in animals and men* (1932) presents a broadened picture of behavioristic doctrine. For the flavor of the early polemics, Watson and McDougall's little volume reporting their debate, *The battle of behaviorism* (1929), is invaluable. A comprehensive volume on the various facets of the mind-body problem was edited by Feigl, Scriven, and Maxwell (1958). Secondary sources, mostly critical, are Woodworth's *Contemporary schools of psychology* (1948), Heidbreder's *Seven psychologies* (1933), Murphy's *Historical introduction to modern psychology* (1949), and Roback's *A history of American psychology* (1952). Stevens's classic paper (1939), "Psychology and the science of science," relates the behavioristic trend to logical positivism and operationism and is a most useful historical treatment. An especially interesting and provocative paper, using Kuhn's concept of paradigm clash, is that by Burnham (1968). A treatment of behaviorism from a highly sympathetic point of view is found in Spence's paper "The methods and postulates of behaviorism" (1948). A book which has been hailed as a scholarly and balanced assessment of the impact and present status of behaviorism is Zuriff's *Behaviorism: A conceptual reconstruction* (1985). Finally, Cohen's (1979) biography *John B. Watson: The founder of behaviorism* is both very interesting and a source of much more information about Watson's life than was previously available.

END NOTES

Dimensional Descriptions of Behaviorism

Behaviorism, like structuralism, takes clear positions on the dimensions provided by Watson. However, on important factors the behavioristic position was opposite to the structuralistic position and often similar to that of the associationists, from whom Watson borrowed so freely. One can also see the functionalist heritage reflected in some behavioristic stands.

Conscious Mentalism–Unconscious Mentalism. J. B. Watson would have preferred to forget all about R. I. Watson's first dimension. J. B. wanted nothing whatever to do with mentalism, which he regarded as a holdover from the old philosophy. Thus this category is really not applicable to behaviorism. Nevertheless, some people might place him closer to the unconscious end of the dimension, since he so vehemently denied the relevance of consciousness for behavior and would therefore by default become something of an unconscious "mentalist."

Content: Objective vs. Subjective. On this dimension there is no need to quibble. Objective content is what *defines* behaviorism. It rejects the possibility of subjective content in a science of psychology and therefore takes the most extreme objective position on this dimension.

Determinism–Indeterminism. John B. Watson was such an extreme determinist that his position was attacked on precisely this point.

Empiricism–Rationalism. Again there is no doubt; Watson was an empiricist, an extreme empiricist in his later writing. This is one place in which we see the close relationship to associationistic psychology.

Functionalism–Structuralism. Watson was more a functionalist than a structuralist, in keeping with his training at the University of Chicago. However, his great interest in structure in the anatomical sense might be interpreted as giving him a moderate position on this dimension.

Inductivism–Deductivism. Watson was a strong inductivist. He made little use of deductive logic or of rational principles. He produced no systems of postulates and no equations.

Mechanism–Vitalism. We have argued that Watson need not be called a mechanist because of his determinism; however, in the sense that mechanism is the opposite of vitalism, Watson was a strong mechanist. He wanted to get all kinds of ghosts out of the human machine, even the ghost of mind or consciousness. He was clearly against the "something extra" implied by vitalism. For Watson, all psychological phenomena were ultimately reducible to physical and chemical principles.

Method: Objectivism vs. Subjectivism. The critics claimed that there was some hidden subjectivity in Watson's acceptance of verbal behavior, but at least the fact that he tried to hide it showed that he very much wanted to be a pure objectivist in method!

Molecularism–Molarism. Not all behaviorists were molecularistic—Tolman and Lashley are examples—but Watson was, although his molar definitions of many stimuli and responses made him less a molecularist than many would think on the basis of his beliefs about the adequacy of an S-R psychology.

Monism–Dualism. Watson, like most behaviorists, was a materialistic (physicalistic) monist. The behaviorists who admitted the existence of consciousness were generally "weak" dualists who denied consciousness any causal efficacy.

Naturalism–Supernaturalism. Watson's fond dream was to make psychology an indisputably natural science. He disliked supernaturalism intensely.

Nomotheticism–Idiographicism. Watson recognized some individual uniqueness, but his famous claim that he could make anything of any healthy infant was a denial of the importance of that uniqueness. Watson's environmentalism made him a nomotheticist. The laws of conditioning and behavior were, for Watson, quite general laws which could be used to control the behavior of anyone.

Peripheralism–Centralism. The behaviorists were the prototype for peripheralism. Watson even tried to bring thinking out to the vocal cords, where it could be more easily observed. Although he seemed to be happy that society was unable to regularize his visceral responses, that was an exception, a rare case in which the events of his private life probably preempted his professional beliefs.

Purism–Utilitarianism. Watson believed in, and demonstrated, the usefulness of psychology. Had he been allowed to remain within academic psychology, there is little doubt that some version of behavior therapy would have developed about 30 years earlier. As events actually occurred, Watson's most convincing demonstrations of the usefulness of psychology involved advertising.

Quantitativism–Qualitativism. On this dimension Watson was less extreme than, for example, Thorndike. In his textbooks, however, he showed a quantitative tendency in his descriptions of how to determine the quantity of saliva in a conditioning experiment. Quantification was, for Watson, just part of good scientific practice and not something which he needed to emphasize strongly.

Rationalism–Irrationalism. Watson was closer to the irrationalistic position on this dimension because of his rejection of a rationalistic approach and because of his acceptance of irrational, arbitrary, events as determiners of behavior. There was slight rationalism in little Albert's fear of rats, since it resulted from a rather arbitrary connection between seeing a rat and hearing a loud, frightening noise.

Staticism–Developmentalism.   Developmentalism describes Watson's behaviorism better than does staticism. Behavior was so much a result of environmental influence that it could not be static. The environment changed it too much over time.

Staticism–Dynamicism.   On this second type of staticism contrast, behaviorism appears more static. The stimulus-response formula leaves little room for dynamic factors. In fact, Watson's determinism and molecularism would place him rather far toward the static side of this polarity.

Coan's Factors

Behaviorism is like structuralism and associationism in being restrictive. It restricted psychological study to objective study, but beyond this limitation there was little restriction. Any behavior was fair game for scientific study, and certainly purism was no part of Watson's motivation. Nevertheless, behaviorism was analytic, structural, and objective, as we would expect a restrictive school to be on the basis of Coan's study. Behaviorism had some similarity to structuralism and associationism in its elementarism. All three schools tended to be quantitative in approach, with behaviorism a little less extreme than associationism. Behaviorism is as *apersonal* and *static* as structuralism. Behaviorism, as conceived by Watson, was as *exogenistic* as associationism.

GESTALT PSYCHOLOGY

Gestalt psychology was born with a paper by Max Wertheimer (1880–1943) on apparent movement (1912), a report of work by Wertheimer, Wolfgang Köhler (1887–1967), and Kurt Koffka (1886–1941), the cofounders of the new school. Gestalt psychology cleared away some of the old problems in psychology and pointed to the importance of new ones. Its rejection of the artificiality of much of the psychological analysis of the day led to an acceptance of problems closer to everyday-life experiences.

The problem of how elements are organized into wholes was central to Gestalt psychology. Wertheimer later stated what he believed were the laws of such organization. The Gestalt type of examination and explanation of perceptual phenomena, such as afterimages and apparent movement, was begun. Learning theorists were forced to consider Gestalt principles of organization, and the concept of insight, in their own theories. We have already encountered Thorndike's principle of belongingness as an example of the Gestalt influence.

Gestalt psychology was especially prone to be misunderstood. It was a product of European culture (Table 7-1 lists some of the most important persons in the school), and the early papers were published in German. Fortunately, its founders remained active in the field, and when they, as well as many developers of Gestalt psychology, came to the United States after fleeing Hitler's Germany, they were able to clarify the Gestalt position and to make its principles available in English. Thus Gestalt psychology avoided prolonged misinterpretations such as occurred with Wundt's psychology.

The early misunderstandings of Gestalt psychology have lessened. Köhler's book (1947) was especially helpful because of the simplicity of its exposition. In it Köhler pointed out (p. 168) that Gestalt psychology does not reject analysis in general. Many American psychologists had felt that the Gestalt derogation of artificial introspective

TABLE 7-1
IMPORTANT FIGURES IN GESTALT PSYCHOLOGY

| Antecedent influences | Gestaltists | | |
	Pioneers	Founders	Developers
Franz Brentano (1838–1917)	G. E. Müller (1850–1934), Göttingen	Max Wertheimer (1880–1943), Frankfurt	Kurt Lewin (1890–1947), Berlin
Ernst Mach (1838–1916)	Erich R. Jaensch (1883–1940), Göttingen	Kurt Koffka (1886–1941), Frankfurt	Raymond H. Wheeler (1892–1961), Kansas
William James (1842–1910)	David Katz (1884–1957), Göttingen	Wolfgang Köhler (1887–1967), Frankfurt	Egon Brunswik (1903–1955), Berkeley
Alexius Meinong (1853–1920)	Edgar Rubin (1886–1951), Göttingen		Roger Barker (1903–), Kansas
John Dewey (1859–1952)			
Christian von Ehrenfels (1859–1932)			
G. F. Stout (1860–1944)			

analysis implied a rejection of all analysis. Köhler also pointed out that the Gestalt opposition to quantitative statements was a prescription for psychology because of its youth, not an objection to the ultimate desirability of quantification.

This improved understanding of the Gestalt position, and the interaction of Gestalt psychology with the more American brands, have resulted in the general acceptance of several fundamental Gestalt ideas even in the originally unfriendly climate of American psychology. Acceptance of the Gestalt point that there are wholes which lose much of their identity and importance when they are analyzed into parts has helped to make the study of relatively unanalyzed global variables more respectable in experimental psychology. The size of the unit of analysis is now most often regarded as something to be selected for the sake of convenience and adjusted to fit the particular problem under investigation. This position is different from the behaviorist tendency to reduce molar acts to molecular units of analysis. If psychologists do analyze situations in terms of molecular variables, they recognize the need for what may be called *combination laws*. These laws specify the relationships between the several simple variables and tell how they combine to produce the molar behavior. It is no longer considered sufficient to specify the relationships between single independent variables and the dependent variable, "other things being equal." Situations can be understood

Max Wertheimer (1880–1943), who was the oldest of the three men credited with founding the Gestalt school. It was his inspiration about apparent movement that brought the three together in Frankfurt-am-Main.

Wolfgang Köhler (1887–1967), one of the three original Gestaltists. He fled the Nazis and spent much of his professional life at Swarthmore University.

Kurt Koffka (1886–1941), one of the three originators of Gestalt psychology. Like the other two, he emigrated to the United States and spent many years at Smith College.

completely only when we know how the several relevant variables interact. The Gestalt point that new phenomena are created (emerge) in complex situations is accepted.

The Gestalt psychologists accepted a phenomenological description of experience, a description based on what was given directly rather than on elements analyzed out of that experience. This has encouraged the use by others of direct, naive reports of untrained subjects. Since the phenomenological report contains meanings directly, it is no longer necessary to quibble about stimulus errors, which presumably arise from prior knowledge about the stimuli. The report, with its meaning, can be accepted as it is given. Since the wholes given in phenomenological experience are assumed to be legitimate phenomena in their own right, concern for breaking experienced wholes into constituent elements has virtually disappeared.

THE ANTECEDENTS OF THE GESTALT MOVEMENT

When one speaks of the antecedents of modern psychological systems, Wundt is usually mentioned first. He was the father to be rejected by each new adolescent. His elementaristic position was a target for Gestalt psychology, just as it was for functionalism and behaviorism. However, he was an antecedent in a more direct sense; his principle of creative synthesis was an early concept that implied some recognition of the difference between wholes and the sum of their parts. This concept was much like John Stuart Mill's mental chemistry. Both men recognized that new characteristics might emerge from the combination of elements into wholes. Neither, however, did enough about his notion to satisfy the founders of Gestalt psychology.

Franz Brentano, whom we have discussed in relation to Wundtian psychology (Chapter 4), believed that psychology should concentrate upon the process or act of sensing rather than upon the sensation as an element. He used introspection, but his introspection tended toward the naive phenomenological variety. He considered Wundt's introspection artificial and strained. Thus he anticipated the Gestalt method of introspection and made the direct, naive expression of experience respectable. However, he did not emphasize the emergence of new phenomena with increasing complexity.

Carl Stumpf (1848–1936) was another antecedent of Gestalt psychology, but he bore a very peculiar relationship to its founders. Köhler (1920) dedicated a book to Stumpf, from whom he had received his doctorate; Koffka was also a student of Stumpf, as was Kurt Lewin, who developed his own brand of Gestalt psychology. Wertheimer got his degree with Külpe at Würzburg but studied with Stumpf and was associated with him for years at the University of Berlin. Yet Stumpf, who was so closely associated with these four chief figures in Gestalt psychology, denied having any systematic influence on the new movement (Hartmann, 1935, p. 32). It seemed that Stumpf was positively anxious to disown any influence. Both Stumpf and Külpe, however, deviated in important ways from structuralist orthodoxy. Both used some variation of the traditional introspective techniques or problems, and Stumpf in particular may have helped to transmit Brentano's more tolerant style of introspection to the Gestaltists. Boring (1950, p. 595) reports that Brentano and Husserl had won Stumpf over to phenomenology.

Most of the other antecedents had some more direct intellectual relationship to Gestalt psychology, although none of them could have had a closer personal relationship than Stumpf. Ernst Mach (1838–1916) was a physicist who came into the history of psychology by the back door. He was interested in the new psychology and contributed to it both in theory and in experiment. He insisted that sensations form the basis of all science. This was a point that a physicist could make as well as a psychologist, for it relates to the general question of epistemology. Yet in his study of the nature of sensations, Mach was led to postulate the existence of two entirely new types of sensation: sensations of space form, as in a circle or any other geometrical form, and sensations of time form, as in a melody. These sensations of space form and time form Mach correctly (according to the Gestalt psychologists) stated to be independent of their elements. For example, circles can be red, blue, large, or small and lose nothing of their circularity. Similarly, the notes of a melody can be played in another key without any alteration of their time form.

Christian von Ehrenfels (1859–1932) shared with Mach an interest in the new psychology. Although he was a philosopher for the most part, he elaborated Mach's psychological notions of the new elements into a theory and called it *Gestaltqualität*. In his analysis of the new sensational elements, he was faced with the question of whether they were really new. Could the new qualities be reduced to combinations of the other qualities? He decided that although the qualities depend upon the elements arranged in a certain pattern, they are nevertheless immediately experienced and do not inhere in any of the component elements. They are present in the mind and not in the physical elements.

According to Boring (1950), "At first the Gestalt psychologists did not realize what a respectable and competent ancestor they had in von Ehrenfels, but presently they discovered him, and when he died in 1933 the *Psychologische Forschung* printed a brief but fitting recognition of his role" (p. 608). Similarly, Heider (1973) says that the Berlin Gestaltists singled out von Ehrenfels as a significant forerunner of their own theories. However, the original development by Wertheimer, Köhler, and Koffka seems to have occurred before they were aware of von Ehrenfels and his work.

Mach and von Ehrenfels postulated new elements, but they were not Gestalt psychologists. We miss the point of the Gestalt revolution unless we see that its precursors were in reality merely carrying on in the old atomistic tradition. They discovered new elements and did not eschew elementarism as the Gestaltists did. They were aware of the problems of the older formulation, but they gave an entirely wrong solution, from the point of view of Gestalt psychology. They complicated rather than simplified.

Alexius Meinong (1853–1920) gave the same wrong answer that von Ehrenfels had given. He was a pupil of Brentano and the leader of the Graz school of psychology. He elaborated the ideas of von Ehrenfels and changed his terminology but added nothing essentially new. His methodology tended toward the phenomenological, so that in this way he anticipated Gestalt. The break of the act psychology of Brentano and the psychology of the Graz school with the academic tradition was not clean enough.

Helson, in his article "Why did their precursors fail and the Gestalt psychologists succeed?" (1969), makes nearly the same point: "First and foremost, it was a radical movement. I once referred to the Benussi group as the left-wing Gestalters with their assumption of higher processes to account for whole qualities, and Koffka said: 'No, we are the radicals in rejecting such processes,' and he was, of course, right" (p. 1007).

The Benussi group to which Helson was referring was made up of students and other associates of Vittorio Benussi (1878–1927), who was himself a student of Meinong. They, like the other predecessors, failed to take the radical step; they failed to reject elementarism. However, Benussi performed a long series of experiments on perception in an attempt to clarify the question of whether Gestalt properties were really different from sensations. Had he rejected the question and accepted Gestalts as given in perception, he would have been the founder of the Gestalt school. As it was, he became a respected and friendly opponent of the Gestaltists (Heider, 1973).

These schools did not flourish and gain adherents as Gestalt psychology did later. Thus they provided antecedents for Gestalt psychology in an intellectual, systematic, sense, but there was no continuity between the personnel of these earlier groups and the originators of Gestalt psychology. The fundamentals of the new position thus coalesced by the very process that Gestalt psychology was later to advocate as the basis of learning—an historical insight.

Several psychologists at Göttingen were also important precursors of Gestalt psychology. G. E. Müller directed the laboratory there and supported a program of introspective research that resembled the Gestalt phenomenological approach. He was later to claim (Müller, 1923) that there was really nothing new in the Gestalt approach to perceptual theory. The research of three other men in his laboratory lent support to his contention. Had these men had the inspiration to make their results the basis of a school, the names of Gestalt psychology's founders might have been Erich R. Jaensch (1883–1940), David Katz (1884–1957), and Edgar Rubin (1886–1951). All three men were working on and publishing phenomenological investigations in 1911 or 1912, which was the year Wertheimer published his results and launched Gestalt psychology. These three were young men, almost exactly the same age as Wertheimer, Köhler, and Koffka. The fact that all six of these young psychologists were working on similar radical ideas at about the same time lends credence to Boring's belief in a *Zeitgeist*.

Jaensch was working with visual acuity, and he showed that large interacting systems had to be considered in the discussion of acuity. The elementary atomistic approach would not do. Katz had already published an investigation of color in 1907, and in 1911 he published an extensive monograph on color. It contained a careful phenomenological description of the different kinds of colors: surface colors, volumic colors, and film colors. He described the conditions under which each type of color could be observed and did *not* try to explain the different types of colors by recourse to the combination of sensations of color with some other elements, as the Wundtians would have. Rubin did not begin his work until 1912, the year the Gestalt school was founded. He developed the distinction between figure and ground in his phenomenological investigations. He noted that commonly part of the total stimulus configuration stands out, while part of it recedes and is more amorphous. He produced several demonstrations in which the figure and ground can be reversed. Rubin did not publish until 1915, but then the Gestaltists pounced on his work and appropriated it to their system. It provided another instance of evidence which required the consideration of the totality of stimulation for its explanation.

Meanwhile, others were being beckoned by problems similar to the one so ingeniously solved by the Gestalt triumvirate. In England, G. F. Stout (1860–1944) raised questions about the whole-part relationship. He was concerned chiefly with form and concluded that "an element which is apprehended first as part of one whole, and then as part of another, is presented in two different points of view, and so far suffers transformation" (1902, p. 71). He thus stated clearly the Gestalt point that there exist wholes which influence the mode of existence of their parts.

Even earlier, William James in the United States had challenged psychological atomism. He said, "The traditional psychologist talks like one who would say a river consists of nothing but pailsful, spoonsful, quartpotsful, barrelsful, and other moulded forms of water. Even were the pails and the pots all actually standing in the stream, still between them the free water would continue to flow" (1890, vol. I, p. 255). Like the water, the stream of consciousness for James had a reality independent of its atomistic analysis.

Curiously, James also used an analogy that was almost exactly like one used by Köhler many years later:

> In a sense a soap bubble has parts; it is a sum of juxtaposed spherical triangles. But these triangles are not separate realities. Touch the bubble and the triangles are no more. Dismiss the thought and out go its parts. You can no more make a new thought out of ideas that have once served you than you can make a new bubble out of old triangles. Each bubble, each thought, is a fresh organic unity, sui generis. (1890, vol. I, p. 279, footnote)

Had James elaborated his point sufficiently, Gestalt psychology might have had an earlier founding.

We have already met another American who was surprisingly close to Gestalt principles, although his point was made in another context. John Dewey, in his reflex-arc paper (1896) was advocating a field approach, a study of the whole situation in itself, a discarding of the artificial analysis into stimulus and response. The reflex arc was seen to be an organic unity, losing its meaning and reality in the analysis.

The very atmosphere of thought just prior to the founding of Gestalt psychology seemed to be permeated with the notion of fields, which in psychology became the notion of organic wholes. Thought of this sort was not limited to psychologists and philosophers. For example, E. B. Wilson, a leading biologist, said that the cell must not be regarded as an independent unit, the only real unity being that of the organism.

THE FOUNDING OF THE GESTALT SCHOOL

Max Wertheimer, the oldest of the founders, was born in Prague in 1880. He studied law there before turning to psychology. He studied with Stumpf and Friedrich Schumann (1863–1940) before taking his degree with Külpe at Würzburg. Early in his career, Wertheimer became embroiled in a controversy with C. G. Jung of psychoanalytic fame. His son Michael (Wertheimer, 1982), now a psychologist at the University of Colorado, explains that the issue was which man, Jung or Wertheimer, had first suggested the use of the association test to detect criminal knowledge. It seems that Max Wertheimer first used the test to identify criminals, although Jung was the first to use it to identify "complexes" of ideas which were involved in neuroses.

Wertheimer was apparently financially independent. After obtaining his degree summa cum laude, he spent some time at Prague, Vienna, and Berlin. He was on his way to a summer vacation, although he had no formal employment to vacation from, when he showed up at the Psychological Institute in Frankfurt am Main in 1910. He had just arrived on the train and stopped at a store to buy a toy stroboscope (Harper, Newman, & Schab, 1985). At his hotel, he made some preliminary observations before going to the institute to find more subjects. Schumann, his friend and teacher from Berlin, was there, and he let Wertheimer use his recently constructed tachistoscope. Two other graduates from Berlin, Wolfgang Köhler and Kurt Koffka, were soon helping Wertheimer study apparent movement. The young assistants, then about 23 and 24, were happy to help the venerable Wertheimer, who was 30 that year, by serving as subjects. Later, they were joined by Koffka's wife, Dr. Klein-Koffka, who also became one of the regular subjects. The phenomenon which gives us motion pictures had long been difficult for psychologists to interpret. The problem was how to explain, using sensations as elements, the perception of movement which arose from a series of stimuli, none of which themselves moved.

Wertheimer worked with a number of experimental arrangements. One involved the use of two slits, one vertical and the other inclined 20 or 30 degrees from the vertical. When light was thrown first through one slit and then through the other, the slit of light appeared to move from one position to the other if the time between presentations of the two lights was within the proper range. Wertheimer found that an interval of about 60 milliseconds was optimal. If the interval was longer than about 200 milliseconds, the light appeared to be stationary, first at one position, then at the other. If the interval was too short, 30 milliseconds or less, both lights seemed to be on continuously. Wertheimer gave the apparent movement the name *phi;* he wished to give it a neutral name that would emphasize its independent character as a phenomenon in its own right. Pure phi was movement that occurred in the absence of any impression of an object that moved.

It was clear that the phenomenon could not be a result of the summation of simple sensations. An elementarist would have great difficulty convincing anyone that the addition of a second stationary stimulus to a first stationary stimulus should add up to movement, but that is exactly what happened. The founders of Gestalt psychology were extremely astute men, and they were working with an experimental paradigm which encouraged them to look at the total situation, the pattern of events, in seeking an explanation for the phenomena they discovered. It was apparently Wertheimer's insight about that explanation which so excited him that he stopped his journey at Frankfurt (Boring, 1950).

In his monograph describing the research, Wertheimer rejected all the traditional explanations of apparent motion, saying, in part, "There is no internal reason why something that is psychologically 'dynamic' should have to be deduced *a priori* from something 'static' " (Shipley, 1961, p. 1082, translated from Wertheimer, 1912). An attempt to analyze apparent movement into simpler sensations, in the orthodox Wundtian manner, would destroy the reality of the phenomenon as such. Apparent movement would not be found to exist except in situations where prescribed *relationships* between elements held.

Wertheimer implied that at the psychological level, apparent motion should be "left alone" and recognized as a whole-phenomenon in its own right. Then, in a strategy that was often used by Gestalt psychologists, he turned to the physiological level and suggested some plausible hypotheses about physiological events which might account for the phenomenological observations. He thought that the neurological events that corresponded to the static stimuli might give rise to a spreading excitation, and "Then there would occur a kind of *psychological short-circuit* from a to b . . . the circular disturbance from b now occurs, then excitation flows over (a physiologically specific event), the direction of which is given by the fact that a and its circular disturbance occurred first" (quoted in Shipley, 1961, p. 1085).

It was not easy to arrive at the "simple" conceptions responsible for the beginning of Gestalt psychology. Its principles were completely counter to most of the academic tradition of German psychology. To regard a complex experience as having an existence of its own was revolutionary. To maintain, as Wertheimer did, that the *primary* data of perception are typically structures (*Gestalten*) was heresy to the German introspective tradition and to its American counterpart, which was already flourishing under Titchener. Structures, for these psychologists, were things to be broken down into elements, which were primary.

In addition, Wertheimer thought that it was legitimate for introspectors to use simple, naive descriptive words. He maintained that local sensations should not be expected to concur with local stimulation, because both are part of a field, a whole, which influences the individual parts in a way which depends upon the structure of the whole.

Köhler and Koffka joined Wertheimer as vociferous advocates of the new psychology. As Köhler (1942) said in his obituary for Koffka:

> Those were years of cheerful revolt in German psychology. We all had great respect for the exact methods by which certain sensory data and facts of memory were being investigated, but we also felt quite strongly that work of so little scope could never give us an adequate psychology of real human beings. Some believed that the founding fathers of experimental psychology had done grave injustice to every higher form of mental life. Others suspected that at the very bottom of the new science there were some premises which tended to make its work sterile. (p. 97)

This last point concurs with one stated brilliantly by William James and cited in Chapter 5.

With such cheerful revolutionists, the movement gained momentum. There were many in Germany, as in America (e.g., Helson, 1925, 1926), who were dissatisfied with the artificiality and paucity of results of the older psychology. Gestalt psychology quickly gained support from them. These restless psychologists were happy to find a way to avoid the proliferation of elements needed to explain each new complex experience. They did not believe that the legitimacy of the phenomenological approach, or of emergent real phenomena, could any longer be denied. This was the primary assumption of the developing school. Let us look further at the set of tenets developed by the new psychology.

THE TENETS OF GESTALT PSYCHOLOGY

The Whole-Part Attitude

The attitude of Gestaltists toward wholes is one of the most difficult concepts which psychologists need to grasp. We must therefore devote the most careful attention to it. Certainly the distinction Gestaltists make between a whole and the sum of its parts is not new. The Chinese sage Lao-Tse is said (Hartmann, 1935, p. 9) to have expressed in 700 B.C. the notion that the sum of the parts is different from the whole. Also, Skinner (1938, p. 29) has contended that the question of whether the whole is different from the sum of its parts is a pseudoproblem. On the other hand, Weiss (1967) entitled a long and beautifully illustrated article "1 + 1 ≠ 2 (One plus one does not equal two)," and there is no doubt whatever that he considers it a meaningful problem. Many have been concerned with it, and it seems to justify whatever investigation is required in order to understand the nature of the questions raised.

Max Wertheimer had this to say about the whole-part problem as it occurs with respect to the given in experience (Wertheimer, 1938): *"The given is itself in varying degrees structured (Gestaltet), it consists of more or less definitely structured wholes and whole-processes with their whole-properties and laws, characteristic whole-tendencies and whole-determinations of parts. Pieces almost always appear as parts in whole processes."* (p. 14).

Wertheimer was, of course, pointing to the importance of structure, but he was doing more than that. Even an associationist or a structuralist could accept that. Wertheimer was indicating a kind of logical *priority* of the whole. Consider an example provided by Orbison (1939) and reproduced here as Figure 7-1. The two squares are "objectively" identical in size, with all sides straight. Yet in perception the structure of the whole makes them appear different. It does not make sense to a Gestaltist to say that the two squares appear first as parts and then make up different wholes. The very nature of their existence as parts is determined by the wholes.

Analogies from other fields which demonstrate the importance of structure and the difference between wholes and the sums of parts are common. One of the oldest and most familiar is water, which is quite different from a *mixture* of its elements, hydrogen and oxygen. Water has emergent qualities, that is, qualities that emerge only in the combination of its elements. We can know about the characteristics of the compound water only by studying water directly; the characteristics could not be predicted by a knowledge of the characteristics of the elements alone. Although advances in physical theories may now make such predictions possible, those advances could not themselves have occurred without observations of the properties of wholes.

FIGURE 7-1
An illustration of the dependence of perception of a part upon the pattern of the whole. (*Adapted from Orbison, 1939, p. 42.*)

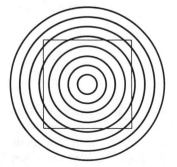 

C. S. Smith, a materials scientist, in a review of the status of his own field (1968), made several statements which indicated that physical scientists were increasingly being forced to recognize the importance of organized wholes in their study of materials:

> The main characteristic of today's science of materials is a concern with properties and the dependence of properties upon structure. This is exactly where the story began. The history of materials has been a long journey in search of knowledge in strange and difficult terrain, finally to return to the familiar scene with vastly better understanding. . . . Matter cannot be understood without a knowledge of atoms; yet it is now becoming evident that the properties of materials that we enjoy in a work of art or exploit in an interplanetary rocket are really not those of atoms but those of aggregates; indeed they arise in the behavior of electrons and protons within a framework of nuclei arranged in a complex hierarchy of many stages of aggregation. It is not stretching the analogy much to suggest that the chemical explanation of matter is analogous to using an identification of individual brick types as an explanation of Hagia Sophia. The scientists' laudable striving to eliminate the evidence of the senses has sometimes produced a senseless result. (p. 638)

To eliminate any doubt that Smith (1968) was talking about the whole-part problem, look at a later excerpt:

> The immense understanding that has come from digging deeper to atomic explanations has been followed by a realization that this leaves out something essential. In its rapid advance, science has had to ignore the fact that a whole is more than the sum of its parts. (pp. 643–644)

Polanyi (1968) has strongly argued that biology is not reducible to physics and chemistry, because the existing morphology of an organism, which provides the boundary conditions within which the physical or chemical laws operate, is physically and energetically indistinguishable from other no less probable morphologies that have not happened to come into existence. Thus the way in which the organism behaves is dependent upon it own characteristics, *as well as* upon the laws of physics and chemistry. This argument is valid, and it applies even to the much simpler aggregates of the materials engineer, as discussed above.

Köhler's *Die physischen Gestalten* (1920) is a relatively clear statement of the Gestalt view of the whole-part relationship, although such a complex and many-faceted problem is difficult to explain simply. Köhler said in part:

> Let us consider under what conditions a physical system attains a state which is independent of time (i.e., a state of equilibrium or a so-called stationary state). In general we can say that such a state is reached when a certain condition is satisfied for the system *as a whole*. The potential energy must have reached a minimum, the entropy a maximum, or the like. The solution of the problem demands not that forces or potentials assume particular values in individual regions, but that their total arrangements relative to one another in the whole system must be of a certain definite type. The state of process at any place therefore depends in principle on the conditions obtaining in all other parts of the system. If the laws of equilibrium or stationary state for the individual parts can be formulated separately, then these parts do not together constitute a *single* physical system, but each part is a system in itself.
>
> Thus an electric circuit is a physical system precisely because the conditions prevailing at any given point are determined by those obtaining in all the other parts. Contrariwise, a

group of electrical circuits completely insulated from each other constitutes a complex of independent, single systems. This complex is a "whole" *only* in the mind of one who chances to think of it as such; from the physical standpoint it is a summation of independent entities. (Köhler, 1920, as translated in Ellis, 1938, pp. 18–19)

Weiss (1967) gives several commonplace examples of complexly interrelated systems best regarded as wholes. One lovely visual example is a spiderweb. Changes made by the spider near the center of the web have effects that literally *can be seen* to reverberate throughout the web, as when a garden spider vibrates its web in response to a disturbance. Multiple interconnections between all parts of the web account for its action, but these interconnections defy analysis into parts; hence, "the whole is different from the sum of the parts."

As a contrasting type of example, consider a collection of 500 marbles scattered on a floor. Assume that one of the marbles strikes another with considerable force. Multiple hits would almost certainly follow. Nevertheless, this "system" is different from the first one, and the changes in marble position are, at least in principle, analyzable into a series of interactions between individual pairs of marbles. In contrast, the spiderweb provides no place for us to sink in our analytic teeth and constitutes a real system rather than the kind of pseudosystem provided by the marbles.

Implications for a World View

G. W. Hartmann has pointed out that there are two extreme views of the physical world and the role of systems within it. One view is that the world is composed of independent additive parts whose total constitutes reality. The other view is that everything is related to everything else and there are no independent systems. The Gestaltists held neither of these extreme views, although they leaned toward the latter. They recognized that there are systems which may be considered independent for practical (including practical scientific) purposes. Hartmann (1935) concluded: "Both evils are avoided as soon as one recognizes that *the laws of science are the laws of systems,* i.e., structures of finite extent—a generalization applicable to both physics and psychology" (p. 42).

The Gestaltists, then, wished to extend these ideas about physical systems to psychology. They maintained that in biology and psychology, as in physics, there are phenomena whose character depends on the whole field. In visual perception, for example, the thing seen was thought to be a function of the total, overall retinal stimulation rather than of the stimulation of any specific local point. Unfortunately, the nature of the psychological field is not always clear.

In 1955, at the American Psychological Association meeting in San Francisco, the physicist Robert Oppenheimer said that he had no idea what a "psychological field" could mean. The statement drew laughter and applause from the audience of American psychologists. Apparently many of them did not know either and felt that there might be no such thing or that the concept of psychological field is overworked and ill-defined. Oppenheimer (1956) continued, putting the matter quite politely:

But probably between sciences of very different character, the direct formal analogies in their structure are not too likely to be helpful. Certainly what the pseudo-Newtonians did with sociology was a laughable affair; and similar things have been done with mechanical notions of how psychological phenomena are to be explained. . . . I know that when I hear the word "field" used in physics and in psychology I have a nervousness that I cannot entirely account for. (pp. 133–134)

Despite the doubts of Oppenheimer and of many others, Köhler's statement about systems, quoted above, seems simple and reasonable enough. The real question is whether or not field-like theories can be meaningfully applied to psychology. Let us examine the question: "What meaning can wholes, systems whose parts depend on the whole, or fields, have in psychology?"

One of the key issues is the determination of what constitutes an isolated system. The Gestalt contention has been that fields or systems are widespread in psychology and that the elementaristic analysis of structuralism or behaviorism destroys the meaningful relationships these fields might have in psychological laws. At the same time, the Gestaltists have not denied that the proper use of analysis is necessary. How can we determine whether a particular field can be further analyzed without destroying the very relationships we intend to study? It seems that the only way to do so is by attempting both analysis and the use of the unanalyzed field in the construction of psychological laws. The decision about which method should be used will eventually be made on a pragmatic basis. If the molar, Gestalt approach leads to more useful laws, and if no further analysis is necessary, then this approach will be adopted for the particular purpose. On the other hand, if this approach does not succeed, further analysis will be necessary.

Factor analysis has been a very important tool for determining the degree and kind of system with which one is dealing. There are now several sophisticated multivariate techniques for determining interrelationships within complex sets of variables. If many measures of system behavior can be taken, analysis of the matrix of interrelationships may reveal significant aspects of the system's structure. There seems to be a trend in Germany for psychologists to study some qualitative Gestalt problems using multivariate analysis. Such analyses are becoming increasingly popular in American psychology as well. Many years ago, L. L. Thurstone was already known for his multivariate analyses. Gulliksen (1968) said of him:

For the last 25 years of his study, Thurstone typically investigated 40–60 variables at a time in order to get good leverage on the interrelationships among them. It may be said that this is the greatest legacy he has left us: the emphasis on both accurate experimentation and accurate analyses in the multivariate situation that is essential to psychology. (p. 800)

Modern mathematical techniques for studying dynamic systems involving many variables demonstrate that Köhler was quite correct in his contention that equilibrium conditions depend upon some condition in the system as a whole. These mathematical techniques are quite powerful. Specifically, some systems can be represented by a set of linear differential equations. The coefficients of the equations can, in turn, be written in a matrix. It is then characteristics of the *matrix as a whole* that determine whether or not the system will be stable and, if it is, what kind of stability it will manifest. Thus some of the Gestalt contentions have a very precise interpretation, and Köhler's contention is correct.

Modern catastrophe theory, as developed by René Thom (1975), is a mathematical development which deals with how systems can change suddenly from one stable equilibrium to another. A remarkable characteristic of such changes is that they occur at different places if one moves in different directions. It is as though one would encounter the "same" cliff at different places, depending upon whether one was traveling east or west. Changes are delayed past the "midpoint" as one moves in either direction, a property that is called "hysteresis." Since perceptual changes often occur suddenly, one might expect that catastrophe theory should apply to them and that they should show delay, or hysteresis, effects.

In this context, consider the following quotation from Shipley's (1961) translation of Wertheimer's 1912 paper:

> An effective arrangement for obtaining the phi-phenomena in a definite field, also appeared in a simple way in the following experiments: I presented a rather long horizontal line as one object and a line standing on its middle as the other. . . . When the middle line stood inclined towards the right—by about 20° to 80°—under the given conditions of exposure ($t = 70$ms), a rightward rotation.. . . . occurred under normal circumstances (that is, upon the first exposure of this arrangement), i.e. in the sense of the acute angle. When the line was inclined towards the left—by about 100° to 170°—then, correspondingly, a leftward rotation occurred. . . .
>
> If the exposures were now given one after the other, so that *a* was successively exposed first inclined to the right at about 30°, then inclined at 40° and then at 50°, and so on, one could go *far beyond* 90° without a reversal occurring in the direction of apparent motion. For example, the setting at 120° still produced a rightward rotation, over the longer stretch, through the obtuse angle. . . .
>
> When one is set on a definite direction (or a definite rotation to one side) one often tries vainly to rid oneself of the rotation towards this side, appearing in so very unlikely a position. It is no use: the phenomenon may sometimes appear, for example, in the extremely unlikely position of 160°! (pp. 1053–1054)

It is apparent from the foregoing that Wertheimer and his colleagues had stumbled upon a demonstration of catastrophe theory about 60 years before that theory was developed. Some of the intuitive claims of Gestalt psychology about the nature of sudden changes in systems seem strikingly consistent with Thom's catastrophe theory.

GESTALT PSYCHOLOGY AND PHYSIOLOGY

In his 1912 paper, Max Wertheimer had no sooner said that apparent movement need not be explained in terms of its "elements" than he turned to an explanation in terms of presumed underlying physiological events. He suggested that when the temporal relationships were within the right range, excitation from one object jumped over to the excitation generated by the next object presented. Thus Wertheimer immediately revealed his deep interest in physiology and foreshadowed the persisting preoccupation of Gestalt psychology with physiological (brain) explanations of perception and behavior.

Unfortunately, physiology often served only a hypothetical role. In the absence of direct observation, it was easy to postulate just the physiological "field" needed to "explain" the observed results. In physics, a field is an inference made directly from the movements of particles within a portion of space. From Oppenheimer's remarks, cited earlier, we may gather that "field" does not mean exactly the same thing in psychology as in physics. If it did, we would in both cases have a mathematical description which would predict new movements in the field, and that is all we would have. The physical field has the necessary mathematical properties but no existential properties.

In psychology, a similar situation *may* obtain. By *perceptual field* the careful psychologist may mean nothing more than certain antecedent-consequent relations and the verbal or mathematical description of a state of affairs which would allow the derivation of the observations. The concept of field is most likely to be used where the consequent (verbal report or other behavior) does not depend in a point-to-point fashion upon the local characteristics of the stimulus. If "field" is used in this strict sense, as a mathematical device for describing relationships, psychological fields resemble physical fields. If the psychological field does not allow predictions, it is essentially meaningless. A psychological field, used thus strictly, is many times more "physical" than most physiological "fields." The latter are likely to be pure assumptions, based on no physiological observations at all. If the physiological field is recognized as a model which helps in making predictions, there is nothing wrong with this situation. It makes no difference to its predictive power whether the field is thought to be physiological or not. The only problem is that some readers may be misled into believing that the physiological field is derived from physiological evidence.

Our picture of how the brain behaves is still quite incomplete. The early ablation work of Franz and Lashley demonstrated that the brain must act in some very complex manner, a conclusion that no one has had the courage to question. Lashley favored the view that whole patterns of neural activity, rather than localized activity, determine behavior. Yet Lashley, Chow, and Semmes (1951) performed experiments whose results also brought into question the Gestalt view that electric field activity in the brain underlies perception. Lashley and his coworkers undertook to short out any field currents in the visual cortex of the monkey by placing silver foil on the cortical surface or by placing metal pins in the striate cortex. They found no deterioration of visual discrimination performance, and they concluded that cortical fields are probably not related to visual perception. This type of experiment was later extended (Sperry & Miner, 1955; Sperry, Miner, & Myers, 1955), again without affecting visual discrimination.

Köhler (1958) did not think that Lashley's procedures had been adequate to short out the postulated cortical currents. However, Sperry and his coworkers had literally segmented the cortex by inserting sheets of mica. Köhler said that these workers had so damaged the brain that no theory of brain action could account for the continued visual discriminative ability. He suspected that some extraneous cues might have been available, so that the discrimination was not genuinely visual.

Thus the attempt to maintain a field theory of cortical action has not been abandoned, nor have attempts to explain brain action without field concepts (Hebb, 1949, 1959). Whatever the final explanation, there is no field explanation which is accepted at the present time. The popular holographic views of Karl Pribram (1971) are fieldlike in the sense that memory is hypothesized to be distributed throughout the brain rather than localized in a limited area. Certainly Pribram's view is more Gestalt than associationistic.

The description of brain fields given by the Gestalt psychologists has thus depended largely upon data from perceptual, not physiological, experiments. Prentice (1959, p. 451) cited some physiological research, but the results were not overwhelmingly impressive. We must conclude that the Gestaltists' physiological statements should be regarded as models intended to make possible the prediction of results on the psychological (behavioral) level. It is not always clear that these predictions could be made.

An instructive instance is the theory of cohesive and restraining forces. Cohesive forces are tendencies of excitations in the cortex to attract one another if nothing restrains them. Restraining forces prevent such movement; these "conservative" forces result from the immediate presence of the stimulus. For example, if there are two lights, A and B, in the stimulus field, restraining forces will keep them in place. But if A and B are alternately on and off and are in an appropriate spatial and temporal relationship, cohesive forces will make them appear to move back and forth between their actual locations.

Brown and Voth (1937) demonstrated the interactions between cohesive and restraining effects in an experiment on apparent motion. They made a direct and explicit analogy between the forces in the visual field and the field forces of physics. In one of their experiments, four lights were arranged in square pattern and flashed on, one at a time, successively around the square. As the rate of succession increased, apparent movement was perceived from one position to the succeeding position. As the rate increased further, the path of the movement became curved until the path appeared circular, rather than square. Further, the perceived path of movement had a diameter too small to intercept the actual positions of the lights.

This phenomenon was said to result because cohesive forces were greatest at an optimum time interval and the vectors of attraction between successive lights summated to produce the curved path of movement. The locus in which the attractive forces work is presumably the brain, while the restraining forces are thought to be more likely retinal. However, Brown and Voth were not very concerned about the physiological locus of the forces; what they wanted to do was to make predictions by assuming forces in the visual field, and they succeeded, in a general way, in making those predictions. However, they present no equations for their field or for their vectors, and their predictions are based on informal geometric arguments which support only qualitative predictions. This is a typical state of affairs for Gestalt psychology.

Isomorphism

Gestalt theorists have often made easy inferences from stimulus-response observations to physiological events because they accept the principle of isomorphism. An isomorphism is a 1:1 relationship, assumed in this case to hold between brain fields and experience.

Köhler stated an isomorphism between experienced space and brain events as follows (1947): *"Experienced order in space is always structurally identical with a functional order in the distribution of underlying brain processes"* (p. 61). Woodworth (1948, p. 135) used an analogy, the relationship between a map and the country it represents, to clarify what the Gestaltists meant by isomorphism. The map and the country are not the same, but their structure is identical in the sense that we can read off the characteristics of the country from the map. But this identity is a very restricted one; for example, the colors on the map are not the same as the colors of the country. At the same time, the isomorphism does not depend on the physical condition of the map; that can be folded or unfolded, or even wadded up, without destroying the isomorphism. It is interesting that the human cortex is folded, not to say wadded, so the Gestaltists were wise to choose a type of relationship which is unaffected by such arrangements. The Gestaltist assumes that we shall eventually be able to read off information about this contorted mass of brain from what we know of experience, and vice versa; we just need a better set of instructions for map reading.

The doctrine of isomorphism leads easily to another way of approaching the whole-part problem. To recapitulate, the Gestaltists emphasized whole properties and a phenomenal approach to perception. Thus they would expect to find physiological structures that corresponded to these whole properties. J. J. Gibson, who spent much of his life in studying perception, reached conclusions which had a Gestalt flavor. He showed that the most adaptive informational properties of our stimulus world require a complex description which we might well call "holistic." These psychological facts now have their physiological counterparts. Maturana, Lettvin, McCulloch, and Pitts (1960), in their classic article, described units in the frog's optic tract which responded when stimuli had complex sets of characteristics, including the right curvature, size, and movement (like a fly!), but did not respond under other conditions. It is clear that a physiology or psychology which studied only local responses to local stimulation would find it impossible to deal with such complex properties. There are probably myriad unknown examples of nerve nets that extract complex features from stimuli, in humans as well as in frogs. We know there are, if we accept isomorphism.

Thus the doctrine of isomorphism reflects a view of the value of introspection which leads us in quite a different direction from that of the structuralist or behaviorist. For Gestaltists, experience is just the other side of physiology and therefore becomes their "royal road" to knowledge of physiology. For structuralists, experience was studied for its own sake, with little thought of its relationship to physiology. For the behaviorist, experience was of little interest.

Nativism-Empiricism and the Contemporaneity Principle

Both of the components of the Gestaltists' isomorphism presently exist; the physiology and the correlated experience are available for immediate study. Nobody would be confused about the physiological side of this duality. We recognize that past physiology is not influencing what is presently happening physiologically. Of course, something that *happened* in the past, like a brain injury, may affect present physiology, but the present condition of the brain completely determines what it can and will do right now.

The Gestaltists wanted to convey this same clarity about the relationship between past and present to the psychological side. The principle of isomorphism says that present experience is explicable solely on the basis of present physiology. There is, in a sense, no looking back, despite the emphasis of other systems, like associationism and psychoanalysis, on the importance of the past. The past is important *only* because it affects present conditions, only because it is "represented" in the present. Thus if we understood the present physiology completely, we would, because of isomorphism, understand present experience completely. Nothing would be left out of the immediate causal account. A study based on past events would always be handicapped because of the distortions worked on earlier events by later ones, and there would always be the necessity to account for the relationship between these past events and the physiology of the organism.

Köhler (1938) stated part of the case against past experience as an exclusive explanatory principle as follows:

> It would be extremely unfortunate if the problem were thrust aside at this point as being after all only another case of the influence of past experience. No one doubts that past experience is an important factor in *some* cases, but the attempt to explain all perception in such terms is absolutely sure to fail, for it is easy to demonstrate instances where perception is not all all influenced by past experience. Fig. 1 is an example. We see a group of rectangles; but the figure may also be seen as two H's with certain intervening lines. Despite our extensive past experience with the letter H, it is, nevertheless, the articulation of *the presented object* which determines what we shall see. (p. 58)

Here is Köhler's Figure 1:

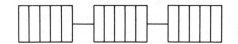

Köhler was not insisting that past experience is irrelevant to present perception, nor was he insisting that perceptual behavior is innate. There are three types of variables that may influence perception: genetic, historical, and present. Nativism is commonly understood to be the position that genetic variables completely determine present perceptual responding. The Gestalt position is not nativistic in this sense. The Gestaltists have simply insisted that the historical variables do not *completely* determine perceptual response and have concomitantly emphasized the other two classes of variables.

THE ATTITUDE TOWARD ANALYSIS

We have said that Gestalt psychology began as a revolt against the allegedly artificial analysis of the introspectionist. Nevertheless, the Gestalt psychologists recognized that analysis is at the very heart of science. The objection was not to analysis as such but to a particular kind of analysis. Köhler (1947) said that if we analyze as the orthodox introspectionists do, then those experiences that are most important will be neglected completely. Common experience, the experience of everyday life, is not to be found in the introspectionist's psychology. Köhler did not argue that the introspectionist's findings are unreal, just that the reality is contrived and artificial. Gestalt psychologists have objected not to the artificiality of the laboratory as such but to the artificiality of a stilted type of method and a sterile conception. The early Gestalt psychology was not an applied psychology but a psychology whose results apply to real experience. No doubt this attitude made it easier for later developers of Gestalt psychology like Kurt Lewin to make the transition to very applied work in social psychology.

The Gestaltists have also been interpreted as rejecting quantification within psychology. Their feeling was not that quantification is illegitimate or unnecessary but that it is often premature. They have held that psychology should first concern itself with important qualitative discoveries. The attitude toward quantification *as such* was not negative, but the attitude toward quantification *for its own sake* was quite negative. The feeling is summed up in Köhler's statement (1947) that "one can hardly exaggerate the value of qualitative information as a necessary supplement to quantitative work" (p. 49). He went on to say, of his own work on learning: "Everything that is valuable in these observations would disappear if 'results' were handled in an abstract statistical fashion" (p. 50). This is one aspect of Gestalt psychology with which our most famous operant conditioner, B. F. Skinner, could sympathize; Skinner claimed never to have designed an experiment in advance, and he showed little interest in statistical tests of significance. Both he and the Gestaltists want reliable results which do not need that kind of testing.

Koffka (1935, pp. 13–15) gave a more thorough and sophisticated treatment of quantification, making similar points. He rejected the antithesis felt by some to exist between quantity and quality, concluding that "the quantitative, mathematical description of physical science, far from being opposed to quality, is but a particularly accurate way of representing quality" (p. 14). Koffka would therefore agree that psychology must eventually express its laws in quantitative form in order to reach maximum precision.

EMPIRICAL STATEMENTS

Principles of Organization

The best-known empirical statements made by the Gestalt psychologists are the six principles of perceptual organization stated by Wertheimer (1923). These principles are "proved" via demonstration. Hochberg and McAlister (1953) commented on the status of the laws of organization: "Empirical study of the Gestalt principles of perceptual organization is, despite their great heuristic value, frequently made difficult by their subjective and qualitative formulation" (p. 361). Three examples of these laws are:

1 *Proximity.*   Elements close together in time or space tend to be perceived together. For example, the lines in figure 7-2a tend to be seen as three pairs of lines rather than in some other way.

FIGURE 7-2
Examples of perceptual factors in Gestalt psychology.

2 *Similarity.* Like elements tend to be seen together in the same structure, other things being equal, as in Figure 7-2*b*.

3 *Direction.* We tend to see figures in such a way that the direction continues smoothly. This factor is illustrated in Figure 7-2*c*.

Wertheimer recognized that the laws of organization were far from final or complete. He suggested some of the work that needed to be done to improve them when he said: "What will happen when *two* such factors appear in the same constellation? They may be made to cooperate; or, they can be set in opposition. . . . In this way, it is possible to test the strength of these factors" (1923; as translated in Ellis, 1938, pp. 76–77).

Koffka, writing 12 years later (1935), could still say: "A measurement of the relative strength of these factors would be possible, as Wertheimer has already suggested, by varying these relative distances" (p. 166). It must be a very difficult task, however, to study the interactions among all the principles of organization, since this task is still not completed. This situation is a common one in psychology; that is, some significant independent variables are known, but the exact functional relationships between the independent variables and the dependent variable or variables are not known. The Gestaltists therefore proceeded, with respect to their laws of organization, in just the way they criticize in others. Demonstrations were constructed wherein the individual factors could be shown to operate, *other things being equal*. The laws of combination of the factors, and their relative strengths, are missing. An attempt to determine a more holistic description of the laws of perception might well have been one of the Gestaltists' first orders of business.

Learning Principles

Gestalt psychologists have not worked nearly so extensively in learning as in perception. However, they have done some highly suggestive studies in learning. Köhler's *The mentality of apes* (1925) was based largely on his study at the anthropoid station at Tenerife in the Canary Islands, where he had been marooned during World War I.

It was natural that Köhler saw the problem-solving process in quite a different way from the behaviorists and associationists, or even the functionalists. Gestalt psychology is based on the premise that perception is determined by the character of the field as a whole. What is more natural than that the Gestaltists should explain learning and problem solving in an analogous fashion? That is just what Köhler did. Problem solution for him became a *restructuring* of the perceptual field. When the problem is presented, something necessary for an adequate solution is missing. The solution occurs when the missing ingredient is supplied so that the field becomes meaningful in relation to the problem presented. For example, one of the chimpanzees in Köhler's experiment was given two sticks which could be joined, enabling him to reach a banana that could be reached in no other way. After many futile attempts to reach the banana with one stick by itself, the chimp gave up and continued to play with the sticks. When he "accidentally" joined the two sticks, he immediately reached out with his new tool and got the banana. The missing perceptual ingredient for the solution had been applied. The perceptual field had been restructured.

The Gestaltist would want us to notice that the missing *ingredient* in the solution was not a missing *element*. All the elements were always present, but they were not "seen" in the right way. Our very language, in using the word *seen* in this context, tells us what a close analogy exists between perception and problem solving.

Just as "good" perceptual figures are stable, so learning, once achieved through this insightful restructuring, is stable. The Gestaltists regarded some kinds of learning as requiring a single trial, with the performance being easily repeatable without further practice.

Much Gestalt work has concerned problem solving rather than learning. The two areas can be distinguished roughly. Problem solving involves the combination of already learned elements in such a way that a solution is achieved. Learning is usually concerned with the acquisition of relatively simpler, more discrete responses. The distinction is to some extent arbitrary, as is certainly clear from Köhler's experiments with apes, which could be considered either learning or problem solving.

Wertheimer's *Productive thinking* (1945) suggested effective methods for problem solving. He applied the Gestalt principles of learning to human creative thinking. He said that thinking should be in terms of wholes. One should take a broad overview of the situation and not become lost in details. Errors, if inevitable, should at least be good errors, errors with a possibility of success, not blind errors made without regard to the limitations of the situation as a whole upon acceptable solutions. Just as learners should *regard* the situation as a whole, so teachers should *present* the situation as a whole. They should not, as Thorndike had done to his cats, hide the true solution or the true path and require errors. One should not be required or even allowed to take a single blind step but rather should always be required to keep the goal and the requirements for success in view.

Duncker (1945) performed an extensive Gestaltist analysis of the problem-solving process. He analyzed the factors in the situation and in the problem-solving procedure which determine difficulty of solution. Like Wertheimer, he believed that the tendency of the subject to restrict the possible solutions is one of the most serious obstacles to successful performance. He devoted a great deal of attention to discussion of fixedness of response. The inevitable errors played some role because thinking might not regress to the original ideas about possible solutions when leads were found to be false. Thus errors could sometimes direct further responses rather than simply being eliminated. The requirements of the problem situation "ask for" a solution with the required attributes; that is, responses are determined by the total situation, the problem field. Duncker's classic monograph contains many ingenious ideas and examples but has the usual Gestalt characteristic of being largely nonexperimental and programmatic.

Most modern techniques of instruction are designed to prevent errors, as Wertheimer suggested they should be. For example, programmed instruction, which is an outgrowth of quite another tradition, is designed to eliminate errors. This type of instruction is not based on Gestalt theory but on repeated experiences with what works best. Similarly, "errorless discrimination," as developed by Terrace (1966), is a very effective way to teach simple sensory discriminations to animals. Modern cognitive psychologists both minimize errors and maximize motivation by training from the last steps in a sequence of goal-directed behaviors toward the first, so that the learner experiences the goal immediately and always works toward it. Wertheimer's suggestions thus seem to be supported, after decades of additional work.

The Gestaltists have generally emphasized the *directed* character of behavior in problem-solving situations. Thorndike emphasized trial-and-error learning, as though the behavior of the animal in the situation were blind and random. Köhler and Wertheimer pointed out the blindness of Thorndike's situation. They believed that the random nature of the activity inhered not in the animal but in the situation. A good solution is possible only if an overview of the situation is available to the animal. In Thorndike's puzzle-box situation, only the experimenter can see the overall situation. The animal is *reduced* to trial and error by the situation, but to say that learning in general is by trial and error is itself an error.

Thorndike, a favorite Gestalt target, had stated that learning is a gradual process of elimination of errors with the accompanying fixation of the correct response. The Gestaltists said that more frequently, learning is not gradual at all but is rather a process involving insight. We might think of insight as a sudden shift in the perceptual field. There seems to be no basic theoretical reason why the Gestaltists should say that the perceptual shift should be sudden rather than gradual, but Köhler's observations indicated to him that sudden learning does occur. It is also true that perceptual changes tend to occur fairly quickly, so the Gestalt tendency to identify perception and learning encouraged a belief that learning would occur quickly.

Four behavioral indices of insight learning are usually cited: the sudden transition from helplessness to mastery, the quick and smooth performance once the correct principle is grasped, the good retention, and the immediacy with which the solution can be transferred to other similar situations involving the same principle. Once Köhler's chimpanzees joined the sticks to reach a banana, they joined them in other situations for reaching other objects.

The disagreement about whether learning is continuous, as Thorndike thought, or sudden, as the Gestaltists thought, was called the continuity-noncontinuity controversy in learning. According to the continuity position, each trial or reinforcement contributes some increment of response strength. This assumption is denied by the noncontinuity position, which emphasizes sudden discontinuous increments, such as are associated with insights, rather than a slow building up of strength.

In this controversy, as in many similar controversies, there is no winner or loser. Both continuous and discontinuous improvements in performance occur. A complete learning theory will have to deal with both types of changes. The variables affecting learning will all have to be related to performance, and different values of the independent variables will produce continuous and discontinuous learning curves.

Spence (1940) showed that Hull's theory, which treats *learning* as continuous, can predict sudden increments of *performance* if the constants in his equations are chosen properly. For example, if there is a sudden shift in the number of hours of food deprivation from one trial to the next, there will be a sudden increment in performance. The Gestalt assertion is just that such sudden changes can occur, although presumably as a function of other variables besides shifts in deprivation. The Gestalt learning theorist is then faced with the task of writing the equations needed to make a Gestalt learning theory as sophisticated as its competitors, which can now predict "Gestalt" phenomena.

Insight is supposed to involve restructuring of the situation as a whole. Thus it is predicted, from Gestalt theory, that animals will sometimes respond to relationships between stimuli rather than to local stimuli. This is exactly what is said to occur in perception, where the percept depends upon the whole field rather than upon local stimulation. As in perception, behavior should depend on the situation as a whole.

The transposition experiment is an example of the action of this principle. An animal is trained to respond to the darker of two gray cards; food is always found behind this dark card. The traditional associative explanation of what has happened in training is that the dark card is associated with reward, so that the animal approaches it. The lighter card has no association with reward and is not approached. However, when the dark card is put with a still darker card, the animal under some conditions chooses the new darker card, even though responding to it has never been reinforced. Koffka (1935) said that in looking at the two cards, a *step* is perceived from lower to higher brightness, and the animal responds to the step. Thus the whole field must be considered in making predictions.

Spence (1937b) derived the observed relational response by introducing gradients of generalization of reinforcement from the reinforced card to other values of gray and gradients of inhibition from the lighter card to other values. If the generalization curves are given appropriate shapes, the animal should respond to the new card rather than to the previously reinforced one, because the new card is suffering less inhibition from the previously nonreinforced card. The significant aspect of Spence's transposition theory was that it not only explained transposition but also predicted that transposition should *not* occur when the new test stimuli were too far away from the training stimuli. It was then demonstrated that transposition often failed under such conditions.

Spence never derived the underlying gradients of excitation and inhibition from experimental observations; he merely assumed the gradients that he needed in order to account for transposition effects. Hearst (1968) showed that *empirically derived* gradients could be used to predict discrimination behavior with moderate success. Even so, the general Gestalt point is again made. The combination of simple elements presents an emerging complexity which requires new laws for its description. In this case, new equations are required for describing generalization gradients and methods of combining them.

Krechevsky (1932) noted that animals tended to persevere over a number of trials with systematic responses. For example, the animal might respond in terms of a position habit and then suddenly shift to a choice of the brighter of two stimuli. These consistent tendencies he called *hypotheses,* by analogy with a problem situation in which a human being tries out various alternative solutions until the correct one is found. This finding lent some support to the Gestalt claim that animals did not respond blindly or randomly as they searched for the solution to a problem. Spence (1936), however, observed that the word *hypothesis* is just a name for a persistent response tendency whose history of reinforcement we do not know. Harlow (1951) pointed out that the typical paradigm for insight learning is one in which we do not know the past experience of the animal with the component parts of the problem. Insight did not occur in some experiments in which the subjects were animals without such previous experience.

Levine (1970) demonstrated that human subjects who are led into generating hypotheses belonging to a class that is not relevant to the solution of a problem may persist for 100 trials or more in making errors. This is for problems as simple as "The black card is correct, and the white card is incorrect." If subjects were responding in terms of a simple reinforcement theory, they should solve the problem immediately. Levine's experiments provided convincing evidence that human beings, at least sometimes, behave in a way more easily consistent with a Gestalt view of learning than with associationist alternatives.

Thus Gestalt psychology has pointed to interesting learning phenomena, but it has not worked out detailed principles of learning. Gestalt interpretations have sometimes ignored critical background factors that might help to account for the observed outcomes on the basis of simple behavioral principles. The Gestaltists' theorizing has often been highly general, and their explanations ad hoc.

Despite these weaknesses, Gestalt psychology has made a decisive contribution to the areas of learning and problem solving. Modern cognitive psychology—and Levine's work is an example—takes its heritage directly from Gestalt psychology as well as from the information-processing tradition which is related to computer and communication systems. Cognitive psychology is making more and more inroads in the field of learning and in doing so is carrying out the program of Gestalt psychology. The founders of Gestalt psychology virtually told the fortune of modern psychology.

THE DEVELOPMENT OF GESTALT PSYCHOLOGY

Kurt Lewin's Vector Field Theory

Kurt Lewin (1890–1947) is among the most significant contributors to psychology. He was a brilliant researcher, as recognized even by his severest critics. The series of experimental studies which he directed at the University of Berlin in the 1920s is a model of theoretical creativity and imagination coupled with appropriate methodology. Later, in the United States, he was the acknowledged leader among those doing innovative social research. Lewin was also an ingenious theorist. He is best known for his development of vector field theory, which he applied to the behavior of persons rather than to perceptual fields.

Although Lewin was associated with the most active center of Gestalt psychology, at Berlin, he was not closely associated with the orthodox issues. His own systematizing took him in new directions, at first in the direction of motivational effects and later toward social psychology, in particular attitude change and leadership. In a letter to Köhler that constitutes the preface to his book *The principles of topological psychology*, Lewin (1936) probably expresses his relationship to Gestalt psychology most succinctly: "I have tried my best to destroy the myth that Gestaltists do not attack each other" (p. viii). Thus Lewin may have felt most like a member of the group when he was criticizing it.

Lewin's early research was concerned largely with motivational problems of individual subjects, which led to an interest in problems of personality organization. His later efforts in social psychology included the beginning of the group dynamics movement and assistance in the development of *action research* (i.e., research directed at producing changes in the behavior of groups of people). In between these two phases, he was concerned with problems of the nature of learning, cultural factors in personality development, and child development. In all of these diverse areas Lewin used the same fundamental approach: an emphasis always upon the psychological, rather than just the environmental, factors in the situation. This emphasis is related to the earlier Gestalt distinction, most explicitly made by Koffka, between the "behavioral" and the "geographical" environments. The crux of the distinction is that the effective meaning of environmental conditions depends upon more than merely physical attributes; that is, a description in terms of such factors alone is inadequate. An individual's *perception* of the physical attributes determines how that individual will react.

Lewin's Career   Kurt Lewin was born in Prussia in 1890 and received his higher education at the Universities of Freiburg, Munich, and Berlin (Ph.D., 1914). He was thus present during the formative years of the Gestalt movement. After a 5-year interlude of military service, he returned to Berlin and remained in various academic capacities until 1932, when he came to the United States. He spent that year as visiting professor at Stanford, and the following 2 years at Cornell. The decision to establish permanent residence in this country was made as a consequence of the rise of Nazi power in Germany, where his Jewish ancestry might well have led to his demise. Lewin went to the Child Welfare Station of the University of Iowa as professor of child psychology in 1935, and finally to Massachusetts Institute of Technology in 1944. In this last appointment he was director of the Research Center for Group Dynamics, a position which he had held for only 3 years at the time of his early death in 1947.

Marrow, in his biography *The practical theorist* (1969), describes Lewin as an enthusiastic, charming, and intellectually scintillating man. He was as far from the popular image of the German professor as Wundt and Titchener were close to it. Marrow describes him as being so democratic that he was a sort of natural American. He was very close to his students and in the habit of making unannounced visits to their homes. Through them, as well as through his own research and conceptualization, he has left an indelible mark on American social psychology.

Roger Barker reported to Marrow that Lewin never had any conception of when to stop once he had begun a stimulating discussion. Only the excuse that he had to get home to his wife saved Barker from complete exhaustion on many occasions. Perhaps that level of intensity accounts in part for Lewin's death of a heart attack when he was only 56.

Lewin's major publications were journal reports and contributions to various collections of papers. His papers have been collected in four small volumes. The first two of these, *A dynamic theory of personality* (1935) and *Principles of topological psychology* (1936), represent the European phase of his career; the last two collections, *Resolving social conflicts* (1948) and *Field theory in social science* (1951), report the later, American, phase.

Topology and Hodological Space Lewin selected topology, a relatively new geometry, as a mathematical model for psychological processes. This was a natural development arising from the use by the earlier Gestaltists of topological analogies to describe isomorphism. Topology is a geometry in which spatial relationships are represented in a nonmetrical manner. Positional relationships between areas or regions are maintained in spite of changes in size and shape. The primary concern is with connections between bounded regions and with their spatial relationships. For example, one area will remain inside another despite stretching and distortion. Brown (1936) gave a simplified introduction to Lewin's use of topology.

Lewin thought that positional relationships were the best representation of the structure of psychological relationships. However, the topological model had a serious limitation: It lacked directional concepts. To represent direction, Lewin invented a new qualitative geometry (1938), which he named *hodology* (from the Greek *hodos*, which is translated as "path"). He used *vectors* in hodological space to represent dynamic directional factors in psychological relationships.

Cartwright (1959, pp. 61–65) reported that later researchers substituted a new mathematical tool, the linear graph, for Lewin's topology plus hodology. On the planar maps which Lewin used to represent life spaces, no more than four regions can have mutual boundaries. This limits the complexity of structure which can be represented on two-dimensional maps. On a linear graph, an indefinite number of points (which replace regions in the hodological representation) can be interconnected. The linear graph can also represent asymmetrical relationships, as when movement can occur from region A to region B, but not back to region A. For example, one can move from not having a college degree to having one, but not back. There is no natural way to represent these asymmetries on the map.

Life Space Lewin's objective in adapting and inventing such geometries was to clarify his conceptualization of the psychological field, or *life space*. The life space is most simply defined as the totality of effective *psychological* factors for a given person at some particular time. It consists of a number of differentiated *regions,* which represent significant conditions in the person's life. Although the totality of factors is emphasized in definitions such as the above, in actual practice only the most relevant ones are ordinarily included in diagrammatic presentations of the life-space concept.

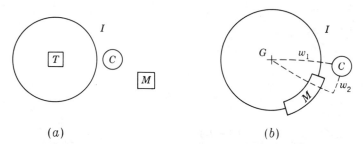

(a)   (b)

FIGURE 7-3
Situation in which a young child wishes to reach a toy that lies inside a circular barrier: (a) physical situation; (b) psychological situation. C, child; T toy; I, barrier; M, mother; G, goal; w^1, w^2, paths. (*Source: Lewin, 1936, p. 147*).

Let us illustrate Lewin's distinction between physical and psychological representations by an example from his writing. Figure 7-3a shows the physical situation, and Figure 7-3b shows the psychological representation, where a goal object (toy) is placed out of reach within a circular area.

Direct physical approach to the goal via path $w1$ is not possible, but psychological locomotion via path $w2$ is effective if mother can be persuaded to obtain the toy. Although a physical barrier is present in this example, the same psychological situation might be produced if the barrier were a verbal restriction, especially for an older child. In similar situations, the barrier might consist of personal or intraorganismic factors like politeness in a child trained not to take things without asking, or timidity, or fear. In these cases the physical picture would show no barrier, but the psychological representation of this slice of life space would look very much like that shown in Figure 7-3b.

A more complex example of a life space is portrayed in Figure 7-4. Here Lewin depicted a series of locomotions involving an occupational choice by a young man. Lewin (1936) pointed out that the passing of the college entrance examinations, while not a physical locomotion, represents a "real change of position in the quasi-social . . . life space. . . . Many things are now within his reach which were not before" (p. 48). It is this kind of crossing from one region to another that is emphasized in the life-space schema. Note that this is another example of the kind of directionality with which Cartwright was concerned; the exams, once passed, cannot be unpassed.

Important dimensions of the life space, as Lewin conceptualized it, are its temporal and reality characteristics. As children grow older, their life spaces become increasingly differentiated into regions, and they develop clearer temporal and reality-irreality

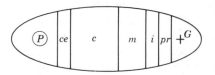

FIGURE 7-4
Situation of a boy who wants to become a physician. P, person; G, goal; ce, college entrance examinations; c, college, m, medical school; i, internship; pr, establishing a practice. (*Source: Lewin, 1936, p. 48*)

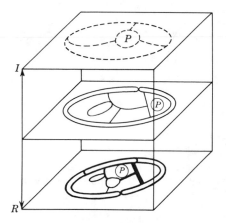

FIGURE 7-5
Representation of different degrees of reality by
an additional dimension of the life space. *R,* more
real level; *I,* more ideal level; *P,* person. In a level
of greater reality the barriers are stronger and the
person *P* is more clearly separated from the
environment. (*Source: Lewin, 1936, p. 200.*)

dimensions. For example, children begin to plan for the future as well as to respond
more effectively in longer time units. Further, they begin to use imagery and fantasy
and thus to live, in some degree, on an irreality level. There they are less restricted
in behavior by the usual barriers of the real world.

The reality dimension is illustrated in Figure 7-5, in which Lewin showed three
levels of this variable in the life space. Lewin considered this dimension highly significant in a psychological analysis, and he paid considerable attention to it. He did
not believe that an absolute reality or irreality dimension was tenable. What at one
instant may be considered reality may be altered by new events and experiences.
Furthermore, as the individual matures, the reality-irreality dimension broadens and
becomes more differentiated (Lewin, 1936, p. 204).

Perhaps the most widely known Lewinian contribution within the life-space framework is his conceptualization of conflict. He described three basic types of conflict
that produced frustration: approach-approach, approach-avoidance, and avoidance-
avoidance. Approach-approach conflict occurs when an individual wishes to achieve
two goals, only one of which is obtainable. An example is having two invitations for
the same evening. Approach-avoidance conflict occurs when a goal has both desirable
and undesirable features, as when one wants the money but not the effort involved in
a job. An avoidance-avoidance conflict is present when two anticipated consequences
are both undesirable. A typical example would be the necessity either to accept an
unwanted invitation or to offend an esteemed friend. This last type of conflict is
characterized by a vacillation between the alternatives or by an attempt to escape the
situation ("leave the field"). One might literally leave town for the weekend.

One misinterpretation of Lewin's life space occurs often enough to demand discussion. This is that the life space is the same as the phenomenal world of the person
who occupies the life space. That is not true. Lewin intended the life space to be a
representation of the factors which influenced the behavior and perception of the
individual. Some of these factors might be quite unconscious. Thus the life space is
a conceptual device in the service of the scientist. The phenomenology of the individual
may be either close to or rather distant from the life space as conceptualized by the

psychologist. If an individual believed too many things that were not true, his or her phenomenology might be quite unlike the life space. Although the life space is intended to represent the *concrete* reality in which the individual is immersed, it also shares an *abstract* quality with theories like Hull's.

Lewin's System   Lewin never produced a completely integrated system; when he was not busy with methodological problems in field theory, he worked on a number of different empirical and theoretical problems. All of them involved somewhat the same general type of working assumptions and procedures and to a great extent the same constructs. However, no serious attempt was made by Lewin to coordinate these concepts into a grand scheme (cf. Cartwright, 1959). The systematic development that he did produce tended to be loose and flexible, as indicated in the following criticism of his learning theory by Estes (1954):

> This informal development of coordinating definitions in use enables the theorist to give plausible accounts of concrete situations, but with no possibility of having the theory refuted by the outcome of the behavioral situations, since the correspondence between theoretical and empirical terms is adjusted in accordance with the empirical findings and is never formally incorporated into the system. Flexibility is obtained at the cost of testability. (p. 332)

We have chosen the series of researches involving Lewin's assumption of the *tension system* to give the flavor of his work. These studies were all based upon implications of the one central concept. Lewin himself has provided a theoretical account of these researches, emphasizing the formal assumptions and derivations (Lewin, 1940, pp. 13–28; 1944, pp. 4–20). Our treatment follows this account as well as the more informal description given by Deutsch (1954, pp. 199ff).

The background for Lewin's development of the construct of the tension system goes back to his first psychological research (Lewin, 1917). He was interested in refining some of Ach's earlier research (Ach, 1910) on the strength of the will. The general procedure had been to establish associations of nonsense syllables through repeated pairings and then to evaluate the strength of the voluntary factor, manipulated by instructions, by opposing it to the habitual tendency. (Hilgard, 1956, pp. 258ff., gives a description of this research and its theoretical rationales.) Lewin finally rejected Ach's attempt to supplement the association factor with such new constructs as set and determining tendency, constructs which were in the tradition of the Würzburg school. He felt that Ach had not gone far enough in his interpretation. Lewin substituted two voluntary factors for an association and a voluntary factor. He said that association per se provided no motive power. That power had to be accounted for in some other way. As he later put it:

> Dynamically, an "association" is something like a link in a chain, i.e., a pattern of restraining forces without intrinsic tendency to create a change. This property of a need or quasi-need can be represented by coordinating it to a "system in tension." By taking this construct seriously and using certain operational definitions, particularly by correlating the "release of tension" to a "satisfaction of the need" (or "reaching of the goal") and the "setting up of tension" to an "intention" or to a "need in a state of hunger," a great many testable conclusions were made possible. (Lewin, 1940, p. 14)

The first formal effort to test the tension-system proposition thus developed by Lewin was the dissertation research done by Zeigarnik (1927) under his supervision. Her experiments were based on the assumptions that (1) tension systems would be established in subjects who were given simple tasks to perform and (2) if such tension systems were not dissipated, as would normally occur with the completion of the tasks, their persistence would result in a greater likelihood of subsequent recall of the names of the tasks. Her results in several experiments substantially confirmed this prediction. Interrupted tasks were generally better recalled than completed tasks. There is an extensive experimental literature (Alper, 1948; Deutsch, 1954) concerning this interesting phenomenon, the so-called Zeigarnik effect.

The next experimental test of the tension-system construct was performed by Ovsiankina (1928). She showed that subjects would more often voluntarily resume interrupted than completed activities; for example, they would be more likely to start another jigsaw puzzle.

Following the confirmatory results of these first studies, more tests were performed. Among the better known are the studies of Lissner (1933) and Mahler (1933) on the role of substitute activities as dischargers of tension; of Hoppe (1930) and J. D. Frank (1935) on success and failure as related to "level of aspiration"; and of Karsten (1928) on "physical satiation," which concerns the problem of reduction in performance as a function of continued repetition. A summary of these and related studies was written by Lewin (1935, pp. 239ff.). The fruitfulness of the tension-system construct is well attested by the manner in which these concepts and problems have been used in personality theory (Deutsch, 1954).

Lewin's later concern with systematic problems of social psychology is illustrated by his wartime research on food habits (Lewin, 1943b; 1951, chapter 8). Lewin asked why people eat what they do. The interaction of psychological factors (e.g., cultural tradition, individual preference) and nonpsychological factors (e.g., food availability, cost) was investigated in the framework of a so-called channel theory. According to this viewpoint, most of the food that appears on the table is eventually eaten by someone, so the question reduces to the channels by which food is obtained for family use. The two major sources of food in the United Stated during World War II were store purchases and gardening (minor channels were country buying, home baking and canning, and the like). Lewin emphasized the role of the "gatekeeper"—usually the housewife—as the individual who determines for each channel how much of each foodstuff shall be procured and taken through the stages of preparation for eating.

The psychology of the gatekeeper, as Lewin phrased it, thus became a focal point of this research. Although several interesting questions were asked in the pursuit of the problem, we shall outline only one that received considerable attention. That is the question of the most effective procedure for changing opinions. Attention focused on individual versus group procedures. Lewin pointed out (1951, chapter 10) that an a priori expectation might well be that single individuals, being "more pliable" than groups of like-minded persons, should be easier to convince. An opposite conclusion, however, is supported by the preponderance of research on a variety of social problems. Standards are much easier to change and keep changed as a result of group discussions. In practical settings, when a group has problems, for example with race relations, it is best to work with the group as an intact unit.

One illustrative study concerned attempts to increase the consumption of fresh milk. Individual and group discussions of equal length were compared, with no pressure used in either. The results showed clearly that homemakers' compliance with the desired change was greater following the group procedure. Similar results held for other foodstuffs (like evaporated milk and orange juice) and for different social problems (such as productivity among factory workers). A public commitment to a new course of action generally produces more permanence of changed attitudes or behaviors. In some cases, the degree of change may even increase over a period of time following the experimental manipulations; when this happens, there is said to be a "sleeper effect." The conditions under which the sleeper effect occurs are quite restrictive. Greenwald, Pratkanis, Leippe, and Baumgardner (1986) have taken the history of study of this effect as their prototype of theoretical development. These authors believe that theoretical development is, to a very significant degree, a matter of progressive delineation of exactly when specific phenomena—like the sleeper effect—are and are *not* observed.

The research on food choices is a good example of the way in which Lewin's work combined theoretically important questions with practically significant problems and procedures. Food acceptability was of great importance when Lewin started his research during wartime. As the world's population increases, the problem may become even more acute. More generally, group processes are important to the well-being and survival of humanity. Enduring interest in group processes can be traced, to a very great extent, to Kurt Lewin (Bradford, Gibb, & Benne, 1964).

Lewin's Contributions   Lewin has few peers as both a creative conceptualizer and an ingenious experimenter. It was largely his ability to reflect his theoretical insights in concrete empirical studies that accounts for his preeminence. This ability was apparently based, at least in part, upon his insightful observations of everyday life. For example, his conceptualization of the tension system in relation to memory (Zeigarnik effect, above) is said to have been suggested by his observation that waiters in Berlin restaurants had a remarkably accurate memory for the amount of each bill, but only until it was paid (Hartman, 1935, p. 221).

Lewin's specific contributions to psychological theory included concepts like level of aspiration, which has enjoyed widespread acceptance in the field of personality and motivation. His classification of types of conflict is known by all psychologists and is used in research by many.

Finally, Lewin's pioneering efforts in social psychology would be enough to guarantee him a prominent place in the history of psychology. His early research in social psychology in the United States is exemplified by the pioneer studies (Lewin, 1939; Lippitt, 1940; Lippit & White, 1943) on behavior in social climates that were experimentally manipulated. For example, leadership techniques were experimentally varied in boys' clubs. Laissez-faire, democratic, and autocratic techniques were compared, and various types of behaviors, such as aggressive, were correlated with the different social climates that resulted (Lippitt & White, 1943). These studies opened up a new area of research and influenced educational and social practices (Cartwright, 1959).

The final phase of Lewin's research, in group dynamics, occurred when he was more of an administrator and supervisor. In *Resolving social conflicts* (1948), Lewin reported on experimental efforts to change social behavior in real everyday situations (such as interracial factory workshops). It is unfortunate that his death at only 56 prevented him from contributing further to this type of research.

The lines of work started by Lewin certainly did not stop with his death. He was one of those rare individuals who are in tune with the times that are to come 25 to 50 years later. The problems connected with social influence and leadership are still under active study. Field observations, which so often gave Lewin his inspiration, are now a standard source of psychological data (Willems & Rausch, 1969). His concern, late in life, with psychological ecology probably provided part of the impetus for Barker's book on that topic (1968). Even his attempt to find parallels between different fields, best seen in his attitude toward field theory and his attempt to use mathematical formalism, may have provided part of the general background for the development of general systems theory (see Buckley, 1968, for papers in this area). Kurt Lewin was one of the germinal figures for modern psychology.

Few psychologists have been as eager as Lewin to contribute to the solution of social problems. Part of his practical interest is traceable to his own personal experience. He was in the German army in World War I and experienced the disaster that was postwar Germany. His mother died as a victim of the Nazis during World War II, and he felt the long arm of anti-Semitism even in the United States. It was a Jewish religious group concerned with the elimination of prejudice that funded the Research Center for Group Dynamics which Lewin founded at MIT. Circumstance and temperament combined in him to form a unique combination of theoretician and man of action—the practical theorist. No wonder, then, that his interests encompassed leadership and prejudice and that he devoted so much attention and ingenuity to methods of changing behavior.

So great was the effect of Lewin as a human being and as an investigator that one could call American social psychology a Lewinian development. However, Lewin's theory and the earlier Berlin developments have been almost forgotten. He changed his interests between his early and late years, and the early work was neither easily accessible nor easily understood. A book by de Rivera (1966) collected the early dissertations, related them to their theoretical background, and added some new theoretical suggestions. However, there is to date no marked indication of a renaissance in interest in the neglected early work of Lewin.

Brunswik's Probabilistic Functionalism

The psychology of Egon Brunswik (1903–1955) is difficult to categorize. He was not an S-R theorist, although he moved in the direction of behaviorism after he came to the United States. His research on the perceptual constancies was often related to orthodox Gestalt psychology, but Brunswik himself (1949, p. 57) explicitly denied any such historical or conceptual relationship. We will make of Brunswik an unwilling Gestaltist in our discussion, primarily because he persistently and successfully considered the totality of interacting factors in his research and conceptualizations. He consistently emphasized distal stimuli and behavioral consequences, as contrasted to proximal stimuli and responses. Thus Brunswik accepted the fundamentals of the Gestalt approach and fits into this category as well as into any other.

Brunswik's Career   Egon Brunswik was born in Hungary, where he received an unusually varied education. He was trained as an engineer and passed the first state examination before shifting to the study of psychology at the University of Vienna. There he was much influenced by contacts with the logical positivists in the so-called Vienna Circle. He studied psychology under Karl Bühler and took his doctorate in 1927. In the meantime, he passed the state examination for teaching mathematics and physics.

After several years of various academic appointments, a critical turning point in Brunswik's career occurred during the 1933–1934 academic year. E. C. Tolman, while visiting in Vienna, met Brunswik and was very impressed with him. Two years later Brunswik received a Rockefeller Fellowship and, largely at Tolman's instigation, was invited to serve as visiting lecturer and research fellow in psychology at the Berkeley campus of the University of California. In 1937, he returned to Berkeley as an assistant professor. He stayed there until 1955, when, after years of illness, he ended his own life.

Brunswik's Research   Brunswik is best known in psychology for his research on visual constancy factors, usually referred to as *thing constancy*. This research program was well begun in Europe and played a major role in attracting Tolman to Brunswik. The heart of Brunswik's thing-constancy research is the dichotomy between the physical nature of an object and its sensory representation. The extent to which the perceptual effect tends to approximate the more remote physical (distal) or the more immediate sensory (proximal) value is the fundamental problem of this kind of research. For example, consider a table. As a distal object, the table has a certain determinate physical length; as a proximal object it also has a certain length, determined by the physical distance occupied by its image on the retina. The physical, or distal, dimension remains stable, while a wide variety of conditions, such as distance or angle of view, affect the proximal dimension.

The major conclusion from Brunswik's thing-constancy research was that there is almost always a compromise in experience, or, more operationally, in the subject's reported judgment, between the distal and proximal values. Normally the subject tends to approximate more closely the distal, or real, characteristics of the object in spite of the various distorting conditions; hence the term *thing constancy*. The index of the distal influence (Thouless's "regression to the real") is called the *Brunswik ratio*. This ratio is unity when constancy is perfect, that is, when perceived factors such as size, shape, and brightness are independent of distance, angle of tilt, luminous flux, or other proximal variables. On the other hand, when the proximal (in this case, retinal) stimulus completely determines the perception, the Brunswik ratio is zero. Thus the ratio reflects, on a scale ranging from 0 to 1, the degree to which the distal (object) aspects of the stimulus situation determine perception.

A specific example of thing constancy is size constancy: the tendency to see things as the same size regardless of distance. If the perceived size of the object departs just as much from the retinal size as the actual object size departs from the retinal size, then constancy is perfect and the Brunswik ratio is 1.

In subsequent research Brunswik extended this basic methodology to new problems. First, within the area of perception, he brought into his experiments such variables as monetary value. For example, in one experiment (Brunswik, 1934, pp. 147–150; see also Brunswik, 1956, p. 78) the experimenter asked subjects to make comparisons between cards containing varying numbers of coins of varying sizes and monetary values. In accordance with the basic principle repeatedly demonstrated in the simpler research, judgments of equality between stimuli were compromised to some extent by each of the three variables. Later, under the influence of Tolman and American neo-behaviorism, Brunswik became interested in instrumental behavior as well as in perception (cf. the early collaborative paper, Tolman & Brunswik, 1935). Brunswik had noted that organisms could use varying cues to arrive at the same knowledge of an object; Tolman had noted that organisms could use various behavioral means to reach the same ends. The two joined their ideas in a paper and expressed their common core of ideas in the concept of *vicarious function,* which meant that cues or behaviors could act vicariously for each other.

Brunswik (1939b) also attacked the problem of *partial* or *intermittent* reinforcement. He thought that the all-or-none reward situation that had been used almost exclusively in learning experimentation up to that time failed to represent normal situations. Accordingly, he varied the proportion of reward to total trials in the two ends of a standard T maze. The rat subjects cooperated by choosing each side in rough proportion to the probability of reward in the two ends; that is, the rats "probability matched."

Brunswik's System The probabilistic functionalism that Brunswik came to feel most adequately systematizes psychological problems was a direct and logical outgrowth of the research program outlined above. Brunswik's system is *probabilistic* since it holds that the perceptual and behavioral goals in the natural environment are usually related only probabilistically to cues and responses. The system is a *functionalism* because it is concerned primarily with the degree of success, or achievement, in perception and instrumental behavior.

An illustration of Brunswik's systematic thinking is his conceptual framework (1939a) in which a succession of temporally and spatially ordered "levels" or "layers" of variables is envisioned. These range from the temporally most remote (those furthest back in the past of the individual) through manipulable physical objects (distal stimuli) to the outer physical areas of the organism (proximal stimuli) and thence to intraorganismic functions and states. On the response side, a comparable array is conceptualized, from proximal reactions through distal effects (achievements in regard to environmental objects) to long-range successes and ultimate products of the individual's life span. These relations are represented in Figure 7-6. Brunswik used his conceptual framework to describe psychological systems. For example, both structural and Gestalt psychologists, according to Brunswik's analysis of the situation, confined themselves primarily to the study of the relationships between proximal stimuli (level *a* in the scheme of Fig. 7-6) and intraorganismic events and dispositions (level O). Classical behaviorism studied *a-A* relationships for the most part. Psychoanalysis would be described as concentrating on *c-O* relationships. The concentration of a functionalism or a molar behaviorism would tend to be on *b-B* relationships (the *O* level may also enter into nearly any systematic position).

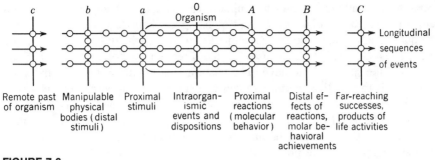

FIGURE 7-6
Scheme of the organism in its surroundings. (*Source: Brunswik, 1939a, p. 37.*)

Leeper (1966), in a generally balanced and friendly critical review of Brunswik's contribution, points out that Brunswik was prone to take too simple a view of what others were doing. Thus each of the groups referred to in the previous paragraph might find something objectionable in Brunswik's description of its efforts. However, his characterizations demonstrate an important and unique feature of his thought: he integrated history, methodology, and research into one conceptual structure.

Brunswik's lens model (1952), shown in Figure 7-7, illustrates the way in which a great variety of different but interacting processes can be initiated from a single focal factor (such as an object in the stimulus situation in perception research or some aspect of a learning problem in instrumental behavioral research). It also shows how a similarly differentiated array of response processes mediated within the organism may focus into a single perceptual or instrumental achievement. For an illustrative commonplace application of the lens model, consider the behavior of a baseball player who is

FIGURE 7-7
The lens model: Composite picture of the functional unit of behavior. (*Source: Brunswik, 1952, p. 20.*)

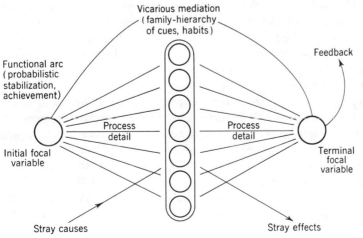

attempting to catch a high fly ball (the "initial focal variable"). Many perceptual cues emanate from the ball in flight as a result of its speed, height, and distance. These must be quickly taken into account by the fielder, who is estimating its trajectory and ultimate destination. Such "stray causes" as the direction and force of the wind and the position of the sun may also have to be taken into account. On the response side, the fielder needs to mobilize energies so that movement toward the ball can be timed properly and must avoid interference from teammates, fences, and the like. An instrumental achievement like catching a difficult fly ball (the "terminal focal variable") is thus seen to be dependent upon the successful coordination of many "process details" on both the perceptual and response sides.

Leeper (1966, p. 423) suggested that Brunswik's thinking would be better represented by a two-lens model, rather than the single-lens model he actually used. The single lens was fine as long as Brunswick was concerned only with focusing cues in bringing about a stable central representation of the object. However, if the focusing of different behaviors on goal attainment is also to be represented, a second lens is needed, with the central response between them, the distal stimulus on the left, and the distal achievement on the right. Brunswik was taking a bit of poetic license in his simpler representation, combining two lenses and an organism into a single element which was, literally speaking, inadequate to carry out its assigned function.

Brunswik felt that the double convex model represented the manner in which an organism is able to mobilize its functions so as to maximize its use of cues emanating from distal stimuli and achieve a reasonable amount of success in its control of the environment. He felt that problems of distal relationships should be studied first, before problems of mediation by intraorganismic detail processes were investigated. He criticized those who used intervening variables, and in particular the early Gestaltists, for moving in toward the center of the organism when he thought they should be moving outward into the environment. Postman and Tolman (1959) made it clear, however, that Brunswik had no absolute prejudices against physiology but felt that psychology's original duty lay with distal investigations. In this respect Brunswik's position was remarkably close to Skinner's.

Hursch, Hammond, and Hursch (1964) followed up Brunswik's suggestion that the relationships represented in the lens model could be more precisely studied by using multiple correlation methods. Their techniques make it possible to determine how well a subject could do on the basis of various ecological cues and how well the subject is actually using the available cues. They show how their analysis can be applied to a case of probability learning and to a case of clinical inference.

The same techniques have been used in other experiments (C. R. Peterson, Hammond, & Summers, 1965; Summers & Hammond, 1966). Naturalistic studies generally are now regarded as more respectable, and new statistical techniques—for example, multiple analysis of variance, which handles the large numbers of dependent variables typical of naturalistic studies—are continually being developed. The ubiquitous computer now simplifies making the extensive computations that are required, and problems which were prohibitively laborious 30 years ago are now within easy reach. If Brunswik were alive today, he would likely be turning out volumes of reports on naturalistic research.

Brunswik felt that research involving particular mechanisms should wait until the fundamantal achievement principles are worked out, because there is a high degree of substitutability among such mechanisms. On the response side, for example, a rat can depress a bar in many ways, and the Guthrie and Horton (1946) cats could tip a pole in many ways, all of which opened the door. In these cases, the terminal—focal— effect is the same regardless of the mechanism used to bring it about. Brunswik's suggestion that we study the overall situation first is typical of what Gestalt psychologists would suggest.

The same relationship of interchangeability among mechanisms may be illustrated on the perceptual side by the variety of cues that mediate visual depth perception (Postman & Tolman, 1959, pp. 511ff.). The distal stimulus here is represented as a focal point, shown on the left in the double convex lens model of Figure 7-7. A variety of different kinds of physical energies, represented by the diverging lines of the lens model, serve to produce the proximal distance cues (retinal disparity, accommodation, convergence, linear perspective, and the like), which are represented by circles in the center of the model. Intraorganismic mediating processes relate each proximal cue to the terminal perceptual event, in this case the distance judgment.

Several interesting points are suggested by this kind of analysis. The *ecological validity* of cues (or habits) is defined as the degree of correlation between each such proximal condition and the value of the distal stimulus. For example, the ecological validity of retinal disparity is generally higher than that of accommodation or convergence as a cue to distance. This means simply that retinal disparity is a more effective cue, correlating more highly with physical distance. But it is not essential; other cues can substitute for it and mediate depth perception. In its normal adjustment to the flux of events in the environment, the organism needs to have considerable flexibility with regard to which cues or habits are given the greatest weight. The necessarily probabilistic nature of the terminal focal events (perceptual and instrumental) is clearly indicated by this analysis. As Brunswik (1955a), said:

> The general pattern of the mediational strategy of the organism is predicated upon the limited ecological validity or trustworthiness of cues. . . . This forces a probabilistic strategy upon the organism. To improve its bet, it must accumulate and combine cues. . . . No matter how much the attainment is improved, however, distal function remains inherently probabilistic. (p. 207)

Brunswik and Kamiya (1953) reported a preliminary study of the ecological validity of one of the Gestalt principles of organization. They studied photographs of natural objects to see how often elements in proximity belonged to the same *objects*. If proximal elements belonged to the same object with high probability, the functional usefulness of the principle of proximity in perception would be demonstrated. Organisms that organized elements into wholes while taking the principle into account would tend to perceive the environment correctly. Brunswik and Kamiya found that there is a tendency for proximate elements to belong to the same object, but the tendency is relatively weak. This result is in perfect concordance with Brunswik's general claim that our behavior is necessarily probabilistic and that it needs to be guided by multiple cues. This research on proximity indicates that organisms could learn to organize elements via their experiences with the environment, but it is also possible that the visual system has "learned" the principle through evolutionary selection.

Brunswik's Emphasis on Representative Design Perhaps the most far-reaching aspect of Brunswik's conceptual formulation was his increasing emphasis on the need for psychology to use what he called *representative,* rather than systematic, design in its experimentation (Brunswik, 1956). This emphasis follows directly from the probabilistic functionalism which he developed. As long as rigorous control of variables is practiced, in the orthodox systematic design used by most psychologists, there will be serious limitations on the degree to which experimental results are representative of the natural behavior of the subject. In order to permit a more adequate analysis of the organism's achievements in relation to the environment, seen by Brunswik from his functionalistic position as the primary problem for psychology, a wider sampling of effective variables must be used, even if this means less rigorous control in the usual sense.

As a corollary to this position, the general laws aimed at in orthodox systematic research would have to be replaced by statistical statements in which only probability values can be expressed. Such statistical expressions concern the probabilities with which the various conditions sampled are found to correlate with the achievements of the organism in dealing with the environment. In representative designs, correlational techniques replace the statistical tests of differences that are usual in systematic designs.

Although the positive side of these methodological proposals is reasonably clear, Brunswik's criticisms of the orthodox type of experimental design may require further explanation. He felt that any experiment which deals with only one variable at a time, in the classic manner, is hopelessly inadequate to present a realistic picture of the organism's behavior. Although the recent trend toward multivariate design is a step in the right direction, it was in Brunswik's lifetime only a small and seriously limited one. Furthermore, the variables ordinarily manipulated were proximal rather than distal ones, in the conceptual framework described above; from Brunswik's point of view, this places the emphasis on the wrong kind of investigation.

Brunswik was also highly critical of the way in which variables were artificially "tied" and "untied," as well as "interlocked," in the orthodox systematic design. Although a detailed description of these problems is beyond the scope of this volume, the general point is that a truly representative design should permit a freer covariation among factors (see Postman & Tolman, 1959, pp. 516ff., for a presentation of this argument).

This point can be illustrated by the relatively simple example diagrammed in Figure 7-8, which Brunswik (1955a, pp. 194ff.) developed on the basis of a problem suggested earlier by E. B. Holt (1915). Imagine a flock of birds flying (1) over a green field (dashed arrow) and (2) southward (solid arrow). For the flock at the left of the figure, these two, variables are confounded, or tied. Merely returning the birds to point (○) does not resolve the confounding, nor does adding new subjects from the same population. The typical technique used to untie these two variables in systematically designed experimentation is called *diacritical* by Brunswik. It is indicated in Figure 7-8 by the movement of the birds to a new position (●), so that the two alternative

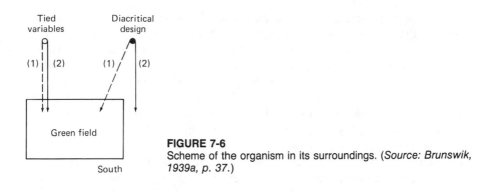

FIGURE 7-6
Scheme of the organism in its surroundings. (*Source: Brunswik, 1939a, p. 37.*)

interpretations can be clearly separated, that is, have different consequences. Birds either fly to the green field, and not directly south, or they fly south and thereby miss the green field. But, Brunswik (1955a) pointed out:

> We soon discover that southwardness is still tied to such factors as the general area of start, temperature and other climatic conditions, topographic landmarks, magnetic cues, and so forth; and so is the greenness of the field to its squareness or size. What we have accomplished in diacritical design is to separate or "split" an original encompassing cluster into two subclusters of tied variables; but we have not really "isolated" our variable as it may have seemed at first glance, and therefore are not yet entitled to speak of its attainment as a constant function. (p. 195)

For Brunswik the only satisfactory solution to this kind of problem would be a truly representative design in which a more adequate sampling of situational variables is possible. A partial solution would not be enough. Brunswik later (1956, p. 27) provided a simple example of the inadequacy of such artificial untying of variables in systematic design. In an experiment on judgment of personality traits, subjects were placed in identical body positions and given identical clothes to wear. While this experimental procedure controls for the influence of these two variables, it also makes impossible the assay of any normal interactions between the personality traits estimated and such factors as body tone and dressing habits. This typical experiment is incompletely designed, according to Brunswik. For completeness, one would have to include a much wider range of important variables in the behavior sampling (that is, have subjects take different positions and wear different clothes, while continuing to study the other variables).

The problem posed is indeed like the problem posed for the pollster asked to assess public opinion. One would like to sample the whole population, but that is impractical. The pollster therefore settles for a "representative sample" of the population. In the same way, the experimenter might like to sample all the variables, and all the inter-relationships between variables, in order to arrive at psychological laws. It would then be possible to use a systematic design, which would indicate all the interrelationships between variables. But such a procedure is far more difficult even than sampling a complete population of people. Thus the experimenter, too, must take a sample, and the most useful sample to take is not one that is arbitrarily chosen but one that characterizes the variables and their values and interactions *as they occur in the actual environment*. Even if we could do a complete systematic experiment, we would not know what organisms would do until we studied the contexts in which they would behave. Thus representative designs are necessary in principle as well as in practice.

J. J. Gibson (1904–1979) spent much of his professional life looking at Brunswik's "actual environment" to try to find out what properties of our surroundings carry the most constant and reliable information. His point of view was also functionalistic in that he viewed the senses as means for gathering information that was useful for the organism rather than as passive receptors that recorded whatever was present. One desirable characteristic of an information-gathering system would be that it concentrates on information which varies least under changes in variables which do not matter to the organism. Along these lines, Gibson (1966) said: "Above all, it should be remembered that the informative variables of optical structure are *invariant under changes in the intensity of illumination and changes in the station-point of the observer*" (p. 242). If one considers the infinitude of changes in illumination and station-point (the position from which an object is viewed) that take place during the life of an organism, it is clear that a system which preserved or responded to the results of such changes would have a tendency to overload. From this point of view, the structuralist concern with the analytic details of local stimulation was misguided if scientific interest is to be focused on the same things that are important in the lives of organisms. The organism, in order to function through a reasonable lifetime without being overloaded with information, must be constructed so that it focuses on invariants. These invariants turn out to be fairly complex relational properties of wholes. Thus efficient stimulus description must be molar stimulus definition, and the Gestaltists rest their case.

All of this means that the concept of constancy in perception has to be rethought. That is, *local* stimulation should not be expected to coincide with local response, for both are parts of a total field. The influence of that field determines the nature of the response to every local stimulus which is present. Thus the organism should be expected to see the same object as having the same characteristics regardless of its distance. Failure of constancy then becomes unexpected, and constancy becomes routine.

Brunswik's Contribution to Psychology   Brunswik's analysis of design problems is almost certain to have a continuing influence upon the future course of psychological science. There is evidence that his position is being implemented outside the experimental study of perception in which it originated. One example is K. R. Hammond's (1954, 1955) demonstration of the importance of representative design in clinical psychology. Research on the diagnostic use of test scores is criticized for not sampling adequately the personality characteristics of the examiners and the situational variables involved in the test administration. Frequently the range of examiners is severely limited, even to a single person, for the express purpose of eliminating variability in results. Such application of the typical systematic design unfortunately has not prevented investigators from generalizing their results to a presumably wide range of examiners and situations, as well as to a population of individuals. Extension of the principles of representative design to other experimental and clinical situations would seem to be indicated, regardless of the extent to which one accepts Brunswik's criticisms of orthodox systematic design.

It is possible to accept Brunswik's plea for more representative designs without denying the value of orthodox designs where the latter are appropriate, Leeper (1966) thinks that Brunswik did himself a disservice by overstating the case against systematic experimentation. In medical research, for example, one may be quite concerned with the effects of curative agents on particular diseases, and systematic design may be appropriate, sufficient, and efficient in answering the questions that arise.

Other criticisms of Brunswik's methodological points have centered on his apparent opposition to research on mediational mechanisms and his apparent assumption of a basic nonuniformity or nonuniversality in behavioral laws (Hilgard, 1955; Postman, 1955). We have already encountered the attempt by Postman and Tolman (1959) to clarify Brunswik's attitude on the study of mediational mechanisms. On the second point, Brunswik has taken pains to say that he did not think that behavioral laws are fundamentally probabilistic but only that their establishment is necessarily limited to statistical or probabilistic expression. As he has put it: "The crucial point is that while God may not gamble, animals and humans do, and that they cannot help but to gamble in an ecology that is of essence only partly accessible to their foresight" (Brunswik, 1955b, p. 236).

With the increasing influence of ethology on psychology, some of Brunswik's methodological points begin to look prophetic. However, ethology and comparative psychology show signs of beginning to fit together in harmony, just as we believe that systematic and representative design principles are destined to fit together. The pendulum must swing much farther before it will reach a point that would please Brunswik, but it is still swinging. We might wonder why it has taken so long. Hammond (1966, p. vi) suggests one reason: In the United States, Brunswik had only one student who completed a dissertation with him. Tolman (1966) tells us that Brunswik had to curtail his contacts in his last years, and Leeper (1966) bemoans the fact that Brunswik worked too much alone. Hammond's memorial volume, which contains the three papers just cited among several others, is helping to bring Brunswik's contribution to the attention of psychologists.

Eventually Brunswik will be recognized for the great thinker he was. He was deeply admired by the students who knew him, though they would not, or dared not, do dissertations with him. Besides his methodological contributions, Brunswik contributed substantially to our understanding of the perceptual constancies. He started the study of probability learning. He demonstrated how one might weave all one's work into a single piece. These achievements give him a significant place in the history of psychology.

Barker's Ecological Psychology

Roger G. Barker (1903–) is one of the few psychologists who have behaved as if they had ever heard of Egon Brunswik. Hammond (1966, p. 317) describes one of Barker's papers as a unique reconciliation of Brunswik's environmentalism with Lewin's interest in central processes.

Barker also combined Brunswik's attitude toward data collection with Lewin's type of interest. Brunswik collected much of his data in the natural environment, but he was interested primarily in perception. Lewin and his students collected much of their data in contrived situations, but they were interested primarily in motivational and social variables. Barker collected data about social interactions in natural field settings, and Barker and his students and coworkers have looked as closely at the environment as they have at the people in the environment. His results are the most convincing argument that could be made for his procedures.

Barker's Career   Barker never had the advantages attached to being a member of two cultures, as Brunswik and Lewin did. He received all his academic degrees from Stanford University (Ph.D., 1934). He met Lewin when Lewin came as a visiting professor in 1932, and later took a postdoctoral fellowship with him at Iowa. Their association led to their publication of the classic laboratory study of frustration and regression in children (Barker, Dembo, & Lewin, 1941). After serving as an instructor at Harvard in 1937–1938, an assistant professor at Stanford from 1942 to 1945, and a professor at Clark University from 1945 to 1947, Barker settled down as a professor at the University of Kansas. Barker and a colleague, Herbert F. Wright, established the Midwest Psychological Field Station in Oskaloosa, Kansas, in 1947. Barker's place in this volume is based largely on his first 20 years of work at the Midwest Station and at a station established in 1954, and operated on a periodic basis, in Leyburn, Yorkshire, England. Comparisons between the findings at the two stations contribute to the fascination of the observations made by Barker and his coworkers.

Barker's Research   Although Barker has made methodological discoveries and contributions to our theoretical attitudes as well, these have grown so naturally out of his research that we are justified in putting all of our emphasis there, just as he has done. We have seen that Barker has close conceptual and personal ties to Lewin. In some respects, their research too went in similar directions after they left Iowa. Lewin had been forced to take a close look at the "social ecology" when he was doing research on how food finds its way to the table. Lewin, however, tended to pull people out of their natural settings for his study and manipulation, and Barker did not.

Barker felt that Brunswik tended to overemphasize the disordered and probabilistic nature of the environment. However, at other times Brunswik's intuitive evaluations were prophetic of the empirical findings of Barker, as when he said:

> Ecological generality of experimental or statistical results may thus be established along with populational generality. In fact, proper sampling of situations and problems may in the end be more important than proper sampling of subjects, considering the fact that individuals are probably on the whole much more alike than are situations among one another. (Brunswik, 1956, p. 39)

Barker went out and sampled situations and subjects in the ecologies of Kansas and Yorkshire. When he reported, 22 years after Brunswik's statement, what he had found, he did not have to guess, as Brunswik had. Barker's (1968) summary was:

> The environment is seen to consist of highly structured, improbable arrangements of objects and events which coerce behavior in accordance with their own dynamic patterning. When, early in our work at the Field Station, we made long records of children's behavior in real-life settings in accordance with a traditional person-centered approach, we found that some

attributes of behavior varied less across children in settings than across settings within the days of children. We found, in short, that we could predict some aspects of children's behavior more adequately from knowledge of the behavior characteristics of the drugstores, arithmetic classes, and basketball games they inhabited than from knowledge of the behavior tendencies of particular children [Ashton, 1964; Barker & Gump, 1964; Rausch; Dittman, & Taylor, 1959, 1960]. It was this experience that led us to look at the real-life environment in which behavior occurs, with the methodological and theoretical consequences that are reported in this book. (p. 4)

One can only be grateful that Barker and his coworkers were led to look closely at this "real-life environment in which behavior occurs," for the results of that work have the kind of unself-conscious beauty seen in the well-fed Hereford cattle admired around Oskaloosa, Kansas. The data presented by Barker to illustrate molar units of individual behavior exemplify the general sturdy empiricism of the approach. Five-year-old Maud Pintner is in Clifford's Drugstore:

> Maud sat at the fountain waiting to order the treat her mother had promised her. On the stool next to Maud was her two-year-old brother, Fred; her mother sat beside Fred.
>
> 2:48 P.M. From her jeans pocket Maud now took an orange crayon. She brushed it across her lips as if it were a lipstick.
>
> Maud then leaned over, sliding her arms along the counter, as she watched a man serve a strawberry soda to his blond, curly-headed, three-year-old girl.
>
> Maud seemed fascinated by the procedure; she took in every detail of the situation. (Barker, 1968, p. 146)

From this, two molar units of behavior, called *behavior episodes,* were abstracted: *pretending to use lipstick* and *watching girl eat soda.* The isolation of these units, which might at first appear to be a simple task, is both difficult and of critical importance if effective field work is to be done. Barker (1968) says of behavior episodes: "Like crystals and cells that also have distinguishing attributes and limited size-ranges, behavior episodes have as clear a position in the hierarchy of behavior units as the former have in the hierarchies of physical and organic units" (p. 146).

Barker favors the gathering of data uncontaminated by the operation of the psychologist on the situation. The psychologist in the field can act as a transducer (and hence gather T data, rather than the O data gathered by the psychologist who operates in the situation). Barker illustrates the possible misleading conclusions that may be drawn from O data. His strictures are made doubly impressive by the fact that he uses his own classic study as the horrible example! Barker says:

> Experiments have provided basic information about the consequences for children of frustration, as defined and contrived in the experiments, e.g. Barker et al. (1941). But Fawl, who did *not* contrive frustration for his subjects, but studied it in transducer records of children's everyday behavior, reported (Fawl, 1963, p. 99): "The results . . . were surprising in two respects. First even with a liberal interpretation of frustration fewer incidents were detected than we expected. . . . Second . . . meaningful relationships could not be found between frustration . . . and consequent behavior such as . . . regression."

> In other words, frustration was rare in children's days, and when it did occur it did not have the behavioral consequences observed in the laboratory. It appears that the earlier experiments simulated frustration very well as defined and prescribed in theories, but the experiments did not simulate frustration as life prescribes it for children. (Barker, 1968, pp. 144–145)

Brunswik would no doubt have loved to have this Fawl-Barker commentary as an example of the weaknesses of systematic design. However, we should not *equate* Barker's preference for T data with Brunswik's preference for representative design. Brunswik did not say that data should be gathered in an undisturbed environment, and his research was not much like Barker's. Brunswik did follow subjects around in their daily routines, but he disturbed and manipulated those routines whenever he wished.

Nevertheless, Brunswik's and Barker's attitudes converge in suggesting the need for a thorough study of the ecology in which human beings grow and behave. Barker has not hesitated to make this point forcefully and directly. He says that it is ironic that we know the percentage of each element to be found in the earth's crust but do not have similar knowledge about man's *behavioral* surroundings. Barker makes his contribution to this effort by cataloging the "behavior settings" of Oskaloosa, Kansas. His appendix lists 220 behavior settings, from abstract and title company offices to x-ray laboratories. These are all public behavior settings; one misses, for example, Maud Pintner's living room. We await the Masters and Johnson of Oskaloosa, Kansas, to fill in the ecological picture.

In order to survey behavior settings, Barker had first to define a behavior setting, to discover or invent its identifying attributes. We shall list only the first three of seven attributes. First, a behavior setting consists of one or more standing patterns of behavior. Barker says that such patterns are clearly located in time and space, and he gives basketball games, worship services, and piano lessons as examples. Second, a behavior setting consists of standing patterns of behavior and milieu. That is, the setting includes the surroundings as well as the behavior, and the surroundings may be man-made (such as buildings) or natural (such as trees). Third, the milieu is circumjacent to the behavior—that is, the milieu surrounds the behavior, rather than vice versa. The interested reader is invited to consult Barker (1968) for the remaining defining characteristics as well as for the details of other aspects of his data and theory.

Finally, Barker considers the interactions between behavior settings and the behaviors of the people who inhabit them. We might expect him to see the behavior setting as a field and the persons in it as particles, on the basis of an analogy with physics. Instead, he borrows an almost opposite analogy from Heider and likens the behavior setting to a "thing" and the people who inhabit it to a "medium." An example of a thing is a stone, which can be thrown into a pond, the medium. The medium, although it has characteristics of its own, is more flexible than the thing and so adapts itself to it. People in general adapt themselves to behavior settings, partially because of the intervention of "environmental force units." But those are another part of the story, and we cannot tell it all. We shall conclude with the comment that Barker's work combines in a rare way the imaginative approach of the field theorist with the persistent empiricism which seems to have been most often connected with associationistic psychologists. Both his descriptive schemes and his theory of behavior settings show great promise for stimulating further work in ecological psychology. The availability of usable descriptive categories makes Barker one of the few psychologists rich enough to give away the following tidbits, among others, on a single page (1968, p. 141): Disturbances occur in a child's experience at a median rate of 5.4 per hour, half of the disturbances being occasioned by adults; the units of the Midwest children are shorter on the average than those of comparable "Yoredale" children; the Yoredale children receive devaluative input from adults four times as frequently as the Midwest children.

Barker's Contributions   It would be a serious injustice to regard Barker as a follower of Lewin and Brunswik who had simply worked out some elements of their programs. He cites each of them as often to reveal their errors as to express appreciation for their guidance. For example, one of Barker's most insistent themes is that the environment is organized into unique and unlikely patterns. Describing it as probabilistic or chaotic leads us in exactly the wrong direction. It turns out that the texture of the environment is highly patterned and that this structured environment coerces our behavior. Humans do not ingeniously organize a "blooming, buzzing confusion"; they respond appropriately and sometimes apparently unwillingly to a surrounding structure.

Barker (1969) has repeatedly called for the creation of tools appropriate to the task of studying the interdependence of human beings and their environment. Three very basic things are needed: archives, field stations, and statistical techniques that are appropriate to naturalistic studies. We have already said that the statistical techniques are in a phase of rapid development. Many of the archival problems are also being solved through the creation of better databases and via the development of communication and computer techniques that put distant archives literally at the fingertips of investigators. Field stations remain in short supply and will continue to do so until financial support becomes more readily available. As the tools for naturalistic research continue to develop, Roger Barker will continue to deserve credit both for pointing out what was needed and for doing more than his share of work toward producing it.

Although Barker has not produced truly encompassing theory, he showed us one way to describe the environment and the place of people in it. Perhaps even more important, he demonstrated that a naturalistic orientation need not lead to mere fuzzy thinking and a lack of empirical research. His study of Maud Pintner applying lipstick should help us to see that the gigantic flywheel of any society is not just James's habits, but also the behavior settings which, Barker has reminded us, every society provides.

GESTALT PSYCHOLOGY AS A SYSTEM

Definition of Psychology

The orthodox Gestaltists regarded psychology as being primarily the study of the immediate phenomenal experience of the organism. They included all areas of psychology within their scope, but they began with perception. Later Gestaltists—Lewin,

Brunswik, and Barker—paid increasing attention to behavior. Nevertheless, there was sometimes a tendency for Gestaltists to pay more attention to the relationships between antecedents and perception than to those between perception and behavior. The Gestaltists certainly differed from the behaviorists, who skipped the way station of perception to study the relationships between antecedents and behavior directly.

Postulates

Helson (1933) summarized the postulates of Gestalt psychology, and they can also be winnowed out of the original sources. Here we present only a few of the most basic postulates, some of which we regard as primary and some as secondary.

Gestalt psychology, like behaviorism, has only one primary postulate which has commanded wide acceptance. This is the belief that the whole is primary and has properties different from a sum of parts. A brief discussion cannot do this issue justice, but what follows is a summary of what has been said at more length earlier in the chapter. The whole dominates the parts and is the primary reality, the primary datum for psychology, the unit most profitable to use in analysis. The whole is not the sum, or the product, or any simple function of its parts, but a system whose character depends upon all of itself.

The secondary postulates, like those of behaviorism, are not necessary to Gestalt psychology, although its founders made them a part of *the* Gestalt psychology that developed. The most important of these is the isomorphism principle. A related principle is the contemporaneity principle. More specific secondary principles related to the whole-part attitude are the laws of organization. The noncontinuity postulate regarding learning has already been discussed as secondary.

None of the Gestalt postulates were entirely new. Even the basic postulate had been anticipated. The thing that made Gestalt psychology new was itself a Gestalt. It was the detailed organization and interrelationship of things that the Gestaltists said about the whole-part attitude as it affected psychology that distinguished their system from the philosophical forerunners who had made a case for emergence, and from the psychological forerunners who had made a case for phenomenology.

Mind-Body Problem

The Gestaltists, like most psychologists, tried to evade this issue by pointing to the unity of the organism and maintaining that there was no real problem. However, their recognition of experience and their use of the principle of isomorphism implied some kind of dualism, for isomorphism must be a relation between two sets of events. Isomorphism itself implies no particular subvariety of dualism. Since the Gestaltists attempted to make light of the problem, and even to deny any underlying dualism, the dual-aspect view seems most consistent with their position. This view provides two aspects that can be put into an isomorphic relation, while recognizing only one basic reality, which leaves the organism unitary and integrated.

Prentice (1959) expressed the Gestalt desire to avoid the issue:

Let me say once and for all that the concept of isomorphism is not an attempt to solve the mind-body problem in its usual metaphysical form. It takes no stand whatsoever on the question of whether "mind" is more or less "real" than "matter." Questions of reality and existence are not raised at all. Mind and body are dealt with as two natural phenomena whose interrelations we are trying to understand. . . . It comes nearest, perhaps, to what has sometimes been called the "double aspect" theory, the view that cortical events and phenomenal facts are merely two ways of looking at the same natural phenomenon, two faces of the same coin, as it were. (p. 435)

However, Prentice has apparently not been allowed to have his say "once for all," since R. I. Watson (1968) says that "by his statement of isomorphism Köhler was offering his particular solution to the age-old mind-body problem. Isomorphism was his way of integrating the mind with the rest of the world" (p. 448). Obviously, it is not easy to agree on what constitutes a stand on the mind-body position.

Nature of the Data

Immediate, unanalyzed experience obtained by naive introspection furnished the bulk of the data for Gestalt psychology. The "given," as they called such experience, was used as data. Behavioral data were also used, notably in the fields of learning, problem solving, and social interaction.

Because the behaviorists were concentrating on quite a different point, and because they deemphasized experience, one might not notice that both systems tended to accept the same kinds of data and that both groups were making a point that converged on the same criterion for acceptability of data. The behaviorists, although they rejected consciousness as an object of study, accepted verbal behavior as data when there was consistency and agreement within a given experimental situation. The Gestaltists, although they accepted experience and consciousness, rejected a certain kind of analysis of that experience. They retained what was given in consciousness. Now, the verbal behavior related to that "given" was very nearly the same as the class of verbal behavior which was acceptable to a behaviorist. Wertheimer, when he talked about the given, talked about trees and windows. Watson, when he wished to make the point that consciousness was not part of science, contrasted it with things that were: contents of test tubes, things that he could see and feel and lift. Both were using a language appropriate for describing objects. A long history of usage has demonstrated that we can agree about the meaning of such a language. Thus, although the two schools started from quite different perspectives, they tended to accept about the same kinds of data as being of interest in their kind of psychology. The Gestaltists were more tolerant; they could afford to recognize the results obtained with the structuralist kind of introspection, even though they regarded them as largely irrelevant. The behaviorists, whose whole existence was based on this methodological point, could not. Looking at the other end of the spectrum, the Gestaltists were also more tolerant than the structuralists, who did not regard Watsonian behaviorism as a true psychology. The

Gestaltists were perfectly willing to study behavior, but they wanted to relate it to psychological fields, not just to environmental variables.

Principles of Selection

For the Gestalt psychologist, every part of the field played some role in perceptual structuring. Thus the problem for the Gestaltist was not so much how the given was selected as how it was structured. Why, out of all the possible alternatives, did the actual structure emerge? One principle was that in a given perceptual whole, part of the perception will be figure and part ground. Rubin's laws governing the selection of the figure state how this segregation takes place. Wertheimer's laws of organization are also laws of selection in the same sense; they explain the particular form taken by the figure. Neither Rubin nor Wertheimer worked out the laws in great detail. J. J. Gibson's later work (1966) has done much more to specify the properties of stimuli which make them available as invariants for the organism's use. Maturana et al. (1960) used objective physiological measures to discover some of the properties of stimuli that were responded to by the frog's eye. Maturana and his coworkers found that the frog's eye contains cells that respond only to small curved moving objects within a circumscribed receptive area. That is, these cells "select" only those objects possessing the right *set* of complex properties. Gibson argues that such complex invariants are the primary stimuli for most human perception. All of this work fits neatly into the Gestalt tradition. None of this leads to a denial of the role of experience in determining which perception or which behavior would be selected. However, it does place more emphasis on the current situation, and it does draw attention to the complex relational properties of the situation as determiners of response.

Principles of Connection

The problem of connection takes a different form for Gestaltists. Since elementarism was rejected, one form of the problem of connection could be ignored. It is not meaningful to reconstruct wholes by connecting elements which are already parts of the whole. The Gestaltists believed that the *bundle hypothesis* was completely fallacious. The bundle hypothesis treated complex perceptions as though they were a bundle of simple perceptions and treated meaning as though it arose from such a bundling. Thus one of the Gestalt principles was negative; it was that the bundle hypothesis is invalid and that therefore one of the problems of connection is an artificial problem arising from an artificial analysis. The laws of organization are not principles of connection, for organizations are not elements connected. The laws state what structures will arise, not what elements will be connected.

It follows that Gestalt psychology would have more to say about how elements would be *related* in a particular whole than about how elements would be connected. The extensive work of Johansson (see Hochberg, 1957) on relative movement in two or more objects provides interesting examples. The general and surprising finding is that when the objects have a common component of movement, that component will be "partialed out" of the total movement and seen as a movement of a common frame. The remaining component of the total movement will be seen as movement of the separate objects relative to each other. What makes this surprising from a nonGestalt point of view is that neither the perceived movement of the "frame" nor the remaining relative movement component need exist in the objective stimulus! Two movements that do not exist are seen, and no movement that does exist is seen. However, this constructed movement makes for a simple description of the total movement, a "good" Gestalt. This is reminiscent of the situation in which Gestalt psychology originated, wherein two stationary objects give rise to the perception of movement.

Another form of the problem of connection cannot be avoided by any system. This is the problem of the connection or relationship between antecedents and consequents in laws. The Gestaltists stated that the relationships are dynamic and that the significant relationships are between fields.

CRITICISMS OF GESTALT PSYCHOLOGY

Gestalt psychology has been criticized chiefly for its nebulous character. Many hard-headed scientists have maintained that it does not really assert anything. This criticism may be at least partially justified. Harrower, one of Koffka's students, may be typical of the Gestalt school in her attitude toward the problem of definition of terms (1932):

> Much criticism has accrued to Gestalt theory for its use of the term "organization," which has not yet been sufficiently rigorously defined to meet the demands of many psychologists. And if, in the realm of perception, where as yet it has been predominantly employed, one meets with the criticism of its vagueness and ambiguity, how much more open to attack will be its preliminary appearance in investigations concerning the higher mental processes.
>
> And yet we deliberately give no precise definition of our use of the term, for with Dewey we believe that "Definitions are not ends in themselves, but instrumentalities for facilitating the development of a concept into forms where its applicability to given facts may best be tested." And since we believe that the concept is already in such form as to make it applicable to our facts, we leave more precise definition until experimental results can contribute towards it. (p. 57)

Harrower's cool bow in the direction of definition does not help in bringing experimental facts to bear. Psychologists need to have some way of distinguishing an organization from a nonorganization if they are to carry out empirical investigations on the subject. However, non-Gestaltists who are allegedly much concerned with definition may not have done much better. The often conflicting uses of words like *stimulus* and *response* are examples. Koch (1954) shows how a single author uses the words in inconsistent ways. The Gestaltist may just be more cautious, preferring to await more data before settling upon the meanings of words.

Gestalt psychology has been criticized for having too high a ratio of theory and criticism to experiment and positive empirical statements. Gestalt psychologists have certainly been experimental, but the devastation wrought by their criticisms has not always been repaired quickly by their positive statements. A closely related criticism is that Gestalt psychology has little predictive power. Gates (1942), in defending Thorndike's identical-elements theory of transfer of training, has presented a criticism which, if justified, invalidates the Gestalt theory of transfer:

> The Gestaltists somewhat similarly insist that transfer depends upon "insight." The objection to these views is not that they are wrong, but merely that they are too vague and restricted. To say that one transfers his learning when he generalizes is not saying much more than "You generalize when you generalize." "You get transfer when you get it." We must go deeper than that. In a scientific sense, no theory of transfer is a full or final explanation, but the Thorndike formulations at least point to a number of factors, observation and study of which enable us to improve learning. (p. 153)

Gates's criticism applies especially to the field of learning, where the associationists, functionalists, and behaviorists have presented some fairly specific theories. The Gestaltist has said, in effect: "Your theory is inadequate for the following reasons, and an adequate theory must take the following form." But the Gestaltist has often not said what the specific statements of the theory should be. This situation is being remedied by modern cognitive theorists, who have carried out studies using basic premises and methods which are consistent with the Gestalt approach.

When Gestaltists are more specific, they, like any other theorists, open themselves to other kinds of criticism. We have already mentioned Estes' criticism of Lewin's learning theory. London (1944) also criticized Lewin, in this case for his use of topological concepts in his hodological psychology. London claimed that Lewin had misappropriated and misused these concepts, had merely borrowed the terminology and some gross conceptualizations, and had failed to use the set of fundamental topological relationships needed to make the analogy meaningful. In answering this objection, Lewin argued that those who apply a mathematical model need coordinate only some of the conceptual relationships with empirical processes. He said (1951): "There can be no other meaning and no other proof of the applicability of these geometries to psychology than the fruitfulness of predictions based on such coordination" (p. 22). The issue between London and Lewin was: Did the topological model as appropriated by Lewin retain enough logical structure for it to retain any deductive power? If it did not, London's criticism was well taken, and there are no genuine predictions based on the coordination of topology and psychology. The evidence seems to us to indicate that Lewin's predictions were based on informal arguments and prior observations rather than on deductions within topology. Even so, the topological model may have had useful motivational and heuristic functions for Lewin and his students. Marrow (1969) says that they often carried on animated discussions in Lewin's home with the aid of a litter of paper and colored pencils which they used to make topological diagrams! Such a procedure may be important and valuable, even in the absence of formal rigor.

Other critics (Deutsch, 1954; Estes, 1954) have criticized Lewin for failing to define terms like *person* or *life space* clearly. A related complaint is that he concentrated too much on the central aspects of psychology and ignored the motor aspects, which meant that his concepts were not operationally defined. Brunswik (1943), who one might have expected to be a friendly critic, held that Lewin's life space suffered from "encapsulation into the central layer," which meant that it was "post-perceptual and pre-behavioral." Lewin's reply to this comment was that he did not think that psychology needed to study the objective physical and sociological factors which do not have implications for behavior. However, he was willing to study those objective factors which are potential determiners of the life space; this kind of study he called *psychological ecology* (Lewin, 1943a).

To summarize, their critics claimed that Gestaltists had too high a ratio of criticism to positive theory, and in turn too high a ratio of theory to empirical grounding. This makes Gestalt psychology look more nebulous and more programmatic than most systems. There is probably a grain of truth in the criticisms, but we must credit Gestalt psychologists with being uncommonly astute critics, creative theorists, and ingenious experimenters. They have always been a forward-looking group, and today's psychology shows many features inherited from Gestalt psychology.

Some other criticisms of Gestalt psychology are difficult to support and probably relate more to the complexities of the Gestalt position than to defects. For example, it has been said that Gestalt psychology is mystical or metaphysical. Actually, it seems as much a natural science as behaviorism. Heider states the Gestaltists' attitude very clearly (1970): "They abhorred vitalism because it implied the presence of a mysterious metaphysical agency that reaches into the world of nature from outside and is somehow made responsible for the order of the world as we perceive it" (pp. 135–136).

Weiss (1967) sums up the source of, and reply to, this kind of objection as follows:

> The unorthodox dissenters usually phrased their argument in the age-old adage that "the whole is *more* than the sum of its parts." Look at this phrasing and you will discover the root of the distrust, and indeed, outright rejection, of the valid principle behind it. What did they mean by stating that "an organism is *more* than the sum of its cells and humors"; that "a cell is *more* than its content and molecules"; that "brain function is *more* than the aggregate of activities in its constituent neurons"; and so on? As the term "more" unquestionably connotes some tangible addition, an algebraic plus, one naturally had to ask: "More of what? Dimensions, mass, electric charges?" Surely none of those. Then what? Perhaps something unfathomable, weightless, chargeless, nonmaterial? All sorts of agents have indeed been invoked in that capacity—entelechy, *elan vital,* formative drive, vital principle—all idle words, unpalatable to most scientists for being just fancy names for an unknown X.
>
> Unfortunately, in their aversion to the supernatural, the scientific purists poured out the baby with the intellectually soiled bath water by repudiating the very aspect of wholeness in nature that had conjured up those cover terms for ignorance. (p. 801)

One of the specific objections to the speculation found in the Gestalt system has been to its physiological assumptions. The principle of isomorphism has made these speculations all too easy. However, speculation is a useful part of every system. The Gestaltists have often admitted that their physiologizing is speculative. It has no effect on the validity of their experimental results and has stimulated experimentation.

The criticism that Gestalt psychology is antianalytic has already been countered in the discussion of the Gestalt attitude toward analysis.

The experimentation of Gestalt psychologists has been criticized for being poorly controlled, nonquantitative, and nonstatistical. Experimenters have been accused of giving subjects cues which affected learning in unknown ways and of ignoring possible effects of past experience. It is true that the Gestaltists' level of sophistication in experiments has not always been up to the level of their criticism and metatheoretical suggestions. However, they believe that qualitative results must come first. Thus the experiments have purposely been nonquantitative and nonstatistical in most cases. Since so many new areas have been explored, or old areas explored from new points of view, it is natural that some experiments have been preliminary and tentative. Later workers in the Gestalt tradition, such as Lewin, Brunswik, and Barker, have continued to perform very ingenious experiments and observations while improving methodology to the extent possible in field settings. Anyway, criticism of Gestalt experimentation, even if valid in some cases, cannot be a criticism of Gestalt psychology in general but only of particular Gestalt products. Gestalt psychology does not advocate poorly designed experiments. Poor experiments have been done under the aegis of every school but with the blessing of none.

Some other criticisms have little substance. It has been said that Gestalt psychology was not new. This can always be claimed, but (1) Gestalt psychology was as new as any school has ever been, and (2) the criticism is irrelevant to the merits of the system as it stands. The criticism that Gestalt psychology set up straw men to attack in each of the older systems is also irrelevant; such criticism might help in the defense of the older system but has nothing to do with Gestalt psychology's positive program.

THE CONTRIBUTIONS AND PRESENT STATUS OF GESTALT PSYCHOLOGY

The approach of Gestalt psychology has had a tremendous, though still often unrecognized, influence upon psychology in general. Its insistence that a whole system should be examined before beginning its analysis is now widely accepted. Naturalistic experimentation has finally become popular, and the impetus for its development comes from Gestalt psychology as well as from ethology. Conditions of system equilibrium are recognized as important subjects for study; the Gestalt psychologists were a half century ahead of most psychologists in pointing out the need to study system stability and instability. The resurgence of cognitive theory owes much to Gestalt psychology, which pointed to the importance of central processes from its inception but particularly after Köhler's work with apes.

Thus Gestalt psychology was extremely important because of its metatheoretical and methodological contributions. Yet the experiments done or inspired by Gestalt psychologists were also necessary to illustrate the usefulness of the more general claims, and experiments are always unquestioned contributions in their own right.

Hochberg (1957) reviewed a number of experimental results in his report of a symposium on the Gestalt revolution; we have already mentioned the Johannson experiments on perceived motion. Another set of experiments by Ivo Kohler of Innsbruck is also particularly interesting. He created several types of disturbances to normal stimulation and observed perceptual and behavioral adaptations to the disturbances. In one representative experiment, the left half of each lens of a pair of spectacles was made blue and the right half yellow. Then, when the spectacles were worn, white objects to the left of center were seen as blue and white objects to the right as yellow.

When the eyes were turned to the left, the world tended to look blue; to the right, yellow. After long adaptation, objects remained constant in color despite eye movement. Then, when the glasses were taken off, the world appeared yellow with eyes left and blue with eyes right! This fact illustrates a relational determination of color which is *completely* independent of local stimulation. Gestalt psychology could hardly have asked nature to provide a clearer demonstration of the inadequacy of the "mosaic hypothesis."

It was suggested that Ivo Kohler's results could be summed up as an elimination of invariable relations in order to achieve a maximum amount of information via a description which eliminated unneeded complexity. Thus in the blue-yellow spectacles experiment it would invariably be the case that blue light would be received with eyes left, and yellow light with eyes right. The common blue or yellow bias could be filtered out in perception without loss of information, and it was. The resulting "normal" perception was quite relational and thus in keeping with Gestalt views.

These experiments show that local stimulation may not be correlated well with local sensation. Though Kohler's observations emphasize the importance of perceptual learning, this direction of emphasis does not contradict Gestalt precepts. The Gestaltists tended toward nativism because an antidote was needed. The structuralists and associationists too often hid behind the skirts of past associations whenever empirical facts belied what their elementaristic analyses led them to expect. Now that structuralism is gone and associationism is tinged with cognitivism, the Gestalt position on nativism-empiricism can relax to a more neutral position.

The evidence gathered by Land (1959), apparently independently of any systematic preconceptions, gives additional support to the Gestalt antimosaic hypothesis. Color perception, according to Land, is to a large extent independent of the nature of the stimulation of individual retinal receptors. The perception of color depends upon relationships over the whole retina. Land believed that information about colors is gathered, and colors are therefore seen, because objects of different colors reflect different proportions of "warm" and "cool" light. Thus negatives exposed through filters that screen long-wave (warm) and short-wave (cool) parts of the spectrum differently contain information about the colors present.

An interesting demonstration follows. Land exposed two black-and-white negatives to the same scene, producing one negative that had been exposed through a long-wave filter and one that had been exposed through a short-wave filter. When the two developed negatives were put into projectors and superimposed on a screen, a rich array of colors appeared, despite the fact that there was no color in either negative! This demonstration could hardly provide more dramatic support for the Gestalt antimosaic hypothesis. This does not mean that Land's color theory supports Gestalt color theory; Land believed that his results demanded a reformulation of all color theories. Walls (1960) disagreed with Land; he held that traditional explanations in terms of contrast and induction could handle the observations. Regardless of who turns out to be closest to the truth on this point, Land's direction of attention to these color phenomena vindicates the general Gestalt emphasis.

Gestalt psychology, then, is not just a useful failure like structuralism. Until Wolfgang Köhler's death in 1967, it still had a founder as a leader. Its propositions, especially those which concern the whole-part relationship, involve complexities that still require working out, and that has kept scientists interested. Modern systems theory and modern statistics, aided by computers, are developing some of the techniques required for dealing with organized complex systems.

Köhler lived to see the Gestalt whole-part attitude accepted by many. Psychology has also accepted the essential correctness of the contemporaneity principle, but many psychologists still emphasize historical variables because they are easier to observe. Gestalt psychology has stimulated significant work within the orthodox areas of general psychology (e.g., Asch, Hay, & Diamond, 1960, on verbal learning; Katona, 1940, on memory).

The attitudes of Gestalt psychology have been assimilated by cognitive psychologists. Gestaltists tended to be centralistic, to emphasize organization in memory, and to concentrate on the use of principles rather than on the influence of habits. All of these tendencies are consistent with modern developments in computer modeling. We cannot credit the Gestalt position directly with the development of the cognitive or computer-oriented approaches, but it is easy to see the intellectual similarities. Thus the current great activity in these areas strengthens our belief in the importance of the conceptions originally presented by the Gestaltists.

Lastly, Gestalt psychology has contributed to psychology via its sharp criticism of other systems. It forced reexamination and revamping of every system which wished to stand in opposition to it. It has pointed to phenomena which existing systems could incorporate only after they modified fundamental features of their theories.

SUMMARY AND CONCLUSIONS

Gestalt psychology originated in Frankfurt am Main, Germany, between 1910 and 1912. Wertheimer, Köhler, and Koffka arrived at their basic position as a result of Wertheimer's insight and their confirmation of it in experiments on apparent movement (phi phenomenon). Their psychology was more phenomenological than that of Wundt; they accepted introspection but changed its character. One of their basic objections to the old psychology concerned its artificiality of analysis. They disliked the quest for the elements of experience and noted that the simple combination of elements was inadequate to produce the features of the whole. The *whole* in psychology, as in physics or chemistry, required laws of its own, and psychology should try to find these laws.

For the Gestaltists, the laws of science were the laws of systems. They set out to apply their points of view to the fields of perception and learning. In perception, they put forth the laws of organization. In learning, they found the same kinds of principles. They objected to the overuse of past experience as an explanatory concept both in perception and in learning. Learning and problem solving were seen in relation to restructuring of the perceptual field. Only influences on this field that were presently active could be used in the explanation of perception and behavior. Many Gestalt criticisms of structuralistic and behavioristic psychology have been accepted as cogent, and these criticisms have forced the reformulation of those theoretical positions. The fundamental Gestalt principles have been developed in quite different directions by

Kurt Lewin, Egon Brunswik, and Roger Barker. Gestalt psychology is thus still an active force in contemporary psychology.

FURTHER READINGS

G. W. Hartmann's *Gestalt psychology* (1935) is a fine source for the student who seeks information about, and appraisal of, Gestalt psychology in a single book. It gives excellent historical background and a good explanation of the basic systematic position. Köhler's *Gestalt psychology* (1947) is the most readable of the primary sources by the three founders; Koffka's *Principles of Gestalt psychology* (1935), while less readable, is more thorough. Koffka's book is the most comprehensive treatment in English by one of the founders. Wertheimer is represented in English by the posthumous *Productive thinking* (1945), which is brief and incomplete. For translations of early papers, Ellis's *A source book of Gestalt psychology* (1938) is, as the title suggests, a classic source for some of the most important of the basic Gestalt writings. Henle's *Documents of Gestalt psychology* (1961) is also a valuable source of similar materials. Prentice's article entitled "The systematic psychology of Wolfgang Köhler" (1959) is an easily available summary. Köhler's *The task of Gestalt psychology* (1969), prepared for posthumous publication by Solomon Asch, Mary Henle, and Edwin Newman, presents a broad review of the Gestalt movement and includes an introductory eulogy by Carroll Pratt. Henle has also (1971) edited a collection of papers by Köhler. An article by Crannell (1970) is an interesting tidbit because of its descriptions of Köhler's personal courage in the face of Nazi persecution. Fritz Heider (1970) provides some good background for Gestalt theory, including descriptions of Meinong and Benussi. Hochberg's (1957) summary of the Cornell symposium is a succinct appetizer for those who are curious about the kind of perceptual work which has been done with a Gestalt methodology. Weiss's article (1967) can be recommended for those who still do not believe, that under some conditions $1 + 1 \neq 2$. Marrow's *The practical theorist* (1969) is an excellent and entertaining introduction to Kurt Lewin. De Rivera's book *Field theory as human science: Contributions of Lewin's Berlin group* (1976) is what the title says it is and serves as an excellent supplement to Marrow. The best place to start with Egon Brunswik is Hammond's *The psychology of Egon Brunswik* (1966). Hammond is an excellent "translator" and might help enough that one can enjoy Brunswik's own *Perception and the representative design of psychological experiments* (1956), a brilliant, important, and difficult work. Barker is perfectly capable of putting his own best foot forward, as he does in his interesting and readable *Ecological psychology* (1968).

END NOTES

Dimensional Descriptions of Gestalt Psychology

Conscious Mentalism–Unconscious Mentalism   The Gestaltists recognized both conscious and unconscious mentalism. They accepted their own kind of introspection, and they used introspective techniques in the analysis of learning and problem solving, as well as in the analysis of perception. However, the concept of psychological field included both unconscious and conscious influences; that is, they recognized unconscious influences in the causation of behavior. Today's Gestalt therapy, which shares some attitudes with traditional Gestalt psychology, combines a psychoanalytic emphasis on the unconscious with a Gestalt eye for the present situation. After considering all of these factors, we would rate Gestalt psychology as putting a little, but only a little, more than average emphasis on conscious mentalism.

Content: Objective vs. Subjective   The Gestaltists accepted both objective and subjective content and in this respect would be in a perfectly neutral position. However, their tendency to get "encapsulated into the central layer" in some of their perceptual studies justifies us in placing them, in practice, somewhat toward the subjective end of this dimension.

Determinism–Indeterminism   Gestaltists join with others in the scientific tradition in favoring determinism. Perhaps they were a little less vehement about their determinism than the behaviorists and so would be rated as a little further from the deterministic pole; however, their clear antivitalism, among other things, leaves no question as to their basic acceptance of a deterministic position.

Empiricism–Rationalism   The Gestaltists appeared rationalistic in contrast to most of their peers, particularly because they argued that past experience was not a sufficient explanation of present experience and/or behavior. This very reasonable claim was mistakenly taken by many to mean that the Gestaltists were rationalists. They were not; they were just more neutral than extremists like the associationists.

Functionalism–Structuralism   Gestalt psychology attempted to take a functional position, but at times the emphasis on perceptual structure and on organization seemed to give it a structural flavor. This impression was abetted by the attention given to the present moment, as we see in the contemporaneity principle and the principle of isomorphism. Thus we hesitantly ascribe a degree of structuralistic emphasis to Gestalt psychology.

Inductivism–Deductivism   The Gestalt psychologists, like all scientists, made use of inductive techniques. However, the time they spent on criticism and theorizing (or metatheorizing) seems to put them in a deductive mode a substantial part of the time. If the ratio of theory to experiment was high, as claimed by their critics, then they earn a rating toward the deductive pole.

Mechanism–Vitalism   We have seen that the Gestaltists rejected vitalism with great vehemence; however, they did not accept mechanism with equal vehemence, so we place them at about the middle of this dimension.

Methods: Objective vs. Subjective   We know that Gestaltists were tolerant of both objective and subjective methods; thus they belong in the middle here, but because of contrast effects with the more objective schools, they look a little more subjective than average.

Molecularism–Molarism   We can't miss here. The essence of the school was its molarism.

Monism–Dualism   It seems that everyone wants to be regarded as a monist, but only the behaviorists have consistently refused to talk about mind in their science. The Gestaltists talked so much about experience, and recognized a kind of duality so clearly in their principle of isomorphism, that we place them somewhat toward the dualistic position.

Naturalism–Supernaturalism   The critics might find tinges of supernaturalism in the Gestaltist's claim that new phenomena emerged in wholes, which were more than the sums of their parts, and so on; but the Gestaltists were nonetheless strongly naturalistic.

Nomotheticism–Idiographicism   The Gestalt insistence that wholes had an uniqueness of their own makes them appear more idiographic than the typical school. But they were looking for general laws, like all scientists, and are thus basically nomethetic. They may nevertheless have seen more impediments to finding simple general laws because of their recognition of how multivariate and interactive situations were.

Peripheralism–Centralism   There is little doubt about the Gestalt emphasis on central processes. That is one reason for the debt owed to Gestalt psychology by modern cognitive psychology. Most Gestaltists preferred to try to predict behavior from a knowledge of central events rather than from a knowledge of environmental circumstances. Thus Gestalt psychology rates as the most centralistic of the schools.

Purism–Utilitarianism   The original Gestaltists were academic purists, but the developers were much more utilitarian. We would still tend to rate them slightly toward purism.

Quantitativism–Qualitativism   We have seen that the Gestaltists were not really antiquantitative; however, their emphasis on the importance of qualitative study—an emphasis neglected by most of their competitors—places them toward the qualitative end relative to others.

Rationalism–Irrationalism   The emphasis on intellectual ability, even in the chimpanzee, and on rational approaches to problem solving places Gestalt psychology somewhat toward the rationalistic pole.

Staticism–Developmentalism   Most Gestalt studies were cross-sectional, and their contemporaneity principle forces us to rate them toward staticism, despite the fact that this seems out of character with the generally dynamic nature of the system.

Staticism–Dynamicism   The psychological field, the perceptual field, the brain field— they were all regarded as dynamic. The Gestaltists also emphasized motivation, as one expects from those with dynamic leanings.

Three dimensions which seem to be particularly important in describing Gestalt psychology are molarism, centralism, and, to a lesser extent, purism.

Gestalt Psychology Compared to Other Systems

With respect to Coan's (1979) first three dimensions, concerned with the distinction between a generally analytic and a generally synthetic approach, Gestalt is consistently synthetic. It does not strongly emphasize objective data, tends toward the qualitative, and is decidedly and critically molaristic. Thus Gestalt psychology is in these respects at the opposite pole from associationism and behaviorism, with functionalism in the more moderate position.

On Coan's second set of three dimensions, Gestalt psychology has a fairly close kinship with functionalism and is distant from associationism. It is more personal in orientation (we have mentioned some tendency toward the idiographic) is highly dynamic, and is more endogenistic than most systems. Despite some slight indications to the contrary, Gestalt psychology tends in general toward the functional rather than toward the structural.

Gestalt psychology surely belongs toward the fluid, rather than the restrictive, pole of the most general of Coan's descriptive dimensions. It was too radical and too open to be restrictive. Gestalt psychology helped to open up psychology to new methods and new attitudes, for which psychology will be forever in its debt.

PSYCHOANALYSIS

Psychoanalysis is the most widely known psychological system, especially among nonpsychologists. Although it has been rejected by many academic psychologists, it has been more popular in other scientific and technical areas, in literary and artistic circles, and with the lay public. Recently some of the previously recalcitrant academic psychologists have become more interested in, or at least tolerant of, psychoanalysis. Controversy now surrounds the system because of questions about one of Freud's theoretical changes of mind: his shift from an emphasis on real childhood sexual abuse to an emphasis on fantasized sexual abuse as a key focal factor in neurosis.

The body of psychoanalytic writing is enormous. Freud's collected works alone, in their English translation, run to twenty-four volumes. Members of the Chicago Institute for Psychoanalysis published 3000 articles between 1963 and 1983 (Pollock, 1983). These two facts are evidence enough that we must present an extremely synoptic treatment.

Our discussion of psychoanalysis will have a critical tone. However, this should not be taken as a denial that Freud, his followers, and the rebels who nevertheless continued to follow an essentially psychoanalytic course made and continue to make an enormous contribution to psychology. Despite all objections to his theory, in 1962 Freud was rated by American psychologists as by far the most eminent psychological theoretician of all time (Coan & Zogona, 1962). It is very likely that he would still be rated as the top theorist. The reader should bear this in mind when reading criticisms of psychoanalysis. Criticisms are indications of flaws which need to be eliminated if psychoanalysis is to gain greater acceptance by the scientific community.

Table 8-1 lists the more important names associated with psychoanalysis.

TABLE 8-1
IMPORTANT FIGURES IN PSYCHOANALYSIS

| | Psychoanalysts | | |
Antecedent influences	Founders	Rebels	Developers
G. W. Leibniz (1646–1715)	Josef Breuer (1842–1925)	Alfred Adler (1870–1937)	Karen Horney (1885–1952)
Johann Wolfgang Göthe (1749–1832)	Sigmund Freud (1856–1939)	Sandor Ferenczi (1873–1933)	H. S. Sullivan (1892–1949)
Johann Friedrich Herbart (1776–1841)		C. G. Jung (1875–1961)	Anna Freud (1895–1982)
Arthur Schopenhauer (1788–1860)		Otto Rank (1884–1939)	Erich Fromm (1900–1980)
Gustav Theodor Fechner (1801–1887)			
Charles Darwin (1809–1882)			
Jean Martin Charcot (1825–1893)			

HISTORICAL ANTECEDENTS OF PSYCHOANALYSIS

Psychoanalysis fell upon the world like a bomb. The shock of some of its concepts and principles was so great that most people regarded it as entirely new. Yet it, too, had many antecedents—so many that they again resign us to the fact that there is rarely anything entirely new in the world of ideas.

The development of psychoanalysis involved two kinds of influences. There was the intellectual tradition in which Freud can be placed, and there was another set of more personal influences on Freud. Let us consider the former first.

Early in the eighteenth century, Leibniz developed a new kind of theory about the elements of reality. His elements were called *monads,* and they were quite unlike the mechanistic atoms of Democritus, who thought that the world was merely passive atoms in the void. Leibniz's monads were not material in the usual sense but could better be described as centers of energy. Each such center was independent of the others, with a source of striving within itself; a monad was a center of motivation, a self-moved entity. Activity thus became the basic requirement for being. Freud took a decisive step in his career when he turned away from the mechanistic tradition, in which he had been nurtured scholastically, to the more dynamic tradition represented by Leibniz.

Leibniz also pointed to the unconscious and to degrees of consciousness. A century after Leibniz, Herbart worked these concepts into a mathematics which described the conflict of ideas as they strive to become conscious. Freud thus was not the first to "discover" the unconscious; his unique contribution was his detailed characterization

Alfred Adler (1870–1937), one of Freud's earliest disciples and the earliest defector. Adler founded individual psychology after his break from Freud.

Carl Gustav Jung (1875–1961) became Freud's "crown prince" but later separated from Freud and founded his own brand of psychoanalysis, called analytic psychology.

Sigmund Freud (1856–1939) with the members of his "committee" in 1922, when psychoanalysis was well established, and the year before Freud was found to have oral cancer. Back row, left to right: Otto Rank, Karl Abraham, Max Eitingon, Ernest Jones. Front row: Sigmund Freud, Sandor Ferenczi, Hans Sachs.

of the unconscious and its mode of operation (Ellenberger, 1970). Freud (1938, p. 939) himself yielded precedence to Schopenhauer for the ideas of repression into the unconscious, resistance to the recognition of repressed material, and the roles of these processes in the genesis of mental disturbance. However, Freud said that he developed these same ideas without having read Schopenhauer.

Freud attended the lectures of Franz Brentano, who was a very popular lecturer in Vienna. No doubt Brentano introduced him to the Liebnizian mode of thought, for Brentano based his own psychological system on *activity* rather than on elements.

The German romantic scientific tradition played a somewhat more direct role for Freud. Schelling and Göthe were two of the most important figures in this tradition. Freud said that he decided upon a scientific career after hearing a poem of Göthe's called "Nature." Ellenberger (1970) points out that Göthe did not actually write the poem, but in any event Freud probably saw his way to power through an extremely deep understanding of nature (Jones, 1953).

Freud's formal training was in marked contrast to the romantic tradition. Ernst Brücke, with whom Freud studied for years at the Vienna Physiological Institute, was in the mechanistic school associated with Helmholtz. Brücke, Ludwig, and Du Bois-Reymond joined with Helmholtz in an antivitalistic pact when all were in their twenties (Boring, 1950, p. 708). They intended to force acceptance of the belief that there are no forces within living bodies that are not in nonliving bodies. Part of what motivated Helmholtz to write his paper on the conservation-of-energy principle was a desire to show that there is no unique energy unaccounted for within the organism considered purely as a physical system. Perhaps contact with this tradition later helped Freud to view the dreams and fantasies, wit and errors, of humans as determinate, and to formulate his own version of the determinacy of human behavior, which he called *psychic determinism*. Helmholtz also developed the concept of "unconscious inference" to explain how we reach conclusions in perception via a quasilogical process which does not appear in consciousness. Helmholtz's concept may have helped Freud to see the importance of the unconscious.

Freud was no doubt reinforced in his determinism by his reading of Charles Darwin's evolutionary thesis and discussion of it with others in the institute and the hospital where he studied for his medical degree. He tended to take a biological view of man in accord with Darwin's biological view, and many of his ideas drew directly upon evolutionary theory. One example is the death instinct, which Freud said depended upon speculation about the origins of life. Freud's ideas about the tremendous importance of sexual motives can hardly have been independent of evolutionary thinking, in which reproduction is the central issue.

Hughlings Jackson combined a physiological and an evolutionary outlook in a way that influenced Freud. Jackson said that nervous systems achieve, through evolutionary development, a hierarchical structure in which the higher structures are more complex, but less completely determined than the lower structures. The precise interconnections of the higher structures are then developed during the life of the individual. In nervous diseases, Jackson thought that there was a process which he called *dissolution,* the approximate opposite of the process of evolutionary development. Freud, in turn, apparently patterned his idea of regression after Jackson's dissolution (Herrnstein & Boring, 1965, p. 248).

Two somewhat conflicting traditions, which we may refer to as the romantic and the mechanistic, thus influenced Freud. The romantic and mystical side was strengthened by Freud's religious background, which contained strong mystical components. The Jewish writings also attributed a mystical significance to sex (Bakan, 1958).

Gustav Fechner had the same mechanistic-romantic conflict as Freud. Fechner finally solved it by being rigorously scientific about a somewhat mystical problem, the mind-body issue. It seems that the kind of genius peculiar to psychology has often been of this type. Among others who have "naturalized" some theretofore mystical phenomenon are Darwin (natural selection and evolution), Ebbinghaus (memory), and Pavlov (associations in behavior). Ellenberger (1956), among others, has shown in detail that there was a direct relationship between Fechner and Freud. Freud admired Fechner and was familiar with his writings. Freud's concerns with the intensity of stimulation, with mental energy, and with the topographical concept of mind were related to Fechner's prior work.

THE LIFE OF SIGMUND FREUD

Sigmund Freud (1856–1939) is almost universally considered a giant among psychologists, even by those who think he was a misguided giant. For that reason, and because his system was based to an appreciable extent on his observations of himself, his life deserves a closer look than we have afforded most of our "founders."

Freud was born in what is now Pribor, Czechoslovakia, on May 6, 1856. His father, Jacob, was primarily in the business of dyeing and dressing wool cloth at that time; there is no information as to how he supported his family later, after they moved to Vienna by way of Leipzig. Pribor was at that time Freiberg, Austria. The family had arrived in Vienna by the time young Sigmund was four. Freud was reared primarily by his young mother, who was closer in age to him than to his father. Some scholars have suggested that Freud's later ideas about the Oedipal conflict could be related to this experience. Ironically, Freud believed that his mother was Jacob's second wife and identified himself with the Biblical David partly for that reason. In reality, she was Jacob's third wife (Ellenberger, 1970); for a very short time, he had a second wife at about the time the family went briefly to Leipzig. Historical study has so far revealed very little about this shadowy second wife.

It soon became clear that Sigmund had great academic aptitude. He eventually decided upon medicine as a career, although he neither liked the practice of medicine nor identified himself closely with the medical profession. He postponed taking the medical examinations while he spent his time working under Brücke in the Physiological Institute on problems that were purely scientific and thus more friendly to his temper. He hoped eventually to become a professor of anatomy rather than a physician. He finally gave up hope of academic advancement and decided to take his medical examinations and training at the hospital in order that he might enter private practice as a physician. Brücke had apparently helped him to arrive at this decision. Freud's Jewishness may have impeded his advancement, but another factor was simply the greath length of time that typically elapsed before positions became available.

Even prior to his taking the examinations for the medical degree, Freud felt an interest primarily in neurology or psychiatry among the medical specialties. In the hospital, his feelings were reinforced. From 1880 on, he wavered between the study of the anatomy of the nervous system and the study of psychiatry. He published many papers on anatomy, among them one concerning a new method of staining nervous tissue and a paper containing the germ of the neuron theory. At one time he became interested in cocaine and suggested its efficacy to one of his colleagues, who discovered its anesthetic properties. Freud was intensely disappointed that he had missed the opportunity to make this discovery and achieve the fame that attended it. He was more interested in cocaine's potency as a tranquilizer, and he recommended its use to friends. One substituted a cocaine addiction for a prior addiction, and Freud received reprimands from his colleagues rather than the recognition he so much desired.

From the 1870s through the early 1890s, Freud was befriended by Josef Breuer, a practicing physician. Breuer gave his impoverished younger colleague money as well as advice and friendship. The two later were estranged at about the same time that Freud became closely attached to another physician, Wilhelm Fliess. The Fliess association led to an usually close relationship during the years when Freud was formulating his ideas about psychoanalysis.

In 1885, Freud obtained a grant to study in Paris. He studied under Charcot, a famous Parisian hypnotist, teacher, and authority on hysteria. Freud already had some interest in hypnosis as a method of treatment, and the interest was strengthened by Charcot. Back in Vienna, Freud reported to his colleagues what he had learned about hysteria and hypnosis. His report was not taken as a revelation by the Viennese Medical Society, and the young pioneer was embittered. Ellenberger (1970, p. 448 ff.), however, finds no evidence that Freud was rejected or isolated, and sees Freud's feelings at the time as probably neurotic.

The young Freud continued to use hypnosis in his practice to supplement massage, baths, and the mild kind of electrotherapy then in vogue. He later discontinued the latter, commenting that the only reason he disagreed with those who attributed the effects of electrotherapy to suggestion was that he did not observe any results to explain. This sort of ironic humor was typical of Freud's approach to life and himself, and served as a balance to some of his less stable personality traits.

By 1895, he had lost interest in anatomy. He and Breuer had published *Studies in hysteria,* which marked the beginning of the psychoanalytic school (Breuer & Freud, 1895). He wrote no more articles or books on neurology, with the exception of one encyclopedia article in 1897.

It was about this time, too, that Freud became estranged from Breuer and established Fliess as his mentor—in spite of the fact that Fliess was two years his junior and intellectually his inferior. Freud was highly dependent upon Fliess during this most neurotic period of his life. He was overdependent, jealous, sometimes domineering, overly concerned with death, and hypochondriacal.

In 1897, Freud began a full-scale self-analysis. One of its results was the growth of his ability to stand on his own feet. Fliess and Freud had a disagreement in 1900, perhaps over some of Fliess's highly speculative ideas about the periodicity of behavior. Freud later attributed their alienation to an analysis he had made of Fliess's choice of occupation. The final separation followed several years later; Freud had been indirectly responsible for the plagiarism by one of his own patients of Fliess's ideas on bisexuality, and had refused first to acknowledge any responsibility and then later to apologize.

Perhaps the greatest milestone in Freud's career was the publication of *The inter-pretation of dreams* in 1900 (see Freud, 1950/1900), two years after the death of his father. According to Jones (1953, p. 324) and Freud's own interpretation, the necessary freeing of the unconscious could occur only after the father was gone. Not long after this he began to gain recognition and soon had gathered around him a group of collaborators. His role became that of the father rather than of the son. Gustav Jung, Alfred Adler, Otto Rank, and Sandor Ferenczi were first disciples and then rebels. Various difficulties in personal interaction usually started the rebellion, and the young psychoanalysts were intolerant of disagreement within their ranks. At one time a committee of the faithful was formed, composed of Karl Abraham, Max Eitingon, Sandor Ferenczi, Otto Rank, Ernest Jones, and Hans Sachs. The committee was to further analytic work. Freud gave each member a setting for a seal ring like the one he wore.

Through the committee and an ever-growing body of publications, Freud became successful and widely known. One of the first marks of his international recognition was G. Stanley Hall's invitation to speak at Clark University's twentieth anniversary celebration in 1909. Freud spoke, as did Jung; among the analysts present were Ferenczi, Jones, and A. A. Brill, while Titchener, James McKeen Cattell, and William James were among the academic psychologists who attended. James Putnam, a pro-fessor of neurology at Harvard University, became a steadfast friend of analysis at this time.

Jung later returned to the United States for further lectures. He reported that he had little trouble in getting analytic doctrine accepted if he ceased to emphasize sex so heavily. This statement widened an already existing breach between Jung and Freud. It is not possible to summarize briefly the reasons for their final break, but those who are interested in this fascinating subject can now watch Jung's defection pass before their very eyes by reading the published correspondence between Jung and Freud (see McGuire, 1974).

Freud's recognition and success continued to grow, but his troubles were far from over. He had to deal with almost continuous dissension within the analytic ranks, while supporting himself, his wife, their six children, and a sister-in-law. World War I brought hardship and anxiety, as Freud's sons Martin and Ernst were called to the front. Still Freud worked, and his fame grew. When the war ended, he attracted many English and American students who helped to keep him going when Austrian money was of little value. He continued to expand and modify his theories and to regulate the rapid expansion of psychoanalysis. One of his devices for control was his volu-minous correspondence, wherein he admonished and praised his followers.

In the fateful year 1923, a cancer was discovered in Freud's mouth. It is highly probable that Freud's cancer was connected with the fact that he typically smoked twenty cigars a day. Parts of his palate and upper jaw had to be removed, so that he had to wear a prosthesis to separate his mouth from his nasal cavity and to make eating and talking possible. Freud accepted the series of operations and almost constant pain that attended the last sixteen years of his life with his characteristic blend of realism, pessimism, and fatalism.

Finally, 1938 brought the long-dreaded invasion of Austria by the Nazis. Hitler himself visited the city in triumph. Freud's books were burned, and his children were detained and questioned by the Gestapo. Still Freud did not wish to leave his home at Berggasse 19, the place at which he had created, founded, and nurtured psychoanalysis. Ernest Jones and Princess Marie Bonaparte, both Freud's dear friends, cajoled and pleaded with him on the one hand and with the Nazis on the other, and enlisted the help of many others, including Ambassador Bullitt of the United States. Finally both sides were convinced, and the Nazis released Freud after bleeding him of everything they could get their hands on. Freud was required to sign a paper absolving the Nazis of all blame, saying he was perfectly free to stay and continue his work. His only request was to add one sentence; he is said to have written "And I can heartily recommend the Gestapo." His ironic humor had not deserted him even in age and extremity!

In England he was welcomed as a hero and was soon made a member of the Royal Society, as Newton and Darwin had been before him. Americans can be proud that prominent citizens of Cleveland sent him a four-page telegram inviting him to settle there and guaranteeing plush accommodations, money, and the warmest of welcomes. It is not likely that Freud considered this kind offer seriously, since he had a long-standing prejudice against America despite the intense pleasure his visit to Clark University had brought. His visit had unfortunately been accompanied by an illness which he attributed to American cooking and accommodations, and he felt uncomfortable with the language and manners of the Americans.

Freud had not been in England long before his cancer recurred, and the series of operations and treatments began again. Despite almost continuous pain and discomfort, he worked almost to the end, and died in peace and honor on September 23, 1939. He was spared the knowledge that four of his sisters, who stayed behind in Austria, would be killed by the Nazis.

THE FOUNDING OF PSYCHOANALYSIS

The germ of psychoanalysis appeared in a paper, *Studies in hysteria,* published by Breuer and Freud in 1895. Freud had met the older Breuer in the late 1870s. They shared a strong scientific interest, and both were interested in hypnotism as a therapeutic device. Breuer soon after had an interesting case, Fraulein Anna O., whom he treated in 1881 and 1882; that fall he told Freud about it. The highly intelligent girl had come to Breuer with multiple symptoms, including paralysis of three limbs, contractures, and a tendency to dual personality. In the course of the treatment, it was found that if she related every occurrence of a symptom all the way back to its origin, the symptom would disappear. Anna O. retraced these occurrences while in a kind of transition state between her two personalities. Breuer then began to hypnotize her daily so that she could rid herself of the symptoms faster. She christened the method they had discovered the "talking cure" or "chimney sweeping." The idea of catharsis was very much in the air in Vienna at the time (Ellenberger, 1972), and it is possible that Anna O. and Breuer brought that idea from the theater to the therapy room. Breuer devoted an hour or more a day for over a year to her. Legend, deriving from Freud and Jung through Jones, had it that Breuer and his patient became inordinately fond of each other and that when Breuer was to terminate the treatment Anna O. went into the throes of hysterical childbirth, whereupon Breuer fled, taking his jealous wife on a second honeymoon during which a real daughter was conceived.

Ellenberger (1972) found that, honeymoon or no, the legend is mostly moonshine. The documented chronology proves that none of Breuer's daughters could have been conceived at the corresponding time. More important, Anna O. was far from cured when Breuer stopped treating her, as reported in a previously unknown case history discovered by Ellenberger in the sanitarium at Kreuzlingen in Switzerland, where Anna O. was treated after Breuer stopped seeing her. This puts the beginning of psychoanalysis under something of a cloud, since Anna O. had been regarded as a prototype of a cathartic "cure."

Anna O., whose real name was Bertha Pappenheim, later became so well known that Germany issued a commemorative stamp in her memory, in recognition of her work with children, prostitutes, and Jewish relief. Lucy Freeman (1972) even wrote a somewhat novelized biography of her in English. Thus, although Breuer did not cure her completely, she later became well enough to lead a noteworthy life.

Freud was very interested in her case and urged Breuer to publish it. However, the full-scale *Studien über Hysterie* (Breuer and Freud, 1895) followed the close of the case by 13 years, and even the preliminary report took 11 years.

Meanwhile, in 1885, Freud studied with Charcot. Charcot was famous for his treatment of hysteria and other functional nervous diseases by hypnosis. After several months, Freud returned to Vienna and resumed private practice. It was at about this time that he abandoned electrotherapy. He also observed that not all his patients could be hypnotized, and, perhaps feeling that his technique was deficient, he went to study at Nancy with Bernheim for a few weeks. He took along a patient in whom he had been unable to induce a deep trance, but Bernheim also failed.

Despite this setback, Freud was impressed with what he saw at Nancy, especially by his observation that a posthypnotic suggestion could be carried out, even though the suggestion was forgotten. He was probably equally impressed with the demonstration that the patient would remember the suggestion after sufficient insistence on the part of the hypnotist. This may have encouraged him to believe in the efficacy of suggestions given during the ordinary waking state.

Freud now began to modify his techniques with patients in whom he could not induce hypnosis. He was determined to save the talking cure. He insisted that the patients would remember the origins of symptoms, even though they were not hypnotized. He supplemented his insistence with suggestions that patients would remember when Freud pressed upon their foreheads. At this stage, Freud was exerting a great deal of guidance on the patients' processes of association. One patient told him that he was interrupting too much and that he should keep quiet. This suggestion was the final impetus that converted Freud from the hypnotic trance to free association as a method of treatment.

By the time the *Studies* appeared, Breuer and Freud were in possession of many of the ideas that were to provide the basis for psychoanalysis. Several of the ideas had come from Breuer's observation of Anna O., and others from Freud's observations of hysterical patients. The first of these ideas was a conviction of the importance of unconscious processes in the etiology of the neuroses. This conviction came partly from the observation that symptoms often seemed to be expressions of events which patients could not remember or of impulses of which they were unaware. The influence of posthypnotic suggestion which the subject did not at the moment remember may have contributed to the belief in the strength of unconscious processes.

Freud was convinced by this time that sex plays a dominant role in the psychic aberrations of the neurotic. Breuer did not share Freud's certainty on this point, and their disagreement seems to have resulted in what Freud considered some underplaying of the theme in their publication. Charcot had apparently remarked at one time that a certain type of case always has a sexual basis. Freud also claimed that Breuer and a gynecologist named Chrobak had made similar remarks about nervous disorders. Freud observed that most of his hysterical patients reported traumatic sexual childhood experiences, often with members of their own families. He concluded that no neurosis is possible in a person with a normal sex life.

The importance of symbolism was also recognized by Freud at this time. Symptoms seemed to be distorted, but symbolic, representations of repressed events or conflicts. In the case of Anna O., the symbolic relation between the origin of the symptoms and the symptoms themselves was clear to her and to Breuer when she was able to recall the origin. The symptoms were not chosen arbitrarily.

In every case, the situation at the time the symptom originated had involved strong impulses to do something which had been opposed by forces preventing Anna O. from carrying out her wish. For example, she might want to cry in the presence of her father because of her grief over his illness and yet be unable to cry for fear he would become upset about his condition. The repressed impulse might later manifest itself in symbolic form, as an inability to see. The existence of contradictory tendencies was evidence of the importance of conflict in the creation of symptoms and in the production of neuroses in general.

As the preceding discussion implies, an acceptance of the unconscious is intertwined with the notion of repression into the unconscious. Under ordinary circumstances, undesirable impulses and memories are pushed into the unconscious and are forgotten and unavailable as conscious materials. Only through their recovery and working out (*abreaction*) can the patient be cured.

In his quest for the origins of symptoms, for the repressed material represented by the symptoms, Freud was forced further and further back into childhood. His belief in the importance of childhood experiences in the production of neuroses was growing. Many of these childhood experiences were sexual; in hysteria particularly, Freud found reports of early sexual experiences. However, he believed that these experiences gained their traumatic force only after the patient had reached puberty. He had not yet been driven to his later opinions about the early genesis of sexuality in childhood.

The last, and possibly most important, discovery was the transference relation. We have already seen that Breuer became fond of his patient (countertransference) and that she also became fond of him. It seemed that the patient transferred to her therapist the feelings that she earlier had for other people, especially her parents. At some stages of the therapeutic relationship, these feelings might become strongly negative. In either case, the patient was able to live through, to work out, the impulses that had earlier been incapable of expression. The transference could thus become one of the most useful tools of the therapist.

On the other hand, transference might strike a chill into the heart of the timid. It may have been Breuer's anxiety about the transference he had elicited in Anna O. that led him to leave the field that he and Freud were starting to open up. There was also the controversy about the importance attributed to sexuality. Since he could not decide whether sex was really so critical or not, Breuer chose to leave psychoanalysis to Freud.

FREUD'S SYSTEM

We now leap over the developmental phases to present a thumbnail sketch of Freud's later system. We should distinguish between the structure of constructs that Freud developed, with which we will be primarily concerned, and psychoanalytic techniques viewed as therapy or as sources of empirical data. These facets of psychoanalysis should be evaluated separately, just as the question of whether or not aspirin is effective should be kept separate from explanations of how it works. Much confused criticism of psychoanalysis is the result of a failure to separate the therapy from the theory. Positive results of the therapy do not necessarily support the theory, and vice versa.

Freud did not suddenly develop the ideas to be presented here, nor did he continue to adhere to an idea if it seemed to him to contradict evidence that he gathered in his work. For example, he changed his position on hysteria profoundly after he concluded that in many cases the traumatic sexual incidents reported by his patients had not occurred. Before that, he had resisted all attempts by others to get him to change his position. Masson (1985), after reviewing the archival evidence, maintained that Freud was correct in the first place and that the patients *were* abused as children. R. I. Watson (1968) has also studied this theoretical change:

> A short time after he gave this paper the horrible truth began to dawn on him—these seductions in childhood, in most, but not all instances, had never actually occurred.
>
> A lesser man might have hidden his mistake and tried to forget it. A less clinically acute individual might have "bravely" confessed his error and turned to other more profitable matters. Freud did neither. . . . Was not the very fact that their fantasies took the form of sexual matters evidence that there was a sexual tinge or basis to their thinking, and was he not, consequently, right in emphasizing the sexual basis of their difficulty even though the situations which they had described had actually never taken place? Despite the temporary setback, this "mistake" was actually later to be seen as an advance. (p. 467)

Whether Watson is correct, or even if Masson's claim that Freud was suppressing the truth is true, there remains a strong kernel of truth in Freud's position: sex plays a very central role in the human psychic economy. And if Freud suppressed the truth in this matter, it was certainly uncharacteristic of him. He typically showed great courage and an extreme insensitivity to criticism from outside the psychoanalytic movement. However, he was sensitive to self-criticism, and his system was accordingly flexible. Seldom did he present his theories as certainties; rather, they were usually presented as tentative conclusions that seemed to be supported by his clinical data. It is largely this resistance to external criticism and his feeling that experimental support for his notions was not necessary that gave him the reputation of being cocksure and dogmatic about his conclusions.

Freud had a surprising attitude about the reality of his conceptions. He might, when being self-consciously corrrect about methodology, admit that his concepts were convenient fictions invented for explanatory purposes, but his usual attitude was that he was dealing with real things. For example, he once used Janet's statement that the unconscious was a "manner of speaking" as an example of Janet's low level of understanding (Jones, 1957, p. 214). Freud apparently regarded the unconscious as a country he was exploring rather than a mythological realm he was constructing for the purpose of explanation. Perhaps Freud's background in neurology was conducive to the belief that he was working with *real* structures.

The Psychic Apparatus

As we have already seen, Freud believed that he found two "states" within the "country." The states were called *conscious* and *unconscious*. Different kinds of laws determine what happens in these two states. The unconscious operates according to a set which Freud called the *primary process,* and the conscious according to the *secondary process*. Ordinary logic applies to the latter but not to the former. The mechanisms that can be observed in dreams characterize the action of the primary process. Some of the things that can occur under the actions of this process are the *condensation* of several thoughts into a single symbol, the *displacement* of an impulse or affect from one symbol to another, the *timelessness* of dreams, and *conversion* of an impulse into its opposite. The illogicality of the dream is characteristic of the primary process as a whole.

Part of the energy for the mental apparatus is called *libido;* its source is in biological tensions, and certainly the most important of these to the mental economy is sexual. Most of the sexual energy derives from the erogenous zones, bodily areas especially sensitive to stimulation. The *id* is the primordial reservoir of this energy and, being unconscious, operates according to the primary process. Various instincts which reside in the id press toward the discharge of their libidinal energy. Each instinct, therefore, has a *source* in biological tensions, an *aim* of discharge in some specific activity, and an *object* which will facilitate the discharge.

The id operates according to the *pleasure principle*. In general, the elimination of tension is what defines pleasure, although it is not always clear whether it is the elimination of all tension or the maintenance of a constant level of tension which is pleasurable. Departure from a low level of tension or any heightening of tension is unpleasurable. One should remember that the id operates *only* according to the pleasure principle; it does not, for example, distinguish between the hallucinatory fulfillment of a hunger need and the actual fulfillment of the need. It is like a drug addict who cannot distinguish between a feeling of well-being and genuine well-being. However, tensions do not remain reduced except through contact with objects that are in reality appropriate.

Accordingly, another psychic structure develops and complements the id. It is called the *ego*. The ego operates according to the laws of the secondary process and, in contact with reality, pays attention to the *reality principle*. That is, it is an evaluative agency which intelligently selects that line of behavior which minimizes pain while maximizing pleasure. The ego is still in the service of the pleasure principle, as modified by the reality principle, and sometimes it temporarily turns aside the gratification of individual needs to increase overall gratification.

As a result of contact with cultural realities, especially as embodied in the parents, a third mental agency, the *superego,* develops. It functions as a suppressor of pleasurable activity in the same way that external agencies did during its formative years. It has two subsystems: a conscience that punishes behavior and an ego ideal that rewards it. The conscience brings about feelings of guilt, and the ego ideal brings about feeling of pride. The superego is unlike the ego (which ultimately serves the pleasure principle, and only postpones gratification) in its attempts to halt certain pleasurable activities. The operation of the superego is largely unconscious, and a large part of its operation therefore follows the laws of the primary process.

Freud came to the conclusion that the instincts active throughout the psychic apparatus could be divided into two groups: the *life instincts* and the *destructive instincts*. The latter were more commonly called the *death instincts,* since their aim is the death of an individual. Freud viewed the instincts as conservative; that is, they aim for a return to a previous state and thus explain the *repetition compulsion* which manifests itself in some behavior. Since living matter arises from dead matter, the ultimate previous state must be a state of complete quiescence, or death. The death instincts work for disintegration of the individual, while the life instincts work for the continued integration of the individual. The death instinct is the part of Freud's theory least frequently accepted by other analysts, perhaps as much because of its implied pessimism as because of lack of evidence. Many articles in analytic publications have been unfavorable to this Freudian conception (Jones, 1957, p. 276). The life and death instincts had the advantage for Freud of giving him a pair of opposite elements in conflict. Freud was quite fond of the dualistic mode of thought, preferring it to either monistic or pluralistic conceptions.

The energy in the service of the life instincts was called the *libido;* the energy that activates the death instincts was given no special name. As the individual ego develops, more and more of the available psychic energy comes under the dominion of the ego rather than the id, which originally directs it. The ego attaches the energy to psychic representations of external objects; such an attachment is called a *cathexis*. The kind of object cathected depends upon the instinct which has energy available. The distribution of energy over the instincts is flexible. In the original version of analytic theory, the distribution was assumed to change gradually, so that more and more energy was available for the self-preservative instincts of the ego and less and less for the sexual instincts of the id. This version made the basis of conflict the self-preservation versus the sexual instincts, rather than life versus death.

In the course of an individual's development, there is a stage at which much of the libidinal energy is cathected onto the parent of the opposite sex. In the case of the boy, this leads to the development of the Oedipal conflict. Like the mythical Oedipus, the boy loves his mother. He is also jealous and resentful of his rival, the father. His sexual feelings are directed to the mother, but the child is blocked from direct expression of the instinctual urges toward incest. Because of his impulses, which are repressed, the boy has a fear of castration by the father. It is at this time that the urges toward the mother are repressed into the unconscious—so strongly repressed that all sexual urges enter the latency period. They emerge again at puberty, when the increase in sexual tensions is sufficient to upset the psychic economy and allow the impulses to overcome the repressive forces. Freud thought that his discovery of the Oedipal conflict was a major contribution to psychoanalysis. One of the presuppositions necessary for its acceptance is the belief that sexuality is developed very early in life, and that belief has become a hallmark of psychoanalysis.

Treatment of Neurosis

Let us now consider the implications of the psychoanalytic position for the treatment of neurotics. We should remember that this discussion reversed the process as it occurred; the theory grew out of the therapy and the observations that attended it, rather than vice versa.

In treating neurotics, ordinary methods of gathering information about the genesis of symptoms will not work. We have seen how unwelcome memories and impulses are repressed by the ego at the behest of reality, or by the superego. They are not conscious. They are not even available in the in-between zone that Freud called the *preconscious,* from which they might be summoned with sufficient effort. Any attempt to recollect them will be met by *resistance;* accordingly, a special method, such as hypnosis or free association, is required. Dreams, since they are governed to a considerable extent by the primary process, are an avenue to knowledge about the unconscious, provided they are interpreted correctly. Correct interpretation depends upon the knowledge that the function of dreams is to fulfill wishes; since the id does not recognize the difference betweeen hallucinatory and actual satisfaction of wishes, the existing psychic tensions may press toward discharge in dreams. In order to determine the precise meaning of the dream—that is, in order to uncover the hidden (latent) impulses expressed—patients are instructed to give their associations to the elements of their dreams. In this way, dream symbols can be related to their meanings and the repressed material brought to consciousness.

The analysis of resistance to recall of repressed materials is one of the most difficult and most important tasks of the analyst. If the resistance is too strong, the patient continues to refuse to recognize the existence of the repressed material even when the analyst presents it verbally. It is only when the patient can overcome the inner resistance and accept the analysis that improvement becomes possible. Overcoming the resistance brings the impulses under the control of the ego, where they obey the laws of the secondary process. As its dominion is enlarged, the ego is strengthened, and the patient's impulses become accessible to rational control. The patient cannot be freed from the rule of the pleasure principle, but more overall gratification can be obtained once the impulses are also made to conform to the reality principle.

The overcoming of the resistance is made possible, at least in some cases, by the transference to the therapist of a considerable portion of the libidinal energy. This energy is therefore available to the therapist for application of counterforce to the resistance. In turn, the transference itself becomes an object of analysis and must be overcome before the patient is independent and can be said to be cured.

In overcoming the resistance and in tracing the significant repressed material, the patient must be forced to recall material that goes further and further back into childhood. The childhood years are critical in the development of every individual. If a person becomes fixated at some early stage of sexual development or returns (*regresses*) to an earlier stage in the face of later trauma, the scene is set for the development of neurosis. The early experiences that are most likely to be punished, and hence repressed, involve sex. Therefore, the significant material that will be recovered will concern sex. Even more specifically, we can say that the Oedipal conflict and its resolution will be central to the analysis, and the patient's insight into it will be central to recovery.

It is clear in all of this that the symptom is of interest to the Freudian primarily for its symbolic value, as an initial clue that can finally lead the analyst and the patient to the true difficulty. Investigating symptoms to find causes was for many years so much a part of all therapies that it did not even need to be mentioned. It is only in the last 30 years or so, since behavior modifiers in significant numbers began to work *directly* on the elimination of symptoms, that Freud's attitude toward symptoms has been questioned. Are symptoms themselves the problem of the neurotic, or are they only symbols of a deeper-lying problem? That is indeed a fundamental issue, and a clear decision on it would probably help to resolve much of the conflict between psychoanalytic and behavior therapies.

Freud seemed to feel that the iron rule of determinism could be broken if the impulses could be brought under the sway of the secondary process. In this way the patient would substitute *self*-control for impulse control. Freud was less concerned with the question of determinism within the secondary process, although his followers (including his daughter Anna) have spent a great deal of time in the study of ego processes. For Freud, human hope of improvement lay in becoming truly rational. Insight was not a sufficient condition for being cured, but it was a necessary condition. The insight had to be "deep," that is, to involve genuine emotional acceptance of the analysis, not just an intellectual parroting of words.

Freud's emphasis on rationality resulted in a rather strange combination of positions on determinism. In most respects he was an arch determinist. He is famous for his work in the determination of errors in speech and writing, in forgetting, and even in losing objects. He presented evidence that the apparently chance nature of these events conceals the fact that the error reveals the unconscious motivation of the person who has erred, forgotten, or lost something. A published example (Freud, 1938, p. 75) concerns a member of the United Daughters of the Confederacy, who, in concluding her eulogy of Jefferson Davis, said, "the great and only President of the Confederate States of America—Abraham Lincoln!" A previously unpublished example was recently provided by a young woman who said to an admirer who clearly lusted after her, "One reason I like you is that I know you'd never try to make me do what I want to do." In explaining such "slips," Freud was enlarging the presumed realm of determinism; but in helping his patients to achieve ego control, Freud was trying to free them from its grip.

THE REBELS

Four important members of Freud's early group first occupied favored positions and then disagreed with Freudian beliefs and established rival factions. These men were, in order, Adler, Jung, Rank, and Ferenczi. Their defections have been used by opponents of psychoanalysis to demonstrate either that there is no consistency among psychoanalysts or that Freud was a despotic tyrant who brooked no opposition. As we might expect, the charges were neither wholly true nor wholly false. There were both fundamental agreements and fundamental disagreements among the five men presently being considered. As to the personality factors, these are difficult to assess; in every case, some of the blame can probably be laid at each doorstep.

Levinson's research (1978) has thrown an interesting new light on the relationship of Freud to his disciples. Levinson finds that it is typical of young adults that they find a mentor, just as Adler, Jung, Rank, and Ferenczi found Freud. And it is also typical that an intense mentor relationship ends with strong conflict and bad feelings. The younger person finds the mentor critical and demanding, and the older person finds the younger touchy, rebellious, and ungrateful. Thus we have probably tended to think of the successive rebellions of Freud's disciples as unusual, when in fact they are exactly what should have been expected. With this foreword, we now turn to the four men and the modifications they proposed.

Alfred Adler

Alfred Adler (1870–1937) was a Viennese physician who early attached himself to the Wednesday night group that started meeting with Freud in 1902 to discuss psychoanalysis. Adler and Wilhelm Stekel (1868–1940) were Freud's two earliest followers, and they withdrew from the society in successive years (1911 and 1912). Stekel had contributed to the field of symbolism but, according to Jones (1955, p. 135), had no scientific conscience and formed no school of his own after he left the fold of psychoanalysis.

Adler's case was quite different. He made a greater contribution to psychoanalysis, formulated a partially independent theory of behavior, and set up a rival school.

The difficulties between Freud and Adler became intense after Freud insisted that the Swiss analyst Carl Gustav Jung be made president of the international association. The Viennese were jealous of their positions, since they had been the first followers.

Then, the year after the international meetings in 1910, it was decided to hold discussions and debates about Adler's theories. After the discussions, the disagreements about theory seemed both obvious and serious, and Adler and his faction resigned from the Wednesday Society before the end of 1911. Adler named his rival school *individual psychology*.

Freud had at first tolerated or even welcomed Adler's contributions. Adler initially stressed organ inferiority in the backgrounds of neurotics. At first blush, this seems a more biological view even than Freud's. However, appearances are deceptive in this case, for Adler emphasized the psychological reaction to either real or *imagined* organ inferiority, rather than the biological facts themselves. *Compensation* for this inferiority accounts for the nature of many neurotic symptoms and helps to determine the individual's *life style,* the way in which he or she deals with problems in general. The analysis of the compensatory mechanisms was seen by Adler as the major task of both the theory and practice of analysis.

Although Adler emphasized the conflict between masculinity and femininity as very important, his views on sexuality were very different from Freud's. He saw the overcoming of femininity by both males and females ("masculine protest"), rather than sexuality in itself, as the important thing. The will to power was thought to be the greatest motivating force in people's lives, and sex at times was a symptom of this will. The sex act represented a domination of the female, rather than simply the running off of sexual impulses.

The will to power and need to overcome inferiority arise, according to Adler, because of the conditions of life that universally apply for human infants. The infant is not a small sexual animal whose incestuous desires must be repressed, but a small and helpless organism whose every need must be ministered to by relatively powerful adults. Necessarily, then, the infant develops feelings of inferiority relative to these adults and must strive to overcome this inferiority and rise above dependent status. The Oedipal conflict, if it exists at all, should be understood as a conquering of the mother, rather than as a direct expression of any infantile sexuality.

Adler thus shifted the emphasis away from inborn biological instincts and energies and toward the social relationships within the family as the children grow up. He concluded that the position within the family (such as eldest daughter, second son, youngest child) is extremely important in determining how an individual deals with reality (i.e., life style). Sibling rivalry is bound to occur and affect personality. In Adler's theory, we see that the important conflicts often occur between the individual and the environment rather than within the individual as Freud had held.

Adler presented a more hopeful view of the human being than was typical of the orthodox analysts. He saw a person not as a group of segments at war with themselves but as an integrated, striving individual. He laid less stress on the uncovering of the unconscious and its dark forces. He regarded human beings as largely conscious and creative, living partly by adherence to a "fictional future," which consists of possibilities presently believed in. Such possibilities, though they may never come to pass, can nevertheless direct behavior. An example might be the precept "Your reward will be in Heaven."

Adler and his school made therapy a shorter process and, at least sometimes, dispensed with the Freudian couch. Practical applications of Adlerian theory to educational and social problems helped to popularize the theory, as did the ease with which such terms as *inferiority complex* and *sibling rivalry* were assimilated into the lay language. Adler's theory is generally closer to common sense than Freud's.

Carl Gustav Jung

Relationship to Freud. Carl Gustav Jung (1875–1961) was a Swiss psychiatrist who became interested in Freud's theories after reading *The interpretation of dreams,* which appeared in 1900. Jung visited Freud and his Wednesday Society in Vienna in 1907, and the two men immediately became strongly attached to each other. Freud soon viewed Jung as the crown prince of the psychoanalytic movement. In 1909, as we have seen, Jung accompanied Freud to America for the Clark University lectures and later returned to America alone to give additional lectures. At the first meeting of the International Psychoanalytic Association, Jung was elected president. Freud wanted a younger man who was not a Jew to head the new movement so that anti-Jewish sentiment would not impede its progress. On these grounds, Jung seemed the logical choice. The Viennese, who were nearly all Jews, were jealous of their own priority in the movement. They also believed that Jung was himself anti-Semitic. But Freud overcame their objections, and Jung was elected.

Soon after, the relationship between Jung and Freud began to weaken. Jung was not performing his presidential duties as well as Freud had expected. He deemphasized sex in his lectures and in his therapeutic analyses, and he changed the concept of libido. Personal frictions were straining the relations between the two men as they privately accused each other of neurosis, and rivalry developed as both of them nearly simultaneously became interested in the psychology of religion. In January 1913 they agreed to discontinue their personal correspondence. By 1914, Jung had withdrawn completely from the movement. He never resumed his former friendship with Freud, and he soon founded a new school which he called *analytic psychology.*

Basic Attitudes and Methodology. Jung had early assumed that there must be some physical changes which account for the development of schizophrenia. In this he was emphasizing a contemporaneous factor rather than an historical factor as Freud was in the habit of doing. Although Freud at that time agreed with Jung about this particular point, he would not have agreed in general with Jung's emphasis on the present situation, rather than on the past, in the study of neuroses. Jung was more like the Gestaltists, and Freud more like the behaviorists, on this issue. Not only did Jung emphasize the *present* as important, but also he believed that one must understand the future, the potentialities of human beings, in order to make sense when talking about them. Human goals and intentions were to Jung as important in directing human behavior as was personal history. He deplored Freud's study of causality exclusively in terms of the past and thought Freud's theorizing too reductive and mechanistic. Jung later suggested (Jung & Pauli, 1955) a principle called *synchronicity* for those events which occur together in time but do not cause one another. For example, Jung's archetypes, which are primordial images based on inherited response tendencies, are supposed to fulfill themselves psychically and physically within the real world at the same time, although the two manifestations are not causally related. According to van der Post (1975), Jung thought that cause and effect were themselves parts of a more encompassing whole which accounted for both. Events occurring at the same time shared the temporal properties of that given moment in the universal unfolding and hence were, in that sense, more closely related than were effects and their causes.

Jung changed his position on scientific methodology as time passed. At first, he wanted to bridge the gap between academic psychology and psychoanalysis, using the association experiment as one tool for the purpose. Later, Jung lost interest in "proving" analysis through traditionally conceived experiments. He and his followers turned more to the study of mythology and art as more useful methods of revealing the form of the unconscious. Jung became the most negative of the leading analysts toward the traditional methods of empirical science.

Jung's therapy, in accordance with his basic views, put less stress upon the past of the individual and more upon the present situation and desires for the future. Jung saw the human being as more creative and less a passive recipient of environmental influences than had Freud. Jung was accordingly more optimistic in his psychology. Freud saw Jung's therapy as something that might be expected from a priest, with moral exhortation, appeals to willpower, and an attempt to develop human yearnings after the divine (Freud, 1938, p. 975). Jung believed that primitive human urges might be channeled into a quest for self-actualization or for the divine; if the energy were not recognized and used properly by the ego, it might so warp a person's functioning that neurosis or psychosis would result.

Jung's interest in the divine and the similarity of some of his views to religious views are not difficult to understand. Jung's father was a minister, and Jung never strayed far from his upbringing. Rather, he traded conventional views for his own quite unconventional ones but never gave up the essence of his theological beliefs. As he grew older, he turned increasingly from the scientism of his early years back to a position more consonant with the beliefs of his childhood.

Basic Energies and Instincts.   Jung's views about basic human energy were closer to a commonsense conception than Freud's. He regarded the libido as a general biological life energy, not necessarily predominantly sexual. Where Freud saw sexual energy concentrated on different body zones at different stages (oral, anal, phallic, latency, genital), Jung saw the life energy simply manifesting itself in the form which was at the moment most important for the organism. At some times eating was a predominant activity; at others, elimination or sex. The early concentration of gratification on the oral zone was accounted for by the relation of the oral zone to eating rather than to the pleasurable sensations (conceived of by Freud as sexual in the broad sense) which arise from oral stimulation. Jung did not like Freud's lumping together of all pleasurable sensations as sexual.

Since he did not conceive of the basic energy as altogether sexual, Jung was free to reinterpret analytic observations that had previously been assumed to represent sexual strivings. The Oedipal conflict was interpreted in a new way by Jung, as it had been by Adler. For Jung, the nutritive functions become important in the child's attitude toward the mother. These become overlaid and combined with sexual feelings as the child develops in sexual functioning. Combined with these feelings are certain primitive unconscious predispositions to react toward the mother. The Oedipal relationship is then not based, as Freud thought, almost exclusively on sexuality.

Jung transferred concepts from physics almost directly into dicta about psychic energy. He did not believe that psychic energy can be destroyed any more than physical energy can. If the energy is used in some psychic function, the amount available for that function will decrease, but it will reappear in the form of increased energy available for some other function. If the energy disappears from one psychic system, it will reappear in some other. This view is not very unlike Freud's; he, too, talked of the reappearance of unused psychic energy in other forms, as when sexual energy is sublimated and used for artistic creativity. Jung did not believe that the sum of the available psychic energy remains constant, for energy can be exchanged with the external world through such activities as muscular work and the ingestion of food. Energy, since it can flow from one psychic system to another, tends to move from the points of higher energy toward the points of lower energy. The system, in short, tends to reach a state of balance, although such a state cannot be maintained permanently. Even if a temporary balance were to be reached, it would soon be upset by exchanges between some psychic system and the external world. For example, if most of the available energy were concentrated in the personal unconscious, the latter would tend to share energy with other systems, such as the ego. Then an exchange with the external world might occur. The ego would further increase its energy supply from that source, and the direction would now reverse to replenish the personal unconscious.

Views on Psychic Structures. C. S. Hall and Lindzey (1957) wrote an excellent brief summary of Jung's position.

> The total personality or psyche, as it is called by Jung, consists of a number of separate but interacting systems. The principal ones are the *ego*, the *personal unconscious* and its *complexes*, the *collective unconscious* and its *archetypes*, the *persona*, the *anima*, or *animus*, and the *shadow*. In addition to these interdependent systems there are the *attitudes* of introversion and extraversion, and the *functions* of thinking, feeling, sensing, and intuiting. Finally, there is the *self* which is the fully developed and fully unified personality. (p. 79)

Jung's concept of ego is something like the lay idea of a self-concept. It is the conscious mind in contact with reality, and it contains the conscious memories. It is felt to be the center of identity and personality. Jung's ego is also similar to Freud's ego.

The personal unconscious is the region just "interior" to the ego. Since it is in contact with the ego, materials may be repressed into it directly from the ego. The personal unconscious resembles a blend of Freud's unconscious and preconscious. The contents of the personal unconscious are available to consciousness and include both materials which have come into the unconscious as a result of repression of personal experiences of the individual and materials which originated in the collective unconscious.

The collective unconscious lies deeper than the personal unconscious. In this dark and misty region are those things which human beings have inherited phylogenetically. Some of the more distinct things that are inherited are called *archetypes*. Archetypes are predispositions to perceive, act, or think in a certain way. They are formed as a result of the experiences of our forebears, and they include symbols as well as dispositions to act. Since the presumed experiences are universal, the archetypes are also universal. Jung discovered their existence as a result of his study of the myths and art of several ages and cultures. Certain symbols were common to all, despite the presumed lack of any direct exchanges between the cultures. Examples of these universal archetypes are those representing birth, death, the hero, man, woman, child, and God.

Four archetypes are better developed than any of the others: the persona, the anima, the animus, and the shadow. These are so well developed that they have become separate personality systems. The *persona* is the mask presented by an individual to society; it is feminine in women and masculine in men. It may or may not conceal the true personality.

Balancing the persona are the *anima,* which is the feminine part of man, and the *animus,* which is the masculine part of woman. These archetypes constitute Jung's recognition of human bisexuality. They evolve, like any other archetypes, as a result of universal racial experiences. The anima is the result of man's experiences with woman, and the animus is the result of woman's experiences with man.

The *shadow* consists of that part of the unconscious that was inherited from man's prehuman ancestors. It is the animal instinct. Immoral and passionate impulses emanate largely from the shadow. When these impulses appear in consciousness, they may be expressed or repressed. In the latter case, some of the materials of the personal unconscious come from the shadow, up through consciousness, and back down into the personal unconscious.

A fifth well-developed archetype, the *self,* is the most important one of all. Jung found this archetype represented in various cultures by a symbol which was called the *mandala* or *magic circle*. It represented human striving for unity, wholeness, and integration of personality. Jung accordingly made the self a separate system, changing from his earlier conception of the self as equivalent to the whole psyche. The self holds all the other systems together. It apparently strives for oneness of the individual with the world through religious experience as well as for oneness of the psychic systems within the individual. The self can appear only as the other psychic systems become separate enough to require integration, which does not occur until middle age. Some of Jung's disagreements with Freud were based on this "breaking point" in middle age. Jung thought that Freud might be essentially correct about the importance of sexual motivation before middle age, but he believed that Freud had simply ignored what happened after this point had been passed, when the self developed and sex became a subsidiary consideration.

Jung identified two attitudes toward the world: extraversion and introversion. This is the best-known part of his system. In extraversion, most of the individual's attention is directed to the external world; in introversion, to the internal world. Usually the ego and the personal unconscious have opposite attitudes, since both attitudes are always present to some extent somewhere in the personality. The nondominant attitude tends to be repressed. The stronger the conscious expression of one attitude, the stronger the unconscious development of the other. Sometimes an upset allows the libido attached to the unconscious attitude to overwhelm the repression, and the dominant attitude is overcome.

Finally, there are the functions, any one of which may be dominant. Jung's definitions of *thinking, feeling, sensing, and intuiting* do not differ from the common meanings. Jung did not think that there was anything arbitrary about the statement that there are exactly four functions; this was simply a matter of fact as far as he was concerned. Generally, two of the functions predominate at the expense of the other two, and the latter are then developed unconsciously, just as in the case of a repressed attitude. If an individual is described in terms of function and attitude, we have a sort of typology. A feeling-intuiting introvert might be a prophet or a monk. Jung seems to have thought of himself as a thinking-feeling introvert, although van der Post (1975) believed that intuiting, rather than thinking, was Jung's strongest function. In any case, all functions and both attitudes are necessary for successful living, so there are no pure types. The integrated individual has all these factors acting in harmony; people who are nearly pure types are seen as pathological.

Contribution and Evaluation. Jung is difficult to evaluate. When Freud was alive, Jung and all other analysts were in his shadow. Even though Freud is gone, he remains the father of all psychoanalysis. In addition, Jung is difficult to comprehend. As Jones (1957) has said, "Then his mentality had the serious flaw of lacking lucidity. I remember once meeting someone who had been in school with him and being struck by the answer he gave to my question of what Jung had been like as a boy: 'He had a confused mind.' I was not the only person to make the same observation" (p. 32).

Although Jones may have been biased because of his special friendship with Freud, there does seem to be some justification for his attitude. Jung's own statement (1956) about one of his works seems appplicable to many: "It was written at top speed, amid the rush and press of my medical practice, without regard to time or method. I had to fling my material hastily together just as I found it. There was no opportunity to let my thoughts mature. The whole thing came upon me like a landslide that cannot be stopped" (p. xxiii). A book so written could hardly be easy for the reader. In addition to the style problem, the English-speaking reader had the problem of translation until 1966, when the last of eighteen volumes was translated.

Even when the difficult problems of reading and understanding Jung are resolved, others remain. Jung's dislike for traditional scientific methodology makes his views foreign to psychologists who like statistical or laboratory proof. If such proof is demanded, Jung can be dismissed.

In 1929, Jung himself offered an assessment of the status of psychology, including that of his own system: "Our psychology is the more or less successfully formulated confession of a few individuals, and so far as each of them conforms more or less to a type, his confession can be accepted as a fairly valid description of a large number of people" (reprinted in Hillix & Marx, 1974, pp. 372–373). Jung makes it quite clear that he intends this comment to apply to psychoanalysis as developed by Freud and Adler, as well as to his own system. Thus there would be at least three sorts of people, each reasonably well described and explained by a different psychoanalytic theory.

At first blush, this seems to be a peculiar sort of science in which there are no general laws. There are only limited laws which apply to an appropriate set of persons. However, Diesing (1971) describes this procedure exactly as one of his four "methods of discovery" in the social sciences. It is part of the holistic method, which begins with concrete data, discovers themes in the data, then constructs typologies (which are theories of limited scope), and finally develops a general theory which accounts for all the types. Within this context, psychoanalysis would be seen as an intermediate stage of scientific development, which might lead eventually to a general theory of the kind aspired to by most scientists.

Jung's importance has grown within recent years. He outlived Freud by 22 years, and his works were translated into English soon after his death. His ideas are novel and provocative. They are based in part upon Oriental religion and philosophy, in which there has been a surge of Western interest. His view of the human being is a refreshing antidote to Freud's pessimism. His views seem more acceptable to women, and women played a crucial role in the Jungian school and the development of Jungian theory. Jung's position affords a comfortable resting place for those who are surfeited with the scientific approach and its results. Jungian psychology fits well with modern existentialism and even with mysticism. These movements have strengthened one another.

It is significant that Jung's scientific training was not as long or as intense as Freud's. Thus Jung was more easily able to accept a view inconsistent with traditional science. Freud had faced and passed many fearful tests of courage, but he never conceived the possibility of flying completely and purposely in the face of organized science. Jung did. That will be his downfall or his salvation. Jung was erudite and enthusiastic, and his followers were loyal and dedicated once they understood him. We cannot predict what the coming years will do to the popularity of Jung's psychology.

Rank and Ferenczi

Although their views and contributions were not identical, we will discuss Otto Rank (1884–1939) and Sandor Ferenczi (1873–1933) together because they published together and because their defections from Freud were related, although Rank's schism from Freud was earlier, more severe, and more complete than Ferenczi's. Neither has approached the stature of Freud, Adler, or Jung, although their contributions to psychoanalytic theory and practice were significant.

In 1922, Rank began to present his ideas on birth trauma. In addition, he and Ferenczi were collaborating on a book entitled *The development of psychoanalysis* (Ferenczi & Rank, 1923). The book advocated the possibility of shorter therapy and stirred considerable dissension among analysts. Even more disturbing was the book Rank later wrote alone, *The trauma of birth* (1929). Freud reacted quite positively to the book at first, but he was later ambivalent about it. Complicating the picture was Rank's aversion to Jones; Freud apparently did not know whose side to take in these disagreements. A series of declarations of independence by Rank followed by declarations of friendship finally resulted in Rank's complete separation from Freud and the orthodox analytic movement.

Initially, Ferenczi showed some hostility to the members of the committee and was disappointed by his treatment at party congresses. He was never elected president by a full congress. However, his final separation from Freud was neither so early nor so dramatic as that of Rank. He simply drifted away from the other analysts, partly because of his therapeutic beliefs. There was little or no bitterness between him and Freud, at least until near the end of Ferenczi's life in 1933; by that time Ferenczi's physical illness may have affected his mind (Jones, 1957, p. 176).

Rank's background—or lack thereof, medically speaking—contributed a professional issue to psychoanalysis. He had come from a technical school to the Wednesday Society and had there been encouraged to attend the university. His application of psychoanalysis to cultural developments endeared him to Freud. Rank thereby swayed Freud in favor of lay analysts. Freud had never identified with the medical profession himself and did not see any absolute necessity to study medicine before practicing analysis.

Rank's more direct contribution was connected largely with the birth trauma. In a sense, Rank was pushing Freud's concern with the early years to its logical conclusion. He saw the neuroses as originating in the trauma of birth, when the child experiences a forcible and painful expulsion from the comfort of the womb into the terrors of the world. This trauma, he believed, is never forgotten. The "separation anxiety" that results from the birth trauma is basic to neurotic symptoms. The clash of will between child and parent that later attends the growing-up process is also important. The job of the therapist, then, is to alleviate both the guilt of the patient over this clash and his or her anxiety over separation. In order to get the patient to work hard during therapy and in order to ensure that the patient does not become overdependent on the therapist, a definite date is set for the separation of therapist and patient. The therapy is then terminated at the agreed time, and the patient develops in therapy the ability to function alone after this time.

One interesting sidelight on Rank's theory is connected with Freud's usual dislike of statistical treatment of data. The only known exception to this aversion occurred when Freud was in a critical mood toward Rank's theory; he suggested (Jones, 1957, p. 68) that he would never have proposed the theory without prior statistical evaluation of the mentalities of those who were firstborn, had difficult births, or were delivered by Caesarean section.

Sandor Ferenczi made no theoretical modifications as sweeping as Rank's. His chief defections were in therapeutic technique. He shared with Rank the belief that it is not always necessary to exhume the historical origins of neurotic symptoms; thus a briefer therapy should be possible. Ferenczi thought that the warm relationship with the mother was missing in the lives of most of his neurotic patients and that the therapist should supply the missing element. Accordingly, he coddled patients, holding them on his lap and kissing them at times (Jones, 1957, pp. 163–164). Freud saw this as opening the door to therapeutic techniques which could discredit psychoanalysis completely, and Ferenczi was hurt by Freud's doubts. However, he would not be dissuaded from his belief that *acting out* the unconscious problems is the way to mental health, and he continued to use his unique therapy until his health became so poor that he could no longer work. Compared to the primal therapy or nude marathon of the 1970s, Ferenczi's procedures appear quite conservative.

LATER DEVELOPERS OF PSYCHOANALYSIS

After the first surge of development and rebellion in psychoanalysis, there arose a second generation of psychoanalytic theory, closely related to the first generation but branching out in directions that generally were logical developments of the original ideas. By now, there have been thousands of workers trained in psychoanalysis. We have space to consider only two, who must serve as representatives of all those who bridged the time between the earliest days of psychoanalysis and the present time. If there is a common theme in these representatives, it is that the human being cannot be understood separately from society. In making this point, the newer theories necessarily pay less attention, relatively speaking, to biological factors. This relative neglect of instinctual factors sets these theories apart from Freudian and Jungian theory. The newer theories have also paid close attention to ego functioning, which brings them a step closer to modern cognitive psychology and a step away from Freudian views.

Karen Horney

Karen Horney (1885–1952) was trained entirely within the field of psychoanalysis. German by birth, Horney studied medicine at the University of Berlin. She received her psychoanalytic training at the Berlin Psychoanalytic Institute under Karl Abraham and Hans Sachs. Abraham was one of the members of Freud's "committee." Horney stayed at the Berlin Institute from 1918 until 1932, when she became one of the early emigrants to the United States. When she arrived during the Great Depression, she found that American neuroses refused to conform to the Freudian model. Money, more often than sex, was found at the center of these American neuroses. That finding helped to lead her away from biological factors and toward social factors in neurosis.

Horney was associate director of the Chicago Psychoanalytic Institute, taught at the New York Psychoanalytic Institute, and conducted a private practice in psychotherapy. Her efforts to break away from orthodox psychoanalysis led to the formation of the Association for the Advancement of Psychoanalysis, of which she was dean.

Horney's theoretical emphasis is reflected in the titles of three of her books: *Neurotic personality of our times* (1937), *Our inner conflicts* (1945), and *Neurosis and human growth* (1950). Her ties to psychoanalysis are obvious in two other book titles, *New ways in psychoanalysis* (1939), and *Self-analysis* (1942).

Horney's social theory flies the banner of *basic anxiety*. She believed that the essential factor in personality development is "the feeling a child has of being isolated and helpless in a potentially hostile world" (1937, p. 79). Horney's concept of help-lessness as experienced by the infant does not have the universal flavor that Adler assigned to it. It provides a predisposition for the future development of pathological conditions, without necessarily leading to a striving for superiority. It does produce a desire for security.

The home environment and the social structure within the family receive by far the greatest emphasis in Horney's theory. In this structure and the child's reaction to it, Horney believed she had the key to the development of an individual's personality structure. The predominant reason that basic anxiety develops from parent-child re-lationships is the absence of genuine love and affection, and this can almost invariably be traced to neurotic parents. It should be noted, however, that Horney defines neurosis as any deviation from normal, efficient behavior. The term is not used to indicate pathology unless that is explicitly stated.

The child responds to basic anxiety by developing some strategy of behavior, called a *neurotic trend,* in an attempt to overcome the anxiety. It is this character structure arising from the reaction to basic anxiety which accounts for neurotic symptoms. It is *not,* as Freud had claimed, a frustration of the sexual instinct. Horney maintained that sexual difficulty is the result, and not the cause, of conflicts. Furthermore, it is not a compulsion to repeat experiences based on unchanged, repressed childhood experiences: "There is no such thing as an isolated repetition of isolated experiences; but the entirety of infantile experiences combines to form a certain character structure, and it is this structure from which later difficulties emanate" (Horney, 1939, p. 9).

The child also develops an idealized self-concept by internalizing the aspirational levels and ethics of others in the culture. This concept develops without regard for the child's own potentialities or limitations. Consequently, in trying to reach these ideal goals, the child is curtailed both by personal limitations and by limitations imposed by the culture. In other words, a person's basic conflict is between self-realization and self-idealization. The idealized self becomes a crutch for neurotic persons. They come to believe that they *are* their idealized picture. This solution brings a temporary reduction of anxiety but in the long run increases it. The attempts of neurotics to live up to their idealized, unrealistic picture of themselves result in new conflicts and consequently in greater tension. The only real conflict which Horney recognized is that resulting from the present situation and the demands it makes upon the individual.

The devices which the person uses to face conflicts (neurotic trends) are generally unrealistic and lead to some degree of neurotic behavior. These may be classified into two categories: (1) those which have their roots in the early developmental period and which demonstrate a discernible etiology, and (2) those which are a reaction to some situational stress and are usually transitory (Munroe, 1955). A vicious circle develops once these neurotic trends are initiated. Anxiety causes an original behavior, whose inadequacy, in turn, leads to further anxiety which initiates another cycle.

In attempting to find security, individuals use three types of behavioral patterns: moving toward people, moving against people, or moving away from people (Horney, 1945). Fundamental to these three types of behavior are the need for affection, the need to exploit people, and the need for self-sufficiency. There are personality types corresponding to the type of behavior selected: compliant, aggressive, and detached. Again one must be cautious not to assume that an individual uses only a single type. Vacillating from one situation to another, a person uses the behavior most efficient for the specific situation. The exclusive use of a single type of behavior, regardless of the situation, is an index of neurosis.

The compliant individual relies upon other people; is ostensibly loving, kind, and loyal; and finds personal criticism devastating. Cynicism, a philosophy of the survival of the fittest, and extreme independence characterize the aggressive personality. The detached individual is perfectionistic, uncreative, and lacks interpersonal relationships.

Horney emphasized only two of the many unconscious defense mechanisms: rationalization and externalization. Rationalization is used in the Freudian sense, except that it is explained in the context of the social theory of Horney; that is, it is concerned with the whole organism and is not related to Freud's instinctual personality components. Externalization is merely a more general term for projection. The whole organism participates in an attempt to explain *every* motive and action externally, not just the undesirable ones.

Horney was optimistic about the possibility of avoiding neurotic reactions, as one tends to be when one believes that social factors are of preponderant importance. A secure and loving home would be insurance against the development of a neurotic character structure. Those, like Freud, who emphasize biological factors find it harder to be optimistic. If conflict is based on hereditary factors, change is likely to be slow and difficult. Horney's more hopeful views, like Adler's, were welcomed as a relief from the oppressive pessimism of the orthodox Freudian assumptions. She attempted to point the way to better families, to better societies, and, through them, to better people. Despite her long-term association with the training of analysts, Horney never formed a cohesive school of followers, nor did her theoretical views inspire research directly. As time passes, Horney's important contributions will probably become less associated with her name and more a part of the general *Zeitgeist* of psychology.

Erich Fromm

Erich Fromm (1900–1980), like Horney, was born and trained in Germany and emigrated to the United States. He studied sociology and psychology at the Universities of Munich and Frankfurt, and at Heidelberg, where he took his Ph.D. His psychoanalytic training was mainly at the Berlin Psychoanalytic Institute.

After his emigration in 1933, Fromm was not firmly identified with any one institution. He lectured at the Chicago Psychoanalytic Institute, and he taught at numerous other institutes and universities in the United States. After 1951, he was a professor at the University of Mexico and director of the Mexican Psychoanalytic Institute. He spent some time each summer in New York City, while maintaining a primary residence in Mexico City.

Fromm's major contributions to neo-Freudian analysis were presented in *Escape from freedom* (1941), *Man for himself* (1947), and *The sane society* (1955). These books (cf. Fromm, 1961b) express the relationship of the larger segments of society to the individual. Partly because of their relationships to the political upheavals of the time, they attracted more attention from nonpsychological scientists and from the lay public than did the works of any of Fromm's peers.

Fromm was a greater admirer of Marx (Fromm, 1961a) than of Freud (Fromm, 1959), and he could as well be labeled a Marxist personality theorist as a Freudian personality theorist (see Hall & Lindzey, 1970, p. 130). Fromm believed that our political organizations no longer provided the firm direction and secure framework which they did when the units of political organization were smaller and people had less freedom to determine their own fates. People today suffer from a feeling of insecure aloneness engendered by their lack of a framework. They desire to actualize their self-potential and develop a feeling of belongingness.

Fromm's basic premise that an individual attempts to escape from freedom and return to a more secure existence first gained public notice in his appropriately titled *Escape from freedom*. Children's physical condition at birth and shortly thereafter makes their survival dependent upon their environment in general and upon their mothers in particular. Children are soon weaned from early postnatal surroundings, and they gradually achieve more and more independence. However, the accompanying amount of strength necessary to augment their independence and to cope with the elements of society is conspicuously lacking. Moreover, human beings alone have the power to reason and imagine, and with the acquisition of this power they have lost the animal's ability to react to nature instinctively, intimately, and directly. Thus people find themselves in a unique position, separated from their fellows by political conditions and from the rest of nature by being human. Their first reaction to this situation is to try to recapture their earlier form of security. Upon finding this physically impossible and socially inefficient, they attempt other means. The two most common solutions are *authoritarianism* and *humanism*.

Broadly defined, authoritarianism is that which externally imposes a set of standards on society. It may be exemplified by a totalitarian state, or dictatorship, or belief in a supreme being. These solutions are inadequate because they do not permit individuals an opportunity to realize their potentialities. Frustration and hostility against the imposed conditions are then mobilized.

Fromm believed that humanism is a better solution. All the possibilities of human life have a chance to develop through love of fellow human beings and through mutual cooperation. In a humanistic society, all people would be brothers and sisters and no one would be alone.

Fromm identified four ways of escaping the isolation and insecurity prevalent in modern society. He referred to them as types of *orientation*, or relatedness. These types of orientation are receptive, exploitative, hoarding, and marketing. In addition, there is the healthy, or productive, orientation. No person exhibits a pure orientation. However, it is possible to manifest one type so that it subordinates all others.

The *receptive* orientation "is often to be found in societies in which the right of one group to exploit another is firmly established" (Fromm, 1947, p. 79). Individuals with this type of orientation sacrifice everything to maintain their identification with the group or the leader. They expect to receive something gratis, and when adversity occurs they are extremely rebellious and aggressive, exhibiting behaviors not unlike those of a spoiled child.

The philosophy of "might makes right" characterizes *exploitative* individuals. The value which they place upon an object is directly proportional to the value which others place on it. They would feel no compunction about taking some object for no other reason than that it is highly prized by another.

The *hoarding* orientation is what one might expect it to be. Individuals with this orientation are frugal, impecunious, and miserly. Security is evaluated in terms of tangible physical wealth.

The last orientation, *marketing,* was associated with the advent of modern capitalism. Its emphasis is centered upon such superficial objectives as keeping up with the Joneses and the related social climbing.

Fromm (1964) later added the *biophilous* type, who is in love with life. If love of life is frustrated, a person with this orientation may become *necrophilous* (attracted to death).

As society now stands, it is necessary to warp the individual to some extent to fit the needs of society. Though this necessity cannot be circumvented, Fromm sees hope in societies which give each individual a chance to develop into a fully human creature within these limits. Fromm named his ideal society a *humanistic communitarian socialism.* His desperate concern for the development of such a society, born at least partly out of his own flight from Nazism, put him in the forefront of the psychology of his time. Psychology has only in the last 20 years or so experienced a relatively complete social and political awakening. Every conception of the human being has implications for the kind of society in which people can live comfortably. For example, Skinner has tried to specify the nature of his Utopian society and to tell us how to get "beyond freedom and dignity." But few psychologists have devoted as high a percentage of their efforts to clarifying the significance of politics for persons and of persons for politics as Erich Fromm. One of our missions must be to study this problem, and Erich Fromm tried hard to show us the way.

SYSTEMATIC FEATURES OF PSYCHOANALYSIS

Because of the differences between the positions of Freud, the rebels, and the developers, there is no single system of psychoanalysis. However, there are important commonalities even among the most disparate of the positions, and we shall try to keep these commonalities in the focus of the discussion to follow. Where there are conflicts, we will present Freud's system rather than some compromise position.

Definition of Psychology

Although Freud was not within the psychological tradition as such, psychoanalysis was probably, to him, the only psychology worthy of the name. He was interested in developing a systematic framework but not in stating definitions. His followers did not differ from him on this point. At one time Freud distinguished psychoanalysis, but did not define it, by its concern with resistance and transference; at another time he said that the distinguishing mark of an analyst was concern with sexual factors. We will follow Freud in being content with pointing out some salient features of psychoanalysis, providing an implicit definition of psychology from an analytic view. Psychoanalysis is a discipline which began in the study of neurosis through the techniques of hypnosis, dream analysis, and free association. It emphasizes unconscious motivational conditions. It has broadened its fields and methods of study to include anthropological investigation, laboratory experiments, testing techniques, and the study of normal persons, cultures, and cultural records. Rapaport (1959) said that psychoanalysts do intend to define psychology in a way that allows psychoanalysis to encompass it:

> Finally, in the late thirties, forties, and fifties, the influence of psychoanalysis and of the psychoanalytic ego psychology expanded to the whole of psychology, first through projective techniques into clinical psychology, then into experimental clinical psychology, and finally into experimental psychology proper. Thus the original claim of comprehensiveness for this theory is gradually being realized. (p. 79)

Several basic assumptions are made by analysts, and these assumptions must be included as a part of the definition of the school; only those who accept some minimum number of them are accepted as analysts. These assumptions are examined next.

Basic Postulates

According to Munroe (1955), nearly all varieties of analysts accept four basic assumptions. First, the psychic life is *determined*. Second, the *unconscious* plays a dominant role in determining human behavior, which previously had been thought to follow rational patterns of determination. Third, the most important explanatory concepts are *motivational* (i.e., "dynamic"). Many different behavioral manifestations can be explained by recourse to a single underlying motivational concept. The emphasis is on the purposiveness of action rather than on more mechanical S-R connections. Fourth, the *history* of the organism is of extreme importance in determining contemporary behavior.

More orthodox analysts usually accept several additional postulates, which may be summarized as follows. The basic drive is sexual and has its foundation in the biology of the organism. The manifestations of this primal biological energy include the various instincts. There is a basic conflict of life and death instincts. A structural, topographical model is needed to explain unconscious activity; Freud's id, ego, and superego are the usually accepted structures. Parental relationships with the young child account for the neuroses. The individual goes through various stages of libidinal development— oral, anal, phallic, latency, and genital. The defense mechanisms under the control of the ego protect the individual from psychological harm. Finally, dreams, slips of the tongue, wit, and various errors have symbolic meaning related to repressed sexual content.

Although we have called the above assumptions *postulates,* the term should not be taken to mean formal logical axioms. Freud was an inductive thinker, at least as he conceived his own creative process. He did not see himself as postulating at all but merely as reporting or summarizing the results of his observations. His reaction to Janet's saying that the unconscious was a manner of speaking shows that Freud did not like to have his concepts treated as postulates. The behavior of many of his followers indicates a similar feeling. However, it does not matter how concepts are viewed as long as they play a useful part in theory.

Nature of the Data

The basic data of psychoanalysis come from the therapeutic setting. They are the data of verbal report, a type of introspection. Although psychoanalytic introspection is markedly different from the structuralist type, it shares similar difficulties, sometimes in exaggerated form. If psychoanalytic introspection is supposed to give information about past events, then the original stimuli for the verbal report occurred months or years previously. Many of the hypotheses of psychoanalysis are about relationships between present behavior and events in the patient's past. Some critics (e.g. Skinner, 1954) think that one of the main contributions of psychoanalysis was its emphasis on the causal importance of events in the life of the individual. Yet there have been few direct studies of these events. The data are the *current* verbal productions of the patient. We have seen that Freud was puzzled when he concluded, after checking the reports of his patients against the reports of other family members, that many of the events reported by the patients could not have occurred. Freud then decided that the report was its own justification that the event was important for therapy. While Freud may not have been correct in either conclusion, Ezriel (1951) has argued on the basis of such reasoning that analysis is *not* an historical method. It seems that he is correct, since the analyst works on the assumption that *reports* about the past are what is important. Operationally speaking, the analyst has nothing to do with the past of the patient. Looked at from this perspective, Freud's emphasis on "the past" and the rebels' emphasis upon the present become the same. Psychoanalysis is a dynamic, not a genetic, method, working with contemporary, rather than with genetic, data.

The relationship between the data and the theory of psychoanalysis is thus not altogether clear. If the theory is about genetic factors, then most of the data are highly questionable. The past events must be *inferred* from the kind of data collected. We remember from the criticisms of structural psychology that psychologists have generally not been content to trust human memory for more than a few seconds, even under strictly controlled conditions. If the data are recognized for what they are—appropriate to statements about the present only—then the form of Freudian theory would seem to require modification. This kind of criticism is, of course, less relevant for Jung or even Adler, since they both recognized the importance of including the present and a representation of the future in their theoretical presentations. Even in their cases, however, many of the hypotheses are about the past—in Jung's case, even the phylogenetic past, about which no direct observational data are available.

A second difficulty arises necessarily from the nature of the therapeutic relationship. Many of the statements made by patients must be kept confidential. Analysts must play the role of therapist during an analytic session and can take the detached role of scientist only after the session is over. They may forget, or they may select only confirmatory data. What a patient says may be influenced by previous statements of the analyst. Freud himself taught his patients some analytic theory in the therapeutic process, although he did not teach them as much in later years; such learning may have inclined the patients toward behaving in accordance with theory. Thus the confirmation by a patient that, for example, the analysis of a dream is correct is of little value. The patient has participated in the interpretation under the influence of the therapist and knowing something about the psychoanalytic theory of dreams. The net result of all these difficulties is that it is very difficult to gather convincing data which relate psychoanalytic theory to the events of therapy.

One might wish to ignore the need to evaluate the relationship between the "microstructure" of the therapeutic interaction and psychoanalytic theory and to concentrate on the relative successes of psychoanalytic therapies and other therapies. However, such comparisons have their own pitfalls. For example, Nash, Frank, Imber, and Stone (1964) found a huge effect of beginning treatment. The effect was visible regardless of treatment type and started even before treatment began. Sloane, Staples, Cristol, Yorkston, and Wipple (1975) found that both behavior therapy and psychoanalytically oriented therapy accelerated improvement relative to carefully selected control subjects. However, they also found that the behavior therapists made just as many interpretations as the psychoanalytic therapists! In the literally hundreds of studies of therapeutic outcome that have now been done, a typical finding is that less than 10 percent of the variance in outcome is related to patient, therapist, or technique variables (Hartley & Strupp, 1983; Rosenthal, 1983; Smith, Glass, & Miller, 1980). The outcomes of these studies reinforce our point that therapeutic studies in their present form cannot test theory.

Frank (1974) hypothesized on the basis of earlier studies that the demonstrated, but nondifferential, success of psychotherapy rested upon a few simple factors common to all therapies. For example, all therapies involved a relationship with another person that made the patient expect help and aroused emotions. Each therapy also furnished a rationale for the patients' suffering and later improvement, new information about the patient and the world, and experiences leading to increased feelings of competence and mastery.

Since it seems impossible to demonstrate the superiority of psychoanalytic therapy, we might expect behavior therapists to ignore it. We have already seen that they do not; in addition, Lazarus (1971) found that ten of twenty behaviorists who were themselves in therapy were in psychoanalytic therapy, with the rest scattered across a number of other types of therapy, none of which was behavioral! It seems that psychoanalytic therapy remains a highly viable alternative, even among those we might expect to be its most sophisticated critics and competitors.

The therapeutic situation is not the only "naturalistic" setting in which observation relevant to psychoanalytic theory have been made. Kardiner (1939), Mead (1950), and Malinowski (1950) have gleaned relevant data from primitive societies. These data have sometimes bolstered the system and sometimes necessitated its modification; for example, the data have not supported the supposed universality of the Oedipal complex (Toulmin, 1948).

Hilgard (1952) has reported data from human subjects in laboratory or classroom situations. These data are concerned with isolated portions of psychoanalytic theory, as is necessary in any closely controlled study. Still absent is the painstakingly detailed longitudinal study which would be needed to give sound underpinning to psychoanalytic genetic assumptions. Pumpian-Mindlin (1952) pointed out the need for such research to be carried out by a psychoanalytic institute.

Psychoanalytic theory has been tested even in animal experiments. Sears (1943) reviewed the early research in this genre. A disproportionately large number of these studies involved tests of fixation or regression, and the results were somewhat discouraging. However, Fisher and Greenberg (1977) reported a much greater degree of validation of Freudian principles, even within the experimental framework involved in Sears' original survey.

Horwitz (1963) points out that psychoanalysts are often sublimely uninterested in such experiments. Too often the hypotheses investigated are trivial, or the experimental investigator has not taken the trouble to get more than a most superficial knowledge of psychoanalytic theory. Under these conditions, the attitude of the analyst is certainly understandable. However, the overconcern with a limited number of concepts may be as much an indication of weakness in the theory as of weakness in the investigators. Too many psychoanalytic statements are so general or so ambiguous that they are difficult or impossible to test.

New York University psychologist Lloyd Silverman (1976, 1983) has performed a large number of laboratory research studies and has reviewed similar research by other investigators. The results are mixed, but they favor the psychodynamic hypotheses of psychoanalysis by a ratio of at least 3 to 1. Silverman's research design calls for the presentation of subliminal stimuli designed to elicit, unconsciously, aggressive or calming effects. For example, a picture of a snarling man and the statement "Cannibal Eats Person" were reported to produce transitory increases in "ego pathology." The positive stimulus "Mommy and I are One" is reported to relieve the pathological symptoms of subjects in a variety of experimental settings. Silverman interprets these results as demonstrating the soothing effects of the unconscious fantasy of gratification produced by the stimulus. Control subliminal stimuli (e.g., "People are Walking") typically produce significantly smaller behavioral effects. Double-blind procedures are used, so that neither the biases of the experimenter nor those of the subject can affect the results. Although Silverman's results remain controversial (Adams, 1982), it is significant that the basic Freudian ideas are being subjected to this kind of laboratory test so that they can be evaluated on experimental as well as theoretical and clinical grounds.

Another laboratory research program has been conducted by Howard Shevrin and his associates at the University of Michigan Center. They also use subliminal stimuli but measure the effects by evaluating psychophysiological recordings. Shevrin and Dickman (1980) describe the research and its results, which are generally in accord with Freudian theory.

Still another project is directed by Reyher (1977) at Michigan State University. Stories containing stimuli for socially unacceptable sexual or aggressive impulses are given to subjects under hypnotic induction, with key words emphasized in posthypnotic suggestion. Behavioral disturbances are subsequently assessed as a function of the presentation of selected stimulus words, certain of which (the key words) are related to the impulses and others of which are control (unrelated) cues. Statistically reliable differences in support of psychoanalytic propositions have been reported in these studies.

Mind-Body Position

Freud was a modern in this respect; he did not much concern himself with the question. Jones (1953, p. 367) said that passages could be quoted from Freud which would place him in any one of several philosophical mind-body positions. Freud self-consciously declared himself a psychophysical parallelist; he held that psychical processes cannot occur in the absence of physiological processes and that the latter must precede the former. He thus assigned some priority to the material, a priority that may have been held over from his student days when he espoused a radical materialism.

Principles of Connection

Since psychoanalysis developed outside of academic psychology, it might not have treated the problem of connection as such. However, we have already seen that Jung made a good deal of association in his early work. Even earlier, the free-association method became a key feature of psychoanalysis. One can ask how it happens that associations are connected in such a way that they provide, as Freud said of the dream, a "royal road to the unconscious."

The principles of connection are of several kinds. First, there are the classic principles of contiguity, similarity, and opposition (contrast). These principles all refer to contiguity, similarity, and contrast *in the experience of the individual*. Although the acceptance of these classic principles makes available a rudimentary learning theory, Rapaport (1959) explicitly says, "If we must single out an outstanding limitation of this theory's claim to comprehensiveness, then we should choose its lack of a specific learning theory" (p. 79).

The more important principles of connection are those which relate to motivational factors. In an association, the similarity or opposition may be one of motive or feeling, rather than a matter of the objective stimuli. A recognition of this fact enables analysts to recognize connections which are not apparent to academic psychologists. The determination of associations by these factors also explains why the patient's "free" associations involve material relevant to the patient's basic problems. These problems beget motives which in turn control the associations.

Still other and more complex principles are needed to explain why certain symptoms arise from associated problems and why certain manifest content arises from its latent content in the dream. These are the special principles of symbolism mentioned earlier: distortion, displacement, and condensation. Finally, there are the defense mechanisms of the ego, such as rationalization and projection. They explain the connections between some overt behaviors and their motivational bases. The complexity of these principles of symbolism and defense has made them the subject of extended analytic investigation.

Principles of Selection

Motivation is the key to selection as well as to connection. In most systems, the principles of selection and connection are the obverse of each other. Analysts have emphasized the selectivity exercised in the movement of material into consciousness from the preconscious and unconscious more than they have the selection of stimuli in the environment. The selection of an idea or memory depends upon the dynamic balance between repressive forces and the instinctual forces that are striving to get the repressed material expressed. Repression acts selectively to remove material from consciousness, and resistances act to keep out the emotionally toned material. The job of the analyst is to redistribute the available libidinal energy so that the repressive forces of the ego or superego are lessened relative to the expressive forces. Often the libido attached to the repressed material is so strong that it forces its own selection for acting out in disguised form; for example, repressed hostility may be expressed through its projection onto other persons, who are then thought to be hostile. The ego is continuously selecting appropriate repressed materials for such symbolic expression. The principles of connection are also involved in selection. These principles must determine the symbols that must be selected in order to give vent to repressed impulses.

We see from such examples that Freud developed in detail principles of selection and connection for cases that had previously been regarded as arbitrary and lawless. He extended the principles to the unconscious, where different laws were required, and this extension is at the heart of his system.

Research involving the so-called new look in perception, which is no longer very new, has been concerned with the effects of motivation on the perception of objective stimuli. Such selective perception has been demonstrated in the laboratory (Erdelyi, 1974) and represents an extension of analytic thinking from memory to perception. Although the interpretation given to some of the experiments has been questioned (e.g., Goldiamond, 1958), there can be no doubt that variables which were earlier thought irrelevant to perception have received careful study, and they do turn out to have significant effects. An example of the results is the finding that more time is required for the perception of a taboo word than for the perception of a neutral word. The analytic interpretation would be that an unconscious ego-defensive mechanism tends to inhibit perception of guilt-arousing words.

CRITICISMS OF PSYCHOANALYSIS

Immorality

Both the lay and the religious publics have sometimes been vindictive toward psychoanalysis, especially the orthodox Freudian type, because of its alleged irreligiosity, amorality, and overemphasis on sex. It has been said that Freud reviled and desecrated religion and childhood. Freud was not personally religious, and he attempted to explain religiosity in scientific terms. It is also true that Freud extended the concept of sexuality into childhood and advocated less repressive attitudes toward sex, including realistic sex education.

Regardless of Freud's personal feelings and his statements on these subjects, such criticisms are altogether irrelevant to the truth or falsity of his scientific hypotheses. If one regards Freud's pronouncements on these subjects as philosophical rather than scientific, then one can reject them on the basis of values rather than on the basis of validity. A reader who does not like Freud's pessimism about life can reject it for more optimistic views, but such acceptance or rejection is again independent of scientific considerations.

Origins

Several critics have pointed out relationships between Freud's personality or background and the theory he evolved. For example, some might read Bakan's book (1958) as a denunciation of psychoanalysis, since it points out in a clear and scholarly way the relationship between Jewish mysticism and psychoanalysis, with side excursions into Freud's messianic feelings and their implications for theory. It is no rarity to see the Oedipal part of analysis explained by recourse to Freud's own relationship with his young mother, or to see his tendency to oppose traditional views reduced to a reaction to his membership in the Jewish minority.

Ellenberger (1970) suggests that Anna O. was simply a classic case of hysteria, in the sense that her symptoms were the effect of suggestion more than they were symbolic reactions to traumatic events. If this were true of her and of many other patients—suggestibility is a pervasive problem—then the foundations of psychoanalysis would be very weak. Freud, of course, became acutely aware that the reports of his patients might be fabrications, but he appears not to have considered the possibility that part of the symptomatology of analytic patients might be created by the analyst.

Thus the data of psychoanalysis are not so convincing as most scientific data. If a critic claims that an analytic belief is only an outcome of the personal experiences of the theorist, it seems reasonable to expect the defender of psychoanalysis to show that the belief also rests upon some firmer foundation of acceptable data.

Theory

No complete psychological system provides an adequate theory. Psychoanalysis is certainly no exception. We must take a very broad view of theory even to consider that there *is* a psychoanalytic theory. There are many empirical generalizations, and some parts of psychoanalytic theory constitute rudimentary models. Walker (1957) outlined the nature of the unconscious as a scientific model. Rapaport (1959) discussed four separate models and one combined model.

Freud regarded himself as only a beginner, and his system as only a beginning. Perhaps the analogy between psychoanalysis and phrenology (Dallenbach, 1955) is not so unfair as it first appears to be; both disciplines brought about important changes in scientific attitudes. Bakan (1968) has meanwhile convincingly defended the virtue of phrenology, so it is no longer necessary to be offended by an analogy between psychoanalysis and phrenology, no matter how accurate it may be.

Since no psychological theory of great scope is satisfactory, one cannot reasonably criticize psychoanalysis for imperfections. The more justifiable question becomes whether a particular theory is ever likely to *become* a good theory. Rapaport (1959) expressed pessimism by doubting that the theory could ever be confirmed by generating and testing predictions. Horwitz (1963) is more optimistic and does not see why testing is impossible in the long run. A damning statement, if it continued to be true, was made in a review by Ford and Urban (1967):

> Similarly, although 30 to 40 psychoanalytic articles and books have been examined, they are not emphasized here. Our examination of that literature gives the strong impression that little substantive development is underway. . . . There is little substantive novelty in these writings, and they are likely to be of interest only to followers of the particular view represented. . . . These books, the psychoanalytic literature this year, and our reading of that literature during the last few years lead us to the conclusion that the innovative steam has gone out of the psychoanalytic movement. Major theoretical and technical advances in the future will probably come from other orientations, although the theoretical contributions of the past will continue to be influential. (p. 333)

It is now 20 years since Ford and Urban rendered that verdict, and there is nothing that compels disagreement with its essentials. Psychoanalysis, which has recently been approved as a division within the American Psychological Association, seems to be more in a period of consolidation than in a period of innovation. The work of people like Silverman, which has been mentioned above, is some cause for believing that psychoanalytic propositions may be confirmed or disconfirmed, but there is not a great deal of "innovative steam" with respect to theoretical development in this work or in the other research intended to test psychoanalytic hypotheses.

As is almost always the case, empirical studies apply to limited parts of the theory, not to the theory as a whole. Yet, as Skinner says "You can't expect a Freudian to say, yes, I will admit that Freud's only contribution was in demonstrating some unusual causal relations between early experience and the present behavior. He loves . . . the various geographies of the mind and all of that stuff" (quoted in M. H. Hall, 1967, p. 69).

One of the empirical questions which has recently been reopened is concerned with Freud's radical reversal of the original hypothesis that childhood sexual trauma is the determining event for adult neurosis, specifically hysteria. We have already alluded briefly to this question. Recently released correspondence between Freud and his friend and confidant, Wilhelm Fliess, clearly demonstrates the former's vacillation over and ultimate rejection of his initial hypothesis. In September 1897, Freud indicated that he no longer believed the sexual-seduction hypothesis. Nevertheless, in December of the same year he wrote about a case which "speaks for the intrinsic authenticity of infantile trauma." Ultimately, however, he renounced the hypothesis and turned to fantasized sexual trauma in childhood as the key factor in neurosis.

Two factors have been emphasized by Freudian scholars as responsible for this radical reversal. One common speculation is that Freud was reacting to the extremely unsympathetic treatment that his ideas received from some of his most eminent colleagues. For example, renowned sex pathologist Richard von Krafft-Ebing is quoted as having pronounced the child-seduction account a "scientific fairy tale." Freudian scholar Jeffrey Masson (1985), the most controversial figure in the recent uproar over Freud and his ideas, has claimed that such criticism was "simply too much for Freud. He retreated."

Freudian scholars point also to what they claim was an attempt to absolve Freud's own father from any charges of sexual abuse of children. This hypothesis is allegedly suggested by allusions in some letters written to Fliess by Freud, such as the phrase "not excluding my own" immediately after the comment that fathers are often blamed in patients' memories of sexual trauma in childhood.

Critics of Freud's turnaround on this issue also hold that the orthodox theory has just not been productive. For example, Jeffrey Masson, (Remnick, 1984) argued that "Freud began a trend away from the real world that . . . is at the root of the present-day sterility of psychoanalysis and psychiatry throughout the world" (p. 66).

Farrell (1951) listed several propositions which at that time seemed to be better confirmed than the one we have just discussed. Infants do obtain pleasure from oral or genital stimulation, manual masturbation is more frequent among preschool boys than girls, and small children exhibit extensive pregenital play. Other propositions he regarded as disconfirmed: that all small girls have penis envy and wish to be boys, and that all children exhibit sexual attraction and attachment for the parent of the opposite sex and sexual jealousy of the parent of the same sex. A third class of propositions is regarded as untested or untestable, such as the hypothesis about substitutability of erogenous zones.

Farrell's treatment illustrates the necessarily piecemeal nature of the confirmation process, especially as applied to informal theories. Extensive theories cannot be confirmed or disconfirmed as a unit. We must, however, agree with Farrell that "psychoanalytic theory is, qua theory, unbelievably bad." However, theories are seldom if ever discarded before they are replaced by a better theory. Walker's comment (1957) was that psychoanalysis fills the need for a model that will "go anywhere, do anything, and be good at dealing with people" (p. 122). Horwitz (1963) says, along the same lines, that it is the implicit feeling of clinicians "that psychoanalysis is not the best theory of human behavior, it is the *only* theory" (p. 429).

Criticisms of Therapeutic Outcomes

Toulmin (1948) said that "if a fully-fledged analytic explanation is not part of a successful cure, we do not regard it as a 'correct' explanation; therapeutic failure is as fatal to an explanation in psychoanalysis as a predictive failure is to an explanation in physics" (p. 29). We must disagree with Toulmin on this point. A psychoanalytic explanation could be correct but the course of the illness irreversible because the analyst cannot control the situation well enough to bring about a cure. The physicians who treated Freud probably attributed his cancer to his cigar smoking and were probably correct, but they could not cure him. Astronomers cannot change the orbit of Mars, despite their presumably accurate knowledge about the laws of moving bodies. Theories can be criticized on the basis of outcomes only if it can be shown that the theory was applicable and perfectly applied to the case, and if the theorist was able to manipulate all circumstances at will.

Lack of Control

This criticism has been implicit in several of the other criticisms. The control we are speaking of here is not the control astronomers would lack if they wanted to move Mars; it is the control of variables in order to isolate the factors which are relevant to some outcome. That is, in the language of experimental psychology, the analyst must work with too many uncontrolled variables. It is not possible to isolate influences on a patient one by one, but lawful relationships must somehow be disentangled from the complex matrices of lives as patients happen to live them. The analyst cannot be sure that descriptions of the past, or even of the present, are adequate, relevant, or accurate. It is impossible to back up and see what would have happened if events had been changed in some way. One cannot try out the effect of some single manipulation on the patient's future behavior, for there is no way to isolate people from a multitude of other influences. No wonder it has been said that the situation is uncontrolled!

A common answer to this criticism is that analysts have proceeded through *clinical validation*. This seems to mean that successive confirmations of a theoretical prediction within the clinical setting constitute acceptable demonstrations of the accuracy of the principles involved. If so, the argument is unsound. We have to know what alternative explanations are possible and eliminate each alternative through appropriate controlled changes in the situation. Otherwise, however large the number of clinical validations, it is possible that the same artifacts continue to give the same outcomes. In reality, it is unlikely that clinical validation would be even as systematic and careful as we have pictured it. It is difficult to imagine a clinician finding enough cases that test the same prediction to permit several repetitions of a test of some hypothesis.

It is easy to criticize, but not so easy to suggest improved methods for testing psychoanalytic propositions. This is partly because of the state of the theory. A necessary step, requiring a huge amount of labor and ingenuity, is the improved definition of terms and the formalization of the theory. A prior step, then, would be to provide operational definitions for terms that occur in isolated propositions, so that these will be testable. Mullahy (1948, pp. 316ff.) gave several examples of the needs for clarification and for the elimination of contradiction.

Other steps besides the clarification of theory need to be taken if the evaluation of the theory is to be improved. Investigations of the verbal behavior of subjects could be made more systematic by using procedures like Stephenson's (1953) Q sort, which is a compromise between the free analytic situation and more objective personality tests. Stephenson has shown that his technique can be used to test analytic propositions.

Psychoanalytic propositions can also be further tested through more extensive observations of everyday life. Social caseworkers can observe real-life characteristics of people and relate their observations to the events in therapy. We have already said that behavioral observations unrelated to therapy are also needed. Although Freud thought that the best way to get information about the psychic apparatus was to study cases in which it was malfunctioning, we also need more information about the genetic events in the lives of normal people.

Horwitz (1963) provides suggestions on how studies within the therapeutic situation might be improved, and reports as follows on some ingenious and careful studies:

> The treatment study, long the subject of post-dictive study, is now becoming the locus of predictive studies. Bellak and Smith (1956) have reported a carefully controlled study of short-term predictions concerning the expected developments in the analytic treatment of patients whose preceding hours had been carefully studied by a group of analyst-predictors who were not themselves treating the patient. Wallerstein, Robbins, et al. (1956, 1958, 1960) have initiated a long-range study of both process and outcome in which a major method is the formulation of predictions prior to beginning treatment. A key feature of this investigation is the formulation of the theoretical assumptive base for each prediction in an effort to validate and extend psychoanalytic theory. (p. 431)

Dogmatism and Cultishness

We have already had some discussion of this point in other connections; for example, we saw the sense in which Freud was dogmatic and the sense in which he was not. We have met the "committee," composed of men who might almost be called disciples; Eitingon, for example, always made a "pilgrimage" to see Freud on the latter's birthday. There are other points which might suggest cultishness; it became accepted that only the analyzed could analyze, as though one had to be initiated in a trial by fire before one could carry the analytic word.

These characteristics indicate why psychoanalysis from the outside has seemed almost as much a religion as a science. Again, the argument has nothing to do logically with the value of the theory or the therapy, but it has something to do with the acceptance of the theory by those who feel that science is not a cult. Agreement with a gospel, or subjective evaluations of persons, should have nothing to do with the evaluations of scientific propositions, and psychoanalysts have sometimes seemed to use these forbidden criteria.

An interesting form of dogmatism is the criticism by analysts of their detractors. A critic who refuses to accept some aspect of psychoanalysis is said to be manifesting resistance. We see this in Freud himself; when he wished to show why Adler was wrong, Freud (1938) said: "I shall, therefore, use analysis only to make clear how these deviations from analysis could take place among analysts" (p. 964). No doubt Adler analyzed Freud in return, to show why he had resisted Adler's new ideas.

Loss of Humanism

A radically different kind of criticism of the contemporary American psychoanalytic movement has come from within analytic ranks, specifically from Viennese-born, American immigrant Bruno Bettelheim, long a leading psychoanalyst and child psychologist. Bettelheim (1982) said, "As a child born into a middle-class, assimilated Jewish family in Vienna, I was raised into an environment that was in many respects identical with the one that has formed Freud's background" (p. 52). Although he came along some 50 years later, he felt that there had been no significant changes in the culture he absorbed in his Viennese education, grade school through university. Moreover, he was an avid reader of all of Freud's work in its original language.

When he came to the United States, Bettelheim was greatly disturbed by the differences and omissions he found in the English translations of Freud's works. He argued that, largely because of these changes in meaning, the humanistic facets of Freud's thinking, which Bettelheim considers of much greater importance than the scientific, have been lost. The result has been that Freud's fundamental ideas have been distorted and misinterpreted by psychoanalysts and psychiatrists as well as by others.

The decidedly humanistic orientation of much of Freud's language—for example, the German expression *Seelentatigkeit*—was generally lost in translation, the neutral phrase "mental activity" being the common rendition of this word, rather than the more accurate "activity of the soul." Such errors in translation were in part a function of the natural ambiguity in many of the German expressions that Freud used. Moreover, Freud himself seems to have been deliberately ambiguous—for example, never defining the key term *soul*.

The pervasive mistranslations are responsible, according to Bettelheim, for the generally fallacious views of Freud's ideas. It is difficult to promote Freud's fundamental objective—to encourage self-understanding by removal of self-destructive tendencies—when his ideas are not accurately presented. The result has been overemphasis of the dark side of the psyche and neglect of the positive forces in society and self.

Sympathetic analysts have also argued that other facets of European psychoanalysis were lost in the American version of the system. The generally apolitical tone of American psychoanalysis contrasts sharply with the political and general cultural interests of Freud himself. Resistance to this depoliticization was most marked in the case of European analyst Otto Fenichel, who emigrated to the United States after the Nazi takeover. The regular letters that Fenichel sent to six other analysts relocated in the United States (a total of 119 *Rundbriefe* over a 12-year period) have been closely examined by Russell Jacoby (1983).

Jacoby's book identifies two other effects of the Americanization of the psychoanalytic movement. First, there is the relative decline in the number of women actively engaged in psychoanalysis. Although approximately 30 percent of the analysts who emigrated from Europe to the United States were women, they constitute a much smaller proportion of contemporary American analysts. Second, Jacoby complains about the sterility and near unreadability of American psychoanalytic prose, a criticism related to that more strongly advanced by Bettelheim.

THE CONTRIBUTIONS OF PSYCHOANALYSIS

Psychoanalysis continues, paradoxically, to be often rejected as a scientific system at the same time that it is regarded as an outstanding contributor to science. Freud is treated as a pioneer, or prescientist, more than as a scientist. He called himself a conquistador. Whatever he is called, he is recognized even by his critics as a great man, perhaps the greatest genius within psychology. He contributed to many fields, but predominantly to psychology.

Freud stimulated thinking about, and observation of, neglected aspects of psychology: the significance of the unconscious in determining behavior, the widespread importance of psychic conflict, childhood, the irrational, and the emotional. He personally made acute observations throughout a long life of daily work and contributed hypotheses or facts—we cannot yet be sure which are which—about broad areas of human behavior.

He developed provocative explanations of behaviors, such as errors and dreams, previously considered outside the realm of scientific explanation. The fact that such areas were examined and such explanations developed by a serious worker was important regardless of the correctness of the explanations.

Even in technique and methodology, areas in which psychoanalysis is often criticized for falling short of traditional criteria, Freud either made contributions or reinforced points made by others. His development of methods of free association and dream analysis for the study of unconscious processes has been compared with the invention of the microscope for studying cellular processes. Equally important, his emphasis on the study of unconscious processes preceded and reinforced the behaviorist and Gestaltist point that structuralist introspection was severely inadequate to reveal the psychology of the complete human being. One could argue that Freud made incidentally a point that became the central thesis of behaviorism. In this sense, psychoanalysis has been a source of great optimism. With its methods, psychology can become a full-fledged science and seems capable of developing techniques for overcoming any barrier. Without Freud, that conviction might have been slower in growing.

C. S. Hall and Lindzey (1957) stated that Freud's use of internal consistency as a method of checking hypotheses was one of his most important contributions to research strategy. This involves cross-checking a hypothesis by examining a large number of different indicators. If all indications are consistent, the hypothesis is regarded as verified. This method is applicable only when there is a large amount of data on a single case. And psychoanalysis has contributed intensive studies of individual cases unlike those available anywhere else. Although Freud himself published only four case histories of his patients, many other analysts have also contributed.

Another contribution is not easily weighed. Psychoanalysis added to the popularity of psychology and psychiatry with the lay public. The average person's vocabulary includes analytic words from all schools, and most people use some analytic modes of thinking about the behavior of others, and perhaps even occasionally about their own. Psychoanalysis has thus made the public aware of the importance of psychology, where other systems have not.

Psychoanalysis sometimes presents explanations of normal and neurotic behavior in a language and at a level which people believe they understand. It deals with practical situations in an exciting and challenging manner. Its method and theory contrast markedly with the slow, tiresome, painstaking program characteristic of most scientific research and theory construction. Therein lie both its appeal and its weakness.

REANALYZING FREUD

A wealth of newly released material bearing on Sigmund Freud's development of psychoanalysis has recently become available to scholars and researchers. The result has been a searching reanalysis of Freud's personal and professional lives.

Most prominent among these new materials is the release of the unexpurgated text of the 284 known letters that Freud wrote to Wilhelm Fliess over the 15-year period of their close friendship. Publication of these and other Freudian materials over the next several decades has been arranged by Harvard University Press. Freudian scholars have increasingly chafed at the many restrictions now in the process of being lifted; for example, only 168 of the letters to Fliess have been published, and many of these were substantially cut for reasons of confidentiality.

Sigmund Freud Archives, Inc. has also reached an agreement with the Library of Congress to open up its treasure trove of Freudiana to the public over the next few years. There is to be a complete public cataloguing of the approximately 150,000 items in the collection (plus 400 taped interviews with surviving friends and patients which have recently been added to the collection). Also in the works are the initial publication of Freud's teenage letters to a close friend and the first full publication of his letters to disciples Karl Abraham and Ludwig Binswanger.

Finally, awaiting compilation for subsequent publication are the 200 letters exchanged between Freud and his fiancée Martha Bernays (only 100 of which have been published previously) and the 1500 letters exchanged between Freud and Sandor Ferenczi, one of his most brilliant, and critical, disciples.

SUMMARY AND CONCLUSIONS

Psychoanalysis deals with the interesting and mysterious, yet practical and important, regions of human existence. That gives it an almost irresistible fascination, one which may yet prove fatal rather than constructive. Its adherents have hung together in a kind of cult, through good times and bad. The Chicago and New York institutes of psychoanalysis, appropriately enough, were both founded at the beginning of the Great Depression, in 1931, and have persevered for over 50 years through good times and bad. Psychoanalysis is sufficiently esoteric that its intricacies are not understood by many people who are not analysts. Still, some of its terms have enriched the lay vocabulary, probably more than from any other psychological system.

Psychoanalysis is more an art, philosophy, and practice than a science. The theory is loose and nebulous, sometimes even apparently self-contradictory. The therapy has not demonstrated any greater effectiveness than other kinds of therapy, and yet it retains a kind of mystique. The data and methodology which gave rise to psychoanalytic theory are inadequate from the point of view of traditional natural science, and analysts have sometimes shown little interest either in improving the theory or in improving the evidence supporting it. However, analytic theory has changed in response to new observations in therapy, and experimental tests of one or another key proposition are appearing in increasing numbers.

Many of the modern variations on Freud's theory continue to follow Adler down the path of increased emphasis upon cultural factors, although there are new indications of a possible rapprochement with the developing science of sociobiology (Wenegrat, 1984). Much effort has gone into study of the nature and genesis of ego functioning; this is the area of study which promises the greatest compatibility with academic psychology. Jung is typical of the analysts who put increased faith in the unity and creative potential of the self. Psychoanalytic theory has been a powerful force since 1900, and some of its basic ideas continue to be accepted. Among these are the defense mechanisms, the unconscious, and the importance of sexuality.

We should not derogate the positive contribution of psychoanalysis. It opened up new areas of investigation, gave impetus to motivational research, and pointed to the importance of childhood and genetic factors in the determination of personality. It provided valuable and intensive empirical observations, and continues to do so; and it worked out the nature of the defense mechanisms. All of these contributions are gratefully accepted by otherwise unfriendly psychologists.

Our final observation concerns the marked resurgence of interest in psychoanalysis. Officially sanctioned by the American Psychological Association at a relatively late date (1980), by the acceptance of a Division of Psychoanalysis and the sponsorship of a journal, psychoanalysis has become a training objective of an increasing number of clinical psychologists. Those seeking analytic training within a psychoanalytic setting have been stymied by the resistance of the American Psychoanalytic Association to accepting nonmedical trainees, and there are growing pressures for some kind of accommodation on this problem.

This renewed interest is curious because it comes when the status of psychoanalysis within American medicine generally, and within psychiatry particularly, has been at a very low ebb. There are currently fewer than 3000 psychoanalysts practicing in the United States, and many of these are concentrated in the east, particularly in New York City. Moreover, only about 3 percent of medical school graduates select psychiatry as a specialty, and a very small proportion of these turn to psychoanalysis. It would be an ironic development indeed if the future of the psychoanalytic movement depended upon the support of nonmedically trained psychologists, but such a situation seems to be an increasingly realistic possibility.

FURTHER READINGS

Jones's three volumes *The life and work of Sigmund Freud* (1953–1957) continue to be a classic source on psychoanalysis. Jones has written an absorbing biography that will infuse large quantities of information about psychoanalysis painlessly into the unwary brain. Trilling and Marcus (1961) have abridged Jones's work. C. S. Hall's *Primer of Freudian psychology* (1954) is just what the title claims it is and provides a solid introduction to Freud's system. Hall and Lindzey, in their *Theories of personality* (1970), do the same thing for all the important psychoanalytic theorists. Munroe's *Schools of psychoanalytic thought* (1955) is a friendly psychologist's look at psycho-analysis—and a friendly psychologist has been hard for psychoanalysts to find at some times in the past. Ellenberger's *The discovery of the unconscious* (1970) is a scholarly work that puts all of dynamic psychology into historical and cultural perspective and is particularly good at showing the contributions of French psychologists like Janet and Charcot, who have been relatively neglected in the present chapter. Bakan's *Sigmund Freud and the Jewish mystical tradition* (1958) is a scholarly and readable account of how Freud's theory was related to his cultural background. *A general introduction to psychoanalysis* (1943) is probably Freud's own most readable book. Rapaport's (1959) chapter gives a systematic overview of psychoanalysis from a generally positive and optimistic point of view. Evans and Koelsch (1985) outline Freud's personal introduction of Americans to psychoanalysis at the 1909 Clark conference. Silverman's chapter (1983) in Masling's book *Empirical studies of psychoanalytic theories* is a good brief introduction to the research done in the style of Silverman's own work. Leak and Christopher's (1982) synthesis of psychoanalysis and sociobiology illustrates the continuing attempt to broaden the application of psychoanalytic theory and to integrate it with other types of theory. For the flavor of what American psychoanalysis is up to these days, the *Annual of psychoanalysis,* published since 1973 by the Chicago Institute for Psychoanalysis, can be recommended. For the work of other analysts, see the references cited in the relevant parts of the present chapter.

END NOTES

Dimensional Descriptions of Psychoanalysis

Conscious Mentalism–Unconscious Mentalism   This is a dimension on which nearly all analysts agree; an emphasis on the unconscious is the very stuff of which psychoanalysis is made. Although conscious mentalism plays a role in the psychic economy, no other system of psychology puts as much emphasis on the unconscious as psychoanalysis.

Content: Objective vs. Subjective   Psychoanalysts, although they work with subjective material, recognize the importance of objective content as well. We have seen that in one respect they support a behaviorist position because they recognize the inadequacy of the structuralist type of introspection. Despite these caveats, we agree with most raters, who see psychoanalysis as more subjective than most systems.

Determinism–Indeterminism   We rate psychoanalysis as highly deterministic, but there are those who disagree with our position. A belief in psychic determinism is a fundamental feature of psychoanalysis; however, we understand the temptation to rate Freud's psychology as somewhat indeterministic because of what at first appears to be a somewhat mystical flavor.

Empiricism–Rationalism   All systems of psychology have their empiricist features, and psychoanalysis is no exception. The theory is grounded on observations, mostly in therapeutic contexts but including a broad range of situations. However, there is also a high percentage of speculative content, and that leads us to put psychoanalysis closer to the rationalist pole than most systems.

Functionalism–Structuralism   The pragmatic and dynamic features of psycho-analysis made it look functional, but there is also a great emphasis on the "psychic apparatus" which gives it structural tendencies. We place psychoanalysis almost exactly in the middle on this dimension.

Inductivism–Deductivism   As with empiricism–rationalism, we recognize both features in psychoanalysis but place it closer to the deductive pole. Analysts like Jung and Rank, with their sometimes unsupported speculations, incline us to that conclusion.

Mechanism–Vitalism   Freud's preeminence forces us to put psychoanalysis closer to the mechanistic pole, but the unclarity of the mind-body positions taken by Freud and other analysts gives us some pause; closer to mechanistic, then, but by no means as close as behaviorism or associationism.

Methods: Objective vs. Subjective   Psychoanalytic methods are more subjective than psychoanalytic philosophy; we therefore put psychoanalysis close to the subjective end of the continuum because of its almost exclusive reliance on verbal behavior, which in turn relies upon the possibly distorted memories of emotionally disturbed people.

Molecularism–Molarism   Analysts work at a relatively molar level of behavior, but they do try to analyze it, often getting to rather molecular levels in the process. So we put it on the molar side, but close to the middle.

Monism–Dualism   Psychoanalysts seem to be most comfortable with one of the varieties of dualism. Freud was typical in claiming to be a psychophysical parallelist. Probably psychoanalysis is as dualistic as any system.

Naturalism–Supernaturalism   Jung furnishes the only hint of supernaturalism to be found among the famous analysts, and that is only a hint. We think Freud deserves credit for "naturalizing" behavior which earlier was seen as quite mysterious and thus perhaps supernatural. Thus psychoanalysis goes close to the naturalistic pole, along with all other systems of psychology.

Nomotheticism–Idiographicism   Psychoanalysis, like Gestalt psychology, looks for general laws, but looks for them in individual situations–in this case in individual persons. Thus it occupies a middle ground on this dimension.

Peripheralism–Centralism   What could be more centralistic than the quest for hidden motives, old traumas, and the contents of dreams and fantasies? Psychoanalysis is probably closer to centralism than any other school.

Purism–Utilitarianism   Psychoanalysis was born in a utilitarian situation, even one where money changes hands! It is the most utilitarian of our systems in practice, although functionalism may have had a slightly more utilitarian philosophy.

Quantitativism–Qualitativism   Statistics has, historically, been little used by psychoanalysts, although that situation has changed. We still know of no mathematical psychoanalytic theories, and we rate psychoanalysis quite close to the qualitative pole.

Rationalism–Irrationalism   Here there is no contest. Freud, probably more than any other analyst, emphasized the irrationality of much human behavior and the power of the id. Certainly psychoanalysts as a whole outdo all others in their belief in irrational factors.

Staticism–Developmentalism   This is a more difficult choice than it would first appear, given the dynamic character of part of psychoanalytic theory. The problem is that Freud put so much emphasis on the permanence of the effects of early childhood experience that it gives the theory a static aspect. Thus we would score psychoanalysis only a little toward the developmental end of this dimension.

Staticism–Dynamicism   The dynamic character of the psychoanalytic view of events over the short term puts psychoanalysis much farther toward the dynamic pole on this dimension.

The three dimensions that seem most important in describing psychoanalysis are probably unconscious mentalism, determinism, and irrationalism. However, dynamicism is also a reasonable choice.

Psychoanalysis Compared to Other Systems

Psychoanalysis, like Gestalt psychology, tends toward a synthetic, as contrasted with an analytic, approach. With respect to the three subproperties of the synthetic approach (Coan, 1979), it uses subjective data, is qualitative, and prefers molar to molecular variables. It is also like Gestalt psychology, and contrasts with associationism and behaviorism, in that it leans toward the functional rather than the structural, because it is highly dynamic overall. It is not highly endogenistic, but it does recognize instinctual factors (markedly so in the case of Jung). Its positions on the three subfactors thus place psychoanalysis with the more functional systems.

PART TWO

CONTEMPORARY THEORIES

PSYCHOLOGICAL THEORY

INTRODUCTION

Newton in physics, Darwin in biology, and Freud in psychology have become almost magical names because of the importance of their theories. Yet we have been critical of Freud's theories, Newton's theories have been displaced for many purposes by Einstein's or Bohr's or someone else's, and Darwin continues to come in for his share of criticism and modification. It seems that theories are neither simple nor permanent, and we need to look carefully at theoretical issues before proceeding to study of more recent developments in psychological theory.

In saying this, we are repeating a conclusion reached much earlier by philosophers of science who were upset by the overthrow of much of Newton's theory. They wondered where earlier theoretical developments had gone wrong, and they tried to analyze and restructure the theory of theory—metatheory—in an attempt to avoid some of the errors of the past. An analysis of theory in any field quickly leads to the realization that theories are all expressed in language. Theories are attempts to predict or explain empirical observations, and explanations are verbal. The language used may range from quite ordinary everyday language to specialized logical or mathematical languages, like the hodological geometry adapted by Kurt Lewin and discussed in Chapter 7. No matter what sort of language is used, certain problems must be faced if the language is to become part of a successful theory. Thus the first step in theoretical analysis is to examine what these linguistic problems are and how some of the most serious errors in the use of language can be avoided. In the present chapter, our direction of movement will be from theories expressed in ordinary language (Freud's theory is an outstanding example) to theories which make use of more formal languages (in psychology, some modern learning theories, information theory, signal detectability theory, and neural network theories are examples). We will examine the types of problems involved, without going into the details of any theory; the examination of particular theories will be the subject of later chapters. As the first step in this process, we will review the nature of the linguistic process as it occurs in all kinds of human activities, ranging from the making of pies to the making of the most abstruse psychological theories.

GENERAL PROBLEMS OF LANGUAGE

Stevens (1951) wrote an article examining the relationship between language and theory which has become a classic within psychology. He used C. W. Morris's (1938) distinction among three interrelated subareas of the general topic of the use of signs to organize his discussion. The general area was to be called *semiotics*. The three specific subareas were *semantics, syntactics,* and *pragmatics.* Semantics is the study of the relationship of signs to objects. Syntactics is the study of the relationship of signs to each other. Pragmatics is the study of the relationship of signs to their users. Any theory which uses signs—and they all do—must relate its signs to objects and events, must relate signs to each other according to specified rules, and must be usable by those who have an interest in the theory. Thus every theory has its semantic, syntactic, and pragmatic aspects.

Semantics

Stevens first defines semantics as the study of the relationship of signs to objects. Later he says that meaningful signs must refer to objects or to *events*. If Stevens had limited meaningful terms to those that denoted objects, he would have left us with little to say! We could point to a chair and say "chair," but the meaning of "sit" would remain forever a mystery, since sitting is not an object.

Many books have been written on the subject of semantics. It is no simple matter to assign a meaning even to an apparently simple word like *of*, although native speakers of English have a good intuitive notion of what it means. Bridgman's (1927) philosophy of science, which became known as *operationism,* took as its single core problem the assignment of meaning to scientific concepts. Bridgman (1927) insisted that the meaning of a scientific concept must be reducible to a set of operations. Operationism was a proposed solution to the semantic question of how signs should be brought into relationship with objects or events. Some interpretations of operationism may have been too restrictive. Critics pointed out that much theoretical activity may occur at a very abstract level and involve the manipulation of signs which are in themselves empirically meaningless. Thus some, but not necessarily all, signs must eventually make contact with observations if the theory containing the signs is to be considered meaningful. If operationism were used to limit the freedom of the theorist to proceed on this basis, it would do science a disservice.

In response to such criticism, Bridgman (1952) broadened the concept of *operation* to include pencil-and-paper operations with purely abstract symbols. He thus made it clear that "abstract" operations were admissible and that meaning was therefore partly a matter of syntactical, as well as semantic, considerations.

Operationism promoted a great concern with the semantic problems of scientific theories. Scientists, and particularly psychologists, became more acutely aware that their terms needed to be carefully coordinated with specific empirical observations. If a term was not directly defined empirically, there had to be a defensible rationale for using, within a theory, terms which were only indirectly defined through other terms.

Verbal definitions can be used to assign meanings to terms. A dictionary is a sort of "semantics machine" which tells us about the meanings of words. Before there were written dictionaries, older people had to "tell" younger people through precept and example what oral and written signs meant. There are differences between this "living dictionary" and a written version that we should consider. People can clarify the meanings of words through all sorts of nondictionary operations like pointing and demonstrating. Without outside reference a written dictionary is useless. To appreciate this, try using a dictionary in a foreign language of which you have no knowledge. Although all the words in it are defined, it is no good to you because you have no external referents for any of the words to get you started. You can easily use a dictionary in your own language because you already know enough words *independently of the dictionary* that you can use them to understand the remaining words. An actual example of this is that the language of ancient Egypt could not be translated until the Rosetta stone was discovered in 1799. This stone had parallel inscriptions in Greek and in ancient Egyptian characters. Since the Greek was already understood, the Egyptian could at last be decoded.

The dictionary problem is exactly analogous to the theory problem in psychology. Operational definition is the Rosetta stone of scientific theory. Without external definitions of at least some of the terms of a theory, the whole theory stands as devoid of meaning as Egyptian hieroglyphics before the Rosetta stone came to light. However, not all hieroglyphics had to be coordinated with Greek terms. Once some of the hieroglyphics were understood, the meanings of others could be determined by using internal relationships to deduce the meanings of additional signs, in the same way that we deduce the meaning of an unknown English word from its context. Modern science allows the theoretician freedom to use some terms that have no direct relationship to empirical observations, as long as other logically related terms in the theory are tied to observations.

Some of these issues will arise again on the following pages, since all aspects of the study of language are interrelated. Semantics is closely related to pragmatics, because it is the users of language who relate symbols to things, and to syntactics, which tells users how to relate signs to one another.

Syntactics

Syntactics is the study of the relationships of symbols to each other. Developers of a language determine these relationships in accordance with the demands of the context in which the language will be used. This is true whether the language is a natural language or a special logical or mathematical language. Thus the syntax of a language is determined by pragmatic considerations, and we see again that all subareas of language study are interrelated. Syntactics, however, concentrates on that aspect of language which involves only symbols and their manipulation.

Syntactics is thus the study of the rules by which symbols are related to each other. Common examples with which most people are familiar include grammatical rules in ordinary language and algebraic rules in mathematics. More esoteric examples include the rules for the manipulation of symbols in formal logic, and more homely ones include the rules for playing games like chess and bridge.

Syntactics is an attempt to deal with abstract systems as such. In a sense, it is a study that turns the world on its head, for the most concrete "objects" with which this study deals are the abstractions (symbols) which science uses to understand the rest of the world. Notice also that scholars in this field of study use language just as other scholars do, so they are in the somewhat peculiar position of having to use language to talk about how language ought to be used. This is not the only reflexive relationship with which psychologists are familiar; we must use consciousness to study consciousness, behavior in studying behavior, and so on. Syntactics contributes to *metatheory,* since the uses of language affect our ideas of what theories are or what they should be as abstract systems.

Games are a useful way of illustrating what is involved in the study of syntactics. The reason is that games have explicitly stated rules which govern how the pieces in the game may legitimately relate to each other and to the arena in which the game is played. A good illustrative game is chess. One need not know how to play chess to recognize that each piece in the game is allowed only certain moves. The pieces are like the symbols in a purely syntactic system. The positions of all the pieces are like a statement in a syntactic system, which could be a scientific theory. The rules of the game are like syntactic rules which regulate how one position can be transformed into another. Moves or transformations which are not allowed by the rules are illegal, and illegal transformations result in nonsensical positions or nonsensical statements.

Systems like the algebra of real numbers are similar to chess in many respects. They are symbolic games which include rules for "moves" and have as a goal the production of new "winning" combinations. In mathematical and logical games, any new combination may be interesting. However, the most appealing part of the game seems to be the ability to make a sequence of legal manuevers that ends in the "proof" of a theorem which is regarded as important by the other players. In mathematics, the theorems or conjectures that are important can often be put to use in some more practical endeavor, for example, in generating an unbreakable code or in finding a way to break an "unbreakable" code.

The continuity between what we regard as a game, like chess, and what we regard as scientific theory, like a theory of elementary particles, has recently been demonstrated in a very surprising context. A few years ago Rubik's Cube was a faddish "toy." Its "legal" moves are defined by what one can do without disassembling or distorting the cube; that is, its legal moves are defined by its structure. These moves can also be described abstractly, and one could thus manipulate an *imaginary* Rubik's Cube.

Now for the surprise. Rubik's Cube is an excellent model of the behavior of the elementary particles called quarks (Golomb, 1982). The way the "cubelets" rotate matches the production of quarks, antiquarks, and mesons. One can also produce *three* quarks with the cubelets, which corresponds to producing a proton or neutron. The color of the cubelets models a property also called color in quarks, and the position (above or below) of the cubelet models a property of quarks called "flavor."

The Rubik's Cube metaphor for quark behavior, like the model in any useful theory, thus reflects many aspects of quark behavior. Both the physical Rubik's Cube and the abstract model are, in a sense, equivalent representations of quarks, although one or the other might be easier to use and understand. In any model, whether physical or abstract, the critical features are syntactic. That is, predictions from a model depend on how the parts of the model relate to one another. In a natural language, prediction is based on the grammatical constraints on what can be said using the concepts of the language.

There are some cases in which the model can no more be translated into an abstract system than can the system being represented by the model. In such cases, it may still be easier to experiment with the model than with the thing being modeled. Consider the rat as a "model" for human response to nicotine. The rat may be a very useful model on which we can experiment and from which we can predict human responses to nicotine or other drugs. But in this case the usefulness of the model does not depend on its being more abstract, for we cannot describe the rat's metabolism any more easily than the human's. We do not know rat syntax any better than we know human syntax. Nevertheless, for the rat to be a useful model, the relationships between its parts must reflect the relationships between human parts; it seems that the two must have a similar syntax, even though we cannot describe it.

Manipulators of symbols are scientists only if they use symbols to model some aspect of the world external to the symbols. The essence of science is the establishment of new relationships between sets of symbols and the world outside the symbols. Scientists may invent new symbols and a new syntax, but their work as scientists is not finished if they do only that. If they have only invented a new symbolic system or proved new theorems within established systems, they are logicians or mathematicians. To become a scientist, one must relate the symbols, and operations with the symbols, to objects or events external to the symbolic system. That is, the scientists must coordinate abstract systems with observations. An empirical scientist attends to semantics, not just to syntactics. Pure syntacticists can divorce themselves from such empirical concerns.

Pragmatics

Pragmatics is the study of the relationships between signs and the users of signs. Semantics and syntactics cannot be studied apart from pragmatics, because signs are related to each other, and to observations, only through the mediation of the users of signs.

Users of signs are trained to think or to do certain things in the presence of sequences of signs. Syntactics describes agreements about what sequences are regarded as meaningful by the users of signs. Semantics tells us what the user should think or do in the presence of each meaningful sequence. It would be more accurate to say "Syntactics (or semantics) *tries* to tell us, etc.," since there is so much unfinished business in the realm of language. In any case, the point is that language cannot be understood independently of its relationship to users of the language. Perhaps that is one incontrovertible point that can be extracted from Skinner's book *Verbal behavior* (1957). For Skinner, language was clearly a matter of stimulus (for a listener) and response (for a speaker) and was to be understood, like any other behavioral problem, in terms of the reinforcements which attended the linguistically related behaviors of speakers and listeners.

From this point of view, language is a pragmatic business indeed. Skinner thinks that we must study how language *functions* if we wish to understand any aspect of it. His attitude may remind us of the attitude of Thomas Kuhn, who studied the history of science in order to find out how science proceeded. He did not study the philosophy of science alone in an attempt to find out how it *ought* to proceed. Skinnner would have us start with pragmatics, not syntactics, if we want to find out how language is used. Natural languages like English, German, Russian, or Chinese have passed the test of usefulness over many centuries. Languages are like scientific theories in that they continue to evolve. New words and new usages emerge to cover new situations, and some words become archaic as they are no longer needed.

Even the oldest scientific theories are newcomers compared to natural languages. However, they are subject to the same kinds of tests for usefulness. Simple theories, like simple statements in natural language, are easier to use. In both cases, brevity is the soul of wit. Very straightforward practical considerations account for scientists' preference for the simpler of two alternative hypotheses or theories.

This concludes our introduction to the areas of study in the field of linguistics as envisioned by Morris and reported by Stevens. Stevens later (1968) described science as a "schemapiric" activity. He saw science as an activity that establishes relationships between symbols (*schema-*) and empirical observations (*-piric*). In this chapter we have taken a position very consistent with Stevens's description. We now turn to a description of theory by Feigl. Every aspect of language we have discussed has its counterpart in Feigl's picture of scientific theory. Since Feigl is concerned with more formal theories, what he says will help us in our progression of study from informal theories couched in natural language, like those of Freud and Darwin, to the more modern formal theories like those found in the fields of learning and perception.

A PICTURE OF THEORY: FEIGL'S DIAGRAM

Herbert Feigl (1970) described his view of theory as "classical." By this he meant that it was an older view, but he may have also meant that it was, like Greek art, classical in its simplicity. We reproduce his sketch of theory in Figure 9-1. It is a useful framework around which we can organize further discussion of the nature of theory.

First, let us note the relationships between Feigl's diagram and Stevens's areas of language study. Feigl has a postulate set, indicated by interconnected circles, which "hovers" high above the "soil" of observation, indicated at the bottom. The postulates

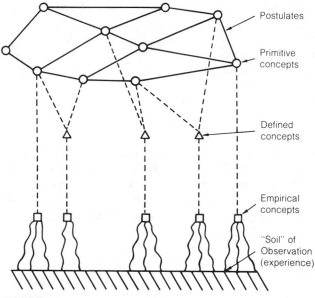

FIGURE 9-1
A classical view of theory. (*Adapted from Feigl, 1970.*)

lead to theorems, which are indicated by connections between the "primitive concept" circles and "defined concept" triangles or connections between the defined concepts. The circles and triangles representing the elements of the syntactic system are like the words of natural languages or the symbols in mathematical languages. Feigl derived this "picturesque" view of an "uninterpreted calculus" floating freely above an observation plane from Campbell (1920), who had a very similar view of theory.

The elements of Feigl's calculus may be defined via rules which relate the elements to each other. However, elements need not have a definition relating them to the outside world in order to have meaning; that is, some elements may be made meaningful via strictly *internal* definitions. Their core meaning is syntactical. However, in a scientific theory some portion of the abstract elements must be given *external* meaning by relating them to empirical concepts. Feigl indicates such coordinations in his diagram by lines linking the hovering syntactical system with empirical concepts.

Feigl calls the hovering syntactical system a *calculus* because he intends for it to enable us to calculate something, to enable us to generate hypotheses and to make predictions, perhaps even quantitative predictions. The study of how we interact with the abstract system to make the calculations is part of pragmatics.

We can choose whatever calculational system we wish. New games are frequently invented, and so are new nongame syntactical systems. Most such systems generate little interest, but occasionally something like the kind of calculus jointly invented by Newton and Leibniz comes along and arouses so much interest that priority fights break out about it, and we argue about whether Newton, Leibniz, or perhaps Isaac Barrow deserves most of the credit for inventing it. Although the syntactical system to be used for a scientific theory can be chosen arbitrarily, the *ultimate* choice of such a system is based on considerations of interest and usefulness.

Exactly the same things can be said about the external definitions of the terms of the theory. Theoreticians can try any definitions they wish, or invent or use any other calculus and define elements just as they wish, both internally and externally. We can ignore the completed theory if it does not fulfill our criteria of usefulness. We can refuse to consider it at all if its definitions and postulates are not clear. However, it would not be wise to reject a theory just because it was too unusual or nonintuitive in its postulates or definitions.

In Feigl's picture, definition is not portrayed as a one-step process. Rather, Feigl interposes what he calls empirical concepts between the abstract system and the soil of observation. Then the theoretical terms are coordinated with the concepts, rather than being coordinated directly with the observations. These empirical concepts are thus themselves abstractions. However, such concepts are developed "from below" rather than "from above" in terms of Feigl's picture. "Response rate" is an example of an empirical concept which is meaningful independently of any theory and is developed "from below." Response rate is an abstract characteristic of many different responses that, superficially, may be as dissimilar as pigeon pecks and page turning.

Measurement operations would be used to connect empirical concepts (like response rate) to observations made in an experiment or field study. Thus, in the case of measurements, we are dealing with one type of operational definition. Operational definitions are not limited to this type of grass-roots measurement operation, but such measurement is a clear example of operational definition. If the operations for establishing response rate are clearly specified, and if response rate is given no meaning aside from the specified operations, then the operationist would not object to the use of the concept.

A theory builder might decide that one of the elements in a theory could usefully be defined as, or coordinated with, response rate. He or she could then coordinate other elements from the abstract calculus that was being used with other empirical concepts for operations which influence response rate or which might be influenced by response rate. If the calculus truly calculates, the theory builder can then make predictions about how various values of other variables would be related to response rate or what the effects of response rate on other variables ought to be, or both, depending upon the structure of the theory. At that point, the theoretician would have a scientific theory which could be tested by performing experiments or making observations to see whether or not the predictions of the theory were correct.

All the problems of "coordination" of the syntactical, calculus part of Feigl's diagram should by now be recognizable as *semantic* problems. They are the theoretical analog of the general linguistic problem of assigning meaning to words. The fields of operational definition and measurement are subfields of semantics, if the latter is broadly defined. Since pragmatics suffuses the other linguistic areas of study as well as the study of theory, it is not identified with a part of Feigl's diagram; rather, it is an aspect of the whole diagram.

Feigl's diagram also fits in perfectly with the definition of theory given by another philosopher of science, Paul Diesing (1971). Diesing defines a theory as "a model with one or more interpretations." In this definition, Diesing means by model exactly what Feigl means by a "calculus"; it is an abstract system which can be used to make predictions about events. The definitions which connect the model to observations, plus the observations themselves, constitute what Deising means by the "interpretation." Diesing's view of theory is thus very consistent with the picture presented by Feigl. Feigl's calculus is the same as Diesing's model, and the whole Feigl diagram corresponds to what Diesing means by theory. If the same model (for example, algebra) were given a different "interpretation" (applied to the psychology of learning rather than to computing atomic weights), then we would have to draw a different picture to portray the new connections between the model and empirical concepts.

A theory enables predictions (made by manipulating the abstract calculus or model) and makes it possible to check the predictions (by making the corresponding manipulations on the "interpretation" and observing whether or not the results conform to prediction). In this book, we use the terms "model" and "theory" as Diesing uses them. Other authors do not always follow this usage. The most common alternative is probably to interchange the meanings of model and theory. There is nothing wrong with defining terms in other ways, since everyone presumably has an equal right to choose definitions. However, readers should be on the alert when reading about psychological theory, in order to ascertain just how a particular author defines the terms in question.

Now we have looked at a global picture of what a full-blown theory involves, as seen by Feigl and Diesing. Psychologists have made attempts, beginning with the work of Clark Hull, to produce such theories. The early attempts led to criticism, largely justified, of the nature of these attempts. We now turn to the types of considerations which are appropriate when a theory is systematic, explicit, and formal, by contrast with early theories like Freud's.

THE STRUCTURE OF A THEORY

The following discussion summarizes the thinking of a group of outstanding psychologists (Estes, Koch, MacCorquodale, Meehl, Mueller, Schoenfeld, and Verplanck, 1954) and tries to simplify it so that it will be applicable to actual, rather than just ideal, psychological theories. We will begin by looking at some questions directed at the empirical "interpretation" with which the theory is concerned.

One of the questions about a theory concerns the area to which the model applies. Some of the most familiar areas covered are learning and personality. Within these general areas we find more specific limitations on what is covered. For example, some theories of learning might deal with all of classical conditioning, or all of verbal learning, while others might concentrate on the changes in probability of being correct about a specific word as a result of a single trial. Some personality theories might be quite encompassing, and others more limited. To be specific about the area covered, one could look at the independent and dependent variables with which the theory deals. One also needs to know just how the theoretical concepts are coordinated with the data.

Methodological Characteristics

The preceding questions are closer to the soil of observation than are the following questions, which deal more with the syntactical character of the theory, that is, with the nature of the model or calculus. One can ask, first, whether or not all the terms of the model have a proper internal definition. Second, are the rules for manipulating the statements within the model explicit and clear? Third, how were the postulates and the rules for their manipulation constructed from previous observations or related abstract systems? For most psychological theories, it would be very difficult to answer these questions.

A more fundamental question would be whether or not there *is* any explicit model or calculus. For many psychological theories, the answer is no. Such "theories without models" are usually the familiar informal theories couched in natural language. Nearly all personality theories are of this kind. In such cases, it is not possible to determine the logical status of all the statements. Some might be implicit postulates, and others might be statements of observed relationships between empirical concepts. Such informal theory is not to be derogated and may be entirely appropriate to the stage of development within a given field of psychology. We have seen in Chapter 5 that functionalists tend to prefer informal and unpretentious theories, and we will give an example of such informal development later in this chapter.

Where there is a model, one can proceed to questions about how the model has been related to the empirical area under study. If there is no complete model, this cannot be done, at least not without preliminary work. If a particular informal position seems to involve some implicit model, the model could be made explicit. Incomplete parts of implicit or explicit models could be filled in. However one attains a model for analysis, once that step is finished, one can ask questions about its logical properties. For example, are its postulates (or axioms) stated explicitly, clearly, and quantitatively? Are the assumptions consistent and independent? How does one derive theorems from the postulates? Few psychological theories can support these questions without further development. But some can, and the number that can increases every year. Producing a theory that *can* support such questions is a worthy goal for the aspiring theorist.

Exacting theorists assume that fully axiomatized systems are desirable. It is difficult to disagree with this viewpoint, but full axiomatization is seldom practical. Some empirical systems are so complex that axiomatization is not feasible at present, and it may be a waste of time to try it. None of us should be disappointed if our initial attempts go awry. We are temporarily out of our depths with the warm, pulsing, protoplasmic, unpredictable psychological objects with which our theories must try to cope. Thus readers will find in the following chapters, as in the preceding ones, that rigorous psychological theories are rare jewels and hence the more to be treasured.

Empirical Content and Adequacy

Whether or not there is an identifiable model, and whatever its logical properties (or lack thereof), one can ask questions about the usefulness of the theory. Does it suggest experiments? Predict new phenomena? Has it had any striking successes or failures? How does it stack up against competing theories for the same general empirical phenomena? A theory might have many logical weaknesses and still be the best available. That has often been said about Freud's theory.

Many psychological "theories" are mere programs for building theories. Even so, they may be useful if they are good programs. There may be techniques for theory construction, or even attitudes toward theory construction, which can be of use. Development in any science is gradual and, according to most analysts, progressive. Thus programs are critical to this gradual development, and theories themselves develop gradually under the guidance of more general paradigms or research programs.

If, on the other hand, a theory is clear and well developed, the questions about empirical adequacy can be more detailed. An accurate prediction of new phenomena would be impressive. Even an explanation of known phenomena would be better than nothing. The *aim* of theory is the correct prediction and explanation of all phenomena in the empirical area to which the theory applies. That goal has not yet been reached even by limited theories, let alone by encompassing theories like those in the personality area. Whatever its success rate, the theory should be sensitive to empirical findings. If a theory makes bad predictions, the theory should be changed. Here the point is that even a bad prediction is better than no prediction at all, for the bad prediction may point toward improvements. If a theory cannot predict, empirical observations cannot affect it. If empiricial observations cannot affect it, then the theory fails the most critical test of all: It is not testable, and in that sense it is not a scientific theory at all.

NONLINGUISTIC FEATURES OF SCIENCE

So far we have been directing our discussion almost exclusively to the linguistic features of science. However, Kuhn (1970), among others, has argued that science is by no means all language. Language does not even succeed completely in conveying the nature of the thought that presumably underlies it. And students do not become scientists solely by reading textbooks and reports, any more than one becomes a carpenter by reading a manual on carpentry. This is expressed in the Chinese proverb that says, "I hear, and I forget. I see, and I remember. I do, and I understand."

What are these indescribable things that the neophyte scientist has to learn? One thing is the ability to discriminate. Just as the chef must know when a dish is properly cooked by observing its color, texture, and tenderness, so the scientist must learn what to observe and what observations indicate that the desired outcome is being achieved. Before the observations can begin, the scientist must know how to conceptualize problems and set up experiments or take advantage of naturalistic opportunities. In learning what to observe, one is learning to direct attention to relevant features and to ignore others which might seem more important to the uninitiated. This type of learning is sometimes summarized by saying that a scientist has a "trained" or "prepared" mind. Röntgen's mind was prepared when he saw a tube glowing when it should not have been glowing, and he immediately used the observation to discover x-rays. Perhaps one weakness of written reports is the fact that they do not list everything that should *not* be seen!

Scientists must sometimes learn habits of manipulation as well as habits of observation and conceptualization. They must learn what apparatus to use and how to use it. Occasionally they may need manipulative skills rivaling those of a surgeon or a helicopter pilot. It is difficult to bring about new phenomena without some technical skills, and a part of the business of science is the creation of entirely new phenomena. Biologists, for example, are busily providing us with modified life forms by recombining genes. The world is already replete with other human-created phenomena like the jet plane, television, the hydrogen bomb, the computer, nuclear power, and plastics. Such examples remind us of one undoubted advantage of experimental research over naturalistic observation: naturalistic observation is an effective technique for finding out what *is,* but only experimental research can tell us efficiently what *might be.* The furor about research recombining and transforming genetic materials tells us that both the friends and the foes of experimental research share the belief that experimentation can greatly accelerate the rate of development of new life forms, just as experimentation in the past has accelerated the rate of development of new inanimate forms. Bacteria which produce insulin for human diabetics are already hard at work, and they are only the beginning of a biological revolution.

Finally, science as practiced by human beings may well depend in ways that we can hardly imagine on our own unique human characteristics, nonlinguistic as well as linguistic. Francis Bacon expressed this general problem in his discussion of the various "idols" to which human thought is subject. Bacon (1605/1857, Part 3) pointed out that human thought is not independent of our natures as individuals and as members of the human species: "For the mind of man is far from the nature of a clear and equal glass, wherein the beams of things should reflect according to their true incidence; nay, it is rather like an enchanted glass, full of superstition and imposture, if it be not delivered and reduced." It is almost commonplace today, as Bacon was suggesting, to say that our thoughts and perceptions have their subjective, as well as their objective, sides.

Our discussion leaves little doubt that the linguistic activities of scientists are balanced by a host of activities and considerations which are not primarily linguistic. Bacon's idols are worshipped by the theoretician as well as by the observer, and as much by the psychologist as by the physicist. However, none of these difficulties invalidate science and its theories; rather, they constitute a set of obstacles to be recognized and counteracted to the best of our ability.

THE UNFOLDING OF PSYCHOLOGICAL THEORY

Psychologists have devoted increasing attention to the development of explicit and precise theories over the last 50 years. As the theories have become more precise, they have necessarily become more limited. Hull, who will be discussed in the upcoming chapter, was probably psychology's most representative bridge between the earlier global systematic thinkers and today's theoretical thinkers. He attempted a comprehensive precise theory, and that goal was not within reach in his lifetime.

As R. I. Watson (1967) said, there are likely to be both dominant and counterdominant positions on any issue within the same historical period. At present, there is a counterdominant position on the desirability of constructing extensive or formal psychological theory. Followers of Skinner believe that too much attention devoted to formal theory diverts effort away from the main business of psychology, which they believe is empirical study. The latter is regarded as certain to lead to better and more reliable theory than a too-hasty formal approach. These psychologists support a Baconian, inductive, approach both to science and to theory construction.

Opposition to formal theory also comes from the "Third Force," a loose alliance of humanists, existentialists, and phenomenologists. They reject theories that they regard as overly mechanistic. Formal theorists are seen by this group as slavish followers of admired physical scientists. They believe that psychologists should recognize that they are *not* physicists. The human being is a dynamic and evolving cultural product, the laws of whose behavior are, at least in part, self-constructed and variable from time to time and from place to place. Any attempt to formalize such fluid laws is foolish and wasteful. We should, according to this view, develop a looser and more human science. Although our own biases tend toward the more traditional view of theory, we believe that we and the reader should keep an open mind and be tolerant both of failures to achieve a good formal theory and of those who have a very different view of the whole enterprise.

In summary, good theories must be accountable for and sensitive to observations. That is, if they seem to contradict observations, intuitions, or even common sense, their adherents should be able to say why. If the theory fails to make predictions, it is not a good theory. Even a bad prediction is better than no prediction, for a bad prediction can guide revision of the theory. Theories should have heuristic value, suggesting both additional theoretical development and empirical observations that test predictions of the theory. Theories are probably neither provable nor refutable as a whole, but they must be explicit and definite in their predictions. Finally, ideal theories should be esthetic in their simplicity.

THE EXPERIMENTAL DEVELOPMENT OF CONSTRUCTS

Intervening Variables and Hypothetical Constructs

One of the problems faced by theoreticians is how the concepts of the theory should be chosen, defined, and used. Informal theorists seem generally to induce their concepts from observations rather than from primitive concepts within some theoretical system. For example, Freud derived his theoretical concepts from his clinical observations. He probably believed that he "saw" superego, id, ego, and libido in his patients. However, the exact relationship between the concepts and the observations is difficult or impossible to describe. To take one example, the superego was a complex structure and was presumed to affect many, if not all, behaviors. Its role in any given behavior was not, however, absolutely clear, and it was easier to explain the role of the superego after a behavior had occurred than to predict what the role of the superego, or the behavior, would be in advance. It appeared to many students of theory that Freud's implicit model was too flexible to be testable. The informal model could account for *any* behavior that occurred and therefore was not testable and not scientific.

This critical position is very much like the position taken by MacCorquodale and

Meehl (1948) in their classical paper on *hypothetical constructs* (HCs) and *intervening variables* (IVs). Their reaction to constructs like Freud's *ego* or *superego* was largely negative. They said that such concepts were HCs because they carried *surplus meaning* not justified by the observations on which they were based. MacCorquodale and Meehl preferred the IV type of construct. The IV was defined as having complete operational clarity; its meaning was to be completely determined by an observed relationship between antecedent variables and responses.

It did not take critics long to respond to MacCorquodale and Meehl. A "horrible example" of an IV is intelligence, defined as "what intelligence tests measure." Advocates of the use of "richer" HCs would point to the emptiness of such usage and ask why one would want to give a test in the first place or how one could tell an intelligence test from some other test. Part of the argument seems to be about whether or not constructs must be embedded in a model that relates them to other constructs. The rest is about whether there is, or should be, an implied relationship to other empirical concepts. We obviously have other ideas about intelligence beyond our knowledge that it is a score on a specific test of intelligence. There are even theories of intelligence and a host of studies that correlate various measures of intelligence with other variables. Part of the difficulty, and one source of the arguments about HCs and IVs, is that so much theoretical activity in psychology has remained at an implicit and intuitive level. We can seldom determine exactly what surplus meaning is connected with a construct, what part of that surplus meaning is connected with some implicit model, and what part is connected with related empirical relationships. This problem is just as severe with Freud's concepts as it is with "intelligence," and the reverse is also true.

The HC has been much more popular than the IV in psychology. The reasons for this seem clear; if one is to have a theory, as defined in this chapter, then one must use HCs. If a concept has a specified relationship with other concepts in some model, then it *must* have excess meaning. That is, manipulations within the model will produce predictions about observations not yet made. Manipulations involving the concept will thus produce "excess meaning" beyond observations previously made. That is the very essence of theory.

The "Learned Helplessness" Construct

Inductive theorists, many of whom are admirers of Skinnerian techniques, proceed by gradual enrichment of the meaning of operationally defined constructs (IVs). This is the procedure admired by MacCorquodale and Meehl. One example of this generally functional type of research begins with an experiment by Mowrer and Viek (1948). They shocked hungry rats before offering them food on a stick presented between the floor bars of the cage. Rats in an experimental group could turn off the shock by jumping off the floor. Matched control rats received exactly the same intensity and duration of shock as the experimental subjects but could do nothing to turn off the shock. The experimental rats ate more food than the controls. This behavioral difference could not be attributed to any physical difference in the shock. Thus Mowrer and Viek attributed it to a "sense of helplessness" in the control rats. This construct would be an IV as long as its meaning is strictly confined to the S-R relationships. However, the very name of the construct may endow it with a meaning in addition to what would be suggested if we called it "factor X."

Marx and Van Spanckeren (1952) used a similar experimental design but changed the experimental situation. Instead of shock, they presented intense high-pitched sound to rats prone to have seizures in the presence of such sounds. Side-by-side cages were placed under a centrally located sound source. Upright poles were placed in each cage. Rats in the experimental cage were able to turn the sound off by tilting the pole. The pole in the control cage had no effect on the sound. Rats in the control group had more seizures and had them faster. Marx and Van Spanckeren attributed this difference to a "sense of control" in the experimental rats—the other side of Mowrer and Viek's "sense of helplessness." Thus the second experiment enriched the meaning of this construct, regarded as an IV, by demonstrating that it was related to another set of experimental operations. Many later experiments on the "learned helplessness" phenomenon, some of which will be discussed in Chapter 11, illustrate the increasingly rich meaning of this particular theoretical construct.

Most psychological theory construction probably still proceeds on this informal, "bottom-up" basis. The meanings of constructs are simultaneously enriched, clarified, and made more specific by conducting a series of related experiments. The constructs may eventually become part of some more encompassing and more formal theory of the type discussed in this chapter and to be exemplified by Hull in the following chapter. Meanwhile, even informal constructs suggest additional experiments which provide new information and lead to the development of still other constructs. They also guide observations, sometimes in unusual directions; without Freud's theory, it is unlikely that the study of dreams would have been as active!

SUMMARY

Theories involve language. Hence an understanding of the problems of semiotics, which subsumes syntactics, semantics, and pragmatics, is necessary. Feigl's diagram of the classical view of theory helps to connect the study of language to the study of theory. But the classical view has been criticized as too idealized, particularly because it too cleanly separates the abstract portion of the theory from its empirical underpinnings. Theory determines and corrects observation, and vice versa. The notion of a theory-independent "soil of experience" is questionable. Nevertheless, the classical view of theory is serviceable as an ideal, and one historical trend in psychological theory has been toward the kind of formal, precise, and limited theory that is consistent with Feigl's diagram. There is, however, an opposing trend which rejects the formalistic enterprise on the grounds that it has been blindly and unwisely borrowed from the physical sciences. Science also has nonlinguistic features which require the acquisition of perceptual and manipulative skills and allow the intrusion of subjective and intuitive components. The typical role of theory in psychology is probably less formal and more intuitive than our previous analysis may suggest; one example of this is research on learned helplessness. It is premature to reject any viewpoint, whether theoretical or antitheoretical.

FURTHER READINGS

Marx and Goodson (1976) have collected many useful articles, some of them their own, relevant to the concerns of this chapter in their *Theories in contemporary psychology*. Stevens and Feigl present their classical viewpoint in that book, and Feyerabend and Marx present two versions of the necessary correctives in the light of modern criticism and experience. For some interesting historical insights into the social psychology of the empirical segment of the psychological research enterprise, see Danziger's (1985) article on the experiment as a social institution. *Criticism and the growth of knowledge,* edited by Musgrave and Lakatos (1970), treats some knotty problems in the philosophy of science, especially as they relate to the questions raised by Thomas Kuhn. The book also provides clear connections between general systematic issues and more specific problems in the construction and correction of theories, but unfortunately none of the theories are psychological. Stephen Toulmin's *Human understanding* (1972) presents a very attractive view of science as an evolutionary process, using the ideas of variation and selection in a detailed and serious way to apply to the evolution of scientific concepts. Each of these sources presents a multitude of additional sources for those who want an introduction to the worlds of philosophy of science and theory construction.

CHAPTER 10

S-R AND S-S THEORIES: HULL VS. TOLMAN

INTRODUCTION

One of the most classic confrontations in American psychology was the one between the S-R reinforcement system proposed by Clark Hull and the S-S system of Edward Tolman. Their theoretical disputes are of great historical interest. The particular points that were so vigorously argued during the middle decades of this century, when the controversy was at its peak intensity, are no longer being directly contested. However, the study of this confrontation will amply repay us because of the many lessons provided. Moreover, some of the issues were not really resolved and thus still suggest problems to be solved.

What is *not* now being actively debated is the fundamental theoretical point that was at issue in the Hull-Tolman confrontation: whether learning is best interpreted as an S-R reinforcement or an S-S type of associationism. Perhaps the first lesson to be drawn from this period of intense theoretical debate is that too much repetition of such *total* theoretical opposition is not useful for a fledgling science like psychology if we hope for a steady advance toward the solution of the theoretical problems that face us.

It is difficult for today's student of psychology, mindful of a number of theoretical oppositions but accustomed to tolerating different points of view in experimental and theoretical programs, to appreciate the intensity of the theoretical disputation of this earlier period. The emotional fervor that accompanied much of the S-R versus S-S confrontation was in some ways more like a religious or political than a scientific confrontation. On the positive side, nevertheless, a spurt of experimentation was directly stimulated by the theoretical arguments. Much of this research would almost certainly not have been performed without the theoretical controversy. On the negative

Clark Hull (1884–1952), who developed the best-known formal theory of learning. Hull tried to pattern his S-R hypothetico-deductive system along the same lines as Euclid and Newton.

Edward Chace Tolman (1886–1959), a purposive behaviorist whose S-S theory was the leading alternative to Hull's for many years of exciting experimental and intellectual competition.

side, the collapse of the primary theoretical issues produced a general disillusionment with theory. This disillusionment has only recently ended, as new theoretical perspectives and issues emerge (cf. the "cognitive revolution," Chapter 13).

HULL'S S-R REINFORCEMENT THEORY

The main lines of modern S-R reinforcement theory were laid down by Clark L. Hull. He had the help of several other psychologists, notably Kenneth Spence and Neal Miller. Both of them were associated with him at Yale University, and both helped to determine the way in which Hull's theory developed. Spence especially was consistently interested in the form of the theory, and trained and sent forth from Iowa a large number of theoretical devotees. Miller not only worked directly with the theory but also extended it to the explanation of personality.

Hull's Career

Clark L. Hull (1884–1952) was born in New York and reared on a farm near Sickles, Michigan. Throughout his childhood and early adult years he was beset by illnesses, and he suffered from poor vision all his life. In young adulthood, polio left him crippled in one leg. He believed that much of his motivation derived from his handicap; however, there is reason to doubt that this is the whole story. His own "idea books" refer to his hope that he might some day achieve prominence, fully seven years before he contracted polio (Hays, 1962). Hull showed his mechanical ingenuity even in responding to his handicap. He built a prosthesis for walking, using discarded buggy springs as the main components, and could walk almost without a limp.

Hull's education was interrupted both by these physical problems and by lack of money. He taught in the one-room rural school near his home and in a Kentucky normal school, to repair his financial shortfalls. Nevertheless, he managed to earn his bachelor's degree at the University of Michigan, where Pillsbury was a dominant influence. Pillsbury may have influenced Hull in the direction of behaviorism, since he was far more functional than his own mentor, Titchener, had been.

Hull completed his doctoral research at the University of Wisconsin. His dissertation was a study of concept formation (Hull, 1920). He was 34 by the time he completed his own personal obstacle course that led to the Ph.D. His idea books (Hull, 1962) show that he was often concerned that this late start might prevent him from achieving the greatness to which he aspired. At one stage he expected to have only six creative years left. Then he raised his estimate to eleven upon reading of the advanced ages at which men like Kant and Leibniz had created great works. When he made his 11-year estimate, he actually had 20 productive years left!

After receiving his Ph.D., Hull stayed on at Wisconsin as a member of the psychology staff. One of his early research efforts concerned the effects of tobacco smoking on efficiency. These much-cited experiments (Hull, 1924) were remarkable for their control of the sensory factors involved in smoking (such as the warmth of the air produced by a pipe). The control of suggestibility by concealing whether tobacco was really present presaged Hull's later concern with hypnosis and suggestibility.

As a result of being assigned a course in tests and measures, Hull surveyed the literature in that field and eventually published an important early text, *Aptitude testing* (1928). He did not continue these activities, however, because of what he later called his "pessimistic view as to the future of tests in this field" (1952, p. 151). Here again Hull's idea books provide us with justification for doubting his assessment of his own motives, since he says in an idea book of 1929 that he still plans to do "a grand experiment on a huge scale" (1962, p. 827), with the intention of constructing a universal aptitude battery. Hull's discussions there convey the clear impression that the aptitude work was merely being deferred until later because he thought of it as the kind of work that he could do when he was older and less creative.

Hull's next persistent research interest was in hypnosis and suggestibility. He became involved because he had to present academic lectures and laboratory work to medical students. He spent ten productive years in research on suggestion, supervising a large number of senior theses. By his own count, some twenty persons engaged in the research, which was reported in thirty-two papers. He stated (1952) that his interest in hypnotic research was not encouraged after he moved to Yale. He encountered medical opposition there, but not at Wisconsin. He published a classic book, *Hypnosis and suggestibility* (1933), at the end of this phase of his career.

Hull's third and final major research interest was learning theory. He studied Anrep's translation of Pavlov's *Conditioned reflexes* (1927) and became progressively more interested in learning and general behavior theory. In 1929 he became a research professor at Yale's Institute of Psychology (which shortly thereafter became the Institute of Human Relations). Thenceforth he turned to the development of behavior theory on a full-scale basis. He continued zealous and devoted work on this most important part of his contribution to psychology, despite declining health during the last years of his life, until his death in 1952. He left behind a band of students as devoted to him as he had been to them.

The Development of Hull's System

Hull published a series of brilliantly conceived theoretical papers on conditioning during the 1930s. One of the best known was his presidential address before the American Psychological Association, entitled "Mind, mechanism, and adaptive behavior" (1937). The general purpose of these papers, exemplified in the title cited, was to show how basic conditioning principles might be extended to complex behavioral processes. As a methodological, rather than a metaphysical, behaviorist, Hull did not deny the existence of mental phenomena. However, he thought mental phenomena *needed explaining,* rather than that they themselves were useful as explanatory devices. He therefore proposed to give as complete an explanation of action as possible, and he hoped that his theory would someday help to account for consciousness. Hull thought that the behavioral approach to mental phenomena had not had a thorough trial. He wanted to give it a trial that would either succeed or show that the approach could not work.

A brief excursion into the field of verbal rote learning followed his early theoretical work. Here Hull enlisted the aid of a group of mathematicians and logicians, as well as psychologists, and they gave a logically rigorous quantitative analysis of the kind of rote verbal learning first studied by Ebbinghaus. Although the book that emerged from this effort was hailed as a landmark in the development of scientific psychology, it has seldom been read, less often understood, and unproductive of research. The *Mathematico-deductive theory of rote learning* (Hull, Hovland, Ross, Hall, Perkins, & Fitch, 1940) thus remains a monumental but relatively fruitless model of psychological theory construction.

Hull's next major publication, *Principles of behavior* (1943), had quite the opposite effect. Its appearance marked the beginning of an era of psychological research in which Hull became the unquestioned leader of learning research in this country and one of the most controversial figures in the field. In *Principles of behavior* Hull attempted to lay down the framework for a comprehensive theory of all mammalian behavior. He outlined a set of postulates and corollaries, logically interlaced in the hypothetico-deductive style that he considered the correct mode for scientific theorizing.

Although many psychologists did not think that the book fulfilled the great promise of Hull's early theoretical papers, it nevertheless had an enormous influence on research in learning. Hull became by far the most-cited writer in that field. Untold numbers of master's theses and doctoral dissertations were tests of the implications of Hull's theory. Up to the time of his death in 1952, Hull remained the dominant figure in learning theory.

A major factor in the success of *Principles of behavior* in stimulating research was its detailed spelling out of the postulate-corollary set. Hull deliberately laid out the system as explicitly as he could in order to expedite empirical checking. This explicitness was probably the most important feature of his systematic endeavor. Never before had a theorist succeeded in being so complete and precise in formulating a psychological theory.

Perhaps the most important subject-matter aspect of Hull's theorizing was its reconciliation of Thorndikian effect with the conditioning paradigm and methodology of Pavlov. Hull incorporated the effect principle—now called *reinforcement*—into the conditioning framework. He did not agree with J. B. Watson that frequency and recency of response were sufficient principles to account for learning. Hull's emphasis on effect was evident in the last organization of his postulate set. Hull (1952) began with introductory postulates that dealt with "unlearned stimulus-response connections" (postulate I) and "stimulus reception" (postulate II). He then stated the key principle of reinforcement, first described as the *law of primary reinforcement,* as follows:

Postulate III. Primary Reinforcement

Whenever an effector activity (R) is closely associated with a stimulus afferent impulse or trace (s) and the conjunction is closely associated with a rapid diminution in the motivational stimulus (S_D or S_G), there will result an increment (Δ) to a tendency for that stimulus to evoke that response. (1952, pp. 5–6)

Immediately following were corollaries dealing with secondary motivation and secondary reinforcement. Postulate IV stated the law of habit formation, with number of reinforcements as the independent variable.

Hull's last books were *Essentials of behavior* (1951) and *A behavior system* (1952). The latter work attempted to extend the use of quantitative methods within the system and to extend the domain of the system in accounting for individual behavior. A final contemplated work on social behavior was never begun. Hull, who was very ill for some time before his death, did not live to read the galley proofs of *A behavior system.*

Hullian Methodology

Objectivity   Hull was first and foremost a behaviorist. He rejected metaphysical behaviorism, with its denial of consciousness, but fully and enthusiastically endorsed methodological behaviorism. Hull was considered the archobjectivist of the 1940s both by his followers, who reveled in this identification, and by his opponents, who chose it as a point of attack. In pursuing his behavioristic program, Hull tried to use concepts that were reducible, at least in principle, to physical terms.

Hull (1943) gave physicalistic definitions of stimulus and response; stimulus was defined in part as "stimulus energy in general, e.g., the energy of sound, light, or heat waves, pressure, etc." (p. 407). Koch (1954) showed that Hull's operations with stimuli did not, however, at all conform to this definition. In practice, a stimulus was a part of the environment which the *experimenter* discriminated and responded to.

Thus Hull, like most objectivists, did not follow physicalistic definitions in his experimental work. However, even his critics have typically found Hull's data language objective enough.

Hull's theory contained a number of explicit intervening variables. Such variables are logical constructs postulated to help account for the relationship between input and output. They correspond to the circles and triangles in Feigl's diagram in Chapter 9. Hull made sure that his intervening variables were connected to observable antecedent conditions like number of reinforced trials, stimulus intensity, and hours of deprivation. The intervening variables were interconnected with each other and, finally, with the properties of responses. Thus Hull's variables were intended to be anchored in antecedent and consequent conditions. To the extent that the anchoring and the theoretical interrelationships were clearly specified, the intervening variables were sure to have a clear meaning. If theoretical predictions then coincided with observed data, the intervening variables could be said to "summarize" the observed relationships.

Although Hull and his followers usually called his theoretical variables "intervening variables," they were clearly hypothetical constructs in the sense in which Mac-Corquodale and Meehl (1948) used the term (see Chapter 9). They had a great deal of excess meaning because they were part of an extensive theory. Hull used that theory to make predictions of new phenomena, which is in itself evidence that the constructs had meaning which went beyond the observations from which they were induced. It is important to remember that it is possible to have a whole range of construct types. At the completely operational end are the "E/C" intervening variables (Marx, 1951) whose meaning is limited to whatever is needed to account for the observed difference between experimental (E) and control (C) conditions. At the opposite end are constructs which are completely hypothetical and have no empirical anchorages whatever. Such constructs are scientifically meaningless. These are the constructs to which Mac-Corquodale and Meehl really objected. In between the extremes are constructs with anchorages in empirical observation and surplus meaning of some kind. Even the in-between constructs differ over a wide range in the ratio of empirical to theoretical meaning. Hull recognized that his constructs had a great hypothetical component, which is why he put so much emphasis on empirical anchorages; he recognized the danger of getting too far from an empirical base.

Hypothetico-deductive Form Hull was greatly impressed by the elegance of formal mathematical systems, such as those developed by Euclid and Newton. As his interest in developing a general behavior system grew, he determined to model it upon these examples. The result was that he tried to build a formalized and comprehensive behavior theory of a "hypothetico-deductive" type. Formal postulates and corollaries were proposed, and theorems followed as deductive consequences. Such a system is hypothetico-deductive because it begins with *hypotheses* which are well enough connected in a logical system so that their consequences can be *deduced*. The deductions (theorems) are related by the theorist to statements of empirical observations which should follow under the specified conditions. The validity of the empirical predictions is checked by experiment. If the predictions are verified, the hypotheses are retained; if they are false, some postulates require modification or rejection.

In *Principles of behavior* (1943), Hull laid down sixteen primary principles as postulates, and a large number of corollaries. In the 1951 revision of the system, a total of eighteen postulates and twelve corollaries was produced. In accordance with the hypothetico-deductive procedure that Hull intended to follow, these primary principles were to be used deductively to predict secondary principles such as the goal gradient and latent learning.

Formulation of Postulates   The focal point of Hull's theoretical thinking was the conditioned reflex, as conceptualized by Pavlov. Hull regarded it as a kind of simplified learning situation which was admirably suited for experimental analyses. The findings could then be extended to other, more complex, phenomena. Hull made the extension by basing the axioms of his system on experimental findings from conditioning experiments. For example, Hull's postulate II in his final system states the value of the ascending "molar stimulus trace" as a function of time since stimulation in this equation (1952, p. 5):

$$\dot{S}' = 465{,}190 \times t^{7.6936} + 1.0,$$

$\dot{S}'$ reaching its maximum (and termination) when t equals about .450 second.

Hull stated his individual equations formally, carefully, and precisely. Although the precision was sometimes misleading, the symbols used were carefully defined. The above equation, as well as the others in postulate II, was based directly on empirical relationships observed in conditioning experiments.

Koch (1954, pp. 70ff.) believes that Hull erred in basing his postulates too directly on data. The history of science suggests that most successful abstract postulates are several steps removed from the functional forms seen directly in data. Thus Koch believes that postulates induced from the data of particular experiments have little chance of being useful in a general theory. This view contrasts sharply with the view that theorists *should* proceed from limited, data-based, formulations which eventually can be combined into more global theories.

Such use of conditioning experiments as a source of axioms is, in any case, a distinct and critical change from previous behavioristic practice. Watson had used the conditioned reflex only grossly, as an element from which more complex behaviors could be constructed by chaining such elements together. It is clear that Hull's theorizing was a great leap forward in sophistication of theoretical methodology, for he used the conditioning situation as a source of abstract relations which could be combined into a general theory.

Derivation of Theorems   An example will illustrate how Hull used some prior empirical knowledge, one or more primary principles (postulates or corollaries), and some deductive derivation combined with a little quantification to produce theorems that could be tested empirically. Consider the problem of the order of elimination of blind alleys in maze learning, as by a rat. It had long been known that the blind alleys closest to the goal are eliminated first, a principle Hull (1932) called the "goal-gradient hypothesis." Hull put this empirical fact into a logical form by assuming that the reaction potential of any response is a function of its distance in time from the reinforcing event (in this case the reaching of the food incentive in the goal box). Thus Hull's (1952) corollary iii, delay in reinforcement (*J*) reads:

A. *The greater the delay in reinforcement of a link within a given behavior chain, the weaker will be the resulting reaction potential of the link in question to the stimulus traces present at the time.* (p. 126)

This principle, the logical derivation of which was given (Hull, 1952, Ch. 5), led to a number of predictions for multidimensional maze learning (Hull, 1952, Ch. 9). Among these were the propositions that a long blind alley, since it entails a greater delay of reinforcement, will be eliminated more quickly than a short blind alley (theorem 104, p. 282) and that the rate of locomotion through the maze will become progressively faster for the later, compared with the earlier, parts (theorem 110, 1952, p. 285). Now it is important to note that neither of these two predictions could be generated directly from the first empirical result itself, the observation of a gradient of error elimination. It *could* be logically derived from the general principle of delay of reinforcement, which was developed from the empirical data. Such logical deduction of many new and different predictions from a smaller number of key principles is a major contribution of a hypothetico-deductive system. Hull's *A behavior system* is full of such derivations, with quantitative calculations, and so it is a better example of hypothetico-deductive methodology than was the more programmatic *Principles of behavior*.

Hull's system was not static. His formal theory underwent an almost continuous series of revisions. He did not take his own quantitative statements too seriously, and he said that he could not be certain of the value of a single parameter in his equations. He was content if the qualitative predictions of his theory were verified even if the quantitative predictions were far from the mark.

Quantitativeness   Although Hull did not have much faith in the specifics of his quantitative statements, he thought that theoretical progress in psychology must come as a consequence of the successful use of quantitative methods. He did his best to make his own theory quantitative in form. In *Principles of behavior,* most of the "quantification" was only programmatic. Many postulates had no mathematical form or lacked numerical values for the constants. Hull was acutely aware of the shortcomings of this 1943 system. He continued to strive for genuine quantification, and he published five articles which reported the progress of this work. One basic experiment (Felsinger, Gladstone, Yamaguchi, & Hull, 1947) was a study of the latency of response to a manipulandum. Latency was measured from the time that a cover was removed to make the manipulandum available. Thurstone's method of paired comparisons was used to estimate the amount of $_sE_R$ (reaction potential) giving rise to the response.

There are some unavoidable problems associated with the attempt to quantify the variables of a complex theory. Whenever intervening variables, which cannot be directly observed, are involved in a theoretical chain, rational decisions involving an element of guesswork must be made about the quantitative interrelationships between all the variables in the theory. There is no escape from this requirement. Guesses which produce a useful general theory require great creativity, plus some luck. Logan

(1959, pp. 303–306) gave a concise example of the general method by which Hull proceeded to combine empirical observations with rational guesses to produce his version of a quantitative behavior theory. A look at Hull's system will show that he would have needed unusual luck and creativity if his quantitative statements were to have the least chance of being correct.

Summary of the System   Hullian theory deals with three types of variables: the stimulus (antecedent or input), the intervening (intraorganismic), and the response (consequent or output). The following abbreviated account is intended to give a little of the general nature and flavor of the system. The basic constructs and interrelationships of the system are presented diagrammatically in Figure 10-1. For a more detailed exposition, the reader should consult one of the original sources referred to above, or a more specialized secondary source (e.g., Bower & Hilgard, 1981; Koch, 1954; Spence, 1951a, b).

The input variables to Hull's theory are such objective factors as number of reinforced trials, deprivation of incentive, intensity of conditioned stimulus, and amount of reward. These factors are directly associated with processes hypothesized to function within the organism: intervening variables of the first order. Examples are habit strength $_sH_R$ as a function of number of trials N; drive D as a function of drive condition, such as deprivation of incentive C_D; stimulus-intensity dynamism V as a function of stimulus intensity S; and incentive reinforcement K as a function of amount of reward W.

FIGURE 10-1
Simplified diagrammatic representation of the Hullian system. See text for explanation of symbols and relationships.

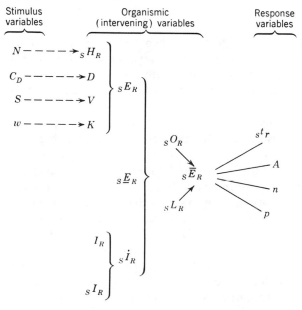

Certain of these direct, or first-order, constructs are assumed now to coalesce into a smaller number of second-order intervening variables. The major construct is reaction potential, or response evocation $_sE_R$, which is a joint function of $_sH_R$, D, V, and K. Also to be considered at this level are generalized reaction potential $_s\underline{E}_R$, which is a function of the amount of similarity of the present conditioned stimulus to ones previously experienced for which habit strengths have been established, and the aggregate of the negative reaction tendencies $(_s\dot{I}_R)$. The latter construct is a function of reactive inhibition I_R and conditioned or learned inhibition $_sI_R$, both of which are the direct consequence of work performed in the response.

At the final level, the higher-order intervening constructs then are net reaction potential $_s\bar{E}_R$, a function of the two excitatory factors and the one inhibitory factor just mentioned, and two more speculative and less well-specified constructs which modify its action. These are the oscillation $_sO_R$ and threshold $_sL_R$ of reaction potential. Finally, on the output side, there are four major measures of the strength of response: latency $_st_R$, amplitude A, number of responses to extinction n, and probability of response p.

A number of stimulus-trace concepts, such as the drive stimulus S_D and the fractional anticipatory goal stimulus s_G, supplement the theory. They are of great importance but were omitted from our description so that the essentials could be presented more simply.

Also of great importance, but not included in the summary diagram, are a number of secondary principles which Hull developed in an attempt to bridge the gap between the complexities of molar behavior and the abstracted simplicity of his postulate set. Most important among these are the *habit family hierarchy* and the *goal gradient*. The latter has already been described above; the former refers to the presumed ordering, according to their relative strengths, of the set of responses that can be elicited in any given stimulus situation.

Systematic Issues   Anyone who aspires to build a theory of behavior like Hull's must face a number of very difficult problems. There is a very low probability that these problems could be solved today, let alone when Hull was alive. However, we can defer criticism of Hull's aspirations until later and look first at the nature of the problems which those aspirations led him to face.

One early problem is to decide which independent and dependent variables will be used in the theory. Some guidance is available from experimental practice, but many decisions will remain. For example, will it be profitable to try to predict all response variables from the same theory? Hull tried to predict latency, amplitude, number of responses to extinction, and probability of response from the value of a single intervening variable. Skinner believes that rate of response is the best, if not the only, measure to use. Accordingly, he has studied primarily free operants, responses like bar pressing which the animal is free to repeat "at will." Hull studied primarily controlled operants, responses for which the experimenter controls opportunities for response emission, as in a runway. His decision to relate his final intervening variable, net generalized reaction potential, to four response measures made it legitimate to ask whether these measures were perfectly correlated as the theory said they should be.

Hull could have avoided embarrassing issues of this kind by making predictions of only one response measure, but he would have lost a great deal of generality in doing so.

Similar problems had to be faced at the level of the intervening variables. For example, there is Hull's decision to have a single excitatory learning construct, $_sH_R$. If a theorist were working on this problem today, he might feel it necessary to have distinct constructs (or distinct subtheories) for different kinds of learning; for example, food-motivated learning might be distinguished from sex-motivated learning within the theory.

A very general problem connected with intervening variables concerns what we might call their *reality status.* We have been describing Hull's intervening variables as "organismic," which implies some physiological commitment. A more neutral description would be simply that the intervening variables are intratheoretical, which they indubitably are, rather than intraorganismic, which they may or may not be.

Even after the constructs of a system are isolated and their general type decided upon, there remain problems concerning the definition of each construct and the specification of construct interrelationships. As an example of such problems, we might take the innocuous-looking N, the number of reinforced trials. What is a reinforced trial?

Hull first specified that if a trial were to be reinforced, it had to be followed by need reduction. There were difficulties with this definition. First, need reduction was likely to be quite slow and thus did not seem to provide the close temporal contiguity between response and reinforcement expected to be necessary for effective strengthening. Second, it was not easy to know whether or not need reduction had occurred. It could be tempting to postulate need reduction whenever a response had been strengthened, but this would not provide the necessary independent basis for the construct. Third, consequences like handling or escape strengthened responses, despite the fact that they had no obvious need-reducing properties. Additional difficulties are discussed later in this chapter.

For these and perhaps other reasons, Hull then decided that a reinforcer had to reduce a drive stimulus rather than reduce a need. This definition had the potential for remedying the first and third difficulties above, but the possibility of circularity remained. Hull had exactly the same sort of problem that Thorndike had encountered with respect to his law of effect, and they needed to resort to the same kind of solution. Any residual looseness in the definition of reinforcement makes the concept of N imprecise and thereby affects all related concepts in the theory.

The specification of construct interrelationships is just as fertile a source of problems. The habit construct, $_sH_R$, can serve as an example. In Hull's early theory, several input variables influenced habit. Habit, in its turn, influenced reaction potential. Since habit was thought to be capable only of slow and continuous change, it was not possible to derive sudden shifts in performance from the theory. But such shifts occurred in the latent learning experiments, as detailed later in this chapter, so a change in the theory was needed. Hull changed the construct interrelationships to make the input variables D (drive) and K (incentive) affect $_sE_R$ (reaction potential) rather than $_sH_R$. It was then possible for the theory to account for the rapid change in response strength which had empirically been observed to occur following changes in deprivation or incentive.

We are not saying that Hull changed the construct interrelationships *in order* to explain latent learning, although there would have been nothing wrong with doing so. Koch (1954) and Hilgard and Bower (1966) agreed that the change was actually made so that $_sH_R$ could be more easily quantified.

Hull's precise statement of relationships between constructs helped to create additional controversies. Let us take $_sH_R$ as an example again. Its mathematical relationship to number of trials (N) was postulated to be as follows:

$$_sH_R = 1 - 10^{-aN}$$

Trials were assumed to be evenly spaced, and the constant a was thought to be approximately 0.03 in numerical value (Hull, 1951, p. 32).

This clear mathematical statement implies that each trial imparts an increment to the strength of $_sH_R$ and thus indirectly to the tendency to respond. Although this is not truly a continuous function, since N takes only discrete values, Hull's theory was called a continuity theory to distinguish it from the view that learning is basically sudden, an all-or-none process. The latter view would be exemplified by the Gestalt position, which was that learning is sudden and insightful and thus noncontinuous. The starkness of Hull's mathematical statements made disagreements stand out nakedly. Controversies about continuity versus noncontinuity and about latent learning raged for years.

Criticisms of the Hullian System

The criticisms of Hull's system were searching and vehement. As a leading neobehaviorist, Hull inherited much of the criticism that had earlier been directed at Watson. Much of this criticism was based on fundamental methodological or theoretical differences in taste. The volume and quality of Hull's work shielded him from any charge that he lacked ingenuity, originality, or persistence. Nevertheless, the solid critical points lodged against Hull merit attention.

Synthetic Approach As we have seen, Hull attempted to work out a comprehensive theoretical account of mammalian behavior over a very short span of years. He had to put together the pieces of his behavioral puzzle before much of the necessary research had been done. In Hull's defense, however, it must be said that he used whatever empirical evidence he could find and persistently tried to create more.

Hull wished to emulate the formal elegance of the systems of Euclid and Newton, but he faced problems of greater complexity and may not have had as much background for his work. The elegance of a beautifully integrated formal system hides the fits and starts involved in the development of the final product. It may be that theory develops faster in the long run if initial efforts are not very ambitious. It is often said that Hull's approach to the exceedingly complex problem of behavior was too optimistic, but we should remember that Hull recognized the shortness of life and tried to do as much as he could within its confines.

Particularistic Approach   One of the most persistent criticisms from sympathetic sources was that Hull relied too much upon particular values of critical variables within special experimental circumstances. The problem of generality, always a knotty one in behavior theory, was noted early by Koch (1944, p. 283) in his review of *Principles of behavior,* and by Hilgard and Bower (1966, p. 186), who cited the dependence of Hull's system upon particular constants from rat bar-pressing and human eyelid experimentation.

An example of the extreme particularism of some of Hull's theorizing, in the sense of dependence upon specific experimental setups, is his provisional definition of the *wat* (honoring Watson) as the unit of reaction potential;

> The wat is the mean standard deviation of the momentary reaction potential (E) of standard albino rats, 90 days of age, learning a simple manipulative act requiring a 10-gram pressure by 24-hour distributed trials under 23 hours' hunger, water available, with reward in the form of a 2.5-gram pellet of the usual dry dog food, the mean being taken from all the reinforcement trials producing the habit strength from .75 to .85 habs inclusive. (Hull, 1951, p. 100)

It seems unlikely that generalization from a situation involving such particular values of food weight and manipulandum pressure to other animal behavior situations would be successful, to say nothing of generalizing to more complex behavioral situations with higher mammals such as humans. Thus while Hull's specificity is in some respects admirable, the aspirations of his theorizing seem far beyond its achievements. Hull himself stated increasing reservations about the generality of his theory in his later writing (see Koch, 1954, pp. 167ff.). This is also evident in the more cautious tone of his final work (Hull, 1952).

The only answer to these criticisms is that the results will determine whether or not the approach is effective. This is also the only answer to the more general criticism made of S-R theorists: that they oversimplify complex behavioral problems. Until we try, we cannot be sure whether an approach such as Hull's will lead us to an adequate account of the complexities of mammalian behavior, and the only scientific way to find out is to try.

Logical Weakness   Probably the most telling criticism of Hull's theory was the demonstration that his system was not the tightly knit, logical one that he intended it to be and that many believed it to be. Hull sometimes failed to build in logically necessary connections between his constructs. A number of careful critical analyses demonstrated this. Koch's (1954) analysis is devastating because of its extremely detailed documentation and logical sophistication (in spite of an unsympathetic and sometimes unfair tone). The easy testability of construct relationships that Hull envisioned was shown to be largely illusory. Cotton (1955) also gave a persuasive and beautifully presented demonstration of the impossibility of making predictions from

Hull's theory as Hull had presented it. Even when "friendly" assumptions were made in the attempt to make derivations possible, difficulties remained. We are forced to conclude that Hull's theory was logically incomplete.

Hull's Contributions

Objective Terminology and Methodology   Hull's own life was that of a scientist and scholar, a life of the mind. But in his psychology he determined to start with action, stay with action, and see how far action would carry him. His terms, therefore, were not new names for old concepts. *Reactive inhibition, habit strength, reaction potential*—these terms had some of their creator's active vitality, ringing forth with the promise of carrying out the evangelical behavioristic program thrust upon the incredulous world at Watson's psychological revival meeting. The type of methodology implied by these terms will not be forgotten, whatever the fate of the theory in which Hull embedded them.

We believe that Hull's most important contribution to psychology was his demonstration of the value of setting one's sights upon the ultimate goal of a thoroughly scientific and systematic behavior theory. He lived his own scientific life in pursuit of that goal, and thereby influenced even those who disagreed most vehemently with the details of his work. Few psychologists have had so great an effect on the professional motivation of so many researchers. He popularized the strictly objective behavioristic approach as it had never been popularized previously.

New Problem Areas   Hull opened new areas in a rather peculiar sense. He did not develop important new pieces of apparatus or initiate research in previously untouched areas. Rather, he conceived new ways of viewing problems and suggested new relationships to be studied. He was a theoretical psychologist, just as some physicists are theoretical physicists. Unfortunately, he was a theoretician preceded by no Einstein, Newton, Copernicus, or perhaps even Archimedes in the field of psychology. Nevertheless, when he formulated a postulate or derived a theorem from his potulate set, other investigators performed experiments to test the predicted relationships. For example, when Hull stated his belief about the shape of the generalization gradient, research quickly focused on determining the correctness of the stated shape. The very attempt to formalize a theory of behavior forced Hull and his coworkers to see what must be known before the formalization could be completed. Key concepts such as stimulus and processes such as reinforcement had to undergo intensive examination.

Although Hull was most strongly attacked by cognitive theorists and field theorists, in one respect his system was more a "field theory" than was typical of those called by that name. Hull specified as many of the relevant variables as he reasonably could, and he stated their hypothesized mode of interaction. This high degree of theoretical specificity goes far beyond the speculative use of conditioning by the early behaviorists and is more concrete than anything offered by Hull's critics, who tended not to specify the characteristics of the psychological field precisely (Estes, 1954).

Finally, Hull was criticized for giving too much direction to research effort. He concentrated work on the solution of the theoretical problems which he thought needed to be resolved if behavior theory was to make significant advances; naturally, those were the questions which needed to be answered in order to complete his own theory. However, some critics thought that we could not yet afford to decide the direction of research on formal theoretical grounds. Rather, those empirical areas should be studied which produce results that are interesting in themselves. We believe that both of these contrasting views have some merit. Fortunately, there are many psychologists available to explore both paths. Part of Hull's contribution was that he showed how the high theoretical road could be taken.

Hull's Place in History

Clark Hull's place in psychological history seems to be assured. He was one of those rare people whose influence was so great that they redirected a science. He found psychology still wrestling with broad systematic issues, mostly of metatheoretical significance, and he left large numbers of psychologists doing experimental analyses of his postulates and theorems. Hull's theory was far easier to criticize than the broader issues had been, and his clear formulations revealed gaps that made criticism almost superfluous.

It is paradoxical that Hull changed metatheory by being concerned with theory. His predecessors, the earlier behaviorists, had done their utmost to turn psychology away from verbal issues and toward more empirically fruitful problems. But this never quite came off. Hull brought it off with a positive effect. He was certainly deeply and intelligently concerned with metatheory, and the system he created is the "grandest" ever attempted in the behavioristic tradition. His distinction is that he did not stop there. He made a persistent, even if largely unsuccessful, attempt to push on into the tangled unknown where specific issues are resolved and thereby gave psychological explorers a better feel for what a psychological theory should be.

Another paradox is Hull's lack of rigor. His system had the appearance but not the reality. He never had time to smooth out wrinkles. Neither did any of the other of psychology's greatest figures. If anyone in psychology is excessively afraid of being wrong, that person has published no extensive theory. Hull, even though he strove for rigor, had to stand with those who had no such fear. In this rather peculiar way, he carved his niche in history between the systematists and those following him who will construct more rigorous behavior theories.

For a time, it seemed that Hull had made of psychology his own private domain. In the early 1950s, he was cited far more often than any other psychologist in the *Journal of Experimental Psychology* (Ammons, 1962), and his *Principles of behavior* (Hull, 1943) was the most frequently cited publication, with its nearest rival cited less than a fourth as often in the four journals tabulated. Between 1930 and 1950, Hull was regarded as the leading psychological theorist (Coan & Zagona, 1962, p. 319). Later, however, his fall from favor was rapid. The pendulum of theoretical style swung rapidly toward primarily inductive procedures, but there are signs that it is swinging back. Mathematical modeling (partially as represented in computer stimulation) has again become popular, and there is no denying Hull's priority and early dominance in this type of endeavor.

TOLMAN'S PURPOSIVE S-S BEHAVIORISM

The important contribution of Edward C. Tolman (1886–1959) to the development of behaviorism was noted in Chapter 6. He emphasized a *molar* interpretation of behavior as *purposive* (Tolman, 1932) throughout his long and illustrious career. Although Tolman did not develop a definitive theory, his system, with its cognitive, or S-S, position on learning, has been extremely influential. Tolman was the most acceptable of the behaviorists to nonbehavioristically oriented psychologists. His system was a seemingly paradoxical combination of elements from behaviorism and Gestalt psychology. In Tolman's later papers (for example, 1949a), he professed an admiration for the field-theoretical views of Kurt Lewin and adopted some of his theoretical positions.

Tolman's Career

Edward C. Tolman was born in Massachusetts and took an engineering degree at the Massachusetts Institute of Technology. He switched to psychology, in which subject he received a Ph.D. in 1915 from Harvard. He was an instructor in psychology at Northwestern University from 1915 to 1918. He then moved to the University of California, where he established a rat laboratory. During World War II Tolman served for 2 years (1944 and 1945) in the Office of Strategic Services. In 1950, at the age of 64, he demonstrated his patriotism in a different way by leading the fight against the state loyalty oath. During the next 3 years, while the issue was being resolved, Tolman held appointments at the University of Chicago and at Harvard.

Tolman's deep humanness, which made him beloved by his students, still showed through in the conclusion to his final published statement:

> I have liked to think about psychology in ways that have proved congenial to me. Since all the sciences, and especially psychology, are still immersed in such tremendous realms of the uncertain and the unknown, the best that any individual scientist, especially any psychologist, can do seems to be to follow his own gleam and his own bent, however inadequate they may be. In fact, I suppose that actually this is what we all do. In the end, the only sure criterion is to have fun. And I have had fun. (1959, p. 152)

Tolman the man was thus something of a maverick and a dissenter. We shall see that the system, like the man, resisted being fitted easily into preconceived categories.

Tolman's System

Tolman's system was loosely formulated in his first and most important book, *Purposive behavior in animals and man* (1932). At the time that he was working on it, little effort was expended to organize the major ideas into an integrated system.

Predictions about experimental outcomes were not related to one another in a logically rigorous manner. Thus Tolman was long considered a programmatic theorist. MacCorquodale and Meehl (1954) formalized his principles with much more rigor and detail. In his final work (1959), Tolman himself presented a more organized picture of his system.

The primary principle in Tolman's systematic thinking about behavior is that the organism, in its purposive activities, uses environmental objects and develops *means-end readinesses* with regard to them and to their roles in relation to its behavior. The italicized phrase is but one of many awkwardly compounded terms which Tolman coined early in his career and used consistently in his writing. This one is particularly emphasized in his "Principles of purposive behavior" (1959). The term is roughly synonymous with *cognitions* or *expectancies*. It refers to the kind of learning which Tolman thought was central to behavior: sign learning. Briefly put, the organism learns "what leads to what." Like the Gestalt theorist, Tolman felt that the actual behavior is relatively unimportant; the primary determiners of action are central. They are not peripheral determiners, as the typical S-R theorist would have us believe.

In his statement of 1959, Tolman presented a schema for each of five representative situations: simple approach to food, simple escape from electric shock, simple avoidance of electric shock, choice-point learning, and latent learning. These five paradigms demonstrate several aspects of Tolman's late thought. First, a superficial similarity to the Hullian system is apparent. To some extent, however, Tolman's logical interrelating of concepts was induced by the form of presentation requested by the editor of the book in which it appeared. Formalization may also have been encouraged by the earlier effort of MacCorquodale and Meehl (1954), who had already put Tolman's thinking into a near-Hullian form.

Second, and more important, Tolman's final formulation illustrates the central role played in his theory by cognitive constructs. Two major constructs were: the means-end readiness, a pure acquired cognitive disposition, and the expectation. The former is "pure" in the sense that it endures independently of the present motivational state of the organism. That is, the organism may know where food is whether or not it is hungry. The expectation, on the other hand, is the concrete product of the means-end readiness. It is a cognitive event that applies specifically to a current situation. Tolman (1959) summed up the two concepts:

> A means-end readiness, as I conceive it, is a condition in the organism, which is equivalent to what in ordinary parlance we call a "belief" (a readiness or disposition) to the effect that an instance of this *sort* of stimulus situation, if reacted to by an instance of this *sort* of response, will lead to an instance of that *sort* of further stimulus situation, or else, that an instance of this *sort* of stimulus situation will simply by itself be accompanied, or followed, by an instance of that *sort* of stimulus situation. Further, I assume that the different readinesses or beliefs (dispositions) are stored up together (in the nervous system). When they are concretely activated in the form of expectancies they tend to interact and or consolidate with one another. And I would also assert that "thinking" as we know it in human beings, is in essence no more than an activated interplay among expectancies resulting from such previously acquired readinesses which result in new expectancies and resultant new means-end readinesses. (pp. 113–114)

Tolman conceded that this formulation was weak because it lacked a solid basis in specific empirical measures. He recognized the difficulty of implementing his constructs operationally, but at the same time he repeatedly pointed to what he saw as a comparable weakness in the Hull-Spence r_g - s_g construct.

Although the concept of cognition, however phrased, is the key to Tolman's system, he considered other types of concepts and other kinds of learning. In his effort (1949b) to cover the major types of learning processes, he pointed to the following six "types of connections." *Cathexes* are affective properties acquired by objects: they resemble Lewinian valences. *Equivalence beliefs* are the cognitive representations of subgoals, secondary reinforcers, or impending disturbances. *Field expectancies,* which were earlier called sign-Gestalt-expectations, are representations of the environment that make possible latent learning, behavioral shortcuts, and so on. *Field-cognition modes* are the higher-order functions that produce field expectancies through perceptual, memorial, or inferential processes. *Drive discriminations* are the demonstrated abilities of animals to behave differently under different deprivation conditions. Finally, *motor patterns* are responses and combinations of responses (skills).

Tolman made only the sketchiest effort to indicate the kinds of laws, or empirical relationships between variables, that might relate to these various kinds of learning. No laws were suggested, for example, for the important field-cognition modes or drive discriminations. A simple contiguity principle, following Guthrie, was accepted for motor patterns. Hullian need reduction was considered to be at least partially responsible for cathexes and equivalence beliefs. And no definitive interpretations were offered for the key concept of field expectancies, although Tolman explicitly denied that the reinforcement principle played more than an incidental role in their formation.

One of Tolman's "models" (1959b) contained three major constructs: the *need system,* closely related to orthodox drive notions; the *behavior space,* closely related to Lewin's life space; and the *belief-value matrix,* which consists of hierarchies of learned expectations concerning environmental objects and their roles in relation to behavior.

These brief sketches of Tolman's approach indicate the tentative and preliminary nature of his system. He seldom felt sure enough of his ground to suggest lawful relationships, or even logical relationships, between the variables of his system. Even the variables changed from time to time, perhaps because his thought matured and grew more complex. Tolman (1959) was acutely aware of the questionable status of some aspects of his system: "I think the days of such grandiose, all-covering systems in psychology as mine attempted to be are, at least for the present, pretty much passé. . . . I have an inveterate tendency to make my ideas too complicated and too high-flown so that they become less and less susceptible to empirical test" (pp. 93–94).

Tolman did not produce this kind of system because of his metatheoretical principles or his methodological ignorance, but because he was the kind of person he was. In his early work (1938), he had specified in some detail the variables which he felt were significant in determining behavior and had indicated the kind of "standard" experimental situation in which their values might be determined. He was also early concerned with a prototype of experimental design intended to identify the functional interrelationships of independent, intervening, and dependent variables. Thus Tolman espoused a strict empirical methodology designed to uncover lawful relationships between variables, but he did not always carry his beliefs over into practice. The amount of tedium involved may well make such a program impractical for anyone to carry out. Certainly it was not Tolman's kind of fun.

Tolman's Experimentation

The kind of experimental research performed by Tolman is well illustrated by an early study on insight learning in the rat (Tolman & Honzik, 1930). An elevated maze with three alternative paths to the goal box, as shown in Figure 10-2, was used. The three paths were of different lengths. In preliminary training, path 1, the shortest, was sometimes blocked. The animals then learned to use the next shortest path, path 2. Note that paths 1 and 2 share the final part of the direct runway to the goal box. During training trials the block had been placed close to the starting place (e.g., at A), well before the common segment of paths 1 and 2. For the test trials, the block was moved to position B, toward the end of the common segment and close to the goal box. According to the insight prediction, the animal would now turn to path 3 rather than to the previously preferred path 2, since path 2 was also blocked. A noninsight, simple S-R view would predict the choice of the next strongest response in the hierarchy established in training—that of running down path 2. Most of the animals chose path 3, thus supporting Tolman's cognitive or expectancy position.

Modifications of this early experiment have been reported a number of times (Hilgard & Bower, 1975, p. 154; Bower & Hilgard, 1981, pp. 337–338). Although insight occurred in some cases, apparently minor changes in apparatus or arrangements sometimes produced a failure in insight. A long-standing joke in psychology had it that Tolman's rats were much more insightful than Hull's. Be that as it may, Deutsch (1960) developed a "structural" model, superficially unlike Tolman's rough models, which made predictions about when insight should or should not occur. An experiment

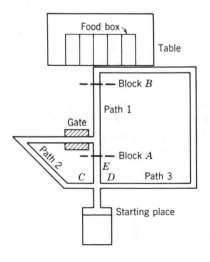

FIGURE 10-2
Maze used to test insight in rats. The paths become established as a hierarchy according to length: path 1 preferred to path 2, and path 2 preferred to path 3. If path 1 is closed by block A, the rats run by path 2. If path 1 is closed by block B, the rats run by path 3 if they have insight that the barrier closes path 2 as well as path 1. (*Source: Tolman & Honzik, 1930, p. 223.*)

by Deutsch and Clarkson (1959), using the same basic procedure as Tolman and Honzik, confirmed the predictions of the Deutsch model. This situation is reminiscent of Spence's earlier model, which enabled the prediction of the occurrence or nonoccurrence of transposition (see Chapter 7). In both cases we see genuine progress. Other ideas of Tolman's also may have helped to point in the direction of progress. In the Deutsch-Clarkson "non-insightful" condition, the animals experienced frustration in the goal box, and Tolman and Gleitman (1949) had shown that rats were quite capable of avoiding the route to a box in which they had been shocked, even though the shock did not follow *running* to the box. Perhaps, in a loose system like Tolman's, we can always find another idea or another experiment to account for new results.

Criticisms of Tolman's System

The most frequent criticism of Tolman's work has already been indicated: that he failed to develop a logically integrated theory. In this respect his own comments may be instructive. In refusing to comment on a requested distinction between his use of immediate data language and construct language, Tolman (1959) noted that "I myself can neither get very interested in nor completely understand such more refined logical distinctions" (p. 149). Perhaps his lack of interest in problems of logical relationships accounts in part for the programmaticity of his systematizing.

One important criticism which Tolman shared with Lewin was that he paid insufficient attention to relating overt behavior to central states. Guthrie, for instance, commented that Tolman leaves the rat "buried in thought" (Guthrie, 1935 p. 172). This weakness in Tolman's system may be seen as part of his general lack of specificity, but it also reflects his concentration on central, rather than peripheral, processes.

Finally, as a representative of a kind of commonsense approach to behavior, Tolman has received criticism from more tough-minded psychologists. His alleged mentalism drew some fire, largely as a result of the kind of language Tolman used and the centralist nature of his constructs. In answer to such attacks, he defended his own basic adherence to behavioristic methodology. Even the more sympathetic of Tolman's critics, however, have entertained some doubt on this score. Thus MacCorquodale and Meehl (1954) noted "a certain affinity for the dualistic," even though they did not mean "even to suggest that he is anything else [than a behaviorist] consciously or unconsciously" (p. 185). In considering this criticism, Tolman (1959) could offer a partial explanation:

> Although I was sold on objectivism and behaviorism as *the* method in psychology, the only categorizing rubrics which I had at hand were mentalistic ones. So when I began to try to develop a behavioristic system of my own, what I really was doing was trying to rewrite a commonsense mentalistic psychology . . . in operational behavioristic terms. (p. 94)

Tolman's Contributions

In spite of the undeniable programmaticity of his systematizing, Tolman has had a great influence upon the course of psychology. He leavened the behavioristic loaf in its early formative period. Although his emphasis on a molar point of view along with his acceptance of purpose was never quite accepted by some behaviorists, his modifications made behaviorism more understandable and acceptable to many others. Tolman thus saved for the consideration of the science of psychology concepts which might otherwise have been discarded completely because they were not easy to define operationally. The verdict of history has clearly favored Tolman, particularly in the case of "purpose"; the science of cybernetics has objectified and precisely defined what it is for a machine to have purpose, so that there are few left in or out of psychology who would maintain that the concept is unacceptable.

The influence of Tolman's cognitive, S-S, learning system has also been very great. For two decades his cognitive position offered the major alternative to the Hullian need-reduction theory. Much of the learning experimentation and literature tried to pit cognitive theory against reinforcement theory. Thus in reviewing the learning literature for the first issue of the *Annual Review of Psychology,* Melton (1950) said that "These past twenty years of experimental-theoretical development have been increasingly under the influence of the opposed theoretical systems of Tolman and Hull" (p. 9).

We have already mentioned in Chapter 7 Tolman's long-time associate at the University of California, David Krechevsky (later Krech) as a contributor to the cognitive tradition. His hypotheses about hypotheses in rats agreed nicely with Tolman's viewpoint. Levine (1970) worked out more detailed accounts of how hypotheses ought to be related to prior experience in human subjects and how they should then control behavior. Several ingenious experiments were in excellent agreement with his predictions—and with a Tolmanian type of thinking.

Tolman has influenced psychology though his long-standing support of the rat as a laboratory animal and appropriate subject even for the study of the field-theoretical and centralist thinking which he espoused. Such use of this favored laboratory animal by Tolman was undoubtedly responsible for some of the acceptance accorded "rat psychology," despite the indifference or resistance of many other psychologists. Tolman's position on this issue was stated in a delightful essay. Here Tolman, always humorous and self-effacing, is at his best. The concluding sentences (Tolman, 1945) are especially noteworthy:

> What, by way of summary, can we now say as to the contributions of us rodent psychologists to human behavior? What is it that we rat runners still have to contribute to the understanding of the deeds and the misdeeds, the absurdities and the tragedies of our friend, and our enemy—*homo sapiens?* The answer is that, whereas man's successes, persistences, and socially unacceptable divagations—that is, his intelligences, his motivations, and his instabilities—are all ultimately shaped and materialized by specific cultures, it is still true that most of the formal underlying laws of intelligence, motivation, and instability can still be studied in rats as well as, and more easily than, in men.
>
> And, as a final peroration, let it be noted that rats live in cages; they do not go on binges the night before one has planned an experiment; they do not kill each other off in wars; they do not invent engines of destruction, and, if they did, they would not be so inept about controlling such engines; they do not go in for either class conflicts or race conflicts; they avoid politics, economics, and papers in psychology. They are marvelous, pure, and delightful. And, as soon as I possibly can, I am going to climb back again out on that good

old phylogenetic limb and sit there, this time right side up and unashamed, wiggling my whiskers at all the silly, yet at the same time far too complicated, specimens of *homo sapiens,* whom I shall see strutting and fighting and messing things up, down there on the ground below me. (p. 166).

Of the many more specific contributions that Tolman made, two early ones deserve mention. One is his invention in 1936 of the intervening-variable paradigm, later adopted and more thoroughly implemented by Hull. An intervening variable, as we have seen, is an intratheoretical function that is postulated to help in accounting for behavior. An example might be the presumed intraorganismic variable hunger, which, if the stimulus situation allows, may lead to eating. Although Tolman had apparently intended a purely summary usage of intervening variables, he eventually renounced a purely summary use in favor of the less strictly operational "hypothetical construct" (see Marx, 1963, Chaps. 1 and 5). He later stated: "My intervening variables are generally speaking mere temporarily believed-in, inductive, more or less qualitative generalizations which categorize and sum up for me various empirically found relationships" (Tolman, 1959, p. 97). He further observed that they are not "primarily neurophysiological . . . but are derived rather from intuition, common experience, a little sophomoric neurology, and my own phenomenology" (1959, pp. 98ff).

The second contribution was Tolman's distinction between learning and performance. He early pointed out that learning alone is not sufficient to produce behavior; the motivational conditions must also be appropriate. The distinction between learning and performance has been important throughout the subsequent development of learning theory and research. Tolman credited Blodgett, who performed the first latent-learning experiment, for having forced this distinction on him and also noted (1959, p. 149) that Lashley had anticipated him.

Tolman must also be credited with helping to open up significant areas of research. The most important, described later in this chapter, was the latent-learning paradigm, which throws open the question of the effect of reinforcement on learning. Second was the transposition problem, which concerns the dependence of learning upon relative vs. absolute cues. Third was the continuity-noncontinuity issue, which concerns the nature of the effect of each trial on learning. Each of these problem areas also related directly to the theoretical opposition between Tolman and Hull.

Finally, we should mention Tolman's influence through his students and admirers. Z. Y. Kuo, who has already been mentioned as an early behaviorist, had this to say about Tolman in his last publication in English:

My major professor, the late E. C. Tolman, exerted a great influence on me; although I was never an adherent of his psychological views, his exceptional tolerance and the way he encouraged his students to develop and express views that opposed his own greatly strengthened the skeptical attitude toward everything I read that I had acquired earlier in China. In a joking, yet approving manner, Tolman often said to other students in my presence: "Kuo has an Oedipus complex against all authorities and a strong tendency toward negativism." (1967, p. viii)

Kuo's comments on Tolman came 44 years after he left Berkeley to return to China. No more need be said regarding students' opinions of Tolman.

THE CONFLICT OF THEORIES

Having presented the theoretical systems of Hull and Tolman separately, we can now consider their major contrasts on key issues. Some such comparisons have already been suggested, but the following pages provide a more concentrated and systematic review of the differences between the two theories and how some of these differences were resolved.

The "Crucial Experiment"

Study of the so-called "crucial experiment," sought as a way to settle the confrontation between S-R and S-S perspectives, offers an interesting and instructive lesson in theory testing. Questions such as "Is there one basic learning process?" or "Is reinforcement necessary and sufficient for learning?" are examples of the kinds of issues faced by opposing theories. They are also the kind of broad issues whose resolution has often been sought by means of some single completely convincing experimental demonstration. Is any one experiment likely to be sufficiently "crucial" to provide a clear-cut answer to such questions? Probably not. Questions such as these and the experiments that they have spawned are now generally seen as too simplistic. Answers to broad questions require a converging set of experimental demonstrations to cover all perspectives.

Nevertheless, the concept of the crucial experiment can be useful, as a kind of psychological "holy grail," if it produces important research. This research need not be ultimately conclusive, or "crucial," in order to have great value. In science the frontiers are never-ending. They expand as our knowledge accumulates, and a succession of seemingly "crucial" experiments may thereby be indicated. Opposing theoreticians make slight modifications in their theories or interpretations of empirical situations in order to encompass contradictory results, and science marches on. Today's crucial experiment becomes tomorrow's historical incident; such a process is probably inevitable.

The discussion of latent learning later in this chapter provides some excellent illustrations of the role of crucial experiments. As we shall see, the really *crucial* factor may not be so much the experiment itself as the subsequent accommodation of the alternative theories to the experimental results. The results themselves are generally accepted—especially, of course, as replications accumulate—by all the proponents of varying theoretical persuasions. Then, if sufficient theoretical accommodation occurs, there will eventually be a blurring of initially outstanding differences, and the theoretical issue no longer commands much active interest.

Contrasting Assumptions

As the earlier descriptions indicate, Hull and Tolman made radically different working assumptions. Some of these assumptions were necessary for the development of the type of theory involved, but others were characteristic of the scientific personalities of the two theoreticians.

For Tolman, the most significant feature of behavior was the *act,* or the achievement, rather than the particular muscular responses, which were emphasized by S-R theorists; in other words, Tolman was a *molar,* and Hull a somewhat less molar, behaviorist. The purpose of the act was assumed by Tolman to be most important, but, as we have seen, purpose was behaviorally defined. Hull made no assumptions about purposes, although he did include in his system the concept of goal, as in the goal-gradient hypothesis. Thus Tolman gave purpose a central role in all behavior, while for Hull it played a distinctly secondary role.

Hull assumed the critical factor for learning to be the *reinforcement* of S-R relationships. Although he was ultimately to give up this position, largely as a result of the empirical achievements of cognitive researchers (as described below, for the latent-learning problem), early in his career Hull adapted the Thorndikian law of effect as the primary learning principle; Pavlovian or classical conditioning was assumed to be interpretable within this reinforcement framework (Hull, 1935, 1937).

For Tolman, the critical factor in learning was the S-S relationship—the learning of "what leads to what." The consequences of responses (the "reinforcement" of the S-R theorists) were accepted as learning cues, but only in a secondary sense—only, that is, because they have stimulus components. Thus the finding of food in the goal box of a maze tells the rat where to find the food, rather than strengthening the particular responses leading to the goal box as in Hull's theory.

As a consequence of these two differing sets of working assumptions about behavior and the perceptual process, two equally opposed positions were taken on the problem of how best to view the product of learning. For Tolman, learning led to knowledge; indeed, it *was* knowledge. A *cognitive map* is built up by the consequences of an individual's observation of S-R, as well as of S-S, relationships in a given situation. The concept of the cognitive map most directly relates to the manner in which geographical features become encoded, of course, but equally functional "maps" were held to be acquired to help the individual run through other kinds of "mazes"—social and academic, for example. Thus one's experiences could be used in handling social invitations or in successfully passing over hurdles in a tough college course.

For Hull, on the other hand, the primary consequences of learning were S-R relationships. Acts, as defined by Tolman, do occur, and achievements might well result from them, but the basic behavioral changes called learning were best described in terms of the responses themselves and the consequences that strengthened or weakened them.

Delineation of these contrasting sets of assumptions about behavior and learning is useful in helping us understand the initially quite divergent theoretical superstructures that the two theorists built. But there are additional lessons to be learned from this classic confrontation. For one example, consider the fundamental question of the role of reinforcement in learning. Hull was forced to relinquish this once-critical principle under the cumulative force of the negative results reported, mainly by cognitively oriented researchers. This fact, however, is relevant only to Hull's theory and any similar theories, and not to various other applications of the reinforcement principle such as Skinner's operant-conditioning approach (cf. Chapter 11). Moreover, even if reinforcement is not the dominant factor in learning as Hull initially assumed, this fact does not mean that it plays no part at all, even in habit formation. There is a very serious danger that researchers and theorists will overreact to such demonstrations of the inapplicability of some particular position and tend then to ignore other, more limited theoretical applications of the principle.

Latent Learning

The results of experiments on latent learning are generally regarded as most definitive in differentiating the Hullian S-R and the Tolmanian S-S theoretical positions. The basic question under investigation was whether learning can occur in the absence of reinforcement, as for example from mere exposure to a stimulus situation in the manner postulated by Tolman to be sufficient. As we have seen, Tolman distinguished between learning, or habit *formation,* and performance, or habit *expression* in behavior; thus the learning that Tolman expected to occur in the absence of appropriate motivating and/or rewarding conditions for performance was labeled "latent" because its expression in performance would occur only after such appropriate conditions were introduced (at test).

The research on latent learning generally employed the subject of most convenience at the time—the laboratory rat—and some form of maze for its training and testing.

Findings and Counterfindings   Thistlethwaite's (1951) comprehensive review of research on latent learning distinguished four fundamental research designs. In the Type I design, control rats receive their usual food reward after traversing the maze, but equally hungry experimental rats—those assumed to show the "latent" learning—are given food reward at the end of the maze only on selected later trials. The experimental question is whether or not they will then perform, on subsequent trials, in approximately the same manner as the continuously rewarded control rats; if they do, they will have demonstrated the kind of acquisition of knowledge of the maze that Tolman predicted could be developed in the absence of reinforcement.

This design was first systematically used in Tolman's laboratory by Blodgett (1929), who also introduced the term "latent learning" to refer to the expected positive results. Blodgett fed his two experimental groups for the first time, at the end of their daily runs through the six-unit T-maze, on the third and seventh days, respectively. The experimental rats showed a large reduction in errors on the first run immediately following the introduction of the food reward, so that Blodgett felt justified in concluding that they had indeed learned, "latently," in the absence of earlier reinforcement. A similar but even greater improvement was shortly thereafter reported by Tolman and Honzik (1930) in an experiment using the same basic design with a fourteen-unit T-maze.

In the Type II experimental design, the experimental animals are allowed to explore the maze, usually for a considerable period of time, before being tested and compared with controls that have not been given the same pretest exploratory opportunity. The presumption is that in the absence of the usual kind of reinforcement, S-S learning will nonetheless occur and will therefore facilitate the test performance of the experimental subjects. At test, in this design, the experimental animals are either given the typical sessions of test trials or are first placed in the goal box directly and allowed to eat and then given one or more test trials.

The results of a number of different experiments using this design were generally positive. Experimental animals performed on test trials with fewer errors then controls, which were usually given equivalent exploratory time but in a different maze pattern. Thus both Haney (1931) and Daub (1933) reported superior performance by experimental animals tested under the typical conditions, and Buxton (1940) and Seward (1949) reported similar results for experimental rats given goal-box prefeeding.

Thistlethwaite (1951) concluded that the amount of latent learning shown in Type II experiments varied positively with the complexity of the maze (because more complex mazes provided more cues to be learned, and these would then be relatively more helpful at test) and the degree to which the reward used was "demanded" (because more highly valued rewards would increase the degree to which latent learning is manifested).

The last two designs used either weak (Type III) or strong (Type IV) irrelevant motivation in training. Spence and Lippitt (1940) found that rats initially trained while satiated on food and water nevertheless learned the locations of these two incentives (a different one in each end of a one-unit Y-maze), as demonstrated by a significantly high percentage of correct choices on test trials conducted under either water or food deprivation. A similar result was later reported by Meehl and MacCorquodale (1948).

Most of the failures to find latent learning—or "irrelevant incentive learning," as Thistlethwaite (1951) labeled his Type III and Type IV designs—have been reported for the strong irrelevant motivation condition. Spence and Lippitt (1940) suggested that "latent learning does not occur in the situation where the animals perceived the subsequent test goal object (food) while motivated for another goal object (water), but latent learning does occur where complete satiation presumably did not predispose animals toward any particular goal directedness in the experimental setup during the training series" (p. 429). Kendler (1947) later found no evidence of latent learning for animals trained under thirst or hunger motivation. In other experiments (Grice, 1948; Kendler & Mencher, 1948), negative results were reported when the reward was placed on both sides of the T-maze and also (Gleitman, 1950) when thirsty rats found water on both sides and food on only one side during training.

Because of the complexity involved in Type IV designs, we forgo any more detailed description of these experiments. After surveying a large number of them, Thistlethwaite (1951) concluded that "irrelevant-incentive learning seems to occur most readily under the following conditions: weak irrelevant motivation, hunger rather than thirst as the irrelevant drive, weak position preferences, symmetry of reward during training, free rather than forced trials, discriminating contact with the undesired goal object, previous exploratory or need differentiation exercise, and large amounts of training under conditions which do not produce strong asymmetrical preferences" (p. 120).

Explanations and Counterexplanations   The preponderance of results from latent learning experiments, especially those conducted with Type I and Type II designs, left little doubt but that the basic S-S proposition is correct. In the absence of any reinforcement of the type explicitly defined by Hullian theory, laboratory rats are clearly able to learn a great deal about the environment. Some of the features thus learned enable them to deal effectively with the test situations determined by experimenters, so that "latent" learning is demonstrated.

Even this clear-cut picture, however, has not gone unchallenged. For example, some S-R theorists have argued that reinforcement may be present. What can these hidden reinforcing agents be? Two that have been suggested by diehard proponents of S-R theory are (1) escape from the apparatus (the rat during training is, of course, typically removed from the maze at the conclusion of its run), and (2) satisfaction of curiosity. There is no doubt that curiosity plays a role in rats as well as in the higher mammalian forms, such as monkeys and apes, in which it has been systematically investigated. Nevertheless, the very abrupt reductions in error and time scores that have been found to accompany introduction of reward are difficult to explain on the basis of such conjectures. In any event, more direct experimental manipulation of these suspected reinforcers is needed before they can achieve much credibility in the latent learning situation. Moreover, they have been critically evaluated, and found wanting, by a number of researchers (Buxton, 1940; Hilgard, 1948). One of the major arguments against the escape-reinforcement factor is that in some experiments (e.g., Seward, 1949) there was simply no basis for any differential association of escape with left or right T-maze responses (the ones used in tests).

In experiments in which the rats were fed in the goal box just prior to test trials, Hull (1935) has pointed out that the correct response might be "essentially a case of the perseveration of a goal reaction . . . from one stimulus situation to a closely following one" (p. 243). However, control conditions manipulated by both Buxton (1940) and Seward (1949) eliminated this factor, at least as a complete explanation of the positive results.

Seward (1947, 1949) has shown that latent learning can be derived from S-R principles with the help of a central "surrogate response," but the reinforcement principle is not involved in this formulation.

A reinforcement explanation of correct test performance of animals satiated during training (Type III design) was attempted by MacCorquodale and Meehl (1948). Their explanation depends upon the assumption that differential (right or left) turns in the single-unit T-maze are conditioned to fractional consummatory responses elicited in training by the irrelevant rewards. Maltzman (1950) published a similar interpretation. Again, however, this conjecture has not been adequately tested, and its credibility awaits direct experimental demonstration.

In yet another attempt to salvage some form of reinforcement principle, Meehl (1950) suggested that the abrupt improvement in test performance associated with the sudden introduction of reward in the latent learning experiments might be due to the increment in strength of a habit that had been minimally established during training. In support of this supposition he pointed to the evidence from Type I designs (e.g., Blodgett, 1929) of slight improvements in performance even during the latent (training) phase. However, contradictory evidence is available in such experiments as Herb's (1940), in which animals made training responses contrary to those which were presumably being lightly reinforced but were nonetheless subsequently performed at test.

The various theoretical suggestions advanced by reinforcement theorists to account for the complex but generally positive results of Type III and Type IV experiments are too involved to permit a description in these pages; the interested reader can consult the reviews by Thistlethwaite (1951), MacCorquodale and Meehl (1954), and Hilgard (1956).

THE ELUSIVE RESOLUTION

For Hullian theory, the most striking change stimulated by the demonstration of latent learning was the removal of magnitude of reinforcement (K) as a determinant of habit strength ($_sH_R$). Thus, in Hull's final system (1952), the acquisition of habit can occur under minimal reinforcement conditions; the abrupt improvements in performance typically found at test in latent learning experiments are then readily explained on the basis of correspondingly large increments in reaction potential ($_sE_R$), which is tied directly to magnitude of reinforcement.

On the S-S side, modifications by Tolman of his original sign-Gestalt theory were also made on the basis of the empirical results obtained in the latent learning research. For example, Tolman recognized the difficulty the laboratory animals apparently had in discriminating among drives, and suggested that such learning may be different from the acquisition of "field expectancies" (Tolman, 1949b). Tolman (1948) also accounted for the generally poorer latent learning found under strong irrelevant drives by postulating the development of weak or narrow cognitive maps under "too strongly motivating or too strongly frustrating conditions."

Although these shifts in both S-R and S-S theory were, of course, more or less directly attributable to data from the latent learning experiments, those data had many facets with implications for other, more particular theoretical issues (for example, the ways in which drive states and incentives interact in association with instrumental conditioning). Nevertheless, interest in these side issues seems to have been relatively dormant over the past several decades, as psychologists concerned with learning and motivation have turned their attention increasingly to other problems, mainly those concerned with memory.

This fact is especially ironic in light of the reasonable plea made by Thistlethwaite (1951) for more closely coordinated research designs. The directions in which science develops are indeed difficult to predict, much less to legislate in advance. Perhaps in the future we shall find renewed interest in some of these now largely dormant theoretical issues. In the meantime, with the major point of contention substantially resolved, largely because of the accommodation of S-R theory to the data, the blurring of theoretical differences between S-R and S-S positions has left little interest in this once pivotal theoretical problem.

THEORETICAL CONSEQUENCES

Discouragement of "Grand Theory"

Probably the major single consequence of the Hull-Tolman theoretical controversy was a general loss of interest in what has sometimes been called "grand theory." Both of these theories were designed to encompass a very broad spectrum of behavior. While

Tolman's theory was certainly less detailed and less pretentious than Hull's, it was developed to cover essentially the same behavioral ground.

It is interesting that both of these systematists were animal researchers, whereas the focus of research in learning and related topics has recently shifted to human subjects and primarily human problems. This shift has occurred mainly as a result of the great spurt of interest in cognitive problems, for which humans are more appropriate subjects (although the steady growth of interest in animal memory is by no means an insignificant trend). The obviously great variety and complexity of cognitive functions in humans have probably helped to keep psychological researchers from too rapid a return to global theories of behavior. Nevertheless, there are some signs of a resumption of interest in theories of increasingly broad range (for example, the application of evolutionary theory to behavior; cf. Goodson, 1973). It may well be that we shall soon be seeing a wave of more ambitious theories reminiscent of the type that Hull and Tolman developed several decades ago.

Limited Theory

The decline in grand theory has been accompanied by the growth of more limited theories. These were at one time called "miniature theories," in contrast with the grand theory of the earlier era, but this term does not seem to have caught on.

Two kinds of such limited theories may be identified. First, there are the mathematical models, which generally undertake to account for a circumscribed set of behaviors; second, there are what are sometimes called *functional* theories. Their major characteristic is a focus on the mechanism by means of which some behavioral process can be explained (e.g., the interference theory of forgetting).

A most important methodological advantage that limited theory has over the more ambitious type of theory is that it encourages a more gradual and more soundly based development. Because empirical tests of a more limited type are indicated and are more readily carried out, this kind of theory stays closer to the data. As a result it is likely to have fewer wide and questionable gaps to strain its theoretical concepts and their arrangement. Furthermore, combination of small theories (e.g., theories accounting for different types of memory or learning) is feasible once sound empirical bases are secured for the component theories, and the degree of commonality of the different mechanisms postulated can be more readily ascertained.

Limited theories therefore not only permit but also encourage a slow and sure growth that is more difficult for grand theory. We have already mentioned the severe logical problems which prevented rigorous testing of Hull's theory. MacCorquodale and Meehl (1954) found Tolman's theory even less ready for testing. Thus we have seen in the Hull-Tolman confrontation that backing up to cover problem areas is an inefficient way to proceed.

All of this should not be construed to mean that we are opposed to hypothesis and speculation. Not at all. We think psychology badly needs new insights and perspectives, and these require not only creative thinking but also a willingness to be wrong. But theoretical speculation is most effective in a context that also stresses reasonable empirical checks and balances, and for this reason limited theory has much to offer psychology.

SUMMARY AND CONCLUSIONS

Two of psychology's most influential theorists were Clark Hull and Edward Tolman. The opposition of Hull's S-R reinforcement theory and Tolman's S-S, cognitive, system was a classic theoretical confrontation during the middle decades of this century. Although psychology remains in debt to both of these extraordinarily ingenious and productive men, there is no longer much interest in the pivotal difference between the theories: whether learning is better regarded as the strengthening of S-R connections or as the acquisition of cognitions such as expectancies. In terms of the specific experimental problems spawned by the confrontation, it is clear that on balance the Tolmanian cognitive approach had the better of it. The latent learning problem in particular helped to force drastic changes in the initial Hullian S-R system. However, Spence's treatment of the transposition problem, discussed in Chapter 7, was a demonstration of the power of S-R theory.

An important consequence of the theoretical disputation was a period of disenchantment with such "grand theory" as had been offered by Hull and Tolman. Avoidance of large-scale theory resulted in a greater concentration on limited theoretical efforts. There is nevertheless a continuing place for large-scale theory, and there is some indication of renewed interest in more global theoretical vistas.

Finally, we want to reiterate our appreciation for the enormous contributions made by both Hull and Tolman to contemporary psychology, in spite of the loss of interest in the particular theoretical issues about which they disagreed. Their approaches to psychology and the results they produced are enduring legacies, even though the theoretical structures which provided their inspiration are no longer of immediate interest.

FURTHER READINGS

For an understanding of Hull's system, the most useful of his books are *Principles of behavior* (1943) and *A behavior system* (1952). His paper on conditioning theory (1937), cited in the text, outlines the development of his thinking, and his autobiographical statement (1952) is unusually frank in dealing with personal factors in his career. His *Hypnosis and suggestibility* (1933) represented perhaps the greatest single advance ever made in the study of hypnosis, although it is of limited relevance in the present context. Koch (1954) can be consulted for a brilliant but overly negative analysis of the weaknesses of Hull's effort. Tolman is well represented by his early *Purposive behavior in animals and man* (1932), his *Collected papers in psychology* (1951a), and his final statement (1959). The formalization of Tolman's system by MacCorquodale and Meehl (1954) is well worth consulting, in part because it shows how further formalization of a programmatic theory can proceed.

CHAPTER 11

FURTHER DEVELOPMENT
OF S-R THEORY

In this chapter we examine some other S-R theories which either accompanied or followed Hull's pioneering effort. Although these theories share a common S-R character and behavioristic orientation, they differ in important ways. Some of them, such as Guthrie's and Skinner's, were contemporaneous with Hull's theory; others are neo-Hullian in that they generally follow the line of theoretical development initiated by Hull but branch off in some new directions. These theories are both competitive with and complementary to the cognitive theories (Chapter 13) that have succeeded Tolman and the field theorists (Chapter 7) of the earlier era.

THE DEFINITION OF STIMULUS AND RESPONSE

A definition of stimulus and response is needed if we are to understand what S-R psychology involves. It is easy to produce such definitions but difficult to procure agreement about them. The definition chosen will determine what is meant by S-R psychology.

One issue is whether the stimulus should be defined independently of the response or as "that which produces a response." We have already mentioned that John Dewey in 1896 deplored the artificial analysis of the reflex arc into stimulus and response. Skinner (1938) agreed in the sense that he thought it useful to consider a stimulus and a response to be any situational and behavioral aspects of a context that could be shown to enter into an orderly functional relationship. Gibson (1960) was critical of this kind of formulation and pointed to the possibility that it would lead to circularity; that is, the stimulus might become whatever was needed to bring about the response, leaving no independent term to explain the occurrence of the response. Hocutt (1967)

Burrhus Frederic Skinner (1904–   ), probably the world's best-known psychologist and a dyed-in-the-wool behaviorist. His work has led to important applications as well as to a distinctive methodological position.

defended relational terms of this type against the charge that they were meaningless. Among Hocutt's examples of such concepts are those of husband and wife, neither of which can be defined independently of the marriage relation. Despite their lack of independence, it remains meaningful to speak of a wife as something like "the female partner in a marriage relationship."

Even if a stimulus is conceptualized initially as independent of responses and is defined in terms of physical energies, it will be of continuing interest only if it does in fact enter into some relationship with a response. It would seem that S-R psychologists need only be careful to have a means of identifying stimuli and manipulating them; they can then ascertain whether the independently identified stimulus enters into relationships with independently identified responses.

A second important question concerns the relative level of molarity of definition of stimulus and response. On the stimulus side, we have encountered a version of this problem in the contrast between the structuralists' molecular view and the Gestaltists' molar view. Brunswik's lens model and his scheme of the organism in its surroundings are clear expositions of some of the possible definitions of both stimulus and response. Brunswik's general argument tends toward molar definitions for psychology, at least at the outset. The typical S-R psychologist, as a descendant of the more molecular and analytic associationistic school, is probably more molecular than Brunswik would wish.

A third definitional question concerns the inclusiveness of the definitions of stimulus and response. Specific questions related to this issue would include: "Is perception a response?" "Is deprivation a stimulus?" "Is an injection of androgen a stimulus?" Because he believes that such things do not fit the definitions of stimulus and response,

Skinner does not think of himself as an S-R psychologist (Evans, 1968, p. 20; Skinner, 1966, p. 12). On the other hand, Kimble (1967), who uses the terms *stimulus* and *response* more inclusively, concludes: "Thus the facts of psychology turn out to be Ss and Rs, a state of affairs which suggests with a certain insistence, that the laws of psychology must be reducible to these terms and that an S-R psychology is an inevitability" (p. 76).

Thus there is some disagreement about whether one must be an S-R psychologist because there is disagreement about what S and R are. We will see later that cognitive psychologists believe that one *cannot* be a strict S-R psychologist if all the facts of behavior are to be accounted for.

We believe that it is useful to regard a stimulus as an event capable of stimulating a receptor. Only stimuli that are related to responses will be of interest; however, if stimuli cannot be identified independently without relating them to responses, they become mere convenient inventions providing a pseudo explanation of responses. Thus an explanation of behavior as caused by some unobservable "internal stimulus" is not a genuine explanation. It is at most a promissory note, until a satisfactory account of the behavior can be produced.

No position need be taken on the level of molarity of definition of either stimulus or response; that is a matter of convenience rather than of "correctness." We do not believe that S and R should be defined so inclusively that they become indistinguishable from antecedents and consequents; hence we are closer to Skinner than to Kimble on this issue. However, we think that it may sometimes be useful to regard inner processes, like perception, as analogous to responses. It is sometimes necessary for an S-R theorist to postulate inner stimuli, but care should be taken to move toward objective identification of such postulated entities.

CATEGORIES OF S-R THEORY

Contemporary S-R theory can be divided into two broad classes which differ in the role accorded the reinforcement, or response-strengthening, process. The first of these classes may be called *S-R reinforcement theory*. Both of the two major subtypes of this theory afford reinforcement a central role, but they interpret the nature of this role differently. Many psychologists, like Hull, have interested themselves in the mechanism of the reinforcement process; some form of need or stimulus reduction has been most often identified as the necessary and sufficient condition for reinforcement. Others, like Skinner, have stressed the importance of reinforcement without commitment to the underlying nature of the process. This view may be classed as *descriptive S-R* theory, since the fact of reinforcement is accepted in a descriptive or theoretically neutral sense.

The second class of modern S-R theory is generally called *contiguity theory*. Following Guthrie, contiguity theorists hold that all that is essential to learning is contiguity of stimulus and response. Reinforcement, in the sense of presentation of a so-called reinforcing stimulus such as food or money, is important because it changes the stimulus situation and so preserves associations already established. Modern contiguity theory is a refined associationism.

The S-R reinforcement theorist emphasizes the effect of reinforcement upon a connection which has already occurred, much as Thorndike did. The contiguity theorist largely ignores this aspect of reinforcement, attending, rather, to the *stimulus* characteristics of reinforcement. Guthrie, for example, was fond of asking what an aversive stimulus made the organism do, and he and the other contiguity theorists also looked closely at what rewarding stimuli make organisms do.

Several writers have suggested combinations of the two major views. Their two-factor theories will also be treated briefly. With the exception of Mowrer's version (1960a), they present few new theoretical positions but rearrange the points already present in the two major positions.

All the different S-R theories have a great deal in common, probably more than theories of perception or personality. For one thing, they are all primarily *learning* theories.

Nearly all S-R theories now distinguish between learning and performance, with some variables affecting only the latter, but learning remains central. Because of the important role that learning has played in these theories, it is often very difficult to distinguish between learning theory and general behavior theory. Hull, for example, considered himself a general behavior theorist and thought of learning constructs as central but not exclusive determiners of performance. Most psychologists, however, have thought of Hull as a learning theorist because he has been concerned primarily with behavior *changes*. Similar statements apply to most of the theorists to be discussed in this chapter.

A second characteristic common to all S-R theorists is their *neobehaviorism*. The most marked difference between neobehaviorism and Watsonian behaviorism is the greatly increased theoretical sophistication of the former. Watson, Weiss, and Holt were content with making gross generalizations based on very limited empirical evidence. Today, however, detailed justification as well as empirical evidence is demanded by and of neobehaviorists.

CONTIGUITY THEORY: GUTHRIAN ASSOCIATIONISM

Guthrie's Career

Edwin R. Guthrie (1886–1959) was for several decades the leading exponent of a simple contiguity principle of learning. Throughout a long period, while first one and then another opposing school developed, Guthrie held steadfastly to a small number of strict associationistic principles. His patience was finally rewarded by the appearance of statistical models of learning based largely upon the Guthrian pattern. However, Guthrie's own position remained that of a prophet and overseer, rather than that of an active experimentalist or producer of detailed theory.

Guthrie stayed at one school, the University of Washington, throughout his entire academic career (1914–1956). He had less than the usual formal training in psychology, having been trained instead in philosophy and mathematics. He took his doctoral degree in 1912 at the University of Pennsylvania, after having earned degrees earlier at the University of Nebraska. With one major exception (Guthrie & Horton, 1946), he preferred writing and argumentation to experimentation. His several books, especially *The psychology of learning* (1935, rev. 1952) and *The psychology of human conflict* (1938), are full of persuasive anecdotal supports for his general associationistic principles but contain little controlled evidence.

Watson's doctrines so influenced Guthrie that he became a thoroughgoing behaviorist, although he differed from Watson on many theoretical details. Guthrie's interest in psychology was apparently kindled during his graduate training by the philosopher E. A. Singer, although he had also been exposed very early to one of Wundt's earliest American students, Harry Wolfe, while attending high school. Guthrie said that his year's collaboration on a textbook with the psychologist Stevenson Smith (Smith & Guthrie, 1921) gave him "invaluable training" in psychology. He retained his early interest in problems of philosophy of science throughout his career. His final major work (Guthrie, 1959) shows a continuing interest in general methodological questions, such as the relationship between logic, language, and scientific progress.

Guthrie's Basic Principles

Guthrie believed that a few primary principles are sufficient to account for the fundamental facts of learning. His most famous principle is popularly referred to as *one-trial learning*. Guthrie held that S-R associations, as the basis of learning, are established by contiguity per se in a single pairing of stimulus and response. He early (1935) stated this principle as follows: "A combination of stimuli which has accompanied a movement will on its recurrence tend to be followed by that movement" (p. 26). A related principle is: "A stimulus pattern gains its full associative strength on the occasion of its first pairing with a response" (p. 30). Guthrie (1959) offered a final simplified version: "What is being noticed becomes a signal for what is being done" (p. 186). This statement reflects his concern with the active role of the organism (the old problem of attention). In his final paper he also placed increased emphasis on the problem of patterning in stimulus complexes (cf. Guthrie, 1959, pp. 186ff.).

His early distinction between acts and movements enabled Guthrie to hold to his basic one-trial-learning principle and still account for the fact that behavior change typically requires repeated pairings of cue and response before it can be reliably predicted that the response will occur in the presence of the cue. According to Guthrie, the basic connections are between stimuli and movements, but *acts*, rather than *movements*, are usually measured. An example of an act would be serving a tennis ball into the service court. Every separate movement which is necessary in order to bring this result about is an example of what Guthrie meant by a movement. While observable in principle, these movements are not easily noticed and are generally overlooked in theorizing. However, anyone who has had tennis lessons is painfully aware that such movements must sometimes be considered and carefully learned, especially when complex coordinations are involved.

This does not mean that movements are equivalent to the contractions of individual muscles. In a sense what Guthrie means by movement is itself a kind of behavioral result. It is a result in terms of what is happening to a part of the organism, but it does not necessarily produce an effect on the environment. Guthrie's level of movements is not the most molecular level of description that could be used. As Guthrie (1959) says: "A description of the action of the individual muscles concerned would be hopeless confusion" (p. 183).

The situation is similar on the stimulus side. Guthrie regarded a complex stimulus as a collection of a great many stimulus components, with not all components present on every occasion. The net result of this complexity of stimulus and response components is that many presentations of the gross stimulus and many occurrences of the gross response (the act) are required before satisfactory regularity can be found in the behavior being measured. That is so because large numbers of the stimulus and response components have to be involved in the conditioning process. If exact replications of stimuli and responses could be achieved, single presentations would be sufficient to produce perfect conditioning.

For Guthrie, the process of conditioning was as follows: Aspects of the total stimulus situation present on a given trial become associated with a successful movement, that is, with a movement that is part of the sequence constituting the successful "act." The successful movement causes movement-produced stimuli, which, along with external stimuli present in the environment (which may have been altered by the movement), are associated with a subsequent successful movement. This chain of movements linked by movement-produced stimuli constitutes an act. When the act is terminated, it must result in the removal of the relevant stimuli if it is to be retained. Otherwise, other movements would become associated with the same stimuli.

On a subsequent trial, when different aspects of the total stimulus situation are present, the subject will engage in random behaviors until the act is again performed successfully. The movements constituting the act on that occasion are consequently associated with the stimulus complex present during the second trial. The associative process will recur on additional trials until successful movements are conditioned to all aspects of the stimulus situation. When this point is reached, conditioning is complete, and the act will occur smoothly, whatever aspect of the stimulus situation happens to be present.

Finally, it should be noted that Guthrie thought that learning occurs through pure contiguity of stimulus and response. This might be considered a misguided view of the process of forming associations, since it is obvious that reinforcers have an important role in learning. Guthrie had no need to deny that reinforcers are effective; his theory simply accounted for their effectiveness in an ingenious and different way. The reinforcer was presumed to change the stimulus situation in which the response had just been made. The original stimulus situation, prior to the presentation of the reinforcer, therefore cannot be disconnected from the response just made and connected to a new response. The connection is thus preserved because of the stimulus change produced by the presence of the reinforcer. Unlearning, or extinction, is really the learning of different responses to the same stimulus, according to Guthrie. He is therefore able to present a beautifully parsimonious and consistent picture of both learning and extinction.

Guthrie was more than merely an astute critic and propounder of simple generalizations illustrated by fluent anecdotal stories. He stood by his theoretical guns, consistently espousing a contiguity principle as the basis of all learning. He supported his emphasis on movements as the crucial response elements by experimental studies of stereotypy (Guthrie & Horton, 1946) and showed how well stereotypy observed by other experimenters can be subsumed by his theoretical analysis. Guthrie demonstrated the theoretical roles that can be played by mediating mechanisms like movement-produced stimuli. This ingenious mechanism is much like Hull's fractional anticipatory goal response in that both serve to forge links in the chain of behavior. Finally, Guthrie did not say much because he did not believe that he had enough information to say much. Thus he made a small target. In 1958, the year before his death, Guthrie, the consistent psychologist, received the American Psychological Foundation Award in recognition of his distinguished contributions. These contributions have not stopped with his death; William K. Estes modeled his influential statistical association theory on Guthrian principles.

W. K. ESTES' GUTHRIAN MATHEMATICAL MODEL

W. K. Estes (1919–) is a highly successful pioneer among contemporary psychologists who have used mathematical models for learning. Estes was born in Minneapolis, Minnesota, on July 17, 1919. He attended the University of Minnesota, where he received the Ph.D. degree in psychology in 1943. While a graduate student, he worked both with S. R. Hathaway on the development of the Minnesota Multiphasic Personality Inventory and with B. F. Skinner on operant conditioning problems. His dissertation was a study of the effects of punishment. Soon after graduating, he volunteered for service in World War II and did research on flexible gunnery and clinical work as an officer in the Pacific. At the end of the war, in 1946, he went to Indiana University, where he climbed through the academic ranks before leaving for Stanford in 1962. He was a professor there until 1968, when he went to Rockefeller University; then, in 1979, he went to Harvard, where he now is. Estes was awarded the American Psychological Association's Distinguished Contribution award in 1962, and he has done enough research and writing since then to justify the award all over again.

Estes' first statement of the preliminary version of his statistical association model was published in 1950. Somewhat later efforts are summarized in a comprehensive article (Estes, 1959a). Here we will consider the orienting attitudes involved in his early efforts, together with the basic assumptions underlying the model.

Estes is one of an increasing number of psychologists who apply mathematics to psychology. His orientation is quantitative, operational, physicalistic—generally hard-headed, as one might expect of a mathematical modeler. He is also frankly behavioristic. His views on learning theory are often similar to Guthrie's. His theory assumes that a "stimulus" is decomposable into elements and that the termination of a stimulus is the reinforcing event.

With respect to this contiguity aspect of his theory, Estes' later position was less clear than his initial one. He said: "In brief, our answer to the question 'reinforcement or contiguity?' is simply 'both.' Whether we can have our cake and eat it and still not grow fat is a much more difficult question" (1959b, p. 405). In spite of this apparent hedging, Estes leaned toward contiguity assumptions. He later developed a theory which regards learning as an all-or-none process at the level of observable responses, and supported it with data from human paired-associate learning (Estes, 1960; Estes, Hopkins, & Crothers, 1960). The stimulus pattern to be learned either is or is not associated with the correct response on a particular trial. There is also a probability that the association will be forgotten, so that a correct response on one test will be followed by an incorrect response on a subsequent test (in some situations the correct response can also occur by chance, although it has not been learned). If the correct response is *not* learned on a particular trial, the theory predicts that there will be no increase in the probability that a correct response will be made to the stimulus on a subsequent test.

We present Estes' earlier version of statistical association theory because it is more consistent with Guthrie's classical theory and because it is applicable as often as the later theory. Bower and Hilgard (1981) also continue to treat Estes' stimulus sampling theory as the best example of the mathematical approach.

For Estes, learning was a statistical process. The observable stimulus was conceived of as decomposable, for theoretical purposes, into a set of stimulus elements. According to this model, not all elements are available on a single trial; that is, on any given trial the organism is assumed to contact only a sample of the population of elements. If a particular element is sampled on a trial and some reinforced response terminates the trial, that element will be conditioned (connected) to that response as a result of that single pairing. Any stimulus element can be connected to only one response at a time. Extinction occurs, then, whenever the stimulus elements become connected to some response other than the previously reinforced one. The response measure used is probability of response, which is certainly in keeping with the generally statistical approach.

The proportion of elements that is sampled on each trial is called theta (θ). If we know theta, the question becomes "What effect will a single trial have on the probability of making a specified response?"

To answer this question, we must consider the possible "states" of the elements. For theoretical purposes, the two relevant states of an element at any moment are (1) connected to the response being observed or (2) connected to some other response. Let X represent the number of elements conditioned (connected) to the response in question. If S is the total number of elements, then $S - X$ of the elements will be connected to some other response. If a correction procedure is used, so that the subject continues to try until the correct response is made on each trial, then it turns out that a constant proportion of the remaining *unconditioned* elements will be attached to the correct response on each trial.

Estes follows up on this kind of thinking to derive a "difference equation" which describes the increase in the probability of response to be expected on each trial. From this, he derives a general equation for the probability of response on *any* trial, provided that θ and the probability of response on the first trial are known. This general equation provided a good fit to acquisition data obtained from rats in runways, T-mazes, and bar-pressing experiments (see Estes, 1959b, for details). This simple model is one of the earliest and best known of the modern, largely post-Hullian, miniature models.

Even though the model has been successful in fitting some data, problems remain. First, there is the question of determining θ, the proportion of elements sampled. The determination cannot be made directly by observing an overt stimulus sampling process. No correspondence is established between the theoretical stimulus elements and observable elements of any experimentally defined stimulus. Even if such a correspondence existed, it is difficult to visualize how one could determine what proportion of elements an organism sampled on a given trial. The determination of θ must, then, be indirect. That value of θ is chosen which provides the best fit of the theoretical curve to acquisiton data. At this first stage, the model becomes, in one sense, superfluous; that is, if success in fitting a curve to the data were *all* the model provided, the theorist would be little better off than if he or she started out directly in quest of a curve. However, the *type* of curve sought is determined by the equation derived within the confines of the model, and it is encouraging that a curve of the simple type described above can provide a good fit to the data, even with the freedom to choose θ so that the best fit is obtained.

If the value of θ which is obtained in one situation also applies to other situations, that is a very substantial gain. Estes has shown that values of θ do have some generality from one learning situation to another; for example, a θ obtained in a situation with one number of possible responses has been shown to generalize to a situation with another, larger, number of alternative responses.

Estes' theory is but one of many mathematical developments, but it is typical of the group. Modern theories in the field of learning tend to share its hardheaded and specific approach. Its clarity and logical consistency allow us to see what it is and is not doing, and its failures are as obvious as its successes. Estes has done on a small scale what Hull tried, less successfully, to do on a large scale. Thus Estes is the heir of Hull as well as of Guthrie; probably both of his precursors, despite their differences, would applaud his efforts.

REINFORCEMENT THEORY

Kenneth Spence

Spence's Career   Kenneth W. Spence (1907–1967) was the primary developer of theory in the Hullian tradition. He took his doctoral training at Yale and was strongly influenced by his association there with Hull, although he took his degree under Yerkes. Spence worked for 4 years at the Yale Laboratories of Primate Biology in Orange Park, Florida. From 1938 to 1964 he was at the University of Iowa, where he was a very active researcher in learning and motivation and supervised the training of a large number of distinguished psychologists. In 1964 he moved to the University of Texas, where he remained until his death at the age of 59. While at Iowa he published a number of theoretical papers with Gustav Bergmann, the philosopher. Spence's major works are *Behavior theory and conditioning* (1956) and *Behavior theory and learning: Selected papers* (1960). The former was based on his 1955 Silliman lectures at Yale; Spence was the first psychologist to be honored by an invitation to deliver these lectures.

Research Achievements   Spence's first important research and theorizing dealt with the problem of discrimination learning (1936; 1937a, b). He produced a classic demonstration of how a conditioning theory involving positive and negative reaction tendencies interacting algebraically can account for the primary data of discrimination and transposition. His disagreement with the Gestaltists about the explanation of these phenomena (see Chapter 7) is an excellent illustration of opposing approaches to psychological explanation. On one side Spence was operating in the reductive mode characteristic of associationistic psychology, of S-R psychology as a more modern version of Hull, and of Spence himself. The principle of parsimony, as expressed in Lloyd Morgan's canon, is one of the first principles of theorizing for this tradition. Spence's theorizing on discrimination and transposition serves as an inspiring model of simplicity and clarity for exponents of this general approach. Hull's early work on the derivation of complex behaviors from conditioning principles was similar in this respect.

Following his early development of theory applicable to simple discrimination learning, Spence directed or supervised research projects on eyelid conditioning, latent learning, transposition, secondary reinforcement, and "anxiety" as measured by a questionnaire technique (Spence, 1960). His work, much of it in collaboration with Janet Taylor Spence, on the relationship between anxiety and learning is often quoted in articles on personality.

One of Spence's preoccupations in his later work was with isolating cognitive factors in human eyelid conditioning studies. Earlier work had demonstrated apparent qualitative differences between eyelid conditioning in humans and in other animals. Human subjects typically extinguish conditioned eyeblinks in a strikingly small number of trials, typically one or two, while animals continue to make conditioned responses for up to hundreds of trials. Spence and his students masked the true nature of the experiment for human subjects by telling them that their experimental task was to learn verbal materials while being "distracted." The "distractors" were the conditioned and unconditioned stimuli of the eyeblink experiment. Under such conditions, with their cognitive apparatus occupied elsewhere, the extinction behavior of the human subjects paralleled the behavior that had earlier been seen only in the animal subjects (Spence, 1966).

This aspect of Spence's work ties in with the history of psychological systems in an interesting way. For one thing, the experimental situation is especially designed to reduce one aspect of the human subjects' functioning to the level of animal functioning. Since Darwin, those working in a reductive tradition have often had to face the charge that they were trying to reduce human capabilities to the level of animal abilities. Spence's work on eyelid conditioning thus exemplifies at the experimental level a reductive tendency which too frequently took place only at a theoretical or metatheoretical level. At the same time, the attempt at reduction forced a clear recognition of a qualitative difference between human and animal functioning. The differences, like the similarities, have too often remained nebulous. In following up on Hull's reductive program, Spence found factors which, at least at this time, cannot easily be accounted for reductively. Thus, like many honest scientists, he obtained data which in some sense supported those who held opposing viewpoints about human nature.

While he recognized his debt to Hullian theory, Spence pointed out the differences between his theory and Hull's (see especially his 1956 book). He was less concerned with the comprehensive formality with which Hull endowed his work and more concerned with the quantification of variables. He did not share Hull's enthusiasm for physiological suggestions and speculations, feeling that until physiology had more to offer psychology it should be kept out of behavior theory. He said (Spence, 1956, p. 57) that he had not accepted the Hullian requirement for need reduction as the essential component of the reinforcement process; he made no specific physiological assumption about the nature of the action of a reinforcer. Finally, he was much more cautious than Hull in "hazarding a set of theoretical postulates on the basis of a minimum of empirical data" (Spence, 1956, p. 58). Spence also intended to restrict the applicability of his own work to the experimental situations from which his data came. Although he adopted the basic Hullian approach and many of the theoretical constructs, he put less emphasis on the postulational approach and modified some of the postulates that he did accept.

Spence treated the key motivational variables differently from Hull. Both assumed that there was a multiplicative relationship between motivation and habit in the production of response. Spence, however, theorized that incentive and deprivation *added* to produce motivation; Hull had incentive and deprivation in a *multiplicative* relationship. Spence's formulation allowed for the occurrence of a response even when either incentive or drive was at zero, as long as the other factor was not at zero. Hull's multiplicative relationship called for a zero value of reaction potential when either incentive or drive was zero. It is difficult to test this relationship, however, since it is not easy to be sure that incentive or drive is completely absent. Neither is it easy to choose between the additive and multiplicative assumptions by doing a parametric study in which D and K are varied. One reason is that the relationship between D, K, and reaction potential depends on the scales of measurement of all three. Another is that D is assumed to be related to fractional anticipatory goal responses and the stimuli produced by them. Thus motivation has a learned component, and the relationship between drive, incentive, and reaction potential is further complicated.

Spence also took a different view of reinforcement from Hull's. In his later work, he assumed that habit formation was not dependent on reinforcement. He suggested a two-factor learning theory which is precisely reversed from the usual one. Usually, contiguity factors are assumed to account for classical conditioning, and reinforcement factors for instrumental conditioning. Spence's contiguity explanation for instrumental conditioning does not necessitate any change in the basic form of the theory; it simply changes the definition of what constitutes a trial for the purposes of the theory. For Hull, a trial was a *reinforced* trial. For Spence, reinforcement did not matter; it mattered only that the response was performed in the presence of the stimulus. On this issue, Spence's position resembled Tolman's. Spence was interested in Tolman's competing theory and was close to Tolman in some of his methodological attitudes (Kendler, 1967).

Neal Miller

Miller's Career Neal E. Miller (1909–) is another of Hull's remarkably productive students and associates. Miller's reputation for empirical investigation is unsurpassed, but he has not neglected theory either. He and John Dollard followed up one of Hull's interests, integrating learning theory with psychoanalytic theory in their book *Personality and psychotherapy* (Dollard & Miller, 1950). This book was apparently a direct outgrowth of Hull's seminars of 1936 and 1937 on the relationships between these apparently diverse areas of psychology. In turn, there is little doubt that the book helped to pave the way for later developments in behavior modification.

Miller has also done more than enough work to make up a complete career in physiological psychology. Some of his physiological studies, and many of his behaviorial studies, are reviewed in his article in the Koch series (N. E. Miller, 1959).

Research and Theoretical Contributions Some of Miller's experiments have involved electrical stimulation of brain centers; some, feeding animals through fistulas; and some, preloading the stomach with different substances before the animal is allowed to eat or engage in instrumental behaviors. Still other studies were examinations of feeding without any nutritive consequences, several involved the behavioral effects of drugs, and, finally, there was the famous series of experiments on the operant conditioning of the autonomic nervous system.

It is not surprising that Miller was led to a careful consideration of the starting and stopping of behavior. For one thing, he was aware of the fact that under certain conditions, electrical stimulation of centers in the brain will be alternately started and stopped by rats free to do both. For another, he knew that feeding may sometimes be started by brain stimulation or stopped by stomach loading, and that feeding may *not* stop when it "should" if an animal has lesions in the hypothalamus.

Thinking about "go" and "stop" mechanisms may in turn have helped to lead Miller to his theoretical views on the nature of reinforcement. He was also exposed to some of Sheffield's ideas (Haber, 1966, pp. 98ff.). Sheffield suggested that an *increase* in drive, produced directly or indirectly by reward, might account for learning better than the decrease in drive or drive stimulus required by Hull. At one time, Hull and Miller would both have embraced the view that reinforcement is effective because it reduces the intensity of drive stimuli.

Miller later suggested (1963) that reinforcing operations are effective because they activate a "go" mechanism. Responses occurring when the mechanism is activated are intensified and increase in rate, according to Miller's view. Learning requires only contiguity between stimulus and response, but learning is increased by increases in the intensity or frequency of the pairing. Reinforcement (activation of the "go" mechanism) increases learning because it increases the opportunity for contiguity to produce learning.

This ingenious proposal is similar to the suggestions of several other theorists. It bears a striking resemblance to Guthrie's theory, in that contiguity alone is supposed to suffice for learning (see the discussion earlier in this chapter). Thorndike's "confirming reaction" resembles Miller's "go" mechanism; the latter, however, is presumed to affect learning indirectly through an increase in performance. That is the way Tolman would have seen the problem, while Thorndike had suggested a direct effect on the strength of connections. Sheffield's (1954) so-called drive *induction* theory of reinforcement (so named to contrast with Hull's drive *reduction* theory) is also similar in several respects. Several of these ideas share the feature that they emphasize the reinforcer as a stimulus rather than as an aftereffect.

Some of Miller's later research was on the conditioning of autonomic responses through the use of operant techniques (N. E. Miller, 1969). This work treats a problem which was central for Hull. We have seen that Hull accepted the Thorndikian principle of effect as a basic condition for learning. Hull had rejected his own earlier tentative commitment to contiguity (as in classical conditioning) as a sufficient condition for learning. Miller's work, which showed that the autonomic system was surprisingly susceptible to modification via effect learning, supports Hull's later formulation, albeit indirectly. This work of Miller's helped to stimulate interest in biofeedback, since it encouraged the belief that the autonomic system could be brought under voluntary control if we knew what responses were occurring in that system. Artificial feedback given to humans in attempts to condition the autonomic system has produced mixed results; ironically, replications of Miller's early work in this area have also met with mixed success (Bower & Hilgard, 1981, p. 258). Effects comparable in size to those obtained in the early experiments have not reappeared, especially those on heart rate. The reasons for the replication difficulties are still being sought.

At about the same time that Miller seemed to be enlarging the scope of behavior which could be modified through reward learning, Brown and Jenkins (1968) reported that more behavior than was previously realized could be controlled via the arrangement of simple contingencies. They "shaped" key-pecking by illuminating the key just prior to delivering food to hungry pigeons. No response was required, but the pigeons pecked persistently anyway. They were conditioning a voluntary response by using a classical conditioning procedure! We seem to be in danger of losing some of the traditional distinguishing characteristics of classical and operant conditioning, specifically that classical conditioning deals with autonomic responses and operant conditioning with voluntary responses. The distinction may be simply a distinction between response-independent schedules ("classical") and response-dependent schedules ("operant") (Staddon & Simmelhag, 1971). It may be that somatic and autonomic nervous system activities are never independent, even in curarized animals (Goesling & Brener, 1972).

M. Ray Denny

Career Maurice Ray Denny (1918–) was born in Terre Haute, Indiana, on November 5, 1918. He received his B.S. and M.A. degrees from the University of Michigan, and his Ph.D., under Kenneth Spence, at the University of Iowa in 1945. After one year at the University of Oklahoma as an instructor, Denny went to Michigan

State University as an assistant professor. He has been there ever since, except for brief sojourns at the University of Michigan, Indiana University, the University of Wisconsin (both at Milwaukee and at Madison), and the University of Guelph. He retired formally in 1983 but continues to do research and teach informally at Michigan State University, where at any given moment he is as likely as not to have a rat in his hand.

Research and Theory Denny's theory was developed in collaboration with a number of his students, notably J. L. Maatsch and H. M. Adelman. Since Denny did his doctoral work with Kenneth Spence, it was natural that he and his students would be interested in Clark Hull's theory. Maatsch, in his master's thesis, was testing some implications of Hull's ideas on reactive inhibition and conditioned inhibition. He found that, contrary to expectation, there was no discernible decrement in running speed on a trial immediately following another trial, whether or not the preceding trial was reinforced. This seems to contradict the presence of *either* reactive inhibition or conditioned inhibition. Extinction occurred, as demonstrated by increases in running time, only when a cue was present which indicated that no reinforcement would be forthcoming on that trial.

Denny and his students capitalized on the Maatsch observations to develop a general theory of learning and extinction. The fundamental idea shared components with several earlier theories, including Pavlov's, Guthrie's, Hull's, and Amsel's frustration theory (to be discussed later in this chapter). The theory is called "elicitation theory" (Denny, 1971) and is characterized as a classical conditioning analysis of operant or instrumental learning. It is clear that this description of Denny's theory is reminiscent of Hull's use of classical conditioning principles to derive the laws used in his general behavior theory. Denny's theory is much simpler and is based on a phenomenon observed in classical conditioning (response elicitation) rather than on laws extracted from study of the independent variable–dependent variable relationships found in the classical conditioning paradigm.

The essence of elicitation theory is the Guthrian, Pavlovian belief that what is learned depends only upon the occurrence of a response in the presence of a stimulus. The difference between Guthrie's theory and Denny's is that Guthrie failed to exploit the *stimulus* properties of reinforcers. For Guthrie, the primary role of the reinforcer was that it changed the stimulus situation and protected the S-R connection from being replaced. For Denny, the reinforcer is important because it *elicits* approach, which is in most cases the response to be learned. Guthrie recognized the importance of what *aversive* stimuli made the organism do; Denny extended the same type of thinking to positive reinforcers. Extinction for Denny consists in the elicitation of a competing response by stimuli present on extinction trials. It is therefore possible to vary resistance to extinction by varying the response made to the *absence* of reinforcement during extinction trials.

Experiments by Adelman and Maatsch (1955, 1956) provided striking confirmation for the predictions of elicitation theory. A group of animals allowed to jump out of the goal box onto a ledge during extinction trials showed little sign of extinction even after 100 massed trials. Animals allowed to recoil from the goal box extinguished more quickly than animals extinguished in the usual way (retained in the goal box for 20 seconds). Subsequent experiments have sometimes confirmed these early findings (W. E. Bacon, 1965; Cotton, Lewis, & Metzger, 1958; Gray, 1969) and have sometimes failed to confirm them (Theios & Bower, 1964; Marx, 1967a, b).

As with all other theories we have discussed, we thus cannot reach an unequivocal conclusion about its essential correctness. Denny's theory, like Guthrie's, is attractive in terms of its simplicity. It gives a parsimonious account of the basis for all learning, both classical and operant, including both learning for positive reinforcement and learning involving aversive stimuli. It deserves more of a hearing than it seems thus far to have received, despite its support by a sizable and enthusiastic band of Denny's students.

SKINNER'S POSITIVISTIC PSYCHOLOGY

Skinner's Career   Burrhus Frederic Skinner (1904–) has had a career remarkable for its breadth of interest and exceptional ingenuity of experimental operations. His intellectual curiosity has refused to be contained within any specialized area. He has analyzed verbal learning, trained pigeons to guide missiles, developed teaching machines, studied the effects of schedules of reinforcement on behavior in great depth and detail, and designed what he thinks would be an ideal society. The ingenious apparatus to his credit includes an automated baby-tending device, used with one of his own children and later marketed commercially. His ideal society was depicted in his novel on a Utopian theme, *Walden two* (1948b).

Skinner got his doctoral degree in psychology from Harvard in 1931. After several years of postdoctoral fellowships, he taught at the University of Minnesota (1936 to 1945) and at Indiana University (1945 to 1947), where he was chairman. He returned to Harvard in 1947, and, although he is now formally retired, he continues to use Harvard as a base. During the 1930s and 1940s Skinner's influence was less than that of Hull and Tolman, but it soon became far greater (Coan & Zagona, 1962). His influence on younger psychologists has always been strong, and he continues to be the leader of the operant psychologists. There is no perceptible lessening in his productivity, as indexed by frequent lectures both at university colloquia and at meetings of psychological associations. He is currently concerned with the decadence of American society, which produces a culture with too few significant behavioral contingencies, and with the possibility of nuclear holocaust. Despite his busy schedule, he continues to be a gracious and accommodating conversationalist both with friends and with the many strangers who seek his company at every gathering.

Skinner's System

Skinner is best known for his insistence upon a descriptive and atheoretical approach to behavioral research. He has long felt that psychology's stage of development is too primitive to justify elaborate formal theorizing. Skinnerians often state that when theories are developed and espoused, personal satisfactions from confirmations of theory become the issue, rather than acquisition of facts. Skinner believes that more effective progress toward the prediction and control of behavior can be obtained through a careful collection of data. The "functional analysis of behavior" has been his objective. Relationships among variables are to be discovered via experimental techniques. Eventually, Skinner believes, sufficient empirical relationships will be established to justify the formation of some limited theories or more comprehensive empirical generalizations, but these must be prepared with caution. Such integrative principles should be allowed to develop gradually, not forced prematurely.

Skinner is not against all theory, and he no doubt believes that psychology is more nearly ready for theory now than it was over half a century ago when he entered the field. At any rate, he has said: "But I look forward to an overall theory of human behavior which will bring together a lot of facts and express them in a more general way. That kind of theory I would be very much interested in promoting, and I consider myself to be a theoretician" (quoted in Evans, 1968, p. 88). In fact, Skinner has taken pains to emphasize his interest in the right kind of theory, subtitling one of his books (1969) *A theoretical analysis* and detailing in its preface the numerous theoretical articles he has written. It is dangerous to overgeneralize with Skinner, just as it is with Titchener, Thorndike, or any other great figure in the history of psychology. Brilliant thinkers seldom take positions as extreme as the positions ascribed to them by incautious critics.

A second methodological emphasis of Skinner has been his insistence upon a thorough analysis of the behavior of single organisms, coupled with his disinclination to use large groups of subjects. Large numbers of subjects have too often been used, he contends, to cover up a lack of experimental controls. With adequate controls, a single subject, or at most a small number of subjects, should be sufficient to demonstrate orderly effects. The use of large groups, he says, also leads indirectly to other difficulties. When a large group is used, the experimenter usually attends primarily or exclusively to statistical properties of the group rather than to the behaviors of the individuals within it. Individual variations may then be lost, and the statistical measures may not describe the characteristics of *any* of the individuals within the group (Sidman, 1960). Skinner does not believe that such large-group experiments are likely to lead to a science in which the prediction and control of the behaviors of individual organisms are possible. On the other hand, when large amounts of data from a single animal are collected under stringently controlled conditions, the results will be clearly replicable with other individuals. No statistical techniques will be necessary. In this connection, Skinner claims that as far as he knows, no student of his ever "designed an experiment" (Evans, 1968, p. 89).

Third, Skinner has objected particularly to physiological speculation in the guise of theory. He has been against what he has considered excessive and futile physiologizing; when physiological data have more concrete points on which behavioral observations can turn, they should be permitted to influence psychology, but not before. This generally aphysiological attitude was shared by Spence, and together they contributed to the prominence of the "empty organism" era in recent psychological thinking. Even on this issue, it is easy to overdramatize Skinner's attitude. His opposition to too much physiologizing seems to be largely a matter of self-discipline. He says:

"I have never said anything against the study of physiology, and I feel that I have done my best to facilitate it by clarifying the problems that the physiologist has to deal with. At the same time, I don't want to borrow support from physiology when my formulation breaks down" (Evans, 1968, p. 22).

A fourth major methodological characteristic of Skinner has been his emphasis on operant, as contrasted with respondent, behavior. Skinner early distinguished between responses made as a direct result of stimulation (Pavlov's unconditioned responses are a good example) and responses emitted by the organism in the absence of any apparent external instigation (operants). The eliciting stimuli for the latter are unknown. The free operant is an operant whose emission does not directly preclude successive emissions of the same response; its study has been especially favored by Skinnerians. The free operant is exemplified by bar-pressing in rats and key-pecking in pigeons. Both organisms are usually studied in a "Skinner box" (Skinner prefers that it be called an operant chamber). These boxes are insulated against noise, and temperature and lighting are closely controlled. Data gathered under such controlled conditions tend to be more uniform and replicable than the data that are otherwise available. Skinner has typically used the rate of emission of a response as his dependent variable. Both the responses and this measure are relatively uncomplicated. A cumulative recorder directly produces a cumulative frequency curve of responses as an experiment progresses.

The free operant as the object of study, the use of rate as the primary datum, and the cumulative recorder as an instrument—these three, in Skinner's view, constitute a unique combination that makes for progress. Rate becomes a meaningful measure only when free operants are being studied and the cumulative recorder efficiently displays rate characteristics over an extended period of time. The experimenter can see what is happening to rate almost as soon as it happens and can change procedures if that seems appropriate. Skinner (1966, p. 16) points out how important it was in chemistry to use dull, colorless weight as a measure as a way of bringing order out of chaos in that field, and he believes that dull, colorless rate will do the same thing for psychology.

Major Contributions

Shaping One of Skinner's most enduring interests has been the training of organisms. Quite early in his career, he developed the training technique called *shaping*. Shaping depends upon presenting rewards to the trainee, whether human or animal, contingent upon a graded series of responses approximating the desired response. For example, we might wish to teach a rat to climb a ladder. At first, the animal might be reinforced merely for facing toward the ladder; later, it would be required to move toward the ladder; then, to touch the ladder, then to get on it, and finally to climb it, in each case in order to receive a reward. Two of Skinner's early associates, Keller and Marian Breland, helped in the development of shaping techniques (Skinner, 1977). They worked with him on what was later called "Project Pigeon" under the auspices of General Mills in Minneapolis. They were well along in teaching pigeons to guide a bomb toward a target when the development of atomic weapons ended the war and removed the urgency from this research. After the project was declassified, a fascinating account was written by Skinner (1960).

The training of animals for shows has been one application of shaping techniques. The Brelands themselves left the academic field to become pioneers in this use of operant techniques (Breland & Breland, 1951, 1961). Skinnerian techniques are now used in virtually every zoo and marine animal show in the United States. Of course, many of these techniques were used long before Skinner gave them a name and a rationale.

Superstitious Behavior   Skinner found that animals sometimes developed orderly behaviors even though they were not rewarded for particular responses. Hungry pigeons developed repetitive behaviors when they were simply given food at regular intervals regardless of what they did. He called such behaviors *superstitious* (Skinner, 1948a) because of their apparent resemblance to human behaviors like carrying a rabbit's foot or refusing to change the clothes one had worn during a winning baseball game. When the delivery of reward is not contingent upon engaging in any specified behavior, the schedule of reinforcement is called *noncontingent* (or *incontingent*). In such a situation, some response which just happens to precede reinforcement early in the session will often be fixated and become predominant in the behavioral repertoire of the animal during the experimental period. This was presumed to occur because one or two early reinforcements increased the rate at which the particular response was emitted, thus making more and more likely its occurrence just prior to subsequent reinforcements. The particular response strengthened, such as wing flapping, neck craning, or leg raising, varies from one animal to the next. Probably the outcome of the procedure depends on the interaction between the animal's initial repertoire in the situation and the schedule of reinforcement delivery. Herrnstein (1966) reported a study in which the animal was first taught a response on a fixed-interval schedule and then shifted to a noncontingent schedule. This procedure gives experimenters control over the animal's repertoire, at least in that it allows them to decide which response shall be of highest frequency when the noncontingent condition is initiated. Under these conditions, Herrnstein found that the high-frequency response was maintained at a rate well above the operant level over the course of many sessions. This result, however, probably depends upon the relationship between the contingent conditions and the noncontingent conditions, since Edwards, West, and Jackson (1968) found that response rates fell fairly rapidly when noncontingent conditions were instituted.

Staddon and Simmelhag (1971) showed that the careful study of superstitious behaviors could be very instructive. They studied several behaviors that occurred in a noncontingent reinforcement situation. They found, among other things, highly consistent sequences of behavior. Component parts of these sequences never occurred "out of position." Their work tends to highlight the stimulating aspects of the reinforcer (see the discussion of Denny's theory, above), since "interim" behaviors occurred repeatedly but *not* in close proximity to the delivery of the reinforcer. It thus appears that the Skinnerian explanation of superstitious behavior may put the emphasis on the wrong features of reinforcement.

Schedules of Reinforcement There is no absolute difference between the non-contingent situation and the contingent situation. Skinner noted that the link between response and reinforcement in most operant work is simply a temporal relationship; as he says: "The response produces food only in the sense that food follows it—a Humean version of causality" (1966, p. 14). He is also aware that superstitious behaviors arise from response-reinforcement relationships not specified by the experimenter, and he has generalized this thinking to contingent conditions: "It is characteristic of most contingencies that they are not precisely controlled, and in any case they are effective only in combination with the behavior which the organism brings to the experiment" (1966, pp. 20–21).

Thus Skinner's concern with superstitious behavior is related quite directly to his even earlier work on the problem of reinforcement scheduling in operant conditioning. His early emphasis on intermittent reinforcement (1938) culminated in the exhaustive volume *Schedules of reinforcement* (Ferster & Skinner, 1957). He worked first with the rat in the Skinner box, subsequently with the pigeon in a comparable chamber, and ultimately with human subjects. Use of children as subjects in operant conditioning studies involving various reinforcement schedules has become a very important feature of behavioral research, involving psychologists of varying degrees of adherence to Skinnerian principles.

A number of examples from everyday-life situations illustrate the effectiveness of intermittent reinforcement in controlling behavior. One of the most apt is the control of behavior exercised by the occasional payoff of the slot machine. The increasing number and success of state lotteries show that even the government is willing to take advantage of behavioral principles to fleece a gullible public. No doubt vicarious reinforcement plays a role in these confidence games, but that theoretical quibble is of little practical significance in these contexts. Reinforcement is often scheduled intermittently in less intentionally manipulative contexts as well; the child's behavior *sometimes* produces approbation in the parent, the fisherman *sometimes* catches fish, and the student does not always do well on examinations.

In laboratory investigations of the effects of different schedules of reinforcement, four major types have been used. These are *fixed interval* (FI), in which the first response made after some fixed period of time is reinforced; *variable interval* (VI), in which the first response made after some variable period of time is reinforced; *fixed ratio* (FR), in which the first response made after some fixed number of previous responses is reinforced; and *variable ratio* (VR), in which the first response made after some variable number of prior responses is reinforced. The two variable schedules (VI and VR) and the fixed-ratio schedule (FR) characteristically produce steady and high rates of responding. The FI schedule ideally produces more cyclical cumulative performance curves featuring bursts of responses just preceding the usual reinforcement time, with pauses or very low rates of response just after reinforcement. This pattern of responding gives the cumulative curve its "scalloped" appearance.

Schoenfeld, Cumming, and Hearst (1968) suggested a classification scheme for schedules of reinforcement defined in terms of strictly temporal variables. The critical properties of schedules are presumed to be the length of the period during which reinforcement is available and the total "cycle length," which includes the period of unavailability as well as the period of availability. If the animal responds during the period of availability, the reinforcement is delivered; otherwise, it isn't. These authors found that response rate increased when, for a fixed total cycle time, the period of availability was increased. Conversely, rates decreased when availability time decreased.

This work and Skinner's own thinking would seem to be pointing toward a description of contingencies couched in more basic terms than those now used. Describing a schedule as "fixed-interval 15 seconds" leaves out critical properties of the relationship between reinforcement delivery and the organism's behavior. It also encourages a distinction between such a schedule and a fixed-ratio 25-response schedule, whether or not such a distinction is important in a particular context. Finally, the similarities which may exist between intermittent reinforcement schedules and free food delivery on a noncontingent schedule tend to be obscured. A general description in terms of more basic properties of the various schedules as they relate to the organism's responses should make it possible to describe all schedules within a single encompassing framework.

Verbal Behavior   Skinner has also been interested in a systematic analysis of verbal behavior. His conceptualization of human language has been controversial but influential. His major publication in this field was *Verbal behavior* (1957). According to Skinner's interpretation, language as verbal behavior is basically similar to other behavior and can be best understood when viewed in this general framework.

Skinner describes verbal behavior as behavior whose reinforcement is mediated by another organism that has been specifically conditioned to mediate such reinforcements. Verbal operants, like other operants, are recognized because of a relationship to an antecedent condition, typically a controlling stimulus. An example of a functional relationship between an antecedent variable and a verbal response would be one's writing, under the appropriate conditions, "chair" as a response to an objective, real chair. Such responses are called *tacts* by Skinner because their controlling variable is *contact* with an object, event, or property of an object or event. If a person says "coffee" because he or she is deprived of that substance, to Skinner that person is emitting a *mand* because of his or her *demand* for the appropriate reinforcer. Skinner believes that the appropriate course of investigation of language involves just the functional analysis of the relationship between antecedents and verbal behavior. The organism makes no real contribution to verbal behavior but is best regarded as a locus through which variables act.

Although Skinner's analysis has come in for severe criticism, there is little doubt that it has had a stimulating effect. Skinner's break with conventional accounts of verbal behavior largely preceded, and probably contributed to, the several attempts to teach the rudiments of human language to chimpanzees.

Behavioral Technology   Skinner's utopian *Walden two* of 1948 displayed his interest in applying behavioral technology to improve society. Much later, *Beyond freedom and dignity* (1971) challenged our society to do something about itself by using the behavioral techniques discovered by Skinner and others. No doubt Skinner was being deliberately provocative when he suggested that freedom and dignity, two of America's most holy cows, are in the way of progress toward a better world. We will reserve comment on whether those cows belong on the street or on the table. However, we do know that Skinner had the attention of the nation, for the book was on the best-seller list. It also succeeded in being provocative, since it evoked strong comments from then Vice President Spiro Agnew (Goodall, 1972). We have seen no rush to apply Skinner's ideas, however.

Many others of Skinner's ideas have been taken more seriously. For example, Skinner receives a great deal of credit for contemporary interest in programmed instruction, some of which he deserves. We might consider the following, quoted in Boring and Lindzey (1967):

> In a window of the little apparatus showed a four-choice question to which students responded by pressing the key corresponding to the answer they thought right. If it was, the next question turned up, but if not, they had to try again until they did find the right answer— meanwhile a counter kept a cumulative record of their tries. Moreover (two features no device since has had) if a lever were raised, the device was changed into a self-scoring and rewarding testing machine: whatever key was pressed, the next question turned up, but the counter registered only rights; also when the set on a reward dial was reached, a candy lozenge was automatically presented. (p. 232)

Surprisingly, this quotation is not from Skinner's autobiography but from Sidney Pressey's, and the machine described was exhibited in 1925, before Skinner went into psychology. However, teaching machines did not catch on until much later, and they have truly hit their pace only with the advent of the cheap and practical computer. It is interesting to ask why. The machines themselves have certainly undergone changes, but some successful machines have been very simple—no more complex than Pressey's much earlier machine. Modern exponents of programmed instruction would probably insist that the materials are now better organized and that the technical features of the organization are responsible for the increase in the acceptance of programmed instruction.

It is nevertheless interesting to consider the possibility that the reason for Skinner's success in popularizing this approach to learning, where Pressey had failed about 30 years earlier, is that Skinner had better reasons to believe that the technique ought to work. Further, he had a cohesive and enthusiastic group of followers, and Pressey did not. The principles of operant conditioning were working in the control of animal behavior, and concurrent efforts indicated that they would work for the control of human behavior. Thus a *Zeitgeist* was developing within which programmed instruction could thrive. It was probably Pressey's fate to be a little too far ahead of his time in 1925.

Similar considerations apply to Skinner's role in the development of the behavior-modification movement. Kalish (1977) is one of those who have pointed out that most of the concepts central to behavior modification were developed by Thorndike, Pavlov, or J. B. Watson. Yet the use of behavior-modification techniques remained rare, and there was no "movement" before Skinner was there to lead the movement. Now books on the subject are legion, studies countless, and the practice ubiquitous. Ullman and Krasner (1965) provided one of the earlier summaries, reporting a host of cases in which operant techniques had been used to modify the behaviors of patients ranging from disturbed children to psychotic adults. Skinner has participated in and nurtured this development from the beginning, but his critical role has been in providing the intellectual justification.

Criticisms of Skinner's System

Positivism Skinner's positivism has invited attack. Critics have maintained that Skinner is deluding himself if he believes that theory has no value. Theory is inevitable. Every experiment and observation is in some way planned, based on hunches or ideas at the very least; therefore, say the critics, it is better to bring the presuppositions out into the open and formalize them; then they can be recognized and challenged. In addition, formal theory in the older sciences has provided a generality of explanation which Skinner's fact gathering alone can never achieve.

Further, the *efficiency* of the atheoretical approach has been questioned. The book *Schedules of reinforcement* (Ferster & Skinner, 1957) has been used as an example of the dangers of too inductive and positivistic an approach. It summarized about 70,000 hours of continuously recorded behavior of individual pigeons, during which time the pigeons emitted approximately a *quarter billion* responses. The data are presented in a total of 921 separate figures with almost no interpretive, or even summarizing, comment. This procedure accords well with Skinner's (1959a) belief that the scientist should be brought into direct contact with data, but it does not agree so well with the scientific temperament of those whose immediate interests are in general principles.

Skinner has several replies available. First, he is not antitheoretical. He is only against certain types of theories, either those which are premature or those which are attempts to avoid empirical work or *genuine* explanation. He does believe that theories may guide investigators into unprofitable efforts to confirm or disconfirm them, when they might better devote themselves to the exploration of interesting empirical situations. Theories should be primarily inductive, not based on logical guesses. Theories *should* be an end product of scientific endeavor, and they should be proposed only as the data are ready to support them. Second, Skinner would probably insist that presuppositions need to be kept to a minimum if they cannot be avoided altogether. Premature speculation, even if it is not misleading, is a waste of time. In the worst cases, it will be misleading, a waste of time both directly and indirectly, and a source of personal involvement and controversy.

Peripheralism This argument against Skinner has two major facets. One involves his aphysiological bias; this is largely a matter of taste. If one prefers not to think in physiological terms, surely that is one's privilege. The other involves his refusal to posit intervening psychological processes such as Hull's habit strength or inhibition or Spence's incentive motivation. Here too the issue is one of personal preference, but difficulties arise when one side attempts to force its views on the other.

We have already noted in passing Skinner's own contention that he is not against real physiological psychology. He is only against the practice of taking refuge in physiological terminology when behavioral accounts break down. The use of merely verbal explanations, whether physiological, mentalistic, or anything else, is discouraged by Skinner.

In some cases, Skinner or his followers may have waxed too enthusiastic in their efforts to purify psychological language by eliminating terms like *emotion, motivation,* and *perception.* These much-abused terms may be highly variable in meaning and yet have some core of useful meaning. If so, the critics would have a legitimate claim that some problems were being neglected because of a positivistic insistence on purity of language. The reply might be that the problems of nature eventually insist that attention be paid to them. Meanwhile, there are plenty of problems suggested by concepts with demonstrated meaningfulness. Would the critic rather devote time to issues that are assuredly meaningful or to problems that have no clear meaning?

Excessive Extrapolation   Skinner has often gone well beyond his data, as in his proposals about human problems in *Science and human behavior* (1953) and many other publications. On this issue he is somewhat vulnerable; the whole spirit of his methodology revolves around the notion of sticking close to observed facts, but his generalizations to human behavior very clearly go far beyond the observations of the laboratory.

Cook (1963) criticized Skinnerians for too literal an application to programmed learning of techniques appropriate in the operant conditioning chamber. For one thing, there is a great deal of evidence that humans need *not* make an overt response in order to learn and in fact often do better if no overt response is required (Hillix & Marx, 1960; Rosenbaum & Hewitt, 1966; Rosenbaum & Schutz, 1967). Further, they may do as well when they are told in advance what the correct response is (a prompting procedure) as they do when they are reinforced after making the correct response. Both of these findings about human learning contradict assumptions made by operant conditioners prior to their discovery and thus are instances of premature extrapolation of operant principles from animal behavior to human behavior.

Account of Verbal Behavior   The best-known criticism of Skinner's work is by Chomsky (1959). In his famous thirty-two-page review of *Verbal behavior*, Chomsky analyzed Skinner's formulation with great care and criticized it with great effectiveness. He devoted a great deal of attention to the terms *stimulus, response*, and *reinforcement*, since these are critical terms in Skinner's account of verbal behavior. Serious problems arise with the use of each of the three terms as they are employed in the analysis of verbal behavior. We shall note here only some difficulties with the use of the term *reinforcement*, but similar difficulties arise with the other two words as well.

Chomsky noted that in bar-pressing experiments the reinforcer is an identifiable stimulus and that statements about reinforcement therefore have a meaningful referent. This in turn makes it meaningful to use the concept of reinforcement in the explanation of behavior. However, Chomsky contended that the extension of the concept of reinforcement to the explanation of verbal behavior is completely unjustified. In support of his criticism, he cited from Skinner a number of examples in which the term *reinforcement* did not refer to an identifiable stimulus. Skinner often used "automatic self-reinforcement" (not identifiable as a stimulus) as an explanation of why verbal behavior is maintained. "Future reinforcements" are also appealed to at times, as when a writer is said to be reinforced because of the effect his work will have on future generations. Chomsky (1959) said of such usage: "In fact, the term is used in such a way that the assertion that reinforcement is necessary for learning and continued availability of behavior is likewise empty" (p. 37).

Despite the astuteness that they both demonstrate, Chomsky's review is like Koch's (1954) review of Hull's work in that, from one point of view, they are both unjust. The reason is that Hull and Skinner were being programmatic and were bound to be inaccurate in many details. It was Hull's explicit intention to set up hypotheses which could be proved wrong by others. Chomsky might reply that the defects in detail in Skinner's account are so great that the whole program of application of operant principles to verbal behavior becomes meaningless. Chomsky may be correct; in the midst of the current "cognitive revolution," there seems to be more interest in pursuing Chomsky's program than in pursuing Skinner's.

Nevertheless, Skinner's verbal behavior program is defensible. Bem and Bem, although they are not greatly impressed by Skinner's viewpoint, indicate the direction such a defense might take. In comparing Skinner's *Verbal behavior* and Lenneberg's *The biological foundations of language* (1967), they say: "Both works, in short, constitute plausibility arguments for particular views of verbal behavior" (1968, p. 497). Skinner clearly stated that this was the way in which he viewed his analysis of verbal behavior, and he could easily extend this argument to his other extrapolations. If they are accepted as merely suggestions stemming from his conceptual framework, they may serve at least as an intellectual stimulant. The extent to which simple principles can be applied to complex situations and processes cannot be safely prejudged.

Skinner is confident that the pendulum of opinion will swing back and award the victory to him:

> What the psycholinguists miss is any conception of a functional analysis as opposed to a structural analysis of verbal behavior. . . . They lean very heavily on the mentalistic psychology, and they are going to be let down because there is no such psychology. But as I said earlier, now they are postulating innate ideas, and that is next to worthless, if not a little bit comical. But I am in no real hurry, I have had my say. I am not interested in arguing with them at all. When all their mythical machinery finally grinds to a halt and is laid aside, discarded, then we will see what is remembered fifty or a hundred years from now, when the truth will have all been brought out in the open. (quoted in Hall, 1967, pp. 69–70)

MacCorquodale agrees with Skinner. After chastising Chomsky for what he sees as a misunderstanding of Skinner's purpose, MacCorquodale (1969) says:

> Unfortunately for his purposes, Chomsky did not grasp the differences between Skinnerian and Watsonian-Hullian behaviorism, and his criticisms, although stylistically effective, were mostly irrelevant to *Verbal behavior*.

> He was simply wrong. This is a *great* book. (p. 841)

Environmentalism   Skinner's position in *The behavior of organisms* (1938) was often interpreted as quite environmentalistic. He put a good deal of stress on the ubiquity of learned behaviors and seemed to have great faith in the power of operant procedures—a faith which has, for the most part, been justified by events. However, the Brelands, while training many species of animals, made some observations that led them to depart to some extent from Skinnerian views on operant conditioning. The Brelands noted (1961) several failures to teach the behaviors desired. For example (see Breland & Breland, 1966, pp. 67–68), raccoons, pigs, squirrel monkeys, and other animals often have trouble letting go of a token which they are learning to insert into a food dispenser, much as a miser has trouble letting go of money. The Brelands believed that more primitive food-related behaviors were activated on earlier trials and that these more primitive behaviors interfered with the performance of the operant response. They described this "instinctive drift" as follows:

> The general principle seems to be that wherever an animal has strong instinctive behaviors in the area of the conditioned response, after continued running the organism will drift toward the instinctive behavior, to the detriment of the conditioned behavior and even to the delay or preclusion of the reinforcement. (Breland & Breland, 1961, p. 684)

The Brelands, although they were nurtured by Skinner in the environmentalistic tradition which has been a common feature of the behavioristic outlook, were prominent among psychologists responsible for a swing back toward nativism. This change was initiated by the ethologists and nurtured later by sociobiologists, and it has gone far enough to be itself vehemently opposed by new defenders of the importance of the environment.

Lockard (1971) documented that part of the nativistic trend which was most closely related to animal behavior. He detailed the contributions of ethologists like Lorenz and Tinbergen, as well as that of the Brelands. His conclusions come through clearly in statements like the following:

> Scientifically speaking, only two pieces of information were needed to bring behavior into the modern synthesis of the new biology: the fact that behavior has a genetic basis, thus making it heritable and therefore subject to natural selection; and the fact that behavior, or rather, particular behaviors, are adaptive—that they bear intimate relationships to particulars of the environment such that some kind of advantage results. The genetic basis of hundreds and hundreds of particular behaviors has been demonstrated beyond doubt, and the adaptive significance of particular behaviors has been demonstrated in hundreds of cases. (Lockard, 1971, p. 171)

Another student of Skinner's, R. J. Herrnstein (1977a, b) also interpreted the findings of the Brelands as contradicting Skinner's views. Fortunately for Skinner, he is still here to stem what Herrnstein called the "rising tide of anti-Skinnerianism" (1977a, p. 593), and we do not need to guess what Skinner's reply would be to critics of his environmentalism.

His first retort is that his extreme environmentalism does not exist. Skinner's position on the issue has no doubt shifted over the years, just as everyone else's has or should have. In an extensive article (1966), Skinner described his position on the phylogeny and ontogeny of behavior, and he very explicitly recognized the importance of phylogeny at that time. He refused to go overboard in either direction at that time or later: "Phylogeny and ontogeny are friendly rivals and neither one always wins" (1977, p. 1009). He pointed out examples in which learned behaviors intrude on instinctive behaviors, as well as vice versa, and concluded: "Civilization has supplied an unlimited number of examples of the suppression of the phylogenic repertoire of the human species by learned behavior. In fact, it is often the very function of a culture to mask a genetic endowment" (1977, p. 1007). Clearly, Skinner needs no defense from us on this point; he is more than capable of taking care of himself.

Neglect of Statistics Skinner and his followers are usually not interested in statistical tests. Their attitude is probably best represented by Sidman's (1960) book, *Tactics of scientific research*. The preferred methodology within this tradition involves intensive and carefully controlled investigation of a small number of individual subjects. The search is for reliable functional relationships, and reliability is established by demonstrating the same functional relationship in several *individual* organisms, preferably under different conditions. The statistical approach uses larger groups of subjects and examines quantitative indices of the group's performance. As we said earlier, Skinner does not believe that we are likely to arrive at laws by following the statisticians' procedures. The issue is, like most such issues, debatable. At the least, the Skinnerians have forced important questions into the spotlight, where they can be carefully reconsidered. Some aspects of operant methodology are unquestionably useful, and on some issues concerning the relationships between group and individual functions the Skinnerians are demonstrably correct. Those who advocate an overtly statistical approach are probably correct when they maintain that Skinnerians must make statistical decisions. One example is deciding whether or not rate of responding has stabilized; another is deciding whether experimental manipulations have produced a reliable effect.

Skinner's Role in Contemporary Psychology

The extent of Skinner's systematic contributions to modern experimental psychology is nicely summarized in the formal citation accompanying the American Psychological Association's Distinguished Scientific Contribution Award granted him in 1958. This citation is as follows:

> An imaginative and creative scientist, characterized by great objectivity in scientific matters and by warmth and enthusiasm in personal contacts. Choosing simple operant behavior as subject matter, he has challenged alternative analyses of behavior, insisting that description take precedence over hypotheses. By careful control of experimental conditions, he has produced data which are relatively free from fortuitous variation. Despite his antitheoretical position, he is considered an important systematist and has developed a self-consistent description of behavior which has greatly increased our ability to predict and control the behavior of organisms from rat to man. Few American psychologists have had so profound an impact on the development of psychology and on promising younger psychologists. (*American Psychologist*, 1958)

Skinner has become the grandest of psychology's grand old men. "Mr. Behaviorist" has probably endured more unjustified and uninformed attacks than any other living psychologist, but the charm and modesty of his personality have survived with no visible impairment.

There is probably some abatement of enthusiasm for the Skinnerian position, as cognitive psychology increasingly attracts the attention of eager young psychologists. However, there are still plenty of enthusiastic Skinnerians, and neither their *Journal for the Experimental Analysis of Behavior*, established by operant psychologists in 1958, nor their more recently established *Journal of Applied Experimental Analysis* shows signs of being short of papers. The popular press has long recognized Skinner as the greatest of the contemporary behaviorists (e.g., *Psychology Today*, September, 1983), and many regard his theoretical views as serious competitors to Freud's. He has revivified and extended the strictly behavioral position. He has perpetuated the vision of psychology initiated by J. B. Watson with a style which is, if anything, cleaner and purer than Watson's.

Skinner remains the most important of the true behaviorists, sticking to his metatheoretical position despite the slings and arrows of the many critics of the purely objective approach.

We believe that Skinner would be pleased with that assessment.

SYNTHETIC (TWO-FACTOR) THEORIES

It has been clear for a long time that the Thorndikian and Pavlovian procedures for studying S-R learning differ in the operations employed. In the Pavlovian procedure, the unconditioned stimulus follows the conditioned stimulus, whatever the subject in the experiment does. In the Thorndikian procedure, the reward is presented only if the subject has previously engaged in the behavior required by the experimenter. This basic difference in procedure implies some corollary distinctions. In the Pavlovian paradigm, the conditioned stimulus, which comes to elicit the conditioned response if learning occurs, is an identifiable stimulus manipulated by the experimenter. The unconditioned stimulus elicits an identifiable unconditioned response. The unconditioned response in the Pavlovian studies was nearly always an involuntary response mediated by the autonomic nervous system. The conditioned response typically resembles the unconditioned response, if the two are not identical as measured in the experiment. The Thorndikian procedure is different in all the above respects: there is no experimentally identified conditioned stimulus, the response elicited by the reward is not of great interest, the experimental arrangements do not "force" the performance of the unconditioned response to the reward, the response to be learned may not be at all related in form to the response made to the reward, and the responses of interest are mediated by the "voluntary" nervous system.

A consideration of these operational differences between Pavlovian (classical) conditioning and Thorndikian (instrumental) learning leads one to question whether different laws of behavior modification are involved in the two situations. For example, one might ask whether stimulus associations, as in Pavlovian conditioning, and stimulus-response associations, as emphasized by the Thorndikian procedure, are formed by different basic processes.

Rescorla and Solomon (1967), in their review of the literature on two-factor learning theories, stated that three different sets of variables are usually implicated by those who think that there are two basically different processes. The three sets are the class of responses affected by the process, the effective reinforcers involved, and the results of the learning process.

The most common distinction based on response characteristics has been that classical conditioning involves autonomic responses, while instrumental learning involves somatic (skeletal) responses, but a number of other distinctions have also been suggested.

It is more difficult to find a basis for distinguishing the kinds of reinforcers, but it has been suggested that the "rewards" used in instrumental learning have an affective character, while Pavlovian reinforcers do not. Again, several bases for a distinction between the reinforcers have been proposed.

Finally, among the several possible distinctions between the "products" of learning is the suggestion that classical conditioning involves stimulus-stimulus connections, while instrumental learning produces stimulus-response connections. There is no highly convincing empirical evidence that compels adherence to any of these theoretical distinctions, but there is not sufficient evidence to reject them either. However, we have seen above that there is increasing evidence which brings the most popular response distinction into question.

The most popular theoretical strategy has been an attempt to reduce the two operationally different procedures to a common theoretical framework which can explain both. Hull, for example, accepted the laws of Pavlovian conditioning as basic but modified the most common conception of the process in his emphasis on the necessity for drive reduction to occur if learning is to be successful. The more complex, and therefore less popular, solution is to assume that there are two different processes involved and propose a theory which relates the two processes. If this approach is chosen, it is natural to assume that classical conditioning involves contiguity as a basic process and that instrumental learning involves reward as a basic component.

Jerzy Konorski

Polish neurophysiologist Jerzy Konorski (1903–1973) is generally credited with the first systematic distinction between instrumental and classical conditioning. Although Konorski received medical training and the M.D. degree and regarded himself primarily as a neurophysiologist, much of his research centered on strictly behavioral problems, mainly conditioning.

In 1928 Konorski, then a medical school student, published his first scientific papers jointly with Stefan Miller, another medical student with whom he collaborated (Miller & Konorski, 1928; English translation, 1969). Their research used a single dog subject. Miller and Konorski found that if the dog's leg were passively flexed following a conditioned stimulus, only on trials on which food was delivered, the conditioned stimulus would later spontaneously elicit the leg flexion. On the other hand, so to speak, if the leg were passively flexed only on trials involving some aversive stimulus, such as blowing air into the dog's ear, the conditioned stimulus would produce only a progressively greater extension of the leg.

Having only recently discovered and been excited by Pavlov's research, Miller and Konorski called the reflex they had demonstrated a Type II conditioned reflex, in order to separate it from the orthodox Pavlovian reflex, called Type I. In this paper they not only fully discussed the salient differences between the two types of reflex but also described the procedures to be followed in avoidance and omission training and their relationships to instrumental reward and punishment training.

In his posthumously published autobiography, Konorski (1974) provides a most entertaining and instructive account of this early research conducted with Miller. They obtained from a sympathetic professor at the Free Polish University the use of a small room in a third-floor apartment. They improvised a "Pavlovian stand" from two square stools and used a piece of cardboard with a hole cut in it for a screen through which food reward could be delivered. They then purchased a dog, which they named Bobek, at the marketplace. In order to record the dog's responses they used rolls of toilet paper, because it "was both cheap and convenient, provided that it was relatively smooth and did not have any transversal perforations. You can imagine the comical picture presented by two serious young men going to a paper store and asking to be shown all of the possible varieties of toilet paper, scrutinizing them thoroughly, and choosing the one which fulfilled both conditions" (Konorski, 1974, pp. 187–188).

In later papers Miller and Konorski showed that the same results as they had with passive leg flexion occurred when electric shock was used to force a leg flexion or the experimenters simply waited for the dog to flex the leg.

After receiving his medical degree, Konorski was invited to spend some time in Pavlov's laboratory. The two years (1931 to 1933) spent there familiarized him with the intricacies of the superficially simple classically conditioned reflex but did not convince him of the correctness of Pavlov's theoretical views. Konorski later became head of the department of neurophysiology at the Nencki Institute in Poland, a position that he managed to retain in spite of political vicissitudes. His two major books were *Conditioned reflexes and neuron organization* (1948), and the more ambitious but less empirically constrained *Integrative activity of the brain: An interdisciplinary approach* (1967), in which he follows the neurophysiological lead of Sherrington rather than of Pavlov.

One example of Konorski's later work illustrates his research productivity and his theoretical insightfulness. Ellison and Konorski (1964) trained hungry dogs to panel push repeatedly in order to produce a signal that was followed by food reward. These dogs showed a classically conditioned response, salivation, to the signal for food but not to the signal initiating their instrumental panel-pushing response. A similar dissociation between classically and instrumentally conditioned responses was reported by Williams (1965). It thus appears that there can be considerable independence between these two fundamental forms of learning. However, whether they can ultimately be reduced to some single underlying mechanism is, of course, a more difficult and less readily resolved question.

Halliday (1979) has examined the paradoxical neglect of Konorski and Miller by western psychologists, which occurred despite two early papers, published in English (Konorski and Miller, 1937a,b), that were concerned both with their own research and with a critical comparison of it with Skinner's alternative conditioning dichotomy (operant and respondent conditioning). Moreover, these papers were described both in Skinner's *The behavior of organisms* (1938) and in Hilgard and Marquis's *Conditioning and learning* (1940), books widely read by experimental psychologists of that time.

For a variety of reasons, mainly perhaps relating to changes in the psychological *Zeitgeist* (e.g., the coming into favor of the concept of inhibition, which was central to Konorski's theoretical thinking), Konorski has received increasing attention from western psychologists. This story is interestingly told by Halliday (1979). His summation of Konorski's contemporary significance is that Konorski, speaking over an interval of more than a generation, addresses current issues better than the American behaviorists of only 25 years ago.

Other Two-Factor Theorists

Several two-factor learning theories have been advanced over the past half century or so. These proposals were anticipated by Thorndike's early (1911) distinction between what he called "associative shifting" (classical conditioning) and "trial and error learning." As has been mentioned, Skinner (1938) distinguished between Type S (or respondent) and Type R (operant, or instrumental) conditioning, and Schlosberg (1937), accepting "conditioning" as a generic term for classical or Pavlovian conditioning, suggested "success learning" for the alternative form. Finally, Hilgard and Marquis (1940) coined the terms that have come to be most generally accepted, classical and instrumental conditioning.

A suggestion for a different kind of two-factor theory has been made by Spence (1956). As he pointed out, one might develop his suggestion into a two-factor theory "exactly the opposite of the well-known two-factor theory espoused by Schlosberg, Mowrer, and others" (p. 151). Reinforcement would be accorded the determining role in the case of classically conditioned responses, which are emphasized in Spence's systematic theory, rather than in instrumental behavior.

O. H. Mowrer Perhaps the most comprehensive attempt to elaborate two contrasting forms of learning has been made by O. H. Mowrer (1907–1982). Actually, Mowrer published two different versions of two-factor theory. His initial version became, and has remained, the best-known two-factor theory because of the tightness of his reasoning, the empirical work which buttressed his suggestions, and the length and number of his publications on the subject (e.g., 1947). Mowrer contrasted conditioning and "solution learning." The acquisition of emotions, meanings, attitudes, and the like is mediated through simple contiguity of stimuli—conditioning. Overt instrumental learning—solution learning—occurs through reinforcement or law-of-effect learning. Because Mowrer was originally a strong Hullian reinforcement theorist, his shift to two-factor theory was surprising, and his theory was criticized by his earlier collaborator, Neal Miller (1951), among others.

An even more ambitious two-factor theory was subsequently advanced by Mowrer (1956, 1960a, b); it is a drastic revision of his earlier theory. Actually, it is no longer "two-factor" in the original sense. Mowrer came to accept only conditioning, or sign learning, as the single basic learning process; solution learning is regarded as a special, derived case of conditioning. In this respect Mowrer's later theory involves a return to Hullian principles. This theory is still two-factor, however, in that it stresses two types of reinforcement. *Decremental reinforcement* refers to the need-reducing kind of process stressed by Thorndike and Hull in their theories; *incremental reinforcement* refers to the growth of "fear" with consequent avoidance of excessive stimulation.

This theory was developed mainly by means of an extension of the secondary-reinforcement principle. Mowrer assumes that when a hungry animal obtains food, response-produced stimuli become conditioned as secondary reinforcers, as "promising" stimuli which arouse "hope." In this "feedback theory of habit," as Mowrer calls it, hope is thus conditioned in fundamentally the same way as fear is conditioned in aversive learning. The parallelism is stated by Mowrer (1960b): "A conditioned stimulus not only makes the subject salivate; it also makes him *hopeful*, just as surely as a stimulus which has been associated with the onset of pain makes a subject *fearful* (p. 8).

Comments on Two-Factor Theory

It is still too early to say whether learning will eventually be subsumed under a single set of laws or under two or more sets of laws. Rescorla and Solomon (1967) cite a number of studies which demonstrate interactions between classical and instrumental conditioning arrangements. Changes in the rate of instrumental responding can be produced by the introduction of conditioned stimuli previously used in the Pavlovian context. Such empirical demonstrations do not prove that there are two kinds of learning, but they do show that it is profitable to study the relationships between situations in which stimulus *contiguity* is arranged (Pavlovian) and situations in which a response-reinforcement *contingency* is arranged. Two-factor theories may not turn out to be "correct," but they have the virtue of alerting us to such relationships.

Two-factor theories should also help us to remember that it is always the organism, and not some "autonomic learning system" or "somatic learning system," that is involved in the learning process. Kendon Smith (1954) long ago suggested that autonomic conditioning might occur only as a by-product of somatic learning and is therefore in a sense an artifact. Theorists like Neal Miller have tried to eliminate this possibility by showing that animals learn autonomic responses even though they are under the influence of curare, which is intended to block all somatic responses. But Black (1967) reports that instrumental avoidance learning also occurs under curare, even though the avoidance response could not occur during the learning sessions! And Goesling and Brener (1972) showed that the effects of somatic learning prior to curarization were manifested in autonomic learning *after* curarization. Considering all these complexities—and there are cognitive effects to be added—it seems best to suspend judgment about the number of fundamental types of learning while we wait for future clarification.

CONTEMPORARY DEVELOPMENTS IN S-R THEORY

Amsel's Frustration Theory

One of the most prominent of the neo-Hullian efforts is the frustration theory developed by Abram Amsel (1922–). Frustration is regarded as an active, invigorating, aversive condition rather than as a merely passive state as most earlier theorists like Hull and Tolman had thought. Amsel was a student of Spence, and he developed his frustration theory (1967) along lines parallel to those used earlier for reward learning. A primary frustration reaction (R_f) and consequent aggressive or other short-term persisting effects are assumed to result from nonreward when the organism expects reward. There is also classical conditioning of fractional frustration responses r_f to prior and concurrent stimuli. The S_f cues constitute anticipatory frustration and tend to elicit avoidance responses.

The most popular apparatus used in research on Amsel's frustration theory has been a double, or two-link, runway. The subject, ordinarily a laboratory rat, is trained to proceed from the start box into which it is placed and on down the runway and into a goal box. After a short interval during which food is consumed (or frustration presumably builds up if the anticipated food reward offered on earlier trials is not available), a door leading from this first goal box is opened, allowing access to the second runway and its goal box at the end. The speed at which the subject proceeds through this second runway serves as a measure of the hypothesized frustration effect (FE).

When a 50 percent schedule of reinforcement in the first goal box is used, following some initial training with continuous reward, the typical result is that progressively faster running in the second alley (greater FE) occurs on the trials on which no reward is given in the first goal box. An especially impressive opposite result was reported by Amsel and Ward (1965). They found a progressive *reduction* of the FE in animals given discriminative cues for *nonreward* in the first runway, indicating the importance of the anticipation of reward, and consequent frustration, in the more typical situation.

Another interesting but more complicated experiment was reported by R. R. Ross (1964), who confirmed the predictions of frustration theory in a situation involving several responses, with subjects trained under either partial or continuous reinforcement conditions. Frustration was shown to act as a cue for transfer of responding from training to test conditions, and animals trained to make a response to frustration which was incompatible with continued responding extinguished quickly.

Amsel's frustration theory is not the only viable theory of extinction; Capaldi's sequential discrimination account is an attractive alternative with which Amsel's theory makes little conceptual contact. Moreover, there are results which seem inconsistent with frustration theory (Levy & Seward, 1969). Nevertheless, Amsel's theory has demonstrated its applicability and provided a solid base for further development.

Logan's Micromolar Theory

An entirely different type of neo-Hullian theory has been developed by Frank Logan (1924–), yet another Spence doctoral student who worked at Yale during the final years of Hull's life. Logan (1956, 1960) stressed the need to look more closely than

Hull did at the particular features of learned responses, such as their speed and amplitude. The molecular analysis of molar responses led to the term *micromolar*. The intensive features of responses are poorly correlated under ordinary learning conditions, and they can be differentially strengthened under special learning conditions.

Logan's (1960) results indicate that his highly specific approach to responses is fruitful. Organisms can be trained to optimize the various intensive characteristics of their responses (i.e., latency, speed, and amplitude) if these characteristics are closely correlated with some dimension of the reinforcement situation. Thus the forcefulness of a response like bar pressing, which is not ordinarily correlated with reinforcement, can be increased if greater amounts of reward are presented for more forceful response.

Logan's micromolar theory serves an important integrating function in learning theory. Bower and Hilgard (1981) say that its primary importance is the "conceptual housecleaning" which it provides for learning theory. A good example of this service is the way in which the micromolar approach accommodates the basic relationships between Skinnerian schedules of reinforcement and response rate. The similarity between Logan's differential reinforcement of intensive features of the response and Skinnerian shaping is also evident. Further indications of the usefulness of Logan's approach are that it applies to both classical and instrumental conditioning and that it fits with commonsense notions of everyday-life learning situations in which specificity of response is necessary.

Harlow's Primate Research

Harry F. Harlow (1905–1981) was trained as a comparative psychologist in the Stanford University laboratory of Calvin Stone. From 1950 to 1952, he was Chief of Human Resources Research for the U.S. Army; he had been instrumental in setting up the Army's human factors research program. He was a long-time researcher and research administrator in the primate laboratories of the University of Wisconsin at Madison. After he retired from Wisconsin, he spent many more active years at the University of Arizona before his death in 1981.

Harlow is an especially difficult researcher to place in any one systematic or theoretical category. He was not a Gestalt psychologist, yet his "learning-set" experiments helped to support and popularize the Gestalt interpretation of learning. He was not a clinical psychologist, yet his "surrogate-mother" research with young rhesus monkeys led to seminal insights into important developmental and personality problems. And he was not an avowed S-R psychologist, although we have placed him in this chapter because of the S-R character of his "error-factor" learning research. More than anything, perhaps, Harlow was a functionalist, because he was dedicated to solving behavioral problems and did not pay much attention to systematic labels. However he is labeled, Harlow was a major contributor to psychological research.

Harlow's early research on learning sets (Harlow, 1949, 1950) demonstrated the extremely rapid discrimination learning of which rhesus monkeys are capable. These subjects were given a series of short (six trials) and relatively simple two-choice object-discrimination problems, with correct responses rewarded by the providing of a raisin. The important finding was that the monkey subject was able, with increasing proficiency, to use the right/wrong feedback on the first trial as a guide to subsequent object choices (say, between a "correct" box and an incorrect shoe). A correct response on the first trial by a sophisticated monkey led to immediate repetition of that selection. An incorrect response led to an immediate change of the choice. Different pairs of common objects (comb, shoe, and the like) were used on successive problems. Harlow called the discrimination ability shown a "learning set" and felt that the theoretical significance of the progressive improvement in the ability to benefit from the first-trial feedback was that the subjects could "gradually learn insight" (Harlow, 1949, p. 56). This conclusion incorporates the Gestalt insight phenomenon into a kind of modified S-R theoretical framework. The Gestaltists believed that insight was incompatible with such a framework, but Harlow demonstrated the continuity between the two points of view.

Harlow's immediately following research was designed to uncover the kinds of factors, which he called "error factors," that needed to be eliminated before the proper learning set could be established. Unfortunately, each new investigation seemed to indicate a different array of such error factors, and there seemed to be little underlying relationship among them. It remained for one of Harlow's students, Marvin Levine (1959, 1963), to propose a unifying account of these phenomena; Levine adapted the cognitive concept *hypothesis* to account for each of the particular error tendencies evidenced as well as for the much more generalized correct tendency, the learning set itself. A succinct but clear and comprehensive review of this unusual mix of traditional (S-R-like) and cognitive theoretical features is provided by Gholson and Barker (1985).

Harlow's later research dealt with developmental failures in rhesus monkeys (Harlow, 1962). Infant monkeys deprived of normal social interactions with other monkeys were found to be inadequate in subsequent sexual behavior, and infant monkeys provided with "surrogate mothers" were found to be inadequate mothers. This work on surrogate mothers is much better known than Harlow's earlier discrimination-learning research, involving as it does issues like "love" in infant monkeys. It also had considerable theoretical impact at the time, since the infants clearly preferred a cloth mother to a wire mother associated with feeding. This preference violated expectations derived from the idea that food reinforcement should be preferred to tactile stimulation.

Harlow's developmental research is clearly related to our next and final example of an S-R development, the work on "learned helplessness." The failure of Harlow's deprived infant monkeys to show subsequent normal sexual and maternal behaviors indicates a kind of specific behavioral "helplessness" that is clearly due to the absence of appropriate environmental stimulation, whereas the learned helplessness next discussed is the consequence of noxious environmental intervention.

The "Learned Helplessness" Phenomenon

"Learned helplessness" is a final illustration of a development in S-R theory which goes far beyond its own stimulating conditions. It also illustrates how the developing product can challenge S-R theory and force it to broaden both its assumptions and its scope. This concept differs from our previous examples because it developed directly out of empirical research. The results of the research were both unexpected and difficult to reconcile with the theoretical framework within which the research was initiated.

In the prototypical experiment (Seligman & Maier, 1967), dogs were harnessed in a typical experimental setting. Subjects trained under learned helplessness conditions were given a series of sporadic and unsignaled, highly painful electric shocks. Neither avoidance of nor escape from these shocks was permitted; nothing the animals did had any effect on the programming of the shocks. A second set of dogs received identical electric shocks but were able to terminate them by pushing a panel. On the following day all the subjects were tested in a standard two-way shuttle box. In this situation both escape and avoidance responses were permitted. The dogs could jump over a hurdle between the two compartments and thereby escape or, if they responded to a signal, avoid the shock. Typical learning of the avoidance response was found in the dogs that had been able to terminate their shocks on the previous day. However, the dogs that had been unable to escape the shocks on the first day performed extremely poorly, behaving as though they were still helpless to influence the outcome. The term "learned helplessness" expresses the presumption that they had learned to do nothing because of the trying and stressful conditions of the first task.

Earlier demonstrations of the importance of the ability to control aversive stimulation had been reported by Mowrer and Viek (1948) for rats allowed to eat in a shock-avoidance situation, and by Marx and Van Spanckeren (1952) for seizure-sensitive rats in a high-frequency sound situation (see Chapter 9), but these researchers did not test the transfer of the deleterious effects of helplessness to other situations.

Extension of the learned-helplessness effect to human subjects has also been reported (Thornton & Jacobs, 1971; Hiroto & Seligman, 1975). The clinical significance of the effect is evident; learned helplessness is related to the problem of human depression.

Maier and Seligman (1976) analyze learned helplessness in terms of motivation, cognition, and emotion. Although there is no doubt some cognitive deficit involved, it appears that the effect is primarily motivational and emotional. The apparent cognitive effect can be regarded as a result of the subject's having "given up." As Thornton and Jacobs' subjects commented, they "had no control over the shocks, so why try?" This kind of generalized apathy transfers all too readily to subsequent stressful situations.

The clinical implications of the learned helplessness effect are described in Seligman's 1975 book and in an article by Abramson, Seligman, and Teasdale (1978). Its theoretical interpretation has been in terms of "superstitious learning" of competing responses during training (Levis, 1976; Black, 1977). Experiments with rats (Weiss, Glazer, & Pohorecky, 1976) add some credence to this interpretation. However learned helplessness is ultimately interpreted, it will require a broadened S-R framework if it is to be accommodated within the S-R approach.

SUMMARY AND CONCLUSIONS

In this chapter we have surveyed several developments within the general framework of S-R theory. They are neobehavioristic and concentrate on the problem of learning. They are most clearly distinguished on the basis of their treatment of reinforcement.

E. R. Guthrie has been the most influential of the American contiguity theorists. He argued that what is called "reinforcement" operates by protecting S-R connections, formed by contiguity per se, from unlearning. Others have argued that reinforcement increases contiguity (Tolman, N. Miller) or brings about the response to be learned (Pavlovians). W. K. Estes has cast Guthrie's contiguity theory into mathematical form, and this has stimulated growth in mathematical modeling in general.

Reinforcement theorists propose some connection-strengthening or response-strengthening mechanism for reinforcement. They have presented a varied set of approaches to learning. Kenneth Spence, Neal Miller, and Ray Denny have played several variations on the Hullian theme, as have Abram Amsel and Frank Logan.

B. F. Skinner's psychology largely replaced Hull's and is in turn being displaced to some extent by cognitive approaches. Skinner believes that theory should be developed inductively and gradually, rather than all at once on the basis of a priori postulates which tend to prescribe what data are to be gathered and how. Skinner seems gradually to be taking a more positive attitude toward theory, perhaps because psychology is maturing. He has been an innovative behavioral technologist, working with language and programmed instruction, as well as a researcher and theorist.

Several two-factor theories supplement the contiguity and reinforcement positions. Beginning with the early demonstration of two apparently independent types of conditioning by Polish researchers Miller and Konorski, these theories typically combine the contiguity and reinforcement positions. The most recent approach by O. H. Mowrer is novel in that it takes contiguity as basic but distinguishes two kinds of reinforcement.

Studies of learned helplessness have broadened the S-R perspective and have suggested clinical implications of learning experience, going beyond the now classical use of behavioral techniques in therapy.

An important conclusion from the wide variety of approaches outlined is that no one procedure can be guaranteed to be more productive than any other. Each approach will help to motivate and organize research. Which kind of research or theory is eventually seen to be most significant must await the verdict of history.

FURTHER READINGS

Guthrie is well represented by his two basic books, *The psychology of learning* (1935) and *The psychology of human conflict* (1938). Estes' early (1950) paper presents the basis of his statistical approach. Spence's adaptation of Hullian theory is given in his *Behavior theory and conditioning* (1956) and in the volume of collected papers, *Behavior theory and learning* (1960). Neal Miller's early work is represented by his 1944 and 1948 papers, his later work by his 1958 and 1964 articles. Of Skinner's many papers and books, the most important early sources are his introductory textbook *Science and human behavior* (1953) and his collected writings, *Cumulative record* (1959b). His utopian novel *Walden two* was published in 1948. His most controversial book was probably *Beyond freedom and dignity* (1971), and his life and career are extensively described in his autobiographical volumes (1976, 1979, 1983). The sources cited in the text are brief enough to serve as introductions to the various two-factor theories and to Amsel, Denny, Logan, and the learned-helplessness literature. Harlow's learning set and error factor work is reviewed in his 1959 article, and his developmental research on affection in his book *Learning to love* (1973). Broader coverages of most of these topics can be found in Koch's *Psychology: A study of a science,* Volume 2 (1959), which contains papers on the Hullian system and its derivatives by Logan and Miller, Guthrie's final systematic paper, Skinner's "Case history in scientific method," and an excellent detailed account of statistical theories up to that time by Estes. Finally, Bower and Hilgard, in their scholarly *Theories of learning* (1981), describe in impressive detail all the theories we have covered.

CHAPTER 12

COMPUTER INFLUENCES

When this chapter was first written in the early 1960s, there was much talk of a computer revolution in psychology, but the chapter was written on a typewriter. Now the author (W.A.C-H.) is writing on a computer keyboard, while his wife composes a test on a second computer in another room. Two computers are replacing two cars in the American dream, as the latter replaced a chicken in every pot. If there is no nuclear war, there will come to be more computers than cars. Thus the superlatives of computer revolutions and computer consciousnesses and computer servants have been replaced with the trivialities of word processors and database systems and spreadsheet programs and integrated software. At the very time that the benefits of computers are coming within our reach, their significance seems to be forgotten; AI (artificial intelligence) has become a buzzword, but now nobody seems to know what it means.

In this chapter, we will try to restore some of the original sense of wonder about computers by pointing out some fascinating connections between philosophy, mathematics, computers, and psychology. The rich interfaces between these disciplines are among the most challenging intellectual territories in the world. But it is sometimes difficult to recognize these challenges; one of the problems is to remove the familiarity from the commonplace so that we can see its significance in a fresh light.

THE MATHEMATICAL CONNECTION

Mathematics is a particular form of logic, which is a linguistic activity. The subject matter of mathematics includes quantities, magnitudes, and relationships between terms. Immanuel Kant said that an area of study was as scientific as it was mathematical, and psychology, according to this criterion, is becoming more scientific at a rapid pace.

Computers use the logical, mathematical linguistic mode. Philosophers, logicians, and mathematicians have naturally had a great deal to say about the capabilities of computers and of people, both of which entities fall within their bailiwicks. Can computers, in principle, do everything that people can do, including being intelligent and conscious? Does all thought take place in linguistic form? If a question can be asked, does that mean that it can be answered? It turns out that some of these questions can themselves be answered, and the answers are surprising. But before we turn to these broader issues, let us review the properties of Estes' model and introduce another useful model. This will help later in examining philosophical questions about the computer-human relationship.

In Chapter 11 we described the early work of Estes. It illustrates the use of mathematics to make science more rigorous, precise, rich, and logical. Estes made some very simple assumptions about the nature of learning and then, via a deductive process, derived an equation which allowed him to make exact predictions about the rate at which organisms should learn. The shape of the learning curve was completely determined by these logical considerations. Estes found it easy to coordinate probability in his model with an empirical concept, probability of response, in the manner depicted in Feigl's diagram shown in Chapter 9. Measurement is the general term for setting up relationships between abstract terms in a calculus or model and empirical observations. Only if measurement succeeds can an abstract system, no matter how aesthetic, rich, or parsimonious, have empirical applications. Estes' one-element model has been valuable because it suggests easy-to-make measurements of probability that test predictions of the model (Bower & Hilgard, 1981, p. 238).

There are two opposite directions from which theorists can come in relating a mathematical system to an empirical system. They can apply existing mathematics to the empirical system without changing the mathematics. Hull and Estes both took this path. Since most scientists are not professional mathematicians, this is the path most frequently taken. Only in the case of Lewin's attempt to use topological concepts (Chapter 7) did we see an attempt to modify the model in the process of applying it to a psychological problem.

Lewin's work shows that, in principle, a theorist might begin from the other direction and try to construct a mathematical model to fit the empirical area of interest. Hull and his collaborators (Hull et al., 1940) developed a special postulational structure in their attempt to account for the phenomena of rote learning. The resulting logical model was too formidable to be of much practical use and so aroused little interest. These examples would lead us to believe that psychologists are generally better off if they use existing mathematical systems rather than trying to invent new ones. History indicates that viable mathematical models are both relatively simple and in a continuing state of intimate interchange with empirical results. As psychologists become more sophisticated with mathematics and computer simulation, the requirement for simplicity may be relaxed, but the second requirement is not likely to become any less stringent.

Mathematics is useful to science because it provides convenient and conventional deductive apparatus for prediction and generalization. There are many types of mathematics, as well as many possible ways to relate each type to empirical problems. One does not need to ask whether it is appropriate to use mathematics, because the ability to generalize is useful, and because mathematics, as conceived of by scientists, is just a tool for accomplishing that.

We now turn to the uses of information theory by psychologists. Information theory is based on traditional mathematical techniques and has proved to be quite striking both in its range of application and in its usefulness within that range.

INFORMATION THEORY

Information Measures

According to Norbert Wiener (1948), no one person can be credited with the development of a measure of information: "This idea occurred at about the same time to several writers, among them the statistician R. A. Fisher, Dr. Shannon of the Bell Telephone Laboratories, and the author" (p. 18). However, Shannon worked most persistently on the theoretical development of information theory and has been most responsible for disseminating the ideas of information theory (e.g., Shannon, 1951; Shannon & Weaver, 1949).

The intuitive arguments that underlie the definition of an information measure can be presented simply. Shannon was concerned with real communication systems, since he was an employee of Bell Telephone. A communication system contains at least a transmitter, a communication channel, and a receiver. A fundamental requirement for developing a theory of communication was the development of a measure of information.

First, assume that only a limited number of alternatives can be communicated via any communication system. For example, assume that an English-speaking radio announcer is transmitting words. We can regard the announcer as choosing from all possible English words a single word to transmit at each interval of time. Until the word is spoken, a person at the receiving end is uncertain about what word will be spoken, but the receiver knows that some English word will be chosen. Seen in this way, the process of information transmission can be treated as a process of reducing uncertainty. If there is no uncertainty remaining after a message is sent and received, then the amount of information transmitted is the same as the amount of uncertainty that existed initially. It seems reasonable that the amount of initial uncertainty should be made proportional in some way to the number of possible messages that might conceivably be sent; the more alternatives there are, the harder it would be to guess which would be sent.

Shannon noted that it would be possible to number all the alternatives using the binary number system. If there were sixty-four alternative messages, any of which might be sent, we could number them in binary notation from 000000, through 000001, etc., to 111111. A six-place binary number is needed to express all the alternatives that would be coded by the decimal numbers 00 through 63.

In general, we can designate 2^N different alternatives with N columns of binary numbers. In the above example of 64 alternatives, we have $2^6 = 2 \times 2 \times 2 \times 2 \times 2 \times 2 = 64$. Shannon lets the number of columns of binary digits required to number the possible messages be the number of units of information. These units of information are called bits, an abbreviation of *bi*nary digi*ts*. If you are told which of 64 possible alternatives is true, you have received six bits of information.

This definition of information measure allows us to express it as a logarithm. In the case we are examining, 6 is the logarithm to the base 2 of 64, because we took 2 as the base which we raised to the 6th power to obtain the 64. (A logarithm is the power to which we raise some base in order to obtain the number in question.) We can express this in conventional mathematical notation as $\log_2 (64) = 6$; verbally, the logarithm to the base 2 of 64 equals 6. We can, therefore, find the number of bits involved in selecting one of a set of equally probable alternatives by taking the logarithm to the base 2 of the number of alternatives. Shannon used H to stand for the number of bits, so the definition becomes $H = \log_2 (N)$.

The use of the simple definition of the number of bits, $H = \log_2 (N)$, is justified only if every message in the set of messages is equally likely to occur. In many cases some messages are more likely than others. "It's snowing" is less likely, and therefore more informative, than "It's sunny" if one lives in southern California. Shannon treats less likely events as more informative in his more general expression for the amount of information contained in receiving a particular message, $H = \log_2 (1/P)$, where P is the probability that the message in question will occur. For example, if an honest die is rolled, the probability that any side will turn up is 1/6. Thus the information in any single roll is the logarithm of 1 divided by 1/6 = 6; a table of logarithms to the base 2 tells us that $\log_2 (6) = 2.58$, so $H = 2.58$ bits. If the die is heavily loaded, it may be that a 1 would come up only 1 time in 16; in this case, when it did come up it would give us $\log_2 1/(1/16) = \log_2 16 = 4$ bits of information. A die that *always* comes up 4 transmits $\log_2 (1/1) = 0$ bits of information when it comes up 4, because we know before we roll it how it will come up.

The context of a message may affect the probability that each possible alternative will be sent. After a particular message occurs, the next message may become very likely; after a q, we definitely expect a u. From the point of view of information theory, we might as well drop all u's after q's, for they add no information in that context. The letter T is often followed by H, but seldom if ever by L. If all symbols from the 26 English letters plus one space were equally likely, each would always carry $\log_2 (27)$, or 4.76, bits of information. As it is, the sequential relationships in English bias the probabilities so much that the estimated information content of continuous text, once the context has been established, lies between 0.6 and 1.3 bits per letter.

Systems of this kind, in which symbols do not carry the maximum possible information, are called redundant. English is therefore estimated to be about three-fourths redundant. Redundancy is not all bad; if information is shared among a number of symbols, the information may be available even though part of the message is missed. For example, the blank in *psychol_gy* can easily be filled in with the missing *o*, for the remaining letters give us sufficient information. In effect, we have the whole message.

Empirical Studies

The foregoing gives enough of the flavor of the orienting attitudes of information theorists that we can appreciate some of the psychological applications of information measures and examine the point of view afforded by the theory. We can ask questions like "What is the capacity of the human being considered as a communication channel?"

Some answers to this question were given soon after information measures were developed. Pierce and Karlin (1957) reported one of the highest rates of continuous information transmission. They had subjects read words aloud as rapidly as possible. The words were read in random order, so that less information would be lost to redundancy. There was, of course, still information lost to sequential effects within the individual words, but it was easy to calculate the information rate because the experimenters had predetermined what the size of the vocabulary was to be. Under these conditions, about 45 bits per second were transmitted.

For a time it seemed that the rate of information transmission by the human channel might be almost independent of the nature of the transmission task, but it soon became clear that this is very far from true. In reading words the information rate equals information per word times words per unit of time. Since the information per word increases with the logarithm of the vocabulary size, larger vocabularies would have to be read proportionately more slowly if the information transmission rate were to remain constant. However, Pierce and Karlin and, even earlier, Sumby and Pollack (1954) found that the reading speed decreases very little as vocabulary size increases. Thus, if the number of syllables per word is held constant, the information rate of reading increases almost as fast as the logarithm of vocabulary size.

In a reading task, subjects transmit information continuously. It is also possible to have subjects observe a single brief presentation of a stimulus and then have them respond at leisure to what was observed. Here the measure is of rate of absorption (and retention) rather than of what we might intuitively feel should be called transmission rate. It may, however, be considered a measure of the channel capacity of the sensory channel involved. G. A. Miller (1956) did an early classic review of studies of human ability to discriminate between stimuli varying along some single dimension; pitch, loudness, pointer position, and square size are examples of the dimensions judged. Surprisingly, the number of values of stimuli which can be discriminated accurately is small, Miller's famous "seven plus or minus two." This number is much smaller than the number of just-noticeable differences along these scales, which might be quite large. However, in the type of situation Miller was discussing, there was no reference stimulus present at the time of judgment, and an absolute discrimination had to be made.

An additional surprising finding was that the spacing along the scale of the values to be discriminated makes little difference in the amount of information transmitted (Attneave, 1959, pp. 67ff.). Garner (1960), however, has found that more information is transmitted by rating scales which use larger numbers of values; the total information transmitted may increase as scale values increase up to 20.

Several experiments (Klemmer & Frick, 1953; Pollack & Ficks, 1953; Pollack & Klemmer, 1954) indicated that increasing the number of dimensions along which stimuli vary increases the number of bits that can be assimilated at a single observation.

Klemmer and Frick, for example, got a transmission value for eight-dimensional stimuli of 7.8 bits, as compared with a value of single-dimensional stimuli of about 3 bits. Quastler, Osborne, and Tweedell (1955) investigated the best combination of number of scales with number of divisions on each scale and found that five or six scales, each divided into five or six scale positions, could be arranged to transmit 12 bits per look. Using three symbols in combination with a dial increased transmission further to 17.6 bits.

MacKay (1952, 1969) made a distinction between two kinds of information content of stimuli which is useful in talking about this set of results and in understanding the way in which humans assimilate information. He called the information carried by the different values along a single scale the *metron* content, and the information carried by the different dimensions the *logon* content. It appears that the metron content increases little after the number of scale values reaches eight, so that additional information can best be carried by increasing the logon content.

Information measures are useful in the study of memory as well as in the study of transmission. Pollack (1954) found that immediate memory span is approximately constant at about seven units, whether the units are binary numbers containing only 1 bit of information per digit, decimal digits containing about 3.32 bits per digit, or letters of the alphabet containing 4.76 bits. It occurred to Smith and Miller (1952) that memory span could be increased if smaller units were coded into units containing more information; at the time of recall, the larger units could be decoded back into the smaller. They had subjects code binary digits three at a time, as follows: $000 = 0$, $001 = 1, 010 = 2, 011 = 3, 100 = 4, 101 = 5, 110 = 6$, and $111 = 7$. After a little practice, subjects could easily code sequences like 111011100010001 into 73421, which was remembered without difficulty. Then subjects could recall the original 15-digit sequence by decoding, thus producing what seemed a remarkable performance to anyone who did not know the procedure. The technique falls only a little short of its theoretical capability of tripling the memory span. This sort of "chunking" is probably a very common feature of human memory and may well account for the apparent increase in memory capacity that occurs when someone becomes an expert in some field. For example, chess experts may remember a whole board position as one chunk.

Information measures have found further application in the description of the perceptual process. Attneave (1954) and Hochberg and McAlister (1953) pointed out the applicability of information measures to Gestalt concepts. They noted that good figures contain less information. It is easier, for example, to predict the continuation of a line from a knowledge of previous portions of the line in a good figure than in a poor one. A circle can be filled in from a knowledge of any short arc, or a triangle from a knowledge of its three corners. Such figures are highly organized, redundant, and "good." Similar informational translations can be given for some of the other Gestalt principles of organization. Information measures are precise measures of organization and should help to bring the qualitative Gestalt principles more fully into the province of quantitative psychology.

Garner (1962) discussed some of the difficulties in making a translation of Gestalt concepts into information terms; problems arise because the Gestalt principles are supposed to apply to single stimuli, whereas information concepts are designed to apply to the characteristics of sets of stimuli. Later, Garner (1966) made a persuasive case for regarding individual stimuli as representative members of a class. He regarded perceiving as analogous to knowing the structure and organization of sets of stimuli. His series of experiments provides an excellent example of the usefulness of the viewpoint provided by information theory, even though very little of the technical apparatus of the theory was used. This seems to be a common feature of narrow mathematical theories; although they have a restricted range, they may suggest useful general approaches to a field.

Posner (1964) is among those who have made extensive use of the information-processing view of human behavior. He suggests, for example, that tasks can be categorized as *conservation* tasks (in which the goal is to transmit information exactly as it is received, as in memory tasks), *reduction* tasks (as in the addition of numbers, in which the goal is to map multiple stimuli into a single response), and *creation* tasks (in which the goal is to make multiple responses to a single stimulus, as in multiple associations). Posner finds predictable empirical relationships between the amount of information transmission required and the adequacy of behavior; for example, reaction time increases as the amount of information reduction increases. Fitts and Posner (1967) organized their book *Human performance* largely around the information model.

Neisser (1964) conducted a series of studies of the process of searching for target words, numbers, faces, and the like in a background of similar items. He found that the search process does not demand that all the information be processed fully and that different tasks may require several different levels of information analysis, from extremely gross to extremely careful. This conclusion can be reached because rates of examination of information differ markedly under different conditions. One of Neisser's more interesting and counterintuitive findings is that experienced scanners can search for multiple targets as quickly as they can search for single targets. For example, an experienced searcher can search a list of any of four names as quickly as for a single name. This kind of search must occur in parallel.

Sternberg (1966) developed an ingenious technique for studying the process of scanning *memory*, rather than scanning external stimuli (see Chapter 13). A subject, having memorized a sequence of symbols, is asked to give a "yes" response if a newly presented symbol was in the remembered sequence and to give a "no" response if it was not. Subjects are asked to respond as quickly as possible. The time required for responding is a linearly increasing function of the number of items held in memory, and it increases in the same way whether or not the probe symbol is an item from the memory set. Sternberg concluded that the search process consists of serial comparisons between the "new" item and those held in memory and that the search is exhaustive even though a match is found (cf. Bower & Hilgard, 1981, p. 359).

Townsend (1974) extended Sternberg's work and paid special attention to the claim that processing in short-term memory is serial and exhaustive. Townsend concluded that a large class of serial and self-terminating models could indeed be eliminated but that several possible models remain. Some parallel models, with appropriate parameter settings, can produce the same predicted performances as serial models.

The foregoing has been a summary of early work using measures and concepts from information theory. We have ignored many important problems as too technical for our overview—for example, the determination of the amount of information transmitted when the transmitter and receiver do not always agree about what message was sent. Attneave (1959) and others who have written books devoted entirely to information theory provide methods for calculating transmitted information, given a knowledge of the inputs to the communication system, outputs from it, and their relationships.

The great strength of information measure is that it is completely general; it applies to every type of "message." The information in binary digits, musical notes, and hormone flow can be measured and compared. The generality is based on the simple but ingenious insight that any finite set of alternatives can be coded by numbering the alternatives. This ability to code any sort of alternative is the foundation stone for the performance of the general-purpose digital computer, which can be programmed to work with moves in a chess game, the simulation of human behavior, or projections for automobile sales. The generality of information measure and of the computer makes both very useful for unifying the points of view of different sciences, like psychology and biology. One can ask questions about whether the quantity of information which is stored in the DNA of the human genome is about the same as the amount contained in a full set of the *Encyclopedia Brittanica*. Before information measures were available, there was no way to answer such a question. (The answer is yes.)

During its formative years, information theory was regarded as a tremendously exciting development, perhaps one which would revolutionize psychology. Now it is just one of our basic tools, like algebra or calculus. Information theory has proved its worth and is as important as, for example, analysis of variance techniques. Those who take an information-theoretic view and whose activities are organized around computers and cognitive psychology have achieved near-paradigmatic status, rivaling and perhaps surpassing in this respect the operant psychologists.

THE COMPUTER IN PSYCHOLOGY

Practical Considerations

Computers have become so ubiquitous in American psychology that it is no longer necessary to describe any but the more remarkable of their capabilities. The changes have taken place very rapidly; a personal computer of today has more computing power than existed in the world 40 years ago. Nearly all mathematical and statistical computations, at least by nonstudents, are now performed by computers. Computers finally, after many years of premature predictions, are playing chess at a master level, although no computer has yet become the champion of the world at this game. Computer operations are routinely performed at a rate of billions per second; a common clock rate in *home* computers now is about 7 million cycles per second. Most departments of psychology have numerous computers and computer terminals at their disposal, and there are few institutions of learning in the United States without access to a computer.

The practical abilities of computers are impressive. They make writing easier for those with a computer or terminal and a word processing program. They make standard statistical calculations trivial, difficult and tedious calculations nearly instantaneous, and erstwhile impossible calculations quite practical. This sort of capability is completely taken for granted. In addition, psychologists increasingly count on the computer to help collect data and control experiments. Many experimenters almost unthinkingly design their experiments so that the data can be collected by computer. The process then continues with computer analysis of data, computer word processing to prepare the manuscript, and computer graphics programs to prepare the figures. In some cases the results are sent to a publisher on disks, or directly over telephone lines to the publisher's computer, which then sets the type. The information can be stored in a computer data bank, which can be accessed by other computers, rather than printed on paper. In the future, increasing amounts of scientific information will be handled only in this more efficient way.

Computers and Philosophy

Thus the speed, patience, and reliability of computers make them wonderful labor-saving devices. When psychologists fully assimilate computers into their ways of working, we can anticipate an ever-increasing deluge of research reports. However, this aspect of computer technology has no more theoretical or philosophical significance than automatic cage-cleaning machines which make it possible to do more animal research. The fact that humans have created computers in their own image makes the computer uniquely fascinating to the psychologist. A computer is humanlike in a functional rather than in a structural sense, at least up to the present time. Androids that mimic human form remain largely a product of science fiction. So far we care little whether the computer physically apes the human being, as long as its answers are "correct," by which we mean the same as a human being would give to the same questions. Thus the computer must be the same as a human being in a logical sense.

At a "molecular" level, there is a logical similarity between human and computer processing elements (Wiener, 1948; Von Neumann, 1958). The classical view of the human neuron had it either responding completely or not responding at all (the "all-or-none law"), just as the computer element was either in one state or in another (expressed as on vs. off, or as 0 vs. 1). Physically, computer elements are larger, faster, fewer, and simpler, at least at the moment. Long ago, as the computer time scale goes, LaBrecque (1970) reported that "Today, microminiaturization has superseded miniaturization, and 100,000 integrated circuits can easily be placed on a single, half-dollar-sized silicon wafer . . . other research aims at developing even more tightly integrated devices, some nearly as compact as the bioelectric system of the human brain" (p. 8). Great progress has been made since LaBrecque wrote those words, and today efforts are directed toward constructing logical elements from individual molecules. When that quest succeeds, we will have substantially outminiaturized ourselves.

We should not lose sight, however, of our primary concern with logical, rather than physical, comparisons. Computer designers want to get the same answers regardless of the physical representation of the logical processes, and they want those answers to remain in agreement with human answers. George Boole (1854) developed an algebra which he intended as an expression of human thought. It turns out that Boole's algebra has found its primary usefulness in the field of mechanized thinking.

It is a two-valued logic based on the notion that elements are either in or out of a set. It works well with binary arithmetic, which works well with the two-valued character of computer elements. Thus Boole's algebra is an abstract model which can be co-ordinated with either human or computer decision processes. It is a perfect example of Diesing's (1971) definition of theory as "a model with one or more interpretations."

The digital computer, like the human being, is able to perform complex tasks using simple elements because complex processes can be broken down into elementary operations which can be performed by simple elements. All possible inputs and outputs (courses of action) can be numbered and are thus ultimately expressible in binary numbers and Boolean algebra. The numbers can be manipulated, compared, and used as a basis for decisions. Thus an Internal Revenue Service computer can reject an income tax return if the information about the individual's income does not agree with information from other sources. A military computer can aim weapons or fire missiles after evaluating threats and computing the paths of targets.

The Limits of Computer Simulation

These behaviors seem all too human; the question becomes whether there are limits to the capabilities of computers so that they cannot simulate all of human behavior. This question is at the hinge of the fascinating logical and philosophical problems mentioned earlier, so let us try to answer it by degrees.

Those with conservative viewpoints on computer capabilities maintain that computers are not capable of intelligent behavior, since they can do only what they are programmed to do. One should not, however, seize this view too eagerly, since "what the computer is programmed to do" may be something like "learn to do this task better." That sounds uncomfortably like what humans are "programmed" to do.

Samuel (1963) wrote a program over 20 years ago which told a computer how to play checkers and how to improve its game as a result of the outcomes of previous games. After the computer had some practice, no doubt a considerable amount, Robert W. Nealy, one of the country's strongest players, played against the computer. His comment was:

> Up to the 31st move, all of our play had been previously published, except where I evaded "the book" several times in a vain effort to throw the computer's timing off. At the 32-27 loser and onwards, all the play is original with us, so far as I have been able to find. It is very interesting to me to note that the computer had to make several star moves in order to get the win, and that I had several opportunities to draw otherwise. That is why I kept the game going. The machine, therefore, played a perfect ending without one misstep. In the matter of the end game, I have not had such competiton from any human being since 1954, when I lost my last game. (Wooldridge, 1968, p. 105)

Wooldridge believes that such computer behavior is adequate evidence of intelligence. Readers can make their own decisions about the adequacy of the evidence. Examples could be given from a number of other fields—chess playing, musical composition, and the like—but essentially the same principles are involved.

Kurzweil (1985) believes that intelligent behavior must combine two attributes: It must be appropriate to the situation, and it must not be totally predictable. He believes that computers are now on the verge of satisfying both conditions. He also points out, however, that the more we understand a process, the less inclined we are to consider it an example of intelligence. Thus checker-playing was considered artificial intelligence in the 1950s, but not now; theorem proving was AI in the early 1960s, but not now. Kurzweil (1985) cites Minsky as saying that if a superior being were to analyze human behavior and understand in great detail how we operate, it might not consider us to be very intelligent either.

We might therefore ask at this point whether or not there are any limits on computer intelligence. Philosophers have long been concerned with limits on *human* intelligence. For example, Kant wondered whether humans could get at absolute knowledge and concluded that they could not; we can contact appearances but not the reality behind them. Wittgenstein (see Kurzweil, 1985) also wrestled with problems of human knowledge and brought forth several pronouncements on the subject. One was "We cannot think what we cannot say." Another was "If a statement can be framed, it can be answered."

These philosophical generalities seem at first blush to have absolutely nothing to do with computers. However, events took a surprising turn, and the disparate areas made unexpected contact through the puzzles and solutions of mathematicians and logicians.

David Hilbert wondered whether it was possible to prove the truth or falsity of any statement in the logical language called the "predicate calculus." The nature of this language need not concern us here, but it was the instrument via which the findings of interest here were made. Alan Turing, a British mathematician, wanted a systematic procedure (algorithm) for proving theorems of the kind that interested Hilbert. He invented the "Turing machine" (1937) to carry out his algorithms. The machine can read a tape containing holes which carry the necessary information. Then the machine can move to the right or left, depending on whether it reads a zero or a one; it can jump to another command; and it can halt. In what was perhaps the ultimate victory for reductionism, Turing proved that his machine could compute anything that any machine, no matter how complex, can compute.

Arbib (1964) notes that Turing's proof implies that *any* well-defined input-output relationship can be simulated by the Turing machine. Thus any relationships described in terms of S-R psychology can be simulated by a simple machine. This is related to a proof by McCulloch and Pitts (1943), who showed that the functions of a digital computer could be carried out by a nerve net, and vice versa. Thus it is reasonable to suppose that the logic of operation of the human nervous system can be simulated exactly by a computer. This conclusion depends, however, on the assumption that the logic of the proofs captured all of the critical properties of the human nervous system. That is a tenuous assumption.

Turing produced another proof that was even more shocking. He found that answers to some perfectly well-defined questions could not be found. Kurzweil (1985) gives an example:

The most famous of these, the Busy Beaver problem, was discovered by Tibor Rado. It may be stated as follows. Given a positive integer N, we construct all the Turing machines that have N states, which is to say N distinct internal configurations (this will always be a finite number); eliminate those that get into infinite loops; and then select the machine that writes the largest number of ones on its tape. The number of ones that this Turing machine writes is called the Busy Beaver of N. Rado showed that there is no algorithm, that is, no Turing machine, that can compute this function for all Ns. The crux of the problem is sorting out those N-state Turing machines that get into infinite loops. If we program what is called a universal Turing machine to simulate all the N-state Turing machines, the simulator itself goes into an infinite loop. (p. 260)

Turing and another mathematician, Alonzo Church, independently postulated that any problem which can be presented to a Turing machine and is unsolvable by the machine is also unsolvable by a human being. Kurt Gödel had already demonstrated that all formal systems of sufficient power generate propositions that cannot be decided. All three men, then, suggest that Wittgenstein was mistaken when he said that any problem that can be framed can be answered.

It has been argued that Gödel's theorem applies to computers but not to people. If this were true, the theorem would suggest limits on the extent to which human thought can be simulated by computers. The argument goes like this: Digital computers are logical machines. As such, they are covered by Gödel's theorem. Human beings are not logical machines; hence they are not covered and not limited. Thus machines cannot completely simulate man.

We disagree that Gödel's theorem applies to computers but not to people. The theorem puts no restrictions on how the logical system is represented—whether by neurons or by transistors, for example—and thus says nothing to limit the possibilities of simulation. Those who seek to put limits on simulation would do better to seek those limits in extralogical areas. Neither Gödel nor Turing nor any other mathematician can produce proofs about the extent to which human experience or human consciousness can be simulated.

All these logical proofs apply both to computers and to human beings. All logical proofs, of course, involve language. Propositions that can be framed in language can be represented in computers or in human beings. The conclusion that computers can, in principle, be as intelligent as human beings seems inescapable. The precise point at which a machine has proved that it is intelligent is a matter for arbitrary decision, and we have already cited Kurzweil's belief that we are constantly raising this criterion. Yet another example can be given from a computer magazine: "Knowledge-based systems aren't intelligent. Rather, they allow for the manipulation and recall of relationships between information instead of the rigid logic traditionally employed." (Barnes, 1985, p. 38).

Barnes, like most people, seems to be reasoning that if she understands what's going on, it can't be intelligent. Perhaps, in a few years, we will be treated to a statement that the world's champion chess-playing entity is a mere unintelligent machine. Among the "unintelligent" knowledge-based systems about which Barnes is speaking are a system which has discovered a molydenum deposit that prospectors had been seeking for 60 years, a system which uses physical data to construct unique new molecular structures, and one which prescribes antibiotics on the basis of symptoms exhibited by the patient.

We believe that arguments about whether computers can be intelligent should have been settled long ago. But logical intelligence is not the only requirement for being human. There may be kinds of intelligence of which the computer is not capable. Only if intelligence is coextensive with the ability to manipulate symbols is it a foregone conclusion that a computer can be as intelligent as a human being. The limitations set by Gödel, Church, and Turing on what questions can be answered and on the power of the systems in which the questions can be framed apply only to systems of symbols. Some human experiences are difficult to express symbolically; for example, how can one express what it is to be in love, or to be nauseated, or to be both at the same time?

Psychologists and computer scientists have devoted little serious attention (as distinguished from science-fictional attention) to the question "Can computers be conscious?" Perhaps the question is too redolent of the philosophical tradition from which psychologists see themselves as emancipated. However, for those who find it meaningful, there is hardly a larger question. Scriven (1963) decided that the question was meaningful and that its answer was yes. His solution to deciding whether or not a computer was conscious sounds simple. Just teach it to understand the question "Are you conscious?" and ask it the question. If it says yes, take its word for it.

Teaching a computer to understand the question would be difficult or impossible. We suggest a somewhat different approach. Progress in science has usually depended upon breaking questions down into smaller parts. We would begin by asking "What are the properties of entities that we call conscious?" Some answers to this question include responsive awareness to the outside world, possession of an inner model of that world, ability to communicate with other entities, possession of a model of the self, the ability to initiate behavior, and continuous analysis of the immediate past (the psychological present). Since there is no definition of consciousness upon which everyone would agree, each person is free to construct his or her own list. We believe that an entity possessing the properties listed above might be accepted as conscious. To our knowledge, nobody is trying to create a conscious computer. The usual science-fiction script has one coming into being accidentally. That could happen, but a conscious computer is likelier to occur as a result of malice aforethought.

A new group of ethical questions, rivaling those that are accompanying advances in biotechnology, would be introduced along with the first conscious computer. Would it be alive? Would it die each time it was switched off and became unconscious? What rights would it have? We can envision the first philosopher-computers speculating in their existential voids, and the first computeristic computers optimistically striving to actualize their potentialities.

All of this must eventually happen if consciousness is simply a matter of interrelationships among parts. If, however, consciousness depends upon the physical constituents of which entities are made, then computers cannot be conscious unless they are made of protoplasm, or are living, or until consciousness is poured onto them, like icing on a cake.

We do not prejudge the question of whether or not computers, or perhaps androids, can be constructed so that they share human experiences; we do believe that this question is separate from the question of computer intelligence. It has been said that man is language, but that statement is simply not true. Humans are without peer as users of language, but it is misleading to speak so loosely that one equates the two. Things as disparate and important as poetry and philosophical puzzles are framed in language, and nobody denies the centrality of language to human endeavors. Still, human existence is not exhausted when we have talked about language; even in our discussion of scientific theory (Chapter 9), in which language plays such a central role, we were careful to point out nonlinguistic features. And of course science is not all of human endeavor, much as we would like to exaggerate its claims to our attention!

Our excursion into computer capabilities and the relationship of computers to humans has helped us to explore some philosophical questions of long standing. Questions can be posed in linguistic systems which cannot be answered within those systems. It is likely that the limitations on computer capabilities with symbolic systems also apply to humans; thus if anything intelligent can be done within those systems, it can be done by humans or by computers. Computer limitations must be sought in other directions, either in limitations on intelligent but nonlinguistic behavior, or in limitations in behaving or experiencing in ways that have nothing to do with intelligence. Consciousness is an aspect of mental life which may have little to do with intelligence. To make a computer more intelligent is not to make it more conscious; the two concepts do not seem to have any definite relationship, although we prefer to believe that human beings are the epitome of both.

At a somewhat more mundane level, it seems certain that computers will continue to play a critical role in psychological research, as distinguished from their role in the more philosophical issues which we have been discussing. Some have suggested (Newell, Shaw, & Simon, 1958; Newell & Simon, 1961) that computer programs can constitute a theory of intelligent human behavior. However, there is a great danger in jumping to the conclusion that because a computer program operates in some particular way, so does the human being. The computer program is like the more traditional mathematical model in this respect; each may allow the correct behavioral prediction to be made, but neither is likely to describe how human beings accomplish what they do.

Kurzweil (1985) has expressed one function of the computer in the construction of cognitive theory very well:

> Before we can run experiments on humans to test alternative theories, we need to have theories to test. One of the best sources for those theories is techniques we have found to work in machines. The fact that an algorithm works in a machine does not prove that the same technique is used in the brain, but it does prove that this is one way that the brain could work, and provides a potential theory that could be subjected to neurophysiological testing (p. 263)

In our upcoming chapter on cognitive psychology, we will see some specific illustrations of the use of computer analogies. For now, we conclude by observing that this analogy has become as dominant a feature of current psychology as behaviorism was in the years between Watson's pronouncements and the end of World War II. We have almost forgotten the precomputer world.

SUMMARY AND CONCLUSIONS

Information theory provides a foundation for the computer revolution, which in turn provides a new foundation for current developments in psychology. Cognitive psychology, which has achieved near-paradigmatic status, often rests on the computer model as its basis. The rigor and precision of mathematical forms of psychology are shared by these computer-related developments. Some philosophical puzzles of long standing have been solved, but others await solutions which must come from outside the realm of logic. It is conceivable that the computer analogy will eventually contribute to our understanding of human consciousness, as developments to the present time have contributed to our understanding of human and computer cognition.

FURTHER READINGS

Raymond Kurzweil's excellent short article (1985), "What is artificial intelligence anyway?" is an introduction to the philosophical problems connected with computers and sketches the views of a person who is solving complex practical problems with computers. For an introduction to the fundamentals, the old books are still good; G. A. Miller's *Mathematics and psychology* (1964) for the general history of mathematical developments; Attneave's *Applications of information theory to psychology: A summary of basic concepts, methods, and results* (1959) for the basic conceptual background of information theory and some early empirical findings; and Miller, Galanter, and Pribram's *Plans and the structure of behavior* (1960) for the use of computer-related concepts in the description of human behavior. Garner's *Uncertainity and structure as psychological concepts* (1962) is excellent as a demonstration of how useful information theory can be in psychological experiments and theories. Wooldridge in his easy piece, *Mechanical man* (1968), provides a nice overview from the point of view of someone who is enamored of the computer revolution. We will suggest readings on more contemporary developments in cognitive psychology following the chapter on that subject.

APPENDIX: DETECTION THEORY

We are relegating one of the most important and useful mathematical developments within the field of psychology to this appendix because its discussion within the body of the chapter destroys the continuity between information theory and computers and cognitive psychology, which is discussed in the following chapter. Also, some previous users of this text indicated that they did not wish to deal with so technical a subject in their courses. Nevertheless, we believe that detection theory has been so important historically, and remains so useful in contemporary psychology, that we should continue to sketch its development for those who do want to cover it.

Detection theory was developed during World War II by engineers who wanted a mathematical description of devices, in particular radar receivers, which were designed to detect targets. Tanner and Swets (1953, 1954) and Smith and Wilson (1953) were quick to adopt the mathematical treatment and apply it to problems in human detection. These theorists and many others have since extended the theory and applied it to areas rather remote from target detection, for example to the description of memory and the optimization of diagnostic decisions.

Egan (1975) describes signal detection theory (SDT) as a combination of decision theory and distribution theory. We will describe part of the decision theory aspect, since it is the most generally applicable, and just touch on the distribution theory aspect in our attempt to indicate the power and range of the theory.

SDT thus involves statistical *decision* theory. A detection involves a decision based on statistical considerations rather than an absolute statement of the form "Yes, I heard the signal." or "No, I did not hear the signal." Detection theory regards the experiment which attempts to determine a sensory threshold as a kind of game between subject and experimenter. According to this view, the subject would always claim to have heard the signal, having heard it or not, if it were known in advance that it would always be presented. This does not mean that subjects should simply be regarded as dishonest; it means that there is no sharp division between detecting and not detecting a signal, and the subject must therefore *always* make a decision based on probabilistic rather than certain information. Subjects should make the best decision based on the information available, whatever the source of the information. They are somewhat like intelligence gatherers, who must rely on uncertain information provided by spies, satellites, newspapers, informants, and so on, in coming to a decision about the intentions of an opponent.

Since decisions must be based on probabilistic rather than on certain information, they are often influenced by the values or costs that may be associated with making them and being right or wrong in the decision. The values and costs associated with being right or wrong about each possible decision determine a *payoff matrix*. If there are only two possible decisions—for example, "Yes, a signal was presented," or "No, a signal was not presented"—the payoff matrix will have only four entries. An example is given in Table 12-1. According to the matrix, the subject gains 10 units (say, 10 cents) for saying it was presented when it was, but loses 5 units (5 cents) for saying it was not when it was. An incorrect decision when a signal was not presented entails a 1-cent loss, but a 1-cent gain results from a correct decision. It is intuitively clear that given this payoff matrix, cases where the probability that a signal was presented is about equal to the probability that no signal was presented should be resolved in favor of it having been presented. More will be gained if this turns out to be right than will be lost if it is wrong; putting it another way, more can be gained by saying "yes" correctly than by saying "no" correctly.

TABLE 12-1
PAYOFF MATRIX FOR DETECTION EXPERIMENT

	Subject's decision	
Signal presented?	Yes	No
Yes	10	−5
No	−1	1

If at first this theory seems not to apply to real-life situations, consider some interesting examples of decision making under uncertain conditions, where values and costs are obviously involved.

Case 1 You are at a party, and you think you detect a possible sign of interest on the part of an attractive person of the opposite sex. The circumstances are such that there will be appreciable embarrassment if you are mistaken.

Case 2 Your wife thinks she hears a burglar downstairs. You do not think it is a burglar. Could you be looking at different value-cost matrices?

Case 3 An airline pilot on a landing approach glimpses something ahead through the haze of wispy clouds. Evasive action will frighten passengers and crew and strew carry-on baggage all around the cabin.

Another factor combines with the payoff matrix in biasing decisions. This is the advance, or a priori, probability that a signal will be presented. Again our intuition tells us that if we know in advance that signals will be presented in nine intervals out of ten, we should say "signal presented" in uncertain cases. The a priori probability, in conjunction with the payoff matrix, determines a criterion—a number—usually called *beta*, with which a number derived from the sensory observation should be compared in order to make the best decision. If the number derived from the sensory input exceeds the criterion, the ideal observer says "signal"; if it does not, the ideal observer says "no signal."

The criterion value is chosen so that some function is maximized. It is assumed that the ideal observer wishes to make decisions such that the greatest gain will be obtained, the most correct decisions made, or some other desirable goal achieved. Peterson, Birdsall, and Fox (1954) have discussed possible goals and have developed for each the equations which combine the a priori probabilities and payoff matrix to determine the optimum criterion value.

Two probabilities must be computed in order to derive the most useful number from the sensory observation. The first is the probability that *if* a signal had been presented, the observed sensory input would have occurred. The second is the probability that the observed sensory input would have occurred if no signal had been presented. The first probability is then divided by the second to form the *likelihood ratio*. This likelihood ratio is compared with the criterion in order to reach an optimal decision, as outlined above. It can be shown that the likelihood ratio contains all the information an observer needs to make an optimal decision. This fact vastly simplifies the decision process, as compared, say, with the necessity to remember exactly what the detailed signal was.

The reader may be wondering at this point what sense it can possibly make to consider the probability that a sensory input would occur if no signal were presented. Such a probability becomes reasonable on the assumption that there is always random stimulation, or noise, present in any sensory system. The name generally given to a sensory system within detection theory is *receiver*. As far as a receiver is concerned, there are two kinds of noise. One comes from the outside world, and the other from the receiver's own workings. When the receiver is a human observer, the internal noise is usually called *neural* noise. Such internal noises could never be completely eliminated, even if it were possible to eliminate noise at the receiver input. The origin of the noise, as far as the performance of the detector is concerned, is irrelevant. Any noise will degrade the performance of the system. Most people have had the experience of hearing unearthly noises emanating from the television set, to which they respond, "Was that the set (internal noise) or the station (external noise)?" The reader by this time should also have noted the possibility that the "unearthly noise" might have been produced by, say, a rock music group—which gives us all the elements for a detection problem, if it is assumed that rock music groups produce signals.

The determination of the necessary probabilities for the computation of a likelihood ratio is not a trivial accomplishment. It is this determination which distinguishes detection theory from decision theory in general. This is where distribution theory comes into the picture. One must determine the nature of the distributions from which the likelihood ratio is to be determined. One basic difficulty in associating a likelihood ratio with a sensory input is that inputs may be given as continuous waveforms, while statistical decision theory is intended to work with discrete numerical measurements. If the waveform has certain properties, it can be characterized, without loss of information, by a limited number of measurements. The number of measurements required depends on the highest frequency present in the waveform (W) and the length of time (T) over which the waveform is to be measured: the number of measurements required is exactly $2WT$. Still other difficulties have to be overcome before the signal and noise can meaningfully be compared: the reader who is interested in the details of this problem may consult Licklider (1959). Green and Swets (1974) also treat this problem, as well as other psychologically relevant aspects of detection theory, in their excellent book.

Figure 12-1 is a general block diagram of the ideal observer as visualized in detection theory. Let us now examine an experimental situation in conjunction with this block diagram in order to get a clearer idea of how detection theorists think about signal detection.

Two general types of situations are usually treated. An observer must say either whether or not a signal was presented within a single fixed time interval or which of

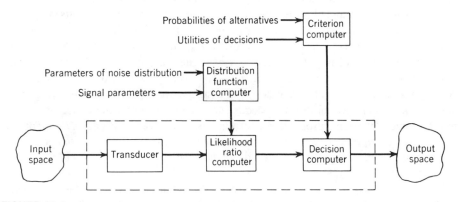

FIGURE 12-1
Block diagram of ideal observer in detection theory. (*Source: Tanner, 1961.*)

several specified intervals contained a signal, knowing that one of them did. It is simpler to talk about the former situation, although it is easier to relate the theory to the latter. In the multiple-interval case, the subject's best strategy is just to choose the interval containing the sensory event with the largest likelihood ratio; the a priori probabilities, the payoff matrix, and hence the criterion are the same for all the intervals. Subject errors in assessing or combining the criterion factors therefore do not affect the decision.

In the other case, in which the subject must say whether or not a signal occurred in a single interval, a number of types of errors may occur. The subject might not use the correct a priori probabilities, might not use the correct payoff matrix, might not try to maximize the desired quantity, or might not combine the factors correctly to do so. In addition, subjects under either condition might not compute the likelihood ratio correctly.

Consider the block diagram as it relates to the single-interval case. It is simplest to assume that the distribution-function computer is given the signal-plus-noise and the noise-alone distributions so that they need not be computed from experience. The distributions must be available so that the likelihood ratio can be computed from its two component probabilities. The signal-plus-noise distribution gives the probability that any given observation would occur on a signal trial. The noise-alone distribution gives the probability that any given observation would arise on a noise-alone trial.

The a priori probabilities that signal plus noise or noise alone will be presented on a particular trial are needed by the criterion computer. The payoff matrix would also be necessary to its computation of the criterion. These quantities would be combined so that some goal would be best achieved. This determines the criterion which must be exceeded by the likelihood ratio in order that the observer say "signal."

With the distributions and the criterion in hand, the ideal observer is ready to begin its observations. An input is presented within an interval. The observer takes the sample through its transducer, which performs the necessary measurements. The output of the transducer is fed into the likelihood computer along with the distribution functions for the two distributions. This information is sufficient for the likelihood-ratio computer to compute its output. The decision computer need only compare the likelihood ratio with the criterion computed by the criterion computer in order to make its decision.

Figure 12-2 illustrates some other concepts of SDT. This figure is based on the assumption that sensory events can be represented along a unidimensional "observation axis." The observations might represent, for example, very faint sounds at the left and very loud sounds at the right end of the axis. Both the N (noise alone) events and the SN (signal plus noise) events are assumed to distribute normally with equal variances. That is, the relative probabilities of occurrence of values along the observation axis are represented by normal probability distributions. We have chosen these assumptions for the sake of simplicity of exposition. The axis and distributions needed for application to a particular detection problem would depend on the actual distributions of the events being modelled.

In our case, the measure of detectability of the signal, d', is the distance between the means of the N and SN distributions, with the units of d' taken to be the standard deviation of the N distribution. We must also compute the criterion value for the

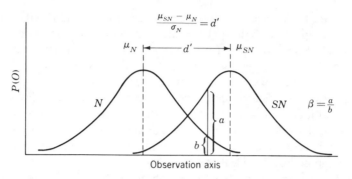

FIGURE 12-2
A visualization of some concepts of the theory of signal detectability. See text for explanation.

likelihood ratio, which we recall is called *beta (β)*. We can then find some point along the observation axis at which the ordinate of the *SN* distribution (*a* in the figure) divided by the ordinate of the *N* distribution (*b*) will equal the criterion value of the likelihood ratio (β). For this case, all observations to the right of that point should be called *signal* and all observations to the left of that point *noise*. Since the two distributions overlap, even an ideal, perfect observer will only "hit" the signal when it occurs *and* the observation associated with signal occurrence happens to fall to the right of the cutoff. The observer will mistakenly say that the signal is presented, even though noise alone is presented (this is called a *false alarm*), if the noise produces an observation to the right of the cutoff. The total probability of a hit is thus given by the area under the *SN* curve which is to the right of the cutoff. Similarly, the probability of a false alarm is the area under the *N* curve which is to the right of the cutoff.

The observer is free to move the cutoff to either the right or the left. Moving it to the right will result in fewer false alarms but also in fewer hits. Moving it to the left will result in more hits but also in more false alarms. We shall see in a moment how movement of the criterion traces out a "receiver operating characteristic" curve. At this point, we should note that the sensitivity (measured by d') and the criterion (β) are separated by detection theory; thus measures of sensitivity are more likely to remain constant over situational changes that might affect a subject's criterion setting.

A perfect performance would be defined by the observation that the subject always said "signal" when a signal was in fact presented and never said "signal" when noise alone was presented. As we have seen, a perfect performance would be possible only if the N and SN distributions had no overlap. The goodness of imperfect performances must always be described as a certain relationship between the probability of a hit, $P_s(S)$, and the probability of a false alarm, $P_s(N)$. Since $P_s(S)$ and $P_s(N)$ can be determined from the value of d', the reverse computation, plus certain assumptions, will give d' if one knows $P_s(S)$ and $P_s(N)$. This is indeed fortunate when d' is to be computed for the human observer, for in this case it is not possible to measure the noise distribution which is presented to the distribution-function computer or, for that matter, to measure the signal-plus-noise distribution. The neural noise cannot be directly measured. Instead, the experimenter computes what d' would have to be for the ideal observer to duplicate the observed values of $P_s(S)$ and $P_s(N)$. The required d' can then be compared with the higher value of d' computed from whatever physical measures the ideal observer would use. Actual observers can never perform better than (and probably never quite as well as) the ideal observer. Thus the theory is "normative" in that it allows us to say how well an observer "ought" to do. Further, the theory allows us to postulate that an ideal observer is limited to less-than-perfect information, and it also allows us to compare this limited performance with that of a human observer; if the limited ideal is very like the human, there is some possibility that the human is actually processing sensory information under the same limitation that we have imposed on our ideal observer.

The d' values so far obtained for human observers have shown good consistency for a given individual over a considerable range of values of a priori probability and payoff matrix. It is this consistency which represents perhaps the greatest victory of detection theory, for this consistency cannot be achieved by the traditional theory based on thresholds. The threshold has been found to vary with conditions. Corrections for guessing cannot eliminate inconsistencies in threshold. Psychophysicists were coming to regard thresholds as significant only under the specified conditions in which the threshold had been determined. The d' measure, with its greater generality, escapes this limitation. If d' has been determined for a particular pair of values $P_s(S)$ and $P_s(N)$, then the pairing of other values of $P_s(S)$ and $P_s(N)$ can be given with greater generality (for a particular subject, as values in the payoff matrix and a priori probabilities are changed).

The ability to do this derives from the fact that d' determines a receiver operating curve, or ROC. Figure 12-3 shows a set of such curves. The diagonal line represents chance performance; we note that an observer who gives no false alarms cannot ever correctly call out "signal." However, an observer willing to call "signal" each time will always be correct *if* the signal is presented and always incorrect if the noise is presented. The diagonal line is the only possible ROC if d' equals 0; as d' increases, the ROC moves further from the diagonal line. There is never any sudden shift to a new level of responding as the signal and noise are made more discriminable, as a naive view of the threshold concept might suggest. Swets (1961) reviewed several versions of threshold theory and showed that the modifications required to bring threshold theory into line with empirical results may so complicate it that it begins to look quite similar to detection theory. Swets (1964) has also collected many of the experimental papers on detection theory into an easily available set of readings.

Detection theory has been useful for predicting results in sensory psychology, particularly in vision and audition (Carterette & Cole, 1962). This is not surprising, since the theory was developed for handling "sensory" problems. An unexpected bonus, however, has been the application of detection theory to problems in memory (Egan, 1958; Banks, 1970; Lockhart & Murdock, 1970). As we have mentioned, the theory has close relationships to the more general theory of statistical decisions and therefore applies in part to games and to statistical testing. Detection theory thus has surprisingly broad application, and its future importance in psychology seems assured. Techniques have been developed which make it possible to apply traditional tests of significance to the parameters of detection theory (Dorfman & Alf, 1968, 1969), thus integrating

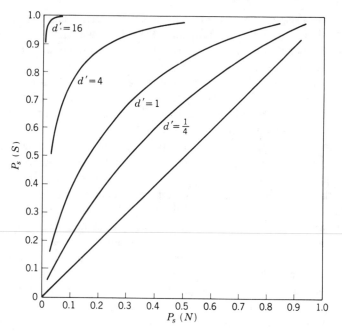

FIGURE 12-3
Receiver operating curves of varying values of *d'*. (*Source: Peterson, Birdsall, & Fox, 1954.*)

it even more closely with traditional statistics. Green and Swets (1974) provide an invaluable bibliography of empirical research using SDT. The bibliography is classified by topics, among them attention, medical diagnosis, memory, and personality. It would be hard to find a better overview of the applications of SDT than browsing through their bibliography and then referring to the articles that struck one's fancy.

Now let us summarize some of the concepts presented so far in this section. The primary datum for the detection theorist is a *decision* made by the observing organism (or observing equipment). The observer is playing a game (in the mathematical sense) and trying to win, rather than describing a sensory experience. If the organism has information that the a priori probability that a tiger is present is equal to 1.00, it does not even listen to present stimuli; it does not introspect; it runs. The observer in the psychophysical experiment is regarded as a similar expression of a tendency for an adjustive organism to use whatever information *should* be related to a decision, with no prejudice that all relevant information is given on a sensory channel on a particular trial. This point of view resembles the functionalist point of view in its emphasis on adaptation, and it is behavioristic in its acceptance of the overt decision as the significant experimental datum. It is modern in its use of a mathematical system as a model; it shows the impact of another modern influence of mathematics on psychology in its relationship to game theory (see Birdsall, 1953). Its realm of relevance is limited, and its specificity is often very high; yet the theory has sufficient generality so that experimental results which had seemed to disagree can be related in a consistent and meaningful way. Despite the fact that the theory is specific and hence sensitive to experimental results, it is not so rigid that it must fall whenever any deviation of experiment from theory occurs; it can be modified to accommodate, to some extent, new and unexpected results.

Both detection theory and information theory represent what may be considered a new middle of the road for psychological theory. They strike a balance between specificity and generality, and between sensitivity and flexibility. Both bodies of theory are quite rigorous compared with the theory and systems of yesteryear, and neither takes all psychological knowledge for its province. Both theories have runners that cross into other gardens; or, to be more accurate, their roots are actually in engineering gardens and their runners in psychology. Finally, they are not isolated from each other or from other theories in terms of the people interested in them, the disciplines involved, or the problems treated. On one level of generality, they have much in common. Both theories deal with signals in a mathematical way, both originated in the study of equipment, and both apply in a most satisfying manner to the study of human beings. Both are heavy in considerations of probabilities of messages or signals, respectively. Neither is divorced from the study of cybernetics—here one could note again Wiener's discussion of information measures in his book entitled *Cybernetics* (1948/1961). As we saw earlier, computers play a role in the thinking of all who are interested in these areas. In fact, there is a very broad sense in which "information theory" or "information-processing theories" can be used to mean those theories which use concepts from all the fields discussed in this chapter: statistical communication theory (informaton theory in the narrow sense), computer simulation, detection theory, and cybernetics. All these theories must come together in the complete robot. If a complete robot existed, it would be a walking model of human behavior.

CHAPTER 13

COGNITIVE PSYCHOLOGY

The so-called "cognitive revolution" of the past quarter century has been extremely influential, and its effects are still growing. The radical behaviorism that played so important a role in the 1940s and 1950s had not been banished but is no longer dominant. The "higher mental functions" of early twentieth-century psychology are once again in vogue. Because cognitive psychology owes much to our forebears, many psychologists with historical interests prefer to speak of a cognitive "renaissance" rather than of a cognitive revolution. Still other psychologists, most of them from the behavioristic tradition, see the current excitement about cognitive psychology as a tempest in a teapot. The consensus view, however, is that the study of cognition is now central to psychology.

This chapter reviews some of the major facets of cognitive psychology. We first consider the problem of definition, outline the distinguishing characteristics of the study area, and relate it to its background. We then present a brief description of some of the most historically significant cognitive researches. The role of consciousness is next critically examined, and problems in both conscious and nonconscious information processing are described to illustrate contemporary cognitive research activities. We conclude the chapter with a discussion of the implications of cognitive psychology and an estimate of its future role.

CHARACTERISTICS OF COGNITIVE PSYCHOLOGY

Cognitive psychology is concerned with central, "mental," structures. That is its big difference from behavioral psychology. Chomsky's criticisms of Skinner's proposals on verbal behavior began with a statement of amazement that Skinner would try to account for the facts of language without postulating any particular structure for the organism. Gestalt psychology, another of the sources of a cognitive approach, postulated physiological structure to account for perceptual and behavioral events. Our computer engineers and programmers have taught us about objective central structures and procedures that process information. The models of human cognition deriving from the computer and information-processing approaches have helped to motivate and justify the growing centralistic tendencies that are at the core of cognitive psychology.

During the very early formative years of cognitive psychology, Great Britain was under the behavioristic thumb less than the United States. Thus two of their famous psychologists can now be seen as harbingers of the new view (Anderson, 1985). The first was Sir Frederic Bartlett, who talked about cognitive structures (schema) even before the first world war. The second was Donald Broadbent, who developed theories of attention after World War II. Once their ideas coalesced with others related to the computer model, new ways of viewing human performance began to emerge. Broadbent emphasized the limited channel capacity which was controlled by attentional mechanisms. Barlett showed how memory can be distorted by schema within which memories fit, and how inference was part of a reconstructive process which produced what passed for memory. The computer model reinforced old Gestalt ideas about the distinction between memory storage and memory retrieval, and, consistent with Bartlett's notions about schema, encouraged the search for the internal representations and structures of memory. Computer data processing shaded over into "cognitive processing" by humans, one example of which was alleged to be the grammatical transformations underlying speech construction and language understanding. All the while, structures were inferred more from objective observations than from introspection, thus demonstrating that a debt was owed to behaviorism.

There is a general picture of the human being that emerges from the cognitive perspective. We are active gatherers of information relevant to decisions. Information from the environment comes in through the senses and is processed (coded) for storage in a systematic, probably hierarchical, arrangement for later use. It is later decoded and combined with other available information so that action can be intelligently guided. The remainder of this chapter will help to fill in this picture.

THE PROBLEMS OF COGNITIVE PSYCHOLOGY

Narrowly defined, cognition refers to knowledge. Broadly defined, however, the term covers practically the full range of mental functions, and a complete cognitive psychology must attempt to answer a corresponding range of questions.

First, there is the question of how knowledge is acquired. We must consider two fundamental psychological functions: (1) perception, the process by which environmental energies are detected and interpreted by the organism, and (2) learning, the process by which new ideas and behaviors are acquired.

Second, knowledge must be retained, if it is to be of any real use to the organism—and this fact brings in the problem of memory. Then the various ways in which knowledge is used have to be considered. To mention some of the more prominent uses, there are thinking and reasoning, both contributing to the enhancement of knowledge (as in "understanding"), and problem solving and decision making, both enabling the organism to deal more effectively with complex situations that call for action.

If knowledge is to be retained and used, then it must be *represented* internally in some form. Two general categories of representation have been suggested. The first is in a perception-based form; for example, we may have visual or auditory images of past events. The general term for memory of particular events is *episodic* memory (memory for episodes). Such memory is probably perception-based to a considerable extent. The second form of representation is in terms of propositions or meanings. This corresponds rather well to *semantic* memory, which refers to abstract representations of the meanings of things, of general principles. This form of representation is probably close to what we mean by a linguistic, abstract, representation. Examples might be our knowledge of mathematics or grammar or scientific laws. It has been suggested that humans develop from a stage in which their representations are almost exclusively perception-based to a more abstract stage, although Anderson (1985) says that this speculation has been difficult to test.

THE INFORMATION-PROCESSING MODEL

Although cognitive psychology can be conceptualized in many ways, the most prominent model derives from the information-processing paradigm. Many cognitive psychologists use this framework to conceptualize their key problems: how organisms collect (perception), code (learning), store (memory), interpret (reasoning), and express (language and other behavior) information.

The information-processing diagram shown in Figure 13-1 is representative of many such efforts by cognitive psychologists to indicate how information might be handled by the human organism. These hypothetical accounts vary in their details, but they often share some key features. Their general similarity to computer flowcharts means that they are well suited to describing the flow of information, and their overall meaning is reasonably clear. However, they often incorporate several functions into single central blocks, and the relationships *among* these functions are not always clear. In this respect, these diagrams reveal the strengths and weaknesses which modern cognitive theories often share with the older Gestalt theories of problem-solving.

As Lachman, Lachman, and Butterfield (1979) point out, "The information-processing approach has . . . provided psychologists with a fundamentally new way of thinking about people . . . viewing the human being as an active seeker and user of information" (p. 10). These authors acknowledge that the approach "seems to work best in accounting for people's ability to accomplish familiar, well-learned operations" (p. 10) but is more limited in other behavioral areas (for example, in individual differences, emotional control, adjustment, and abnormal behavior). They conclude that the information-processing approach cannot explain all features of human behavior but that it does a more adequate job of making sense of some human skills than any alternative approach. Furthermore, the range of its applicability is being enlarged, as by extension to such fields as developmental, social, and even clinical psychology.

This approach has encouraged the development of a more analytic view of the

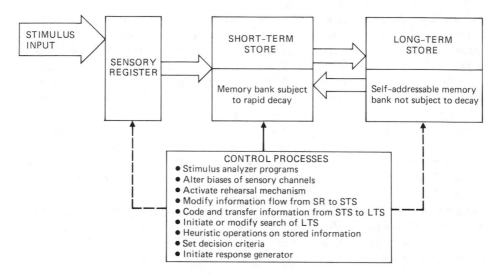

FIGURE 13-1
A flowchart of the memory system. Solid lines indicate paths of information transfer. Dashed lines indicate connections which permit comparison of information arrays residing in different parts of the system; they also indicate paths along which control signals may be sent which activate information transfer, rehearsal mechanisms, and so on.

human as an information-handling system. Memory is broken into several subsystems. A brief "memory" is said to reside in each sensory system. For example, our eyes hold an image for a very brief period, during which information is available to the next stage for further processing. This first stage is called *sensory memory*. Beyond that stage is a postulated second stage which holds the information for a longer, but still brief, period. This stage is the *short-term memory* (STM), and information in this stage is coded in a form different from that of the first stage. Finally, some information is transferred into a third stage, the *long-term memory* (LTM). Here it is held for an indefinite period of time. Some information may never go into LTM, and some information in LTM may not be retrievable. Many studies have examined factors which determine whether or not particular kinds of information will be stored and whether or not it can be retrieved. A general finding is that information which is subjected to "deeper" processing is more likely to be remembered at a later time.

This discussion of processing implies that there are other components in the usual information-processing model. One of these components is a central processor, which manipulates information in a *purposive* manner. Sensory information is combined with the data retrieved from memory in order to solve problems. At every stage, there are limitations on the capacity to handle information; sometimes these limitations are attributable to attentional mechanisms, and sometimes simply to the limited capacity of the channel under consideration. Finally, the decisions of the central executive mechanisms influence the choice of response, and responses are themselves under the control of special mechanisms that sequence and coordinate them. The consequences of responses become sensory feedback which in its turn influences subsequent data processing and later responses.

Significant characteristics of the information-processing model include its analytic nature, the usual serial and sequential picture of events, a hierarchical organization of activity, and inferred central processes, all of which are likely to be represented in the form of a flowchart. Recent versions of this type of model borrow increasingly from computers for their analogies to human cognition. We now turn to an experiment which exemplifies this approach, and then to one which illustrates the involuntary aspects of some cognitive processes.

CLASSIC EXPERIMENTS

Cognitive psychology is so broad that a few experiments cannot represent it adequately. Nevertheless, illustrative work can impart some of the flavor of contemporary cognitive research. The experiments next described, and the research problems discussed later in this chapter, illustrate the kinds of issues that are being investigated.

The series of experiments by Saul Sternberg, already referred to briefly in Chapter 12, have been among the most influential in the field. Sternberg has shown that a simple reaction time measure can help to reveal the structure of very complex mental operations. Our second illustration, the Stroop effect, shows the interplay of cognitive processes below the level of consciousness.

Memory Scanning

Sternberg adapted a technique initially used by F. C. Donders (1862). The original problem was to find out how long it takes the human being to carry out various mental processes (see the discussion of the subtractive procedure in Chapter 2). The time for response in simple reaction-time (RT) tasks was subtracted from the time for response in complex (choice) RT tasks in order to find out how long it took to choose. In a simple RT task the subject only has to make a specified response as quickly as possible when the stimulus occurs. In a choice RT task the subject has to make the same kind of response to one stimulus but withhold response when the other of two alternative stimuli occurs. Donders assumed that the more complex task was composed of independent parts, with the longer RT typically found with the more complex task caused by the simple addition of another mental operation. However, the task was changed between the simpler and the more complex situations, and it was never clear that the assumption that the tasks were independent was warranted. Thus for many years this type of research was out of favor.

Sternberg revived the technique and made it more defensible by changing and simplifying the difference between the conditions being compared. Subjects were required to make the same decision under all conditions. His subjects were first shown a "memory set" containing a number of items—for example, several digits. Then the subjects' task was to indicate, as quickly as possible, whether a test stimulus presented after the memory set had been well learned was a member of the memory set. Thus the subject responded "yes" if the item was part of the memory set and "no" if it was not. Repeated "probe" stimuli were presented, and the subject was told to respond as rapidly as possible, consistent with the requirement to be accurate.

Sternberg discovered that the observed RTs were a consistent positive linear function of the number of items in the memory set. Figure 13-2 shows this relationship. Adding a single member to the memory set produced about the same increment in RT, regardless of the initial number of items, within the range used (typically one through six items); the function was made up of a constant representing the minimal time to respond, plus another constant time for processing each item multiplied by the number of items to be processed.

It is interesting enough that such a simple and consistent mathematical relationship was found, but it is even more interesting that the findings have such clear implications for the cognitive processes which must underlie responding in this situation. As we said in Chapter 12, Sternberg explained that these results are consistent with the assumption that the subject makes an *exhaustive and serial* search of memory. That is, the test item is compared with the memory representation of each of the items in the positive set, one after another. The search continues even if one of the early items in the positive set matches the probe item.

Such an assumption of exhaustive search is counterintuitive, because logically it appears that the search should be terminated as soon as the test digit is matched. Thus a *self-terminating* search would be more consistent with a commonsensical point of view. But the data very definitely indicate that the search is exhaustive. Every item added to the memory set produces the same increment in RT, and the *yes* RTs, which

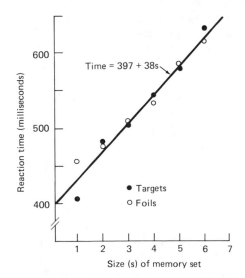

FIGURE 13-2
Time to recognize a digit increases with the number of items in the memory set. (*Source: Sternberg, 1969.*) The straight line represents the linear function that fits the data best.

would be shorter if the search were self-terminating, typically show exactly the same relationship to set size as the *no* RTs, which logically require an exhaustive search.

Once the data required an exhaustive search model, it was easy to find logical arguments to support it. Sternberg estimated that each additional item inserted into the positive memory set required an additional 38 ms of processing time. This means that about 25 to 30 such items can be scanned per second. Sternberg (1969) contended that an item could be scanned faster than a decision could be made about whether a match had been found. Thus it is more efficient to allow the memory scan to run its course, checking every item, and then to decide yes or no only once at the end of the scan, rather than to make a yes/no decision after every item. Sternberg later (1975) pointed out a comparable situation in some telephone exchanges, where computers scan exhaustively because, for them as apparently for people, that is the most efficient procedure.

Sternberg's procedure produced reliable and interesting results, where the method of Donders had failed to do so, because Sternberg worked with a task which did not change except for the addition of items. Donders, and Wundt when he adopted Donders' procedure, changed the *nature* of the processing task as well as the *number* of items to be processed in their version of the subtractive procedure. It now appears that one can subtract *items,* but not psychological *functions,* from one another.

Sternberg's series of carefully controlled experiments was a model of scientific ingenuity and stimulated a host of similar researches on a variety of cognitive problems. The success of his experimental program is reflected in the statement that "over the past decade it has sometimes seemed as though half of the cognitive psychologists in North America were devoting themselves to testing Sternberg's theory" (Lachman, Lachman, and Butterfield, 1979, p. 156).

Sternberg's experiments are excellent exemplifications of the information-processing approach. Sternberg arrived at a clear and aesthetic formulation which included a flowchart describing the comparison of the information in the memory set with the targets and distractors. The flowchart was coordinated with the linear equation describing the relationship between set size and reaction time. Neither the flowchart nor the equation could be obtained via introspection; it is more than doubtful that one experiences the process as involving *exhaustive* search. Thus the results are counterintuitive, and that adds both to their appeal and to the prestige of this approach to cognitive processes.

The Stroop Effect

In contrast to the memory-scan experiments, which make use of rather commonplace mental functions, experiments on the Stroop effect (Stroop, 1935) depend upon a simple but unusual set of circumstances. The subject in such an experiment is told to report the color of a presented cue, typically a word, and to disregard its meaning. Normally, of course, this would be an easy task. However, if the word *yellow* is printed in, say, *blue* ink, the subject is almost invariably inhibited in making the response "blue." Apparently the activation of two conflicting color responses, one cued by the ink color and the other by the color name, interferes with the normally smooth naming of the color. Even noncolor words with strong color connotations, such as *grass* or *banana,* produce a significant slowing in naming a conflicting ink color (Klein, 1964).

Somewhat surprisingly, when the subjects' task is switched to reading the color word ("yellow," in the example above) when it is printed in a different ink color (blue, for example) they can do so without showing the same kind of interference. It may be that most people have had more practice in reading words in several shades or colors than in the opposite operation, so that the response becomes less sensitive to interference from the conflicting color cue (Posner, 1973).

An important conclusion to be drawn from the Stroop-effect research is that there are multiple, complexly interacting activations of names in memory and that such activations are largely unconscious. The Stroop effect shows that subjects are unable to ignore such activations even when they are told that the associations are irrelevant to the task. The Stroop effect is therefore an excellent illustration of the way in which chains of associated memory traces interact quite apart from any conscious intentions.

An indication of the generality of such interactions is the demonstration by Warren (1972) of a Stroop-like effect resulting from the presentation of a word already in an activated condition, or even of a category name of such activated items. In this extension of the Stroop effect, subjects were first shown and instructed to remember sets of three words (for example, maple, oak, elm). They were then shown single words and asked to name the ink color as rapidly as possible. When the subject was shown a word from the memorized set (that is, one of the tree names) or the category name (tree), the color naming was again inhibited.

We conclude our discussion of the Stroop effect with a story for whose veracity we cannot vouch. If seems that a man was accused of being a Russian agent, a charge which he vehemently denied. He claimed to know nothing even of the Russian language. His questioners gave him the Stroop test in the Russian language, which he duly failed; that is, he said "blue" much more slowly when the word was the Russian for "yellow!" If the story is true, the Stroop test has been used to reveal something considerably more applied than the nature of unconscious cognitive processes.

COGNITIVE PSYCHOLOGY AND COMPUTER MODELS

It is no accident that Sternberg buttressed his assumptions about the nature of human information processing by referring to a computer in a telephone exchange. Most cognitive psychologists go about their business with, so to speak, a computer in their heads. It is worthwhile for us to examine why the computer model is so ubiquitous, so attractive, and perhaps so dangerous.

Computers are designed to carry out humanlike functions, so it is only poetic (and cognitive?) justice that we should in turn assume that humans function like computers. The computer model is perhaps the epitome of the analytic approach which characterizes so much of science. When a function is to be automated in a computer, the first step is to analyze the function into components which in turn are analyzed into instructions. Those instructions are themselves defined in terms of even more molecular procedures, which are carried out by the hardware of the computer.

The cognitive scientist often proceeds almost as if he or she were a computer programmer, by making a flowchart of the presumed cognitive activity of subjects in experiments. Even the conventional representation of the flowchart is borrowed from the ways in which computer programmers sketch flowcharts.

The hierarchical organization of today's computers is also often borrowed by the cognitive scientist. In dealing with human behavior, we are faced with the problem of relating global performances to the steps involved in the performance, and these steps are likely to be composed of hosts of still smaller steps. These steps are, at another level, composed of muscular flexions and relaxations brought about by impulses in the peripheral nervous system, which are in turn brought about by activities in the central nervous system. Thus both the study of human activity and the structure of the activity itself manifest a hierarchical structure. As with the computer, study of the human being involves a level of gross performance, a level (or levels) of programming, with a set of more basic instructions at each level, and a level of hardware (even though human hardware is, literally speaking, rather soft and mushy in the parts where data processing takes place). No wonder the computer is such an attractive model.

We can all too easily find homely examples of the parallels between human and computer functioning. When a man wakes up in the morning, he asks his wife how she feels, and she says something like "Fine," or "I have a headache." When a computer is turned on in the morning, it may run a self-diagnostic routine which resides in its read-only memory and beep a number of times to indicate its condition. Only if it finds itself well does it go on to "get out of bed."

One problem in understanding computer operation is to know the basic instruction set of the computer and how more complex programs are constructed out of the basic instructions. In a recent book on cognitive development, Robert Sternberg (1984) says, "I propose to account for intellectual development in terms of changes in availability, accessibility, and ease of execution of a variety of kinds of information-processing components" (p. 164). This is, and has always been, one of the fundamental problems of psychology: that is, what equipment is available in the human infant, and how does development build on this original equipment? What equipment is added as a function of maturation, and what as a function of experience? This is the problem for whose study Piaget is so justly famous, but it is only recently that the computer model has made the nature of the problem seem so clear and its solution of such pressing intellectual interest.

The problem of consciousness, as well as the problem of performance, may be approached via a computer model. As we said in Chapter 12, one can ask whether a computer can be conscious and if it were, how we would recognize it. Are there conscious computers now? Is consciousness possible only in protoplasm, only in living things, or also in inanimate objects which have the right structures? These questions would not be asked, or, if they were, would not be taken at all seriously, if it were not for the remarkable capabilities of today's computers and the promise of ever greater capabilities in the future.

It must be added that many of those most knowledgeable about computers are among the most skeptical of the computer model. The same cautions apply to the computer model that apply to cognitive psychology in general. That is, we must be careful not to ignore the effects of social and emotional factors in human behavior, and an overly logical approach may lead us down barren paths. The computer model, like any other model, is limited and mirrors only a part of human behavior. We should keep that fact before us and at the same time make the fullest possible use of the model.

COGNITIVE VS. S-R APPROACHES

By now our discussion should have suggested some of the major differences between the cognitive and the S-R approaches, provided that the contents of Chapters 10 and 11 were contrasted with those of the present chapter. In the upcoming section, we will make some of the differences more explicit. The two approaches are generally seen as incompatible, but, as with most theoretical conflicts, compromise theories may result in a resolution of the present issues.

Centralism vs. Peripheralism

This is a key dimension on which cognitive and S-R psychologies differ. The cognitive approach is clearly centralistic; cognitions are processes within the organism. The S-R perspective, in contrast, tends to minimize such central components and to concentrate on relationships between environmental cues and responses of the organism.

S-R psychologists, however, differ markedly among themselves in how they regard intraorganismic processes. Some, following the radical behavioristic doctrines of Watson and Skinner, are concerned solely with the S-R relationships themselves and are likely to oppose attempts to measure or speculate about "mental" functions. It is this kind of attitude that accounts for the commonly held belief that cognitive and S-R psychologies are incompatible. Consider, for example, the statement that cognitively "significant issues could not be addressed adequately within the framework of neo-behavioristic psychology" (Lachman, Lachman, and Butterfield, 1979, p. 525).

Bower and Hilgard (1981) argue that there is an ultimate incompatibility between cognitive psychology and S-R psychology. Their claim is that the "terminal meta-postulates" of S-R theory require that all mental operations be isomorphic to S's and R's, and that some behaviors cannot be accounted for in those terms. The direct conclusion is that S-R theory is *in principle* incapable of accounting for all the facts of behavior.

When we consider methodological rather than radical or metaphysical behaviorism (see Chapter 6), a different conclusion can be drawn. The "intervening variable" of early theoreticians (MacCorquodale and Meehl, 1948) clearly referred to the kinds of constructs that contemporary cognitive researchers are using. The methodological behaviorist would point out that it is always some form of behavior, in response to environmental and perhaps internal cues, that identifies the cognitive variables and makes their use possible. Further, a relaxed S-R theory can admit quite complex operations as "responses," and with sufficiently complex internal responses any behavior whatever can be accounted for. It is then unreasonable to argue that there are behaviors which behaviorism cannot explain.

We conclude, therefore, that cognitive psychology is quite compatible with a moderate form of behaviorism, even though it is not compatible with any form of behaviorism which completely rejects central constructs. Many cognitive psychologists consider themselves methodological behaviorists, and they vary over a wide range in the extent to which they rely on introspective techniques. Most of them make little use of introspection. Thus they infer the nature of internal structures from behavior, rather than trying to observe it directly. Sternberg's conclusions about exhaustive search are a good example.

The Complexity Dimension: Interpretations of Language

A major reason for the conflict between cognitive and S-R positions has been the problem of understanding language. This problem was largely ignored by American experimental and theoretical psychologists during the first half century of psychology's existence as a formal discipline. We have already seen that this situation changed in 1957 with the publication of B. F. Skinner's *Verbal behavior,* the first comprehensive attempt to explain language in S-R terms. Skinner's position was that language *is* behavior, and hence no new principles are needed to explain it. That same year Noam Chomsky published his very different account (Chomsky, 1957) in terms of his theory of transformational grammar, which made the hierarchical structure of syntax the focal theme.

Skinner's book aroused far greater interest at the time, at least among psychologists, but Chomsky's (1959) devastating review of that book two years later marked the beginning of cognitive domination in the field. As we indicated in Chapter 11, Chomsky found little substance in the application of S-R principles to language. For example, he pointed out the obscurity of the hypothesized "reinforcement" function as applied to language, and labeled its invocation "a purely ritual function." Although Skinner has continued to hold to his S-R position, the S-R account of language has never really recovered its brief position of eminence. It was many years after Chomsky's criticism before any formal rejoinder appeared (MacCorquodale, 1969, 1970), and the rejoinder has itself received little notice.

There is an important underlying difference between the two approaches in their treatment of complexity. S-R theorists want to reduce complex functions to simpler functions, as far as possible. They therefore attend to those aspects of language that offer a reasonable prospect of such reduction. The typical approach of researchers in the linguistic tradition is to focus directly on complex functions as the most significant features of language. Historically, S-R researchers have studied things like the response strengths of individual words as a function of variables like number of repetitions. The linguist is more likely to study complete sentences and how they are formed and interpreted as a function of grammatical rules. The astonishing ability of human speakers to produce and understand an enormous variety of unique sentences is regarded as probably the most striking feature of human linguistic behavior.

The S-R researcher tends to concentrate on *performance,* the linguist on *competence.* That is, the S-R researcher studies the behaviors actually emitted, in this case verbal behaviors. Cognitive theorists show more interest in the inferred competencies which presumably underlie the observable behaviors. These competencies involve following grammatical rules and the ability to transform underlying meaning into utterances, and vice versa. Cognitivists believe that it is more efficient to study competencies, since a very large number of S-R behaviors should be predictable from a knowledge of a small number of response-generating rules. The competence-performance distinction parallels the learning-performance distinction popularized long ago by Tolman, and similar problems are involved. Learning, like competence, must be an inference from performance, and additional laws are needed to transform learning (or competence) into performance. Anderson (1985) points out that "The exact relationship between a theory of competence and a theory of performance is unclear and can be the subject of heated debates" (p. 306). In principle, the relationship seems to be reasonably clear; competencies are a *part* of a theory of performance. In practice, each type of investigator is likely to ignore the problems studied by the other, so it is not surprising that they seldom agree.

The concentration upon competence and the use of rules accounts for the assumption by many linguists that language ability is innate. In part, this presumption seems to be the result of the difficulty researchers and theorists have encountered in explaining the spontaneity of language behavior in children and in making sense of the rules that govern language. In part, also, it may be the result of discovering the apparent universality of language development in children of all races and cultures; all normal children take about the same amount of time to learn their language and show essentially the same developmental steps in doing so.

The transition from the consideration of adult language to consideration of the development of language in children naturally leads on to the comparative question: What about language in animals? Is there just another developmental step down the ladder to animal language, or is there a qualitative difference between human and animal language? Can animals tell us anything new about the relationship between thought and language? A brief overview of attempts to teach language to animals may give us some ideas about these issues.

Animal Language

The first distinction that needs to be made clear in consideration of this question is that between communication and language. Communication is the broader term, including meaningful signs of various kinds as well as true language. There is no question at all about the reality of animal communication; many types of signs have been studied in many species, sometimes with quite remarkable results. For example, von Frisch (1965) showed that the returning bee's dance in the hive signals information about the direction and distance of discovered nectars. But these behaviors do not show the flexibility of human language. The question is whether they show *sufficient* flexibility to qualify as language. Griffin (1976) believes they do, but others like Chomsky (1972) and Terrace (1979) do not.

What about the recent research demonstrating new levels of communication in the great apes? There is no doubt that each of the subjects whose communication learning has been publicized over the past decade or so has shown a high level of ability to communicate with trainers. However, some of the apparently innovative American Sign Language (ASL) performances claimed for the chimpanzee Washoe (Gardner &

Gardner, 1969) and the gorilla Koko (Patterson, 1978) have been criticized on the ground that there were unidentified cues from the trainers and that the animals' behavior was directed by these cues. Some credence was lent this critical position when Terrace (1979), who controlled for such cues, was unable to find much innovative ASL communication behavior in his chimpanzee, Nim.

The other major techniques used in communication research are using metal-backed plastic chips as symbols (Premack, 1971) and using complex patterns symbolizing words (lexigrams) on a computer keyboard (Rumbaugh, 1977). The computer keyboard technique has probably provided the most convincing demonstration to date that chimpanzees can use representations of objects and events in about the same manner as humans (Savage-Rumbaugh, Rumbaugh, Smith, and Lawson, 1980). Two younger chimpanzees, Austin and Sherman, had been trained to use "Yerkish"—the language of the patterned computer keys. They were required to "name" tools independently of their use. Subsequently, Austin and Sherman were able to name objects correctly with the help of a usage cue (for example, watching a key put into a padlock enabled them to name the key properly, even though just looking at it had not). An older chimpanzee, Lana, who had been trained with other techniques, did not show this ability. Then, on crucial representational tests administered with careful controls, Austin and Sherman were able to categorize new test objects correctly. They even succeeded with photographs of objects like tools and foods. Lana did not do this, even though she was able to label the objects appropriately in terms of their lexigrams.

This research is important because it suggests that a rudimentary form of true language function can be found in the higher apes, even though they lack the great spontaneity shown by human children. The extent to which apes can be trained to use linguistic symbols productively, as humans do, is still under study. It does seem that they can use symbols in a genuinely representational manner, and there is evidence for some spontaneity in chimpanzees who merely observe the use of signing by other chimpanzees.

Despite the demonstration of some language abilities in primates, the consensus among students of animal language is that primate cognitive ability outstrips primate language ability. The comparative perspective thus points to the possibility that cognition in general may be less dependent on language than we thought. Human cognition seems to be linked strongly to language, but we may be unique in this respect. We need to be careful in inferring some sort of symbolic representation in animals whenever they show sophisticated problem-solving abilities. Problems like this make the future of studies in animal language and cognition particularly interesting, and perhaps a clarification of the relationship of language to cognition in animals will clarify the same relationship in people. Eventually, we hope to understand more about the mutual interrelationships of language, cognition, and consciousness in a variety of species.

THE ROLE OF CONSCIOUSNESS

The return of mental problems to psychological favor has resulted in many new empirically grounded questions being asked about the role of consciousness in cognitive psychology. The clear description of consciousness as experience, as well as in relationship to behavior, is now a matter of intense psychological interest and research.

Split-Brain Research

Some of the most illuminating findings from recent research on consciousness have come from the observations of split brains by psychobiologist Roger Sperry and his colleagues (Sperry, 1969). Sperry's award of the Nobel prize for physiology and medicine in 1981, based primarily on this work, is dramatic evidence of the interest aroused by this new approach to the old problem of brain localization.

Sperry's work has demonstrated to nearly everyone's satisfaction that we have been correct since the time of Broca in our assumption that the left hemisphere is more competent than the right for speech in nearly all right-handed individuals. It has come as something of a surprise that the isolated right hemisphere is superior to the left in the solution of most spatial problems. In addition, the right hemisphere has some verbal competence, apparently understanding simple verbal instructions reasonably well. Musically, the right hemisphere is clearly the more competent in most people. Luria, Tsvetkova, and Futer (1965) reported the case of a composer, Professor V. G. Shebalin, who suffered aphasia following a stroke in the left hemisphere but nevertheless continued to compose original works evaluated by critics as of the same quality as those he wrote before his stroke.

Gazzaniga (1981) says of Sperry's work:

> Sperry's dazzling career had its origins in a time when brain scientists, then not so chic, studied the brain because they were interested in how its workings explained behavior. In some sense they were not interested in the brain per se, as are so many current-day neuroscientists. Their experiments constantly focused on discerning something about how the biologic system worked to support behavior, and ultimately the generation of conscious awareness. (p. 517)

In short, Gazzaniga is saying that Sperry took a *psychological,* not a physiological, attitude toward his work. This is an attitude that is appreciated by many of today's cognitive psychologists, who are more interested in what the brain does than in how, neurologically, it does it.

Among the many theoretical products stimulated by this research is Sperry's own (1969) interpretation of consciousness as *supervening,* rather than intervening, in brain physiology. By "supervening," Sperry meant to suggest some kind of overall, or superordinate, control of brain physiology. This is reminiscent of James's contention (1890), already cited in Chapter 6, that "the distribution of consciousness shows it to be exactly such as we might expect in an organ *added* [italics added] for the sake of steering a nervous system grown too complex to regulate itself" (p. 144). It is doubtful that Sperry's statement is any more revealing than James's. Hofstadter (1979) presents a related but somewhat more comprehensible view; he does not regard consciousness as either "supervening" or as being an "added organ." Rather, consciousness is what we see when we study a global level of neural organization, and the nature of this organization may well determine what happens at a more molecular level of neural activity. In this sense, then, "consciousness" may "supervene."

Verbal Reports on Cognitive Functions

Some writers have adopted a more skeptical attitude toward the role of consciousness. Nisbett and Wilson (1977) are typical examples, and they raise several critical questions, specifically about the ability of people to report on crucial cognitive functions which have long been assumed to be available to direct introspection. They argue:

> Subjects are sometimes (a) unaware of the existence of a stimulus that importantly influenced a response, (b) unaware of the existence of the response, and (c) unaware that the stimulus has affected the response. It is proposed that when people attempt to report on their cognitive processes . . . they do not do so on the basis of any true introspection. Instead, their reports are based on a priori, implicit causal theories, or judgments about the extent to which a particular stimulus is a plausible cause of a given response. (1977, p. 231)

Nisbett and Wilson cite many research reports in support of these conclusions. Their conclusions have, however, been questioned by E. R. Smith and Miller (1978) and modified by Ericsson and Simon (1980). Treating verbal reports as "data," these latter authors analyze the sources of the various kinds of verbal reports concerning processes—that is, the mechanisms that generate the reports. They use a model that incorporates short-term memory to make predictions about which kinds of verbal reports will be reliable and which will be found to be unreliable. They conclude that the main inaccuracies that have been reported, and that were documented by Nisbett and Wilson, result from subjects being requested to provide information that was not directly attended to, so that inferences rather than actual memories formed the basis of the reports.

With the continued development of research directly designed to uncover more of the mechanisms underlying both conscious and nonconscious mental processes and their interactions, we may confidently anticipate further refinement of propositions concerning the role of consciousness in cognitive functions. Meanwhile, we turn to the examination of some research indicating that surprising kinds of information processing occur in the *absence* of consciousness.

NONCONSCIOUS INFORMATION PROCESSING

"Subliminal" Stimuli

Obtaining information about the environment from stimulation that is below the standard detection threshold is called "subliminal perception." Whether or not such "perception" is a genuine phenomenon has been difficult to decide. One problem is that it is a technical challenge to show that a stimulus is entirely subliminal while at the same time demonstrating that it was, according to some other measure, effective. American psychologists have tended to be skeptics in this matter, and most of the recently reported positive evidence has come from the more sympathetic European psychologists.

In the 1950s and 1960s, the subliminal perception issue heated up because of the many criticisms leveled at the so-called New Look in perceptual research. Methodological objections were raised against the empirical evidence offered in support of the proposition that personality and social variables can influence basic perceptual processes. For example, Bruner and Goodman (1947) reported that a small coin was perceived as physically larger by poor children than by rich children, but critics said that this result could be produced by the fact that rich children had more familiarity with money and thus might estimate coin size more accurately. However, after many further studies, and after the development of the information-processing conceptual framework, this kind of data has been assimilated into the main line of American experimental psychology (Erdelyi, 1974).

Premature and experimentally unsupported claims for the efficacy of subliminal cues as advertising devices were responsible during the 1950s for further skepticism about subliminal perception. Meanwhile, some solid theoretical, as well as experimental, developments supported the concept. For example, several theories of attention (e.g., Broadbent, 1958) shared the assumption that a selective process occurred *prior to* the conscious recognition of stimuli. That is, the factors determining attention were assumed to be nonconscious.

On the empirical side, there were impressive experimental demonstrations of the need to postulate nonconscious selective screening of stimuli. For example, Corteen and Wood (1972) conditioned subjects to give a galvanic skin response (GSR) to selected words. The subjects were then placed in a dichotic listening situation and instructed to attend to only one of two auditory channels, with one presented to each ear. Corteen and Wood showed that the GSR could be produced by the previously conditioned word cues when they were presented to the unattended ("shadowed") channel. In more recent research (von Wright, Anderson, and Stenman, 1975), the same result was obtained using semantic associates of the conditioned words as the test stimuli, and GSRs were as large for words on the unattended as for words on the attended channel.

Space available in this chapter does not permit a full account of all the lines of evidence on this issue or of the many methodological problems associated with it. Here we will describe the striking, though controversial, results reported by British psychologist A. J. Marcel. He has conducted two lines of research on the problem. His first approach involved what he called "unconscious reading" (Marcel, 1978, 1983). He used a tachistoscope to present words briefly and followed them quickly with a pattern mask composed of a jumble of bits and pieces of letters. Such meaningless masks are intended to preclude further sensory input of information from the masked area. Marcel found that subjects who could not say what words had been presented, or even whether or not a word had been presented, were able to select words on forced-choice tests that were graphically (structurally) and semantically (meaningfully) related to the target word. Their performance was well above chance levels.

These results can be explained by assuming that the visual pattern mask obliterates the neural basis of conscious perception (often called the icon). At the same time, nonconscious visual information processing proceeds. It is this nonconscious processing that is believed to account for the ability of the subject to select from among alternative words those that are similar in structure (e.g., dish) or are associated (e.g., hook) with the target word (in this example, fish).

Independent researchers have thus far been unable to replicate these findings. Either performing effective research on this problem is very difficult, or the early findings were obtained by chance. This issue cannot be decided without further clarifying research by Marcel and his critics.

Marcel's (1983) second line of attack on this problem has produced replicable results (Fowler, Wolford, Slade, & Tassinary, 1981). The technique used in this second line of research involves the "lexical decision" task. The subject is shown a string of letters and asked to decide whether or not the letters form a word. Half of the letter strings form words; half do not. An example of a word string might be "page"; a related non-word string is "dage." The dependent variable is the speed of the subject's decision about the letter string. Marcel's research design used "associative priming." The classical demonstration of priming occurs when the subject is shown a related word as a cue (for example, *stamp* as cue before the target word *mail*). A neutral (control) prime would be an unrelated word such as *bread* or *plant*. Using related words as primes has been shown to increase the speed with which a lexical decision is made.

What Marcel found was that the usual associative priming occurred when an ambiguous word (e.g., *palm*) was used as a cue for the target word (e.g., *wrist*), even after a misleading cue (e.g., *tree*) has been given for the prior string—but *only* if the ambiguous cue (*palm*) was presented subliminally! When supraliminal presentation of the same ambiguous cue occurred so that it could be consciously recognized, no priming resulted. This negative result presumably occurred because the wrong associative chain, cued by *tree*, was activated. Apparently, conscious information processing is limited (unidirectional, in the present situation), whereas nonconscious processing is not so restricted—it permits the essentially simultaneous generation of rapid multiple associations.

Event-Frequency Processing

Our second illustration of contemporary cognitive research is much less controversial but in its way equally exciting. Numerous researchers have been investigating an ability which seems to be quite simple but really is quite remarkable: the ability of human subjects to remember and report how often specific events have occurred, even in the absence of any prior conscious intent to do so or any attempt to count events as they occur (Hasher & Zacks, 1979, 1984).

Such an ability might seem to be commonplace and so hardly surprising. We can agree that it is commonplace, but we would argue that it *is* surprising. Indeed, what makes it surprising is its very ubiquity. All human beings, from childhood through old age, are able to perform at nearly the same level of accuracy (usually around 75 to 80 percent correct judgments, when a large number of items varying in frequency have been presented). Moreover, event-frequency judgment is an ability that seems to be insensitive not only to age but also to a host of other variables that typically have marked effects upon cognitive functions such as free recall. Event-frequency judgments, like judgments of spatial locations and a small number of similar features, are apparently processed automatically, without any conscious intent. When subjects are instructed in advance to keep track of the frequency of specified items (say, words in a list), they typically do no better than uninstructed subjects on subsequent frequency tests. Subjects who try to keep count of the occurrences of several different kinds of events report that they get confused after reaching about three, so that any initial benefits of counting are lost.

IMPLICATIONS OF COGNITIVE PSYCHOLOGY

We conclude this sampling of topics from the vast range of cognitive psychology with an attempt to evaluate its importance for psychology generally and to suggest some of the directions that its future development may take.

This task is difficult because of the breadth of cognitive psychology. As defined by one of its leading researchers, cognition "refers to all the processes by which the sensory input is transformed, reduced, elaborated, stored, recovered, and used" (Neisser, 1967, p. 4). Neisser admits that "given such a sweeping definition, it is apparent that cognition is involved in everything a human being might possibly do; that every phenomenon is a cognitive phenomenon" (1967, p. 10). Practically speaking, we recognize that investigators must establish artificial boundaries in order to manipulate and control the variables in which they are most interested. In any event, there is at least a potential contribution of cognitive variables to all psychological problems. Spence's research on human eyelid conditioning, described in Chapter 11, is a good demonstration of the ubiquity of cognitive variables.

However, the dangers of isolating cognitive (intellectual) functions from the broader social and physical environment in which the human organism lives have recently been emphasized. Norman (1981) puts it this way:

> The human is a social animal, interacting with others, with the environment, and with itself. The core disciplines of cognitive science have tended to ignore these aspects of behavior. The results have been considerable progress on some fronts, but sterility overall, for the organism we are analyzing is conceived as pure intellect, communicating with one another in logical discourse, perceiving, remembering, thinking where appropriate, reasoning its way through the well-formed problems that are encountered in the day. Alas, that description does not fit actual behavior. (p. 266)

The remedy for this state of affairs is, of course, that cognitive psychologists need to pay more explicit attention to such other, nonintellectual variables. This does not mean that research on purely intellectual processes needs to stop, or even that it must slow up. It does mean that there should be more interactive research, such as that relating cognition and affect, and that generalizations drawn on the basis of strictly intellectual operations must be qualified accordingly.

Although cognitive processes by no means constitute *all* there is of psychological interest, they certainly play a most significant role in both behavior and conscious experience. Moreover, their ramifications may be expected to intrude, ultimately, into practically all of the major subject-matter areas of psychology. If it is true that biologically we are what we eat, it may also be true that psychologically we respond and experience in accord with what we *remember*. Memory is the focal function in cognitive processes. Memory may be of perceptions and experiences, or of behaviors and thoughts. However, as the preceding illustrations in this chapter demonstrate, memory is by no means always conscious. The careful experimental separation of conscious and nonconscious memories is a central task for contemporary cognitive psychology. The apparent automaticity of information processing, as illustrated by event-frequency judgments, is common to many cognitive phenomena. It poses a problem whose resolution promises to require a great number of ingeniously designed experiments over the coming decades. Squire (1986) believes that the fundamental breakdown is that between *declarative* knowledge of facts and events and *procedural* knowledge of how tasks are performed. Working out all the interrelationships between different categorizations of memory is one of the most fascinating tasks facing cognitive psychologists.

Another crucial task is the juxtaposition of cognitive and affective processes. The significant role of affect in clinical and personality problems is self-evident. How do affective processes interact with cognitive ones? Beck's (1976) theory of depression is based on the belief that cognitive processes play a crucial role in affective processes. His therapy is intended to change the cognitions of depressed persons, in the belief that more positive cognition will produce more positive affect. The very urgent practical problem of how to alleviate human misery thus motivates research on the connection between cognition and affect.

Another example of a cognition-affect question that needs an answer is provided by proponents of two directly contradictory positions on the affect-cognition issue. Zajonc (1984) has argued for the priority of affective processes and has presented evidence purporting to show the independence, at least under some conditions, of affect from cognition. On the other hand, R. S. Lazarus (1984) has argued for the primacy of cognition, holding that affect depends upon cognition. This issue promises to generate a wealth of experimental data, and it may help to answer some questions connected with Beck's theory and therapy.

Although many worthwhile questions thus exist at the behavioral and theoretical levels, the interrelationship between cognitive research and neuropsychology may well turn out to be the most productive area of investigation. It is doubtful that the phenomenal "essence" of conscious experience will ever be reduced to neurophysiological dimensions. However, the dependence of sensory and other conscious experiences on brain functions may well be uncovered. Increasingly refined relationships between various types of conscious experience and specific types of brain mechanisms can be anticipated. The study of cognitive variables will continue to be an indispensable part of such demonstrations.

FURTHER READINGS

A very economical way to survey cognitive psychology is to read Chapter 13 in Bower and Hilgard's *Theories of learning* (1981, 5th ed.). They give the fundamentals of the cognitive critique of S-R psychology and make most of the distinctions that are central to cognitive psychology. They also give their own brief "further readings," one of which is Estes' *Handbook of learning and cognitive processes* (1975–1978), whose five volumes should sate the most voracious intellectual appetite for academic cognitive psychology. For the less voracious, Norman and Rumelhart's *Explorations in cognition*

(1975) should suffice, or perhaps Anderson's (1985) textbook, *Cognitive psychology and its implications*. Those who are interested in the analysis of language could still hardly do better than to read Chomsky's (1959) review of Skinner's *Verbal behavior* in the journal *Language,* for the battle lines between an S-R and a cognitive approach are drawn nowhere more clearly than there. If you are interested in lateralization, you ought to read something of Sperry (e.g., 1968, 1969). Springer and Deutsch (1985), in their *Left brain, right brain,* provide an easily accessible and balanced perspective on hemispheric lateralization. Less balanced but extremely interesting and provocative is Julian Jaynes's *The origin of consciousness in the breakdown of the bicameral mind* (1976). Two books by Norman Dixon (1971, 1981) provide a lucid account of the subliminal perception controversy. The growing literature on event-frequency processing is reviewed by Hasher and Zacks (1979, 1984). Finally, illustrations of the way in which cognitive research has ramifications for nearly all aspects of psychology can be found for infancy in Mehler and Fox's *Neonate cognition: Beyond the blooming buzzing confusion* (1984), and for animal psychology in Roitblat, Bever, and Terrace's *Animal cognition* (1984) and Kendrick, Rilling, and Denny's *Theories of animal memory* (1985). Recent books by Griffin (1984) and by Ericsson and Simon (1984) examine the question of animal and human consciousness.

14

PSYCHOLOGY AND SOCIETY

OUR CURRENT STATUS

Psychology as a Profession

The splendid isolation of psychology from pressing societal issues can no longer be maintained. The attitudes of the ivory tower which were characteristics of many theoretically oriented scientists a generation or so ago are no longer defensible when animal laboratories are raided and seriously damaged by animal rights activists, and when much of the high cost of our technological tools is paid for through governmental funding. We therefore outline, in this final chapter, some of the societal issues which now concern psychologists. We will present some examples of the place of psychology in, and its relevance to, society.

Beginning from a base of about 4,000 members in 1945, the American Psychological Association (APA) grew to a multifaceted monster of about 60,000 in four decades. The Association originated in 1892 with a group of people who could fit into Granville Stanley Hall's study. In its first 50 years it grew by 4,000; in its next 40 years, by over 50,000.

As psychology has grown and diversified, it has needed more public support and has become more concerned about its image. The APA has recently taken over a popular national magazine, *Psychology Today,* at least partly as a way of giving the public an accurate picture of psychology's relevance to society. Although the number of psychology students, and thus the resources and energy devoted to academic psychology, have increased dramatically, the number of services offered by clinical and other applied psychologists has increased even more rapidly. Hence the balance of power in psychology has shifted steadily from the academic to the applied sector. At the same time, psychology has become increasingly dependent upon government as a source of support for its research efforts. A major criterion for choosing teachers of psychology at major universities has become how successful they are at attracting research funds. The money allocated to the support of psychological research remains very small compared to that devoted to the support of research in the physical sciences; nevertheless, it is beginning to share some of the features of "big science," with its big budgets and complex and expensive equipment. It is unlikely that psychology will ever again be revolutionized by a single man, like Max Wertheimer, using a piece of borrowed equipment.

Psychology has been socially and politically transformed as our society has gone from the palpable horrors of World War II to the impalpable horrors of the cold war. Psychologists from Freud to Jung to Skinner, all across the spectrum of beliefs about the wellsprings of human behavior, have grappled with the apparent irrationality of human political behavior. So far, our "solutions," despite their ingenuity, have not had a dramatic influence on the conduct of practical affairs. However, the grappling has affected psychology in ways which we can as yet see only dimly. It has become as much an article of faith that psychology *cannot* be value-free as it was earlier that all science *must* be value-free. Technology has transformed our intellectual outlook. Behaviorism, as a methodology, has never been displaced; but the simple S-R picture of behavior, deriving from behaviorists and their associationistic cousins, is being increasingly overlaid by a cognitive picture which derives much of its strength from a computer analogy.

Gilgen (1982) found that psychologists still believed that Skinner was the most important person, and his contributions the most important influences, in post–World War II psychology. Thus, prior to 1982 at least, cognitive psychology was not seen as the dominant force in American psychology. However, the computer revolution and associated developments were already rated high by Gilgen's respondents from the APA Division for History of Psychology, who placed the increasing influence of cognitive theory fourth in importance as a postwar development.

Psychologists continue to have serious problems, aside from funding, in their relationship to the larger society. The reasons for this may include the belief of some laypersons that they know as much psychology as they need to know and the fact that the public often mistrusts psychologists' use of animal and human subjects. Particularly since Milgram's experiments of 1963, there have been problems with reconciling the need to do research with the protection of the rights of human subjects. Milgram asked his "teachers" to shock his "learners," who were posing as subjects in an experiment designed to examine the effectiveness of punishment as an incentive to learning. The learners were in reality confederates who pretended to be in great pain but who received no shock. Most of the "teachers" succumbed to pressure from the experimenter and continued to administer ever-increasing "shocks" even when the learner's life was presumably endangered. Milgram's experiments are often misunderstood (we have heard many times that his "learners" really were shocked). The objections to Milgram's work may be based as much on the unflattering picture of the participants' conformity which emerged as on the methods by which the conformity was discovered. In saying this, we do not intend to downplay a legitimate concern with the feelings of subjects who thought they were being pressured to hurt their fellow humans. However, as one contemplates the placid way in which citizens of the world pay for the preparation of their nuclear ovens, one may wonder whether Milgram's conclusions were expressed strongly enough.

Despite the fact that the widespread concern with the rights of subjects may rest partly on misconceptions, the problem is real and deserves continuing attention. Psychologists, like other biological scientists, must be vigilant in the handling of their affairs if they wish to avoid the imposition of even more stringent controls from external sources. Current controls already have their onerous side but seem to be doing reasonably well at safeguarding both human and animal subjects and the researchers who study them.

Psychologists who use objective tests to predict success and failure have their own set of problems. There have been increasing complaints that tests are biased against one or another group, and testers may come into conflict with those who are working for the betterment of minorities. In a protracted court case in California, testing was judged to be prejudicial; minority students were said to be unjustifiably placed in "slow" classes on the basis of the results. At almost the same time, tests were judged not to be prejudicial in an Illinois case. One can anticipate continuing litigation in similar cases, as long as the predictions from psychological test results continue to have less than perfect validity, especially when tests are sometimes administered by people who lack adequate training.

Counseling and clinical psychology continue to prosper. Behavior modification techniques are popular, and clinics for those who wish to stop smoking, lose weight, and achieve independence from alcohol and/or other drugs are increasing in number. This increase in applications of psychology is very important as an indication of the acceptance of our discipline and indicates that we are beginning to develop secure principles and effective techniques, even though we know that much remains to be done in this regard. Industrial-organizational psychology and community psychology are also growing in extent, effectiveness, and acceptance, and we will give one example to illustrate this growth later. However, much work remains to be done in the applied areas as well as in pure research. Consider that society would like to eliminate crime, psychosis, and poverty, to say nothing of war. Despite its patent limitations, psychology is increasingly recognizing the need to work toward such remote goals, as evidenced by the formation of organizations like Psychologists for Social Responsibility. Psychology is not just a science; it is also an art and a profession, and it recognizes that it must earn its place in society. Nearly every issue of the *American Psychologist* expresses our concern with our public image by publishing an interview with or an article by a decision-maker from the public arena, often a member of Congress.

Intellectual Issues

There are also plenty of exciting problems in less immediately applied areas. The technology of genetics has reawakened the ancient problem of the relationship between nature and nurture. The debate about sociobiology and its relationship to theories of behavior and to ethics continues (Singer, 1981; Kamin, 1985). The growth of molecular biology seems to be correlated with the continuation of a nativistic trend, and with heated opposition to that trend, in psychology. Biological boundaries to learning have become so well accepted that the term no longer needs to be enclosed in quotation marks. The question of the extent to which human and animal social behaviors have a genetic basis has never been settled, and probably can never be settled, since all behavior depends on the *joint* action of genes and environment. The question in its usual form is simply not meaningful. In any case, that aspect of the issue seems to have lost much of its passion.

However, Edward Wilson's *Sociobiology* (1975) remains a major publishing event of the last half of the century, partly because of the virulent debate it aroused. One no longer hears that psychology will be encompassed by sociobiology; rather, psychology has incorporated some sociobiological theses while rejecting the more extreme assertions. Some psychologists are content to recognize that all behavior depends to some extent on its genetic basis, but no behavior is determined exclusively by genes. They believe that the laws of behavior must be consistent with a genetic perspective, just as they must be consistent with a learning perspective or a social perspective. There remain, however, those who see sociobiology as a rationalization for the misbehaviors of individuals, for example in the case of rape, and of society, for example in the exploitation of women and minorities. Certainly sociobiology so used would be a threat to society; we do not believe that Wilson intended it to be used in that way.

The neurophysiological approach continues to be of great importance, and it has enriched our understanding of the fundamentals of neural function. For example, Kandel has learned a great deal from the sea slug *Aplysia,* and Alkon from the marine snail *Hermissenda* (S. S. Hall, 1985). Their evidence converges on a belief that blockage of the channels by which potassium leaves the active neuron plays a critical role in conditioning. Other basic events of learning are also gradually emerging from Kandel's and Alkon's studies of their favorite gastropods. Consequently, we are close to having a basic picture of the neurological basis of simple forms of learning.

Interest in consciousness as a subject of study has returned with a vengeance (Humphrey, 1984); even animal consciousness has made a comeback (Griffin, 1984) after a period of neglect following Washburn's (1908) publication on the subject. We noted in Chapter 13 that even speculation about computer consciousness has become at least semi-respectable. Thus, it seems that psychologists now feel capable of encompassing the "softer" areas of study along with the "harder" areas. Our tolerance is increasing as our numbers increase.

SOCIETAL APPLICATIONS OF PSYCHOLOGY

The Fairweather Lodges

There is absolutely no doubt that psychology should contribute to social problems, but that commitment has been accepted in principle far more often than it has been demonstrated in practice. A notable exception to that rule is the set of "lodges" for psychotic patients which developed from the work of psychologist George William

Fairweather (1921–   ). Fairweather was employed at the Veterans' Administration Hospital in Palo Alto when, around 1960, he started studying programs designed to move psychotics into the community. One of his key ideas was that patients, like members of other disadvantaged groups, should be "empowered" to handle their own affairs, and Fairweather systematically examined how such empowerment could be arranged.

He first examined data on length of stay in mental hospitals to find out how long patients stayed and how many stayed for a long period. During this process he looked for variables that were related to length of stay. He found that the most chronic patients were more often psychotic, single, severely incapacitated, legally incompetent, and nonalcoholic (Fairweather & Tornatzky, 1977). Patients who were still in the hospital after a year were very likely to be there after 3 years.

After having identified the serious problem of chronicity and outlined the major variables related to it, Fairweather compared four treatment programs whose goals were to return patients to the community: (1) individual psychotherapy, (2) group psychotherapy, (3) group living, and (4) a work-only program. After 18 months, there were no significant differences among patients in the four treatment programs, but the most chronic patients showed the poorest community adjustment. There was little relationship between measures like the MMPI and community adjustment. Patients who were considered chronic did poorly under all treatment conditions (72.4 percent returned to the hospital by the end of 18 months).

Fairweather then developed an innovative program with the specific goal of returning chronic patients to the community and keeping them there. Lerner and Fairweather (1963) matched psychotics on background experiences and randomly assigned them to an experimental condition with no supervision or to a condition with minimal supervision. Separate wards of patients were established for the purpose of the experiment. Patients made their own decisions about work on the ward and plans for the future. Small-group processes were a focus in both groups; realistic and helpful responses were rewarded, and other responses elicited negative staff feedback.

A longitudinal study over 5 years showed that the innovative groups functioned better than traditional work-only groups in the hospital setting, but the benefits disappeared when group members returned to the community as individuals. This suggested to the investigators that patients needed to be moved into the community as an intact group that would continue to provide the patients with support and resources (Fairweather, Sanders, Maynard, & Cressler, 1969). Thus the next experiment moved a group of patients into the community as a unit. The supportive and democratic patient groups initially cost only one-third what hospitalization cost, and later the group became completely self-supporting and self-managing. Two additional groups were then established, with results similar to those found for the first group (Fairweather, Sanders, & Tornatsky, 1974).

It might be expected that this outstanding success with a social problem would lead to immediate explosive growth in the number of such programs (lodges). That did not happen. There were no quick adoptions of this model by other facilities. Some possible reasons are not difficult to imagine; lodges exist largely or completely without professional help, and professionals must have a job if they are to have a salary. Most people in decision-making roles resist an innovation that would put their staff out of work and reduce their operating budgets. Simple inertia was probably a common factor.

Fairweather then designed another experiment to find out what procedures would be most successful in persuading other institutions to establish lodges. He accordingly became a leader in *dissemination research,* which is intended to find out how any successful innovation can be spread most effectively. This work succeeded well enough that as of 1985 there were 32 programs involving 45 lodges in the United States, primarily in the Great Lakes area, the Northwest, and the South (Mavis & Fergus, 1985). Experience has shown that members in the older lodges tend to move from group employment to individual employment, thus completing the process which traditional programs wished to accomplish.

The Fairweather program makes several points about the relationship between psychology and society. First, psychology does have something to offer society, although its role need not be the traditional one of offering individual therapy; in this particular case, individual therapy was not helpful in the long run. Second, helping society does not mean that the psychologist should turn away from the scientific role; social innovations need solid scientific examination, just as abstract psychological theories need such examination. This point is gaining broader recognition; the editor of *Science* (Koshland, 1985) recently called for routine testing of social innovations before they are implemented on a broad scale. The usual method of implementation involves the passage of a law by Congress, or some other governing body, at the cost of millions of dollars. The innovation may or may not work, is likely to be more expensive than it needs to be, and is very unlikely to be anything like optimal. Psychologists following the Fairweather model could and should play a crucial role in planning and testing future social innovations. They have already made a beginning in this process by establishing programs for diverting juvenile offenders out of the criminal justice system, studying the effectiveness of day care centers for children, and so on.

Eyewitness Testimony

The ways in which psychology can function both as a science and as a service profession are evident in many areas. Research on eyewitness testimony exemplifies more traditional laboratory research which has relevance for a social problem. Elizabeth Loftus has performed some of the best-known experimentation on memory for events. Her basic design involves showing subjects a complex sequence of events; examples are slides or film strips depicting an automobile accident. Subjects are then exposed to misleading information and tested on their memory for the events depicted. The misleading information may be included in the test itself, as in the question "What kind of car was the curly-haired man driving?" when the driver did not have curly hair. Subjects' subsequent descriptions of the driver would, under these conditions, more often include the incorrect "curly haired" feature.

Subjects in such experiments misrecall many of the details about which they have been misinformed. One of the Loftus experiments (1979) presented slides showing stages in an accident in which an automobile struck a pedestrian. The car was driving along a side street toward an intersection. Half of the subjects saw a stop sign, and half a yield sign, at the intersection. Some of the subjects who were shown the yield sign were then asked whether another car had passed the first car while it was at the stop sign. Up to 80 percent of the subjects under this condition later reported a stop sign, instead of the yield sign actually shown, when they described the accident.

Other experiments have examined the factors that make for more or less acceptance of misinformation. Restricting the length of time permitted for observation of the events (Loftus, 1981), or increasing the time between the observation and the misinformation (Loftus, Miller, & Burns, 1978), or imbedding the information in a qualifying clause rather than in a focal or direct question (Loftus, 1981) all lead to greater acceptance of misinformation.

Most attempts to correct the alteration in subjects' memories produced by misinformation have failed (Hertel, 1982). However, subjects sometimes show a marked resistance to accepting misinformation. Factors leading to greater resistance include awareness of bias in the source (Dodd & Bradshaw, 1980), attention to underlying themes rather than superficial features of events (Read & Bruce, 1984), and forewarning about possible misinformation (Greene, Flynn, & Loftus, 1982).

Although the results of research on eyewitness testimony have obvious relevance for the criminal justice system, there has been considerable resistance to making any changes in legal procedures as a result of the research. The applicability of the results has been questioned (Wells, 1978; Yuille, 1980) because the experiments have, for the most part, used slides or films rather than real situations. Some experiments, however, have used "staged" crimes (Malpass & Devine, 1980), and more needs to be done along these lines if experimental results on eyewitness testimony are to be used as a basis for changes in social policy.

Nevertheless, psychology is becoming more involved in legal procedures. One indication of this is the APA's recent approval of a division of psychology and law. Another is that the American Board of Forensic Psychology has been established to certify appropriately trained forensic psychologists. Several joint doctoral programs in psychology and law are already turning out such specialists (Kurke, 1980; Grisso, Sales, & Bayless, 1982). Some functions fulfilled by forensic psychologists are acting as expert witnesses, particularly in questions of competency and dangerousness, and advising on jury selection.

So far, psychology has probably not had a great impact on the legal system, but its effect is likely to increase. As one reviewer recently said, "The influence of any social science on policymaking decisions is often indirect, and it is rare that a single study, or even an entire body of research, would dictate a legal decision or policy" (Roesch, 1984, p. 146). Psychologists may have to play a greater role in bringing about changes in policies as a result of research relevant to those policies, just as Fairweather did in disseminating the results of his research on lodges for psychotic patients.

In conclusion, then, it appears that research on eyewitness testimony is another example of experimentation guided by traditional scientific values, having important theoretical implications, and at the same time being applicable to critical social problems. The distinction between basic and applied research becomes less and less important as we consider the necessity for our experimentation to be carefully designed if society is to accept our conclusions as being well enough established for practical application.

CRITICISMS OF PSYCHOLOGY

As the interests of psychologists have changed, the criticism of mainstream scientific psychology has increased in variety and intensity. This criticism may relate to the shift from a more limited behavioristic psychology to broader cognitive and humanistic perspectives (see Lachman, Lachman, & Butterfield, 1979), or it may be because psychologists are becoming more willing to comment on social and political problems. In some cases, however, the criticisms seem to be motivated by an overgeneralized antiscientific attitude. These criticisms need to be examined, not so much because of their intrinsic merit as because of the damage that their acceptance could do to the image of scientific psychology.

Before we summarize our evaluations of some of these contemporary conflicts, we should make our own biases clear. First, we assume that psychology is a science—a biological as well as social science—and that as such it must use controlled observations whenever possible. The ideal form of such observations is the experiment, although we recognize that experimentation is not possible in all areas of interest. This does not mean that a science, such as psychology, has any exclusive rights to its subject matter. There are always alternative ways of looking at phenomena, and these must be evaluated on their own performance. But we believe that alternative approaches should *complement* science, not replace it.

Second, we assume that scientific progress, perhaps especially in psychology, is slow and tortuous. Progress is often evident only over years, or even decades. The sudden breakthrough that gladdens the heart of the researcher and leads eventually to important applications is apt to come only after a long series of false starts and dead ends. Both public media and, sad to say, scientific textbooks put too little emphasis on the difficulties of research and too much on the final products of the process.

A recent source of methodological attack upon psychology has been the new forms of philosophy of science. The predominant philosophy of science in midcentury was logical positivism. This view holds that progress in science results from building up empirical data, especially in the form of establishing firm relationships among variables. Such relationships are usually called laws which, when explained by interlocking explanatory propositions, become consequences of theories. Positivism is generally seen as offering support to behaviorism, which, as we have seen, was the dominant systematic position in psychology in the midcentury years.

Positivism now has competition from several contrasting positions, most of them stressing subjectivity. In social and behavioral science, interactions between subjects in research and the researchers are carefully examined. The value-free character of data assumed by the positivist and the behaviorist is challenged by those who point to the inevitable biases, cultural and perceptual, of observers (experimenters). Numerous metatheoretical implications for psychology are seen by proponents of these new philosophical positions.

We think that too much attention is paid to the negative side of these metatheoretical issues. Some psychologists tend to forget that metatheory typically follows, rather than leads, empirical investigation. The metatheoretician plays the role of critic, just as does the literary critic or art critic, for those who do the creative work.

The reasons that researchers follow one or another line of inquiry and use this or that type of technique are multiple and not easily categorized. They may, of course, include some metatheoretical factors, but these are most often not only implicit but also relatively unimportant. Certainly they are secondary to the more directly theory-oriented and individualized determining conditions, called *thematic dimensions* by their main proponent, philosopher Gerald Holton (1972, 1978). Compared to such career-long conditions, short-term determinants, like research fads and fashions, are ephemeral and, like metatheoretical considerations, of limited significance.

Our conclusion is therefore that we should not view with great alarm the shifts in metatheory that some psychologists, along with some critics of psychology, are so fond of citing. We should be especially suspicious of statements about research procedures made by those who do little or no research, which seems to be true of many critics. If psychology has shifted its center of interest away from starkly behavioral research toward cognitive problems, it has done so because the results being achieved by using the behavioral approach were less exciting than those promised by the alternative approach, not because of shifts from objectivity in the philosophy of science.

ANTI-INTELLECTUALISM AND THE SUPERNATURAL

Antiscientific protests take many forms. These range from emphasis on the need to pay more attention to sensuous factors to the most orthodox of formal religious dogmas. Although these protests express a common antipathy to the intellectualism of science, they vary markedly in the way in which the opposition is expressed. In evaluating such protests we should keep in mind the restrictions that science places upon itself. We have said that the scientific approach is but one path to knowledge about humans and their world. Its virtues must be recognized, but so must its limitations. Science cannot satisfy all of people's cognitive and emotional needs. Because it is essentially an intellectual effort, it is especially weak in providing emotional support, and this weakness is precisely the strength of various nonscientific and antiscientific doctrines. Religion, art, music, and drama provide humanity with critical supports which are, in themselves, quite independent of science.

Three categories of anti-intellectualism and/or of supernaturalistic beliefs may be distinguished. These are: (1) the familiar varieties of religious belief, which in spite of the dogmatic differences among them are generally marked by faith in one or more supernatural powers; (2) the even greater variety of such psuedoscientific belief systems as astrology, palmistry, and the like, whose conceptual frameworks are usually accepted by adherents on the basis of evidence which scientists consider inadequate; and (3) other forms of anti-intellectualism and irrationalism, some of which have gained unprecedented support from well-educated people, including college students. The consequent upsurge of interest in the occult has found academic expression in the springing up of related college courses, such as on witchcraft. These three categories of anti-intellectualism will now be discussed.

Religious Belief

The recent resurgence of religious fundamentalism may bode ill for psychologists, who have traditionally been a liberal group. However, the key to reconciling science and religion is acceptance of the differences in their roles. Each provides people with a kind of security in a difficult and threatening world. The security provided by religion tends to be more emotionally based, founded as it is on faith, whereas that provided by science is more strictly intellectual. It is true that science as well as religion requires a kind of faith, but this is faith of a different sort. It is not an acceptance of any formal dogma, but rather of a set of such attitudes as skepticism, empiricism, and the tolerance of ambiguity, that are quite different from the attitudes commonly found in those of a religious inclination. If psychology and religion continue to recognize the possibility that they can complement each other, rather than compete with each other, then psychology's social problems will be greatly lessened.

Difficulties arise, of course, when science and religion offer competing interpretations of the same phenomena. A good example of such competition is the effort by fundamentalistic religious groups to promote acceptance of the creationist view of evolution. Forcing schools to give the same amount of time to the Biblical account of creation as to the Darwinian evolutionary theory is an effort to counter what creationists see as an undue sectarian influence. But the belief system of religion cannot appropriately be compared with that of science. We believe that it is more appropriate to treat religious views in courses on religion. If the special creation doctrine cannot be subjected to scientific evaluation, it should not be taught in science courses. If it *is* subject to scientific evaluation, than it clearly lacks supporting evidence, so it is inappropriate to treat it as a viable scientific theory of evolution.

The gaps and inconsistencies in any scientific theory, such as the theory of evolution, are better appreciated by scientists themselves than by others and can be filled in or corrected only by scientific efforts. We conclude that science and religion, like science and art, are radically different kinds of enterprises. Each can study the other from its own perspective, but neither should masquerade as the other. Individuals are free to accept one or the other, neither, or both; in the latter case, it is probably best not to mix the two.

What is the metatheoretical issue raised by religion? Scientists are quite liberal in hypothesizing unobservable forces in order to account for their data, in somewhat the same way that theologians postulate religious forces. But there is a difference in the kinds of logical constraints under which scientists and theologians operate. As long as each enterprise operates under its own rules, there should be a minimum of interference. The danger to scientific theory and scientific aspects of education arises when nonscientific accounts of phenomena are offered as scientific explanations. The best resolution of this problem is to keep the rules of each game explicit and open, and to insist on the maintenance of the appropriate distinction between scientific and religious interpretations.

Pseudoscience

Although they lack the societal credibility of religion, the various forms of pseudo-science are nonetheless powerful competitors with scientific theories. They make up in enthusiasm what they lack in respectability. They are like most religious systems in that they are presented with great certainty. They are unlike them in that their explanations more often compete directly with scientific explanations. Their great advantage in the marketplace of ideas is that they offer simple solutions to complex problems. When some supernatural trappings are added, the pseudoscience may prove irresistible even to many who should know better. A recent Gallup Poll found a surprising increase in the percentage of 13- to 18-year olds who believe in astrology, from 40 to 55 percent over a six-year period.

The fundamental challenge to psychological theory presented by pseudosciences like astrology, phrenology, or dianetics is similar to that posed by religion, but more direct. It seems that the challenges often are presented in the areas with which psychology deals, such as personality theory. We should all make a strong and patient effort to point out the scientific inadequacies of various pseudosciences, but we must not forget to tend our own gardens.

Two special borderline cases deserve mention as demonstrations that it is not easy to distinguish science from pseudoscience. Both the study of extrasensory perception (ESP) and the study of unidentified flying objects (UFOs) have won some recognition within the scientific community but have been regarded as pseudoscientific by most scientists. The difficulty is not with the *search* for extrasensory phenomena or for extraterrestrial intelligence; it is with the *conclusion* that these phenomena have already been demonstrated. Certainly the search for signals from space is proceeding on a systematic and scientific basis, but so far there have been few claims that intelligent signals have been detected.

The most interesting metatheoretical facet of these two belief systems (ESP and UFOs) is their negative character. Note the prefixes in both cases: *extra* and *un*. In the first case, the claim is that perception is *not* all sensory; in the second, that some flying objects have *not* been identified. It has proved to be very difficult to make any positive sense out of such universal negative claims. Although we cannot place these enterprises clearly in the camp of pseudoscience, they have high hurdles to clear before they will gain full scientific credentials. The difficulties are compounded when ESP studies sometimes continue to allow the sender and receiver to be in the same room. It is surprising that even this elementary step to control for possible sensory cues is not taken.

Another persistent and difficult case was presented by Immanuel Velikovsky. He was trained as a psychoanalyst and in addition had early training in mathematics and physical science. He used psychoanalytic ideas, in conjunction with a study of historical and archaeological evidence, to argue for an astronomical scenario which nearly all scientists regarded as preposterous. Velikovsky said that the earth had been subjected to a series of catastrophes within historical times and that these catastrophes had been accurately recorded in the Bible. The Red Sea really had parted for Moses, the earth literally stood still, and manna rained down from Heaven. These events had occurred because of the near approach of Venus and Mars to earth. The resulting catastrophes were not remembered or reported more frequently because of a massive cultural repression.

It might be expected that such unlikely pronouncements would have been quickly rejected by one and all, but that was not the case. Velikovsky's book, *Worlds in Collision* (1950), became a best seller, and his subsequent books on the same general theme also sold well. Part of the reason may have been that Velikovsky was an unusually well-educated man and was able to provide the appearance of strong scholarship to support his assertions. Another source of attraction may have been the religious connection; Velikovsky's theses relied heavily upon the literal truth of Biblical descriptions and thus, like creationism, were attractive to fundamentalists. Finally, Velikovsky made predictions which turned out to be more correct than one would expect from forecasts made on the basis of a crank theory. For example, he said that Venus would be hot, that moon rocks would be magnetized (because they were heated in the presence of a magnetic field when planets approached it), and that Jupiter would be found to be a source of radio noise. These predictions, even though they were accompanied by other inaccurate predictions, made Velikovsky's ideas attractive to many and made it more difficult to discredit him.

Bauer (1985) studied the Velikovsky case in depth, and he concludes, as most scientists did from the beginning, that the "science" of Velikovsky was illusory. However, that does not exhaust the lessons to be learned from his case. Presented with a theory which they considered monstrous, scientists reacted emotionally, sometimes in a manner at least as unscientific as Velikovsky's. Although they pride themselves on the openness of their endeavor, some scientists organized a boycott of textbooks in order to make one publisher withdraw from involvement with Velikovsky. Their arguments seemed designed as much to discredit the man as to discredit his ideas, but science is supposed to consider ideas strictly upon the basis of their own merits. It was a sorry affair, and Bauer spends his time on Velikovsky—and vents his ire on scientists—to prevent a future repetition of similar errors. Psychologists have an obligation to correct pseudoscience, but they must do so without abandoning the methods of their own enterprise.

Irrationalism

The philosopher Charles Frankel (1973) characterized countercultural irrationalism as "a studied and articulated attitude, proudly affirmed and elaborately defended, which pronounces science—and not only science, but more broadly, logical analysis, controlled observation, the norms and civilities of disciplined argument, and the ideal of objectivity—to be systematically misleading as to the nature of the universe and the conditions necessary for human fulfillment." He proceeds to argue that "despite the new language, half jargon and half slang, in which this irrationalism is expressed, the actual assertions on which it rests can be found in classic treatises on mysticism and in the utterances of many traditional philosophers and poets" (1973, p. 927).

In his analysis of this new-old irrationalism, Frankel identifies five fundamental propositions that seem to underlie the thinking of most of its adherents, regardless of their origin. These are:

1   The world has two realms: the apparent and the real. Doubt and disharmony are features of the apparent realm and are dissolved when the coherence of the real world is achieved.

2   Appearance is mistaken for reality because of faulty, biased presuppositions that are imposed on people by their culture and its demands. Thus the prominent counterculturalist, R. D. Laing, made the provocative claim (1967) that "There is no such 'condition' as schizophrenia, but the label is a social fact and the social fact a *political event*" (p. 100; italics in original).

3   Humans reflect the duality of appearance and reality, and it is the attempt of the rational elements to overextend their domain that dehumanizes man. Another prominent spokesman for the counterculture, Theodore Roszak, has argued (1972) that "Our proud, presumptuous head speaks one language; our body another—a silent arcane language. . . . The dichotomy that tears at our personality *is* crude; but I did not invent it. I have only inherited it, like you, from the antiorganic fanaticism of Western culture" (p. 96).

4   Science, which separates subject and object, is not to be trusted, because any such separation is unnatural and wrong.

5   Human problems stem from a loss of the natural harmony between humans and their environment and between their head and their heart.

In demonstrating the unsoundness of these five propositions, Frankel makes a number of points about the metatheoretical issues involved. The pivotal proposition is probably the first one, on the dichotomy of the apparent and the real. Frankel observes that such a dichotomy is routinely recognized by science, which reinterprets the evidence of the senses (the "apparent" realm) into a "real" realm of scientific concept and theory. Frankel (1973) adds "It is passing difficult to understand why the myth persists among many educated people that rational inquiry thins out the world or deprives human experience of its extra dimensions of meaning. Thanks to science, the present world makes available to those who will do their homework subatomic particles, DNA, . . . the Minoan culture, the story of evolution" (p. 927). It is science's removal of the animistic and anthropomorphic features of natural phenomena that is objectionable to the present corps of irrationalists, who may explicitly prefer the "reality" of the dream world to the "appearance" of the waking world (see Roszak, 1972, p. 84).

It should be clear that if the assumptions of the proponents of irrationalism are accepted, a radically different set of metatheoretical standards would follow. There are some less fully committed sympathizers, however, who want to eat their countercultural cake while remaining on an essentially scientific diet. A notable example is the chemist Thomas Blackburn, who has proposed a sensuous-intellectual complementarity for science. His proposal accepts some of the countertechnological arguments, in particular those having to do with the precluding of desirable sensuous experiences by the overly intellectualized functions of science. Blackburn has proposed that we correct this imbalance by accepting the independence of the sensuous or experiential and the abstract or quantitative aspects of science and encouraging them both in a fully complementary relationship. In what he has described as a "feeble fluctuation in the normal curriculum," Blackburn (1971) has on occasion instructed his chemistry students to examine "the colors, smells, textures, and changes of some substances on which they would do a rigorous and abstractly interpreted experiment the following week" (p. 1007).

As we have seen, the recent professional literature, a very small part of which has been cited, is full of doubts and misgivings about the procedures that psychology should use in its research and in its interpretation of findings. Our student bodies contain an even higher proportion of doubters than our professional literature. The general public may have an even more extreme proportion of doubters, and some of them are easily swayed by the spurious arguments of those who deride the experimental and scientific side of science. A leader among critics has been Senator William Proxmire, with his "Golden Fleece" award for researchers who he believes have fleeced the public of money for worthless research. Psychologists have been prominent among recipients of his award. We would not argue that every piece of research is worth the money spent on it, but science as a total enterprise has been highly profitable to society. If psychology is to maintain a viable public image, which will largely determine the size and nature of its research and instructional support, psychologists have to do a much better job of educating the public. We need to present the case for our scientific identity in a clear and forceful manner. However, we must be careful not to oversell psychology. It may be that much of the dissatisfaction with our modest achievements results from their being measured against unrealistically high expectations.

We conclude that there is nothing logically inapplicable or otherwise intrinsically wrong with the scientific method or with its particular techniques. The limitations on psychological science are primarily empirical, having to do with difficulties in identifying and controlling variables; the difficulties are not with our logic. It is also our conviction that many critics of scientific psychology do not really want psychology to be scientific but would prefer to work within its prescientific, or extrascientific, phases (for example, Koch, 1969, 1981). That is fine for those who wish to do it, but their work should then be identified as *complementing* more orthodox scientific approaches rather than as *replacing* them. Those psychologists who prefer the scientific approach could continue to follow a firm and consistent path, staying within the framework of science. Psychology needs to continue to exert a strong effort to build up a body of empirically verified and theoretically interrelated knowledge about behavioral and mental events and their determinants.

SUMMARY AND CONCLUSIONS

The dramatic increases in the applications of psychology over the last 20 years have brought about a greater interdependence between psychology and the larger society. With this has come a greater awareness by psychologists of their social responsibilities. *The American Psychologist* and the APA *Monitor* regularly carry articles by political figures, as well as news on federal legislation which affects psychology.

There is no shortage of problems whose solution depends upon the application of psychological expertise. Although the necessary expertise is not always available, the amount available in most cases exceeds current levels of recognition of its availability. Psychology is sometimes tarred with the brush of "soft science" or even of pseudoscience. It is not easy to avoid these characterizations when psychologists continue to be faced with problems whose solutions require fundamental research which has not yet been done, and are pressured to do the best they can anyway. However, considered as a whole, our discipline is doing well at walking the fine line between overselling and underselling its capabilities.

Tolerance of all aspects of psychology by psychologists also seems to be on the rise; although there continue to be plenty of healthy disagreements, there is a general recognition that the applied and artistic side of psychology depends on a strong basic research component, and a case can be made that the reverse dependency is just as strong. Much work remains to be done by way of communicating the broad scope of psychology to the general public and to other segments of the scientific community. We can expect our image to become clearer with the passage of time, since there is already considerable awareness of the importance of psychological knowledge in the solution of social problems.

On the intellectual front, there has been a shift away from a strict behavioristic viewpoint toward a more cognitive psychology which includes models of central processes and a recognition of consciousness. However, behavioristic psychology still plays a critical role in the overall picture and will ensure that cognitive psychology does not stray too far from the path of operationism. At the same time that consciousness is returning to psychology, even more fundamental work in neurophysiology and neuropsychology is being done with instrumentation of ever-increasing sophistication. Computer simulation of processes ranging from the behavior of single neurons to the behavior of societies will come into much greater favor over the next few years. The intellectual future of psychology, as well as its social future, looks very exciting from our present perspective.

FURTHER READINGS

The best way to keep up on the ever-shifting place of psychology in society is to read two periodical publications of the American Psychological Association, the *American Psychologist* and the newsletter, the *Monitor*. Sources of more general news about science are the publication of the American Association for the Advancement of Science, *Science,* whose News and Comment section will help you keep your finger on the pulse of the general body of science. If one is to understand the place of psychology in its relationship to other sciences, it is critical to get this broader view. Finally, for more long-term perspectives, we suggest Hearst's (1979) *The first century of experimental psychology,* Gilgen's (1982) *American psychology since World War II,* and Sarris and Parducci's (1984) *Perspectives in psychological experimentation: Toward the year 2000.*

REFERENCES

Abramson, L. Y., Seligman, M. E. P., & Teasdale, J. E. (1978). Learned helplessness in humans: Critique and reformulation. *Journal of Abnormal Psychology, 87*, 49–74.

Ach, N. (1910). *Über den Willensakt und des Temperament: Ein experimentelle Untersuchung.* Leipzig: Quelee & Meyer.

Adams, V. (1982). Mommy and I are one: Beaming messages to inner space. *Psychology Today, 16*, 24–36.

Adelman, H. M., & Maatsch, J. L. (1955). Resistance to extinction as a function of the type of response elicited by frustration. *Journal of Experimental Psychology, 50*, 61–65.

——— & ———. (1956). Learning and extinction based on frustration, food reward, and exploratory tendency. *Journal of Experimental Psychology, 52*, 311–315.

Allport, G. W. (1937). *Personality: A psychological interpretation.* New York: Holt.

Alper, T. G. (1948). Memory for completed and incompleted tasks as a function of personality: Correlation between experimental and personality data. *Journal of Personality, 17*, 104–137.

American Psychologist (1958). Vol. **13**, p. 735.

Ammons, R. B. (1962). Psychology of the scientist. II. Clark L. Hull and his "idea books." *Perceptual and Motor Skills, 15*, 800–802.

Amsel, A. (1967). Partial reinforcement effects on vigor and persistence. In K. W. Spence and J. T. Spence (Eds.), *The psychology of learning and motivation.* Vol. 1. New York: Academic Press.

——— & Ward, J. S. (1965). Frustration and persistence: Resistance to extinction following prior experience with the discriminanda. *Psychological Monographs, 79*, No. 4 (Whole No. 597).

Anderson, J. R. (1985). *Cognitive psychology and its implications.* New York: Freeman.

Anderson, R. J. (1971). Attribution of quotations from Wundt. *American Psychologist, 26*, 590–593.

Angell, J. R. (1903). The relations of structural and functional psychology to philosophy. *Philosophical Review*, **12**, 243–271.

———— (1904). *Psychology: An introductory study of the structure and function of human consciousness*. New York: Holt.

————. (1907). The province of functional psychology. *Psychological Review*, **14**. 61–91.

————. (1913). Behavior as a category of psychology. *Psychological Review*, **20**, 255–270.

———— & Moore, A. W. (1896). Reaction time: A study in attention and habit. *Psychological Review*, **3**, 245–258.

Arbib, M. (1964). *Brains, machines, and mathematics*. New York: McGraw-Hill.

Ardrey, R. (1961). *African genesis*. New York: Atheneum.

————. (1966). *The territorial imperative*. New York: Atheneum.

————. (1970). *The social contract*. New York: Atheneum.

Asch, S. E., Hay, J., & Diamond, R. M. (1960). Perceptual organization in serial rote-learning. *American Journal of Psychology*, **73**, 177–198.

Ashton, M. (1964). An ecological study of the stream of behavior. Master's thesis, University of Kansas.

Attneave, F. (1954). Some informational aspects of visual perception. *Psychological Review*, **61**, 183–193.

————. (1959). *Applications of information theory to psychology: A summary of basic concepts, methods, and results*. New York: Holt.

Bacon, F. (1857; originally published 1605). *The works of Francis Bacon: Philosophical writings*. Boston: Houghton Mifflin.

————. (1960; originally published 1620). *The new organon, and related writings*. Edited by F. H. Anderson. Indianapolis: Bobbs-Merrill.

Bacon, W. E. (1965). Resistance to extinction following blocking of the instrumental response during acquisition. *Journal of Experimental Psychology*, **69**, 515–521.

Bain, A. (1855; republished 1886). *The senses and the intellect*. London: Parker.

————. (1859). *The emotions and the will*. London: Parker.

Bakan, D. (1958). *Sigmund Freud and the Jewish mystical tradition*. Princeton, NJ: Van Nostrand.

————. (1968). Is phrenology foolish? *Psychology Today*, **1**, 44–51.

Banks, W. (1970). Signal detection theory and human memory. *Psychological Bulletin*, **74**, 81–99.

Barker, R. G. (1968). *Ecological psychology*. Stanford, CA: Stanford University Press.

————. (1969). Wanted: An eco-behavioral science, In E. P. Willems & H. L. Rausch (Eds.), *Naturalistic viewpoints in psychological research*. New York: Holt, Rinehart, Winston, pp. 31–43.

————, Dembo, T., & Lewin, K. (1941). Frustration and regression: A study of young children. *University of Iowa Studies in Child Welfare*, **18**, 1.

———— & Gump, P. V. (1964). *Big school, small school*. Stanford, CA: Stanford University Press.

Barnes, K. (1985). Expert systems offer advantages in training use. *PC Week*, **2**, No. 23, 38.

Bauer, H. H. (1985). *Beyond Velikovsky: The history of a public controversy*. Urbana, IL: University of Illinois Press.

Beach, F. A., Hebb, D. O., Morgan, C. T., & Nissen, H. W. (Eds.), (1960). *The neuropsychology of Lashley: Selected papers of K. S. Lashley*. New York: McGraw-Hill.

Beck, A. T. (1976). *Depression: Clinical, experimental, and theoretical aspects*. New York: Harper & Row.

Becker, R. J. (1959). Outstanding contributors to psychology. *American Psychologist*, **14**, 297–298.

Bekhterev, V. M. (1913; trans. from the original 1910 Russian ed.) *Objektive Psychologie: Oder Psychoreflexologie, die Lehre von den Assoziationsreflexen*. Leipzig: G. G. Teubner. Republished London: Jarrolds Publishers, 1933.

Bellak, L., & Smith, M. B. (1956). An experimental exploration of the psychoanalytic process. *Psychoanalytic Quarterly*, **25**, 385–414.

Bem, D. J., & Bem, S. L. (1968). Nativism revisited: Review of E. H. Lenneberg's *Biological foundations of language*. *Journal of the Experimental Analysis of Behavior*, **11**, 497–501.

Benjamin, L. J. (1981). *Teaching history of psychology: A handbook*. New York: Academic Press.

Bergmann, G. (1956). The contribution of John B. Watson. *Psychological Review*, **63**, 265–276.

Berkeley, G. (1709). *An essay toward a new theory of vision*. Dublin: Jeremy Pepyat.

———. (1710). *Principles of human knowledge*. Oxford: Oxford University Press.

Bettelheim, B. (1982). Reflections: Freud and the soul. *New Yorker*, March 1, 52–93.

Beveridge, W. I. B. (1957). *The art of scientific investigation*. New York: Vintage Books.

Birdsall, T. (1953). An application of game theory to signal detectability. Technical Report 20, Electronic Defense Group, University of Michigan.

Black, A. H. (1967). Operant conditioning in curarized dogs. *Conditioned Reflex*, **2**, 158.

———. (1977). Comments on "Learned helplessness: Theory and evidence." *Journal of Experimental Psychology: General*, **106**, 41–43.

Blackburn, T. R. (1971). Sensuous-intellectual complementarity in science. *Science*, **172**, 1003–1007.

Blodgett, H. C. (1929). The effects of the introduction of reward upon the maze performance of rats. *University of California Publications in Psychology*, **4**, 113–134.

Blumenthal, A. L. (1980). Wilhelm Wundt—Problems of interpretation. In W. G. Bringmann & R. D. Tweney (Eds.), *Wundt studies*. Toronto: C. J. Hogrefe.

Boice, R. (1977). Heroes and teachers. *Teaching of Psychology*, **4**, 55–58.

Boole, G. (1854). *An investigation of the laws of thought*. New York: Dover.

Boring, E. G. (1933). *The physical dimensions of consciousness*. New York: Appleton-Century-Crofts.

———. (1937). A psychological function is the relation of successive differentiations of events in the organism. *Psychological Review*, **44**, 445–461.

———. (1950). *A history of experimental psychology*. New York: Appleton-Century-Crofts.

———. (1953). A history of introspection. *Psychological Bulletin*, **50**, 169–187.

———. (1964). Cognitive dissonance: Its use in science. *Science*, **145**, 680–685.

———, & Lindzey, G. (Eds.). (1967). *A history of psychology in autobiography*. New York: Appleton-Century-Crofts.

Bottenberg, R. A., Marx, M. H., & Pavur, E. J., Jr. (1976). Differential recall of the problem names and clues as a function of problem solution or nonsolution. *Bulletin of the Psychonomic Society*, **7**, 445–448.

Bower, G. H., & Hilgard, E. R. (1981). *Theories of learning*. 5th ed. Englewood Cliffs, NJ: Prentice-Hall.

Bradford, L. P., Gibb, J. R., & Benne, K. D. (1964). *T-group theory and laboratory method: Innovation in re-education*. New York: Wiley.

Breland, K., & Breland, M. (1951). A field of applied animal psychology. *American Psychologist*, **6**, 202–204.

——— & ———. (1961). The misbehavior of organisms. *American Psychologist* **16**, 681–684.

——— & ———. (1966). *Animal behavior*. New York: Macmillan.

Brentano, F. (1955; orginally published 1874). *Psychologie von empirischen Standpunkte.* Leipzig: Heiner.

Breuer, J., & Freud, S. (1895). *Studien über Hysterie.* Vienna: Franz Deuticke.

Bridges, K. M. B. (1932). Emotional development in early infancy. *Child Development,* **3,** 324–341.

Bridgman, P. W. (1927). *The logic of modern physics.* New York: Macmillan.

———. (1952). *The nature of some of our physical concepts.* New York: Philosophical Library.

Bringmann, W. G., Balance, W. D. G., & Evans, R. B. (1975). Wilhelm Wundt 1832–1920: A brief biographical sketch. *Journal of the History of the Behavioral Sciences,* **11,** 287–297.

———, Bringmann, N. J., & Balance, D. G. (1980). Wilhelm Maxmilian Wundt 1832–1874: The formative years. In W. G. Bringmann & R. D. Tweney (Eds.), *Wundt studies.* Toronto: C. J. Hogrefe. Pp. 13–32.

——— & Tweney, R. D. (Eds.). (1980). *Wundt studies.* Toronto: C. J. Hogrefe.

Broadbent, D. E. (1958). *Perception and communication.* London: Pergamon Press.

Brown, J. F. (1936). On the use of mathematics in psychological theory. *Psychometrika,* **1,** 7–15, 77–90. Also in M. H. Marx (Ed.). (1951). *Psychological theory: Contemporary readings.* New York: Macmillan. Pp. 233–256.

——— & Voth, A. C. (1937). The path of seen movement as a function of the vector-field. *American Journal of Psychology,* **49,** 543–563.

Brown, P. L., & Jenkins, H. M. (1968). Auto-shaping of the pigeon's key-peck. *Journal of the Experimental Analysis of Behavior,* **11,** 1–8.

Brozek, J. (1973). Soviet psychology. In M. H. Marx, & W. A. Hillix, *Systems and theories in psychology.* 2d. ed. New York: McGraw-Hill. Pp. 521–548.

Bruner, J. S., & Goodman, C. C. (1947). Value and need as organizing factors in perception. *Journal of Abnormal and Social Psychology,* **42,** 33–44.

Brunswik, E. (1934). *Wahrnehmung und Gegenstandswelt.* Vienna: Franz Deuticke.

———. (1939a). The conceptual focus of some psychological systems. *Journal of Unified Science,* **8,** 36–49. Reprinted in M. H. Marx (Ed.). (1951). *Psychological theory: Contemporary readings.* New York: Macmillan. Pp. 131–143.

———. (1939b). Probability as a determiner of rat behavior. *Journal of Experimental Psychology,* **25,** 175–197.

———. (1943). Organismic achievement and environmental probability. *Psychological Review,* **50,** 255–272.

———. (1949). Discussion: Remarks on functionalism in perception. *Journal of Personality,* **18,** 56–65.

———. (1952). The conceptual framework of psychology. *International Encyclopedia of Unified Science,* **1,** No. 10, 1–102.

———. (1955a). Representative design and probabilistic theory in a functional psychology. *Psychological Review,* **62,** 193–217.

———. (1955b). In defense of probabilistic functionalism: a reply. *Psychological Review,* **62,** 236–242.

———. (1956). *Perception and the representative design of psychological experiments.* Berkeley: University of California Press.

——— & Kamiya, J. (1953). Ecological cue-validity of "proximity" and of other Gestalt factors. *American Journal of Psychology,* **66,** 20–32.

Buckley, W. (Ed.). (1968). *Modern systems research for the behavioral scientist: A sourcebook.* Chicago: Aldine.

Burnham, J. C. (1968). On the origins of behaviorism. *Journal of the History of the Behavioral Sciences,* **4,** 143–151.

Buss, A. (1973). *Psychology: Man in perspective*. New York: Wiley.

Butterfield, H. (1957). *The origins of modern science: 1300–1800* (rev. ed.) New York: Macmillan.

Buxton, C. E. (1940). Latent learning and the goal gradient hypothesis. *Contributions to psychological theory*, **2** (2).

Campbell, N. R. (1920). *Physics: The elements*. Cambridge, MA: Cambridge University Press.

Capretta, P. J. (1967). *A history of psychology in outline*. New York: Dell.

Carr, H. A. (1925). *Psychology: A study of mental activity*. New York: Longmans.

Carterette, E. C., & Cole, M. (1962). Comparison of the receiver-operating characteristics for messages received by ear and eye. *Journal of the Acoustical Society of America*, **34**, 172–178.

Cartwright, D. (1959). Lewinian theory as a contemporary systematic framework. In S. Koch (Ed.), *Psychology: A study of a science*. Vol. 2. *General systematic formulations, learning and special processes*. New York: McGraw-Hill. Pp. 7–91.

Chomsky, N. (1957). *Syntactic structures*. The Hague: Mouton.

———. (1959). Review of *Verbal behavior* by B. F. Skinner. *Language*, **35**, 26–58.

———. (1972). *Language and mind*. Enlarged ed. New York: Harcourt Brace Jovanovich.

Coan, R. W. (1979). *Psychologists: Personal and theoretical pathways*. New York: Irvington.

——— & Zagona, S. V. (1962). Contemporary ratings of psychological theorists. *Psychological Record*, **12**, 315–322.

Cohen, D. (1979). *J. B. Watson: The founder of behaviorism*, London: Routledge & Kegan Paul.

Cole, M. (1984). The world beyond our borders. What might our students need to know about it? *American Psychologist*, **39**, 998–1005.

——— & Maltzman, I. (Eds.) (1969). *A handbook of contemporary Soviet psychology*. New York: Basic Books.

Comte, A. (1896; first published 1824). *The positive philosophy*. (Trans. by H. Martin). London: B. Bell.

Conant, J. B. (1947). *On understanding science: A historical approach*. New Haven, CT: Yale University Press.

———. (1957). *Harvard case histories in experimental science*. Cambridge, MA: Harvard University Press.

Cook, O. J. (1963). "Superstition" in the Skinnerian. *American Psychologist*, **18**, 516–518.

Corteen, R. S., & Wood, B. (1972). Automatic responses to shock-associated words in an unattended channel. *Journal of Experimental Psychology*, **94**, 308–313.

Cotton, J. W. (1955). On making predictions from Hull's theory. *Psychological Review*, **62**, 303–314.

———, Lewis, D. J., & Metzger, R. (1958). Running behavior as a function of apparatus and of restriction of goal box activity. *Journal of Comparative and Physiological Psychology*, **51**, 336–341.

Crannell, C. W. (1970). Wolfgang Köhler. *Journal of the History of the Behavioral Sciences*, **6**, 267–268.

Dallenbach, K. M. (1955). Phrenology versus psychoanalysis. *American Journal of Psychology*, **68**(4), 511–525.

Danziger, K. (1979). The positivist repudiation of Wundt. *Journal of the History of the Behavioral Sciences*, **15**, 205–230.

———. (1985). The origins of the psychological experiment as a social institution. *American Psychologist*, **40**(2), 133–140.

Darwin, C. (1872). *Expression of emotions in man and animals*. 2d ed. London: J. Murray.

———. (1909; originally published 1859). *Origin of species*. 2d ed. London: Collier.

Daub, C. T. (1933). The effect of doors on latent learning. *Journal of Comparative Psychology*, **15**, 49–58.

Dawkins, R. (1976). *The selfish gene*. New York: Oxford University Press.

Dennis, W. (Ed.), (1948). *Readings in the history of psychology*. New York: Appleton-Century-Crofts.

Denny, M. R. (1971). Relaxation theory and experiments. In F. R. Brush (Ed.), *Aversive conditioning and learning*. New York: Academic Press.

De Rivera, J. (1976). *Field theory as human science: Contributions of Lewin's Berlin group*. New York: Halsted Press.

Deutsch, J. A. (1960). *The structural basis of behavior*. Chicago: University of Chicago Press.

———— & Clarkson, J. K. (1959). Reasoning in the hooded rat. *Quarterly Journal of Experimental Psycholgy*, **11**, 150–154.

Deutsch, M. (1954). Field theory in social psychology. In G. Lindzey (Ed.), *Handbook of social psychology*. Reading, MA: Addison-Wesley. Pp. 181–222.

Dewey, J. (1886). *Psychology*. New York: Harper.

————. (1896). The reflex arc concept in psychology. *Psychological Review*, **3**, 357–370.

————. (1900). Psychology and social practice. *Psychological Review*, **2**, 105–124.

Diesing, P. (1971). *Patterns of discovery in the social sciences*. Chicago: Aldine-Atherton.

Diserens, C. M. (1925). Psychological objectivism. *Psychological Review*, **32**, 121–152.

Dittman, A. T. (1966). Psychotherapeutic processes. *Annual Review of Psychology*, **17**, 57–78.

Dixon, N. F. (1971). *Subliminal perception: The nature of a controversy*. London: McGraw-Hill.

————. (1981). *Preconscious processing*. Chichester, England: Wiley.

Dodd, D. H., & Bradshaw, J. M. (1980). Leading questions and memory: Pragmatic constraints. *Journal of Verbal Learning and Verbal Behavior*, **19**, 695–704.

Dollard, J., & Miller, N. E. (1950). *Personality and psychotherapy: An analysis in terms of learning, thinking, and culture*. New York: McGraw-Hill.

Donders, F. C. (1862). Die Schnelligkeit psychischer Processe. *Archiv Anatomie und Physiologie*, 657–681.

Dorfman, D. D., & Alf, E., Jr. (1968). Maximum likelihood estimation of parameters of signal-detection theory: A direct solution. *Psychometrika*, **33**, 117–124.

———— & ————. (1969). Maximum-likelihood estimation of parameters of signal-detection theory and determination of confidence intervals—Rating method data. *Journal of Mathematical Psychology*, **6**, 487–496.

Duncker, K. (1945; originally published 1935). On problem solving. (Trans. by L. S. Lews). *Psychological Monographs*, **58**, 270.

Ebbinghaus, H. (1913; originally published 1885). *Über das Gedachtnis*. [Reprinted as *Memory*. (Trans. by H. A. Ruger & C. E. Busenius). New York: Teachers College.]

Edwards, D. D., West, J. R., & Jackson, V. (1968). The role of contingencies in the control of behavior. *Psychonomic Science*, **10**, 39–40.

Egan, J. P. (1958). *Recognition memory and the operating characteristic*. Technical Report No. AFCRC-TN-58-51, AD-152650, Indiana University, Hearing and Communications Laboratory.

————. (1975). *Signal detection theory and ROC analysis*. New York: Academic Press.

Ellenberger, H. (1956). Fechner and Freud. *Bulletin of Menninger Clinic*, **20**, 201–214.

————. (1970). *The discovery of the unconscious*. New York: Basic Books.

————. (1972). The story of "Anna O": A critical review with new data. *Journal of the History of the Behavioral Sciences*, **8**, 267–279.

Ellis, W. D. (1938). *A source book of Gestalt psychology*. New York: Harcourt, Brace & World.

Ellison, G. D., & Konorski, J. (1964). Separation of the salivary and motor responses in instrumental conditioning. *Science, 146*, 1071–1072.

Erdelyi, M. H. (1974). A new look at the new look: Perceptual defense and vigilance. *Psychological Review, 81*, 1–25.

Ericsson, K. A., & Simon, H. A. (1980). Verbal reports as data. *Psychological Review, 87*, 215–251.

———— & ————. (1984). *Protocol analysis: Verbal reports as data*. Cambridge, MA: MIT Press.

Esper, E. A. (1967). Max Meyer in America. *Journal of the History of the Behavioral Sciences, 3*, 107–131.

Estes, W. K. (1950). Toward a statistical theory of learning. *Psychological Review, 57*, 94–107.

————. (1954). Kurt Lewin. In W. K. Estes et al. (Eds.), *Modern learning theory*. New York: Appleton-Century-Crofts. Pp. 317–344.

————. (1959a). Component and pattern models with Markovian interpretations. In R. R. Bush & W. K. Estes (Eds.), *Studies in mathematical learning theory*. Stanford, CA: Stanford University Press. Pp. 9–52.

————. (1959b). The statistical approach to learning theory. In S. Koch (Ed.), *Psychology: A study of a science*. Vol. 2. *General systematic formulations, learning and special processes*. New York: McGraw-Hill. Pp. 380–491.

————. (1960). Learning theory and the new "mental chemistry." *Psychological Review, 67*, 207–223.

————. (Ed.). (1975–1978). *Handbook of learning and cognitive processes*. Vols. 1–5. Hillsdale, NJ: Erlbaum.

————, Hopkins, B. L., & Crothers, E. J. (1960). All-or-none and conservation effects in the learning and retention of paired associates. *Psychological Review, 67*, 329–339.

————, Koch, S., MacCorquodale, K., Meehl, P. E., Mueller, C. G., Jr., Schoenfeld, W. N., & Verplanck, W. S. (1954). *Modern learning theory*. New York: Appleton-Century-Crofts.

Evans, R. B. (1972). E. B. Titchener and his lost system. *Journal of the History of the Behavioral Sciences, 2*, 168–180.

Evans, R. B., & Koelsch, W. A. (1985). Psychoanalysis arrives in America: The 1909 psychology conference at Clark University. *American Psychologist, 40*, 942–948.

Evans, R. I. (1968). *B. F. Skinner: The man and his ideas*. New York: Dutton.

Ezriel, H. (1951). The scientific testing of psychoanalytic findings and theory. *British Journal of Medical Psychology, 24*, 26–29.

Fairweather, G. W., Sanders, D. H., Maynard, H. & Cressler, D. L. (1969). *Community life for the mentally ill: An alternative to institutional care*. New York: Aldine.

————, & ————, & Tornatzky, L. G. (1974). *Creating change in mental health organizations*. New York: Pergamon.

———— & Tornatzky, L. G. (1977). *Experimental methods for social policy research*. Oxford: Pergamon.

Falk, J. L. (1956). Issues distinguishing idiographic from nomothetic approaches to personality theory. *Psychological Review, 63*, 53–62.

Farrell, B. A. (1951). The scientific testing of psychoanalytic findings and theory. *British Journal of Medical Psychology, 24*, 35–41.

Fawl, C. L. (1963). Disturbances experienced by children in their natural habitats. In R. G. Barker (Ed.), *The stream of behavior*. New York: Appleton-Century-Crofts. Pp. 99–126.

Fechner, G. T. (1860). *Elemente der Psychophysik*. Leipzig: Breitkopf & Hartel.

Feigl, H. (1970). The "orthodox" view of theories: Remarks in defense as well as critique. In M. Radner & S. Winokur (Eds.), *Analyses of theories and methods of physics and psychology*. Minneapolis: University of Minnesota Press.

———, Scriven, M., & Maxwell, G. (Eds.). (1958). *Minnesota studies in the philosophy of science*. Vol. 2. Minneapolis: University of Minnesota Press.

Felsinger, J. M., Gladstone, A. I., Yamaguchi, H. G., & Hull, C. L. (1947). Reaction latency (str) as a function of the number of reinforcements (N). *Journal of Experimental Psychology,* **37**, 214–228.

Ferenczi, S., & Rank, O. (1956; originally published 1925). *The development of psychoanalysis*. (Trans. by Caroline Newton). New York: Nervous and Mental Disease Publishing.

Ferster, C. B., & Skinner, B. F. (1957). *Schedules of reinforcement*. New York: Appleton-Century-Crofts.

Feyerabend, P. K. (1970). Against method: Outline of an anarchistic theory of knowledge. In M. Radner and S. Winokur (Eds.), *Minnesota studies in the philosophy of science*. Vol. 4, Minneapolis: University of Minnesota Press. Pp. 17–26, 91–92.

Fisher, R. (1966). Biological time. In J. T. Fraser (Ed.), *The voices of time*. New York: George Braziller. Pp. 357–382.

Fisher, S., & Greenberg, R. P. (1977). Stomach symptoms and up-down metaphors and gradients. *Psychosomatic Medicine,* **39**, 93–101.

Fitts, P. M., & Posner, M. I. (1967). *Human performance*. Belmont, CA: Brooks/Cole.

Ford, D. H., & Urban, H. B. (1967). Psychotherapy. *Annual Review of Psychology,* **18**, 333–372.

Frank, J. D. (1935). Some psychological determinants of the level of aspiration. *American Journal of Psychology,* **47**, 285–293.

———. (1974). My philosophy of psychotherapy. *Journal of Contemporary Psychotherapy,* **6**, 115–120.

———. (1983). Therapeutic components of psychotherapy. *Journal of Nervous and Mental Disease,* **159**, 325–343.

Frankel, C. (1973). The nature and sources of irrationalism. *Science,* **180**, 927–931.

Freeman, L. (1972). *The story of Anna O*. New York: Walker.

Freud, S. (1950; originally published 1900). *The interpretation of dreams*. New York: Modern Library.

———. (1938). The history of the psychoanalytic movement. In A. A. Brill (Ed. & Trans.), *The basic writing of Sigmund Freud*. New York: Random House.

———. (1943). *A general introduction to psychoanalysis*. (Trans. by J. Riviere). Garden City, NY: Doubleday.

Frisch, K. von. (1965). Tanzsprache und Orientierung der Bienen. [Dance language and orientation in bees.]. New York: Springer-Verlag.

Fromm, E. (1941). *Escape from freedom*. New York: Holt.

———. (1947). *Man for himself*. New York: Holt.

———. (1955). *The sane society.*. New York: Holt.

———. (1959). *Sigmund Freud's mission*. New York: Harper.

———. (1961a). *Marx's concept of man*. New York: Ungar.

———. (1961b). *May man prevail? An inquiry into the facts and fictions of foreign policy*. Garden City, NY: Doubleday.

———. (1964). *The heart of man*. New York: Harper & Row.

Fuchs, A. H., & Kawash, G. F. (1974). Prescriptive dimensions of five schools of psychology. *Journal of the History of the Behavioral Sciences,* **10**, 352–366.

Galton, F. (1883; originally published 1869). *Hereditary genius: An inquiry into its laws and consequences*. New York: Appleton-Century.

Gardner, R. A., & Gardner, B. T. (1969). Teaching sign language to a chimpanzee. *Science,* **165**, 664–672.

Garner, W. R. (1960). Rating scales, discriminability and information transmission. *Psychological Review,* **67**, 343–352.

———. (1962). *Uncertainty and structure as psychological concepts.* New York: Wiley.

———. (1966). To perceive is to know. *American Psychologist,* **21**, 11–19.

———, Hake, W. H., & Eriksen, C. W. (1956). Operationism and the concept of perception. *Psychological Review,* **63**, 149–159.

Gates, A. I. (1942). Connectionism: Present concepts and interpretations. *Yearbook of National Society of the Study of Education,* **41**, Part II, 141–164.

Gazzaniga, M. S. (1981). Nobel prize for physiology or medicine. *Science,* **214**, 517–518.

Geissler, L. R. (1909). The measurement of attention. *American Journal of Psychology,* **20**, 473–529.

Gholson, B., & Barker, P. (1985). Kuhn, Lakatos, and Laudan. Applications in the history of physics and psychology. *American Psychologist,* **40**, 755–769.

Gibson, J. J. (1960). The concept of stimulus in psychology. *American Psychologist,* **15**, 694–703.

———. (1966). *The senses considered as perceptual systems.* Boston: Houghton Mifflin.

Gilgen, A. R. (1982). *American psychology since World War II: A profile of the discipline.* Westport, CT: Greenwood Press.

Gleitman, J. (1950). Studies in motivation and learning: II. Thirsty rats trained in a maze with food but no water; then run hungry. *Journal of Experimental Psychology,* **40**, 169–174.

Goesling, W. J., & Brener, J. (1972). Effects of activity and immobility conditioning upon subsequent heart-rate conditioning in curarized rats. *Journal of Comparative and Physiological Psychology,* **81**, 311–317.

Goldiamond, I. (1958). Indicators of perception. I. Subliminal perception, subception, unconscious perception. *Psychological Bulletin,* **55**, 373–411.

Golomb, S. W. (1982). Rubik's cube and quarks. *American Scientist,* **70**, 257–259.

Goodall, K. (1972). Tie line. *Psychology Today,* **5**, 24–28.

Goodson, F. E. (1973). *The evolutionary foundations of psychology.* New York: Holt.

Gray, J. A. (1969). Sodium amobarbital and effects of frustrative nonreward. *Journal of Comparative and Physiological Psychology,* **69**, 55–64.

Green, D. M., & Swets, J. A. (1974). *Signal detection theory and psychophysics.* New York: Krieger.

Greene, E., Flynn, M. S., & Loftus, E. F. (1982). Inducing resistance to misleading information. *Journal of Verbal Learning and Verbal Behavior,* **21**, 207–219.

Greenwald, A. G., Pratkanis, A. R., Leippe, M. R., & Baumgardner, M. H. (1986). Under what conditions does theory obstruct progress? *Psychological Review,* **93**, 216–229.

Grice, G. R. (1948). An experimental study of the gradient of reinforcement in maze learning. *Journal of Comparative and Physiological Psychology,* **41**, 137–143.

Griffin, D. R. (1976). *The question of animal awareness.* New York: Rockefeller University Press.

———. (1984). *Animal thinking.* Cambridge, MA: Harvard University Press.

Grisso, T., Sales, B. D., & Bayless, S. (1982). Law-related courses and programs in graduate psychology departments. *American Psychologist,* **37**, 267–278.

Gulliksen, H. (1968). Louis Leon Thurstone, experimental and mathematical psychologist. *American Psychologist,* **23**, 786–802.

Guthrie, E. R. (1935). *The psychology of learning.* New York: Harper & Row.

————. (1938). *The psychology of human conflict*. New York: Harper & Row.

————. (1942). Conditioning: A theory of learning in terms of stimulus, response, and association. *Yearbook of the National Society for the Study of Education*, **41**, Part II, 17–60.

————. (1952). *The psychology of learning*. Rev. ed. New York: Harper & Row.

————. (1959). Association by contiguity. In S. Koch (Ed.), *Psychology: A study of a science*. Vol. 2. *General systematic formulations, learning and special processes*. New York: McGraw-Hill. Pp. 158–195.

———— & Horton, G. P. (1946). *Cats in a puzzle box*. New York: Holt.

Haber, R. N. (Ed.). (1966). *Current research in motivation*. New York: Holt, Rinehart & Winston.

Hall, C. S. (1954). *A primer of Freudian psychology*. Cleveland: World Publishing.

———— & Lindzey, G. (1957). *Theories of personality*. New York: Wiley.

———— & ————. (1970). *Theories of personality*. 2d ed. New York: Wiley.

Hall, G. S. (1904). *Adolescence*. New York: Appleton.

————. (1917). *Jesus, the Christ, in the light of psychology*. Garden City, NY: Doubleday.

————. (1922). *Senescence: The last half of life*. New York: Appleton.

Hall, M. H. (1967). An interview with "Mr. Behaviorist" B. F. Skinner. *Psychology Today*, **1**, 2–23, 68–71.

Hall, S. S. (1985). Aplysia & Hermissenda: Two snails are leading the race to trace the molecules of memory. *Science 85*, May, 30–39.

Halliday, M. S. (1979). Jerzy Konorski and Western psychology. In A. Dickinson & R. A. Boakes (Eds.), *Mechanisms of learning and motivation: A memorial volume to Jerzy Konorski*. Hillsdale, NJ: Erlbaum.

Hammond, K. R. (1954). Representative vs. systematic design in clinical psychology. *Psychological Bulletin*, **51**, 150–159.

————. (1955). Probabilistic functioning and the clinical method. *Psychological Review*, **62**, 255–262.

————. (Ed.). (1966). *The psychology of Egon Brunswik*. New York: Holt.

Haney, G. W. (1931). The effect of familiarity on maze performance of albino rats. *University of California Publications*, **4**, 319–333.

Harlow, H. F. (1949). The formation of learning sets. *Psychological Review*, **56**, 51–65.

————. (1950). Analysis of discrimination learning by monkeys. *Journal of Experimental Psychology*, **40**, 26–39.

————. (1951). Primate learning. In C. P. Stone (Ed.), *Comparative psychology*. Englewood Cliffs, NJ: Prentice-Hall. Pp. 183–238.

————. (1959). Learning set and error factor theory. In S. Koch (Ed.), *Psychology: A study of a science*. Vol. II. New York: McGraw-Hill.

————. (1962). The heterosexual affectional system in monkeys. *American Psychologist*, **17**, 1–9.

————. (1973). *Learning to love*. San Francisco: Albion.

————, Hilgard, E. R., Leeper, R., Skinner, B. F., & Smith, M. B. (1962). American Psychological Association Distinguished Scientific Contribution Awards. *American Psychologist*, **17**, 888–898.

Harper, R. S., Newman, E. B., & Schab, F. R. (1985). Gabriele Grafin von Wartensleben and the birth of Gestaltpsychologie. *Journal of the History of the Behavioral Sciences*, **21**, 118–123.

Harrower, M. R. (1932). Organization in higher mental processes. *Psychologische Forschung*, **17**, 56–120.

Hartley, D. (1749). *Observations on man, his duty, and his expectations*. London: W. Eyres.

Hartley, D. E., & Strupp, H. H. (1983). The therapeutic alliance: Its relationship to outcome in brief psychotherapy. In J. Masling (Ed.), *Empirical studies of psychoanalytical theories.* Vol. 1. London: The Analytic Press.

Hartmann, G. W. (1935). *Gestalt psychology.* New York: Ronald Press.

Hasher, L., & Zacks, R. T. (1979). Automatic and effortful processes in memory. *Journal of Experimental Psychology: General,* **108**, 356–388.

——— & ———. (1984). Automatic processing of fundamental information: The case of frequency of occurrence. *American Psychologist,* **39**, 1372–1388.

Hays, R. (1962). Psychology of the scientist. III. Introduction to "Passages from the idea books of Clark L. Hull." *Perceptual and Motor Skills,* **15**, 803–806.

Hearst, E. (1968). Discrimination learning as the summation of excitation and inhibition. *Science,* **162**, 1303–1306.

———. (Ed.). (1979). *The first century of experimental psychology.* Hillsdale, NJ: Erlbaum.

Hebb, D. O. (1949). *The organization of behavior.* New York: Wiley.

———. (1959). A neuropsychological theory. In S. Koch (Ed.), *Psychology: A study of a science.* Vol. 1. *Sensory, perceptual, and physiological formulations.* New York: McGraw-Hill. Pp. 622–643.

Heidbreder, E. (1933). *Seven psychologies.* New York: Appleton-Century-Crofts.

Heider, F. (1970). Gestalt theory: Early history and reminiscences. *Journal of the History of the Behavioral Sciences,* **6**, 131–139.

Helson, H. (1925). The psychology of Gestalt. *American Journal of Psychology,* **36**, 342–370, 454–526.

———. (1926). The psychology of Gestalt. *American Journal of Psychology,* **37**, 25–62, 189–223.

———. (1933). The fundamental propositions of Gestalt psychology. *Psychological Review,* **40**, 12–32.

———. (1969). Why did their precursors fail and the Gestalt psychologists succeed? *American Psychologist,* **24**, 1006–1011.

Henle, M. (1957). Some problems of eclecticism. *Psychological Review,* **64**, 296–305.

———. (1961). *Documents of Gestalt psychology.* Berkeley: University of California Press.

———. (Ed.). (1971). *The selected papers of Wolfgang Köhler.* New York: Liveright.

———. (1974). E. B. Titchener and the case of the missing element. *Journal of the History of the Behavioral Sciences,* **10**, 227–237.

Herb, F. H. (1940). Latent learning-nonreward followed by food in blinds. *Journal of Comparative Psychology,* **29**, 247–255.

Herrnstein, R. J. (1966). Superstition: A corollary of the principles of operant conditioning. In W. K. Honig (Ed.), *Operant behavior: Areas of research and application.* New York: Appleton-Century-Crofts. Pp. 33–51.

———. (1977a). The evolution of behaviorism. *American Psychologist,* **32**, 593–603.

———. (1977b). Doing what comes naturally: A reply to Professor Skinner. *American Psychologist,* **10**, 1013–1016.

——— & Boring, E. G. (Eds.). (1965). *A source book in the history of psychology.* Cambridge, MA: Harvard University Press.

Hertel, P. T. (1982). Remembering reactions and facts: The influence of subsequent information. *Journal of Experimental Psychology: Learning, Memory, Cognition,* **8**, 513–529.

Hilgard, E. R. (1948). *Theories of learning.* New York: Appleton-Century.

———. (1952). Experimental approaches to psychoanalysis. In E. Pumpian-Mindlin (Ed.), *Psychoanalysis as science.* Stanford, CA: Stanford University Press. Pp. 3–45.

———. (1955). Discussion of probabilistic functionalism. *Psychological Review,* **62**, 226–228.

———. (1956). *Theories of learning.* Rev. ed. New York: Appleton-Century-Crofts.

———— & Bower, G. H. (1975). *Theories of learning.* 4th ed. New York: Appleton-Century-Crofts.

———— & Marquis, D. J. (1940). *Conditioning and learning.* New York: Appleton-Century-Crofts.

Hillix, W. A., & Broyles, J. W. (1980). The family trees of American psychologists. In W. G. Bringmann & R. D. Tweney (Eds.), *Wundt studies.* Toronto: C. J. Hogrefe. Pp. 422–434.

———— & Marx, M. H. (1960). Response strengthening by information and effect in human learning. *Journal of Experimental Psychology,* **60,** 97–102.

———— & ————. (Eds.). (1974). *Systems and theories in psychology: A reader.* St. Paul: West.

Hiroto, D. S., & Seligman, M. E. P. (1975). Generality of learned helplessness in man. *Journal of Personality and Social Psychology,* **31,** 311–327.

Hochberg, J. E. (1957). Effects of the Gestalt revolution: The Cornell symposium on perception. *Psychological Review,* **46,** 361–364.

———— & McAlister, E. A. (1953). A quantitative approach to figural "goodness." *Journal of Experimental Psychology,* **46,** 361–363.

Hocutt, M. (1967). On the alleged circularity of Skinner's concept of stimulus. *Psychological Review,* **74,** 530–532.

Hofstadter, R. (1955). *Social Darwinism in American thought.* Boston: Beacon Press.

Hofstadter, D. R. (1979). *Gödel, Escher, Bach: An eternal golden braid.* New York: Random House.

Holt, E. B. (1915). *The Freudian wish and its place in ethics.* New York: Holt.

————. (1931). *Animal drive and the learning process.* New York: Holt.

Holton, G. J. (1973). *Thematic origins of scientific thought, Kepler to Einstein.* Cambridge, MA: Harvard University Press.

———— (1978). *The scientific imagination: Case studies.* New York: Cambridge University Press.

Hoppe, F. (1930). Erfolg und Misserfolg. *Psychologische Forschung,* **14,** 1–62.

Horney, K. (1937). *Neurotic personality of our times.* New York: Norton.

————. (1939). *New ways in psychoanalysis.* New York: Norton.

————. (1942). *Self-analysis.* New York: Norton.

————. (1945). *Our inner conflicts.* New York: Norton.

————. (1950). *Neurosis and human growth.* New York: Norton.

Horwitz, L. (1963). Theory construction and validation in psychoanalysis. In M. H. Marx (Ed.), *Theories in contemporary psychology.* New York: Macmillan. Pp. 413–434.

Hull, C. L. (1920). Quantitative aspects of the evolution of concepts. *Psychological Monographs,* **28,** No. 123.

————. (1924). The influence of tobacco smoking on mental and motor efficiency. *Psychological Monographs,* **33**(3), 1–160.

————. (1928). *Aptitude testing.* Yonkers, NY: World.

————. (1932). The goal gradient hypothesis and maze learning. *Psychological Review,* **39,** 25–43.

————. (1933). *Hypnosis and suggestibility: An experimental approach.* New York: Appleton-Century.

————. (1935). The mechanism of the assembly of behavior segments in novel combinations suitable for problem solution. *Psychological Review,* **42,** 219–245.

————. (1937). Mind, mechanism, and adaptive behavior. *Psychological Review,* **44,** 1–32.

————. (1943). *Principles of behavior.* New York: Appleton-Century-Crofts.

————. (1951). *Essentials of behavior.* New Haven, CT: Yale University Press.

————. (1952). *A behavior system.* New Haven, CT: Yale University Press.

————. (1962). Psychology of the scientist. IV. Passages from the "idea books" of Clark L. Hull. *Perceptual and Motor Skills,* **15**, 807–882.

————, Hovland, C. L., Ross, R. T., Hall, M., Perkins, D. T., & Fitch, F. G. (1940). *Mathematico-deductive theory of rote learning.* New Haven, CT: Yale University Press.

Hume, D. (1776). *The history of England from the invasion of Julius Caesar to the abdication of James the Second 1688.* Vols. 1–5. Philadelphia: Porter & Coates.

————. (1886; originally published 1739–1740). *A treatise on human nature.* London: Longmans.

————. (1902; originally published 1748). *An enquiry concerning human understanding.* [2d ed.; L. A. Selby-Bigge (Ed.)]. Oxford: Clarendon Press.

Humphrey, N. (1984). *Consciousness regained: Chapters in the development of mind.* Oxford: Oxford University Press.

Hunter, W. S. (1924). The problem of consciousness. *Psychological Review,* **21**, 1–31.

————. (1926). Psychology and anthroponomy. In C. Murchison (Ed.), *Psychologies of 1925.* Worcester, MA: Clark University Press. Pp. 83–107.

Hursch, C. J., Hammond, K. R., & Hursch, J. L. (1964). Some methodological considerations in multiple-cue probability studies. *Psychological Review,* **71**, 42–60.

Irvine, W. (1963). *Apes, angels, and Victorians.* New York: Time-Life.

Jacoby, R. (1983). *The repression of psychoanalysis: Otto Fenichel and the political Freudians.* New York: Basic Books.

James, W. A. (1890). *The principles of psychology.* Vols. I and II. New York: Holt.

————. (1899). *Talks to teachers on psychology and to students on some of life's ideas.* New York: Holt.

————. (1902). *The varieties of religious experience.* New York: Holt.

Jaynes, J. (1976). *The origin of consciousness in the breakdown of the bicameral mind.* Boston: Houghton Mifflin.

Joncich, G. (1968). *The sane positivist: A biography of Edward L. Thorndike.* Middletown, CT: Wesleyan University Press.

Jones, E. (1953; 1955; 1957). *The life and work of Sigmund Freud.* Vols. 1–3. New York: Basic Books.

Jones, M. C. (1924). A laboratory study of fear: The case of Peter. *Pedagogical Seminary,* **31**, 308–315.

————. (1974). Albert, Peter, and John B. Watson. *American Pschologist,* **29**, 581–583.

Jung, C. G. (1956). *Symbols of transformation.* New York: Random House.

———— & Pauli, W. (1955). *The interpretation of nature and the psyche.* New York: Pantheon Books.

Kalish, H. I. (1969). Stimulus generalization. In M. H. Marx (Ed.), *Learning processes.* New York: Macmillan, Pp. 205–298.

————. (1977). Conditioning and learning in behavior modification. In M. H. Marx & M. E. Bunch (Eds.), *Fundamentals and applications of learning.* New York: Macmillan. Pp. 455–490.

Kamin, L. J. (1985). Genes and behavior: The missing link. [Review of Kitcher, P. (1985). *Vaulting ambition: Sociobiology and the quest for human nature*]. *Psychology Today,* October, 76, 78.

Kantor, J. R., & Smith, N. W. (1975). *The science of psychology: An interbehavioral survey.* Chicago: Principia.

Kardiner, A. (1939). *The individual and his society.* New York: Columbia University Press.

Karsten, A. (1928). Psychische Sattigung. *Psychologische Forschung,* **10**, 142–154.

Katona, G. (1940). *Organizing and memorizing.* New York: Columbia University Press.

Kawash, G., & Fuchs, A. H. (1974). A factor analysis of ratings of five schools of psychology on prescriptive dimensions. *Journal of the History of the Behavioral Sciences,* **10**, 426–437.

Kendler, H. H. (1947). An investigation of latent learning in a T-maze. *Journal of Comparative and Physiological Psychology,* **40**, 265–270.

———. (1967). Kenneth W. Spence. *Psychological Review,* **74**, 335–341.

——— & Mencher, H. C. (1948). The ability of rats to learn the location of food when motivated by thirst—An experimental reply to Leeper. *Journal of Experimental Psychology,* **38**, 82–88.

Kendrick, D. F., Rilling, M. E., & Denny, M. R. (1985). *Theories of animal memory.* Hillsdale, NJ: Erlbaum.

Kimble, G. A. (1961). *Hilgard and Marquis' conditioning and learning.* New York: Appleton-Century-Crofts.

———. (1967). *Hilgard and Marquis' conditioning and learning.* 2d ed. New York: Appleton-Century-Crofts.

Kimmel, G. A. (1966). Inhibition of the unconditioned response in classical conditioning. *Psychological Review,* **73**, 232–240.

Klein, G. S. (1964). Semantic power measured through the interference of words with color-naming. *American Journal of Psychology,* **77**, 576–588.

Klemmer, E. T., & Frick, F. C. (1953). Assimilation of information from dot and matrix patterns. *Journal of Experimental Psychology,* **45**, 15–19.

Koch, S. (1944). Review of C. L. Hull, *Principles of behavior. Psychological Bulletin,* **41**, 269–286.

———. (1954). C. L. Hull. In W. K. Estes et al. (Eds.), *Modern learning theory.* New York: Appleton-Century-Crofts. Pp. 1–176.

———. (Ed.). (1959–1963). *Psychology: A study of a science.* 6 vols. New York: McGraw-Hill.

———. (1969). Psychology cannot be a coherent science. *Psychology Today,* **14**, 64, 66–68.

———. (1981). The nature and limits of psychological knowledge: Lessons of a century *qua* science. *American Psychologist,* **35**, 257–269.

Köhler, W. (1920). *Die physischen Gestalten in Ruhe und im stationaren Zustand.* Erlangen: Weltkreisverlag.

———. (1925). *The mentality of apes.* New York: Harcourt Brace.

———. (1938). Some Gestalt problems. In W. D. Ellis (Ed.), *A source book of Gestalt psychology.* London: Routledge & Kegan Paul. Pp. 55–70.

———. (1942). Kurt Koffka. *Psychological Review,* **49**, 97–101.

———. (1947). *Gestalt psychology: An introduction to the new concepts in modern psychology.* New York: Liveright.

———. (1958). The present situation in brain physiology. *American Psychologist,* **13**, 150–154.

———. (1969). *The task of Gestalt psychology.* Princeton, NJ: Princeton University Press.

Koffka, K. (1935). *Principles of Gestalt psychology.* New York: Harcourt, Brace.

Konorski, J. (1948). *Conditioned reflexes and neuron organization.* Cambridge: Cambridge University Press.

———. (1967). *Integrative activity of the brain: An interdisciplinary approach.* Chicago: University of Chicago Press.

———. (1974). Jerzy Konorski. In G. Lindzey (Ed.), *A history of psychology in autobiography.* Vol. 6. Englewood Cliffs, NJ: Prentice-Hall.

——— & Miller, S. (1937a). On two types of conditioned reflexes. *Journal of General Psychology,* **16**, 264–272.

——— & ———. (1937b). Further remarks on two types of conditioned reflexes. *Journal of General Psychology,* **16**, 405–407.

Koshland, D. E., Jr. (1985). Scientific literacy. *Science,* **230**, 391.

Krantz, D. L. (1972). Schools and systems: The mutual isolation of operant and non-operant psychology as a case study. *Journal of the History of the Behavioral Sciences, 8,* 86–102.

Krech, D. (1962). Cortical localization of function. In L. Postman (Ed.), *Psychology in the making.* New York: Knopf. Pp. 31–72.

Krechevsky, I. (1932). "Hypotheses" in rats. *Psychological Review, 39,* 516–532.

Kuhn, T. S. (1970). *The structure of scientific revolutions.* 2d ed. Chicago: University of Chicago Press.

Külpe, O. (1895). *Outlines of psychology, based upon results of experimental investigation.* (Trans. by E. B. Titchener). New York: Macmillan.

Kuo, Z. Y. (1922). The nature of successful acts and their order of elimination. *Journal of Comparative Psychology, 2,* 1–27.

———. (1924). A psychology without heredity. *Psychological Review, 31,* 427–448.

———. (1930). The genesis of the cat's response to the rat. *Journal of Comparative Psychology,* **11,** 1–35.

———. (1932a). Ontogeny of embryonic behavior in Aves. I. The chronology and general nature of the behavior of the chick embryo. *Journal of Experimental Zoology,* **61,** 395–430.

———. (1932c). Ontogeny of embryonic behavior in Aves. II. The mechanical factors in the various stages leading to hatching. *Journal of Experimental Zoology,* **62,** 453–489.

———. (1932e). Ontogeny of embryonic behavior in Aves. III. The structural and environmental factors in embryonic behavior. *Journal of Comparative Psychology,* **13,** 245–271.

———. (1932b). Ontogeny of embryonic behavior in Aves. IV. The influence of embryonic movements upon the behavior after hatching. *Journal of Comparative Psychology,* **14,** 109–122.

———. (1932d). Ontogeny of embryonic behavior in Aves. V. The reflex concepts in the light of embryonic behavior in birds. *Psychological Review, 39,* 499–515.

———. (1938). Further study of the behavior of the cat toward the rat. *Journal of Comparative Psychology,* **25,** 1–8.

———. (1967). *The dynamics of behavior development.* New York: Random House.

Kurke, M. I. (1980). Forensic psychology: A threat and a response. *Professional Psychology,* **11,** 72–77.

Kurzweil, R. (1985). What is artificial intelligence anyway? *American Scientist, 73,* 258–264.

LaBrecque, M. (1970). Very short circuits. *The Sciences, 10,* 8–10.

Lachman, R., Lachman, J. L., & Butterfield, E. C. (1979). *Cognitive psychology and information processing: An introduction.* Hillsdale, NJ: Erlbaum.

Laing, R. D.(1967). *The politics of experience.* Baltimore: Penguin.

Lakatos, I. (1970). Falsification and the methodology of scientific research programmes. In A. Musgrave & I. Lakatos (Eds.) *Criticism and the growth of knowledge.* New York: Cambridge University Press. Pp. 91–195.

Land, E. H. (1959). Experiments in color vision. *Scientific American,* **200,** 84–99.

Lashley, K. S. (1923). The behavioristic interpretation of consciousness. *Psychological Review,* **30,** 329–353.

———. (1929). *Brain mechanisms and intelligence.* Chicago: University of Chicago Press.

———. (1931). Cerebral control versus reflexology: A reply to Professor Hunter. *Journal of General Psychology,* **5,** 3–20.

———, Chow, K. L., & Semmes, J. (1951). An examination of the electrical field theory of cerebral integration. *Psychological Review, 58,* 123–136.

Laudan, L. (1977). *Progress and its problems.* Berkeley, CA: University of California Press.

Lauer, Q. (1965). *Phenomenology: Its genesis and prospect.* New York: Harper & Row.

Lazarus, A. A. (1971). *Behavior therapy and beyond.* New York: McGraw-Hill.

Lazarus, R. S. (1984). On the primacy of cognition. *American Psychologist*, **39**, 124–129.

Leak, G. K., & Christopher, S. B. (1982). Freudian psychoanalysis and sociobiology: A synthesis. *American Psychologist*, **37**, 313–322.

Leeper, R. W. (1966). A critical consideration of Egon Brunswik's probabilistic functionalism. In K. R. Hammond (Ed.), *The psychology of Egon Brunswik*. New York: Holt, Rinehart, Winston. Pp. 405–454.

Lenneberg, E. H. (1967). *The biological foundations of language*. New York: Wiley.

Lerner, M. J., & Fairweather, G. W. (1963). The social behavior of chronic schizophrenics in supervised and unsupervised work groups. *Journal of Abnormal & Social Psychology*, **67**, 219–225.

Levine, M. (1959). A model of hypothesis behavior in discrimination learning sets. *Psychological Review*, **66**, 353–366.

———. (1963). Mediation processes in humans at the outset of discrimination learning. *Psychological Review*, **70**, 254–276.

———. (1970). Human discrimination learning: The subset sampling assumption. *Psychological Bulletin*, **74**, 397–404.

Levinson, D. J. (1978). Growing up with the dream. *Psychology Today*, **11**, 20.

Levis, D. J. (1976). Learned helplessness: A reply and an alternative S-R interpretation. *Journal of Experimental Psychology: General*, **105**, 47–65.

Levy, N., & Seward, J. P. (1969). Frustration and homogeneity of rewards in the double runway. *Journal of Experimental Psychology*, **81**, 460–463.

Lewin, K. (1917). Die psychische Tatigkeit bei der Hemmung on Willensvorgängen und der Grundgesetz der Assoziation. *Zeitschrift für Psychologie*, **77**, 212–247.

———. (1935). *A dynamic theory of personality*. (Trans. by K. E. Zener & D. K. Adams). New York: McGraw-Hill.

———. (1936). *Principles of topological psychology* (Trans. by F. Heider & G. Heider), New York: McGraw-Hill.

———. (1938). *The conceptual representation and measurement of psychological forces*. Durham, NC: Duke University Press.

———. (1939). Field theory and experiment in social psychology: Concept and methods. *American Journal of Sociology*, **44**, 868–896.

———. (1940). Formalization and progress in psychology. *University of Iowa Studies in Child Welfare*, **16**, 9–42.

———. (1943a). Defining the "field at a given time." *Psychological Review*, **50**, 293–310.

———. (1943b). Forces behind food habits and methods of change. *Bulletin of the National Research Council*, **108**, 35–65.

———. (1944). Constructs in psychology and psychological ecology. *University of Iowa Studies in Child Welfare*, **20**, 1–29.

———. (1948). *Resolving social conflicts*. New York: Harper & Row.

———. (1951). *Field study in social science*. New York: Harper & Row.

Licklider, J. C. R. (1959). Three auditory theories. In S. Koch (Ed.), *Psychology: A study of a science*. Vol. 1. *Sensory, perceptual, and physiological formulations*. New York: McGraw-Hill. Pp. 41–144.

Lippitt, R. (1940). An experimental study of authoritarian and democratic group atmospheres. *University of Iowa Studies in Child Welfare*, **16**, 43–195.

——— & White, R. K. (1943). The "social climate" of children's groups. In R. G. Barker, J. S. Kounin, & H. F. Wright (Eds.), *Child behavior and development*. New York: McGraw-Hill. Pp. 485–508.

Lissner, K. (1933). Entspannung von Bedurfnissen durch Ersatzhandlungen. *Psychologische Forschung*, **18**, 218–250.

Lockard, R. B. (1971). Reflections on the fall of comparative psychology: Is there a message for us all? *American Psychologist,* **26**, 168–179.

Locke, J. (1803; originally published 1690). *An essay concerning human understanding.* Vol. 2. (Reprinted from the 20th London ed.). Boston: David Carlisle.

Lockhart, R. S., & Murdock, B. B. (1970). Memory and the theory of signal detection. *Psychological Bulletin,* **74**, 100–109.

Loftus, E. F. (1979). *Eyewitness testimony.* Cambridge, MA: Harvard University Press.

———. (1981). Mentalmorphosis: Alterations in memory produced by the mental bonding of new information to old. In J. Long & A. Baddeley (Eds.), *Attention and Performance.* Vol. 9. Hillsdale, NJ: Erlbaum.

———, Miller, D. G., & Burns, H. J. (1978). Semantic integration of verbal information into a visual memory. *Journal of Experimental Psychology: Human Learning and Memory,* **4**, 19–31.

Logan, F. A. (1956). A micromolar approach to behavior theory. *Psychological Review,* **63**, 73–80.

———. (1959). The Hull-Spence approach. In S. Koch (Ed.), *Psychology: A study of a science.* Vol. 2, *General systematic formulations, learning and special processes.* New York: McGraw-Hill. Pp. 293–348.

———. (1960). *Incentive.* New Haven, CT: Yale University Press.

———. (1970). *Fundamentals of learning and motivation.* Dubuque, IA: Brown.

London, I. (1944). Psychologists' misuse of the auxiliary concepts of physics and mathematics. *Psychological Review,* **51**, 42–45.

Lorenz, K. (1966). *On aggression.* New York: Harcourt, Brace, & World.

Lorge, I. D. (1949). Edward L. Thorndike's publications from 1940 to 1949. *Teachers College Record,* **51**, 42–45.

Luchins, A. S. & Luchins, E. H. (1981). On the inapplicability of dichotomous prescriptive terms to characterize Gestalt Psychology. *Gestalt Theory,* **3**, 5–19.

Luria, A. R., Tsvetkova, L. S., & Futer, D. S. (1965). Aphasia in a composer. *Journal of Neurological Sciences,* **2**, 285–292.

MacCorquodale, K. (1969). B. F. Skinner's *Verbal behavior:* A retrospective appreciation. *Journal of the Experimental Analysis of Behavior,* **12**, 831–841.

———. (1970). On Chomsky's review of Skinner's *Verbal behavior. Journal of the Experimental Anaylysis of Behavior,* **13**, 83–99.

——— & Meehl, P. E. (1948). On a distinction between hypothetical constructs and intervening variables. *Psychological Review,* **55**, 95–107.

——— & ———. (1954). Edward C. Tolman. In W. K. Estes et al. (Eds.), *Modern learning theory.* New York: Appleton-Century-Crofts. Pp. 177–266.

McCulloch, W. S., & Pitts, W. (1943). A logical calculus of the ideas immanent in nervous activity. *Bulletin of Mathematical Biophysics,* **5**, 115–133.

McDougall, W. (1905). *Physiologial psychology.* London: Dent.

———. (1912). *Psychology: The study of behavior.* London: Williams & Norgate.

McGeoch, J. A. (1933). The formal criteria of a systematic psychology. *Psychological Review,* **40**, 1–12.

———. (1942). *The psychology of human learning.* New York: Longmans.

——— & Irion, A. L. (1952). *The psychology of human learning.* 2d ed. New York: Longmans.

McGuire, W. (Ed.). (1974). *The Freud/Jung letters.* Princeton, NJ: Princeton University Press.

MacKay, D. M. (1952). The nomenclature of information theory. In H. von Foerster (Ed.), *Transactions of the eighth conference on cybernetics: Circular feedback mechanisms in biological and social systems.* New York: Josiah Macy, Jr., Foundation. Pp. 222–235.

————. (1969). *Information, mechanism, and meaning.* Cambridge, MA: MIT Press.

McKinney, F. (1978). Functionalism at Chicago—Memories of a graduate student: 1929–1931. *Journal of the History of the Behavioral Sciences,* **14**, 142–148.

Mahler, V. (1933). Ersatzhandlungen verschiedenen Realitatsgrades. *Psychologische Forschung,* **18**, 26–89.

Maier, S. F., & Seligman, M. E. P. (1976). Learned helplessness: Theory and evidence. *Journal of Experimental Psychology: General,* **105**, 3–46.

Malinowski, B. (1950). *Argonauts of the western Pacific.* New York: Dutton.

Malpass, R. S., & Devine, P. G. (1980). Realism and eye witness identification research. *Law and Human Behavior,* **4**, 347–358.

Maltzman, I. M. (1950). An experimental study of learning under irrelevant need. *Journal of Experimental Psychology,* **40**, 788–793.

Marcel, A. J. (1978). Unconscious reading. *Visible Language,* **12**, 391–404.

————. (1983). Conscious and unconscious perception: Experiments on visual masking and word recognition. *Cognitive Psychology,* **15**, 197–237.

Marrow, A. J. (1969). *The practical theorist: The life and work of Kurt Lewin.* New York: Basic Books.

Marshall, M. E., & Wendt, R. A. (1980). Wilhelm Wundt, spiritism, and the assumptions of science. In W. G. Bringmann & R. D. Tweney (Eds.), *Wundt studies.* Toronto: C. J. Hogrefe. Pp. 158–175.

Marx, M. H. (1951). Intervening variable or hypothetical construct? *Psychological Review,* **58**, 235–247.

————. (1956). Spread of effect: A critical review. *General Psychology Monographs,* **53**, 119–186.

————. (1957a). Gradients of error-reinforcement in a serial perceptual-motor task. *Psychological Monographs,* **71**, 1–20.

————. (1957b). Gradients of error-reinforcement in normal multiple-choice learning situations. *Journal of Experimental Psychology,* **54**, 225–228.

————. (Ed.). (1963). *Theories in contemporary psychology.* New York: Macmillan.

————. (1967a). Resistance to extinction as a function of delay of reinforcement and the opportunity to retrace in the runway. *Psychonomic Science,* **8**, 287–288.

————. (1967b). Increased resistance to extinction as a function of the opportunity to retrace in the runway. *Psychonomic Science,* **9**, 397–398.

————. (1978). Transfer of rewarded responses in personality judgements. *Bulletin of the Psychonomic Society,* **2**, 112–114.

————. (1981). Habit activation in human learning. In G. d'Ydewalle (Ed.), *Cognition and memory: Essays in honor of J. Nuttin.* Hillsdale, NJ: Erlbaum. Pp. 87–122.

———— & Goodson, F. E. (Eds.). (1976). *Theories in contemporary psychology.* New York: Macmillan.

———— & Hillix, W. A. (1973). *Systems and theories in psychology.* 2d ed. New York: McGraw-Hill.

————, Marx, K., & Homer, A. L. (1981). Interactions among performance, task, and gender variables in verbal discrimination learning. *Bulletin of the Psychonomic Society,* **18**, 9–11.

————, Pavur, E. J., Jr., & Seymour, G. E. (1977). Differential recall of problems, clues, and solutions from completed and uncompleted tasks. *Bulletin of the Psychonomic Society,* **9**, 322–324.

———— & Van Spanckeren, W. J. (1952). Control of the audiogenic seizure by the rat. *Journal of Comparative and Physiological Psychology,* **45**, 193–200.

Masson, J. M. (1985). *The assault on truth: Freud's suppression of the seduction theory*. New York: Penguin Books.

Masterman, M. (1970). The nature of a paradigm. In A. Musgrave & I. Lakatos (Eds.), *Criticism and the growth of knowledge*. London: Cambridge University Press. Pp. 59–89.

Maturana, H. R., Lettvin, J. Y., McCulloch, W. S., & Pitts, W. H. (1960). Anatomy and physiology of vision in the frog. (*Rana pipiens*). *Journal of Genetic Psychology, 43*, 129–175.

Mavis, B. E., & Fergus, E. O. (1985, September). *Survival in the '80s of the community lodge program*. Paper presented at the meeting of the American Psychological Association, Los Angeles, CA.

Mead, M. (1950; originally published 1928). *Coming of age in Samoa*. Garden City, NY: Doubleday.

Meehl, P. E. (1950). On the circularity of the law of effect. *Psychological Bulletin, 47*, 52–57.

———— & MacCorquodale, K. (1948). A further study of latent learning in the T-maze. *Journal of Comparative and Physiological Psychology, 41*, 372–396.

Mehler, J., & Fox, R. (Eds.). (1984). *Neonate cognition: Beyond the blooming buzzing confusion*. Hillsdale, NJ: Erlbaum.

Melton, A. W. (1950). Learning. *Annual Review of Psychology, 1*, 9–30.

Meyer, M. (1911). *The fundamental laws of human behavior*. Boston: R. G. Badger.

————. (1921). *The psychology of the other one*. Columbia: Missouri Book Store.

Mill, J. (1972; originally published 1818). *The history of British India*. New Delhi: Associated Publishing House.

————. (1829). *Analysis of the phenomena of the human mind*. Vol. 1. London: Longmans.

Mill, J. S. (1956; originally published 1843). *A system of logic*. London: Longmans.

Miller, G. A. (1956). The magical number seven, plus or minus two: Some limits on our capacity for processing information. *Psychological Review, 63*, 81–87.

————. (1964). *Mathematics and psychology*. New York: Wiley.

————, Galanter, E., & Pribram, K. H. (1960). *Plans and the structure of behavior*. New York: Holt.

Miller, N. E. (1944). Experimental studies in conflict. In J. McV. Hunt (Ed.), *Personality and the behavior disorders*. Vol. 1. New York: Ronald Press. Pp. 431–465.

————. (1948). Theory and experiment relating psychoanalytic displacement to stimulus-response generalization. *Journal of Abnormal and Social Psychology, 43*, 155–178.

————. (1951). Comments on multiple-process conceptions of learning. *Psychological Review, 58*, 375–381.

————. (1958). Central stimulation and other new approaches to motivation and reward. *American Psychologist, 13*, 100–108.

————. (1959a). Liberalization of basic S-R concepts: Extensions to conflict behavior, motivation, and social learning. In S. Koch (Ed.), *Psycholology: A study of a science*. Vol. 2. *General systematic formulations, learning and special processes*. New York: McGraw-Hill. Pp. 196–292.

————. (1959b). Some implications of modern behavior theory for personality change and psychotherapy. In P. Worchel & D. Byrne (Eds.), *Personality change*. New York: Wiley. Pp. 149–175.

————. (1963). Some reflections on the law of effect produce a new alternative to drive reduction. *Nebraska symposium on motivation*. Lincoln: University of Nebraska Press. Pp. 65–112.

————. (1969). Learning of visceral and glandular responses. *Science, 163*, 434–445.

———— & Dollard, J. (1941). *Social learning and imitation*. New Haven, CT: Yale University Press.

Miller, S., & Konorski, J. (1928). Sur une forme particuliere des reflexes conditionnels. *Les Comptes Rendus des Seances de la Societe de Biologie*, **99**, 1155–1157. [Translated by B. F. Skinner (1969) as "On a particular form of the conditioned reflex." *Journal of the Experimental Analysis of Behavior*, **12**, 189–199.]

Morgan, C. L. (1899; first edition 1891); *Introduction to comparative psychology*. 2d ed. London: W. Scott.

Morgan, E. (1972). *The descent of woman*. New York: Stein and Day.

Morris, C. W. (1938). Foundations of the theory of signs. *International Encyclopedia of Unified Science*, **2**, 1–59.

Morris, D. (1968). *The naked ape*. New York: McGraw-Hill.

———. (1969). *The human zoo*. New York: McGraw-Hill.

Mowrer, O. H. (1947). On the dual nature of learning: A re-interpretation of "conditioning" and "problem solving." *Harvard Educational Review*, **17**, 102–148.

———. (1956). Two-factor learning theory reconsidered with special reference to secondary reinforcement and the concept of habit. *Psychological Review*, **63**, 114–128.

———. (1959). Review of R. S. Woodworth, *Dynamics of behavior*. *Contemporary Psychology*, **4**, 129–133.

———. (1960a). *Learning theory and behavior*. New York: Wiley.

———. (1960b). *Learning theory and the symbolic processes*. New York: Wiley.

——— & Viek, P. (1948). An experimental analogue of fear from a sense of helplessness. *Journal of Abnormal and Social Psychology*, **43**, 193–200.

Mueller, C. G., Jr., & Schoenfeld, W. N. (1954). Edwin R. Guthrie. In W. K. Estes et al. (Eds.), *Modern learning theory*. New York: Appleton-Century-Crofts. Pp. 345–379.

Müller, G. E. (1923). *Komplextheorie und Gestalttheorie: Ein Beitrag zur Wahrnemungspsychologie*. Göttingen: Vandenhoeck, Ruprecht.

Mullahy, P. (1948). *Oedipus: Myth and complex*. New York: Hermitage House.

Munroe, R. (1955). *Schools of psychoanalytic thought*. New York: Holt.

Murphy, G. (1949). *Historical introduction to modern psychology*. New York: Harcourt, Brace & World.

Murray, E. (1906). Peripheral and central factors in memory: Images of visual form and color. *American Journal of Psychology*, **17**, 225–247.

Musgrave, A., & Lakatos, I. (Eds.). (1970). *Criticism and the growth of knowledge*. New York: Cambridge University Press.

Nafe, J. P. (1927). The psychology of felt experience. *American Journal of Psychology*, **39**, 367–389.

Nash, E. H., Frank, J. D., Imber, S. D., & Stone, A. R. (1964). Selected effects of inert medication on psychiatric outpatients. *American Journal of Psychotherapy*, **18**, Suppl. 1, 33–48.

Natsoulas, T. (1970). Concerning introspective "knowledge." *Psychological Bulletin*, **73**, 89–111.

Neisser, U. (1964). Visual search. *Scientific American*, **210**, 94–102.

———. (1967). *Cognitive psychology*. New York: Appleton-Century-Crofts.

Newbury, E. (1954). Current interpretation and significance of Lloyd Morgan's canon. *Psychological Bulletin*, **51**, 70–74.

Newell, A., Shaw, J. C., & Simon, H. A. (1958). Elements of a theory of human problem solving. *Psychological Review*, **65**, 151–166.

——— & Simon, H. A. (1961). The simulation of human thought. In W. Dennis et al. (Eds.), *Current trends in psychological theory*. Pittsburgh: University of Pittsburgh Press. Pp. 152–179.

Nisbett, R. E., & Wilson, T. D. (1977). Telling more than we can know: Verbal reports on mental processes. *Psychological Review*, **84**, 231–259.

Norman, D. A. (1981). Twelve issues for cognitive science. In D. A. Norman (Ed.), *Perspectives on cognitive science*. Norwood, NJ: Ablex.

———— & Rumelhart, D. E. (1975). *Explorations in cognition*. San Francisco: W. H. Freeman.

O'Donnell, J. M. (1979). The crisis of experimentalism in the 1920s: E. G. Boring and his use of history. *American Psychologist, 34*, 289–295.

Olds, J. (1955). Physiological mechanisms of reward. In M. R. Jones (Ed.), *Nebraska symposium on motivation*. Lincoln: University of Nebraska Press. Pp. 73–139.

O'Neil, W. M. (1968). Realism and behavorism. *Journal of the History of the Behavioral Sciences, 4*, 152–160.

Oppenheimer, R. (1956). Analogy in science. *American Psychologist, 11*, 127–135.

Orbison, W. D. (1939). Shape as a function of the vector field. *American Journal of Psychology, 52*, 31–45.

Ovsiankina, M. (1928). Die Wiederaufnahme unterbrochener Handlungen. *Psychologische Forschung, 11*, 302–379.

Patterson, F. (1978). Conversations with a gorilla. *National Geographic, 154*, 438–465.

Pavlov, I. P. (1906). The scientific investigation of the psychical faculties or processes in the higher animals. *Science, 24*, 613–619.

————. (1927) *Conditioned reflexes*. London: Oxford University Press.

————. (1928). *Lectures on conditioned reflexes*. New York: Liveright.

————. (1932). The reply of a physiologist to psychologists. *Psychological Review, 39*, 91–127.

————. (1941). *Lectures on conditioned reflexes. Vol. 2. Conditioned reflexes and psychiatry.* (Trans. & ed. by W. H. Gantt). New York: International Publishers.

————. (1955). *Selected works.* (Trans. by S. Belsky; ed. by J. Gibbons, under supervision of Kh. S. Koshtoyants). Moscow: Foreign Languages Publishing House.

Perky, C. W. (1910). An experimental study of imagination. *American Journal of Psychology, 21*, 422–452.

Perry, R. B. (1935). *The thought and character of William James*. Volume 1: *Inheritance and vocation*. Vol. 2. *Philosophy and psychology*. Boston: Little, Brown.

Peterson, C. R., Hammond, K. R., & Summers, D. A. (1965). Optimal responding in multiple-cue probability learning. *Journal of Experimental Psychology, 70*, 270–276.

Peterson, W. W., Birdsall, T. G., & Fox, W. C. (1954). The theory of signal detectability. *Transactions of Professional Group on Information Theory, Institute of Radio Engineers*, PGIT-4, 171–212.

Pierce, J. R., & Karlin, J. E. (1957). Reading rates and the information rate of a human channel. *Bell System Technical Journal, 36*, 497–516.

Polanyi, M. (1968). Life's irreducible structure. *Science, 160*, 1308–1312.

Pollack, I. (1954). The assimilation of sequentially-encoded information. *HFORL Memo Report*, TR-54-5.

Pollack, I., & Ficks, L. (1953). Information on multidimensional auditory displays. *Journal of the Acoustical Society of America, 25*, 765–769.

———— & Klemmer, E. T. (1954). The assimilation of visual information from linear dot patterns. *Air Force Cambridge Research Center, Technical Report, 54*, 16.

Pollock, G. H. (1983). The presence of the past. *The Annual of Psychoanalysis, XI*, 3–27.

Popper, K. R. (1970). Normal science and its dangers. In A. Musgrave & I. Lakatos (Eds.), *Criticism and the growth of knowledge*. New York: Cambridge University Press. Pp. 51–58.

Posner, M. I. (1964). Information reduction in the analysis of sequential tasks. *Psychological Review, 71*, 491–504.

————. (1973). *Cognition: An introduction*. Glenview, IL: Scott, Foresman.

Postman, L. (1955). The probability approach and nomothetic theory. *Psychological Review,* **62**, 218–225.

———. (1961). Spread of effect as a function of time and intraserial similarity. *American Journal of Psychology,* **74**, 493–505.

——— & Tolman, E. C. (1959). Brunswik's probabilistic functionalism. In S. Koch (Ed.), *Psychology: A study of a science.* Vol. 1. *Sensory, perceptual, and physiological formulations.* New York: McGraw-Hill. Pp. 502–564.

Premack, D. (1971). Language in chimpanzee? *Science,* **172**, 808–822.

Prentice, W. C. H. (1959). The systematic psychology of Wolfgang Köhler. In S. Koch (Ed.), *Psychology: A study of a science.* Vol. 1. *Sensory, perceptual, and physiological formulations.* New York: McGraw-Hill. Pp. 427–455.

Pribram, K. (1971). *Languages of the brain.* Englewood Cliffs, NJ: Prentice Hall.

Psychology Today (1983). September.

Pumpian-Mindlin, E. (Ed.). (1952). *Pyschoanalysis as science.* Stanford, CA: Stanford University Press.

Quastler, H., Osborne, J. W., & Tweedell, K. (1955). Human performance in information transmission. III. University of Illinois Report R-68, Control Systems Laboratory.

Rank, O. (1929). *The trauma of birth.* New York: Harcourt, Brace.

Rapaport, D. (1959). The structure of psychoanalytic theory: A systematizing attempt. In S. Koch (Ed.), *Psychology: A study of a science.* Vol. 3. *Formulations of the person and the social context.* New York: McGraw-Hill. Pp. 55–83.

Rapoport, A. (1969). *Two-person game theory.* Ann Arbor: University of Michigan Press.

Rausch, H. L., Dittman, A. T., & Taylor, T. J. (1959). Person, setting, and change in social interaction. *Human Relations,* **12**, 361–378.

———, ———, & ———. (1960). Person, setting, and change in social interaction. II. A normal control study. *Human Relations,* **13**, 305–332.

Razran, G. (1949). Stimulus generalization of conditioned responses. *Psychological Bulletin,* **46**, 337–365.

———. (1971). *Mind in evolution: An east-west synthesis of learned behavior and cognition.* Boston: Houghton Mifflin.

Read, J. D., & Bruce, D. (1984). On the external validity of questioning effects in eyewitness testimony. *International Review of Applied Psychology,* **33**, 33–49.

Remnick, D. (1984). Analyzing Sigmund Freud. *The Miami Herald,* February 26, G1, G6.

Rescorla, R. A., & Solomon, R. L. (1967). Two-process learning theory: Relationships between Pavlovian conditioning and instrumental learning. *Psychological Review,* **74**, 151–182.

Reyher, J. (1977). Spontaneous visual imagery: Implications for psychoanalysis, psychopathology, and psychotherapy. *Journal of Mental Imagery,* **1**, 253–273.

Richards, R. J. (1980). Wundt's early theories of unconscious inference and cognitive evolution in their relation to Darwinian biopsychology. In W. G. Bringmann & R. D. Tweney (Eds.), *Wundt Studies.* Toronto: Hogrefe. Pp. 42–70.

Roback, A. A. (1952). *A history of American psychology.* New York: Library Publishers.

Robinson, P. (1984). Review of Jacoby's *The repression of psychoanalysis. Psychology Today,* February, 64.

Roesch, R. (1984). Psychology and the law. In R. J. Corsini, (Ed.), *Encyclopedia of psychology.* Vol. III. New York: Wiley. Pp. 142–146.

Roitblat, H. L., Bever, T. G., & Terrace, H. S. (Eds.). (1984). *Animal cognition.* Hillsdale, NJ: Erlbaum.

Romanes, G. J. (1886). *Animal intelligence.* London: Kegan Paul, Trench, Trubner.

Rosenbaum, M. E., & Hewitt, O. J. (1966). The effect of electric shock on learning by performers and observers. *Psychonomic Science, 5*, 81–82.

———— & Schutz, L. J. (1967). The effects of extraneous response requirements on learning by performers and observers. *Psychonomic Science, 6*, 51–52.

Rosenthal, R. (1983). Assessing the statistical and social importance of the effects of psychotherapy. *Journal of Consulting and Clinical Psychology, 51*, 4–13.

Ross, D. G. (1972). *Stanley Hall: The psychologist as prophet*. Chicago: University of Chicago Press.

Ross, R. R. (1964). Positive and negative partial-reinforcement effects carried through continuous reinforcement, changed motivation, and changed response. *Journal of Experimental Psychology, 68*, 492–502.

Roszak, T. (1972). *Where the wasteland ends*. New York: Doubleday.

Rubin, E. (1915). *Syncopleoede figurer*. Copenhagen: Gyldendalske Boghandel.

Ruckmick, C. A. (1913). The use of the term function in English textbooks of psychology. *American Journal of Psychology, 14*, 99–123.

Rumbaugh, D. M. (Ed.). (1977). *Language learning by a chimpanzee: The Lana project*. New York: Academic Press.

Russell, B. (1945). *A history of western philosophy*. New York: Simon & Schuster.

Sahakian, W. S. (1975). *History and systems of psychology*. New York: Wiley.

Samuel, A. L. (1963). Some studies in machine learning using the game of checkers. In E. Feigenbaum & F. Feldman (Eds.), *Computers and thought*. New York: McGraw-Hill. Pp. 71–105.

Sarris, V., & Parducci, A. (Eds.). (1984). *Perspectives in psychological experimentation: Toward the year 2000*. Hillsdale, NJ: Erlbaum.

Sarton, G. (1952). *A guide to the history of science*. Waltham, MA: Chronica Botanica.

Savage-Rumbaugh, E. S., Rumbaugh, D. M., Smith, S. T., & Lawson, J. (1980). Reference: The linguistic essential. *Science, 210*, 922–925.

Schaub, A. deV. (1911). On the intensity of images. *American Journal of Psychology, 22*, 346–368.

Schlosberg, H. (1937). The relationship between success and the laws of conditioning. *Psychological Review, 44*, 379–394.

Schoenfeld, W. N., Cumming, W. W., & Hearst, E. (1968). On the classification of reinforcement schedules. In A. C. Catania (Ed.), *Contemporary research in operant behavior*. Glenview, IL: Scott, Foresman. Pp. 113–118.

Schultz, D. P. (1969). *A history of modern psychology,* New York: Academic Press.

Scriven, M. (1963). The mechanical concept of mind. In K. M. Sayre & F. J. Crosson (Eds.), *The modeling of the mind: Computers and intelligence*. Notre Dame, IN: University of Notre Dame Press. Pp. 243–254.

Sears, R. R. (1943). *Survey of objective studies of psychoanalytic concepts*. New York: Social Science Research Council.

Sechenov, I. M. (1965; first published 1863). *Reflexes of the brain*. Cambridge, MA: MIT Press.

Seligman, M. E. P. (1975). *Helplessness*. San Francisco: W. H. Freeman.

———— & Maier, S. F. (1967). Failure to escape traumatic shock. *Journal of Experimental Psychololgy, 74*, 1–9.

Seward, J. P. (1947). A theoretical derivation of latent learning. *Psychological Review, 54*, 83–98.

————. (1949). An experimental analysis of latent learning. *Journal of Experimental Psychology, 39*, 177–196.

Shannon, C. E. (1951). Prediction and entropy of printed English. *Bell System Technical Journal.* **30**, 50–64.

———— & Weaver, W. (1949). *The mathematical theory of communication.* Urbana, IL: University of Illinois Press.

Sheffield, F. D. (1954). A drive-induction theory of reinforcement. (Mimeographed, personally distributed.)

Sherrington, C. S. (1947). *The integrative action of the nervous system.* London: Constable, 1906. (Republished with a new foreword and a bibliography of Sherrington's publications: New Haven, CT: Yale University press.)

Shevrin, H., & Dickman, S. (1980). The psychological unconscious: A necessary assumption for all psychological theory? *American Psychologist,* **35**, 421–434.

Shiffrin, R. M., & Atkinson, R. C. (1969). Storage and retrieval processes in long-term memory. *Psychological Review,* **76**, 179–193.

Shipley, T. (Ed.). (1961). *Classics in psychology.* New York: Philosophical Library.

Sidman, M. (1960). *Tactics of scientific research.* New York: Basic Books.

Silverman, L. H. (1976). Psychoanalytic theory: "The reports of my death are greatly exaggerated." *American Psychologist,* **9**, 621–637.

————. (1983). The subliminal psychodynamic activation method: Overview and comprehensive listing of studies. In J. Masling (Ed.), *Empirical studies of psychoanalytical theories.* Vol. 1. Hillsdale, NJ: Erlbaum. Pp. 69–100.

Singer, P. (1981). *The expanding circle: Ethics and sociobiology.* New York: Farrar, Straus & Giroux.

Skinner, B. F. (1938). *The behavior of organisms.* New York: Appleton-Century-Crofts.

————. (1948a). "Superstition" in the pigeon. *Journal of Experimental Psychology,* **38**, 168–172.

————. (1948b). *Walden two.* New York: Macmillan.

————. (1953). *Science and human behavior.* New York: Macmillan.

————. (1954). Critique of psychoanalytic concepts and theories. *Scientific Monthly,* **79**, 300–305.

————. (1957). *Verbal behavior.* New York: Appleton-Century-Crofts.

————. (1959a). A case history in scientific method. In S. Koch (Ed.), *Psychology: A study of a science.* Vol. 2. *General systematic formulations, learning and special processes.* New York: McGraw-Hill. Pp. 359–379.

————. (1959b). *Cumulative record.* New York: Appleton-Century-Crofts.

————. (1960). Pigeons in a pelican. *American Psychologist,* **15**, 28–37.

————. (1966). Operant behavior. In W. K. Honig (Ed.), *Operant behavior: Areas of research and application.* New York: Appleton-Century-Crofts. Pp. 12–32.

————. (1967). B. F. Skinner. In E. G. Boring & G. Lindzey (Eds.), *A history of psychology in autobiography.* New York: Appleton-Century-Crofts. Pp. 385–413.

————. (1969). *Contingencies of reinforcement: A theoretical analysis.* New York: Appleton-Century-Crofts.

————. (1971). *Beyond freedom and dignity.* New York: Knopf.

————. (1974). *About behaviorism.* New York: Knopf.

————. (1976). *Particulars of my life.* New York: Knopf.

————. (1977). Herrnstein and the evolution of behaviorism. *American Psychologist,* **32**, 1006–1012.

————. (1979). *The shaping of a behaviorist: Part two of an autobiography.* New York: Knopf.

————. (1983). *A matter of consequences: Part Three of an autobiography.* New York: Knopf.

Sloane, R. B., Staples, F. R.., Cristol, A. H., Yorkston, N. J., & Wipple, K. (1975). *Psychotherapy versus behavior therapy.* Cambridge, MA: Harvard University Press.

Smith, C. S. (1968). Matter versus materials: A historical view. *Science,* **162**, 637–644.

Smith, E. R., & Miller, F. S. (1978). Limits on perception of cognitive processes. *Psychological Review*, **85**, 355–362.

Smith, K. (1954). Conditioning as an artifact. *Psychological Review*, **61**, 217–225.

Smith, M., & Wilson, E. (1953). A model of the auditory threshold and its application to the problem of the multiple observer. *Psychological Monographs*, **67**, (9), 1–35.

Smith, M. L., Glass, G. V., & Miller, T. I. (1980). *The benefits of psychotherapy*. Baltimore: Johns Hopkins University Press.

Smith, N. K. (1949). *The philosophy of David Hume*. London: Macmillan.

Smith, S., & Guthrie, E. R. (1921). *General psychology in terms of behavior*. New York: Appleton.

Smith, S. K., & Miller, G. A. (1952). The effects of coding procedures on learning and memory. Quarterly progress report of Research Laboratory of Electronics, M.I.T., to Air Force Human Resources Research Laboratories.

Sokal, M. M. (1971). The unpublished autobiography of James McKeen Cattell. *American Psychologist*, **26**, 626–635.

———. (1981). *An education in psychology: James McKeen Cattell's journal and letters from Germany and England, 1880–1888*. Cambridge, MA: The MIT Press.

Spence, K. W. (1936). The nature of discrimination learning in animals. *Psychological Review*, **43**, 427–449.

———. (1937a). Analysis of the formation of visual discrimination habits in chimpanzees. *Journal of Comparative Psychology*, **23**, 77–100.

———. (1937b). The differential response in animals to stimuli varying within a single dimension. *Psychological Review*, **44**, 430–444.

———. (1940). Continuous vs. non-continuous interpretations of discrimination learning. *Psychological Review*, **47**, 271–288.

———. (1948). The methods and postulates of "behaviorism." *Psychological Review*, **55**, 67–78. [Reprinted in M. H. Marx (Ed.). (1963). *Theories in contemporary psychology*. New York: Macmillan. Pp. 272–286.]

———. (1951a). Theoretical interpretations of learning. In C. P. Stone (Ed.), *Comparative psychology*. 3d ed. Englewood Cliffs, NJ: Prentice-Hall. Pp. 239–291.

———. (1951b). Theoretical interpretations of learning. In S. S. Stevens (Ed.), *Handbook of experimental psychology*. New York: Wiley. Pp. 690–729.

———. (1956). *Behavior theory and conditioning*. New Haven, CT: Yale University Press.

———. (1960). *Behavior theory and learning: Selected papers*. Englewood Cliffs, NJ: Prentice-Hall.

———. (1966). Cognitive and drive factors in the extinction of the conditioned eye blink in human subjects. *Psychological Review*, **73**, 445–458.

——— & Lippitt, R. (1940). "Latent" learning of a simple maze problem. *Psychological Bulletin*, **37**, 429.

Spencer, H. (1855). *The principles of psychology*. New York: Appleton.

———. (1961; originally published 1873). *The study of sociology*. Ann Arbor: University of Michigan Press.

Sperry, R. W. (1968). Hemisphere deconnection and unity in conscious awareness. *American Psychologist*, **23**, 723–733.

———. (1969). A modified concept of consciousness. *Psychological Review*, **76**, 532–536.

——— & Miner, N. (1955). Pattern perception following insertion of mica plates into visual cortex. *Journal of Comparative and Physiological Psychology*, **48**, 463–469.

———, Miner, N. & Myers, R. E. (1955). Visual pattern perception following subpial slicing and tantalum wire implantations in the visual cortex. *Journal of Comparative and Physiological Psychology*, **48**, 50–58.

Springer, S. P., & Deutsch, G. (1985). *Left brain, right brain* (Rev. ed). New York: Freeman.

Squire, L. R. (1986). Mechanisms of memory. *Science, 232,* 1612–1619.

Staddon, J. E. R., & Simmelhag, V. L. (1971). The "superstition" experiment: A reexamination of its implications for the principles of adaptive behavior. *Psychological Review,* **78**, 3–43.

Stephenson, W. (1953). *The study of behavior: Q-technique and its methodology.* Chicago: University of Chicago Press.

Sternberg, R. J. (Ed.). (1984). *Mechanisms of cognitive development.* New York: Freeman.

Sternberg, S. (1966). High speed scanning in human memory. *Science,* **153**, 652–654.

———. (1969). Memory scanning: Mental processes revealed by reaction time experiments. *American Scientist,* **57**, 421–457.

———. (1975). Memory scanning: New findings and current controversies. *Quarterly Journal of Experimental Psychology,* **27**, 1–32.

Stevens, S. S. (1939). Psychology and the science of science. *Psychological Bulletin,* **36**, 221–263.

———. (Ed.). (1951). *Handbook of experimental psychology.* New York: Wiley.

———. (1968). Measurement, statistics, and the schemapiric view. *Science,* **161**, 849–856.

Stout, G. F. (1902). *Analytic psychology.* New York: Macmillan.

Stroop, J. R. (1935). Studies of interference in serial verbal reactions. *Journal of Experimental Psychology,* **18**, 643–662.

Sumby, W. H., & Pollack, I. (1954). Short-time processing of information. HFORL Report TR-54-6.

Summers, D. A., & Hammond, K. R. (1966). Inference behavior in multiple-cue tasks involving both linear and nonlinear relations. *Journal of Experimental Psychology,* **71**, 751–757.

Swets, J. A. (1961). Is there a sensory threshold? *Science,* **134**, 168–177.

———. (Ed.). (1964). *Signal detection and recognition by human observers: Contemporary readings.* New York: Wiley.

Tanner, W. P., Jr. (1961). Physiological implications of psycho-physical data. *Annals of the New York Academy of Science,* **89**, 752–765.

——— & Swets, J. A. (1953). A new theory of visual detection. Technical Report 18, Electronic Defense Group, University of Michigan.

——— & ———. (1954). A decision-making theory of visual detection. *Psychological Review,* **61**, EC 401–409.

Terrace, H. S. (1966). Stimulus control. In W. K. Honig (Ed.), *Operant behavior: Areas of research and application.* New York: Appleton-Century-Crofts. Pp. 271–344.

———. (1979). *Nim.* New York: Knopf.

Theios, J., & Bower, G. H. (1964). A test of the competing response-interference theory of extinction. *Psychonomic Science,* **1**, 395–396.

Thistlethwaite, D. A. (1951). A critical review of latent learning and related experiments. *Psychological Bulletin,* **48**, 97–129.

Thom, R. (1975). *Structural stability and morphogenesis: An outline of a general theory of models.* (Trans. by D. H. Fowler.). Reading, MA: Benjamin.

Thorndike, E. L. (1898). Animal intelligence: An experimental study of the associative processes in animals. *Psychological Monographs,* No.. 8.

———. (1905). *The elements of psychology.* New York: A. G. Seiler.

———. (1911). *Animal intelligence.* New York: Hafner.

———. (1913). *Educational psychology.* Vol. 2. *The psychology of learning.* New York: Teachers College.

———. (1931). *Human learning.* New York: Century.

———. (1932). *The fundamentals of learning.* New York: Teachers College.

————. (1933a). An experimental study of rewards. *Teachers College Contributions to Education*, No. 580.

————. (1933b). A theory of the action of the after-effects of a connection upon it. *Psychological Review*, **40**, 434–439.

————. (1935). *The psychology of wants, interests, and attitudes*. New York: Appleton-Century-Crofts.

————. (1936). E. L. Thorndike. In C. Murchison (Ed.), *A history of psychology in autobiography*. Vol. 3. Worcester, MA: Clark University Press. Pp. 263–270.

————. (1949). *Selected writings from a connectionist's psychology*. New York: Appleton-Century-Crofts.

———— & Rock, R. T., Jr. (1934). Learning without awareness of what is being learned or intent to learn it. *Journal of Experimental Psychology*, **17**, 1–19.

———— & Woodworth, R. S. (1901). The influence of improvements in one mental function upon the efficiency of other functions. *Psychological Review*, **8**, 247–261, 384–395, 553–564.

Thornton, J. W., & Jacobs, P. D. (1971). Learned helplessness in human subjects. *Journal of Experimental Psychology*, **87**, 369–372.

Tiger, L. (1969). *Men in groups*. New York: Random House.

Tinker, M. A. (1980). Wundt's doctorate students and their theses 1875–1920. In W. G. Bringmann & R. D. Tweney (Eds.), *Wundt studies*. Toronto: C. J. Hogrefe. Pp. 269–279.

Titchener, E. B. (1898). The postulates of a structural psychology. *Philosophical Review*, **7**, 449–465. [Reprinted in W. Dennis (Ed.). (1948). *Readings in the history of psychology*. New York: Appleton-Century-Crofts. Pp. 366–376.]

————. (1899). *An outline of psychology*. New York: Macmillan.

————. (1908). *Lectures on the elementary psychology of feeling and attention*. New York: Macmillan.

————. (1910). *Text-book of psychology*. New York: Macmillan.

————. (1912a). Prolegomena to a study of introspection. *American Journal of Psychology*, **23**, 427–488.

————. (1912b). The schema of introspection. *American Journal of Psychology*, **23**, 484–508.

————. (1920). Unpublished letter to Walter Pillsbury, University of Michigan Library.

————. (1929). *Systematic psychology: Prolegomena*. New York: Macmillan.

Tolman, E. C. (1927). A behaviorist's definition of consciousness. *Psychological Review*, **34**, 433–439.

————. (1932). *Purposive behavior in animals and man*. New York: Appleton.

————. (1938). The determiners of behavior at a choice point. *Psychological Review*, **45**, 1–41.

————. (1945). A stimulus-expectancy need-cathexis psychology. *Science*, **101**, 160–166.

————. (1948). Cognitive maps in rats and men. *Psychological Review*, **55**, 189–208.

————. (1949a). The psychology of social learning. *Journal of Social Issues, Supplement Service*, **3**, 5–18.

————. (1949b). There is more than one kind of learning. *Psychological Review*, **56**, 144–155.

————. (1951a). *Collected papers in psychology*. Berkeley: University of California Press.

————. (1951b). A psychological model. In T. Parsons & E. A. Shils (Eds.), *Toward a general theory of action*. Cambridge, MA: Harvard University Press. Pp. 279–361.

————. (1959). Principles of purposive behavior. In S. Koch (Ed.), *Psychology: A study of a science*. Vol. 2. *General systematic formulations, learning and special processes*. New York: McGraw-Hill. Pp. 92–157.

————. (1966). Eulogy: Egon Brunswik: 1903–1955. In K. R. Hammond (Ed.), *The psychology of Egon Brunswik*. New York: Holt, Rinehart & Winston. Pp. 1–12.

———— & Brunswik, E. (1935). The organism and the causal texture of the environment. *Psychological Review, 42*, 43–77.

———— & Gleitman, H. (1949). Studies in learning and motivation. *Journal of Experimental Psychology, 39*, 810–819.

———— & Honzik, C. H. (1930). "Insight" in rats. *University of California Publications in Psychology, 4*, 215–232.

Toulmin, S. (1948). The logical status of psychoanalysis. *Analysis, 9*, 23–29.

————. (1972). *Human understanding*. Vol. 1. Princeton, NJ: Princeton University Press.

Townsend, J. T. (1974). Issues and models concerning the processing of a finite number of inputs. In B. H. Kantowitz (Ed.), *Human information processing: Tutorials in performance and cognition*. New York: Wiley. Pp. 133–185.

Trilling, L., & Marcus, S. (Eds.). (1961). *Ernest Jones. The life and work of Sigmund Freud*. Garden City, NY: Doubleday.

Turing, A. M. (1937). On computable numbers, with an application to the Entscheidung's problem. *Proceedings of the London Mathematical Society, 42*, 230–265; **43**, 544–546. Also in M. Davis (Ed.). (1965). *The undecidable*. Hewlett, NY: Raven Press.

Turner, M. B. (1967). *Philosophy and the science of behavior*. New York: Appleton-Century-Crofts.

————. (1971). *Realism and the explanation of behavior*. New York: Appleton-Century-Crofts.

Tweney, R. D., & Yachanin, S. A. (1980). Titchener's Wundt. In W. G. Bringmann & R. D. Tweney (Eds.), *Wundt studies*. Toronto: C. J. Hogrefe. Pp. 380–395.

Twitmyer, E. B. (1905). Knee jerk without stimulation of the patellar tendon. *Psychological Bulletin, 2*, 43–44. (Abstract)

Ullman, L. P., & Krasner, L. (1965). *Case studies in behavior modification*. New York: Holt, Rinehart, & Winston.

Underwood, B. J. (1957). *Psychological research*. New York: Appleton-Century-Crofts.

————. (1966; first published 1949). *Experimental psychology*. 2d ed. New York: Appleton-Century-Crofts.

———— & Eckstrand, B. R. (1967). Studies of distributed practice: XXIV. Differentiation and proactive inhibition. *Journal of Experimental Psychology, 74*, 574–580.

Van der Post, L. (1975). *Jung and the story of our time*. New York: Pantheon Books.

Van Hoorn, W., & Verhave, T. (1980). Wundt's changing conceptions of a general and theoretical psychology. In W. G. Bringmann & R. D. Tweney (Eds.), *Wundt studies*. Toronto: C. J. Hogrefe. Pp. 71–113.

Velikovsky, I. (1950). *Worlds in collision*. Garden City, NY: Doubleday.

Voeks, V. W. (1948). Postremity, recency, and frequency as bases for prediction in the maze situation. *Journal of Experimental Psychology, 38*, 495–510.

————. (1950). Formalization and clarification of a theory of learning. *Journal of Psychology, 30*, 341–362.

————. (1954). Acquisition of S-R connections: A test of Hull's and Guthrie's theories. *Journal of Experimental Psychology, 47*, 137–147.

Von Neumann, J. (1958). *The computer and the brain*. New Haven, CT: Yale University Press.

Walker, N. (1957). Science and the Freudian unconscious. In T. Reik (Ed.), *Psychoanalysis and the future*. New York: National Psychological Association for Psychoanalysis. Pp. 117–124.

Walls, G. L. (1960). "Land! Land!" *Psychological Bulletin, 57*, 29–48.

Wann, T. W. (Ed.). (1964). *Behaviorism and phenomenology*. Chicago: University of Chicago Press.

Warren, R. E. (1972). Stimulus encoding and memory. *Journal of Experimental Psychology, 94*, 90–100.

Washburn, M. F. (1908). *The animal mind*. New York: Macmillan.

Watson, J. B. (1913a). Image and affection in behavior. *Journal of Philosophy*, **10**, 421–428.

———. (1913b). Psychology as the behaviorist views it. *Psychological Review*, **20**, 158–177.

———. (1914). *Behavior: An introduction to comparative psychology*. New York: Holt.

———. (1919). *Psychology from the standpoint of a behaviorist*. Philadelphia: Lippincott. (2d ed., 1924).

———. (1925). *Behaviorism*. New York: Norton.

———. (1926a). Experimental studies on the growth of the emotions. In C. Murchison (Ed.), *Psychologies of 1925*. Worcester, MA: Clark University Press. Pp. 37–58.

———. (1926b). Recent experiments on how we lose and change our emotional equipment. In C. Murchison (Ed.), *Psychologies of 1925*. Worcester, MA: Clark University Press. Pp. 59–82.

———. (1972; first published 1928). *The psychological care of the infant and child*. New York: Arno Press.

———. (1929). *Psychology from the standpoint of a behaviorist*. Philadelphia: Lippincott.

———. (1930). *Behaviorism*. Rev. ed. New York: Norton.

———. (1936). J. B. Watson. In C. Murchison (Ed.), *A history of psychology in autobiography*. Vol. 3. Worcester, MA: Clark University Press. Pp. 271–281.

———. (1967). *Behavior: An introduction to comparative psychology*. New York: Holt, Rinehart, & Winston. [A reissue of Watson (1914), with an introduction by R. J. Herrnstein.]

——— & McDougall, W. (1929). *The battle of behaviorism*. New York: Norton.

Watson, R. I. (1963). *The great psychologists from Aristotle to Freud*. Philadelphia: Lippincott.

———. (1967). Psychology: a prescriptive science. *American Psychologist*, **22**, 435–443.

———. (1968). *The great psychologists from Aristotle to Freud*. Rev. ed. Philadelphia: Lippincott.

———. (1971). *The great psychologists from Aristotle to Freud*. 3d ed. Philadelphia: Lippincott.

Weigel, R. G., & Gottfurcht, J. W. (1972). Faculty genealogies: A stimulus for student involvement in history and systems. *American Psychologist*, **27**, 981–983.

Weiss, A. P. (1917). Relation between structural and behavior psychology. *Psychological Review*, **34**, 301–317.

———. (1925). *A theoretical basis of human behavior*. Columbus, OH: Adams.

Weiss, P. (1967). 1 + 1 ≠ 2 (one plus one does not equal two). In G. C. Quarton, T. Melnechuk, & F. O. Schmitt (Eds.), *The neurosciences*. New York: Rockefeller University Press. Pp. 801–821.

Wells, G. L. (1978). Applied eyewitness-testimony research: System variables and estimator variables. *Journal of Personality and Social Psychology*, **36**, 1546–1557.

Wenegrat, B. (1984). *Sociobiology and mental disorder*. Menlo Park, CA: Addison-Wesley.

Wertheimer, M. (1912). Experimentelle Studien über das Sehen von Bewegung. *Zeitschrift für Psychologie*, **61**, 121–165.

———. (1923). Untersuchungen zur Lehre von der Gestalt. II. *Psychologische Forschung*, **4**, 301–350.

———. (1938). The general theoretical situation. In W. D. Ellis (Ed.), *A source book of Gestalt psychology*. New York: Harcourt, Brace & World. Pp. 12–16.

———. (1945). *Productive thinking*. New York: Harper & Row.

Wertheimer, Michael. (1982). Did Jung invent the word-association test for diagnosing "complexes"? Invited address presented at the Western Psychological Association Convention, April 9, 1982.

Weyer, E. M. (1921). Comment in B. T. Baldwin (Ed.). In memory of Wilhelm Wundt. *Psychological Review*, **28**, 153–188.

Whytt, R. (1763). *An essay on the vital and other involuntary motions of animals*. 2d ed. Edinburgh: J. Balfour.

Wiener, N. (1948). *Cybernetics, or control and communication in the animal and the machine*. New York: Wiley. (2d ed., 1961. Cambridge, MA: MIT Press)

Willems, E. P., & Rausch, H. L. (Eds.). (1969). *Naturalistic viewpoints in psychological research*. New York: Holt.

Williams, D. R. (1965). Classical conditioning and incentive motivation. In W. F. Prokasy (Ed.), *Classical conditioning*. New York: Appleton-Century-Crofts.

Wilson, E. O. (1975). *Sociobiology: The new synthesis*. Cambridge, MA: Harvard University Press.

Woodworth, R. S. (1918). *Dynamic psychology*. New York: Columbia University Press.

————. (1924). Four varieties of behavior. *Psychological Review, 31*, 257–264.

————. (1938). *Experimental psychology*. New York: Holt.

————. (1947). Reinforcement of perception. *American Journal of Psychology, 60*, 119–124.

————. (1948). *Contemporary schools of psychology*. New York: Ronald Press.

————. (1958). *Dynamics of behavior*. New York: Holt.

———— & Schlosberg, H. (1954). *Experimental psychology*. New York: Holt.

———— & Sheehan, M. R. (1964). *Contemporary schools of psychology*. New York: Ronald Press.

Wooldridge, D. E. (1968). *Mechanical man: The physical basis of intelligent life*. New York: McGraw-Hill.

Wright, J. M. von, Anderson, K., & Stenman, U. (1975). Generalization of conditioned GSR in dichotic listening. In P. M. A. Rabbitt (Ed.), *Attention and performance*. Vol. V. London: Academic Press.

Wundt, W. (1894). *Lectures on human and animal psychology*. (Trans. by J. E. Creighton & E. B. Titchener). New York: Macmillan.

————. (1900–1920). *Völkerpsychologie*. Vols. 1–10. Leipzig: Engelmann.

————. (1910). *Principles of physiological psychology*. (Trans. by E. B. Titchener). New York: Macmillan.

————. (1921). *Erlebtes und Erkanntes*. Stuttgart: Alfred Kröner.

Yerkes, R. M. (1943). *Chimpanzees: A laboratory colony*. New Haven, CT: Yale University Press.

Young, T. (1802). On the theory of light and colours. *Philosophical Transactions, 92*, 12–48.

Yuille, J. C. (1980). A critical examination of the psychological and practical implications of eyewitness research. *Law and Human Behavior, 4*, 335–345.

Zajonc, R. B. (1984). On the primacy of affect. *American Psychologist, 39*, 117–123.

Zeigarnik, B. (1927). Das Gehalten erledigter und unerledigter Handlungen. *Psychologische Forschung, 9*, 1–85. [Trans. and cond. as "On finished and unfinished tasks" in W. D. Ellis (Ed.). (1938). *A source book of Gestalt psychology*. New York: Harcourt, Brace & World. Pp. 300–314.]

Zuriff, G. E. (1985). *Behaviorism: A conceptual reconstruction*. New York: Columbia University Press.

Zusne, L., & Jones, W. H. (1982). *Anomalistic psychology*. Hillsdale, NJ: Erlbaum.

GLOSSARY

Abacus A manual computational device using beads that slide on rods; though of ancient origin, an abacus may be used for some operations by an expert at a speed as great as that of a desk calculator.

Abreaction A process of emotional release that occurs with the reliving of past experiences (psychoanalytic); the basic mechanism in catharsis ("talking-out cure").

Abstraction Process of stripping away of concrete properties of objects and events to reduce them, conceptually, to their essential properties.

Act psychology A school of psychology that stressed mental processes rather then the contents of consciousness (Brentano).

Adaptive act Carr's primary unit of behavior, which involves three phases: (1) a motivating stimulus, (2) a sensory situation, and (3) a response that alters the situation to satisfy the motivating conditions.

Adder A device for adding numbers; the adders in electronic digital computers are almost without exception designed to add binary numbers because the adding equipment is much simpler to build for base 2 arithmetic.

Afferent stimulus interaction Hull's postulate that stimuli interact in such a manner that the resulting behavior is more than a mere summation of the behaviorial effects of the stimuli taken separately.

Afterimage The lingering sensation following the removal of stimulation; usually noted in connection with visual stimulation.

All-or-none law Classic principle that a neuron responds completely or not at all.

Analog Having the property of continuous functions, as in the analog computer.

Anal stage The period in an individual's development which is marked by interest in the anal region and which has certain concomitant effects on personality that may be characteristic of the adult individual if fixation at this stage occurs (Freud).

Analysis Separation into constituent parts; conceptually, as in science, as well as physically.

Analytic psychology   Name given Carl Jung's version of psychoanalysis.

And   A commonly used connective in Boolean algebra, $C = A \cdot B$ may be read: "C is true if and only if A *and* B are both true."

Anecdotal method   The use of casually observed events as scientific data.

Anima   A well-developed archetype representing the *feminine* characteristics in men (Jung).

Animus   A well-developed archetype representing the *masculine* characteristics in women (Jung).

Anthropomorphism   The attributing of human characteristics or capacities to other things, especially infrahuman species.

Anthroponomy   A term advocated by Hunter as a name for the "science of human behavior."

Antimosaic hypothesis   The theoretical view opposed to the structuralist bundle hypothesis.

Antiquarianism   Emphasis on the past for its own sake.

Apperception   A clear and vivid perception.

Approach-approach conflict   A conflict which occurs when an individual desires to achieve two goals, only one of which can be obtained (Lewin).

Approach-avoidance conflict   A conflict which is characterized by an anticipated goal which is both desired and not desired (Lewin).

Archetype   Inherited predisposition to perceive or act in a certain way (Jung).

Associationism   The view that mental complexity is produced via learned connections between simple sensations and ideas.

Attensity   Clearness of sensation which varies with attention rather than with the objective characteristics of the stimulus (Titchener).

Attention   Focusing of consciousness.

Autonomic nervous system   The network of nerves and nerve centers mainly serving the viscera and primarily mediating involuntary activities.

Avoidance-avoidance conflict   A conflict which is present when a choice must be made between two anticipated consequences, both undesirable (Lewin).

Axiom   A self-evident truth; a proposition not susceptible to proof or disproof.

Bandwidth   The effective frequency range of a signal or the frequency range to which a particular instrument or channel responds; for example, a particular filter may have a bandwidth of 100 cycles per second.

Basic anxiety   The feeling a child has of being isolated and helpless in a potentially hostile world (Horney).

Behavior episode   A molar response sequence of limited size and range which has constancy of direction and equal potency throughout its parts (Barker).

Behaviorism   Generally, the systematic position that all psychological functions can be explained in terms of muscular reactions and glandular secretions and *nothing more*; therefore, the objective study of the stimulus and response aspects of behavior (Watson). Specifically, (1) methodological (empirical) behaviorism: The view that behavior is all that scientists can study and that strictly objective techniques are therefore required, as in all other natural sciences; and (2) metaphysical (radical) behaviorism: the philosophical position that there is no mind—a kind of physical monism.

Behavior space   Totality of factors affecting behavior for a given individual—similar to Lewin's "life space" construct (Tolman).

Belief-value matrix   Hierarchies of learned expectations concerning environmental objects and their roles in relation to behavior (Tolman).

Belongingness, principle of   The proposition that items are more easily associated if they are related in a recognizable way (Gestalt).

Beta Numerical criterion related to the a priori probability that a signal will be presented in a perceptual judgment situation, and to the values and costs of possible outcomes.

Binary Two-valued, as in the Boolean logic underlying the operation of the digital computer.

Binary number A number to the base 2; in any place the value of the coefficient can be one of only two values, 0 or 1.

Birth trauma The emotional experience of the infant ending its prenatal life (emphasized by Rank as having subsequent effects on personality).

Bit Unit of information, in information theory; abbreviation of "*binary digit.*"

Bond Connection of stimulus and response; hypothetical linkage used to account for the formation of associations.

Boolean algebra Two-valued logic, based on the assumption that any given element is either in or out of a set; the logical basis for the operation of the digital computer (Boole).

Brunswik ratio Relationship of distal (real or physical) to proximal (sensory) representations of an object, indicating the degree to which physical attributes determine any given perception.

Bundle hypothesis The assumption that a complex perception is a group of simple perceptions.

Catastrophe theory Mathematical propositions concerning sudden changes in the equilibrium conditions of systems, possibly exemplified in psychological phenomena (e.g., aggression, perceptual judgments).

Catharsis The psychoanalytic principle of releasing tension and anxiety by emotionally reliving experiences; originally described as the "talking-out cure" (Breuer and Freud).

Cathexis The investing of psychic energy in some object, person, or thing (Freud, Tolman).

Causality Conceptualization of the determination of events by prior events.

Centralism A viewpoint which stresses brain functions in the explanation of psychological phenomena.

Circular conditioned response A conditioned response sequence in which each successive response serves as a stimulus for the ensuing response.

Clinical validation The demonstration of a theoretical principle through successive confirmations within the same clinical setting from which it was derived.

Coded Transformed into other than the original form; for example, the letters of the alphabet might be coded by transforming each into a unique decimal number, which in turn might be coded into binary numbers, which finally might be coded as holes in a punched card.

Cognitive Pertaining to the processes involved in achieving awareness or knowledge of an object; more broadly, pertaining to complex mental activities.

Cognitive dissonance Incongruity between two sets of belief systems, resulting in change of attitude or other behavior so as to minimize the discrepancy.

Cohesive forces The tendency of excitations in the cortex to attract one another (Gestalt).

Collective unconscious That part of a person's unconscious which is inherited phylogenetically and is common to all members of the species (Jung).

Common fate Gestalt priniciple which holds that visual perception tends to group objects together when they seem to be moving in the same direction.

Compensation Development in those areas in which an individual feels inferior, and the attempt to overcome this inferiority.

Compile To translate a program written in a problem language into the language of machine instructions; the problem language is designed to be more natural for the programmer to use than the machine language.

Complex A potentially debilitating belief system held by an individual in spite of contradictory objective evidence.

Computer A device, usually electronic, which carries out a sequence of operations under the control of a stored program.

Conative Purposeful; having to do with motivation.

Condensation The representation of more than one latent element by a single manifest dream element (psychoanalysis).

Conditioned reflex A response that has come to be elicited by an initially ineffective stimulus after that stimulus has been presented together with an initially effective (unconditioned) stimulus.

Conditioning, classical Associative learning in which the reinforcement follows the presentation of a neutral stimulus, whether or not the response to be learned occurs.

Conditioning, instrumental Learning in which the opportunity to engage in one behavior (e.g., eating, observing, or sexual activity) is made contingent upon the performance of the response to be learned (e.g., pressing a bar or passing a test).

Conditioning, operant Instrumental conditioning in which the subject "emits" the learned response in the absence of any particular eliciting stimulus (Skinner); the free operant is a response whose emission leaves the subject in a position to repeat such responses (e.g., pressing a bar in a box, as contrasted with running down a runway).

Conditioning, respondent Classical conditioning, in which there is an eliciting stimulus and in which reinforcement occurs independently of the performance of the response.

Confirming reaction A cerebral function hypothesized by Thorndike as the physiological basis of reinforcement through reward.

Conflict The simultaneous operation of two or more contradictory tendencies; the condition resulting therefrom.

Connectionism The school of psychology which considers a stimulus-response connection or bond to be the basis of all or most behavior.

Conscious Aware of one's own mental activities. Actively experiencing, as in perceiving or thinking.

Conscious mentalism Attention to thinking activities (R.I. Watson).

Consciousness State of awareness of one's own mental activities.

Consensual validation Validation of a symbol or word by agreement on its meaning by a number of people.

Conservation of energy, principle of The proposition that energy is neither created nor destroyed in physical systems but is only transferred into other forms and hence "conserved."

Construct A concept that represents relationships between objects or events.

Contemporaneity, principle of The proposition that only present factors influence present behavior; the past influences behavior only as it is represented in the present (Lewin).

Contentual objectivism Viewing psychological data behaviorally (R. I. Watson).

Contentual subjectivism Viewing psychological data as mental activities or structures (R. I. Watson).

Context theory of meaning The view that the meaning of anything results from the context in which it occurs in consciousness (Titchener).

Contiguity Nearness in time and or space.

Contingent schedule of reinforcement Systematic presentation of reinforcer following some specified response.

Continuity Principle of learning emphasizing small, smooth steps in response changes rather than large discontinuous increments.

Continuum A variable whose values are continuous, that is, such that another value can always be found between any two given values.

Control (1) The method by which extraneous variation is eliminated in science, permitting a less ambiguous assignment of cause-and-effect relationships. (2) The exerting of influence over some variables(s).

Controlled variable A condition whose differential influence on the dependent variable in an experiment is eliminated. This is sometimes achieved by eliminating all variations in the controlled variables (for example, by eliminating the influence of sex by using only one sex) and sometimes by equating the values of the controlled variable for each value of the independent variable (for example, by putting equal numbers of men and women in each group).

Copernican theory Contemporary astronomical view that the earth revolves around the sun.

Corollary A proposition that follows directly from another which has been proved or postulated; a natural consequence which follows, without additional effort, from an action.

Correlation A relationship between two or more variables so that a change in one occurs whenever a change occurs in the other; the degree to which two or more variables are so related.

Creative synthesis The proposition that new characteristics emerge from the combination of elements into wholes (Wundt).

Cybernetics The study of communication and control in animal and machine (Weiner). Control is typically achieved by feeding back information about the results of past activities as input, as in thermostats which control furnaces or as in various homeostatic mechanisms in animals. Sweating and shivering are temperature-dependent examples in humans that parallel the action of the thermostat.

d' Measure of detectability of a signal, in detection theory.

Darwinism Principle of organic evolution systematically propounded by Charles Darwin in 1859.

Data Empirical observations and the records thereof in protocols.

Data processing The manipulation of data, generally for the purpose of making them more comprehensible by revealing hidden relationhips.

Decoded Converted back into a form which had been coded into some other form; for example, if letters of the alphabet were *coded* into numbers, the numbers would be *decoded* into letters of the alphabet.

Deduction A type of reasoning in which one proceeds from a set of given statements, via transformation rules, to generate further valid statements. The classic example goes from the premises "All humans are mortal" and "Socrates is a human" to the conclusion "Socrates is mortal."

Deductivism Emphasis on primacy of deductive investigations (R. I. Watson).

Defense mechanism Unconscious adaptive behavioral device whereby an individual tries to adjust to some real or fancied psychological threat.

Delayed response A response whose performance is permitted only after some set duration of time following the original presentation of the relevant stimuli.

Dependent variable The variable in an experiment whose values are treated as potentially being a function of the independent variable; in psychology, the dependent variable measured is usually some feature of the subject's responses.

Detection theory The theory which treats problems in sensitivity to signals. It is a branch of statistical decision theory and is often called the theory of signal detectability (TSD) or signal detection theory (SDT). Using this theory, it is possible to separate criterion considerations from sensitivity considerations.

Determining tendency A predisposition to behave in a particular manner.

Determinism An assumption that all phenomena can be explained by natural law in a cause-and-effect manner; the view that all events are therefore explicable entirely in terms of relevant antecedent events.

Developmentalism Emphasis on longitudinal changes (R. I. Watson).

Diacritical design The division of intertwined variables into subclasses in an attempt to separate effects (Brunswik).

Digital Concerning discrete rather than continuous values, as in a digital computer.

Dimension An ordered variable with continuously changing values (exemplified by each of R. I. Watson's eighteen prescriptions).

Dimensional analysis The structuring of a total situation into specific continua which are measurable.

Discrimination The process of differentiating between objects or actions; the ability to point to a difference.

Displacement The temporary substitution of a secondary goal for a primary one (psychoanalytic).

Distal effects Alterations of the environment which result from an organism's responses.

Distal stimuli Objects in the environment which produce stimuli at the receptor surfaces of the organism (the latter are proximal stimuli).

Distribution theory Logic underlying the determination of probabilities, as of a given observation arising from signal-plus-noise or noise alone, needed for computation of likelihood ratios in signal detection.

Double-alternation task An experimental design in which the correct responses follow the pattern AABB.

Double-aspect view The metaphysical position in which both mind and body are assumed to be a function of one underlying reality.

Drive (D) A construct used by Hull to indicate a condition of the organism resulting from a deprivation which increases the organism's activity toward a particular class of stimuli.

Drive discrimination The demonstrated ability of organisms to behave differentially under different deprivation conditions.

Dualism The metaphysical position in which both mind and body are assumed to exist.

Dynamic Relating to the motivational forces underlying behavior, as stressed by, for example, psychoanalysis.

Dynamicism Emphasis on change and change-producing processes.

Eclecticism The selection of what seems best from various systems, theories, or procedures.

Ecological validity Extent to which cues aid an organism in accomplishing a successful interaction with the environment (Brunswik).

Ecology, psychological The study of those parts of the environment which play an important role in an individual's life space (Lewin).

Effect, law of The proposition that strengthening of stimulus-response connections, as measured by the increased probability of the occurrence of a response in a particular stimulus situation, results from the action of reward following a response (satisfying aftereffects, as formulated by Thorndike); the original corollary proposition that punishing aftereffects produce a weakening of responses was subsequently discarded by Thorndike.

Effect, spread of The proposition that reinforcement by reward tends to strengthen erroneous responses in close temporal and or spatial contiguity (Thorndike).

Ego (1) The self. (2) That part of mental activity which is conscious and in close contact with reality (psychoanalytic).

Ego-defense mechanism   Any unconscious process which protects the individual from unpleasant reality; an irrational manner of dealing with anxiety (psychoanalytic).

Element   The irreducible unit into which all conscious states can be broken down (Titchener).

Elementarism   The methodological bias that mental and behavioral states and processes should be analyzed as far as possible into their constituent components (structuralism); strongly attacked by Gestalt psychology.

Emergentism   The view that unique properties emerge in combinations of elements and that these properties are not predictable from knowledge of the elements per se. Life and mind, according to this view, would not be completely reducible to physical principles.

Empathy   The sympathetic awareness of an emotional state in another person.

Empirical   Relating to facts and sensory experience.

Empiricism   (1) The school of philosophical thought that believes all knowledge originates in experience. (2) A methodology that emphasizes data and minimizes theoretical inference.

Entropy   In physics, the energy of a physical system which is unavailable for work; in information theory, the average information content of a symbol emitted by a source.

Environment   Totality of energies impinging on an organism from within as well as from without.

Environmentalism   The doctrine that emphasizes environmental factors as crucial determinants of behavior.

Epiphenomenalism   The metaphysical position in which mind is assumed to be a noncausal by-product of body.

Epistemology   A branch of philosophy concerned with the acquisition and the validity of knowledge.

Equilibrium   Stable or resting condition in a system.

Equipotentiality, principle of   The principle stating that within cerebral areas performing the same function all parts are equally capable of carrying on that function (Lashley).

Equivalence belief   A hypothesized state of an organism as a result of which it behaves as though a subgoal were the goal (Tolman).

Erogenous zones   Different zones or regions of the body which are especially sensitive to manipulation (psychoanalytic).

Error factors   The conditions that lead to incorrect responses in learning situations, systematically analyzed in discrimination learning by Harlow.

Ethology   The study of animal behavior via observation in the field.

Eugenics   The science that attempts to improve humankind by selective breeding so as to maximize desirable genetic characteristics.

Evolution, organic   The theory that gradual changes in plants and animals resulting from cumulative environmental influences account for the development of today's diverse species from some simpler common ancestor(s) (Darwin).

Exercise, law of   The proposition that performance of a response improves subsequent performance through practice alone.

Existential psychology   (1) The name often given to structuralism because it treated the elements of consciousness as existent. (2) The school of personality theorists who stress the individual's self-understanding. The term derives from existentialism in philosophy; there the emphasis is on the concrete events in experience and the free will of human beings to choose how they wish to live their lives.

Expectancy   Anticipation of some relationship, such as between two particular stimulus events or between a stimulus and a response (Tolman).

Experience   Conscious (mental) process.

Experience, immediate   Conscious processes in their own right, as studied directly in structural psychology (Wundt).

Experience, mediate   Conscious processes used as a way of knowing about the external "real" world, in physics (Wundt).

Exploitative orientation   A means of escaping insecurity by obtaining objects valued by others (Fromm).

External explanation   Interpretation of some phenomenon in terms of principles extrinsic to it.

Exteroceptor   A sense organ or receptor directly stimulated by energy sources outside the body (e.g., the eye).

Extrasensory perception (ESP)   Responsivity to external events that is not mediated by any known sense modality.

Extraversion   The mode of responding to the world in which the person's attention is directed toward the external world (Jung).

Fact   A verbal statement accepted by a certain group at a particular time (Guthrie).

Factor   A basic condition or variable that is singled out for investigation.

Factor analysis   A statistical technique using sets of correlations; used to extract the underlying dimensions or factors which account for the observed relationships between scores.

False alarm   Identification of noise as signal, in detection theory.

Feedback   In an energy system, the part of the output energy that is returned to the system to regulate further output.

Fictional future   The plans and aspirations a person has for the future and presently believes in (Adler).

Field-cognition modes   A combination of thinking, perceiving, and remembering on the part of the organism which gives rise to a specific way of knowing some characteristic of the environment (Tolman).

Field expectations   A belief by the organism that a particular response to a certain cue or stimulus will produce a particular situation or consequence (Tolman).

Field observation (study)   Scientific research carried out in a real-life situation such as a school, factory, or home.

Field theory   Any psychological theory which attempts to use fields of force analogous to those in physics as an explanation for psychological data.

Figure-ground   A general property of perception; the figure is that which stands out and is attended to, while the ground is that which surrounds the figure and is secondary to it.

Film color   A transparent color which is not substantial and lacks definite localization.

Fixation   (1) Perseveration of a particular response. (2) The persistence of immature behavior or thought processes accompanied by a lack of normal development (psychoanalytic).

Fractional antedating goal response   An implicit goal response which occurs progressively earlier in the response chain, thus providing stimuli which may become conditioned to ensuing responses (Hull, Spence).

Free association   (1) An unrestrained sequence of ideas or thoughts. (2) The technique of having a subject respond with unrestricted verbalizations for clinical purposes (psychoanalytic).

Free operant   *See* **Conditioning, operant.**

Frequency, law of   The proposition that learning is a function of the frequency of occurrence of a response.

Functional autonomy   The performance of a task for its own sake; the drive state is thus independent of the need which gave rise to it (Allport).

Functionalism The psychological system that stresses the function or utility of behavior in adapting to the environment (Angell, Carr, Woodworth).

Generalization (1) The process of extending results or conclusions beyond their initial observational basis. (2) The function whereby a particular conditioned response is made to some stimulus that is similar to the conditioned stimulus (stimulus generalization) or a conditioned stimulus elicits a response similar to the conditioned response (response generalization).

Generalization gradient The orderly differences in effectiveness with which stimuli that have not previously occurred in the conditioning procedure elicit a response, as a function of their similarity to the conditioned stimulus.

Genital stage The final psychosexual stage in the individual's development, in which the individual desires sexual relations with members of the opposite sex (Freud).

Gestalt A figure or configuration which is a whole different from the sum of its parts and which, if analyzed into its parts, is destroyed.

Gestalt psychology The psychological system that stresses the phenomenological study of molar stimulus and response units, with emphasis placed on the primacy of wholes and on the existence of brain fields and configurations (Wertheimer, Koffka, Köhler).

Gestaltqualität Patterns of time and space that are presumed to inhere in the mind and so are independent of physical elements; emphasis thereon is often considered the immediate precursor of Gestalt psychology (von Ehrenfels).

Goal gradient The progressive increment in response strength that occurs as a function of closeness to the goal (Hull).

Hab A unit of learning invented to quantify habit strength; equal to 1 percent of the physiological maximum (Hull).

Habit A learned response to some stimulus or situation.

Habit family hierarchy The ordering by strength of the total set of responses which may occur in a given stimulus situation (Hull).

Habit strength $_sH_r$ An intervening variable representing learning; a function of (1) number of reinforcements, (2) amount of reinforcement, (3) time between stimulus and response, and (4) time between response and reinforcement (Hull, 1943); in the final Hullian system (1951, 1952) only (1) was retained as a determiner.

Hedonism The philosophical belief that behavior is designed to attain pleasure and avoid pain.

Heisenberg principle A mathematical proof that exact simultaneous measurement of the position and the momentum of a single electron is impossible.

Historicist One who wants to understand each period of the past primarily in terms of then-existing phenomena, rather than in terms of present values and knowledge.

Hit Identification of a signal when it occurs, in detection theory.

Hodological space A qualitative geometry of spatial relations, invented by Lewin, which uses vectors to represent dynamic psychological factors.

Holistic Referring to the theoretical belief that an organism must be studied as a whole, since the whole is different from the sum of its constituent parts.

Humanism The general position that the focus and direction of scientific inquiry and interpretation should be determined primarily by human needs and values, especially in the behavioral and social sciences.

Hypothesis (1) A prediction concerning the relationship between variables. (2) A tentative explanation.

Hypothetical construct A construct whose meaning goes beyond summarizing the relationship between the antecedent (stimulus) and consequent (response) conditions which it represents.

Hypothetico-deductive method   A method of theory construction which starts with a few general postulates from which testable theorems and corollaries are derived by rigorous deduction, and then tests the derivations empirically.

Hysteria   The manifestation of such bodily symptoms as anesthesia and paralysis as the result of psychic trauma or conflict.

Id   A psychic structure or process which is the original reservoir of psychic energy and operates according to the pleasure principle (Freud).

Ideal observer   An abstract mathematical construct within detection theory; the behavior of this construct defines the optimal behavior achievable within specified situations amenable to the necessary mathematical treatment.

Ideomotor action   The belief that an idea, unless inhibited by other ideas, will lead directly to motor action (James).

Idiographic   Referring to an individual case or event and to the methodology that stresses understanding individual events rather than seeking general laws.

Idiographicism   Emphasis on intensive investigation of individuals for the sake of understanding them as unique cases (R. I. Watson).

Image   The relatively faint reproduction in consciousness of a previous sensation (Titchener).

Imageless thought   Mental processes or functions which elude introspective analysis.

Incentive   Goal object.

Independent variable   The factor which is manipulated in an experiment so that its influence on the dependent variable can be measured.

Indeterminism   Denial that all events are explicable in terms of antecedent events ("causes").

Individual differences   The totality of diversity exhibited by living organisms in various biological, behavioral, and social measurements.

Individual psychology   The version of psychoanalysis developed by Alfred Adler.

Induction   A mode of logic which proceeds from specific statements to general conclusions.

Inductivism   Emphasis on primacy of inductive investigations (R. I. Watson).

Inferiority complex   The feeling an individual has as the result of real or imagined deficiencies (Adler).

Information   Whatever reduces uncertainty. The receipt of an information-bearing message reduces uncertainty or ignorance by reducing the number of alternative possible messages or by biasing their probabilities so that the remaining uncertainty is reduced.

Information processing   The sensory reception, coding, manipulation, storing (in memory), and retrieval of environmental cues and patterns of stimulation by an organism or a machine.

Information theory   The mathematical theory which deals with the coding, decoding, and transmission of messages.

Inhibition, conditioned   The hypothesized acquisition of inhibitory properties by a stimulus through its repeated association with reactive inhibition (Hull).

Inhibition, reactive   The hypothesized explanation for the decrement of a learned response owing to the effortfulness of the activity (Hull).

Insight   (1) A sudden understanding of a previously insoluble problem. (2) A sudden reorganization of the perceptual field (Gestalt).

Instinct   (1) An innate, complex, stereotyped mode of behaving. (2) Need (Freud).

Instinct, death   The wish of an organism to return to an inorganic state (Freud).

Instinct, life   The desire of the organism to maintain a balance between the anabolistic and catabolistic forces of the body—to maintain life (Freud).

Instructions   Specifications of computer operations to be performed; for example, a computer might have approximately sixty basic instructions to which it can respond, and synthesize the more complex functions from these basic instructions.

Intelligence Adaptive ability of individuals as exhibited by how successfully they adjust to their environment.

Interactionism The metaphysical position in which mind and body are assumed to be two separate entities.

Internal explanation Interpretation of some phenomenon in terms of its own intrinsic functions.

Interoceptor A sense organ or receptor within the organism sensitive to stimuli within the body.

Intervening variable A construct which abstracts the relationship between antecedent (stimulus) and consequent (response) conditions, with no meaning beyond this relationship.

Introspection A generic term for any method which relies upon the subjective report of the subject.

Introversion The mode of responding to the world in which one's attention is directed toward oneself (Jung).

Irradiation The phenomenon of generalization, with the implication of spreading excitatory brain functions (Pavlov).

Irrationalism Acceptance of primacy of emotion in thought.

Isomorphism The 1:1 relationship assumed to hold between brain fields and experience (Gestalt).

Kinesthetic Pertaining to the sense of body movement or position.

Lamarckian evolution The doctrine of the inheritance of acquired characteristics: The belief that the use or disuse of organic structures results in changes which are passed on to the organism's offspring.

Latent learning Learning which is not yet reflected in performance (Tolman).

Law (1) A statement of a regular and predictable relationship between empirical variables. (2) A well-accepted theoretical proposition.

Learning Real or potential change in behavior attributed to training or experience.

Learning set An increased ability to solve a class of problems. Learning sets are acquired through experience with solving a large number of similar problems (Harlow).

Lens model Conceptualization of the interaction of the functional variables affecting behavior (Brunswik).

Level of aspiration The performance level which an individual expects to reach in a given situation and by which he or she judges a performance as a success or failure (Lewin).

Lexigram A geometric pattern symbolizing a word. Duane Rumbaugh used lexigrams on a computer keyboard to allow the chimpanzee Lana to communicate.

Libido Energy in the service of the life instincts (Freud).

Life style The particular manner in which an individual develops in order to deal with reality (Adler).

Likelihood ratio The ratio of the probability that an observed event would occur given one hypothesis to the probability that it would occur given some second hypothesis; within detection theory, the hypotheses are most commonly that "a signal was presented" and that "noise alone was presented."

Linear graph A graph representing an equation of the first degree between two variables.

Linear perspective A monocular depth cue based on the apparent convergence of parallel lines.

Lloyd Morgan's canon Law of parsimony applied to comparative psychology: "In no case may we interpret an action as the outcome of the exercise of a higher psychical faculty, if it can be interpreted as the outcome of the exercise of one which stands lower on the psychological scale."

Logic A set of rules of formal reasoning procedures.

Logical positivism   A philosophical movement headed by Schlick to rid philosophy of metaphysics and to establish a science of science.

Logon content   Information carried by different scales or dimensions (MacKay).

Mandala   The magic circle found in many religious cults, which Jung believed to be symbolic of the human being's striving for unity.

Marketing orientation   A means of escaping insecurity by emulating the social group in which one lives; the individual pretends to be the social ideal (Fromm).

Masculine protest   The desire of both males and females to overcome femininity (Adler).

Mass action, principle of   The principle which states that brain tissues function with an effectiveness which depends on the mass of undisturbed tissue (Lashley).

Materialism   The metaphysical position in which a single underlying physical reality is assumed.

Mathematical models   Calculational systems based on some mathematical formulation; may be applied to empirical problems.

Means-end readiness   A state of selective readiness which endures independently of the present motivational state of the organism and which leads to the acquisition of certain expectancies more readily than to others (Tolman).

Measurement   Use of numbers (quantification) to express the values of variables and their effects.

Mechanism   (1) A purposive response or set of responses (Woodworth). (2) Assumption that life processes are entirely explicable in terms of physiochemical functions.

Mechanistic explanation   Interpretation of phenomena in terms of known or presumed machinelike functions.

Mediational mechanisms   Processes whose effects, as on behavior, are produced indirectly (by mediation) rather than directly.

Memory   (1) Information retained by an organism or machine. (2) System which retains the information.

Mental activity   The generic term for adaptive behavior (Carr).

Mental chemistry   The doctrine that simple ideas coalesce to form new, more complex ideas and lose their individual identity (John Stuart Mill).

Mentalism   *See* **Conscious mentalism.**

Mental mechanics   The doctrine which states that a complex idea is no more than the sum of the simple ideas from which it is formed. (James Mill).

Metaphysics   A branch of philosophy concerned with the identification and understanding of ultimate reality; "above physics."

Metatheory   A set of general rules governing the construction of a theory; a theory about theory.

Method, scientific   The fundamental process by which all science proceeds; it is characterized by conceptual analysis and controlled observation.

Methodological objectivism   Use of techniques open to verification by another observer (R. I. Watson).

Methodological subjectism   Use of techniques not open to verification by another observer (R. I. Watson).

Metron content   Information carried by varying values along a single scale (MacKay).

Mind   Collective name for totality of an individual's thinking and perceptual activities.

Mind-body problem   The puzzle generated by the apparent concomitant operation of mental (conscious) and physical (bodily) functions, and the question how their relationship may be best understood.

Model   Abstract system with logical determinants that can be tested empirically only when their elements have been "interpreted" in terms of observable events.

Model, deterministic Any theoretical position which stresses the complete predictability of a response when antecedent conditions are known.

Model, mathematical learning Any learning theory expressed in mathematical form.

Model, stochastic Any model in which one uses the stochastic assumption, i.e., that in a long series of trials, the probability of an outcome approaches the true probability of that outcome.

Molar Referring to large units of study.

Molarism Preference for large units of description in psychological data (R. I. Watson).

Molecular Referring to small units of study.

Molecularism Preference for small units of description in psychological data (R. I. Watson).

Monad The element of all being, which is indestructible, uncreatable, immutable, and active (Leibniz).

Monism A metaphysical position in which only one basic reality is assumed, either in mind or body.

Morphology The study of biological forms and structures.

Motivation Activating conditions that underlie behavior and mental functions.

Motor conditioned response A voluntary (striped-muscle) response that has been conditioned to some initially ineffective stimulus. *See also* **Conditioning.**

Motor patterns Responses and combinations of responses.

Movement-produced stimuli (mps) Stimuli originating in the movements of the organism (Guthrie).

Nativism The doctrine which emphasizes hereditary factors in the development of an organism, rather than environmental ones.

Naturalism View that natural phenomena can be completely interpreted by principles yielded by study of those phenomena without recourse to any external principles (R. I. Watson).

Naturalistic observation Study of phenomena in their normal state, without experimental or other interference.

Naturalistic view In history, the view that the course of events is determined by the Zeitgeist and historical forces, rather than by great men and women (Boring).

Need Some deficit or want in an organism.

Need reduction Principle that satisfaction of need is crucial in learning (Hull).

Need system Totality of motivational factors affecting an individual (Tolman).

Neoanalytic Referring to relatively new versions of psychoanalysis, rather than to the initial orthodox ones, such as Freudian.

Neobehavioristic Referring to the relatively new versions of behaviorism, in contrast to the early Watsonian.

Neural noise Extraneous internal neural activity in an observer.

Neurosis A personality disorder which is characterized by extreme anxiety; the symptoms are not usually severe enough to require hospitalization.

Neurotic trend The particular approach an individual uses in an attempt to avoid conflict and find security (Horney).

Noise Anything (e.g., meaningless sounds) which interferes with a signal being transmitted.

Nomotheticsm Emphasis on general laws, applicable to more than a single individual (R. I. Watson).

Noncontingent schedule of reinforcement Presentation of reinforcer without regard to the occurrence of some specified response.

Noncontinuity Principle of learning in which large, discontinuous increments in response strength are emphasized rather than small continuous steps.

Non-Euclidean geometry   A geometry using a different set of axioms from those of Euclidean geometry; the most famous example is the geometry used in relativity theory, which rejects the Euclidean postulate concerning parallel lines.

Nonsense syllable   A "meaningless" item most often composed of two consonants separated by a vowel (CVC); developed by Ebbinghaus to reduce variations in learning and memory.

Normal science   The type of science practiced during the period of relatively unquestioned acceptance of a framework ("paradigm") in which scientists work (Kuhn).

Objective set   Perspective that focuses on objects and events as they are seen by others rather than on one's own subjective biases.

Objectivism   *See* **Contentual objectivism, Methodological objectivism.**

Occam's razor   *See* **Parsimony, principle of.**

Occasionalism   A philosophical position on the mind-body issue in which two separate processes are assumed and are correlated by divine intervention.

O data   Behavioral observations made with active intervention of an operator—hence, O (Barker).

Oedipal conflict   The feeling of hostility of the child toward the parent of the same sex and love for the parent of the opposite sex (Freud).

Operant behavior   Responses characterized by their effect on the environment and for which there is usually no known or manipulated eliciting stimulus (Skinner).

Operant conditioning   Conditioning of emitted behavior by establishing a contingency between a response and some consequence (reinforcement schedule).

Operationism   A movement intended to clarify the language of science; an operational definition is any definition in which the meaning of a term is strictly determined by a corresponding set of operations (Bridgman).

Or   A connective used in writing Boolean algebraic equations; typically the inclusive or is used, and $C = A + B$ would then mean "C is true if A is true or if B is true or if both A and B are true."

Oral stage   The first period in an individual's psychosexual development; marked by interest in the oral region (Freud).

Organic evolution   *See* **Evolution, organic.**

Organ inferiority   *See* **Inferiority complex.**

Organism   The individual considered as an integrated totality.

Organismic   Pertaining to any point of view which stresses studying the behavior of the whole organism rather than its parts.

Orienting reaction (OR)   Attentional response—perceptual, physiological, and postural—to novel stimuli.

Paradigm   A more or less inclusive framework of concepts, assumptions, and methods within which some scientific enterprise is carried out during a period of "normal" science (Kuhn).

Parameter   (1) A constant in an equation; the values of the constants determine which curve of a family will represent the relationship between the dependent variable and the independent variable or variables. Parameters in equations would be expected to correspond to the values at which controlled variables have been set in an experiment. (2) Less precisely, a parameter is a particular *value* of a variable; for example one might say that the stimulus parameter was changed in order to produce novelty in the experiment.

Parapsychology   A branch of psychology which studies the psychological aspects of apparently supernatural phenomena.

Parsimony, principle of   The scientific principle that the simpler of two hypotheses should be accepted, other things being equal. It does not negate the acceptance of complex explanations if the data require them. (Also called *William of Occam's razor* and, in comparative psychology, *Lloyd Morgan's canon.)*

Partial reinforcement   Schedule of reinforcement in which reinforcement is provided intermittently rather than continuously following some given response.

Payoff matrix   The pattern of gains (values) and losses (costs) related to being right or wrong in judgments, as in perceptual responses to signals.

Penis envy   The repressed female desire to possess a penis; the female form of castration anxiety (Freud).

Perception   Meaningful apprehension of the environment by means of sense organs.

Performance   Actual behavior; may be contrasted with learning, which refers to behavior potential. Motivation is required to produce performance.

Peripheralism   The explanation of psychological phenomena emphasizing muscular action and other distal events rather than the functioning of the central nervous system.

Permutations   All the possible arrangements of a certain number of different items; each arrangement is called a *permutation*.

Persona   A well-developed archetype which represents a human being's social self (Jung).

Personal equation   Correction for individual differences in reaction time exhibited by astronomers observing stellar transits.

Personalistic view   The belief that the course of history is determined by great individuals and their unique contributions (Boring).

Personality   Unique way in which traits, attitudes, aptitudes, and the like are organized in an individual.

Personification   The attribution of human characters to nonhuman entities.

Phallic stage   The period in an individual's development when the Oedipus complex develops; marked by interest in the penis (Freud).

Phenomenalism   The metaphysical position in which neither mind nor body is considered real and only ideas resulting from sensory impressions are held to exist.

Phenomenology   A method of observation in which experiential data are accepted in a more or less naive manner, without any attempt at analysis.

Phi phenomenon   The name given by Wertheimer to the perception of apparent motion generated by stationary stimuli. *Pure* phi occurs when motion is seen but no *object* is seen in motion.

Phrenology   The belief that mental characteristics can be determined by examining the contours of the skull (Gall).

Physicalism   The philosophical position that all scientific propositions are ultimately reducible to the language of physical science.

Physiologizing   Advancing physiological explanations and conjectures in the absence of definite physiological knowledge.

Physiology   Study of the functions of the various organ systems of the body.

Pleasure principle   Principle that considers only the immediate satisfaction of instinctual desires; governs the development of the id (Freud).

Pluralism   A philosophical position on the mind-body issue in which multiple entities or processes are assumed.

Positivism   A metatheoretical and general scientific position that emphasizes parsimony and operationism in data language and eschews theorizing and inferential commitment; any method designed to produce *positive* knowledge.

Postulate   (1) A fundamental assumption not meant to be tested. (2) A theoretical proposition used within a given logical framework and tested indirectly by means of its empirical implications.

Practitioner One who is engaged in some professional service function at a high level of responsibility, after being more or less intensively trained.

Pragmatics Study of the relationships between signs and their users (Morris).

Pragmatism Validation of a principle through its utility; the philosophical position that that which is useful is true.

Prägnanz, law of The Gestalt principle that a figure will be perceived in its best possible form.

Preconscious That part of mental activity which consists of materials not presently conscious but readily recallable (psychoanalysis).

Preconscious processing Mental (brain) activities which are involved in the handling of sensory information without any conscious representation; such processing may accompany and follow, as well as precede, conscious experience, as when a visual pattern mask blocks out conscious awareness of an event without precluding its nonconscious processing.

Preparadigmatic science Diffuse and tentative beginnings of a science prior to the clear formation of a generally accepted set of concepts, assumptions, and methods (Kuhn).

Prescription The manner in which psychologists tend to answer psychology's most fundamental and persistent questions, as ordered on a continuum, with positive and negative polar extremes (R. I. Watson).

Presentist One who wants to understand the past as it relates to present problems so as better to understand and cope with them.

Primary memory image A lingering memory trace postulated to maintain a sensation for a relatively short time, permitting an accurate introspective report (Titchener).

Primary process A process whose aim is direct and immediate instinctual satisfaction, mediated by the id (psychoanalysis).

Primary qualities Those qualities which are alleged to inhere within the object and to be independent of the perceiver, such as size and shape (Locke).

Primitive term A term which is not defined by any more basic term within a theory.

Probabilistic functionalism Egon Brunswik's position, which emphasizes that both the correctness of perception and the effectiveness of action are only probable. The adaptive, functional relating of distal stimuli to distal effects of responses on the environment is seen as the task of the organism.

Program A sequence of instructions that can be carried out by a computer.

Programmatic Lacking in systematic specificity.

Projection A defense mechanism in which individuals attempt to externalize their own values, faults, and ideas (psychoanalysis).

Proprioceptor A sense organ or receptor sensitive to the position or the movement of the body (e.g., vestibular canal).

Protensity Temporal duration of a sensation or an image (Titchener).

Proximal reactions The peripheral motor responses of the organism, without regard for the consequences on the environment (Brunswik).

Proximal stimuli Stimuli impinging directly on the sensory receptors of the organism (Brunswik).

Psychical satiation A reduction in performance of an activity as a function of the continued repetition of the activity.

Psychic apparatus The various mental structures (id, ego, superego, and the like) hypothesized by Freud to account for normal and maladjusted behavior.

Psychoanalysis (1) A school of psychology developed by Sigmund Freud which places a great deal of emphasis upon unconscious motivation, conflict, and symbolism. (2) A type of psychiatry stressing the free-association technique and long-term, deep psychotherapy.

Psychogenesis The origin and development of mind or behavior.

Psychometrist A person skilled in the administration and scoring of mental tests.

Psychophysical parallelism The metaphysical position in which mind and body are independent and yet perfectly correlated entities.

Psychophysics The scientific study of the relationship between stimuli and sensations.

Psychotherapy Techniques for alleviating maladjustment.

Ptolemaic theory Ancient astronomical view that the earth is the center of the universe.

Purism Seeking knowledge for its own sake (R. I. Watson).

Purposivism The doctrine that behavior is more than purely mechanical and that it is directed toward some goal.

Puzzle box An enclosure which prevents an organism from reaching a goal until a particular device is manipulated (Thorndike).

Qualitative Referring to that which can be distinguished or identified as different in kind.

Qualitativism Stress on knowledge that focuses on differences in kind or essence (R. I. Watson).

Quantification The process of establishing relationships between objects of empirical study and numbers.

Quantitative Referring to that which can be distinguished or identified as different in number or amount.

Quantitativism Stress on measured knowledge (R. I. Watson).

Rationalization A form of projection in which individuals attempt to find justifiable causes for their actions (psychoanalysis).

Reaction potential ($_sE_r$) A construct that indicates the degree of strength of a particular response (Hull).

Reaction time, motor Latency of response made with attention to the response rather than to the stimulus onset.

Reaction time, sensory Latency of response made with attention to the stimulus onset rather than to the response.

Readiness, law of The principle which states that when a conduction unit is ready to conduct, conduction by it is satisfying, providing nothing is done to alter its action (Thorndike).

Reality principle The principle of action imposed by the demands of the environment on the ego, leading to the eventual satisfaction of libidinal drives in such a way that the organism continues to exist (Freud).

Receiver Name for a sensory system in signal detection theory.

Receiver operating characteristic (ROC) curve A function relating the probability of a "hit" (correct report of detection) to the probability of a "false alarm" (incorrect report of detection) in detection theory.

Recency, law of The principle stating that, other things being equal, that which is best remembered is that which was most recently learned.

Receptive orientation A means of escaping insecurity by strong identification with a group or its leader (Fromm).

Reductionism The position holding that complex phenomena should be understood through analysis (reduction) into simpler components.

Reduction screen An opaque screen with one or two small eyeholes, used so that a subject can view stimuli without knowledge of the surrounding illumination.

Redundant Containing repetitious information.

Reflex An involuntary, stereotyped response of a body part to a stimulus.

Reflex arc The simplest functional unit in the nervous system, composed of a receptor, synapse, and effector.

Reflexology The school of psychology which holds that reflexes and combinations of reflexes are the basis of all behavior (Bekhterev).

Regression The return to a former state or condition.

Reinforcement Any process by which a response is strengthened; generally assumed to involve more than mere contiguity of stimulus and response elements.

Relativity theory Presumption of a four-dimensional space-time field for natural phenomena (Einstein).

Repetition compulsion An irrepressible desire to repeat some act over and over (Freud).

Representative design An experimental approach allowing a large sample of variables to change together in a random but known fashion, thus better "representing" the effects of the existing combinations of variables and values (Brunswik).

Repression The unconscious removal of unpleasant thoughts or events from consciousness (Freud).

Resistance Opposition by a patient to the recall of past events, presumably because of unconscious repression (psychoanalysis).

Respondent behavior Response characterized by its identification with a specific eliciting stimulus (Skinner).

Response Any behavior resulting from some stimulus.

Restraining forces Brain excitations preventing the unrestrained action of cohesive forces; usually the result of present stimulation (Gestalt).

Retinal disparity A visual depth cue resulting from the slight difference between the two retinal images in binocular vision.

Retroactive inhibition The interference by a second task with the retention of a previously learned task.

Retrospection Introspection on a past event.

Revolution, scientific Radical and fundamental changes in the framework within which a particular science operates, resulting in a new "paradigm" (Kuhn).

Reward An object or activity that satisfies some motivating condition; often assumed to be necessary for learning (as in Thorndike's law of effect or Hull's S-R behavior system).

ROC *See* **Receiver operating characteristic curve.**

Routine A computer program or part of a program, generally so named because it is designed to carry out a specific function (for example, finding square roots); the word *routine* is ordinarily used if the portion of the program is on the main line of the program, whereas the word *subroutine* is used for units which are called upon periodically from the main program.

Salivary conditioning Process whereby the salivary response becomes attached to some initially ineffective stimulus. *See also* **Conditioning.**

Scaling The construction of an ordered system of measurement to represent any phenomenon.

Schedule, fixed-interval (FI) A program of reinforcement in which reinforcement is given for the first response made after some fixed period of time.

Schedule, fixed-ratio (FR) A program of reinforcement in which reinforcement is given after some fixed number of responses.

Schedule, reinforcement A program indicating how the presentation of some reinforcing stimulus is arranged.

Schedule, variable-interval (VI) A program of reinforcement in which reinforcement is given for the first response made after some variable period of time.

Schedule, variable-ratio (VR) A program of reinforcement in which reinforcement is given after some variable number of responses.

Schema   A fundamental conceptual framework, such as that underlying memory of and reconstruction of a story (Bartlett).

Schemapiric   Description of science as involved in establishing relationships between symbols (*schema-*) and empirical observations (*-piric*) (Stevens).

School   A collection of adherents to a particular systematic position, with varying degrees of temporal and spatial contiguity.

Science   The enterprise by which human beings obtain ordered knowledge about natural phenomena, working with a particular methodology (controlled observation and analysis) and set of attitudes (skepticism, objectivity, etc.).

Science, applied   That part of science which is concerned with investigations believed to have immediate practical utility.

Science, pure   That part of science which is concerned only with the discovery of new facts and the development of theories without regard for the immediate use of such knowledge.

Secondary process   Conscious activity of the ego guided by external reality; it is thus distinguished from the primary-process activity of the id (psychoanalysis).

Secondary qualities   Those qualities alleged to inhere not within the object but within the perceiver, such as color (Locke).

Secondary reinforcement   The strengthening of a response by presentation of a stimulus that does not itself have any direct need-reducing properties but which has occurred contiguously with such a need-reducing stimulus (the primary reinforcer).

Second signal system   Pavlov's name for the complex (secondary) signal system, language, with ordinary conditioning as the first signal system.

Self   (1) An existing picture of an individual's past behavior and experiences as the individual perceives it. (2) A summary name for a set of psychological processes, usually including evaluative and attitudinal functions, involving an individual and that individual's relationship to the world. (3) Construct developed by individuals to account for the integrity and continuity of their experiences.

Self-actualization   Full realization of one's potential.

Semantics   Study of the relationship of signs to objects (Morris).

Semiotics   Study of the uses of signs and symbols, including three major components (semantics, syntactics, and pragmatics) (Morris).

Sensation   A conscious experience which cannot be further analyzed (Titchener).

Sensory isolation   Removal of all or almost all stimulation from an individual for a set period of time.

Separation anxiety   Severe emotionalism resulting from birth trauma and basic to neurotic symptoms (Rank).

Set   A predisposition or determining tendency.

Shadow   A well-developed archetype inherited from the human being's prehuman ancestors; the animal instincts (Jung).

Shaping   A technique used to produce a desired behavioral pattern by selectively reinforcing responses that approximate it or are a part of it.

Sibling rivalry   Competition among offspring (Adler).

Sign   A cue that signals the appearance of some other object or event.

Signal detection theory   *See* **Detection theory.**

Sign learning   Learning of the relationships between signs—what leads to what (Tolman).

Sign significate (sign Gestalt)   An object which gives rise to the expectation that a particular response will lead to a goal (Tolman).

Simplicity   *See* **Parsimony, principle of.**

Skepticism   A refusal to accept propositions without very strong evidence.

Skinner box An operant conditioning chamber; a box provided with a device which the organism can manipulate to produce some type of reinforcement.

Solipsism The philosophical view that one can be certain of nothing but one's own experience, so that the existence of an external world becomes a mere assumption.

Solution learning Overt instrumental learning or problem solving (Mowrer).

Somatic nervous system Network of nerves and nerve centers serving the striped musculature of the body and primarily mediating voluntary activities.

S-O-R Stimulus-organism-response.

Spread of effect Hypothesis that errors occurring in proximity to rewarded responses acquire some degree of strengthening, relative to more distal errors, from the reward function (Thorndike).

State variable A hypothesized condition of the organism which is the result of a past interaction of the organism and the environment, such as deprivation or drug treatment.

Statistical decision theory A theory that specifies how probabilistic decisions, as in perceptual judgments, should be decided.

Staticism Emphasis on cross-sectional or enduring rather than developmental factors (R. I. Watson).

Stimulus Any environmental energy that impinges on an appropriate sense organ.

Stimulus error Paying attention to the properties of the stimulus rather than to the characteristics of the sensation (Titchener).

Stimulus field The totality of stimuli that act on the organism at any given moment (Gestalt).

Stimulus generalization The process whereby some initially ineffective stimulus, not itself used in conditioning, becomes effective in eliciting some response after the conditioning of that response to a stimulus that is similar along some dimension.

Stimulus-intensity dynamism The principle that reaction potential or response amplitude increases monotonically with the intensity of the stimulus (Hull).

Stimulus pool The total population of stimuli from which different samples may be drawn (Estes).

Stimulus-response (S-R) psychology A position whose conceptual framework depends on stimuli and responses.

Stimulus trace The activity in the nervous system which results from stimulation (Hull).

Structuralism The system that stresses the analysis of consciousness into elements through the method of introspection (Wundt, Titchener).

Subjective idealism The metaphysical position in which a single underlying mental or spiritual reality is assumed.

Subjectivism The tendency to base belief on one's own perception and thinking. *See also* **Contentual subjectivism** *and* **Methodological subjectivism**

Sublimation The permanent substitution of a secondary goal for a primary one (Freud).

Superego The psychic structure or process which represents external values, particularly as inculcated by parents. It is roughly equivalent to the conscience (Freud).

Supernaturalism The doctrine that natural phenomena can be completely interpreted only by assuming some external (transcendent) principles (R. I. Watson).

Superstitious behavior Learned responses whose strength depends on adventitious contiguity of the behavior and the reinforcing stimulus (Skinner).

Surface color Color seen as lying on the surface of an object.

Surrogate mothers Artificial doll-like figures, composed of wire or of wire with terry-cloth covers, which were used by Harlow in his research on the role of maternal factors in rhesus monkey development.

Symbol Anything that "stands for" or "means" something else.

Synchronicity The occurrence of events at the same time but without causal relation (Jung).

Syntactics Study of the linguistic relationships among symbols (Morris).

System Ideally, an organization and interpretation of the data and theories of a subject matter, with special assumptions (postulates), definitions, and methodological biases. In psychology, the actual "systems" are primarily sets of suggestions about how to construct a psychology.

Systematic design Classic experimental methodology using rigorous control of variables (Brunswik).

Tabula rasa Blank tablet; usually refers to the doctrine that the mind at birth is blank and is developed through sensory experience.

Talking cure Improvement in adjustment presumably effected by emotional release achieved when one tells one's troubles to another (also called catharsis, "cleansing") (Freud).

Taxis *See* **Tropism.**

T data Behavioral observations made directly as though by a transducer (hence T) rather than an operator (Barker).

Technician One trained to provide technical services for the practitioner or scientist.

Teleology The explanation of behavior in terms of its ultimate utilities in the absence of evidence that these are actually determining factors.

Tension system A motivational factor in which some particular act or set of acts acquires directive influence in behavior until dissipated (Lewin).

Terminal focal event An achievement of the organism, which may be either perceptual or instrumental (Brunswik).

Theorem A statement derived from postulates through the rules of deduction; in science, a statement to be subjected to direct empirical testing.

Theory (1) A group of laws deductively connected. (2) Generalizations beyond the data which are used to bridge gaps in knowledge and to generate research. (3) A model plus one or more interpretations.

Theta The proportion of stimulus elements sampled by an organism on any given learning trial (Estes).

Thing constancy The principle that the perceptual character of an object remains essentially stable in spite of wide variations in its sensory representation (Brunswik).

Third Force Amalgam of humanism, phenomenology, and existentialism envisioned by Maslow as an alternative to behaviorism and orthodox psychoanalysis, the two leading historical forces in American psychology.

Topology A nonmetric and nondirectional geometry of spatial relationships in which boundaries are the critical factors and a variety of tranformations may be achieved; used by Lewin as a model for representation of behavior functions. *See also* **Hodological space.**

Transducer A device that changes energy from one form to another. A radio receiver is a transducer that changes electromagnetic energy into acoustic energy; the human retina transduces light energy into the electrochemical energy of the nerve impulse.

Transference The shifting of emotion from an object or person to the psychoanalyst during therapy (Freud).

Transposition experiment An experiment in which a subject is trained to respond to one of two stimuli which stand in a particular relationship to each other (for example, the stimulus associated with reward is *larger than* the stimulus not associated with reward). During later test trials, typically the stimulus previously rewarded is paired with a stimulus which has the relationship to it which it previously had to the other training stimulus (i.e., the other test stimulus is now *larger than* the previously rewarded stimulus). The question is whether the subject will respond to the relationship (demonstrate transposition) by choosing the new larger stimulus or will respond to absolute stimulus properties by choosing the old, previously rewarded stimulus.

Trial and error   Apparently unplanned but nonetheless not random attempts at problem solving.

Tropism   A forced movement which is a direct function of stimulation, as when a plant turns toward the sun. Now more often refers to plants, with *taxis* the equivalent for animals.

Turing machine   A conceptual device designed to simulate any clearly defined input-output relationship.

Two-factor learning theory   Any theoretical position in which two separate learning processes are considered essential in the acquisition of behavior.

Uncertainty   That property of a set of alternatives which determines its information content; the amount of uncertainty in a set of messages or alternatives is the same as the amount of information transmitted in reducing that uncertainty to zero. Analogous to entropy in physical systems. *See also* **Information.**

Unconscious   The collective term for mental activities of which the person is not aware (psychoanalysis).

Unconscious inference   The drawing of a conclusion, as in perception, in the absence of any reasoning process of which one is aware (Helmholtz).

Unconscious mentalism   Emphasis on the importance of mental activities which occur outside of conscious awareness (R. I. Watson).

Utilitarianism   Seeking knowledge for its applicability to practical problems (R. I. Watson).

Valence   The attractiveness of objects; can be positive or negative (Lewin).

Variable   Usually, any condition or property that may change and be assigned a number. *See also* **Controlled, Dependent, Independent,** and **Intervening variable.**

Vector   Directional force hypothesized to underlie behavioral relationships (Lewin).

Vicarious function   The substitution of one means for another in order to achieve some result (Tolman and Brunswik).

Vitalism   The philosophical position that life cannot be explained entirely in terms of physiochemical principles.

Volumic color   Color seen as occupying volume, as in the case of colored smoke.

Voluntary   Carried out with conscious intention.

Weber-Fechner law   In the more sophisticated form presented by Fechner, a law stating that the intensity of a sensation is proportional to the logarithm of stimulus intensity.

Weber's law   A psychophysical law which states that a noticeable change in a stimulus intensity is always a constant proportional part of the original stimulus.

Zeigarnik effect   The name for the finding that tasks which are not completed are better remembered than tasks which are completed (Lewin).

Zeitgeist   Spirit of the times.

ACKNOWLEDGMENTS

The authors wish to thank the following copyright owners, authors, and publishers for permission to reprint excerpts from copyrighted material:

ABLEX PUBLISHING CORPORATION
Norman, D. A. *Perspectives in cognitive science*. Norwood, New Jersey: Ablex, 1981.

THE AMERICAN ASSOCIATION FOR THE ADVANCEMENT OF SCIENCE
Boring, E. G. When is human behavior predetermined? *Scientific Monthly*, 1957, **84**, 189–196.
Frankel, C. The nature and source of irrationalism. *Science*, 1973, **180**, 927–931.
Smith, C. S. Matter versus materials: A historical view. *Science*, 1968, **162**, 637–644.

THE AMERICAN JOURNAL OF PSYCHOLOGY
Murray, E. Peripheral and central factors in memory: Images of visual form and color. *American Journal of Psychology*, 1906, **7**, 227–247.

THE AMERICAN PSYCHOLOGICAL ASSOCIATION
Coan, R. W. Dimensions of psychological theory. *American Psychologist*, 1968, **23**, 715–722.
Guthrie, E. R. Psychological facts and psychological theory. *Psychological Bulletin*, 1946, **43**, 1–20.

AMERICAN SCIENTIST
Kurzweil, R. What is artificial intelligence anyway? *American Scientist*, 1985, **73**, 258–264.
Skinner, B. F. The experimental analysis of behavior. *American Scientist*, 1957, **45**, 343–371.

ANNUAL REVIEWS, INC.
Adelson, J. Personality. *Annual Review of Psychology*, 1969, **20**, 217–252.
Ford, D. H. & Urban, H. B. Psychotherapy. *Annual Review of Psychology*, 1967, **18**, 333–372.

APPLETON-CENTURY-CROFTS, EDUCATIONAL DIVISION, MEREDITH CORPORATION
Boring, E. G. *The physical dimensions of consciousness*. New York: Appleton-Century-Crofts, 1933.
Boring, E. G. *A history of experimental psychology*. New York: Appleton-Century-Crofts, 1950.

Estes, W. K., Koch, S., MacCorquodale, K., Meehl, P. E., Mueller, C. G., Jr., Schoenfeld, W. N., & Verplanck, W. S. *Modern learning theory*. New York: Appleton-Century-Crofts, 1954.

Heidbreder, E. *Seven psychologies*. New York: Appleton-Century-Crofts, 1933.

Thorndike, E. L. *Selected writings from a connectionist's psychology*. New York: Appleton-Century-Crofts, 1949.

Turner, M. *Philosophy and the science of behavior*. New York: Appleton-Century-Crofts, 1967.

BASIC BOOKS, INC.

Jones, E. *The life and work of Sigmund Freud*. Vol. 3. New York: Basic Books, 1957.

Nagel, E. The nature and aim of science. In S. Morgenhesser (Ed.), *Philosophy of science today*. New York: Basic Books, 1967.

BOLLINGEN FOUNDATION

Jung, C. G. *Symbols of transformation*. New York: Random House, 1956.

BUREAU OF PUBLICATIONS, TEACHERS COLLEGE, COLUMBIA UNIVERSITY

Thorndike, E. L. *Educational psychology*. Vol. 2. *The psychology of learning*. New York: Teachers College, 1913.

CLARK UNIVERSITY PRESS

Murchison, C. (Ed.) *A history of psychology in autobiography*. Vol. 3. Worcester, Mass.: Clark University Press, 1936.

Watson, J. B. What the nursery has to say about instincts. In C. Murchison (Ed.), *Psychologies of 1925*. Worcester, Mass.: Clark University Press, 1926.

Watson, J. B. Recent experiments on how we lose and change our emotional equipment. In C. Murchison (Ed.), *Psychologies of 1925*. Worcester, Mass.: Clark University Press, 1926.

E. P. DUTTON & CO., INC.

Evans, R. I. *B. F. Skinner: The man and his ideas*. New York: Dutton, 1968.

HARVARD UNIVERSITY PRESS

Bridgman, P. W. *The way things are*. Cambridge, Mass.: Harvard University Press, 1959.

HOLT, RINEHART AND WINSTON, INC.

James, W. *The principles of psychology*. New York: Holt, 1890.

HOUGHTON MIFFLIN COMPANY

Platt, J. R. *The excitement of science*. Boston: Houghton Mifflin, 1962.

J. P. LIPPINCOTT COMPANY

Watson, R. I. *The great psychologists from Aristotle to Freud*. (Rev. ed.) Philadelphia: Lippincott, 1968.

THE MACMILLAN COMPANY

Bridgman, P. W. *The logic of modern physics*. New York: Macmillan, 1927.

Horwitz, L. Theory construction and validation in psychoanalysis. In M. H. Marx (Ed.), *Theories in contemporary psychology*. New York: Macmillan, 1963.

Wundt, W. *Principles of physiological psychology*. New York: Macmillan, 1904.

McGRAW-HILL BOOK COMPANY

Prentice, W. C. H. The systematic psychology of Wolfgang Köhler. In S. Koch (Ed.), *Psychology: A study of a science*. Vol. 1. *Sensory, perceptual, and physiological formulations*. New York: McGraw-Hill, 1968.

Tolman, E. C. Principles of purposive behavior. In S. Koch (Ed.), *Psychology: A study of a science*. Vol. 2. *General systematic formulations, learning and special processes*. New York: McGraw-Hill, 1959, pp. 92–157.

Wooldridge, D. E. *Mechanical man: The physical basis of intelligent life*. New York: McGraw-Hill, 1968.

W. W. NORTON & COMPANY, INC.

Watson, J. B. *Behaviorism*. New York: Norton, 1925. Rev. ed., 1930.

Watson, J. B., & McDougall, W. *The battle of behaviorism*. New York: Norton, 1929.

PHILOSOPHICAL LIBRARY, INC.

Bridgman, P. W. *The nature of some of our physical concepts*. New York: Philosophical Library, 1952.

THE PHILOSOPHICAL REVIEW

Titchener, E. B. The postulates of a structural psychology. *Philosophical Review*, 1898, **7**, 449–465.

PRENTICE-HALL, INC.

Konorski, J. & Jerzy Konorski. In Lindzey, G. (Ed.) *A history of psychology in autobiography*. Vol. 6. New York: Prentice-Hall, 1974.

PSYCHOLOGY TODAY

Hall, M. H. An interview with "Mr. Behaviorist" B. F. Skinner. *Psychology Today*, 1967, **1**, 21–23, 68–71.

ROCKEFELLER UNIVERSITY PRESS

Weiss, A. P. 1 + 1 = 2 (one plus one does not equal two). In G. C. Quarton, T. Melnechuk, & F. O. Schmitt (Eds.), *The neurosciences*. New York: Rockefeller University Press, 1967.

THE RONALD PRESS

Woodworth, R. S., & Sheehan, M. R. *Contemporary schools of psychology*. New York: Ronald Press, 1964.

SIMON & SCHUSTER, INC.

Russell, B. *A history of Western philosophy*. New York: Simon & Schuster, 1945.

SPRINGER-VERLAG OHG

Harrower, M. R. Organization in higher mental processes. *Psychologische Forschung*, 1932, **17**, 56–120.

STANFORD UNIVERSITY PRESS

Barker, R. G. *Ecological psychology*. Stanford, Calif.: Stanford University Press, 1968.

THE UNIVERSITY OF CHICAGO PRESS

Kuhn, T. S. *The structure of scientific revolutions*. Chicago: University of Chicago Press, 1962.

Lashley, K. S. *Brain mechanisms and intelligence*. Chicago: University of Chicago Press, 1929.

Ross, D. G. *Stanley Hall: The psychologist as prophet*. Chicago, University of Chicago Press, 1972.

UNIVERSITY OF MICHIGAN

Unpublished letter from E. B. Titchener to Walter Pillsbury. 1920.

VINTAGE BOOKS, RANDOM HOUSE, INC.

Beveridge, W. I. B. *The art of scientific investigation*. New York: Vintage Books, 1957.

WESLEYAN UNIVERSITY PRESS
Joncich, G. *The sane positivist: A biography of Edward L. Thorndike*. Middletown, Conn.: Wesleyan University Press, 1968.

JOHN WILEY & SONS, INC.
Hall, S. C., & Lindzey, G. *Theories of personality*. New York: Wiley, 1957.

The authors also wish to thank the following authors and publishers for permission to reproduce photographs, figures and quotations from their publications:

ACADEMIC PRESS
Rieber, R. W., & Salinger, K. *Psychology: Theoretical-historical perspectives*. New York: Academic Press, 1980.

THE AMERICAN JOURNAL OF PSYCHOLOGY
Orbison, W. O. Shape as a function of the vector field. *American Journal of Psychology*, 1939, **52**, 31–45.

THE AMERICAN PSYCHOLOGICAL ASSOCIATION
Brunswik, E. Representative design and probabilistic theory in a functional psychology. *Psychological Review*, 1955, **62**, 193–217.
Coan, R. W. Dimensions of psychological theory. *American Psychologist*, 1968, **23**, 715–722.
McGeoch, J. A. The formal criteria of a systematic psychology. *Psychological Review*, 1933, **40**, 1–12.

AMERICAN SCIENTIST
Sternberg, S. Memory scanning: Mental processes revealed by reaction time experiments. *American Scientist, 1969,* **57**, 421–457.

CORNELL UNIVERSITY PRESS
Feinstein, H. M. *Becoming William James*. Ithaca, New York: Cornell University Press, 1984.

DR. MOLLY HARROWER
Harrower, M. *Kurt Koffka: An unwitting self-portrait*. Gainesville, Florida: University Presses of Florida, 1983.

INSTITUTE OF ELECTRICAL AND ELECTRONIC ENGINEERING
Peterson, W. W., Birdsall, T. G., & Fox, W. C. The theory of signal detectability. *Transactions of Professional Group on Information Theory, Institute of Radio Engineers*, 1954, **PGIT-4**, 171–212.

IRVINGTON PUBLISHERS, INC.
Boring, E. G., & Lindzey, G. (Eds.). *A history of psychology in autobiography*. New York: Appleton-Century-Crofts, 1967.

LIVERIGHT PUBLISHING COMPANY
Henle, M. The selected papers of Wolfgang Köhler. New York: Liveright, 1971.

McGRAW-HILL BOOK COMPANY
Lewin, K. *Principles of topological psychology*. (Tr. by F. Heider & G. Heider.) New York: McGraw-Hill, 1936.

THE NEW YORK ACADEMY OF SCIENCES
Tanner, W. P., Jr. Physiological implications of psychophysical data. *Annals of the New York Academy of Science*, 1961, **89**, 752–765.

NEW AMERICAN LIBRARY, INC.
Roazen, P. *Freud and his followers*. New York: New American Library, 1974.

PHILOSOPHICAL LIBRARY, INC.
Roback, A. A., & Kiernan, T. *Pictorial history of psychology and psychiatry*. New York: Philosophical Library, 1969.

RANDOM HOUSE, INC.
Hothersall, D. *History of psychology*. Philadelphia: Temple University Press, 1984.

THOMAS NELSON AND SONS LTD
Luce, A. A. *The life of George Berkeley, Bishop of Cloyne*. Westport, Conn.: Greenwood Press, 1968.

UNIVERSITY OF CALIFORNIA PRESS
Tolman, E. C., & Honzik, C. H. *Insight in rats*. Berkeley: University of California Press, 1932.

THE UNIVERSITY OF CHICAGO PRESS
Brunswik, E. The conceptual framework of psychology. *International Encyclopedia of Unified Science*, 1952, **1**, 1–102.

UNIVERSITY OF MINNESOTA PRESS
Feigl, H. The "orthodox" view of theories: Remarks in defense as well as critique. In M. Radner & S. Winokur (Eds.), *Analyses of theories and methods of physics and psychology*. Minneapolis: University of Minnesota Press, 1970.

WIDE WORLD PHOTOS, INC.
Roazen, P. *Freud and his followers*. New York: New American Library, 1974.

JOHN WILEY & SONS, INC.
Hall, C. S., & Lindzey, G. *Theories of personality*. (2d ed.) New York: Wiley, 1970.

WILHELM WUNDT/KARL MARX UNIVERSITY
Photograph of Wundt and his colleagues.

W. P. VAN STOCKUM
Brunswik, E. The conceptual focus of some psychological systems. *Journal of Unified Science*, 1939, **8**, 36–49.

NAME INDEX

Page numbers in *italic* indicate bibliography references.

SUBJECT INDEX